Financing
Income-Producing
Real Estate

Financing Income-Producing Real Estate

A THEORY AND CASEBOOK

Edited by **James A. Britton, Jr.**, CMB, MAI

Chairman of the Board, Dorman & Wilson, Inc.
White Plains, New York

Lewis O. Kerwood

Senior Director
Mortgage Bankers Association of America

Sponsored by
Mortgage Bankers Association of America
Washington, D.C.

McGRAW-HILL BOOK COMPANY

New York   St. Louis   San Francisco   Auckland   Bogotá   Düsseldorf
Johannesburg   London   Madrid   Mexico   Montreal   New Delhi
Panama   Paris   São Paulo   Singapore   Sydney   Tokyo   Toronto

Library of Congress Cataloging in Publication Data
Main entry under title:

Financing income-producing real estate.

    1. Real estate investment—United States.
I. Britton, James A.   II. Kerwood, Lewis O.
III. Mortgage Bankers Association of America.
HD1375.F49   332.6'324'0973   77-21690
ISBN 0-07-007926-9

FINANCING INCOME-PRODUCING REAL ESTATE: A Theory and Casebook

3 4 5 6 7 8 9 0 D O D O 7 8 3 2 1 0 9

This book was set in Times Roman by Book Studio/Phase One.
The editor was James J. Walsh;
the production supervisor was Lester Kaplan.
R. R. Donnelley & Sons Company was printer and binder.

Contents

v

PART TWO CASE STUDIES

Preface

The art of *learning* comes in many forms, styles, and silhouettes. Throughout history man has learned from the printed word, albeit primitive at times. On occasion, the writer and compatriots, if any, will happen upon that "golden moment" when people *really* want to hear what the writer is saying. Too often, though, words are lost to the graveyard of trivia, relegated there because the writer had nothing of importance to say in the first place—only an urge to write!

In the case of income-property financing, however, there seems to be a whole industry—that of real estate financing—striving for professional performance of the highest order, seeking to learn from those of high expertise in the field. To the credit of those who have achieved, they have recognized that the intricacies and the techniques of income-property financing are so broad, so diverse, so comprehensive, so fluid, so changing, and often so elusive that there is no probability of compounding into any one individual every idea or every viewpoint that anyone has ever had on the subject.

Thus, this text has a twofold purpose. It is intended to serve as an introduction for the beginner or anyone not yet familiar with the intracacies of the financing of income-producing properties. It is also intended to be a source of reference to those already active in the field who may seek a greater depth of knowledge in a particular subject area.

Because of the wide diversity of its contents, as well as the breadth of the field itself, it was felt that no one or two authors could fully cover all of the subject matter. For this reason, highly knowledgeable persons in each of the areas were sought out to contribute articles on their specialties. In doing so it was necessary to sacrifice similarity of style for quality of content. This text, therefore, is not to be viewed as a single-author project. It is, instead, the writings of many persons of high reputation in the field, backed by many years of experience. It is our hope that, the industry will reap maximum benefit from this approach.

The history of financing income-producing properties is, in fact, of relatively recent vintage. Its period of rapid growth began its escalation in the early 1950s and has been exploding ever since. If it has had one constant characteristic, it has been that of evolving change. As pressures of supply and demand and of higher and higher interest rates have appeared as obstacles, enterprising mortgage bankers and investors have invented ingenious methods of finance to surmount these obstacles. These methods, many of which are discussed in the text, will be mere starting points for new methods which we will develop tomorrow and in the future.

To all those who have contributed both time and ideas to this project—not only authors but others with whom we have counseled—our sincere gratitude. Unfortunately, a full listing here of all those individuals would simply be too lengthy and impractical.

It would be unfair, however, not to express public gratitude to the special Review Committee, members of which critiqued the manuscript and offered helpful suggestions. This committee consisted of Angelo L. Dentamaro, President & Chief Executive Officer, Latimer & Buck, Inc., Philadelphia, Pennsylvania; Philip J. Ward, Senior Portfolio Analyst, Mortgage and Real Estate Department, Connecticut General Life Insurance Company, Hartford, Connecticut; and Michael P. Galgano, Senior Vice President, Dorman & Wilson, Inc., Long Island Office, Garden City, New York.

Finally, to Douglas Metz, MBA staff writer, our special thanks for his editorial assistance and for guiding us through the labyrinth of the English language.

James A. Britton, Jr.
Lewis O. Kerwood

EDITORS' NOTE

In no instance do capitalization rates and/or interest rates as used imply the status of current market conditions. Such references function only as examples.

J.A.B.
L.O.K.

Part One

Theory

Chapter 1

Fundamental Concepts in Income-Property Financing

Angelo L. Dentamaro

The financing of income-producing real estate, through structures designed and developed exclusively for the production of an income stream, has played an important role in the American economy. Motivated by a desire for return on investment, categorized as *yield*, those financial institutions and individuals who are active in such investments include life insurance companies, commercial and savings banks, savings and loan associations, real estate investment trusts (REITs), pension and welfare funds, and individuals with uninvested capital. In the role as *correspondent*, or as fiduciary intermediary, the mortgage banker's function is to coordinate available capital with development and/or project needs. Among others, property types include apartments, office buildings, regional shopping centers, and a variety of retail establishments, industrial plants, leisure and recreation facilities, and many different special-purpose facilities. Cycles in the production and use of such properties are affected, as is any business, by supply and demand factors of money and consumer markets.

In many financial circles, the era of the mid-1960s through the mid-1970s will be remembered as the era in which the Dow Jones industrial average reached 1000, the era of the Vietnam war, or the era of wage-price controls. For those of us concerned with the production of income-producing real estate, however, this era will be remembered as one of growth and change in the real estate industry. This period has been characterized by the rise of real estate investment trusts, a proliferation of syndications and joint ventures, the advent of limited partnership interests, and the rise and decline of so-called equity kickers. Also, many life insurance companies have left the arena of single-family residential financing to concentrate exclusively on income-producing properties. At the same time, some traditional single-family lenders, such as savings banks and savings and loan associations, have diverted significant portions of their capital to income-property projects.

Thus, the base has been well established for future generations to capitalize on the foundations formed during this decade, a decade that saw both tight money markets and markets in which the availability of funds reached all-time highs.

Perhaps as significant as any of these factors was the introduction of environmental considerations in income-property financing. Currently, the effect of real estate development on the quality of air, water, population, and eye-ear-nose pollution must be considered. For the first time, we find ourselves in need of feasibility studies relating to the effect of development on society. The importance of environmental impact studies is now as significant to development potential as are economic feasibility studies.

The financing of income-producing real estate is not an exact science. Subjective analysis, experience, and an ability to be innovative and creative are essential to growth and opportunities in our industry. Some basic fundamentals, however, remain almost undisturbed. These will be discussed in detail in future chapters as they apply to particular types of income-producing real estate. These basic fundamentals typically cover the characteristics of a project and the analytical techniques for evaluating these characteristics. The characteristics are:

1 Location.
2 Physical property.
3 Sponsorship.

Perhaps the oldest adage in real estate financing is the so-called success formula of *location, location, location*. In recent years, however, this has been tempered with the adage that good locations have been ruined by poor sponsorship and that some projects in marginal locations have been successful because of strong sponsorship. Generally, the location must be suitable for a project under discussion. The location elements which the lender considers are:

1 Proximity to its market.
2 Compatibility with the surrounding environment.
3 Ingress and egress.
4 Visibility.
5 Transportation.
6 Work force.
7 Utilities.
8 Zoning.
9 Physical characteristics of the particular site.

If we ignore any of these elements in an analysis of a particular project, we merely make the task more difficult for those who are responsible for providing financing. In addition, we may be laying the foundation for a financial failure either during construction or after completion of the project. Certainly, there are many examples of project failures due to location deficiencies.

The second characteristic in any project is the *physical property* itself. Here we must consider the size of the facility, parking, drive-by appeal, amenities, physical and mechanical components, functional and economic utility, and all the aspects of physical and economic obsolescence. For most of these elements, common sense may very well be the single most important tool available to you. To illustrate this point, consider an apartment with no bathroom. While this may seem utterly absurd to some, it is no more absurd than an income-producing property without heating and air conditioning in an area that requires it or a supposed full-service motel or hotel without adequate parking and/or eating facilities. The point is that the physical property must be viewed with respect to its designed function, its marketability, and its long-term potential. The analyst must be able to judge it for its appeal in the market today as well as for tomorrow.

An additional area of concern in analyzing the physical property is a technical problem. The components which go into the physical property must be technically sufficient. The analyst is required to have personal knowledge or have available professional expertise for such matters as the adequacy of footings and foundations, heating and air conditioning, load-bearing capacities, lighting, and the more apparent elements concerning ceilings, floors, walls, and windows. The analyst is responsible for making the judgment of whether or not the proposed project is adequate to function successfully as the physical entity it purports to be.

There are two basic categories of income-producing real estate. The first category includes *commercial, industrial,* or *apartment* properties. The other includes those properties described as either *general-purpose, limited-purpose,* or *single-purpose* real estate. The types of properties within the first category are easily recognized, but those within the second category require a further explanation.

General-purpose properties are those for which there is a competitive rental demand with generally accepted physical characteristics that appeal to a broad class of general users. Examples of this type of property are warehouses, most office buildings, and retail stores. A limited-purpose property would be a facility such as a service station, restaurant, theater, or department store capable of being converted to other uses if economically feasible. A single-purpose property would be a facility such as an oil refinery, a grain elevator, or a brick kiln with built-in characteristics that make them inherently difficult to convert for other uses.

For the purpose of simplicity, the elements of both the developer and the manager of income-producing real estate are included under *sponsorship*. The reason for this is that even though the individual, partnership, or corporation that actually develops the real estate may not be the entity that manages the property, collects the rents, and pays the indebtedness, the necessary considerations are often identical. Also, a successful project requires competent developers and managers.

Because of this, it behooves those who are employed in the profession of financing income-producing real estate to cover all aspects of sponsorship. They should be cognizant of the track record of the sponsor, both for development and management capabilities. What other properties has this sponsor produced? Even more significant, what other properties of the same type as the subject property has this particular sponsor developed? Developing includes finding the land, arranging for the actual physical development, arranging for financing, and bringing the concept to actual fruition. It is absolutely necessary to know the amount of real estate actually managed by the sponsorship group, and it is equally beneficial to be familiar with their payment record.

Also included in this fundamental area is the question of the financial stability of the sponsorship group, be it an individual or collective effort. This requires a thorough financial investigation and analysis. In order to be thorough, the corporation and/or partnership and the principal individuals within the legal entity should be looked at carefully to determine their capability to carry a project through to completion. Every effort should be made to obtain the best possible financial information.

The mortgage analyst evaluates the prospects for a project using a series of analytical techniques. They are:

1 Appraising.
2 Underwriting.
3 Structuring the loan.

There are many kinds of appraisals and appraisal techniques, such as those for estate purposes, insurance, condemnation and sale, or acquisition, to name only a few. For consideration here, we are interested in an appraisal for mortgage lending purposes. We are, therefore, concerned with a reasonable *estimate of value* upon which we can base our loan amount. This estimate of value must be acceptable to the lender as well as the many auditors and examiners who must, in turn, be satisfied by the lender.

The information contained in the appraisal report should be consistent. There should not be unexplained differences in areas, sizes, room counts, or any other facts. The appraisal should be logical and based on fact wherever and whenever possible.

The appraisal is always an integral part of any income-property financing submission. Here, again, judgment must be used by the mortgage banker in determining exactly how much importance should be given to the appraisal. It is a fact that some lending institutions are appraisal-oriented, while others place priority or equal emphasis on other factors such as sponsorship and credit. This does not mean that some mortgage bankers and investors accept inadequate appraisals. It merely means that some place less emphasis on the appraisal and more emphasis on other basic fundamentals.

The next analytical technique in the financing of income-producing real estate is underwriting. Of all the elements, this is, perhaps, the most misunderstood and least appreciated in our industry as a whole. It is, however, of paramount importance to lenders. Here, we are involved in the business of *risk analysis*. It is in this area that experience rears its head most often, and it is also in this area that we find the widest divergence of opinion, appetites, and attitudes.

Underwriting involves the melding of specific information on a particular project (sponsorship, physical characteristics, location, appraisal, etc.) with the general information on similar projects with which the individual or institution may have been associated in the past. This melding ultimately results in the decision to make or not to make a loan commitment. If a loan commitment is to be made, the underwriting is the basis for determining ultimate terms. One lender, for instance, seems perfectly at home with "full" loans on shopping centers. Another is willing to consider a shopping center, but only so-called prime centers and only on a very conservative basis. Some lenders will accept luxury apartments, while others find these types of investment totally unacceptable.

We need to know intimately the underwriting patterns of the various lenders. They will vary from property to property and from one geographic location to another, but there are a few which should apply to almost every type of income property. These considerations include the loan-to-value ratio, the debt service coverage, the break-even point, the loan, and the income per unit typical for the particular type of property in question. The analyst may also wish to chart, as a routine matter, appropriate area sizes, parking requirements, and typical amenities.

If one keeps an alert eye on the elements of prudent underwriting, it will become clear for the vast majority of the projects on which one works exactly what is currently acceptable. However, simple guidelines should not be a deterrent to any offering without consideration of its other merits. Consideration of other merits should be tempered with respect to accepted guidelines, but guidelines should never be used alone.

The final technique is structuring the loan. Here the analyst is called upon to make a very significant judgment concerning the *proper amount* of financing that a particular property can sustain. The judgment must be based on a thorough analysis of the project's characteristics. Here, also, the recommended financing must be attuned to the particular lender with whom the mortgage banker is dealing. If, for instance, the property is a nursing home and your one nursing home lender has never made a loan in excess of 70 percent of value or has never made a nursing home loan with less than 1.50 debt service coverage, the mortgage banker must keep those facts firmly in mind when negotiating an application with the sponsor and when recommending a particular dollar amount to the lender. By the same token, if a particular sponsor can accept a certain dollar figure (which you believe is attainable from your lender), but still has a need for a certain constant, then this situation must be faced squarely and honestly. For some, the aim of financing is not necessarily to arrange for a proper level of financing as much as it is to obtain the highest dollar amount at the lowest rate for the longest term. On the other side of the fence, some lenders believe they should strive for the lowest number of dollars at the highest interest rate for a term that keeps the loan classified as a long-term, permanent loan. For many of these lenders, the actual amount of the loan is immaterial.

Fortunately, there are significant numbers in our profession who aspire to place upon any income-producing property a proper level of financing. Fortunately, also, this level will vary between types of lenders as well as between those who typically lend only to particular industries. There are some life insurance company lenders who have had phenomenal success with the financing of industrial properties, or shopping centers, or motels and are, therefore, willing to be more aggressive lenders in those categories than some of their counterparts might be in other companies.

Most experienced individuals in our industry will agree that more projects have failed from overfinancing than from underfinancing, and more sponsors have been driven from our industry because they never acquired the self-discipline of allowing projects to stand on their own merits. Older and wiser heads in our industry can recount tale after tale of the competent sponsor who began counting on the funds from his next project to bail out a previous one. On the other hand, should underfinancing force the sponsor to acquire supplemental, second mortgage financing, his project may be further and unnecessarily destined to failure. In its true concept, of course, the structure of the loan must be reasonable and proper for the particular type of property under consideration, for the particular sponsor and for the particular lender. It is this combination of project, sponsor, and lender whose interests must all be evaluated and equalized if one is to be associated with successful income-producing properties.

In understanding the basic characteristics and analytical techniques of a given project and having these in full control, there remain three areas in which experience and professionalism are necessary to insure an understanding of the particular income property to be financed, that the transaction envisioned is legal and binding, and that the loan remains healthy throughout its term. These three areas are:

1   The preparation of the loan submission.
2   The closing of the loan.
3   The administration of the loan.

Since each mortgage investor has its own philosophy of lending and its own requirements, every effort should be made to comply fully with the investor's desires. The purpose of the loan submission is ultimately to have the lender issue its *commitment*. In order to achieve this ultimate goal, the submission should address itself to those areas previously discussed and, in addition, satisfy each need, current requirement, and objective of the lender. The submission should be complete, accurate, and so thoughtfully prepared as to elicit a favorable response from the lender with a minimum of renegotiation.

In order for the financial transaction to be completed, the loan must be "closed." This requires the availability of legal talent to draft, review, and process the mortgage or deed of trust, leases, surveys, the various certificates of governmental agencies, and to pass judgment on title matters and the legality of the transaction for all the parties within the governing jurisdiction.

After the loan is closed and it becomes part of the mortgage banker's *servicing portfolio*, the continued health of the investment rests, in part, upon the diligence and the competence of the mortgage banker in loan administration. Prompt collection of payments and remittances to the mortgage investor (insuring that real estate taxes and insurance have been attended to) and property inspections are all essential elements of loan administration. Cooperation between the investor and the mortgage banker is imperative to proper loan administration, and a clear and concise understanding of the duties, responsibilities, and expectations of the parties all aid in assuring that the investment is under proper control for the life of the loan.

The astute mortgage banker will convey to the borrower the lender's desires in the area of loan administration so that prompt payment of monthly debt service, taxes, and insurance premiums will come as no surprise to the borrower. Nor will the borrower be surprised by property inspections and the insistence on the part of the mortgage banker from the lender that the property be properly maintained throughout the life of the loan.

Ours is a "people" business, and it is the day-to-day contact and association with builders, developers, financiers, lenders, mortgage bankers, and brokers that makes it the exciting and interesting one it is. Coupled with these personalities is the fact that each and every piece of income-producing real estate is a separate and distinct entity. For the most part, there are no hard and fast rules or bench marks to which we can cling, because each and every person with whom we do business and each and every project to which we address ourselves is different. Ours is not a time-structured industry, but it requires hard work and long hours.

What types of people are needed to bring about a profitable income-producing real estate loan department? It is impossible to establish a profile of a typical mortgage banker, broker, or lender, and it might even be dangerous to try to generalize about certain characteristics which all of us have heard of and perhaps even described when it appeared to be advantageous to us. However, the qualities we see most often, regardless of where the individual fits in our industry, are the following: industriousness, intelligence, hard work, innovation, willingness to learn, receptiveness to new ideas and challenges, a deep and abiding faith in our political and economic systems, and, above all, a desire to become personally proficient.

Successful colleagues in the industry are accountants, lawyers, engineers, architects, and general business practitioners whose backgrounds and formal educations are as varied as one could possibly imagine. We have seen successful individuals in this industry who have no college training at all, and we have seen others who were majors in psychology, political science, business administration as well as the more formal disciplines listed above. There is no distinct profile destined for automatic success in this industry.

Insofar as originations are concerned, you might be wondering who succeeds best. Is it the hard-sell or the soft-sell originator? It is obvious that both kinds can and do succeed. However, the person who does succeed remembers that this is a "people" business, and most of those who have succeeded have been persons who are most able to deal effectively with people.

The field of mortgage banking has evolved through the years from the basic practice of origination and placement of residential loans with various types of institutional investors to highly sophisticated forms of income-property financing to fit ever-changing investor needs.

To meet this challenge, mortgage bankers and institutional investors have had to expand their horizons of knowledge into a variety of fields and endeavors. Today's financing professionals must have a thorough knowledge of the principles of real estate valuation and be proficient in the processing and assimilation of facts in order to properly structure and underwrite loans for income-producing properties. They must also have a knowledge of legal concepts, practical and analytical concepts of planning, construction, and architecture, and, through study and observation, be able to determine if a proposed project is feasible. Investment decisions must be based upon a thorough understanding of economics and movements within money markets.

Still another consideration in income-property lending is a thorough understanding of the cyclical nature of the industry. The cyclical characteristics are caused by, among other things, the general economy, the availability of funds to lending institutions, government fiscal and monetary policy, and supply and demand factors of real estate and certain property types. This means, simply, that there is not always a steady, constant, even flow of projects. Rather, we more often find ourselves with either an overabundance or a scarcity of projects. We operate in valleys and on peaks and not on the level terrain of consistency. This requires self-motivated people who are not only good managers of time, but imaginative and creative to the point of being able to function mentally and physically in what is an ever-changing and nonconstant industry.

There is no substitute for the proper selection of the individual to head an income-property department. Preferably, he or she should be the type of individual who is constantly looking for ways to make a project come to fruition, rather than the type of individual who is a fault finder. This person must be experienced and knowledgeable enough to understand thoroughly the various types of income-producing real estate the department will be working with. He or she must be knowledgeable enough to analyze those projects and ferret out all problem areas and, perhaps more important, to find solutions to those problems. To do so, this individual must possess appraisal skills and be able to visualize the proposed project as a completed, operating, physical and economic entity.

Finally, this individual must be a producer and a performer whose word is bond and whose honesty, judgment, and abilities are accepted without question. Such a person must be able to work effectively with peers as well as with those of lesser experience. This is the person to whom other members of the department must turn to for guidance, for expert training, for direction and for encouragement. This is the person who must also set the professional levels of integrity and competence for the organization as it relates to the financing of income-producing real estate.

If you are a correspondent or a broker and you have such a person to head your department, the next consideration is the matter of outlets for your submissions. You must have a place to go with each submission, and that place must be a lender who not only has funds available, but who is interested in financing the particular type of real estate which you can originate, and who is interested in doing business with you and your firm.

Another area of consideration is to identify the kind of business in which you wish to become involved. This may be done in any one of a number of ways. For instance, one firm may decide to establish an income-property department that deals with FHA-insured financing exclusively. Another firm may decide to establish a department that deals only in conventional projects. Many firms, in fact, have separate departments for each of these functions.

Having decided whether to go the insured or conventional route, one may then wish to categorize the type of business by project type. That is, one may decide to finance only apartments, office buildings, and shopping centers, or to finance any type of income-producing real estate. For the most part, if you surveyed 100 policy makers in our industry, most of them would probably say, "We like to feel that we would consider any type of project that makes sense." As a practical matter, though, this is not the case and it behooves a lender to communicate clearly and concisely to correspondents exactly what types of properties will be considered. In the same sense, if you are a correspondent or broker and do not, in fact, have outlets for a particular type of property, it would behoove you to communicate this to your various sponsors.

Another method of identifying the kind of business in which you wish to become involved is the very simple dollar-amount method. You may, for one reason or another, decide to work only on loans of $1,000,000 or more, or only on loans from $100,000 to $500,000. If you are a lender, the size of your assets and the size of your mortgage loan portfolio may very well dictate the size of loans that you will consider. If, on the other hand, you are a mortgage banker or broker, it is obvious your outlets will determine the size of loans your staff will be working on.

Most observers would comment that you are best advised to work only on makeable deals. Whether you are a mortgage banker, a lender, or a broker, no useful purpose is served in preparing a full loan presentation if the parties know it is not going to be favorably received.

The question of how one gets loans then arises. It is obvious, if you are a lender, that the best way to get loans is to be willing to make loans. Nobody will spend very much time submitting loans to you if they are continually declined or restructured in a manner completely unacceptable to the sponsor. The lender must decide for itself what yields it is willing to accept, what coverages it is willing to accept, what types of properties it is willing to consider, and the dollar limitations under which it must operate. These criteria must then be communicated to the lender's sources.

If you are a mortgage banker or a broker, the only successful way of getting loans is to "go out after them." Few people have been successful in this industry by waiting for the phone to ring. But what does one do and where does one go? In many communities, your commercial bank may not be interested in long-term, permanent financing, but you should be aware that it probably has clients on a continuing basis who do need such financing. Regular, periodic calls to this source may, therefore, prove fruitful, especially if you are able to communicate to the commercial banker the types of projects, sponsors, and dollar amounts you are willing to consider. Every loan originator should know who the major and minor builder/developer sponsors are in their particular area. Regular calls should be made to these sources. Too often, we show up only when we want something—an attitude easily detected. At the same time, no one wants to be an irritant or a pest. In some cases, perhaps, it may be wise to ask whether the other party appreciates being called upon periodically or would rather make some other arrangement for contact. The whole idea is to keep constantly attuned to the markets in which one operates.

Still another source of loans is to work in cooperation with other mortgage bankers. For instance, suppose as a matter of policy you do not work on loans under $1,000,000 and one of your best clients comes in and wants to discuss a $500,000 deal.

If you are attuned to your market, you should know who among your competition could accommodate that type of loan and, rather than tell your cherished client you cannot help, it would be more appropriate to make an arrangement with one of your competitors to handle this type of situation. Some mortgage bankers and brokers have purposely avoided this type of activity for fear of losing clients, but as a practical matter few if any clients have unquestioned loyalty to a particular source and it is probably better in the long run to accommodate your clients, even if it means sending them to your competition. In the final analysis, a client who does not seek out the best, most competent, and capable source of funds may very well prove to have other shortcomings as well.

Ultimately, an originator gets loans by working for them and builds a reputation by delivering. Wherever one sits in on the decision-making process, on whatever side of the street one happens to be working, the final and supreme judgment is always based on whether the deal was made, whether the project was constructed, and whether it is now operating successfully.

Chapter 2

Parties to
the Transaction

David C. Tolzmann

This discussion starts with the basic premise that there are principal parties to any real estate transaction—buyer and seller; borrower and lender, developer partner and money partner; lessor and lessee—and so on. However, there is another cast of characters without whom the principal parties could not successfully consummate their transaction.

A partial listing of these supporting professionals includes:

Mortgage bankers
Real estate brokers
Institutional long-term lenders
Commercial bankers
Real Estate Investment Trusts
Lawyers
Appraisers
Accountants
Leasing agents
Management companies
Title companies
Surveyors

These professionals perform important functions that assist the principals in their negotiations. Each has its own expert role and each is essential to the field of real estate and real estate finance.

MORTGAGE BANKERS

Perhaps the least understood of all in this long list is the mortgage banker. Simply put, the mortgage banker is the catalyst who brings the principals in the transaction together, particularly where financing of the real estate is concerned.

Traditionally, the mortgage banker has served as the *correspondent* or area representative for various institutional lenders, primarily from other sections of the country. The mortgage banker's principal function for the institutional investors represented is to negotiate and offer to those institutions a variety of investments for their portfolios, all of which must meet their individual underwriting criteria.

To accomplish this seemingly simple task the mortgage banker must be thoroughly trained in financial and real estate matters. Broad, in-depth knowledge of appraising, underwriting, negotiating, financial statement and lease analysis, legal matters, in addition to established contacts throughout the real estate community are essential. Knowing and even anticipating institutional investors' investment appetites, a good mortgage banker is one who, above all else, has the confidence of investors. As their eyes and ears in the field, the mortgage banker provides the essential contact between borrower and lender without which the whole system would not function.

REAL ESTATE BROKERS

The real estate broker is licensed (usually by the state and/or municipality) to deal in the sale and transfer of real estate and, consequently, plays a key role in real estate transactions. The real estate broker often controls the site needed for a particular project, and both the developer/borrower and mortgage banker must work closely with the broker in the purchase and rezoning of the land prior to development. The real estate broker is also an excellent source for information on comparable sales.

INSTITUTIONAL LONG-TERM LENDERS

The lender is a principal party to any real estate loan transaction, but it is important to point out how the institutional long-term lender makes the transaction operate. When we discuss the role of the commercial banker and the real estate investment trust later in this chapter, we will be referring to the commitments issued by institutional long-term lenders upon whom the interim lenders usually rely to take out their construction loans. The institutional long-term lender, upon receipt of a proposed investment from a mortgage banker, investigates it, analyzes it, underwrites it, and finally issues a commitment, often with additional conditions, for the purchase of that loan upon completion of the property. Additional conditions often include leasing requirements, certain key tenants, and various legal matters. The issuance of the long-term lender's mortgage commitment triggers the rest of the action that follows. The institutional long-term lender as a group includes life insurance companies, mutual savings banks, savings and loan associations, pension and profit-sharing funds, foundations, endowment funds, and in some cases commercial banks. While not institutional, some *individual* investors supply sufficient funds and are a significant party to a particular transaction.

COMMERCIAL BANKERS

In the traditional mortgage loan transaction, the commercial banker plays the key role of providing construction mortgage funds. Usually, the commercial banker will commit to a construction loan only after the institutional long-term lender has issued a commitment to purchase the loan upon completion of the property. The major share of construction lending is provided by commercial banks, and in recent years the real estate investment trust industry has supplied the balance of these funds. The commercial banker, as construction lender, takes certain normal safeguards to fund as safely as possible the progress of any construction. First, comes a review of the terms of the institutional long-term lender's commitment to be sure there are no problems that cannot be resolved. Then comes a check of the construction contracts and the budgets that have been established in order to ascertain that there are sufficient equity dollars to complete the project. The typical construction lender's pattern would require that equity dollars go into the project before the construction dollars that are secured by a mortgage and by the long-term lender's takeout commitment, making sure always to have sufficient funds remaining in the construction account to complete the project. Because of the enormous resources of the commercial banking system, there have been sufficient funds available to complete most projects under construction. In times of abnormal banking restraints, the shortage of funds and the high cost of construction financing deter a number of projects. Characteristically, construction lenders will make funds available to the developers at an interest rate tied to a floating prime rate. Depending on the credit, the risk involved, and the financial climate at the time, rates range from ½ of 1 percent over prime to a high of 5 percent over prime on a floating basis (plus fees in most cases). Therefore, when prime reaches a high (such as it did in July, 1974 of 12 percent), rates can range from 12½ to 17 percent. So, it is obvious the role of the commercial bank as construction lender is extremely critical to the overall success of a development project.

REAL ESTATE INVESTMENT TRUSTS

The real estate investment trust industry was created by an Act of Congress in 1960, when a law was passed permitting a financing vehicle created for real estate investment purposes to pass all of its profits and losses through to the beneficial interest holders. Simply, as long as 90 percent of the income from the trust is passed on in the form of dividends to the beneficial shareholders, the trust as an entity is not taxed and the benefits are passed on directly to the shareholders. Two basic forms of trusts have developed through this vehicle, one is an equity trust which invests primarily in real estate equities, and the other is a *C and D* trust—a construction and development trust—which is primarily interested in short-term construction loans and land development loans. (A third type of trust, blending a combination of both of the above, also exists.) The C and D trust has become a major competitor of the commercial banker's historic role as construction lender and has brought to the real estate field a new source of construction funds hitherto unavailable to the typical developer. Their basic ground rules follow very close upon the heels of the construction lender as typified by the commercial bank. However, since their rates must be based on a spread between their cost of borrowing and their lending rates, their rates have usually been on the high side of the market spread. When rates continue to rise, the real estate investment trust specializing in construction and development loans comes under increasing pressure to keep rates high to insure adequate yields to its beneficial shareholders. Therefore, in a number of instances, these trusts stretched to obtain high interest-bearing loans and consequently encountered difficulties with high-risk loans. As rates begin to drift lower in any return to ''normal,'' this situation tends to reverse itself.

LAWYERS

Each real estate transaction is usually handled in the closing, and even in the negotiating stages, by lawyers representing the principal parties. Since each case involves a high degree of technical work, and since each transaction is involved with real property, legal experts specializing in real estate matters are essential to insure that both parties are adequately protected.

APPRAISERS

Since real estate values, upon which all transactions are contingent, must be established, the use of a professional real estate appraiser is essential. The appraiser must establish values based on the three approaches—economic value, market value, and physical value—to any piece of real estate. The ultimate valuation is usually a combination of these three approaches. Institutional investors typically require a complete appraisal of the proposed development as part of the loan submission which they consider in underwriting the loan. The construction lender also relies heavily on the value established by the appraiser.

ACCOUNTANTS

Many of the development transactions are extremely complicated and involve not only cash flows, but losses during construction, depreciation, and a myriad of tax considerations. It is essential for all parties involved to have professional accountants who can assist them with their expert knowledge in the accounting and tax fields. Accountants can also be of expert assistance in determining the form of ownership, be it corporation, partnership, or individual proprietary.

LEASING AGENTS

If the property to be constructed involves tenants, someone must develop the proper tenancy for the property. The developer if experienced in leasing, will usually use staff personnel for this function. Many developers, however, utilize the services of a professional organization specifically skilled in the leasing field. Many such organizations combine leasing and management services. The developer and the long-term lender will usually pre-approve a standard lease form and establish all rent schedules. The leasing agent will contact prospective tenants and sign them to the necessary leases.

MANAGEMENT COMPANIES

Once the building or buildings are completed and leased, and the tenants have occupied their spaces, it is necessary to provide for the ongoing management and operation of the properties. An owner/developer with such skills will usually manage the property personally. However, in many instances it is desirable as well as necessary to use outside independent operators. Management companies that specialize in providing ongoing management and operational capabilities for the property have evolved in recent years. Many management companies tend to specialize in one class of property, such as office buildings, shopping centers, industrial properties, or apartments. There are, however, a number of large, nationwide operations that will manage a variety of properties. Special-purpose properties such as motels, nursing homes, and hospitals require management companies which do indeed specialize in that one particular type of property.

TITLE COMPANIES

Since everyone involved in the transaction is desirous that title to a given property be free and clear, the title company plays an important role in searching the title to the property and issuing its report as to the current state of the title, including all exceptions to a clear title. Lawyers for both parties to the transaction then review the preliminary title report and take such steps as are necessary to remove exceptions to the title which are or may be objectionable. The title company also issues its final policy after the transaction is completed and delivers to the owner/developer an owner's title insurance policy and to the lender a mortgagee's title insurance policy. Without such a title policy, transfer of properties would be a much more time-consuming and laborious process.

SURVEYORS

A surveyor is trained to determine the boundaries of a specific property and to put in map form a plat of the property, showing its boundaries and any easements or other known title restrictions. This enables the developer and lender to proceed with assurance that they are building a property within the boundaries of the land owned and, if there are utility or other easements, that they are carefully planning the building so they do not encroach on such easements.

This discussion has identified the many and varied roles which a large cast of characters plays in the development, financing, construction, and operation of income-producing real estate. Needless to say, no transaction involving real estate can be consummated without the expertise and involvement of numerous interested parties, all of whom have a vital role to play.

Chapter 3

Investor Motivation and Investment Risk Analysis

J. Thomas Montgomery

The primary purpose of this chapter is to lay the basis for understanding what motivates investors to invest in anything, to invest in real property, to select one form of real estate investment over another, and to pay a particular price to "buy in."

No investor has to invest in real property: there are many different kinds of investment and very often several different investment positions available within the same property (that is, the equity position, the mortgage position, subordinated land fee, etc.).

"When I use a word," said Humpty Dumpty to Alice in a rather scornful way, "it means just what I choose it to mean—neither more nor less."

Taking that sort of arbitrary liberty, we define:

1 *Capital* as investment funds that flow from savings, retained profits, conversions, and borrowings. By capital is meant cash, its equivalent, the ability to borrow, and all kinds of longer-term financial assets (that is, debt, "hybrid," and equity with "stops in between").

2 *Investor* broadly to include any person or entity with capital to invest in anything. This description would then encompass individuals, partnerships, corporations, financial institutions, REITs, pension funds, etc., both real estate and non-real estate-oriented investors, and debt, equity-oriented investors, and "hybrid." A "hybrid" investment might be defined as one that has the primary characteristic of a debt investment, but is "topped off" with some equity *kicker* features (that is, a convertible debenture or a mortgage with a supplemental interest clause, the latter calculated sometimes as a small percentage of annual gross income in addition to contract interest).

There is no doubt that investors have different investment objectives and constraints. For example, some are restricted by law and regulation (insurance companies, REITs, etc.); some seek highly tax sheltered situations (very high income tax bracket investors); some seek fixed income, secured debt-type positions (by legal restriction or choice); some are "one shot," while others are in the investment market on a continuing basis; some seek highly leveraged, speculative, equity positions; some prefer real estate-oriented investments, while others will consider real estate as only one alternative.

There are five basic concepts that motivate any kind of investor to act, whether the investor is a citizen acting unconsciously at one extreme, or a sophisticated financial institution acting at the other, and whether the investor is acquiring stocks, bonds, real estate equities, or second mortgages. These motivation concepts are the ideal investment, opportunity cost, time value of money, present value estimates, and return on investment (ROI). Let us briefly examine each.

THE IDEAL INVESTMENT

If an investor could have everything, what might the investment look like? Among others, it would have the following characteristics:

1 Absolute certainty of principal with payback assured within the time frame of the investor's expectations.

2 Capital appreciation potential with real dollar growth or simply a hedge against the deeply ingrained expectation of probable long-term inflation.

3 The ability to liquidate (sell) the investment quickly, easily, and without excessive cost, thus enabling conversion to cash in the event of an emergency or perhaps to take advantage of a better investment opportunity.

4 A very high rate of return commensurate with the risk.

5 Certainty of receipts, which would insure "return on" as well as "return of" the investment.

6 Carefree management, requiring little of the investor's time or energy.

7 Available as easy collateral for loan purposes with the ability to pledge quickly and cheaply.

8 Income tax shelter with taxes either delayed or deferred or no taxes of any sort, or even the possibility of excess tax shelter left over.

9 Effective leverage potential requiring a minimum of equity and attractive debt terms, including limited liability.

10 Pride of ownership.

Consider which of these characteristics are generally present in each of the following investments:

The equity position in a high-grade apartment property.

The first mortgage position in the same property.

The land under the same property, subordinated to the first mortgage and then sold to a pension fund.

A share of top-quality stock.

A top-quality corporate bond.

A "tax-free" medium-risk municipal bond.

A deposit in a mutual savings bank.

Raw land five years away from development.

If you were to identify narratively all the future net benefits flowing to each of the above investments, you would find each has ideal characteristics more or less, weighted differently within each alternative.

While no such thing as the "ideal" investment exists, its pursuit may not be as academic as it may sound. This first concept starts to speak to questions such as: What motivates different kinds of investors in the marketplace? What are a particular investor's prime objectives and where can these goals be dovetailed into an available investment opportunity? What secondary objectives is an investor willing to give up to meet the primary objectives?

OPPORTUNITY COST

As you read this chapter you have forever lost the opportunity to do something else (perhaps more worthwhile). In the same way, investments made one way require giving up other ways of using the same funds. No matter how small or unsophisticated any investor is, this thought is always present, even though it may not be identified with the key words "opportunity costs."

The allocation of capital is the "rudder" by which a society, a company, or an investor steers into the future. How is the available, yet limited, pool of capital resources to be divided among competing users or uses? Capital gives its holder a wide array of investment choices; however, no matter how large the amount of capital, any investor has only a limited amount, including access to credit. Everything, including dollars, has a cost in terms of opportunities foregone. Once a decision is made to choose one investment, those dollars may not be available for another.

So, any investor is likely to go through the following thought process before making a decision:

1 My capital is a much sought-after agent in production.

2 What candidates are there for my dollars, which include my ability to borrow?

3 There are unlimited positions in which I can invest. Who says I have to go into real estate?

4 What does the specific investment opportunity have to offer?

5 "Get in line and get up front if you can." If I choose you, the choice has a cost to me in terms of other investment opportunities foregone.

TIME VALUE OF MONEY

The term "time value of money" is an intriguing expression which seems to have many different meanings. It is not easy to define it "head on," so perhaps all one can do is to talk around and about it.

Time is money. Anyone borrowing someone else's capital can expect to pay rent (interest) for its use. Equity investors foregoing other alternatives also hope and anticipate that targeted yields will in fact come on line as predicted over projected time frames. Accordingly, any kind of investment of capital has a time dimension or horizon associated with it; that is, the value of any input of capital today is measured by the contribution it can make to something over time.

In one form or another, this concept certainly has to do with:

The compounding and discounting functions of one dollar—the arithmetic cornerstone of all capitalization methods as well as investment analysis and valuation.

Timing, anticipation, and payback expectations. What happens over time to the injection today of one dollar of any kind of capital into any investment position? In an uncertain world, how fast can and will the capital be recaptured? Any kind of capital invested to create, purchase, or operate an investment has to be "carried." The meter starts and ends the investment life cycle, and it keeps running, whether income of all sorts is being generated or not (that is, the "rent-up" period in a new office building, land not used for productive purposes). Without profitability, capital can erode quickly and the equity investor loses his first because he is a residual claimant.

True effective cost of, and return on, capital can be a very elusive thing: The effective after-tax cost of interest in different tax brackets and the general impact of federal taxes on dollars as they are generated throughout the projection period; or the repayment of borrowed dollars "down the road" with softer, devalued dollars, assuming the level of contract interest rate does not sufficiently reflect inflationary expectations.

PRESENT VALUE ESTIMATES

To an investor buying the equity in a real estate position or anything else, present value estimates indicate how many dollars (both equity and debt) will be or should be paid out to acquire the investment; based on investment objectives present values can also point to a position available in the marketplace at a price the investor is willing to pay. Investors of all sorts buy the future—not history!

Stock prices, sometimes analogous to real estate prices, also reflect investor expectations about the course of future events. Accordingly, stock markets are always discounting the future. An investor buying stock either agrees with the wisdom of the marketplace or elects to challenge it one way or another by buying or selling. An investor buying stocks always tries to find those issues whose current price is below or at least equal to a projected estimate of its present value. As with real estate, the investor should often remember that, although a pot of gold at the end of the rainbow is the goal, the risk of ending up in an investment quagmire is always present. In great part, investment professionalism is the ability to interpret if the current asking price of any investment is adequately discounting for the future.

To repeat, the value of every kind of real or personal property held for investment purposes is the present worth of all future net benefits. The professional real estate appraiser or investment analyst is merely called upon to convert this simple sounding but horribly complex axiom into an arithmetic present value estimate. To do it correctly, the investor should identify:

1 What will be all the future gross benefits flowing from the investment? When and how often will each one occur?

2 What will be all the capital and/or operating costs necessary to generate and trigger the gross benefits, and at what points in time will they be expended?

3 What rates should be used to discount the net benefits back to present worth? Where did the rates come from? How long will they persist? Are they before-tax or after-tax rates? Is there a higher probability that some of the net benefits will come on line as predicted? If so, could an appraiser logically be expected to use a lesser rate, and vice versa? At what rates will the investor be able to reinvest the receipts and how quickly, or does market behavior suggest that receipts appear to merely pass through the particular kind of investment being appraised at a fixed point in time?

4 Over what time frame or holding period does the investor typically hold the investment?

RETURN ON INVESTMENT (ROI)

Return on investment might be defined as the rate of interest (yield) at which the present worth of all the future net benefits equals the original amount of investment —or that rate of interest which equates the present worth of the outflows with the present worth of the inflows. It is interesting to observe that the power of compounding and discounting at different rates over longer time spans can be an awesome thing to behold. Compound interest is one of the most potent forces in the investment markets. It occurs not only in fixed income-type investments (that is, savings accounts, mortgages), but also in the minds of all kinds of equity investors as well.

Capital is brought into being and moved into action by the opportunity to earn yield, either anticipated or contractual. Risk has been defined by some as "the variance between the anticipated and the actual." A discount of interest rate has to do primarily with the degree of risk involved in placing a bet on a potential investment, as well as the degree of probability that each future net benefit will come on line when and as predicted—given the opportunity cost of the investment.

In analyzing return on investment, the investor might array and compare different but similar alternative investment opportunities within something like the following oversimplified sequence:

1 As an investor, what alternatives do I have to invest capital, consistent with my primary investment objectives?

2 Investment opportunities of all sorts have become increasingly complex and numerous.

3 The need for a common measure (ROI)—the benefits as well as the outlays—can be estimated and the results expressed in dollars and then as a percentage.

4 Alternative investment opportunities within the type can then be ranked according to some common measure (ROI), and a ranking or cut-off point will guide acceptance or rejection.

Whether it is realized or not, the unsophisticated investor who buys that 10-unit apartment property is unconsciously thinking ROI, as is a large financial institution in its efforts to formalize this sort of analysis on computers.

In essence, ROI analysis efforts pay tribute to the thought that an investor, when investing in anything (including real estate) does not buy a yield, but rather the assumptions and expectations that create the estimated "paper" yield over a projected holding period. No one ever really knows for sure what the actual yield will really be until the investment is "cashed out" at some future time.

Thus it has been suggested that five basic concepts motivate investors to act. To summarize, they are the concepts of:

The ideal investment.
Opportunity cost.
Time value of money.
Present value estimates.
Return on investment.

Investment analysts face the challenge of mirroring and quantifying these concepts in each investment opportunity. If they do so effectively and consistently, they will become not only the world's best investment analysts, but also its most knowledgeable investors.

INVESTMENT RISKS

During recent years, excellent articles have been published concerning long-standing capital decision-making analysis, valuation, and counseling. Interest and attention in these areas have coincided with an increasing utilization of statistical logic and procedures in real estate situations, made easier by the advent of more economical and understandable computer hardware and investment program software.

The purpose of the next section is to examine the foundational concepts connected with risk as this critical word relates to investor motivation and investment analysis. It is not the purpose of this section to examine the known methods for estimating investment yield (reward, return), or to demonstrate with numbers the little-understood statistical techniques that often are utilized in seemingly frustrating and perhaps even impractical and unrealistic efforts to quantify or measure levels of investment risk, which very few real estate investors attempt to do formally when setting investment objectives or making purchase decisions.

Accordingly, the target of this material is the reader who would like to explore the most basic risk/reward concepts and strategies present in all investor thinking, both within and without real estate, be they emotional or logical. This theme will be developed as follows:

1 Philosophy and nature of investment risk.
2 Risk analysis.
3 Risk management.
4 Risk level measurement.

PHILOSOPHY AND NATURE OF INVESTMENT RISK

Nothing seems to work these days, because there are so many opportunities for failure:

The mails are late.
Some businesses and railroads are on the verge of bankruptcy.
Products fail and people are laid off.
Fuel is uncertain and expensive.
Real estate investments go "belly up."

Failure is a much more complex and elusive notion than most have thought. It is the inability of a mechanism to fulfill the function for which it was designed, and this definition can apply to investors and investments as well as people and things in general. Failure is being recognized at last for what it is: a possibility as well as an acknowledgment that failure and success are opposites, permitting each to be discussed in terms of the other.

Every investor knows there is no such thing as absolute certainty, that there is no way to steal second base and keep one's foot on first base, no matter how low the return or reward. Accordingly, uncertainty is both a threat and an opportunity pointing to a failure/success spectrum that recognizes that investment uncertainty can lead to absolute failure, relative failure, relative success, or absolute success.

Investment Risk

Risk is all-pervasive in the business of making investments of all kinds. It has to do with the capacity to live with and the efforts to control uncertainty. It also relates to future happenings. The income approach to value definition (value is the present worth of future benefits) depends on the future being as the investor or market forecasts it to be. Dissected, this entire approach to value is a study of the risk/reward relation.

Investment risk often has been described as follows:

1 In the eyes of the investor, the notion of risk is related to the uncertainty of achieving a desired result.
2 The chance or probability that the investor will not receive the expected or required rate of return that he desires on an investment.
3 The potential variance between investment expectations and investment realizations; in financial parlance, the difference between *pro forma* prospects and actual results, or, if you will, the difference between the "easy words and the limping deeds."

Risk Taker vs. Risk Averter

Billie Jean King was quoted recently as saying: "No one believes in World Team Tennis. Nobody believes in women's sports. Most people don't believe in anything until after the fact. *They don't want to take the risk.* It's like teaching players to go for it and take the hard shot."

There is no question that emotional and temperamental considerations play a large part in a specific investor's reaction to risk taking. Some investors are risk takers by nature; they not only welcome risk but seem to defy it. Others opt to avoid it at almost all costs. It is probably true that most investors lean toward minimizing risk exposure, preferring relatively lower-return certainty to higher-return uncertainty. Ms. King is no doubt right: most investors prefer the defensive lob to the "gutsy" chance winner down the alley.

It is also often true that an investor tends to become less conservative as wealth increases; furthermore, the attitude toward risk may depend on whose money is "on the line."

Risk Taker by Design

It is logical to hope that the goal of an intelligent, rational investor is not to be a risk taker by nature, but a risk taker by design. The risk taker should ask:

1　What are my specific investment objectives?
2　How much can I afford to lose?
3　How can I recognize, analyze, manage, and measure risk?
4　Are all the remaining risks I cannot manage worth the return I associate with the investment opportunity?

Unfortunately, relatively few investors have specific investment objectives. Even fewer seem to expend much formal effort in analyzing, managing, and measuring risk.

RISK ANALYSIS

Taking his words somewhat out of context from an excellent 1974 speech titled "Uncertainty—Threat and Opportunity," Dr. Carl Spetzler of Stanford Research Institute noted that "uncertainty is running rampant and there seems to be no safe place to hide." He went on to comment that man's ancient recipe for such tremendous uncertainty is simple: "Shift the burden for decision making by consulting oracles, sticking one's head in the sand, calling in astronomers, or reading sheep entrails." He went on to observe that "man's ability to perceive and estimate uncertainty is not developed, and his intuitive abilities to process uncertainty to reach conclusions are virtually nonexistent."

Dr. Spetzler proceeded to describe the reasons for *Homo sapiens'* difficulty in making good judgments about uncertainty:

1　*We think we know more than we do.* As a result, we are surprised too often. The unexpected seems to happen, and we are caught off guard.

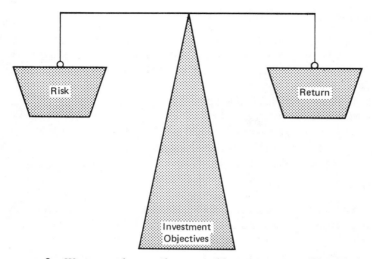

2 *We overvalue easily accessible information.* We simply judge the likeliness of events on the basis of the ease with which we can recall or imagine such events.

3 *We don't revise our judgments in a rational manner.* We are overly conservative information processors and, as a result, fail to extract from data as much information as the data contain. (The human psyche has difficulty dealing with the unpleasant, the improbable, and the unthinkable.)

4 *Our intuition can't deal with complexity.* Under conditions of presumed certainty, we can deal with only about three variables; when uncertainty is added, we have great difficulty coping with just two.

5 *We aren't clear about what we want.* There is great variance among decision makers as to what risks are acceptable, presuming first that all risks are mutually identified and agreed to.

General Categories of Investment Risk

Risk analysis is the orderly process of identifying *all* the uncertainties of any investment opportunity to get a total picture of the downside risks involved—particularly those of a major sort. There are said to be three general categories of risk attached to any kind of investment:

1 *Market risk.* The risk of loss caused by changes unrelated to the intrinsic characteristics of the investment. Real estate does not exist isolated within its own economic, political, and social vacuum. Some examples are:

    a National economic trends, such as unemployment and recession or longer-term inflation.

    b A deteriorating regional economic base.

    c Economic obsolescence, perhaps due to a changing neighborhood environment.

    d Flood, fire, and other natural or man-made disasters.

2 *Business risk.* The risk of loss caused by the intrinsic characteristics of the investment. Some examples are:

a A second mortgage or subordinated land fee.

b Higher-risk properties, such as a seasonal second-rate motel or special-purpose property occupied by an average-credit tenant.

c Functional inutility, lack of quality construction, or simply age in a general-purpose property.

d Those kinds of properties having high operating expense ratios and requiring very specialized kinds of management (that is, nursing homes, hotels).

3 *Money or capital risk*. The risk of losing net income, cash flow, principal, or purchasing power. Some examples are:

a Simply paying too much.

b The availability, terms, and effective cost of financing of all sorts and its effect on present and future value. In 1975, many learned painfully that leverage is always important but not always favorable.

c Recapture or return of capital invested, often referred to as payback expectations. In any uncertain real estate investment climate, how soon does the investor get a return—in terms of real dollars, that is? Do others have a prior claim on income and assets? If so, is the investor personally or corporately liable to any one of them?

d The reinvestment risk. Investment portfolio total return is made up of three elements, not just current yield and investment appreciation. In order to achieve an effective actual total return on any portfolio over a specified holding period equal to the estimated yield to maturity at the time of investment, current income must be reinvested at that yield to maturity. Clearly, future levels and continuity of interest rates and investment yields over the entire investment period are major determinants of portfolio total return.

Emotional vs. Rational Risk Taker

The *emotional* investment risk taker is prone to think:

1 If I always took the time to think about all the risks, I'd never do anything. By the time most investors' thinking crystallizes into consensus, the opportunity for profitable action is gone. Look at the stock market.

2 I could get hit by a truck tomorrow, too. I'm a fatalist. I have a gut feeling based on experience that this is a good deal and, furthermore, I got a hot tip.

3 Forecast the future? If economists, mortgage bankers, and investment analysts are that bright, why aren't they wealthy like me?

4 I'm not like others who can't see the top of the mountain (a high return) for all the trees (risks). If you think this way, put your money in a savings bank or in a box under your bed; don't go into real estate.

On the other hand, the rational, albeit successful, risk taker works quickly and carefully, understands the importance of complete risk identification, and has the insight to extrapolate the possible downside ramifications of all major risks that cannot be avoided. Such a person is not prone to state that the return is worth the risks without carefully analyzing the latter.

RISK MANAGEMENT—TECHNIQUES AND STRATEGIES

It has been said truly that many so-called investors manage money, but that the really successful ones manage risk, the idea being not to avoid risk but to be skilled at identifying it, coping with it, and then living with it under acceptable circumstances.

The risk management concept is paramount in the insurance industry, where the ceding party (the insured) substitutes the certainty of a smaller, known loss (a premium) for the uncertainty of a larger and perhaps devastating loss (for example, death, fire, major illness). Insurance companies that continue to stay in business never risk more than they can afford to lose, never risk a lot for a little, and always consider the odds. Before setting the price of any policy or approving a particular application, actuaries and underwriters are paid, along with others, to seek answers to the following kinds of questions having to do with reducing the chance of loss:

1 What hazards create the risk of loss?
2 Can they be avoided or eliminated?
3 Can any remaining risks be controlled?
4 How can losses be minimized?
5 Is there a need to reinsure the risk?
6 What are the trade-offs and the costs?

Techniques for Managing Investment Risk

Although there is admittedly some overlap, there are essentially three general techniques for managing investment risk. These are:

1 *Avoiding risk*, which means the investor simply refuses to invest after a risk analysis study. Some examples are:
   a Lend $1,000 to my brother-in-law.
   b The risk is the return, and 12 percent is not high enough. (I will buy at a present value or price that reflects a 15 percent return, or I'm not interested.)
   c In unsettled times of great uncertainty, liquidity is favored over commitment. In real estate investment, there is a time for action and a time for patience, when it is prudent to think more about downside risks than upside rewards. (I think the market is overbuilt right now; I'm investing in short-term Treasury bills and corporate commercial paper for the time being.)
   d Individual endorsement or guaranty of a large mortgage. (If I have to be personally liable on the mortgage, I'm not about to buy the equity in that apartment property.)
2 *Tranferring risk*, which means that the investor refuses to consider the investment unless he can unload all or part of the risk on someone else. Some examples are:
   a Fire, flood, and title insurance.
   b Under a high percent-to-value FHA-insured loan, the mortgagee's ultimate recourse is to the FHA with respect to the recovery of any principal;

with a variable-rate conventional mortgage, the lender attempts to shift the major concern with inflationary expectations to the borrower.

c In an era of precipitously increasing construction costs, the developer/landlord attempts to transfer the risk of uncertain leasehold improvement "first" costs to the tenant by simply building the "shell," and via the lease contract, likes to convey the likelihood of escalating ongoing operating "second" cost risks to the tenant, thus maintaining an absolute net overall position.

d Although the timing of the benefits differs widely among different kinds of tax-sheltered investments, the relative amount of risk varies with the tax bracket. Clearly, the 70 percent-tax-bracket investor has the greatest incentive to shelter, because only 30 cents of every dollar is ostensibly at risk; the balance has been shifted, temporarily, to Uncle Sam. (Unfortunately, many tax shelter-seeking investors often become so bedazzled by tax savings that they forget more important real estate investment considerations—that ultimately the piper must be paid.)

3 *Reducing risk*, which means that the investor minimizes or spreads any remaining risk by a variety of tactics. Some examples are:

a *To diversify*. Minimize volatility by spreading the risk with respect to the size, type, and location of investments within a given portfolio. Like mutual funds, REITs originally were devised with the intention of providing diversification for smaller investors desiring to get into real estate.

b *To option*. For a consideration, to temporarily control a real estate investment opportunity that appears outwardly attractive until a complete risk and return analysis can be completed.

c *To hedge*. To inventory land, building materials, and even blocks of permanent mortgage financing for future use, in the face of anticipated price increases.

d *To margin*. Decreasing the investment payback period requirement or increasing the "hurdle" rate return requirement—arbitrary actions that reduce the price the investor is willing to pay to buy into the investment.

e *To participate*. Selling partial interests in either the equity or mortgage investment to others, thus reducing a larger risk exposure via limited partnerships, syndications, etc., in much the same fashion as an insurance company reinsures a portion of a potential larger loss with other insurance companies.

Risk Taker by Design

Modern risk management techniques are not related to being either a generalist or a detail man, an optimist or a pessimist, a determinist or a fatalist, nor do they have anything to do with 100 percent hindsight vision, wearing rose-colored glasses, or making "windshield" appraisals.

Again, the rational investor/risk taker:

1 Specifically delineates the investment objectives as to return and other goals.
2 Identifies all the possible risks, particularly the major ones.

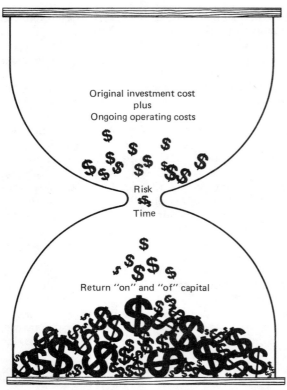

Original investment cost
plus
Ongoing operating costs

Risk

Time

Return "on" and "of" capital

   3 Eliminates certain risks, transfers others, and puts "fences" around some remaining ones by a variety of means.
   4 Decides whether or not the estimated returns and rewards are worth the risks still remaining.
   5 Makes a "go/no go" decision.

MEASURING LEVELS OF INVESTMENT RISK

When once asked what the stock market would do, J. P. Morgan was purported to have said: "It will fluctuate!" Along with deterministic forecasts having to do with the absolute certainty of death and taxes, his prediction appears to have been a safe and continuing one, compared to attempting to select a risk-adjusted rate of return for a given investment opportunity.

   Indeed, *the risk is the rate* and the rational investor not only will think about them both, but in that order. The risk/reward ratio is the relation between remaining potential hazards and hoped-for future benefits.

Investment Yield

Briefly, investment reward means primarily return on investment (ROI), which means yield. Depending on the nature and type of investment under analysis and the method employed, real estate investment yield (%) could be labeled interest, equity dividend rate (R_e), equity yield (Y), discounted cash flow rate of return, before- or after-tax internal rate of return, or a variety of other nicknames.

Within and without real estate finance, there are at least three general truisms that can be stated categorically about any kind of investment yield:

1 It has been defined as that rate of return at which:
  a The present worth of all future net benefits equals the original amount of investment.
  b The present worth of the outflows (costs) equals the present worth of the inflows (benefits).

2 An investor does not buy a yield, but, rather, the risk assumptions and return expectations that create the estimated "paper" yield over a projected holding period (n). The investor never knows for sure what the yield is or was until the investment either matures or is sold.

3 As previously stated, in order for any investment portfolio to achieve an effective actual total return over a specified holding period equal to its estimated yield to maturity, current income must be reinvested at that yield to maturity. Many forget this critical third element of portfolio total return.

Measuring Risk—State of the Art

Dr. Stephen Pyhrr of the University of Texas has done as much market-related research in the area of real estate investment risk measurement as anyone. In a 1972 Toronto address, Dr. Pyhrr said:

> Real estate decision-makers claim they take "calculated risks," but few of them make very clear just how they calculate these risks. Traditionally, because of the difficulties, the dislike, or the lack of knowledge of how to deal explicitly with risk in decisions, most people concentrated on a few key assumptions about the future, examined a few rules of thumb, mulled over the situation, and then decided. Although some of the risk considerations were explicit, most of the mathematics of risk was left to the four horsemen of the implicit decision making apparatus: judgment, hunch, instinct, and intuition.

Very little progress is discernible today in the area of efforts to quantify levels of investment risk in either the actual practice of real estate investment valuation and analysis, or, for that matter, anywhere within the universe of finance. The world of investment continues to slop over with banal generalizations and buzzword-type phrases on the subject. Witness the following:

1 "We would gladly take *more risk* if we thought by doing so we could enjoy a superior performance."

2 "The general objective of portfolio 'X' will be to have its assets managed in a manner intended to maximize total return from both current yield and capital appreciation commensurate with a *moderate level of risk*."

3 "The general objective of the investment functions of this corporation is to manage the assets of its affiliated companies in such a manner as to optimize the rate of return on its assets and to invest prudently but *not take undue risks*."

Response to a 1974 Conference Board survey entitled ''Appraising Pension Fund Investment Performance'' indicated that, if there was a consensus among the great many administered and self-administered pension funds reporting—all of them large and presumably sophisticated, it was clearly as follows:

1 Even if the elements of a successful investment performance can be defined, it is not easy to measure them.
2 Pension fund risk requirements and directives to portfolio managers are usually couched in vague terms. For example, money managers may be advised to invest ''prudently,'' or not to take ''undue risks'' to achieve return objectives.
3 Practically all funds supplying information on performance appraisal made no effort whatsoever to quantify risk levels.

As to a summary of the state of the art, one astute observer of the scene noted recently in the weekly newspaper *Pensions and Investments* that ''Measuring risk has attracted much business and academic talent and investment attention in recent years. If risk could be measured in advance, returns might be better understood. . . . As interesting as this work has been, it is still rampant with problems in application.''

Measuring Risk—Zeroing In

Unfortunately, real estate does not have available to it a Moody's or a Standard and Poor's to place risk quality ratings on each investment opportunity. Envisage a AAA risk rating being attached in advance by outsiders on all available real estate investments of the highest quality, whereas a BBB rating would reflect a risk situation ''of a medium-grade opportunity borderline between definitely sound obligations and those where the speculative elements begin to dominate.'' Other than opinions of lonely valuators and analysts, a given real estate investment opportunity has no early warning system where risk is measured in advance in lettered decibels.

We can say a risk is worth taking if it brings appropriate rewards and/or returns. We can also say that risk level toleration always should relate to investment (portfolio) objectives. Furthermore, any investor's game plan should be to optimize (not maximize) the combination of risk and return, that is, to obtain the highest rate of return at a specific risk level or the lowest risk at a specified rate of return level.

Four Key Words

Any system that attempts to attach numbers to a given level of investment risk has to be concerned with the following four key words, which lend themselves in combination to statistical logic and procedures. They are:

1 *Comparison*. The risk involved in a specific investment is calculated only by comparing that investment to others or to a base kind of investment, for example, a long-term government bond. For instance, we know that a second mortgage is riskier than a first mortgage on the same property and that the level of relative risk exposure between the two depends in great part on the total value of the property.
The so-called *beta* coefficient, a statistical measurement of risk, is essentially a

comparison between the performance of a specific portfolio of common stocks and the stock market in general.

2 *Forecasting*. The future is always a moving target, and forecasting has to do with trying to improve the aim. A forecast is a prediction of the future based on certain presumptions, while a projection is simply an extension of the past. Certainly, one way to reduce the unpredictability of risk is to reduce the margin of error by making better forecasts—there are sampling, interviewing, and other statistical techniques for accomplishing just that.

3 *Probability*. As the weatherman said, "Of course, that 10 percent chance of rain has a 30 percent chance of changing to 20 percent by afternoon."

The only explicit language for measuring uncertainty or risk is probability, and it is possible to be trained in the language and logic of probability without being an expert in the mathematics of statistics.

The theory of probability has to do with the laws of chance. If one can determine what the odds are that an event (a 14 percent yield) will occur in one case, one then can predict with fair accuracy how often it will occur in large numbers of case simulations—particularly with the aid of high-speed computers. Probability has to do with predicting by relying on samples and hoping that the good Lord has not shuffled the deck too badly.

Risk is influenced by both the odds of various events occurring and the magnitude of the rewards or penalties that are involved. Risk can be related to investment or

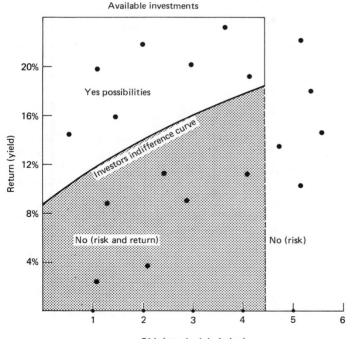

portfolio volatility. Some believe volatility can be displayed as spread on a graph. Accordingly, the level of risk is measured in terms of the dispersion of the distribution of possible or expected yields by means of a simple range or a more commonly used standard deviation.

It is well to remember that risk measurement also has to do with least likely outcomes as well as most probable ones.

4 *Sensitivity*. In July, 1975, Connecticut Blue Cross announced a $5 million operating loss for the first five months of the year. The primary reason for the red ink appeared to be a trend toward ''defensive'' medicine, that is, physicians ordering large numbers of laboratory tests and special hospital services in an effort to preclude the possibilities of later malpractice suits, a highly sensitive matter to physicians.

To oversimplify, sensitivity analysis has to do with improving the quality of input data by paying a great deal of attention to the critical variable(s) impacting on an investment decision, after carefully including and weighing the relative importance of all the factors and variables influencing its outcome.

One commonly used and practical sensitivity technique is the so-called three-level estimate of investment outcome. The analyst simply displays in tiers three predictions of investment yield over the same time, reflecting optimistic, most probable, and pessimistic inputs and outcomes. The resultant spread or range of yield results represents variance or volatility in possible risk, and the rational risk taker/investor ''places his bet'' by attempting to purchase the investment position at a present value that reflects sensible risk analysis conclusions and investment objectives.

SO WHAT!?

Is it really worth the effort for the busy practitioner to expend valuable time and energy to learn more, when a great deal of information is available on these subjects? Too often, this author has listened to unprofessional cop-outs from prominent mortgage bankers (and others). ''If I can't explain it to a borrower or a financial institution, what good is it?'' He also has heard himself and others argue with some degree of logic, uncertainty, and rare conviction that ''very few investors have specific investment objectives to start with, and furthermore, how does one put a number on the level of risk when it is conceded that most investors react to risk temperamentally and emotionally, using words instead of numbers? How is anyone supposed to quantify any process where so little rationale and formal order seem to exist? The rational risk taker, logical decision maker/investor! Has anyone ever met this phantom real estate personality?'' Who is so able among us to measure emotion and so bold as to forecast the future with any degree of confidence? Carried to a logical conclusion, the persuasiveness of this kind of argument would suggest that we dispense with the investment analysis altogether and fly by the seats of our pants!

The Sermon

We know very few things for sure, but we do know that investors of all sorts buy futures and not history. We also know that the present value of any kind of investment is the present worth of all future net benefits. It is our usual charge as appraisers to measure present market value, and as analysts to explain and interpret the actions of real estate investors who are looking ahead and not backward. We have been taught by experience and by our more knowledgeable predecessors and peers to at once respect and question both the inadequacy and the sanctity of data of all sorts. We have been quick to recognize that all too often the tools we have to work with are too few and too simple for use in these more complicated times. Acknowledging the fine line between presumptions and hope, most of us have concluded that there is still no way we can avoid the potential pitfalls of attempting to forecast the future or the frustrations of trying to quantify human behavior, other than to vacate the scene and find some other niche in this imperfect world we share.

In recent years, much has been written but very little new has been developed concerning modern capital and financial market theory and its application to real estate investments. *All* of what the real estate professions have "discovered" more recently has been known for quite some time. The real estate industry has been slow to adapt and update, but it is rapidly catching up; the momentum is strong. On the other hand, it is only fair to observe that relatively few people in the entire universe of investment and finance really understand a great deal about these related subjects, and this indictment is meant to apply to those in the securities and mortgage banking fields, as well as others employed by large and seemingly sophisticated financial institutions, including insurance companies.

To charge that any investment concept, theory, or analytic process is unrealistic can mean that it is. It also can mean that it is valid yet impractical in the sense that neither the mortgage banker, the client, nor the market understands it. If the latter is the case, then the problem becomes one of education and communication. Practical solutions and effective progress always require time, effort, and gradual application.

STATE OF THE SCIENCE

It is suggested respectfully that mortgage bankers and investment analysts who spend time "kicking the tires" of investment-type real estate would do well to gear to the present and anticipate the future by learning a great deal about:

1 *Basic statistics*. These are measurements of central tendency and dispersion, sampling and forecasting techniques, as well as regression, probability, and sensitivity analyses. To utilize the inexact but known methods for measuring levels of risk, it is mandatory to understand the difference between terms such as static risks and dynamic risks, uncertain variables and control variables, indifference curves and preference curves, and efficient frontiers and efficient markets.

2 *Present value estimates*. In terms of real or current dollars, how much is the investment opportunity worth? Which capitalization method is most appropriate to use in estimating the kind of present value being sought? What are the differences between investment value, market value, and net present value? How and when is discounted cash flow analysis used?

3 *Yield estimates*. The risk/return concept is endemic to the entire investment concept. Return means yield. How does the marketplace measure yield for the type of investment being analyzed? What does internal rate of return mean, and how does one calculate it both before and after taxes? Investors have alternatives within and without real estate. For instance, what motivates investors to buy common stocks or municipal bonds? How are present value and yield calculated for such investments?

4 *Computer technology*. It is not possible over any acceptable time span for a human being to manually perform the multiple simulations required by many of the techniques to which I have alluded. Economical hardware and quality commercial software make practical methods heretofore considered impractical, because the calculation time contours have been abbreviated almost to instancy.

However, the major challenge is not an ability to operate sophisticated calculators or mini-computers, or even to comprehend modern statistical, present value, and yield concepts. The real challenges are to make certain that *all* of the necessary input variables are present in any investment analysis program and then to forecast and inject quality data. Never forget that computers merely have a maximum capability to receive, retain, manipulate, and display data as programmed—none can originate data, exercise judgment, or interpret results.

Chapter 4

Negotiating the
Loan Application

Howard M. Stearns, Jr.

The financing of income property is most certainly not an exact science and assumptions can be misleading and costly. However, it is necessary to make a few.

    1   We have specifically identified the parties to the transaction.

    2   We have evaluated the property in question and have decided that it qualifies as security for the recommended loan.

    3   We have, on at least a strong preliminary basis, evaluated the borrower's financial condition and credit standing, and believe it to qualify in relation to the loan being recommended.

    4   We have determined that there are no obvious legal obstructions, such as usury or zoning violations to the making of the loan in question.

The art or function of negotiating and taking a loan application is most definitely a complicated undertaking no matter how simple it may sound or how willing all parties may appear to be. With the above assumptions established, let us proceed to examine the preliminary steps that must be taken before formally negotiating with the borrower.

Determine the Borrower's Real Objectives   This is the most important aspect of negotiating the application—and usually the most difficult. There are many factors which combine to create a loan. Several, but not all, include amount, rate, term, maturity, prepayment option, and personal liability or lack thereof. Obviously, in a world of negotiation and compromise, it is a rare borrower indeed who actually ends up with a loan that incorporates literally every factor desired on an optimum basis. It is, therefore, necessary to determine which factor or factors are most important in order to know where the borrower is most likely to be vulnerable in negotiations.

Examples of this are myriad, but one or two can be outlined to demonstrate the point. A nonprofit corporate borrower does not deduct interest and therefore wants the lowest rate possible. An individual borrower with excess depreciation may want to maximize cash flow. A borrower who plans to expand and refinance a property within five years will not wish to accept a prepayment clause which prohibits any prepayment of the loan during the first ten years.

We must also remember that borrowers—even though they may be corporate entities from a legal standpoint—are individuals and as such are subject to all human frailties such as ego, prejudice, love, hate, and varying moral standards. This, to a greater or lesser degree, contributes to a borrower's real objective.

A mortgage banker once almost failed to sign up an applicant on terms that were definitely ''market'' until he learned that the borrower had bragged at his country club and to his associates that he would obtain a lower rate. His pride would not let him accept the loan rate offered. The problem was resolved by offering the loan at the requested lower rate but with a substantial discount that resulted in the lender's receiving the same yield as was anticipated in the original offering.

Whenever possible, it is wise to spend sufficient time with the borrower and the borrower's associates to get to know and understand them. Keep abreast of market and political conditions which directly or indirectly affect the borrower and, most of all, stay alert to the borrower's attitudes, comments, and responses. This will enable you to identify their real objectives and will go a long way toward clarifying and solving the problem of taking the application.

Determine the Lender's Goals   This is almost identical in importance to the borrower's objective and rates second only because it is somewhat easier to determine. The lender is usually an institution and, as such, many of its requirements are rather inflexibly set by law, practical competition, or company policy. A minimum acceptable yield is usually just that—barring market changes. A percentage of assets which may be invested in certain types of security cannot be exceeded. A set loan-to-value ratio may not be exceeded, although this is not entirely inflexible, since the valuation or appraisal of a security is not a science and is subject to human interpretation.

It is important to stay in constant touch with the investor by mail, phone, and personal contact, and to stay abreast of all conditions affecting the lender's industry to understand as completely as possible the set goals at the time of application.

This is only half the job, however—the easy half! A lending institution is run by individuals with their own likes and dislikes, their own feelings of security or insecurity, and their own interpretations of company policy as well as reflections of company personality. Obviously, a knowledge of their attitudes is extremely important, if not essential, to successful negotiation of the application.

It should be emphasized that institutional lenders vary greatly as to the manner in which they wish to be approached, and ignorance of or deviation from their wishes and/or practices may cause your proposal to be effectively eliminated from serious consideration. Some lenders deal with relatively few representatives or correspondents; others deal with a wider number of brokers; others handle their mortgage and real estate activities directly themselves, and many use a combination of these approaches.

Some lenders prefer to be contacted by phone before a proposal is received; others wish to see it in writing; some welcome you to the home office; and others say ''stay away.''

Your problem is more than half solved once you have defined your borrower's objectives and determined your lender's goals.

Decide What Terms and Conditions You Can Properly Recommend under Any Given Set of Circumstances   The loan being considered may be on one specific piece of real property, but this loan or its terms is most certainly not a fixed, inflexible entity. As pointed out, the parties to the transaction have different goals and needs; also the worth of the property itself can vary widely, depending upon a vast number of varied circumstances. For example, one loan amount may make sense if the borrower is to be personally liable for the debt, but an entirely different amount is necessary otherwise. A loan on a specific type of real estate may be safely made to a borrower who has professional expertise, but it could be a disaster if made to an amateur. Any number of conditions imposed by federal, state, or local entities or by political or ecological considerations may make an otherwise good loan impossible or, at best, give it a much higher degree of risk. An open mind must be maintained and flexibility is the prime condition of negotiation.

Suppose a client phones with some gross and net income figures and asks you if it is possible to borrow a certain loan amount. While the client is still on the phone you can quickly see if you are in the ball park by making some quick calculations. This involves the theory of debt service coverage which is used by some institutional investors.

These investors take the net income figure and relate it to the amount of debt service required at a desired interest rate and amortization period.

To apply this theory one must determine five factors:

DC, or the Debt Coverage ratio desired.
N, or Net income.
DS, or Debt Service.
K, or annual Constant which incorporates both the desired interest rate and amortization period.
L, or Loan amount.

The basic formula for finding the loan amount is:

$$\left[\frac{N}{DC} = DS \right] \div K \times 100 = L$$

Putting this to practical use, let us consider that we have a new apartment house to be built in an area where we believe there should be good demand for it. We are comfortable with the proposed rentals and forecasted expenses, and after deducting a sum for vacancy and rent loss, the net income is estimated to be $54,000 per year. Because of the speculative nature of the project, the lender has determined the need for 1.5 coverage. In other words, the net income before debt service should be one and one-half times the amount needed to service the debt. A competitive interest rate in today's market is 9½% and a 28-year amortization term is equal to a 10.23 constant (or K).

Using the formula to find the loan amount

$$\left[\frac{\$54,000}{1.5} = \$36,000\right] \div 10.23 \times 100 = L$$

$351,907, say $350,000 = L$

Now let us take the same apartment after it has been completed and has two or three years of good experience. The lender feels that the investment would be a safe one with 1.3 coverage rather than 1.5. Let us assume that all of the other factors are the same. Again, using the formula

$$\left[\frac{\$54,000}{1.3} = \$41,538\right] \div 10.23 \times 100 = L$$

$406,045, say $400,000 = L$

In the second example, we are willing to lend more money, because we will settle for less coverage on our debt service with this proven product. Debt service coverage desired is a means of regulating the loan amount.

There are no set formulae for determining the desired debt service coverage. This is a matter of judgment on the part of each lender and some will temper that judgment with personal likes and dislikes. It might also vary with individual loan offerings in the same category. For instance, two loans offered at the same time on garden apartments in Houston and Detroit might, because of the competitive demand in those cities at that particular time, warrant coverages of 1.2 and 1.4 respectively.

In other categories, a lender might consider coverage as low as 1.1 on a loan where there is a net long-term lease to a very strong tenant, requiring no management or future expense to the owner, and further providing for full amortization of the loan during the term of the lease. On the other end of the spectrum, the lender might be seeking debt coverage of 2.0 or even higher where income is of a more volatile nature such as with a resort hotel property.

This does not imply a total disregard of all appraisal principles. The most important key in estimating any loan amount is to accurately determine the net income attributable to the property. This is where the underwriting is done.

Of course, after one has the loan amount, one needs to consider whether of not it qualifies as an investment not exceeding 75 percent of value. Most lenders are restricted to this ratio by regulatory authorities and will require an appraisal for their files with a value estimate which indicates that the loan does not exceed 75 percent. This can also provide you with an additional check as to whether or not your indication makes sense.

To go back to the two examples, a loan of $350,000 will need to be supported by an appraised value estimate of $470,000. And a loan of $400,000 requires $535,000. Using the net income figure of $54,000, it would be necessary to use a capitalization rate of 11.5% to reach $470,000, and 10.1% for $535,000. Can these capitalization rates be supported? If not, then this would be an indication that the loan is in excess of 75 percent or perhaps it does not make any economic sense at all. One word of caution; just because the loan exceeds 75 percent of value does not mean that all lenders will reject it. Some are legally permitted to exceed that percentage figure where debt service is covered by qualified credit and the loan is fully amortized within the term of the lease.

It should be emphasized again that this can be an effective tool, but it is not meant to supplant the established methods of carefully appraising each loan.

LEGAL CONSIDERATIONS

An application is, to an extent, a legal contract. Unfortunately, the laws and customs of the 50 states vary and the enforceability of a contract and its actual form is subject to local law and custom. Included at the end of this chapter are some examples of form applications and authorizations. These are only a few of many used and all have their strengths and weaknesses. It is difficult, however, to find one that is truly perfect.

An application in some form is most always used because it is good business and because it sets the agreement between the parties to writing, decreasing the possibility of dispute and misunderstanding. It is a fact, however, that nothing can replace a strong rapport between the borrower and the mortgage banker and a strong moral commitment on the part of all parties. With many borrowers there can be more value in a handshake than in a signed application. In the event of a change in the situation, they would not consider going back on their word. They value their reputations as being greater than any quick gain that may accrue to them.

A MATTER OF MONEY

Any discussion of a mortgage loan should include consideration of the fee or fees to be exchanged between the parties. A complete understanding of the monetary considerations should be reached prior to the taking of the application, and this understanding should be set to writing either in the application itself or by separate agreement.

Fees may be paid by any party to any party and may or may not be refundable, depending upon their purpose and the circumstances surrounding the transaction. For instance, the borrower in today's economy normally pays a fee to the mortgage banker for securing the loan, but may also be required to pay a fee to the lender. This obviously affects the lender's yield.

It is customary for a fee to be paid by the borrower to the mortgage banker or lender at the time of the signing of the application to indicate the borrower's good faith. This is commonly referred to as a good faith deposit and is refundable to the borrower if the loan is not approved in accordance with the terms of the application. On the other hand, if the loan is approved and the resulting loan commitment is not accepted by the borrower, the fee is retained as liquidating damages and as compensation for expenses incurred. In this event, the fee may be retained by the mortgage banker, by the lender, or split in a manner agreed upon by both.

In the event the loan is approved and a commitment is issued and accepted, the lender usually requires a commitment fee. This fee may be refundable at the time the loan is closed in accordance with the terms of the commitment, or all or part of it may be retained by the lender—once again depending upon prior agreement. This fee may be deposited in cash or in some other form such as negotiable securities, irrevocable letter of credit, or personal or corporate note, depending upon acceptability to the lender.

The fee paid to the mortgage banker is normally for services rendered in obtaining the commitment. It is, therefore, usually due and payable upon delivery of the loan commitment in accordance with the terms of the application, or on terms other than set forth in the application, but acceptable to the borrower. Other arrangements can be made, of course, such as having the fee due at the loan closing or on a deferred basis, but any arrangement should be set forth clearly in writing.

In the case of any refundable fee, thought should be given to the depository. Some states have laws and/or customs that require escrow deposits with title companies or other fiduciary agents. Most well-established mortgage bankers and institutional lenders have sufficient financial integrity to be trusted with refundable monies. Unfortunately, there have been instances in the past where borrowers or prospective borrowers have deposited money with individuals or entities who have been either less than honest or who have run into severe financial difficulties, and the deposit disappeared. It is, therefore, prudent to decide on the depository for the fee as well as upon the fee itself.

Anyone engaged in the negotiation of an application is doing so in anticipation of being rewarded monetarily. Under these circumstances, the matter of money should be totally clarified and understood by all parties.

ACTUAL NEGOTIATION

An example of an actual negotiation might be as follows:

The borrower, Mr. Smith, owns a shopping center and wishes to obtain maximum financing at the lowest possible interest rate. You have determined that the property has a value of $1,500,000 and have reason to believe that your lender will consider a loan of $1,125,000—75 percent of value. You know that an interest rate of 9¾% is probably available but your lender requires 10%. In preliminary discussions with your lender, you point out strongly that 9¾% is available in the marketplace: the lender concurs, but states that the institutional money situation is such that committee approval cannot be obtained at anything less than 10%. Under the circumstances, you work with the lender and obtain an agreement to consider a loan term of 28 years, which is probably three years longer than a normal term for this particular type of property.

Upon arriving at Smith's office, you confidently present the application and, before he has finished reading the first paragraph, he says, "$1,125,000!" The Savings and Loan across the street offered me $1,200,000 at only 9¾%. Your reply might be, "Well, sir, I am not really surprised. Let's take a minute to examine my proposal before rejecting it. I am, admittedly, $75,000 low, but I am prepared to move rapidly and I am in a position to close the loan immediately. I doubt that you could get approval from the Savings and Loan within 60 days because the committee only meets once a month and, if this is true, it would probably take three or four months before you could close. I imagine you are paying an exorbitantly high rate of interest on your land and my fast action will not only stop that, but will, in addition, free up your bank lines for the projects. When the banks are as nervous as they are at the moment, this is an important consideration. In addition, Mr. Smith, I feel certain that the Savings and Loan will require you to be personally liable for all, or at least some portion, of this loan. You will note that my application excludes the possibility of any personal liability. In my humble opinion, this, combined with quick service, is probably worth $75,000."

Mr. Smith may reluctantly accept this without specific comment, but may make some statement to the effect that the quick closing you have offered is really not needed, stating that there is plenty of time to wait for action by the competitive Savings and Loan. Mr. Smith will also, undoubtedly, point out that you are ¼ of a point over the interest rate quoted by the competition. You should then inquire as to the amount of front-end fee to be charged by the Savings and Loan, and let's assume he says 1%, which is the same amount you are going to charge, so that makes no difference. You then counter with, "That's true, Mr. Smith, but if you go with them, who is going to represent you? You will have paid a 1% fee to them and they will be interested only in representing themselves. You pay a 1% fee to me and I will represent you, not only for the time it takes to obtain the commitment but in all negotiations until the loan is closed. In addition, I will be around after the loan is closed to handle any of the eventualities that always arise in connection with an income-producing property." Smith acknowledges this but is not overly impressed and continues to press the point that he is going to be paying you ¼% higher interest. You then suggest that the Savings and Loan will probably limit his term to 25 years. He agrees. You point out that the monthly payments on a loan of $1,125,000, at 9¾%, for 25 years, would be $10,031.25—10.7 constant, which is actually $37.50 a month more than the payments you detailed on your application. You further point out that, since interest is deductible for tax purposes, his cash flow before and after tax considerations will be greater with your loan than with the competition's, even though your interest rate is higher.

Beyond this logic, you point out the extensive knowledge of your investor concerning the type of property and the various problems involved with it, and predict that they will be much more understanding and willing to cooperate throughout the life of the loan. At this point, you stress that timing is of the essence and that if you are to provide the services you have promised, you must have his application immediately so that you can get to work. You might also point out the reality of market flexibility and that it would be advisable to "nail the financing down" before there is any detrimental change in the money market.

"The best laid plans . . ." All of the planning, preparation, and anticipation may go out of the window when you sit down face to face with the borrower to actually take the application.

Any transaction has to start somewhere and it is advisable to have a completed application or authorization letter fully prepared, in the form you prefer, so that it may be presented to the borrower. It is an equally good idea to have a supply of stationery and application blanks with you so that any required revisions can be taken care of immediately and the borrower's signature can be obtained without additional meetings at a later date.

Many books have been written on the art of negotiating and many are well worth reading. Suffice it is to say it is well to be totally honest and realistic with regard to your actual position. Analyze your relationship with all parties and realistically consider how much of the transaction you actually control. Once this has been done, it's up to you. Hold your head high and go forth to meet the borrower with the confidence of sound preparation and solid knowledge of your business and its markets.

One last comment on the subject of actual negotiation. It is virtually impossible to include all aspects or conditions of a loan application. At some point you, the borrower and the lender must take some portion of the deal on faith. This is fine and often even to be desired, since moral obligations are often more binding than those imposed by written conditions. Remember that moral obligation is a two-way street and that you will be expected to back up your promises just as you expect the borrower and lender to back up theirs.

MISCELLANEOUS COMMENTS

A few additional random subjects remain to be dealt with. "Promise her anything but give her—" is a well-known advertising slogan but does not usually hold up well in negotiating a mortgage application. Mortgage bankers and lenders have been guilty of "lowballing." This is the practice of taking an application for an amount or on terms that are unrealistic on the premise that even though the approved loan is not as set forth in the application it can be "sold" to the borrower. This is a technique that sometimes works and is sometimes justified, but it should be avoided because it is normally unnecessary. It usually leaves a bad taste in the borrower's mouth and will generally make the person more difficult to work with later on in the deal in question as well as in any future deals.

Time is an all-important factor in the application process. The borrower may take 18 months to sign an application but upon doing so will expect an answer "yesterday." Borrowers are generally not very patient and lenders are not always very fast. It is up to the mortgage banker to properly analyze the time factor, keep proper pressure on the lender, and give reasonable assurance to the borrower so that the time required to move the application to the commitment level will be reasonable and proper under the circumstances of the specific loan and the property involved.

Lastly, all parties should be prepared for renegotiation. It is a deplorable fact—but fact nevertheless—that your hard-won application will probably be changed by the lender. The lender must deal with a large number of "decision makers" and may make minor changes in the loan. The mortgage banker must be prepared for this and be willing to provide the stability, knowledge, and negotiating expertise to hold the specific transaction together.

In conclusion, the mortgage business is a "people" business. As such, it is not exact, nor is it predictable. It does require constant, top-grade negotiating ability. The application is an all-important first step toward completing the mortgage transaction and the mortgage banker is, in the true sense, the "middle man" in negotiating that application.

EXHIBITS: EXAMPLES OF APPLICATION
AND AUTHORIZATION FORMS

Income-property loan producers throughout the country are split in their opinions as to the use of preprinted application forms or individual authorization letters. The advantage of the individual letter is that it deals with the essence of the particular transaction and may be tailored to various state laws and local customs.

Any application or authorization letter should be carefully reviewed to make certain that it complies with and reflects the spirit of state and federal laws and that it reflects the total understanding of the contemplated transaction.

The exhibits included here are as follows:

Exhibit 1—Mortgage loan application used by a major life insurance company.
Exhibit 2—A printed application used by a leading mortgage banker.
Exhibit 3—An authorization letter for a loan to be submitted to a specific lender.
Exhibits 4 & 5—Exclusive authorization letters to a mortgage banker or broker.

Exhibit 1   Mortgage loan application used by a major life insurance company.

MORTGAGE LOAN APPLICATION

Date _____

To: _____ (hereafter referred to as Lender)

Thru: _____ _____

By: _____ (hereafter referred to as Applicant)

Application is hereby made to Lender for a loan of $ _____ at _____ % annual interest for a term of _____

years _____ months. The loan will carry annual debt service of $ _____ payable in monthly installments

of $ _____ reducing the loan balance to $ _____ at maturity.

Prepayment privilege _____

_____

_____

Personal guarantee of _____

Chattel mortgage on _____

Other provisions _____

_____

_____

_____

Requested disbursement date _____

The proposed loan is to be secured by a first and valid lien on certain real estate fronting _____ feet on

_____ in _____
            (Street)   (City and State)

containing approximately _____ square feet.

Brief description of improvements at disbursement: _____

_____

Use of loan proceeds _____ _____

_____

_____

Amount of equity required _____ Source of equity _____

_____

R 1881c

Applicant hereby agrees:

1. That title and all documents, agreements, or other instruments used in conjunction with this transaction shall be satisfactory to Lender.

2. That there are no Federal income taxes due and unpaid, judgments unsatisfied, or suits pending against Applicant in any court of record and no unrecorded deeds or mortgages, and no outstanding claims, liens or charges against said property whatsoever except as fully described hereafter: _____

_____

3. That there will be no secondary financing on the real estate securing the loan except as fully described hereafter: _____

_____

4. To provide at Applicant's cost and subject to Lender's approval:

   a. a title insurance policy

   b. an engineer's survey

   c. insurance protection against, but not limited to, fire, windstorm, war risk and loss of rents

   d. final plans and specifications

   e. tri-party agreement with approved interim lender

   f. general and or specific assignment of rents and leases

   g. _____

5. To provide, in a form satisfactory to Lender, audited annual reports of the property securing the loan.

6. To deposit with Lender, monthly noninterest-bearing payments equal to 1/12th of the annual real estate taxes.

7. To pay all costs incidental to the proposed loan whether or not the transaction herein contemplated is completed.

8. To pay an origination fee of $ _____ to _____

9. To pay Lender a _____ fee of $ _____

10. To promptly accept a loan commitment issued on the applied for terms and facilitate the closing of the loan in accordance with the provisions of said commitment.

Signed _____
                                 Applicant

_____
                                 Address

Supplemental statements attached include: _____ plot plan of proposed improvements, _____ plans and specifications, _____ breakdown of estimated costs, _____ copy of acceptable contractor's bid, _____ audited operating statements for past _____ years, _____ pro forma projection of expected operations, _____ Applicant's financial statement.

Exhibit 2 A printed application used by a leading mortgage banker.

WAYNE MORTGAGE COMPANY
123 Pine St.
Milford, California

Application is hereby made to Wayne Mortgage   , or its nominee, for a construction and long term
mortgage loan in the amount of $_____ , for _____ ,
with interest at the rate of _____% per annum repayable in equal monthly installments to interest and principal of
$_____ , based on a _____ amortization.

The loan shall be evidenced by a promissory note duly executed by _____
_____

which note shall be secured by a first Deed of Trust, Assignment of Rents, Assignment of Lessor's Interest in Leases
and any other required documents, encumbering property described as:
Address: _____
Legal Description: _____
_____
_____

The note shall be further secured by a Security Agreement (Mortgage of Chattels) and by appropriate Uniform
Commercial Code (California) documents, encumbering all of the personal property located, or to be located, on the
premises, including but not limited to all equipment and furnishings.

It is understood we will be allowed to prepay_____% of the loan in any one year including obligatory
payments, noncumulative, without premium. We are to have the right to pay the loan in full under the following
conditions:
_____
_____
_____

Description of Improvements: _____
_____
_____
_____

Land Cost $_____ Date: _____ Land Value $_____
Purchase Price $_____ Date: _____ Improvement Cost $_____

Annual Income and Expense Statement is attached and made a part hereof. It is understood there will be secondary
financing not to exceed _____ , repayable as follows:
_____
_____

We agree to execute separate loan applications in accord with the terms of this application should Wayne Mortgage
Co. elect to submit this loan to any other lenders of their choice. We warrant that we have not and will not submit
an application to any other source for a period of _____days from date hereof and that, during said
_____ day period, we appoint Wayne Mtg. Co. as our sole and exclusive agent for the purpose of
securing the loan applied for herein. In consideration of the services of Wayne Mtg. Co. , we further agree:

1. To pay a nonrefundable fee of $_____to Wayne Mortgage Co., payable upon execution of
this application, as consideration for appraisal of herein described property; said appraisal shall be solely for the
benefit of lender.

2. To pay a nonrefundable fee of $_____to Wayne Mortgage Co.

3. To pay a standby deposit fee of $_____ , to Wayne Mortgage Co. to be held without interest,
payable upon execution of this application.

4. To act promptly and meet all requirements in order that the loan will be closed _____
_____

Together with this application, we hand you the sum of $_____ , representing the expenses listed under
Item(s) _____above.

The nonrefundable fee, Item No. 2 above, shall be deemed earned and payable at the time a written commitment to make said loan is delivered to us on the terms specified in this application or on other terms accepted by us. Said nonrefundable fee is to be refunded only upon your declination of this application.

The standby deposit, Item No. 3 above, is to be refunded to us, in full, upon recordation of the first Deed of Trust, or upon your declination of this application. In the event the loan should fail to close for any reason other than your declination of this application, said standby deposit shall be retained by you as full and agreed charges for services rendered over and above the charges listed in No. 1 and No. 2 above and we agree that said services are reasonably worth such sum.

ADDITIONAL REQUIREMENTS

We hereby certify that the statements and information contained in this application are in all respects true, complete, and correct to the best of our knowledge and belief.

Date: SIGNATURES

Indicate After Signature
Fed. Tax No. or Soc. Sec. No.

_____   _____   _____

Mailing Address: _____   _____

_____   _____   _____

_____   _____   _____

Phone: _____

Exhibit 3   An authorization letter for a loan to be submitted to a specific lender.

_____ ,19___

Doe and Company
123 Second Street
Philadelphia, PA 19101

                              Re:_ Eastern Annex - DeKalb County, Pa._

Gentleman:

We hereby make application to Westside Insurance Company through
Doe and Company for a first mortgage loan of $2,650,000, 9-3/4%,
payable over 28 years in equal monthly installments of $23,055.
The security will be approximately eight acres improved with
55,000 sq. ft. of GLA plus a 2,500 sq. ft. bank building at
$40,000 per year net.

The commitment will contain alternate provisions to fund as follows:

   1) $2,525,000 with the security including a ground lease to the
      bank at $25,000 per year net as approved by lender.

   2) $2,350,000 excluding the bank site from the security.

The note will contain a prepayment provision which will allow
payment in full during the eleventh year at 105 with the charge
reducing 1% per year thereafter to 101.

The commitment term will be 12 months with full payout based only
on completion according to plans and specifications.

There will be no personal liability on the part of the borrowers.

We understand that we are to pay the actual costs of closing
including title insurance, intangibles, recording tax, survey and
recording charges and that the firm Smith, Jones & Covington will
handle the closing. In addition, we agree to deliver to Westside
Insurance Company upon acceptance of commitment a 2% Bank Letter
of Credit which will be refunded at closing.

We further agree that Doe and Company will have earned on delivery
of commitment a 1% brokerage fee payable 1/2 from the first
construction draw and 1/2 at final closing.

                         Very truly yours,

                         By:_____

                         By:_____

Exhibit 4 Exclusive authorization letter to a mortgage banker or broker.

FINANCING AUTHORIZATION AGREEMENT

The undersigned appoints Strafford Mtg. Co. as exclusive agent from date hereof until 6 P.M. Pacific Standard Time, _____, 19__, to apply on my behalf to any lender Strafford Mtg. Co. selects for financing to be secured by a first lien or encumbrance upon the real'property commonly known as:

Said financing shall be in the face amount of $_____, bearing interest at a rate not to exceed _____% per annum, for a term of _____ years, _____ months, principal and interest payable in _____ installments of $_____, interest included.

The undersigned agrees to execute upon request a written application for such financing on the form in regular use by the lender, and to furnish all information and material and to pay all customary costs and fees required by lender.

In consideration of services rendered, the undersigned agrees to pay Strafford Mtg. Co. a commission in an amount equal to _____ of the face amount of any commitment requested and obtained or any financing agreed upon (whichever is the greater), whether the said commitment or financing be on the same or different terms than those stated herein. A commitment shall be deemed to have been obtained when Strafford Mtg. Co. has secured a responsible firm, person or corporation who is willing to make said financing pursuant to my application, including any changes, amendments or supplements thereto approved by me; none of the latter shall be deemed or considered as a new application. When the commitment is obtained, the commission shall become immediately due and payable.

It is understood that any fees payable to Strafford Mtg. Co . under the terms of this Financing Authorization Agreement are independent of and in addition to any consideration received by you from any source in regard to this property.

I hereby acknowledge receipt of a copy of this agreement.

Dated _____, 19____.

ACCEPTED:
STRAFFORD MTG. CO.

BY:_____   BY:_____

Address:

_____
Address

_____
Telephone

Exhibit 5 Exclusive authorization letter to a mortgage banker or broker.

LOAN AGREEMENT

_____, 19___

    FOR AND IN CONSIDERATION of the services to be performed by ABC MORTGAGE COM-
PANY we hereby employ it as sole and exclusive agent to secure for us a commitment
for a mortgage or other loan on our property known as_____
_____,
City of_____, County of_____, State of_____,
said loan commitment to be in the amount of $_____, payable in _____years,
with interest at the rate of _____% per annum, with payments of $_____ payable
_____ including principal and interest, or any other amount and terms
acceptable to us, to be secured by a first mortgage on the above property.

    PREPAYMENT PRIVILEGE:

    THIS EMPLOYMENT and authority shall continue for sixty days from the date
we furnish all exhibits required for processing the loan or from the date hereof,
whichever is later, and thereafter until withdrawn by us in writing, and we hereby
agree to pay to said ABC MORTGAGE COMPANY , for services rendered _____% of
amount of the loan when commitment is obtained.

    WE FURTHER AGREE to pay for all appraisal fees, title charges, surveys,
attorney fees, recording fees and all other charges necessary to complete this
loan, and to comply with all requirements and to execute all papers required by
the mortgagee or lender for the prompt closing of the loan.

    WE UNDERSTAND and acknowledge that ABC MORTGAGE COMPANY may receive
a fee or fees from the permanent investor with whom the loan covered by this application is placed in connection with the placement or servicing of the loan, and
for services rendered with this loan application. Receipt of such fee or fees by
ABC MORTGAGE COMPANY shall in no way affect the applicant's obligation to
ABC MORTGAGE COMPANY under this application.

WITNESSES:

_____   BY:_____

_____   _____

                           The above employment accepted on the terms
                           outlined herein

                           ABC MORTGAGE COMPANY

                           BY:_____

Chapter 5

The Concept of Appraising Income Property

Charles P. Landt

An appraisal is defined as a report by a qualified appraiser that sets forth a supported opinion or estimate of value, or the process by which an estimate of value is obtained. Appraisals are used in the making of loans secured by real estate for two very simple reasons: (1) the loan should be made in the proper amount in order to insure the safety of the security; and (2) the various laws of states and the federal government require institutional investors to stay within legal loan limits in regard to the ratio of loan-to-value.

In appraising, there are many different types of values. Most of the laws regarding investments by institutional investors use the term *market value*. Market value is defined as the highest price a willing buyer would pay a willing seller for a piece of real estate, neither being forced to act and both knowing the full uses to which the property may be put.

The need to know market value takes the appraiser directly into the marketplace, because a determination must be made of what a willing buyer and a willing seller will do in regard to a particular piece of real estate. In the marketplace, the appraiser is confronted with the task of determining and analyzing the four great forces that either create, destroy, maintain, or modify real estate values. These forces, which motivate human beings, are economic, political, social, and physical.

Thus, an appraisal of real estate is more than just a simple analysis of one particular piece of real property. It involves an understanding of certain laws, life-styles, and customs, and an awareness of the physical factors that affect the particular property.

In the Depression of the 1930s, many financial institutions discovered they had been financing real estate without properly appraising it and, consequently, suffered considerable losses. In 1933, the American Institute of Real Estate Appraisers was organized and one of its first actions was to develop what is called "The Appraisal Process."

The appraisal process is just what the name implies. It is an orderly, well-defined process for the making of an appraisal.

As with any other established process, if it is followed diligently, correctly, and completely, it will be useful, and with an established appraisal process it is possible to come up with a very good estimate of value.

In the appraisal process, there are three approaches to value. They are the cost approach, the market data approach, and the income approach.

The *cost approach* calls for the appraiser to make an accurate estimate of land value and then to determine the current cost of reproducing the building less any accrued depreciation. The net result is the opinion of value established by the cost approach.

The *market data approach* calls for the appraiser to determine what people in the real estate marketplace have paid and are willing to pay for the particular type of property. This is accomplished by analyzing the sale prices of recently sold, comparable properties and comparing each to the subject property so that adjustments can be made. Certainly no two pieces of real estate are alike and certain adaptations have to be made to cause the comparables to conform with the subject property.

Some of the differences that must be looked at for possible adjustments are the date of sale, the purpose of the sale, and the atmosphere surrounding the transaction to determine if the sales price truly represented the definition of market value. Other adjustments can be made for the size, condition, and layout of the physical property, the amount and quality of the income, the location, and other factors as well.

The *income approach* calls for the appraiser to determine how much gross income the subject property will produce based on typical rentals in the marketplace. The appraiser must then establish a vacancy factor and estimate expenses, including taxes, which would be deducted in order to arrive at a figure representing projected net income. This annual net income stream is then converted into a value by the process of capitalization. Capitalization is a method of converting into present value a series of anticipated future installments of net income by discounting them into a present worth using a specific desired rate of earnings.

These three approaches rarely produce the same estimate of value. Because of this and because appraising is not an exact science, there is one final step in the appraisal process. This is called the "correlation" of the three approaches, which consists of reviewing all of the facts gathered, determining once again their accuracy and their sufficiency, and deciding which of the approaches is probably the most accurate. During the process of correlation, the appraiser has three estimates of value which must somehow be converted into one final estimate of market value. Any one or a combination of the three approaches may be appropriate. A decision here is where common sense, judgment, and experience come into play. To simply average the three values produced by the three approaches is totally inadequate and an inaccurate process.

With the three approaches, the appraiser has established a bracket indicating an upper limit of value and a lower limit of value. Somewhere within this bracket lies the final estimate of value. There is a basic principle of value called the *principle of substitution*. This states that no one would pay more for a piece of real estate than it would cost to reproduce that real estate without undue delay. Because of this principle, the cost approach normally tends to set the upper limit of value.

Since the subject of this chapter is appraising income properties, perhaps it would be best to concentrate more on the income approach to value. The appraiser must get all of the pertinent physical facts relating to the property, such as the size of land and buildings, zoning, public or private restrictions, and so forth, and must also determine the highest and best use of the property. If it is unimproved land, it may be for an apartment project, shopping center, industrial or some other type of use.

Once the use is determined, the appraiser should determine how much rent the improved property would command. To do this, the appraiser goes into the marketplace and analyzes the rents of comparable properties, in this way establishing the potential annual gross income. Unless a long-term lease to a very strong tenant is involved, a vacancy and/or collection loss factor must be allowed for. This amount normally would be anywhere from 3 to 10 percent on retail stores and apartments, and in the case of motels up to 35 percent. This vacancy loss is deducted from the gross income and the remainder is called *effective gross income*.

The appraiser must now estimate the expenses involved each year in operating the property, engaging in a considerable amount of research to estimate the annual ad valorem taxes, insurance premiums, management fees, utility costs, maintenance, replacement reserves, and any other expenses. This total expense is deducted from the effective gross income, leaving a net income before recapture.

The term *recapture* formerly was known as future depreciation. An investor in income-producing property is entitled to two things: *return of* money (recapture), and a *return on* money (interest). These two items of recapture and interest are of vital importance in the capitalization process. They may be treated separately or together.

There are many capitalization procedures and it would be impossible to analyze all of them in one chapter. Therefore, we will consider the recapture and the interest as one capitalization rate. The question is, then, where does the appraiser find a capitalization rate? Going into the marketplace permits a determination of what type of return a typical investor seeks on that particular type of property. There are two ways to look at it: (1) the rate of return, if the property were free and clear; and (2) the specific rate of return, if the property were mortgaged and the investor is looking for a certain rate of return on cash flow. This, of course, would take mortgage payments and depreciation into consideration. It is often helpful to use both methods as a cross-check.

Going into the marketplace to find a capitalization rate is difficult but not impossible. This means that the appraiser must locate sales of comparable properties and determine the net income of each in order to arrive at the rate of return. For example, if a property has sold for $1,000,000 and the net income, after recapture, is $100,000 per year, then the rate of return (interest) is 10 percent. To apply this comparable rate to the property being appraised and assume it also has a net income of $100,000, the appraiser would then divide the 10 percent into the net income and arrive at an indicated value of $1,000,000.

To see how the cost approach might apply by using the above example where the indicated value from the income approach is $1,000,000, suppose the appraiser determines that the reproduction cost of the building, less depreciation plus the market value of the land, is $950,000. There is then a $50,000 difference. Let us assume that a long-term lease has been negotiated by the borrower with a quality tenant. Both the quantity and the quality of this income stream have been taken into account in the income approach and can also be taken into account in the cost approach as an indirect value. To determine the value of the mere existence of the lease is a very difficult thing to do, but it must not be overlooked. It entails costs—perhaps considerable costs—in order to put the lease into effect. If the appraiser were to decide that these indirect costs were $50,000, then the cost approach and the income approach would be the same and the indicated market value probably would be $1,000,000.

The above example assumed a single-tenant building, but the same could apply to a proposed apartment project. There are certain direct and indirect costs in building an apartment building. But there are also considerable indirect costs in obtaining tenants for the building in order to produce the income stream and this should not be neglected in the cost approach.

The market data approach should certainly not be overlooked, although it is frequently ignored in appraising for mortgage purposes. The appraiser simply says, "There have been no sales of comparable properties." That statement simply means that the appraiser has not done the proper job, because real estate changes hands daily and it is just a matter of doing the research in order to find out what sales have taken place. The appraiser must diligently investigate the market in order to find the sales and, in effect, make a rough appraisal of each of the comparable properties to compare the physical attributes as well as the ability to produce income to the subject property.

The appraising of real estate for mortgage loan purposes carries a considerable amount of responsibility. Based on the estimate of value and the facts given in the appraisal report, a large sum of money is going to be invested, particularly in the case of income-producing properties. The appraiser must obtain all the facts about the property and all the facts relating to an analysis of the risk, which includes the actions of people in the marketplace. The appraiser must document the facts, analyze them, and submit them in a report in a manner that convinces the reader that an accurate estimate of value has been made.

The entire process is not an easy one in light of the pressure of competition for mortgage loans and the ever present time element. A borrower interested in financing property wants a commitment immediately and, unfortunately, this is seldom possible.

The mortgage banker who originates and submits a loan application to an investor has a fiduciary relationship that requires the origination of loans that are well-secured and supported by an accurate appraisal. A poorly documented appraisal can lead to defaulted loans, which cause a loss in time and money and promote a deterioration of the relationship. A poor appraisal is easy to spot and the person making and/or submitting a below-standard appraisal will soon lose credibility in the eyes of the investor.

Chapter 6

Preparation and Presentation of the Loan Submission

Everett C. Spelman, Jr.

The loan submission, often called the loan package, is a group of documents that are both formal and informal in nature, whose specific purpose is to provide information on a specific mortgage loan offering. It could be likened to a ''prospectus,'' though it is typically more complete in that its representations and statements are supported with exhibits carrying detailed information designed specifically for lending purposes. In short, the loan submission provides all the information necessary to arrive at a knowledgeable decision about the proposal to accept a specific type of collateral as security for the anticipated borrowing.

An analysis of a loan offering requires an examination of a great number of critical details. Often, because of distances involved, the individual responsible for the analysis is unable to keep at hand all the details of a property being offered as security. In addition, since an analysis is based on a general format of loan terms, the amount of information and supporting exhibits can be quite extensive.

A good submission tells a complete story of the loan and its relationship to the property on which the borrowing will apply. It will answer all questions relative to the borrowing and thoroughly detail all the pros and cons of the security.

In some instances, the lender will prescribe the physical order for document presentation, but it should always be remembered that many of these items are interrelated and therefore must be examined together. Also, there are specific items that should be included in all loan submissions. They may be expanded upon, but rarely reduced. Each of these items will be treated in detail, but not necessarily in their order of importance.

LOAN APPLICATION

While some investors do not require an actual loan application document, for others it is the very basis for the entire loan submission. It carries within it the terms and conditions of the borrowing. It is the contractual document that binds the applicant and the lender to the conditions of performance. These terms include, but are not limited to:

1 Loan amount.
2 Rate of interest.
3 Term of loan.
4 Escrow requirements.
5 Prepayment terms.
6 Security offered.
7 Borrower.
8 Type of security documents.
9 Commitment term.
10 Property insurance coverage.
11 Fees and closing costs.
12 Other requirements.

Since the application is a contractual agreement, it should be recognized that any contrived or planned variance between the terms of the application and the ultimate commitment would in all probability void that relationship. Therefore, the application should be drawn carefully, specifying the terms that will be set forth in the loan commitment. In some instances, the loan application may become the commitment or, to some extent, be referred to in the commitment for terms and conditions not specifically referred to in the commitment itself.

The loan application should be prepared with great attention to detail, especially when used as a guideline for the loan submission. It should always be prepared with the ultimate commitment in mind. Since no two borrowers or properties are alike, any special requirements should be specifically set forth to properly reflect the attitude of both the borrower and the lender.

ANALYTICAL REPORT

The analytical report is the information in summary form that is used to underwrite the loan. It may also be known as a loan analysis, a loan brief, or an underwriting report. The items normally covered in an analytical report are:

1 Ownership of security.
2 Description of security.
3 Information relative to the borrower.

4 Information relative to the tenant.
5 Loan terms.

Ownership of Security

This section of the analytical report defines how title to the property will be held. It may be held by a corporation, limited or general partnership, trust, or an individual. Identifying the form of ownership is necessary to determine how the loan documents will be ultimately drawn. It is possible to indicate, however, that the ultimate decision for holding title has not been made but will be accomplished prior to the loan closing.

Description of Security

All real estate is properly identified through the use of a legal description. It is absolutely necessary to provide this formal description somewhere in the loan submission. Logic seems to dictate that the analytical report is the proper place to include it.

In addition to the legal description, the address of the property, including the street address, city, county, and state should be provided. It is also wise to include a brief physical description of the building and the dimensions of the site.

Since additional documents other than the note and mortgage or deed of trust will be used to perfect a first mortgage, such items should be set forth as loan requirements. These items would include but not be limited to:

1 Assignment of mortgage or deed of trust.
2 Assignment of leases.
3 Assignment of rents.
4 Loss payable clause on hazard insurance.
5 Security agreement or chattel mortgage.
6 Recording of leases or short form thereof.
7 Certification of paid real estate taxes.
8 Type of lien (first mortgage, second mortgage, wrap-around mortgage, leasehold loan, etc.).

Information Relative to the Borrower

For many years it was not uncommon to hear the philosophy expounded that there were only three elements necessary to determine real estate value—location, location, and location. This has been refined to the extent of adding two additional dimensions. They are: (1) the borrower and his "track record"; and (2) management.

In order to give the underwriter a feel for the project, a general discussion of the borrower is always in order in any loan submission. In addition to a short background history of the borrower, items that should be discussed include the desire and motivation to develop or acquire the subject property, past experience in development and management, and demonstrated expertise in other real estate transactions. Motivation for real estate investment is often a good indication of its probable ultimate disposition. It is also very important to be aware of other current involvements and the ability to handle projects simultaneously.

You should make it a point to be aware of the borrower's local reputation, including a reputation for handling debt obligations as well as for seeing projects through to completion. Even though this may be nothing more than a broad brush painting of the borrower's character, it can nonetheless give an insight into past dealings and will probably wave a flag to any element warranting further investigation.

A personal knowledge of the borrower's background and reputation is part of the mortgage correspondent's duty as an active participant in the business community. Personal contact with the borrower is extremely important and worthwhile. The knowledge obtained from this contact enhances the correspondent's ability to better negotiate the individual transaction.

Information Relative to the Tenant

In a case where the property is to be rented or leased, some discussion should be devoted to the tenant. This is particularly true where the lease is long-term in nature and even more so when the property is built for a particular tenant.

The points to be covered range from financial capabilities to future potential of the tenant, the tenant's market, and continued demand for present and/or future space. It is not anticipated that a complete financial analysis be undertaken, but exhibits must include both financial and credit information relative to the tenant. This can, of course, be expanded upon if requested by an investor.

Discussion should be directed to the tenant's motivation for occupancy in the subject building and in that particular location, which includes not only the specific neighborhood but the community as well. It would also be proper at this time to examine alternate uses for the space should it be vacated by the present tenant. This is most appropriate, of course, in the case of space leased on a short-term basis.

Loan Terms

Loan terms are set forth in the application, but a more detailed discussion may be warranted. For example, it is not uncommon to construct the payment schedule so that larger payments can be made at a certain time of the year. This is often the case with farm loans, where one annual payment will normally be made against principal and interest. The specific terms of any loan agreement, such as occupancy requirements, holdback and disbursement arrangements, additional security provisions, and/or buy-sell agreements should also be highlighted.

Of prime consideration is the liability of the borrowing entity. Although individual borrowers may execute loan documents, they may be absolved of any liability through a mutual agreement with the lender. Also, it is not uncommon to guarantee a percentage of a loan (such as the top 10 percent of a $1 million loan or $100,000) or to provide for personal liability until such time as the property has achieved occupancy to a breakeven point.

APPRAISAL

The appraisal is an important exhibit in the loan submission. It should help to establish the *fair market value* of the security—an essential factor in determining the appropriate loan amount. In general, the following should be included in an appraisal:

1 Description of the property.
2 Neighborhood analysis.
3 Property utilities and restrictions.
4 The three approaches to value (if appropriate).
5 Correlation.
6 Final value estimate.

It cannot be emphasized enough that the mortgage banker is a risk analyst. A concern for value is only a part of the entire function, which is to determine the potential repayment of the debt within the terms of the mortgage. Value, therefore, must be related to key points such as debt repayment coverage, default point, occupancy, break-even, expense ratios, vacancy ratios, projected income, market acceptability, and other risk considerations.

The appraisal should ordinarily establish the present fair market value, but the underwriter should be able to make a judgment decision as to the future potential disposition of the property from the information provided in the appraisal. Also, the appraisal should specifically refer to any unusual elements of the property such as restrictions, easements, and conditions of arriving at value estimates.

FINANCIAL STATEMENTS

Financial statements are a necessary part of any loan submission. Any analysis of a borrower without financial statements would be incomplete. If the borrower is an individual, it is possible that the statements will not be audited. They must, however, be current (prepared within the last six months) and reflect all assets and liabilities, including any contingent liabilities. With a corporate borrower, it is best to request and obtain audited statements. It is the mortgage banker's responsibility to analyze and be familiar with the income statements and balance sheets in the loan submission, because the investor/underwriter often expects input and guidance from the originating mortgage banker, even when making a personal analysis of the statements.

When dealing with a loan to be made on an existing income-producing property or a property that the owner intends to occupy, the submission should include operating statements for a period of at least the last three years. These statements are important in determining the profitability of a company, the rent or long-term debt that the property can sustain, and the growth pattern of the company, both historical and probable. If the company is a listed firm with either Standard and Poor's or Moody's, then a report should be included.

CREDIT REPORTS

Credit reports provide useful underwriting information insofar as a credit background and an insight into the borrower's repayment attitude and reputation are concerned. These reports can be obtained from reputable credit reporting agencies that specialize in commercial and corporate credit reporting. The company used, however, should be selected from the mortgage banker's own list of approved credit reporting agencies or that of the investor who is to receive the loan submission. If the investor feels that a certain credit report is inadequate or incomplete, it may require a back-up report, resulting in a loss of what is usually valuable time. Your past experience with a certain agency is often the best indicator in a judgment as to whether that agency should be used again.

Also, mortgage bankers who have had past credit experience with the borrower would do well to include their own report in this section of the loan submission. Investors always appreciate thoroughness in a loan submission, and extra input in this area can be very useful.

LEASES

If a property is to be leased, a copy of the lease or leases should be included in the loan submission. An analysis of the lease, prepared by the mortgage banker, should also be included. Since these leases will be reviewed by the legal department, it would be of assistance to the investor/underwriter to have the major points highlighted, thereby allowing a more expeditious review of the submission.

Where a property will have a number of leases, a standard form lease is normally used. This should also be submitted in order that it may be reviewed by the investor to determine if any objectionable points exist.

Since the lease and its term can be an important factor in deciding whether or not to make a loan, its relationship to the mortgage should be considered. If, for example, the building is to be constructed for the occupancy of a specific tenant, the mortgagee may request that the lease be recorded prior to the mortgage. This is done in order to insure that the lease will not be disturbed should a foreclosure occur. If, however, the investor plans to take possession of a property in the event of foreclosure, the lease must be recorded after the mortgage. This procedure allows the foreclosure action to wipe out the leases, thus allowing the investor to control the occupancy of the property. If the investor attaches no particular significance to the leases, it may be suggested that the lease not be recorded.

Many leases contain information that neither the tenant nor the landlord will want made public. This is not unusual, and in such an instance, a short form of the lease may be recorded, thereby providing public notice. This short form reveals no particulars of the lease other than its existence.

For to-be-built projects it is not uncommon to see letters of intent to occupy. These letters of intent are indications of the demand for space in the building and an insight into the market for such space. They should be taken as only an expressed interest in occupancy should the terms and conditions of the lease be satisfactory—no more, no less. They are, however, of value in assessing the future success of a building. Leases and letters of intent are a necessary part of the loan submission.

PHOTOGRAPHS

Photos are an absolute requirement for any expert and complete loan submission. They allow those who are away from the property to gain a feel for it and the surrounding neighborhood. There is nothing very scientific or analytical about photos, but their importance is often so great that it is difficult to give sufficient emphasis to this point. It is probably sufficient to say that photos can, indeed, either make or break a deal!

In a good loan presentation, the mortgage banker must present the photographs as a story being told. The story must cover:

1 The property.
2 The neighborhood.
3 The relation of the property to the neighborhood.
4 Access facts.
5 Project feasibility.

Color photos seem to be the most popular, because they give a feeling of warmth and natural exposure. This does not mean that black-and-white photos are inadequate, but for the minimal additional cost it would seem logical to use color.

Properly displayed photographs should be mounted and placed in an orderly sequence. It is important that the project be displayed as the seller sees it, as it will appear when completed, or as it appears in its present stage.

Aerial photographs should also be included in a loan submission. These can usually be obtained locally through a commercial photographer, often chosen by past experience. The purpose of the aerial photograph, of course, is to relate the subject property to its surrounding community and to certain other areas of the city that may have an effect on the subject. For example, a suburban office property could be shown in relation to the downtown office district, to banks in the area, to freeways or major arterial streets, and to other office buildings or the residential area being served. Aerial views should also be related to a map of the surrounding area as an aid to the underwriter, especially one who is not familiar with the area.

MAPS

The use of maps is mandatory in any loan submission. They should be used to pinpoint the location of the subject property to the major traffic arteries that surround it. The number of maps to be used in a loan submission depends on the number of points that the mortgage banker needs to establish for the benefit of the investor/underwriter. For example, when a property is located in a metropolitan area, the map should cover the entire area, but it should also focus on the relationship of the subject property to other areas of importance and this can often necessitate the use of more than one map. In a small community, it is often wise to use both city and state maps to establish the relationship between that city, the state, and other major populated areas. Also, there may be instances where a certain portion of a map needs to be enlarged to highlight an important, specific area of the city.

In all cases, though, there are certain areas of the city that bear an important relationship to the property in question. The downtown business district is a perfect example of one of these areas. It should always be noted on the map, even if it does nothing more than establish a point of reference for the underwriter.

Maps play the lead role in establishing the location of the subject property to other areas and elements of importance in both the neighborhood and surrounding metropolitan area. They must show the advantages of the subject location in the community as well as the importance of its location with respect to the function that it is to perform. For example, in the case of a medical office building, the location of the area hospital should be noted. Other examples would be office buildings with commercial banking facilities, warehouses and industrial parks with railway accesses and highway systems, and apartments with shopping centers and public transportation.

The flow of traffic into and around the subject property is an extremely important ingredient that maps alone do not reveal. All primary and secondary streets that serve as connecting arteries from highways and other major traffic flow areas to the property must be pointed out to help the underwriter determine the convenience of the subject location, time/distance factors, and the basic character of the approach areas. It should also be remembered that it is easy for a mortgage banker who is familiar with an area to inadvertently ignore traffic flows, so some caution is usually warranted.

To further acquaint the investor/underwriter with the area, it may be wise to develop a strip map that shows those properties in the immediate vicinity of the subject property. This map should depict the relative size of the entire area as well as the size of each individual property shown. For instance, if the subject property is retail in nature, it would not be uncommon to diagram up to six blocks in each direction. It would also be logical to diagram other properties that surround the subject, thereby establishing the character of the neighborhood and showing the relationship of the surrounding properties to the subject. Such a map should be well marked so the viewer can identify each property shown.

In the case of shopping centers, a strip map is an absolute necessity. This map should depict the location of all of the tenants in the center, each in relation to the others. This is important, because some retail stores enjoy benefits from certain types of adjacent merchandisers. Whatever the case, it should be remembered that familiarity is no substitute for the visual recognition that the efficient use of maps can provide.

PLANS AND SPECIFICATIONS

In order to properly evaluate an already completed building, one must have the opportunity to examine the original plans and specifications. These documents give an insight into the concept of the building as well as its physical characteristics.

Many projects, however, are dependent on financing before they can be started. It is, therefore, not unusual to be supplied with outlined plans and specifications. These outlines should be designed to give the underwriter a general idea of the building, its total area, and the quality of the materials and workmanship that will go into the project.

Outlined plans normally include:

1 Plot plan.
2 Floor plan.
3 Wall section.
4 Elevations.

Outlined specifications normally include:

1 Footings and foundations.
2 Exterior walls.
3 Roof structure and finish.
4 Interior walls and ceilings.
5 Floors and floor finish.
6 Mechanical.
7 Electrical.
8 Plumbing.
9 On-site improvements.
10 Special features.

These outlines are not sophisticated enough to be used for the actual construction of the building, but they are quite satisfactory for the purpose of a loan submission and are a logical solution to providing the required information without going to the expense of drafting complete, working drawings. You will want to be sure to advise that, should the loan be committed, the developer will be responsible for providing complete and acceptable plans and specifications before construction on the project can begin. They would, of course, be subject to the approval of the lender, since they must substantially conform to the previously submitted outlines. The final set of plans and specifications is usually prepared in duplicate so the lender may retain one for the files and return the second to the developer as evidence of approval.

It should be remembered that the loan is predicated upon the completion of the building as set out in the final plans and specifications. Therefore, when the project is completed, it would not be uncommon for the lender to require a certification from the project's architect that the building has been completed in a workmanlike manner with substantial conformance to the plans and specifications. Also, if a local agency needs to approve the project prior to occupancy, the lender may further require that this approval be submitted in writing prior to the closing of the transaction.

Since plans and specifications can be quite detailed and often voluminous, a written brief accompanying both would be helpful to the institutional lender. Should a more detailed analysis be required, the lender will probably have a review done by a qualified engineer or architect.

LOAN SUMMARY

In financing income-producing real estate, rules of thumb are constantly being developed. Although they tend to be general in nature, they seem to set the guidelines that we must normally work within and are very beneficial in helping us review the specifics. A good loan summary will usually include a reference sheet of important points so that those who review the case can grasp the concept of the project and its acceptability as security for a loan. This could be done to include details such as:

1 Loan amount.
2 Interest rate.
3 Loan term and amortization period.

4 Land value (per square foot).

5 Building value (per square foot).

6 Loan per square foot (building).

7 Gross income.

8 Expenses (expressed as a percentage of gross).

9 Net income.

10 Debt service (annual constant).

11 Cash flow.

12 Break-even point.

13 Debt coverage.

14 Parking area and ratio.

15 Building efficiency (percentage of net rentable to total gross area).

16 Square foot rental.

17 Land-to-building ratio.

18 Borrower's net worth.

19 Other applicable points.

Even though many institutional investors have their own procedure or format for reviewing a loan and presenting it to their finance committee, this outline of specific information gives the lender's underwriter an opportunity to select specifics and apply them to an assigned space in the underwriting form. This saves time, but more important, it further assures that the originator is aware of the items that are of major importance to proper analysis. The outline helps the underwriter focus on those figures that help in an analysis and discussion of the entire loan submission in an effective and efficient manner.

At this point, some consideration should be given to the length of the completed submission. To believe that a submission with the most information, packaged in a voluminous manner, and placed in an attractive cover is a good loan package is an erroneous opinion. Nothing could be further from the truth. The analyst is primarily concerned with those facts that are essential to the making of a knowledgeable decision that conforms to investment policy. A loan submission that is clear and concise is, without a doubt, much easier to analyze. It also gives the investor the impression that you understand the elements of safety and risk for an institutional investment portfolio. A dressed-up loan submission is no substitute for a quality investment or a keen understanding of the elements of professional real estate lending. Most loan submissions arrive on the underwriter's desk without the benefit of a personal appearance by the mortgage banker, thus every offering must speak for itself. With this in mind, the importance of presenting a loan submission with clear, well-written, and concise thoughts cannot be overemphasized.

LETTER OF TRANSMITTAL

The letter of transmittal is the place where you make a substantiated recommendation for acceptance of the loan. This is the primary function of this exhibit. It can also be used to delineate those items that are included in the submission, if for no other reason than to give a record of what information has been provided. In a sense, this listing acts as a table of contents for the entire loan submission. This is also the best place to discuss items such as fees, servicing, commitment terms, and the probable closing procedure. This letter need not be lengthy, but it should be to the point and inclusive of all pertinent facts.

MISCELLANEOUS

The major elements of a loan submission have been covered. By no means are these all of the exhibits that could be included under each and every circumstance. Others that may be pertinent include:

1   Vacancy surveys.
2   Feasibility studies.
3   Environmental impact studies.
4   Information on the community and/or industry.
5   Area transportation maps.
6   Zoning requirements.
7   Building codes.
8   Schematic drawings.
9   Soil tests.

The information needed to arrive at a sound investment decision is similar for almost all real estate lenders, but questions will inevitably arise as a result of peculiar investment requirements or specific attitudes. Some investors will request more detail than others and the mortgage banker, in the role of correspondent, is obligated to sufficiently research the project so as to make further questions unnecessary. There is no substitute for being completely familiar with the underwriting procedure of the institutional investor. However, should additional information be requested, it should be gathered and made available as rapidly as possible in order to allow for continued and uninterrupted processing.

Chapter 7

Project Feasibility

Karel J. Clettenberg

Any successful real estate development requires a careful analysis known as a *feasibility study*. Traditionally, a real estate project required a developer with an idea and a loan. With these two ingredients, the development process usually followed this pattern:

1 Option or buy land.
2 Draw plans and specifications.
3 Have the project appraised.
4 Obtain financing.
5 Build the project.
6 Hope for success.

Although many of these developments have been successful, there are enough ill-conceived and/or foreclosed projects to warrant a deviation from the traditional development process. This deviation is a feasibility study prior to the expenditure of a great deal of money. A complete feasibility study includes the following steps in the order given:

1 The objectives of the parties involved in the project.
2 The legal environment.

3 The project's market.
4 The costs associated with the project.
5 An analysis of the project's ability to meet the objectives of the parties involved.

The analysis might be terminated, however, with any step that obviates those that follow. For example, an analysis of the legal environment might uncover an impossible zoning situation; therefore, a market study in that location and a cost analysis would serve no purpose.

OBJECTIVES OF ALL PARTIES

A real estate project usually involves a developer and an equity investor (lender). On occasion, there are others such as a passive equity investor. Since the parties have their own objectives, the project must be outlined to correspond to each party.

The lender, or equity investor, has a number of expectations:

Competitive Return on Investment   The lender's return on investment is provided by the interest rate. This rate is determined by risk, the money market, alternative investment opportunities, and so forth.

Return of Mortgage Investment   Lenders eventually want their mortgage investment returned. This is achieved through loan amortization. This expectation plus the interest rate makes up the loan constant.

Extra Returns   In addition to return on and of investment, the mortgage investor might expect some type of extra return. Extra returns are provided by various participation agreements. These agreements usually call for the lender's participation in the project's gross income, net income, or equity.

Portfolio Balance   Another lender objective is portfolio balance, which is the practice of making loans on different types of real estate in different locations.

Risk Management   Any loan carries some risk of loss. The mortgage investor attempts to balance risk against possible returns. The lender can achieve this objective by several methods.

The real estate developer also has a number of objectives. Typically, the developer's primary objective is profit. The feasibility analyst must determine how the profit objective can be measured. For example, the developer's objective could be a given cash-on-cash return (that is, the amount of cash return from profits in relation to the developer's actual cash investment in the property) for a stated payback period. On the other hand, the profit objective might be measured by other considerations, such as internal rate of return, net present value, or a certain profitability index. One developer of apartment property, for example, requires a 20 percent internal rate of return before considering a project. While profit is usually the strongest motive, developers often have secondary objectives. Some examples are:

1 Public relations.
2 Prestige enhancement.
3 Shelter provision on a nonprofit basis.
4 Competition.

If the real estate project includes passive investors, their motives should also be noted by the analyst. Most passive investor objectives can be summarized as a reasonable return and freedom from worry.

The feasibility analyst must identify the objectives of all the parties involved. When these objectives are met, the project can be declared feasible. For example, consider the case of a recent feasibility study on a suburban office building. The lender's objectives were an 11.5 percent constant and a participation in the net income. The developer, on the other hand, wanted to invest very little equity and achieve a certain rate of return. In this particular case, the building was not feasible, because the developer could not achieve a satisfactory rate of return.

LEGAL ENVIRONMENT

The legal environment often imposes a constraint on a project's feasibility, that is, the project's ability to satisfy the stated objectives. A detailed analysis is therefore essential regarding the various codes and regulations that apply to the projected plan.

Communities enact zoning codes in order to direct the course of land development. A zoning code usually indicates the type and density of the land use permitted in a certain location. For example, apartment developments are permitted in certain zones if they do not exceed a certain number of units per acre. Subdivision regulations usually cover such items as the amount of land to be devoted to each use, specific sizes of individual parcels, and standards for sewers, streets, and so forth. Building codes regulate construction materials and methods—for example, what type of material must be used if a wall is to be considered fireproof. In addition to these basic codes and regulations, many governmental bodies are applying environmental regulations to development proposals.

The basic task of the feasibility analyst, then, is to determine if the proposed project can meet its stated objectives within the existing legal framework. For example, consider the shopping center developer whose standard was a certain cash-on-cash return. The feasibility analyst had to determine if this cash-on-cash return could be achieved under the existing zoning and building codes. An analysis of these codes suggested that this objective could not be met and the feasibility study was terminated at that point.

Sometimes a project's feasibility will depend on a change in one of the codes or regulations. A site in a western city, for example, appeared to be an excellent location for a large office complex. Although the market was strong and the office complex would achieve economic success, a zoning change was required. In this particular case, the entire feasibility of the project depended on the analyst's conclusion regarding the probability of a zoning change.

MARKET ANALYSIS

This portion of the feasibility study should determine the type of space needed, the amount of space needed, the price at which the space can be sold or rented, and the absorption rate for the new space. A market study is often confused with an entire feasibility analysis. Although important, a market study is simply a part of a more comprehensive analysis. A typical market analysis focuses on population, income, and employment data. This type of data must be analyzed in light of the proposed development. For example, a market study for an exclusive residential subdivision needs information regarding residents in high income brackets; for a singles apartment complex, it needs data on unmarried adults. The analysis should not stop here, however. A thorough market study involves a three-step procedure: (1) identification of the market segment; (2) determination of the size of the market segment; and (3) determination of the capture rate that can be expected by the proposed project. The following examples illustrate how the procedure has worked in various categories.

Inner-city High-rise Apartments This study involved the development of a high-rise apartment complex in the central core of a large southern city. The zoning code indicated that the site could accommodate 150 apartment units. The site and building costs suggested that each unit would have to rent for at least $400 per month.

Step 1 The market segment that would be attracted to the project would have (a) sufficient income to afford $400 a month rent, (b) no children, and (c) major employment in the downtown area.

Step 2 The size of the market segment was determined by (a) identifying a list of occupations that would allow $400 a month rent and (b) determining how many individuals in these occupations had lived in the downtown area during the past 15 years. Old city directories were helpful here.

Step 3 The capture rate was determined by a questionnaire that was sent to a sample of the households in the market segment. An analysis of the responses indicated how many households might be expected to rent an apartment in the proposed project.

Urban Office Building This case concerned a parcel of land located across the street from the county courthouse in a large southwestern city within a five-minute walk to a Federal Court building. The site and construction costs indicated that the 200,000-square-foot building should rent for at least $8.00 per square foot.

Step 1 The location of this site indicated that the natural market segment would consist of law firms and that they would be (a) primarily engaged in trial work, (b already located in the downtown area, and (c) currently paying at least $8.00 per square foot for their office space.

Step 2 The size of the market segment was determined from a list of attorneys published by the local Bar association. The size of each firm, its type of practice, and its current location were carefully noted.

Step 3 The capture rate—the number of square feet the owner of the proposed building could reasonably expect to rent at $8.00 per square foot per year—was determined by a personal interview with the senior partner in each firm within the market segment.

Residential Subdivision   This analysis involved a 100-acre parcel near a large midwestern city. Subdivision regulations and land costs suggested that the land be developed with single-family homes costing at least $60,000 each.

Step 1   The characteristics of families in this housing market were determined from a questionnaire sent to residents of a comparable subdivision. The responses indicated how many families in this market segment had lived in one of three less expensive subdivisions for at least five years.

Step 2   The total number of families residing in one of these three subdivisions for the last five years was determined from past issues of the city directory, which lists residents according to street address. The percentage of families who had purchased in the comparable, more expensive subdivision indicated the size of the total market segment.

Step 3   The capture rate was determined by analyzing the competitive qualities of existing and proposed subdivisions relative to the total market segment.

Town House Project   This study concerned a proposed 200-unit town house project in a major southern city. The developer wanted to determine the unit mix as well as an equitable price for each type of unit.

Step 1   The market segment was identified as people currently looking at town house projects. A list of prospective buyers was compiled by copying license plate numbers on automobiles parked in front of the models at competitive projects. In this particular state, the name and address of the car owner could be obtained from the license number.

Step 2   The size of the market was projected from a questionnaire sent to each prospective town house purchaser.

Step 3   The capture rate was determined from the responses to the questionnaire and the absorption rate of competitive town house projects.

The market analysis of a feasibility study should result in a projection of how much, and when, income would be received from rents or sales. The projections are the cash inflows that are used in the final conclusions regarding the economic feasibility of the study. Exhibit 1 shows typical cash inflows for a proposed office building.

COST ANALYSIS

This portion of a feasibility study determines the amount and timing of cash outflows during the development and holding period of a project. A typical development would include the following costs:

1   Land costs.
2   Professional fees.
3   Off-site costs.
4   On-site costs.

Exhibit 1 Cash Inflows for a Proposed Office Building

Period	1	2	3	4	5	6	7	8
Type of inflow								
Office space rental	$10,000	$35,000	$40,000	$70,000	$70,000	$70,000	$100,000	$100,000
Parking income	1,000	2,000	8,000	10,000	10,000	10,000	12,000	12,000
Commercial space rental	0	4,000	4,000	4,000	4,000	4,000	4,000	4,000
Miscellaneous income	0	1,000	1,000	1,000	1,000	1,000	1,000	1,000
Total cash inflows	$11,000	$42,000	$53,000	$85,000	$85,000	$85,000	$117,000	$117,000

Exhibit 2 Cash Outflows for a Proposed Subdivision

Period	1	2	3	4	5	6	7	8
Land costs	$1,000,000							
Off-site costs	500,000							
On-site costs	40,000	$ 40,000	$ 40,000	$ 40,000	$ 40,000	$ 40,000	$ 40,000	
Professional fees	30,000							
Advertising	45,000	20,000	20,000	20,000	20,000	20,000	20,000	
Management and supervision	15,000	10,000	10,000	10,000	10,000	10,000	10,000	10,000
Closing costs		8,000	10,000	10,000	15,000	15,000	15,000	15,000
Taxes	40,000	30,000	25,000	20,000	15,000	10,000	5,000	
Total cash outflows	$1,670,000	$108,000	$105,000	$100,000	$100,000	$95,000	$90,000	$25,000

 5   Construction costs.
 6   Advertising costs.
 7   Management and supervision expenses.
 8   Interest expense.
 9   Closing fees.
10   Taxes.

These various outflows must be synchronized with the absorption rate that was indicated in the market analysis. For example, consider the timing of cash outflows for a town house project. First, an initial outflow of cash is required to purchase land. Second, cash is needed for various fees such as appraisal fees. Third, unit construction costs are incurred several months before the unit can be sold. Fourth, cash outflows for sales, commissions, and closing costs are incurred at the time of sale. The timing and amount of each cash outflow will be used in the final analysis. Exhibit 2 shows the typical cash outflows for a proposed subdivision.

ANALYSIS OF OBJECTIVES

As we have seen, the objectives of all parties concerned are the basic premise of a feasibility study. Therefore, the analyst, after following through on the next three steps, must return to these original objectives in order to make sure that each one has been satisfied.

Both the lender's and the developer's profit objectives can be summarized in a cash-flow statement, which is usually regarded as the economic analysis portion of the feasibility study. As noted above, the cash inflows are determined through market analysis, and the outflows are determined by cost analysis. The cash-flow statement is then used to measure the project's ability to meet the profit objectives of all parties. Regarding nonprofit objectives such as image development or portfolio balance, the analyst depends largely on intuition; the report is a subjective conclusion.

The analyst concludes the report by making a statement regarding the feasibility of the plan under consideration. A feasible project is simply one that meets the objectives of all parties.

Chapter 8

Financial Statement and Credit Analysis

James Don Edwards &
Roger A. Roemmich

This chapter will seek to demonstrate how financial statement analysis can be used to analyze the prospective borrower's credit stability, potential cash flow, earning capability, and general ability to repay the loan in arriving at a decision on the loan request.

SOURCES OF CREDIT INFORMATION

The credit-granting-and-collecting function is based on the creditor's evaluation of the customer's ability and willingness to pay the account when due. Among the factors important for consideration in evaluating the creditworthiness of a customer are the financial ability of the customer, the customer's previous credit experience, and the payment record, if any, to the company. Sources of credit information may be either direct or indirect. Direct sources are those derived from the credit customer; indirect sources come from other companies, credit associations, etc.

Direct sources of information provide most of the information necessary for financial statement analysis. Financial statement analysis is extremely useful in evaluating a prospective customer's ability to pay. If the customer is a corporation, direct information can be obtained through the published annual reports of the company's statements by company officials, annual meeting of stockholders, financial statements, and interviews with company management personnel.

Indirect information is useful to a creditor in financial statement analysis as a means of evaluating a company's performance relative to other companies in the same industry. Indirect information on public companies is available in Standard and Poor's *Industry Survey*.

Evaluation of a creditor's willingness to pay and past payment record is beyond the scope of financial statement analysis. This information is available through indirect sources such as Dun and Bradstreet, Inc.; reports by industry mercantile agencies; national credit association report data; other trade association reports; other miscellaneous indirect sources.

SOURCE OF CAPITAL

One of the primary reasons for business or venture failure is insufficient or improper financing. The first step in analyzing the adequacy of financing is to determine the source of the present capital and the capability to obtain capital in the future.

Since it is important to know whether assets have been provided by owners or obtained through the use of debt financing, an analysis of comparative balance sheet percentages is very useful. This advantage is illustrated in Exhibit 1.

The percentage of assets financed through borrowing and the extent of trading on

Exhibit 1

	Company A		Company B	
	Amount	%	Amount	%
Assets:				
Current assets				
Cash	$ 225,365	1.76	$ 253,476	1.73
Accounts receivable	1,362,535	10.61	564,384	3.86
Total current assets	1,587,900	12.37	817,860	5.59
Long-term assets				
Land	8,651,300	67.38	10,873,000	74.26
Building and equipment	4,000,000		5,250,000	
Less: Accumulated depreciation	(1,400,000)	20.25	(2,300,000)	20.15
Total long-term assets	11,251,300	87.63	13,823,000	94.41
Total assets	$12,839,200	100.00	$14,640,860	100.00
Liabilities:				
Accounts payable	$ 275,636	2.15	$ 370,684	2.53
Notes payable	432,284	3.37	205,623	1.40
Mortgage payable	2,532,630	19.73	4,630,000	31.62
Income taxes payable	163,430	1.27	175,233	1.20
Total liabilities	$ 3,403,980	26.51	$ 5,381,540	36.75
Stockholders' equity:				
Capital stock	2,000,000	15.58	3,000,000	20.49
Paid-in capital in excess of par	4,000,000	31.15	5,000,000	34.15
Retained earnings	3,435,220	26.76	1,259,320	8.60
Total stockholders' equity	$ 9,435,220	73.49	$ 9,259,320	63.25
Total liabilities and				
stockholders' equity	$12,839,200	100.00	$14,640,860	100.00

the equity or use of financial leverage is best measured through the *debt ratio*. The debt ratio is computed by dividing total liabilities by total assets. This ratio is an indication of the margin of safety provided to creditors against a reduction in asset values. For example, in Exhibit 1, the debt ratio is 26.51 percent for Company A and 36.76 percent for Company B.

The ratio of stockholders' equity to total assets is called the *equity ratio*. The equity ratio shows that 73.49 percent of the assets of Company A and 63.24 percent of the assets of Company B have been provided by owners.

The percentage of assets provided by owners or stockholders cushions creditors against loss, since by law creditors of a business that fails take priority on claims against the business before funds, if sufficient, are distributed to owners.

The debt and equity ratios are very important indicators of the portion of assets contributed by owners and creditors. We must caution, however, that users of financial statement analysis should note that these ratios measure the margin of safety based upon the recorded asset balances per books of the business. The recorded asset balances are not based upon the value of the assets at the present time but upon the historical or original cost of the asset less depreciation for assets that decline in value through usage in the business. Since the value of assets may differ substantially from the balance per books, we suggest that wherever possible mortgage bankers should ask the prospective borrower to provide evidence of the appraised present value of long-term assets.

Exhibit 2 shows the balance sheets of Company A and Company B based upon appraised values of long-term assets. The debt ratio for Company A is 22.42 percent and for Company B it is 24.66 percent. The equity ratio shows that stockholders' equity accounts for 77.58 percent of the assets of Company A and 75.34 percent of the assets of Company B. Exhibit 2 also shows that assets can decline in value $11,783,920 in Company A and $16,436,320 in Company B before creditors suffer losses.

The primary source of industrial growth in recent years has been undistributed earnings or retained earnings. The ratio of retained earnings to total assets indicates the portion of the existing assets which have been provided by undistributed earnings. In Exhibit 1, note that only 8.60 percent of Company B's assets have been furnished by past operations. This ratio provides evidence of the amount of working capital generated by operations to finance growth and to retire debt.

The ratio of long-term assets to stockholders' equity is often computed as a test of the adequacy of equity capital. A high ratio indicates potential trouble, because the company has committed a large portion of its capital to noncurrent assets, which cannot be used to meet the need for working capital in periods of adversity.

As shown in Exhibit 3, this ratio is extremely high for both Company A and Company B. When this ratio is greater than 1, it means that all of the stockholders' equity and part of the debt financing have been used to purchase long-term assets. As a general rule, the ratio of long-term assets to stockholders' equity should not be greater than 1. A ratio of 1.49 for Company B is especially dangerous when combined with a very low amount of retained earnings. This indicates that the company could experience difficulties in meeting working capital needs in low-income periods. Low retained

Exhibit 2

	Company A		Company B	
	Amount	%	Amount	%
Assets:				
Current assets				
Cash	$ 225,365	1.48	$ 253,476	1.16
Accounts receivable	1,362,535	8.97	564,384	2.59
Total current assets	1,587,900	10.45	817,860	3.75
Long-term assets				
Land (appraised value)	10,000,000	65.84	20,000,000	91.67
Buildings and (appraised)				
and equipment value	3,600,000	23.71	1,000,000	4.58
Total long-term assets	13,600,000	89.55	21,000,000	96.25
Total appraised assets	$15,187,900	100.00	$21,817,860	100.00
Liabilities:				
Accounts payable	$ 275,636	1.81	370,684	1.70
Notes payable	432,284	2.85	205,623	0.94
Mortgage payable	2,532,630	16.68	4,630,000	21.22
Income taxes payable	163,430	1.08	175,233	0.80
Total liabilities	$ 3,403,980	22.42	$ 5,381,500	24.66
Stockholders' equity:				
Capital stock, $10 par	2,000,000	13.17	3,000,000	13.75
Paid-in capital in				
excess of par	4,000,000	26.34	5,000,000	22.92
Retained earnings	3,435,220	22.62	1,259,320	5.77
Unrealized appreciation				
in long-term assets	2,348,700	15.45	7,177,000	32.90
Total stockholders' equity	$11,783,920	77.58	$16,436,320	75.34
Total liabilities and				
stockholders' equity	$15,187,900	100.00	$21,817,860	100.00

earnings suggest that past earnings of this company have not provided substantial working capital.

Our discussion of financial statement analysis relative to the source and adequacy of capitalization has focused on corporate entities. Where individual proprietorships or partnerships seek income-property financing, the owner's equity in personal assets provides an additional margin of safety in making loans, since these forms of business entities have unlimited liability. Personal information such as that shown in Exhibit 4 should be obtained as a means of further illustrating credit worthiness.

Exhibit 3

	Company A	Company B
Long-term assets	$11,251,300	$13,823,000
Stockholders' equity	9,435,220 =	9,259,320 =

Exhibit 4

Personal property (appraised value)	_____
Cash in banks and other savings institutions	_____
Investments (fair market value)	_____
Other assets (list)	_____

EARNING CAPACITY

A very important part of financial statement analysis is the information it provides about the earning capacity of a company. While the owner's or stockholders' equity provides a margin of safety to creditors, the greatest insurance that a company is able to meet its loan obligations is a solid demand for its product and sound management which converts that demand into profits.

Exhibit 5
Comparative Income Statements

	Company A		Company B	
	1974	1975	1974	1975
Sales (000 omitted)	$3,230.9	$3,645.7	$6,345.8	$6,215.6
Other revenue	241.2	313.6	213.3	167.5
Total revenue	3,472.1	3,959.3	6,559.1	6,383.1
Cost of properties sold	2,945.3	3,265.1	6,325.3	6,068.3
Operating expense	100.0	120.0	115.3	106.5
Interest expense	25.0	25.0	10.0	10.0
Income tax expense	180.0	225.0	46.8	104.3
Total expenses	3,250.3	3,635.1	6,497.4	6,289.1
Net income	$ 221.8	$ 324.2	$ 61.7	$ 94.0

Exhibit 5 shows comparative income statements for Company A and Company B for 1974 and 1975. It is important in analyzing earning capabilities to know how a company performs over an extended period of time. Accounting statements are based upon the accrual principle for revenue recognition. The accrual system results in the recognition of income when goods are sold or when services are performed. Although the accrual basis of accounting minimizes opportunity for companies to manage the reported income for an accounting period, some problems do exist in the timing of revenue recognition.

Another important reason for analyzing the trend of revenue recognition is to determine how a company performs in periods of adversity. Many real estate development companies are not sound credit risks, because they experience losses or earn small profits in periods of business contraction. The years 1974 and 1975 are especially useful in analyzing builders or developers of income properties, because they represent lean years for this industry. These comparative income statements show that Company B experienced very low net income in 1974 and 1975. This suggests that, although

Company B may not be a poor risk for continued expansion of existing properties because of the existence of a large amount of stockholders' equity, there are serious indications that the builder may fail in ventures involving the creation of new properties.

Exhibit 6

Ratio or measurement	Method of computation	Company A 1975	Company B 1975
1. Return on total book assets	Net income + interest expense / Investment in assets	2.72%	.75%
2. Return on appraised total assets	Net income before interest expense and taxes / Appraised Assets	3.78%	.95%
3. Return on actual stockholders' equity	Net income / Stockholders' equity	3.44%	1.02%
4. Return on potential stockholders' equity (including unrealized appreciation in long-term assets)	Net income / Stockholders' equity	2.75%	.57%
5. Earnings per share of capital stock	Net income / Shares of capital stock outstanding	$1.62	$ .31
6. Times interest earned (before taxes)	Net income before taxes and interest / Interest expense	22.97 times	20.83 times

Exhibit 6 provides a summary of analytical measurements used in financial statement analysis to assess the earning capacity of a company.

The return on total book assets is the measure normally used in financial statement analysis to assess the productivity of assets. As we noted earlier, in examining the source of business capital, the reported assets per books are based upon the historical cost of assets. Since the historical cost of assets may differ substantially from their value for use in business ventures, we suggest that the commercial loan industry should measure productivity based upon the return on appraised total assets. Where long-term assets have appreciated substantially, the return on appraised total assets is a much better indication of the ability of a builder or developer to generate earnings on new properties or on the expansion of existing properties.

The return on appraised total assets may be used to evaluate the probable effect on net income of business expansion. For example, Exhibit 6 shows the return on appraised assets for Company B for 1975 is .95%. If Company B borrows $5,000,000 to finance a new venture and experiences the same productivity in 1976, then the additional revenue resulting from this expansion is $5,000,000 times .95%, or $47,500. The additional interest expense at 12% is $600,000. Thus, the net loss before taxes due to this expansion for 1976 would be $553,000.

A general rule can be suggested for determining whether expansion based entirely upon commercial loans is likely to result in increased profits for a corporate borrower. The formula is:

$$(a \times r) - (a \times i) = p$$

where a = additional assets created by the loan
r = the estimated return on the additional assets
i = the interest rate on the loan
p = the before-tax profit on the loan

Obviously, the key variable in determining whether a borrower can use the additional capital profitably is r. If r is greater than i, the use of financial leverage or "trading on the equity" will result in increased profits for stockholders. If r is less than i, this use of financial leverage will result in lower profits or losses for stockholders and greater risk for creditors.

The analytical measure return on appraised assets is a very logical means of approximating r. The current return (.95% for Company B) on business assets is measured more reasonably when based upon the appraised value of assets rather than the historical cost of those assets.

The return on stockholders' equity is used to measure the earning power on stockholders' equity. When comparative financial statements are provided for several years, this ratio, combined with the return on assets before interest and taxes, can often provide evidence of the degree of success management has enjoyed in using financial leverage. Exhibit 7 illustrates this approach for Company C. Management was very aggressive in seeking debt financing as a means of expanding existing facilities in 1974 and 1975. The productivity of the assets increased, as witnessed by increased returns on total assets before interest and taxes. The decreased returns to stockholders are caused by interest costs that exceed the return on the additional assets.

It is very important for commercial lenders to examine management's past success in using financial leverage. It provides evidence of the likelihood of future success and suggests when a company may not be able to use additional capital profitably.

Exhibit 7
Company C

		1973	1974	1975
1.	Net income	$ 525,000	$ 495,000	$ 475,000
2.	Stockholders' equity	5,000,000	5,000,000	5,000,000
3.	Net income			
	Stockholders' equity	10.50%	9.90%	9.50%
4.	Return on total assets	10.00%	10.36%	11.08%
	(before interest and taxes)			

The computation of earnings per share of capital stock not only provides evidence of the return per share but, when multiplied by past price-earnings ratios, suggests the potential price for sale of additional capital stock. This method of determining the price at which new capital stock could be issued is not necessary·for widely traded stocks, but provides important evidence for closely held corporations.

When recent earnings have been depressed, most corporations will not issue capital stock as a means of obtaining financing for expansion. Company B's 1975 earnings of $.31 per share would seem to preclude capital stock offerings in the near future. To potential creditors of Company B the depressed 1975 earnings present a risk both as a measure of the company's earnings capacity and as an indicator that debt financing is the most likely source of additional capital. Additional debt financing reduces the relative protection provided by stockholders' equity against reductions in asset values and poor earnings performance.

Since creditors must be primarily concerned with the safety of their capital, the *times interest earned ratio* is a prime index of financial strength. This ratio indicates the number of times (before taxes) interest charges on long-term debt are earned. When providing capital for expansion of existing facilities or construction of new facilities, it is important to determine whether current net income is adequate for covering both the existing interest expense and the additional interest expense resulting from the expansion. This conservative posture is desirable when evaluating the ability to cover interest charges from operating revenues, because positive returns from income-property expansions are frequently not realized in the early life of the development.

CASH FLOW

Sound earnings performance is normally a sign of sound financial position. Companies with a solid earnings record can usually convert those earnings into short-term assets or working capital to meet immediate needs. Even where earnings performance has been

Exhibit 8
X Corporation
Statement of Changes in Financial Position
For the Year Ended December 31, 1975

Funds provided by:		
Operations:		
Net income	$ 320,350	
Add: Expenses not requiring outlay of working capital		
in current period:		
Depreciation	535,200	
Loss on sale of equipment	16,200	
a. Working capital provided by operations		$ 871,750
b. Issuance of capital stock		350,000
c. Proceeds from mortgage loan		1,000,000
d. Sale of equipment		165,325
Total funds provided		$2,387,075
Fund applied to:		
Acquisition of:		
Land	$ 250,000	
Building	1,500,000	
Equipment	350,000	$2,100,000
Payment of dividends		300,000
Decrease in working capital		(12,925)
Total funds applied		$2,387,075

Exhibit 9

Source of Working Capital		% of WC Provided
Operations	$ 871,750	36.52%
Issuance of capital stock	350,000	14.66%
Proceeds from mortgage loan	1,000,000	41.89%
Sale of equipment	165,325	6.93%
Total	$2,387,075	100.00%
Working capital provided by operations		$871,750
Less: Dividends payments	$300,000	$300,000
Working capital available to finance expansion of assets		$571,750

outstanding, it is still important to analyze a company's ability to meet its working capital needs.

Working capital is provided by operations, sale of capital stock, long-term financing, and sale of long-term assets. The ideal situation occurs when operations provide sufficient working capital to meet current needs. When operations do not provide sufficient working capital to meet current needs, the interests of both owners and creditors are best protected by the issuance of additional capital stock to obtain working capital. It is not healthy for a corporation to obtain long-term financing to meet dividend payments, because this capital does not generate additional income to offset the additional interest expense. Thus, the use of long-term financing for dividend payments results in lower earnings available to stockholders and should be contemplated only as a last resort.

Exhibit 8 is X Corporation's Statement of Changes in Financial Position for 1975. This statement is an integral part of financial statement analysis. It provides evidence beyond that in the income statement and balance sheet about the flow of financial resources for a business entity.

Exhibit 9 analyzes the sources and uses of working capital for X Corporation in 1975. The figures show operations provided 36.52 percent of new working capital in 1975. Because of the low cost of using retained earnings, the most desirable source of corporate growth is through expansion based upon internally generated funds. In 1975, X Corporation's operations provided sufficient funds to meet dividend payments and leave $571,750 available for expansion in assets.

Analyzing working capital flow provides sufficient evidence relative to the source and use of working capital, but does not fully answer the question of the adequacy of working capital to meet short-term obligations.

The two ratios frequently used by creditors to determine the ability of a business entity to meet its short-term obligations are the *current ratio* and the *quick or acid-test ratio*. In Exhibit 10, the composition of current assets and current liabilities of X Corporation are detailed for December 31, 1974 and December 31, 1975. The net working capital was $130,988 at December 31, 1974 and was reduced to $118,063 by December 31, 1975.

The current ratio is the traditional measure of a firm's short-term debt-paying ability. X Corporation's current ratio was 1.10 to 1 at the end of both 1974 and 1975. Many lending institutions have traditionally employed a minimum current ratio of 1.5

or 2.0 in determining acceptability for loan purposes. This conservative standard provides a measure of protection against borrowers who are unable to meet short-term obligations, but mortgage bankers must remain cognizant of the differences in collection procedures between firms and the cost to a client of maintaining excess current assets. A company which has a short operating cycle (the time elapsed between investment of cash in inventory to conversion back into cash) needs to maintain less current assets relative to current liabilities than a firm with a long operating cycle. The adequacy of a firm's ability to pay its short-run debts should be viewed as a combination of its earnings capability, its credit rating, and the composition of its current assets.

Those current assets which are easily converted into cash are called quick-assets or cash equivalents. Included among the group of current assets which are classified as quick-assets are cash, accounts receivable, notes receivable (due within the current operating cycle), and marketable securities. The ratio of quick assets to current liabilities is called the acid-test ratio. This ratio measures the ability to meet short-term obligations as they fall due. The acid-test ratio for X Corporation was .52 at December 31, 1974 and .48 at December 31, 1975.

An acid-test ratio of less than 1 is a warning signal which suggests that a company has inadequate liquidity. In order to meet its obligations, X Corporation will have to obtain additional working capital through operations, sale of securities, or through issuance of debt. The current ratio and the acid-test ratio do not provide conclusive evidence that a company will be unable to meet its short-term obligations. They suggest a need for additional working capital, which can be provided by any of the

Exhibit 10
X Corporation

	December 31, 1974	December 31, 1975
Current assets:		
Cash	$ 136,280	$ 75,630
Accounts receivable (net of allowance for doubtful accounts)	526,168	575,160
Notes receivable (due within current operating cycle)	100,000	—
Inventory	675,000	691,325
Prepaid expenses	25,075	—
Total current assets	$1,452,523	$1,342,115
Current liabilities:		
Accounts payable	$ 256,235	$ 158,752
Notes payable (due within current operating cycle)	800,000	800,000
Interest payable	365,300	365,300
Total current liabilities	$1,321,535	$1,224,052
Working capital	$ 130,988	$ 118,063

Current ratio	$\dfrac{\text{(current assets)}}{\text{(current liabilities)}}$	$\dfrac{\$1,452,523}{1,321,535} = 1.10$	$\dfrac{\$1,342,115}{1,224,052} = 1.10$
Acid-test ratio	$\dfrac{\text{(quick assets)}}{\text{(current liabilities)}}$	$\dfrac{\$\ 752,448}{1,452,523} = .52$	$\dfrac{\$\ 650,790}{1,342,115} = .48$

Exhibit 11
Y Corporation

	Net sales	1974	1975
a.	Net Sales	$2,420,000	3,140,000
b.	Average accounts receivable	600,000	920,000
	(Beginning AR + Ending AR)	(300,000 + 900,000)	(900,000 = 940,000)
	2	2	2
c.	Receivables turnover ($a \div b$)	4.03	3.41
d.	Number of days' sales uncollected		
	($365 \div c$) (average receivables)	90.57	106.74
e.	Number of days' sales uncollected		
	($365 \div c$) (ending receivables)	135.69	109.28
f.	Bad debts expense	$128,000	$229,000
g.	Bad debts expense as percentage	5.25%	7.25%
	of net sales		

aforementioned means. When combined with a history of poor earnings performance, low current and acid-test ratios are an important indication of a poor credit risk.

OTHER IMPORTANT FINANCIAL MEASURES

A complete financial analysis must include a determination of the quality of the information included in those statements. As noted earlier, in suggesting that it is more appropriate to evaluate sources of capital and earnings capacity based upon the appraised value of long-term assets rather than the historical cost of those assets, the recorded asset cost may not represent the value of that asset to the business entity.

A very important item for mortgage bankers to analyze is the quality of the accounts receivable. As shown in Exhibit 11, the total amount of accounts receivable increased tremendously from January 1, 1975 to December 31, 1975. Assuming the relative sales levels have not changed significantly in this time period, two plausible reasons for this increase are a loosening of credit standards for sales or that major customers are experiencing financial problems. Either of these explanations is very bad news for Y Corporation.

The number of days' sales uncollected is a measure of the average time necessary to convert receivables into cash. Although it is obvious that the trend is toward slower collection of accounts receivable, it is important to assess the risk attached with average accounts receivable outstanding over 90 days. The National Association of Credit Men estimates that the value of past due accounts receivable declines per the following schedule:

Each $ in Accounts Past Due:	3 Mo	6 Mo	1 Yr.	2 Yr.
Estimated Value	90¢	50¢	25¢	0

The quality of a company's receivables and the soundness of credit policies may also be assessed by examining bad debt experience in recent years. Y Corporation's bad debts expense as a percentage of net sales was 5.29 percent in 1974 and 7.29 percent in 1975. This experience must be examined relative to the experience of other

Exhibit 12

Customer	Amount of receivable	Age of receivable			
		Current	30–60 days	60–90 days	over 90 days
ABC Corporation	$175,000		X		
John Smith	25,000			X	
John Doe	100,000		X		
Z Corporation	150,000				X
Quick Service Co.	50,000	X			

companies in the same industry. Even during 1974 and 1975, when poor collections experience was commonplace, these figures were very high.

Where the collection of accounts receivable appears to be a problem, another avenue may be available to mortgage bankers in assessing the quality of accounts receivable. This avenue is to ask the prospective borrower for a schedule of aged accounts receivable similar to that shown in Exhibit 12. This schedule can provide very good evidence for judging the quality of accounts receivable.

Inventory turnover ratios provide an indication of management's ability to control the investment in inventory. The higher the inventory turnover ratio, the shorter the average time between investment in inventories and the sales transaction. A short cycle from investment in inventory to the sales transaction means the working capital required for investment in inventories is minimized. Exhibit 13 shows the computation of inventory turnover ratios for the Ace Corporation for 1974 and 1975. Inventory turnover ratios for the developers of income properties are normally very low. Thus a potential creditor of Ace Corporation should probably be encouraged by a turnover ratio of 3.01 in 1975 and by the improvement in turnover time on the average property from 164.41 days in 1974 to 121.26 days in 1975.

Exhibit 13
Ace Corporation

		1974	1975
a.	Cost of goods sold	$1,260,000	$1,443,000
	Inventory (beginning of year)	710,000	425,000
	Inventory (end of year)	425,000	535,000
b.	Average inventory	567,500	480,000
c.	Turnover per year ($a \div b$)	2.22	3.01
d.	Number of days' sales in average inventory ($365 \div c$)	164.41	121.26
e.	Number of days' sales in ending inventory	123.14	135.34

The significance of the inventory turnover ratio is minimized if the replacement cost of inventories is substantially different from the recorded inventory cost per financial statements. In such cases it is advisable to ignore the computed inventory ratio in favor of an analysis of the time from the beginning of the latest development projects to their sale.

THE CREDIT DECISION

Fitting all the pieces of financial analysis together to arrive at a decision on the loan request is very difficult. There are many additional factors to consider in evaluating future earnings performance which are not part of traditional financial statement analysis such as: the likely demand for a particular type of product or property; sensitivity to economic fluctuations; effect of technological and environmental changes on a company's business; and competition from existing sources and potential competition from new sources.

Another important point to remember is that the quality of assets reported on financial statements should be carefully assessed. Creditors can and should ask for evidence relative to the value of recorded assets. Such evidence includes appraised values for long-term assets, schedules of aged accounts receivable, and replacement cost information for inventories.

When the parts of financial statement analysis are put into perspective, probably the most important piece of information provided is the source of capital as measured by the debt and equity ratios. With the increasing loan-to-value trend in commercial loans, it is very important to know how great a loss can be sustained by a builder or developer before creditor interests suffer a loss. Although the equity ratio and the margin of safety it represents is important where existing properties are being expanded, it is of much greater significance where a builder or developer seeks a loan for the creation of entirely new properties. The reason for the increased emphasis on the equity ratio is the greater risk attached with new ventures. The existence of an adequate layer of stockholders' equity is one deterrent against creditors' loss on a commercial loan.

From the viewpoint of potential investors, the most important attribute a business can possess is the potential for strong earnings performance in the future. This potential is also very important to creditors, but does not provide the protection that the existence of stockholders' equity does. Potential creditors must remember that existing equity provides certain protection, whereas earnings potential may not be converted into monetary gain. Creditors should use past earnings performance as one barometer of future performance. Since protection of capital is of utmost concern to mortgage bankers, consistent past earnings performance should be given greater weight than dramatic but irregular successes.

When viewed in combination with the amount of equity capital existing, demonstrated consistent past earnings performance is much more necessary when equity capital provides little protection against loss of capital.

Under these circumstances, any loan becomes a very risky proposition. A clear distinction exists in such cases between loans for expansion of existing facilities and loans for creation of new properties. Where existing facilities are being expanded, past earnings performance may sufficiently reduce the risk of loss of capital. Where equity capital provides insufficient protection, the inherent riskiness of new ventures almost precludes creditor's financing the venture. Equity providers have the advantage of receiving substantial compensation when they successfully assume such risks.

Mortgage bankers as creditors normally do not sufficiently share in the profits to warrant the risk assumed in such cases.

The quality of reported assets is an important part of the credit decision. With the possible exception of those cases where sufficient equity capital and strong earnings potential leave little room for doubt as to the desirability of a commercial loan, the quality of accounts receivable and inventories is an integral part of the credit decision.

If mortgage bankers do assume the risk of financing new ventures where inadequate equity capital exists, they should base this decision on the likelihood of strong earnings performance and a short operating cycle for converting inventories into sales and sales into collections.

Cash flow problems have been a major problem for income-property developers in recent years. These cash flow problems have much of their foundation in other factors such as poor earnings performance, inadequate equity capital, and loose sales and credit policies. Nevertheless, it is important to examine a company's working capital flow to determine whether earnings generate sufficient working capital to pay retained earnings and finance part of a company's capital expansion program. It is also desirable to determine whether sufficient quick assets exist to meet current liabilities. When such liquidity does not exist, a company may find it necessary to use emergency measures to meet these short-term obligations.

Determining the advisability of granting a commercial loan for development of income properties is a very complex procedure. Financial statement analysis can provide substantial insight into the creditworthiness of the borrower.

Based upon the premise that the risk of loss of capital and potential interest is the primary concern of mortgage bankers in arriving at a decision on the loan request, the primary financial factors to consider in the financial statement analysis are:

1 Source of capital.
2 Past and future earnings performance.
3 Quality of assets.
4 Cash flow and liquidity.

Chapter 9

Lease Analysis: Some Practical Applications and Techniques

Manuel DeBusk

INTRODUCTION

This chapter is an account of the way in which a prospective mortgagee's interest may be legally and economically affected by lease provisions where either the leasehold or the fee estate to which it is attached is mortgaged. The discussion defines certain ideal lease provisions from the point of view of a mortgage of the fee or a leasehold mortgage. Some remedies to adverse provisions which may be encountered in leases are set out.

It is crucial, however, to realize that laws differ materially between states and that no legal decisions should be made without consulting counsel in the specific jurisdiction in which any subject property is located.

Lease analysis is an exercise in changing points of view. A prospective mortgagee of the fee estate must constantly think of itself as occupying the owner's position through possible foreclosure or other acquisition of title. Where a leasehold mortgage is involved, its point of view will, in many cases, oppose that of a fee mortgagee. The covenants and conditions of any lease should be analyzed by the lender, not only from the standpoint of the landlord or tenant/borrower to perform, but also from the standpoint of the mortgagee as a possible owner.

TYPES OF LEASES TO BE ANALYZED

Leases may be classed as *ground leases, commercial leases*, or *residential leases*. A ground lease is most often a long-term lease of property, which at the outset may be unimproved. Its value to the lessee is the amount of income that it will produce as rent upon improvement and possible subletting. A commercial lease is generally on improved property and provides income to the owner of the property while granting privileges to the tenant in the form of occupying the leased space. The term may be as short as one month to as long as 30 or 40 years, but seldom would the term be longer than the estimated physical or economic life of the improved property. Examples of commercial leases would be for retail business, industrial use, or office space. Because of the length of these leases, tenants are ordinarily required to share in any increase in operating expenses or real estate taxes.

A residential lease may be monthly or longer, but seldom exceeds two or three years. As the term implies, it is for space to be occupied for living quarters. It can be used for single-family houses, but is more often prevalent in apartment complexes.

Leases may also be classified according to whether they antedate or postdate the mortgage in execution. Antedated leases in the absence of a subordination clause are prior in right to subsequent mortgages in most states. Conversely, postdated leases are generally subordinate to the mortgage. The difference is very important to the holder of a mortgage, because foreclosure may "wipe out" the leases on a property and thus eliminate the present income. Depending on the economic facts of the matter, this may or may not be to the advantage of the holder, who might, for example, if the income is uneconomically low, desire to wipe out the contract rent and improve it with something higher. If, on the other hand, the rent is economic, current, and being paid by a responsible and desirable tenant, the holder may desire it to continue.

Subordination may be by separate instrument or may be a covenant of the lease itself. The recital effecting the subordination might be in language similar to this:

> Lessee acknowledges that this lease is and shall be second, inferior, junior and subordinate to any presently existing recorded lien upon the demised premises but lessee's rights under this lease shall nevertheless remain in full force and effect during the term thereof so long as lessee shall continue to perform all of the covenants and conditions of the lease on its part to be done and performed.

An alternative to this kind of covenant of quiet enjoyment might be one in which the landlord or lessor is vested with authority to subordinate the lessee's interest under subsequently executed mortgages, provided that the tenant who pays rent when due and performs all obligations of the lease should continue peaceably and quietly to have, hold, and enjoy the demised premises. In other words, the tenant cannot be evicted. Leases containing covenants of quiet enjoyment should be reviewed with the recognition that in most states they are binding in all respects against the mortgagee after foreclosure.

Postdated leases are subject to the mortgage. Essentially, this means that the mortgagee upon foreclosure has the right of possession against landlord and tenant alike. A mortgagee may demand payment of the rent as a condition for the continuance of the lease. The tenant, however, may refuse payment and regard the lease as terminated upon foreclosure. In some states, a mortgagee may not collect rents in reliance on a postdated lease unless the mortgage so provides.

If protection against the loss of tenants by termination of the lease upon foreclosure is desired, the lender should make certain that the clause contains express subordination of the mortgage to the lease. The mortgage should also provide for assignment of present and future leases to the mortgagee and an assignment of leases and rents. This provides additional security for the mortgage debt and may be either a present assignment or conditioned on default in payment of the debt secured by the mortgage.

STEPS IN ANALYSIS

The steps in analyzing a lease should generally follow the order in which its major provisions are set out in the writing. Sometimes, that may be interrupted by a consideration of the interrelation between several clauses in different portions of the instrument, if this seems appropriate to a proper analysis. Subject matters normally to be expected in a lease include:

The names and addresses of the parties.

An exact description of the demised premises.

The commencement date and termination date.

The amount of rental agreed to be paid and time of payment.

A clause denoting the lessee's acceptance of the premises.

A description of the use to which the premises may be put.

A covenant to comply with all laws, ordinances, and regulations.

A covenant relating to the obligations of the parties with respect to payment of real estate taxes and casualty and other forms of insurance.

A covenant relating to obligations for maintenance by the lessor, the lessee, and to alterations, additions, and improvements.

A covenant providing for the type and location of signs.

Waiver of subrogation substitution of one creditor for another.

A covenant providing for landlord's right of entry.

A covenant relating to the provision of utility services.

Covenants relating to assignment and subleasing.

Covenants concerning the effect of partial or total casualty losses or condemnation.

Covenants relating to the lessee's obligation in the event of a holding over after the expiration of the term.

A hold harmless provision.

A statement of events constituting default.

A statement setting out the lessor's lien, if any.

A covenant for payment of attorney's fees in event of loss.

A covenant of attornment or quiet enjoyment.

Force majeure provisions (a provision to void a contract due to unpredictable occurrences).

Renewal options and terms of options.
Signatures.

PHYSICAL DATA AND TITLE

Complete copies of existing or proposed leases to which all appropriate exhibits have been attached should always be obtained prior to execution of the mortgage. If the lease is an existing one, it should be a fully executed copy together with all exhibits. Concurrently with examination of the lease, there should be some investigation of the financial status of the tenant or (if the lease is a master lease and there are numerous subtenants) cash flow from the property. As in any substantial lending transaction a thorough examination of the landlord's title should be made. Infrequently, the condition of title may be evidenced by a complete abstract of title supplemented to a current date and supported by an attorney's opinion. More often title will be evidenced by title insurance.

DESCRIPTION OF THE PREMISES

This should be taken directly from the landlord's recorded deed or his title insurance policy to assure the accuracy of the estate encumbered. It should include the exact legal description of the portion of the premises to be leased and preferably should incorporate by reference an exhibit which should be an exact plat or diagram showing the area measurements of the premises leased. Commercial and/or shopping center leases may contain a landlord's covenant to provide minimum parking and delivery area throughout the term of the lease. This often entails the grant of a common area easement, or cross easements for ingress, egress, parking, and utilities.

TERM OF THE LEASE

The term of the lease should be specified as commencing on a certain date and, in the absence of a breach of either party, terminating on a certain date. In the case of a ground lease, the term of the leasehold will in all likelihood exceed the term of the mortgage. Where the mortgagee is relying primarily upon the security of the lease, the term of a commercial lease (that is, office buildings, shopping centers, etc.) may equal or exceed the term of the mortgage. If a requirement for occupancy is to be made, it can be included in the term clause. Such a requirement is common for major tenants in shopping centers or office building complexes, for example.

RIGHT TO ENCUMBER THE LEASEHOLD

Such a clause in ground leases is essential to the prospective mortgagee. Language in the lease should make it clear that the lessee may encumber its estate and that the lessee and the lessor are obligated to furnish the mortgagee in writing with all notices given pursuant to the terms of the lease. Notices may relate to delinquent taxes, insurance premiums, special assessments, etc.

SUBORDINATION OF LEASE AND SUBLEASES

While fee mortgages of commercial property may require that the lease be subordinate to the mortgage, such a provision is not mandatory. Credit considerations may, in fact, dictate that the lease not be subordinate, depending on a particular state. Moreover, subordination of the lease cuts off tenant liability in instances of foreclosure in some states, as pointed out above. As a result, some leases recite the priority of the leasehold over the mortgage.

The same rationale may apply in some states in favor of not subordinating master leases or leases on commercial property. In these cases, the mortgagee, upon foreclosure, usually desires to stand in the shoes of its former debtor and to enforce leases according to their precise terms.

Rather than subordinating the mortgage to the lease, a nondisturbance provision may be included, as in the example cited earlier. Nondisturbance language simply obligates the purchaser at a foreclosure sale not to disturb the tenant's occupancy under the lease so long as the tenant is not in default. The advantage of this clause to the mortgagee is that it allows the lease to remain in effect but does not give the tenant superiority in all conflicts between provisions of the lease and the mortgage (for example, the application of fire insurance proceeds or condemnation awards). Where this clause is accepted by the mortgagee, there should be a provision to the effect that the obligation not to disturb does not extend to any subsequent modification of the lease without the mortgagee's prior approval.

CASUALTY PROVISIONS

The most obvious difficulty in casualty is the reconciliation of lease provisions with standard mortgage terms. The primary interest of both parties is to protect the loss funds of a policy against any claims of the mortgagor's other creditors. A second objective of the parties is to provide for allocation of the loss funds. In other words, should they be applied as a credit to the debt or to restoration of the improvements.

Generally, distinctions are drawn between total destruction and partial losses. In the case of the former, it is occasionally possible that mortgagees will require application of loss funds to reduce the debt. Provisions for application of funds in the event of partial losses are by no means uniform. In fact, there is great diversity, particularly in leases of *major tenants*. In either case, the terms *total* and *partial* destruction should be clearly defined. If the mortgage is one secured by leasehold estate, it is more likely that the mortgagee will be agreeable to accepting provisions for restoration rather than application to the debt. Provisions for restoration should also be highly desirable for a mortgagee of either the fee or the leasehold where rentals are determined in whole or in part by a percentage of profits. The interest of landlord, mortgagor, and mortgagee in such case are common ones: to restore the property as quickly as possible so that business activity can resume.

In cases where the lease is already executed and requires that the loss proceeds of hazard insurance policies be applied to restoration costs, the application of proceeds to the loan is precluded unless the tenant can be induced to change this provision. Hazard insurance policies can be endorsed with standard mortgage clauses that permit the loss proceeds to be paid by the insurer to the mortgagee. In all cases, it is imperative that the terms of any policy referred to in the lease be studied for their effect on the mortgagee's interest both as a creditor and as a possible owner of the security in the event of foreclosure.

If a lease provides for application of loss proceeds toward restoration of improvements, it should contain *a force majeure* clause allowing for reasonable or unavoidable delay in effecting such restoration. This would be a delay of a kind occasioned by so-called "acts of God," strikes, equipment shortages, and the like.

From the standpoint of the prospective fee mortgagee, the lease should provide for an option in favor of the landlord permitting the cancellation of the lease for a casualty affecting all or a portion of the mortgaged premises. Leases often refer to a *substantial* portion of the mortgaged premises. If so, a definition of the word "substantial" ought to be included. Further, in the event there is a provision for such an option and it is not exercised, the landlord should agree to pay the loss proceeds to a trustee for restoration of the premises, or to deliver the policy proceeds to the lending institution for application to the debt. The mortgage itself should contain a similar clause reciting that the funds be used for restoration according to the provisions in the lease if the tenant is not in default. Such provisions protect the loss funds against the claims of the landlord's creditors, and if the mortgage specifically provides, these funds can be applied to restoration only after the mortgagee's approval of plans, specifications, architect's progress certificate, and assurances against mechanics' liens. In most instances where there is a substantial loss, it would be treated similar to a construction loan.

CONDEMNATION

When the power of eminent domain is exercised by an authorized agency, three entities, namely, the landlord (lessor), tenant (lessee), and mortgagee, may each sustain injury. In the case of the mortgagee, its damages are to be measured by the extent to which its security is impaired or reduced in value by the taking. If the entire property subject to the lease is condemned, the lease is terminated. The lease should provide in this event that the award for the taking must be applied first to the payment of the mortgage with the remainder to owners of the fee and/or the leasehold estates as their interests may appear.

If there is to be only a partial taking, it is not usually desirable that such an event result in termination of the lease, but that provision be made for adequate protection of each interested party. For example, absent a provision in the lease to the contrary, a tenant is obligated in most states to pay rent for the balance of the term where the premises are only partially condemned. From the standpoint of the mortgagee, provisions must be clear in the lease to the effect that (1) a partial condemnation does not terminate the lease or afford the lessee the right to cancel unless a stipulated minimum portion of the premises is condemned, and (2) tenant's claim against the award be limited by a formula amount in proportion to the extent of the damage of partial condemnation.

Most institutional lenders will stand firm in demanding a full and prior lien against condemnation awards. A landlord may oppose this stand, but the lender could point out that the situation it confronts is equivalent to a hazard loss situation. The lender should, therefore, retain its option to apply the award against either the debt or reconstruction of the improvements just as in a hazard loss situation.

From the standpoint of the mortgage of the fee or of the leasehold, the lease should provide for an express reduction in rent after partial condemnation. Almost any measure of reduction is valid if agreed to. The most objective measure, though, is a percentage of the rent which was payable before condemnation rather than a percentage of the value of the premises which remains after the taking.

In some states, it is possible by statute to condemn real estate temporarily, that is, only the leasehold interest therein. A provision terminating the lease in the event of this type of condemnation is valid. Otherwise, the lessee remains liable for rent payable throughout the term, but he has a claim against the award, which usually is the entire remaining value of his lease as originally written.

RENT, TAXES, INSURANCE, ETC.

A separate provision in the lease should expressly state the tenant's agreement to pay the rent. If no such agreement is recited in the lease, the tenant in some states may argue that payment of the rent is only a condition to the right to occupy the property. The formula for determining the amount of rent in a commercial lease is an important factor in analysis by a prospective mortgagee. Sometimes included in a commercial lease to a retail tenant is some requirement for minimum base rent with an *overage* or *percentage of gross sales* added, the latter figure being the excess over a certain annual income from the tenant's operations in the leased premises. An example of such overage is a retail lease providing for a minimum rent of $50,000 annually plus a 3½ percent overage of the gross sales in excess of $3,000,000. The formula should include the time and installments payable and methods for verification. The mortgagee will want to require appropriate operating statements, but will also want to reserve the right to examine books and records where rent is determined by formula.

Clauses providing for abatement of rent for the landlord's breach of covenant should be closely scrutinized for their effect on a lender.

While the payment of taxes and insurance is usually provided for in separate clauses, the subject overlaps with the payment of rent in net leases. It is not uncommon to find in commercial leases, for example, a clause requiring a proportionate increase in rent where real estate taxes are increased or special assessments levied at any time after the first year of the term. Such a provision, however, sometimes allows the increased amount of tax or assessment to be credited against overage paid to the mortgagee for that year. The lessee who is responsible for payment should agree to pay the taxes before they become delinquent and to provide the lessor with certificates or receipts for payment within so many days after each payment. It is not uncommon to find clauses requiring periodic advance deposits by tenants with landlords to cover taxes and insurance premiums. The mortgagee, of course, may want such clauses to include the provision that the deposits be held by it and that certificates or receipts evidencing payment be forwarded to the lessor and lessee. A clause should be included to require that the mortgagee be furnished with the original current insurance policies and that policies name lessor, lessee, and mortgagee as insureds as interest may appear. Provisions governing the application of hazard insurance loss proceeds are discussed above.

An operational condition frequently found in shopping center leases is the *common area* clause, providing for a proportionate payment by each tenant for costs of maintaining, improving, or constructing areas such as malls, parking facilities, closed circuit television advertising within the area, and "related capital expenses." Such expenses may be voluntarily incurred by the landlord alone or with the consent of a minimum percentage of tenants. A common area clause is an obvious advantage to the mortgagee. Clauses requiring occupancy and operation of the tenant's business for a minimum number of shopping days and hours throughout the term of the lease should always be present in the commercial lease. Such clauses, in effect, help assure the tenant's cash flow and ability to pay the agreed rental.

NONCOMPETITIVE USE PROVISIONS

These clauses most commonly appear in shopping center leases as restrictive covenants. They may be reciprocal in their effects, requiring that the lessor will not lease to another tenant doing the same or a similar type of business and that, in return, the lessee will not open another branch of its business within a reasonable geographic area (the so-called *radius* clause). The clear purpose of such a clause is to limit the production of income to the subject property of the lease, a purpose which the mortgagee will applaud. The lender, in analyzing these clauses, must determine whether the restriction is reasonably limited in time, geographic area, and type of business activity prohibited and whether it may run contra to similar clauses in other instruments. If the restriction is unreasonable in any respect, the mortgagee runs the risk of (1) being struck down by the courts as violative of Federal anti-trust laws, or (2) a breach of covenant by one or more parties to lease resulting in cancellation of the lease. If it is contra to agreements previously made, the conflict could result in claims for damages or stalemate the best use of property which the mortgagee may then own or thereafter acquire.

While there are no definite criteria for reasonable restrictions on a competing use, it is safe for the lender to assume that clauses permitting tenants to disapprove of prospective competing tenants, to limit the floor space of competing tenants, or to control their business operations are probably unreasonable and, therefore, invalid. It is suggedsted that the mortgage contain an option for the mortgagee to accelerate the debt upon breach by the landlord of a covenant barring lease of any part of the premises for a competing use. This provision should be further reinforced by a mortgage clause requiring the mortgagor to perform all covenants and conditions pertaining to the mortagor as landlord. The soundest approach by a prospective mortgagee is to refuse restrictive covenants which prohibit leases for a competing use on property extending outside the immediate geographic area of the subject shopping center, office building, etc. Such covenants are apt to be considered by the courts as unreasonable restraints on commerce and, in any case, will bind the mortgagee-as-landlord too closely in event of foreclosure.

ASSIGNMENT OF THE LEASE AND OF RENTS, SUBLEASING

In some states, either a lessor's or a lessee's interest is assignable. In others, only the landlord may assign its interest in the absence of contrary provisions in the lease. The assignment of a leasehold estate is the conveyance of its entire term without any reservation of an interest in the estate. The sublease of a lease is either the lessee's conveyance of it for a lesser term or a conveyance of the leasehold in which some interest, for example, a reversion, is reserved in the estate. Where there is no clause permitting assignment by the *tenant* in the limiting states, the effect of the nonassignment rule is circumvented by the tenant who subleases for some period within the term of the lease. The landlord's lender will abhor such assignability, since it relies on the strength of tenancies existing at the time of the loan, and will analyze the lease for its validity by seeking a clause which forbids the tenant to assign, mortgage, encumber, sublet, or allow the use of the premises without the lessor's written consent. Clearly, the possibility of assignment or subleasing by either party to the lease will determine the degree to which a mortgage can control the lease and be assured of its value as security for the debt.

The lender, in nearly all circumstances, will wish to take an assignment of the lease and of the rents from the landlord/mortgagor. Such assignment creates a lien on the rents. It should provide additionally that the lease may not be cancelled or modified without the express consent of the mortgagee. Modification should be defined to include payment of rent in advance to the landlord and the landord's consent to assignment or subletting by the tenant. It is further suggested that the assignment stipulate that:

1 "Rents may be collected by the mortgagor unless and until there is a default, whereupon the mortgagee is authorized to collect rents."
2 "The tenant need not join in the assignment instrument to make it effective."
3 "The borrower obligates himself to furnish all tenants with a copy of the assignment."

The assignment should be promptly recorded by the lender.

It is generally believed that these nonmodification provisions in the assignment will bind the tenant, although it is not formally a party to the agreement. Exceptions, particularly those regarding the assignment of rents, exist in a few states, and the laws of the state in which the property is located should be checked by the lender's counsel prior to execution of the assignment.

APARTMENT LEASES

In this type of lease, there is rarely any real negotiation by the parties. A form lease is simply offered by the apartment landlord on a "take it or leave it" basis.

EXPANSION OF IMPROVEMENTS

These clauses frequently found in commercial leases may require the landlord to construct new improvements upon the lessee's demand after a certain level of gross sales is achieved. The parties sometimes recite that they will share the cost of such expansion. Over the long term, such expansion brightens prospects of increased rentals, but the lender must recognize the undesirable possibilities of some varying language in the expansion clause.

The lease should absolve the lender, or anyone claiming under the lender, of any obligation to expand after foreclosure. A side agreement with the tenant will afford this protection as well.

A clause which prevents cancellation or termination of the lease in the event the landlord fails or refuses to expand should be included. This may be difficult to negotiate.

Finally, the lender should demand a clause or side agreement which recites that the lessee will not have a prior lien on the property where the landlord fails to share in the expenses incurred for expansion. The effect of this clause is to preserve the required first-lien status of the mortgage for investment regulation purposes.

DISPOSITION OF SECURITY DEPOSITS

Where the lease requires a deposit of cash, bonds, or stocks, or a pledge of securities for the landlord's security, the mortgagee's concern is to include these as a part of the security for the loan. While the lease itself will probably not provide for disposition of security upon foreclosure, the lender should be aware of two approaches to controlling the deposit. First, if the deposit is in cash, the amount of the loan can simply be reduced by the amount of the deposit. Second, the deposit may be retained by the lender throughout the term of the mortgage or until a specified fraction of the mortgage debt is paid.

New legislation in some states currently requires a landlord to furnish tenants with a written itemizing of documents withheld from the deposit upon termination of the lease. Failure to itemize such deductions carries with it considerable money damages in a subsequent lawsuit, should the tenant succeed in convincing a court that the itemizing is not accurate. A requirement concerning the disposition of security deposits should be included in the lender's commitment letter, particularly when it is issued on the security of an apartment complex, that is (1) the commitment might require that the landlord comply with state statutes concerning deductions from security deposits; (2) such a requirement might further condition the commitment upon the continued existence of a separate account maintained solely by the landlord for the disposition of security deposits (some states require that the landlord pay interest on these security deposits); and (3) periodic statements of this account representing the security deposit of each tenant would then be furnished by the landlord to the lender.

Some leases contain terms by which the tenant is given a prior lien on the property for the value of the deposit. Such a provision should never be accepted by the lender as a creation of a prior encumbrance which may violate statutes regulating mortgage investments.

LESSEE'S OPTION TO PURCHASE

This clause allows a lessee the option to purchase the subject property at a specified future time or upon the occurrence of named conditions. It is imperative that the option itself be subordinated to the mortgage for a number of reasons.

The option clause poses a threat to the required first-lien stature of the mortgage as an investment. Where the lessee exercises the option, it may destroy the priority of the mortgage on the theory that it "relates back" to the time of the prior lease. Furthermore, exercise of the option and subsequent payment of the mortgage debt by the new owner may circumvent the mortgagee's right to the prepayment premium.

The option to purchase may take the form of a *right of first refusal* in the tenant to purchase if the landlord offers the property for sale. In *title theory* states, which regard the execution of a mortgage as primarily a conveyance, not a lien, it is possible that the holder of this option has a right to pay the mortgage debt at the time of foreclosure and take title to the property. In any state, the agreement should set the option price as at least equivalent to the amount of the mortgage debt.

BANKRUPTCY

Language which terminates or modifies the lease in the event of bankruptcy filing or adjudication as to any party is of obvious concern to a lender. Although the power of the trustee in bankruptcy is not well defined as to interests affected by the leasehold, the language of the lease will usually be followed if bankruptcy arises. The most desirable clauses are those which state that the lessor or lessee shall be "entitled to his estate and encumbrances thereon in the event that either party files for bankruptcy or is formally adjudicated as a bankruptcy." The extent to which such clauses control depends in part on the law of the state in which the property is situated.

SURVIVAL CLAUSES

The function of the standard clauses is to preserve the liability of a tenant in default after eviction. Unless the lease contains language to this effect, a tenant's liability to continue to pay rent may terminate upon default. For the mortgagee, a properly constructed clause should preserve tenant liability to pay *rent* upon default for any reason, including the tenant's failure to occupy the premises.

CANCELLATION CLAUSES

A lease which anticipates future construction of improvements on the premises often recites the right of either party to cancel if construction does not proceed according to some approximate timetable. For the lender, either a construction-cancellation clause or a cancellation clause operative upon breach of covenant by landlord is threatening. If either clause is present, the lender should make certain the lease recites an option, upon receiving required notice from the tenant, to cure the breach before cancellation. If no option exists, the lender should obtain a collateral agreement with the tenant which waives the tenant's right vis-á-vis the landlord to cancel the lease for either landlord breach or construction failure.

DOMINO OR KEY TENANT CLAUSES

In the shopping center lease to smaller tenants, the negotiation often ends in favor of a clause by which the landlord covenants that certain larger and more commercially attractive tenants will remain on premises and operate their business. The smaller tenant thus builds the enterprise around a larger business presence. The domino clause is objectionable to a mortgagee, since, if the major tenant cancels or is in breach, the liability of smaller tenants is automatically absolved. The existence of such clauses can destroy the investment potential of the lease as security for the lender. It must be either negotiated out of the lease or effectively neutralized by side agreements with the tenants whom it concerns.

CONCLUSION

The approach of a prospective mortgage lender in analyzing a lease depends largely on three factors: (1) the type of lease involved, (2) whether the lender is prospectively a fee mortgagee or a leasehold mortgagee, and (3) whether the lease is prior or subordinate to the mortgage. The principles discussed above are generalized ones, but they will give the prospective lender a sense of the profound impact which the language of a lease can have on the security for a mortgage debt.

Application of these principles sometimes varies between the so-called *title theory*, *lien theory*, and *intermediate states* in which the property is situated. It varies also with the absolute particulars of the lender's prospective loan and loan security. While there is no substitute for lease analysis by competent counsel representing the lender, the prospective lender should be aware of the impact of the language in leases affecting the security for the proposed loan. Also, it should always be remembered that laws affecting leases are always subject to change—what is valid today may not be valid tomorrow. In many of these areas, there is a question of validity, and litigation is common. When dealing in areas with legal ramifications, the importance of being aware and the use of legal counsel cannot be overemphasized. Through awareness, the economic and legal position of the lender can be strengthened.

Chapter 10

Tax Considerations in Income-Property Finance

Robert M. Fink

INTRODUCTION

Ownership of real estate results in certain income tax benefits which are sometimes referred to as *tax shelters*. The Internal Revenue Code contains provisions that provide for specific tax deductions, and the purpose of said deductions is to encourage the construction of real estate projects. During the period of construction and prior to the time when the real estate is generating an economic profit, the owner receives the benefit of income tax savings representing a return on the equity money invested in the project.

Real estate projects are often syndicated through the utilization of a group of investors who desire a real estate investment, tax losses to shelter other income, and limited liability. The developer shares the income tax losses with investors in return for equity money that may be necessary to fund a project or to fund the payment of the developer's profit.

Some methods of financing are more adaptable to tax-oriented real estate investments. In many cases, the method of financing will improve the income tax benefits.

This chapter will review the tax benefits resulting from the ownership of real estate and also many of the tax problems. The methods and problems of syndicating a real estate project will also be discussed.

It is important to note that the entire area of taxation is in a constant state of flux and change. The politically expedient cry of "close the tax loopholes" is heard with increasing frequency and, indeed, in nearly every Congressional session some adjustments are made in our tax laws. Therefore, specific examples used in this chapter may no longer be applicable due to subsequent changes in the Internal Revenue Code.

In any event, these examples may not apply to the reader, who is cautioned to consult a tax counsel or an accountant for an up-to-date review of any specific problem.

It should also be pointed out that this chapter describes federal taxation matters, and that any matters involving state taxes will vary widely in the different states.

ECONOMIC PROFIT (CASH FLOW) VS. TAX LOSS

General Explanation

The economic profit generated by a real estate investment is often referred to as the cash flow, which is the excess of cash receipts over cash disbursements. An illustration of cash flow is as follows:

Rental income		$200,000
Less: Operating expenses	$80,000	
Debt service (payments on mortgage)	30,000	110,000
		$ 90,000

The taxable income or loss can vary substantially from the economic profit (cash flow). Generally speaking, the taxable income or loss is the economic profit (cash flow) increased by the amount of mortgage debt service pertaining to principal amortization, since such item is not deductible for income tax purposes and is decreased by depreciation. An illustration of the computation is as follows:

Cash flow (above)	$ 90,000
Plus: Principal amortization portion of debt service	4,000
Less: Depreciation expense	110,000
Taxable income (loss)	($ 16,000)

Impact of Financing

Using the same rate of interest, the shorter the term of the loan, the greater the annual debt service payments will be and therefore the cash flow will be reduced. The shorter term will also result in a greater portion of the annual debt service pertaining to principal amortization, which is not tax deductible. An extremely long-term mortgage such as the 40-year FHA mortgage requires less cash for debt service and only a small portion of the annual debt service is attributable to the nondeductible principal amortization during the early years.

The cost of the underlying land is not deductible for tax purposes as an expense, nor does it qualify for depreciation. In an effort to increase the leverage (the portion of the total cost of the project financed) and increase the income tax loss, it is often feasible to sell the land to a lender and lease it back in accordance with the terms of a long-term lease. The annual rent may be equal to the debt service pertaining to the cost of the land or slightly greater, and therefore would have only a slight impact on the annual cash flow. However, the income tax loss will be increased, since the ground rent will be deductible, while the principal amortization pertaining to the cost of the land is not deductible for income tax purposes.

INTEREST EXPENSE

General Explanation

Any interest on the construction mortgage and the permanent mortgage is deductible for income tax purposes. Prior to the Tax Reform Act of 1976, the interest during the construction period could be deducted as an expense or capitalized and amortized over the useful life of the building. When the construction interest was deducted as an expense, a substantial income tax loss would generally result, since the project would not be generating rental income to offset the expense.

The general rule as set forth in the Tax Reform Act of 1976 is that construction interest must be capitalized and amortized over a 10-year period. The full 10-year period is implemented during a transitional period which extends from 1976 through 1988. The following table illustrates the amortization periods during the transition period:

Commercial real estate	Residential real estate	Low-income housing	Amortization period
1976	—	—	*
—	1978	1982	4
1977	1979	1983	5
1978	1980	1984	6
1979	1981	1985	7
1980	1982	1986	8
1981	1983	1987	9
1982	1984	1988	10

*In 1976 construction interest for commercial real estate is currently deducted to the extent of 50 percent and remaining amount is amortized over a three-year period.

A taxpayer on the accrual method of accounting for income tax purposes may deduct interest as it accrues on the outstanding mortgage balance, while a cash-basis taxpayer may deduct interest when paid. Prior to November 28, 1968, a cash-basis taxpayer could prepay and deduct interest for a five-year period. On November 28, 1968, the Internal Revenue Service ruled that a cash-basis taxpayer can prepay and deduct interest for a period of one year. The period of the prepayment is measured at the end of the year in which the payment is made. An illustration of the one-year rule would be where an individual bought a parcel of real estate on February 1, 1973, and gave the seller a promissory note. At the closing, the individual paid the interest for the balance of 1973 and for the entire year of 1974. Assuming the individual is utilizing the cash method of accounting for income tax purposes, he or she could deduct the full amount of interest paid, since only one year is prepaid at the end of the year of payment. The Revenue Ruling issued in 1968 did, however, contain a qualification which limits the deduction of the one-year prepayment to situations where the income of the taxpayer is not materially distorted. Technically, if the taxpayer utilized prepaid interest to eliminate substantially all taxable income, the Internal Revenue Service could disallow the prepayment on the basis of a material distortion of income.

In accordance with the Tax Reform Act of 1976, interest which is prepaid after December 31, 1975, will not be deductible. The amount which is prepaid will be deductible as it accrues on the outstanding indebtedness. However, the new rule does not apply to amounts paid before January 1, 1977, pursuant to a binding contract or written loan commitment which was executed prior to September 16, 1975, and which required prepayments of such amounts by the taxpayer.

It is often necessary to pay points to a lender in order to borrow money. The points are normally payable at the closing and represent additional consideration for the use of money. In such a case, the points represent interest and, prior to January 1, 1976, could be deducted by a cash basis taxpayer if actually paid by the taxpayer. If the lender merely increased the amount of the loan and withheld an amount equal to the points from the loan proceeds disbursed at closing, the Internal Revenue Service takes the position that the points were not paid at the closing but instead are being paid over the term of the loan as the principal payments are made, and therefore the income tax deduction for the points is spread over the term of the loan. In accordance with the Tax Reform Act of 1976, points must be deducted ratably over the term of the loan. However, an exception does exist regarding points paid by a cash-method taxpayer on indebtedness incurred in connection with the purchase or improvement of personal residence. In such case, the points are deducted when paid. The taxpayer will have the burden of proof that the charging of points is an established practice in the geographical area where the loan is made.

Investment Interest Limitation

Due to the extremely beneficial income tax results, many taxpayers incurred large interest expenses in order to finance the acquisition of investment property, which produced little or no current income, with the expectation that the eventual sale of the property will produce a long-term capital gain. The tax benefit resulting from the interest expense was utilized to reduce the income tax liability pertaining to ordinary income such as salary, interest, and other items. The Tax Reform Act of 1969 set limits on the deductibility of investment interest by noncorporate taxpayers in taxable years beginning 1972 and thereafter (*Sec. 163(d)*).

Investment interest includes interest paid or accrued on an indebtedness incurred to purchase or carry property held for investment. The Tax Reform Act of 1969 requires that the investment interest be used to offset specified types of income. The provision in the Tax Reform Act in essence provides a limitation on the amount of the interest deduction. The allowable interest deduction is the sum of the following items:

1 $25,000 exemption.
2 Net investment income. The excess of investment income from interest,

dividends, rents, royalties, net short-term capital gains from investment property, and Section 1245 and Section 1250 gain (depreciation recaptive) over investment expenses, such as straight-line depreciation and cost depletion.

3 Excess of net long-term capital gain over net short-term capital loss. If the net long-term capital gain is utilized to deduct interest expense, the gain is not treated as a long-term capital gain and therefore is taxed at full income tax rates without a capital gain deduction.

4 One-half the excess investment interest over the total of the above items.

The disallowed portion of the investment interest may be carried forward. However, in subsequent years, the limitation must be computed before the carry-over can be utilized. The following is an example of the investment interest deduction limitation:

Investment interest expense		$400,000
Less: Statutory exemption		25,000
		375,000
Less: Investment income	$130,000	
Less: Investment expense	40,000	90,000
		285,000
Less: Long-term capital gain		95,000
		$190,000
50%—Amount Disallowed		$ 95,000
Investment interest allowed		$305,000

Note: The disallowed portion ($95,000) is available as a carry-over to subsequent years.

Generally, income-producing real estate is not considered to be investment property and therefore the interest on the mortgage will not be limited by the investment interest limitation. However, for the sale purpose of the investment interest limitation, property subject to a net lease is treated as investment property rather than business property if (1) the business expense deductions allowed in respect to the property by Code Section 162 (insurance, incidental repairs, and labor) totals less than 15 percent of the rental income, or (2) the lessor is either guaranteed a special return or guaranteed against loss. In the computation of the 15 percent of rental income test, the expenses paid by the lessor, who is then entitled to reimbursement from the lessee, are ignored and therefore not treated as expenses of the lessor. The lessor does have two elections regarding the 15 percent test. All leases on a single parcel of real estate may be aggregated in determining whether a net lease exists under the 15 percent test. The lessor must aggregate the income and expenses on all leased portions of the parcel of land in computing the 15 percent test. The second election is that real property that has been in use more than five years may be exempted from the 15 percent test. This election would cover all real property of the taxpayer which has been in use for more than five years.

This particular limitation has a serious impact on shopping center investments. Since the leased premises are generally on a net lease basis and the expenses, excluding ground rent, generally will not be sufficient to pass the 15 percent test, the entire amount of the interest on the mortgage will be considered investment interest expense.

The limitation also has a serious impact on raw land syndications if the investment is owned by a few individuals and therefore each investor is allocated a large amount of investment interest.

The Tax Reform Act of 1976 modified the investment interest limitation for interest paid after December 31, 1975, on any indebtedness incurred after September 11, 1975. The limitation is more restrictive and the deductible amount is computed as follows:

1   $10,000 statutory allowance plus
2   Net investment income (definition remains the same). No offset of investment interest is allowed against long-term capital gain. The disallowed portion of investment interest is carried over to an unlimited number of subsequent years; however, the deductibility of such amount is subject to the yearly limitation.

DEPRECIATION

General Explanation

Depreciation is the key item in converting an economic profit to an income tax loss. Depreciation for income tax purposes is not the same as depreciation generally used for the purposes of appraising the value of property. The term *depreciation* when used by an appraiser means the estimated loss in value due to physical depreciation, functional or economic obsolescence. For income tax purposes, depreciation is a method of allocating the cost of an asset over its estimated useful life. The Internal Revenue Code provides for a number of accelerated methods of depreciation (Sec. 167).

In light of the changes made by the Tax Reform Act of 1969, the following methods are the authorized accelerated methods of depreciation (*Sec. 167 (b)*):

1   New residential property—The term *new property* means the taxpayer was the owner at the time the first tenant took possession of the premises. *Residential property* means that 80 percent or more of the gross income from the project was from residential dwelling units (apartments).
    a   Double declining balance—The depreciation rate is double the straight line rate, and said rate is applied to the declining balance (cost less accumulated depreciation) of the asset. Assuming a 10-year life, the double declining rate would be 20 percent. The depreciation for the first year would be 20 percent of depreciable costs. The depreciation for the second year would be 20 percent of the cost reduced by the first-year depreciation.
    b   Sum-of-the-years' digits—Each year a new fraction is applied to the cost of the asset. The fraction is determined as follows:
    Numerator   The total of the number of years remaining in the useful life of the asset. Assuming a six-year life, the numerator for the first year would be 6.
    Denominator   The sum of the years included in the useful life. Assuming a six-year life, the denominator would be 21 (1 + 2 + 3 + 4 + 5 + 6).
    c   150 percent declining balance—150 percent of the straight line rate is applied to the declining balance (cost less accumulated depreciation) of

the asset. Assuming a 10-year life, the rate would be 15 percent. The depreciation for the first year would be 15 percent of cost. The depreciation for the second year would be 15 percent of the cost reduced by the first-year depreciation.

    d Straight line—The cost of the asset is divided by the useful life of the asset and therefore a level amount is deducted each year.

  2 Old residential property (apartments)—the term *old property* refers to property where the taxpayer was not the original owner when the first tenant took possession of the project.

    a 125 percent declining balance—A depreciation rate of 125 percent of the straight line rate is applied to the declining balance (cost less accumulated depreciation) of the asset.

    b Straight line depreciation (explained above).

  3 New nonresidential property—*Nonresidential* property is any real estate where more than 20 percent of the gross income is from nonresidential units. Examples of such property would be an office building, shopping center, hotel, and any other commercial-type real estate.

  4 Old nonresidential property—Both terms are defined above.

    a Straight line depreciation—(explained above).

It is quite evident, from the above methods, that new residential property, such as an apartment project, generates larger income tax losses due to the larger amount of depreciation available to the owner.

The Tax Reform Act of 1969 also added a special amortization method for the expenditures to rehabilitate low-income housing. Formerly, capital expenditures to rehabilitate low-income rental housing had to be depreciated over the entire remaining life of the building. The 1969 Tax Reform Act provides a special election to depreciate these expenditures under the straight line method, using a useful life of 60 months (five years) and no salvage value. The election is available only for rehabilitation expenses with respect to low-income rental housing incurred after July 24, 1969, and before January 1, 1975. The aggregate amount of rehabilitation expenditures incurred by a taxpayer with respect to a dwelling unit in a low-income rental housing project that is eligible for the 60-month write-off could not exceed $15,000. The Tax Reform Act of 1976 extended the period for such expenditures to December 31, 1977, and increased the maximum amount per dwelling to $20,000.

In order to compute the annual depreciation expense of an asset, it is necessary to determine the useful life of the asset. The cost of the asset will be depreciated over the useful life of the asset. The shorter the useful life, the greater the annual depreciation will be. The life is based on the estimated period of time the asset will be useful to the taxpayer.

The cost of a building may be allocated to the various components, such as heating, roof, air conditioning, etc. Each component can then be depreciated over its useful life. The utilization of the shorter useful life for the components generally results in a greater amount of overall depreciation.

Another factor to be considered in determining the annual depreciation is the estimated salvage value of the asset at the end of the useful life. The general rule of depreciation is that an asset cannot be depreciated below its salvage value. The declining balance methods of depreciation (200 percent and 150 percent) and the sum-of-the-years' digits method depreciate the asset down to a salvage value. However, when utilizing the straight line method of depreciation, the salvage value must first be deducted from the cost and then the remaining cost is depreciated over the useful life.

Depreciation Recapture

It is quite apparent that depreciation generates tremendous tax savings to those who can afford to invest in real estate. In the early 1960s, Section 1250 was added to the Internal Revenue Code. The purpose of this provision was to reduce but not eliminate the benefits of depreciation resulting from the ownership of real estate. The provisions of Sections 1250 in essence converted the capital gain upon the sale of the property in the future to ordinary income to the extent ordinary income benefits were received through depreciation. Generally, the rules of Section 1250, as originally enacted, provided the following:

1   If property was held for 12 months or less, and was sold after December 31, 1963, the entire amount of depreciation claimed will be recaptured as ordinary income to the extent of the gain recognized.

2   For property disposed of after December 31, 1963, which was held for more than 12 months but not more than 20 months, the entire excess of accelerated depreciation over straight line depreciation would be recaptured as ordinary income.

3   For property disposed of after December 31, 1963, held for more than 20 months but less than 120 months (10 years), the excess of accelerated over straight line depreciation will be recaptured as ordinary income, but the amount of such recapture would be reduced by a percentage equal to 1 percent per month for every month the property is held after 20 months.

During the year 1969 there was much discussion regarding tax reform. The Tax Reform Act as adopted in December, 1969, revised the depreciation recapture rules of Section 1250. Section 1250 still results in the capital gain upon sale being converted to ordinary income; however, the amount is greater for the years where depreciation is claimed after 1969. The depreciation recapture rules as adopted by the Tax Reform Act of 1969 are as follows:

Depreciation claimed after December 31, 1969.

1   Nonresidental property (defined under depreciation methods)—Whenever the property is sold, the excess of the accelerated depreciation claimed over the depreciation that would have been claimed if depreciated on a straight line basis will be ordinary income, but not to exceed the gain recognized. As a result of the Tax Reform Act, a reducing percentage is not utilized in the later years for nonresidential property.

2   Residential property (other than FHA low-income projects)—
   a   If sold during the first 100 months, the entire excess depreciation is recaptured as ordinary income, but not to exceed the gain recognized.
   b   If sold during the second 100 months (8 years, 4 months through 16 years, 8 months), the amount of recapture is reduced by a percentage which is 1 percent a month for every month after the 100th month.

3   FHA low-income projects—The Tax Reform Act of 1969 did not change the

depreciation recapture rules for such projects. Therefore, in the case of such projects, the old rules of Section 1250 will still apply for depreciation claimed after 1970.

In 1976, the depreciation recapture rules were modified by the Tax Reform Act of 1976; however, such amendment only pertained to residential real estate. In accordance with the Act, depreciation on residential real estate claimed after 1975 will be recaptured to the extent of the amount claimed in excess of the amount which would be deductible under the straight line method. The Act also provided that in determining the recapture date in the event of a foreclosure, such date shall be the date the proceedings begin.

The Tax Reform Act of 1976 also modified the depreciation recapture rules regarding low-income housing provided under the National Housing Act (*Sec. 221(d)(3)* and *Sec. 236*) and other subsidized housing such as Section 8 housing and property insured under Title V of the Housing Act of 1945. Depreciation claimed on such housing after 1975 shall be recaptured to the extent of the full excess of accelerated depreciation over straight line depreciation, if the property is owned 100 months or less at the time of the sale. In the event such housing is owned more than 100 months at the time of the sale, the amount of depreciation subject to recapture reduces 1 percent per month.

After determining the extent to which the gain recognized upon sale will result in depreciation recapture pertaining to the depreciation claimed after 1975, the depreciation recapture rules of Section 1250 must then be applied to the depreciation claimed after 1970 and before 1975. Assuming a portion of gain remains which is not subject to recapture, the depreciation rules of Section 1250 must then be applied to depreciation claimed before 1970. Any gain remaining after applying the three recapture rules will be long-term capital gain.

MINIMUM TAX ON PREFERENCE ITEMS

The Tax Reform Act of 1969 imposed a 10 percent tax (in addition to the income tax) on certain tax preference items, and such items will proportionately reduce the amount of earned income subject to the maximum tax of 50 percent. The tax preference items are as follows:

1 Fifty percent capital gain deduction for individuals.
2 The excess of accelerated depreciation over straight line depreciation on real property.
3 The excess of accelerated depreciation over straight line depreciation on personal property subject to a net lease.
4 The bargain element of employees' stock options (on date of exercise).
5 Percentage depletion (the amount of depletion to the extent it exceeds the total cost of the investment).
6 Excess amortization of pollution control facilities and railroad rolling stock.

The minimum tax under the 1969 Tax Reform Act was imposed only on the excess of the taxpayer's tax preference income over $30,000, plus his income tax for the year of computation and the prior seven years.

The intent of the minimum tax was to penalize the taxpayer utilizing accelerated methods of depreciation and the other tax-saving items. The impact of said minimum tax depends upon the individual situations of the investors.

The Tax Reform Act of 1976 modified the computation of the minimum tax and such modification will result in a larger minimum tax liability. The Act added two additional tax preference items for individuals, which are the following:

1 Excess itemized deductions—to the extent the itemized deductions (excluding medical expenses and casualty losses) of an individual exceed 60 percent of adjusted gross income, a tax preference shall result.

2 Intangible drilling expenses—to the extent the intangible drilling expenses (oil or gas investment) deducted by a taxpayer exceed the amount that would be deductible if said expenses were amortized over a 10-year period, a tax preference item will result.

In accordance with the Act, the minimum tax is imposed on the excess of the tax preference items over $10,000 or 50 percent of the income tax liability for such year, whichever is greater. The minimum tax rate has been increased from 10 to 15 percent.

RESIDENTIAL PROPERTY (APARTMENTS) VS. NONRESIDENTIAL PROPERTY

As explained above, residential real estate qualifies for the double declining balance method of depreciation, while the most accelerated method available to the owners of nonresidential property is the 150 percent declining balance. As a result of the available methods, the tax losses generated by residential real estate generally exceed the tax losses generated by nonresidential property. Another factor which contributes to the larger tax losses of residential real estate is the financing. Often, the term of the mortgage for residential property is longer than the usual mortgage term for nonresidential real estate. Often the mortgage term for an apartment project is 30 years, while the term for an office building or shopping center may in many cases be limited to 20 years. As explained earlier, the shorter the term of the mortgage at the same rate of interest, the greater the amount of cash will be which goes toward the amortization of mortgage principal, which is not deductible for income tax purposes.

In many cases, certain nonresidential real estate investments such as shopping centers and office buildings generate a greater amount of cash flow than residential real estate. Said cash flow is substantially tax-free, since the property is generating an income tax loss or the taxable income being generated by the property is generally much less than the cash flow.

CONVENTIONAL MORTGAGE FINANCING VS. FHA-INSURED FINANCING

The maximum term of a conventional mortgage for an apartment project is generally 30 years. An FHA-insured mortgage will generally have a 40-year term. The longer mortgage will result in greater tax losses, but due to certain limitations imposed on

FHA-insured projects, cash flow is much less than the amount of cash flow generated by a conventionally financed apartment project.

The following numbers indicate the section of The National Housing Act which created the programs for FHA multifamily housing projects.

Section 207   The program created under this Section is mainly for the development of luxury-type housing for middle-income families. A project built under this program has no restriction on the income of the tenants, nor does it have a restriction on the rental rates for the apartment units. The mortgage is insured by the FHA, is amortized over a 40-year period, and bears interest at the market rate. The program does not provide for a 10 percent builder/sponsor profit and risk allowance, which is generally provided for in the programs listed below.

Section 221(d)(3)—Rent Supplement   Multifamily housing units built under this program are generally for middle-income and low-income residents. The low-income tenants may benefit by the rent supplement provisions of the section. Assuming the tenant qualifies in accordance with the low-income provisions, his monthly rental figure is substantially less than the market rate for the apartment, and the federal government pays the difference to the owner of the project. The mortgage is amortized over 40 years and is insured by the FHA. The interest rate is the market rate of interest and the maximum mortgage amount is 90 percent of the project's cost. Generally 90 percent of the project's cost is the total construction cost excluding the builder's profit. The 10 percent builder/sponsor profit and risk allowance generally represents the remainder of the project cost.

Section 236   The development of rental and cooperative housing for low- and moderate-income families is encouraged by this program. The mortgage is amortized over 40 years and is insured by the FHA. The maximum amount of the mortgage is 90 percent of the project's cost. Similar to Section 221(d)(3), total project cost includes the builder/sponsor profit and risk allowance. This is approximately 10 percent of the total project's cost. Therefore, the 90 percent mortgage is in essence the total construction cost and cost of the land. The subsidy provided by the government is in essence the difference between a market rate mortgage and a 1 percent mortgage. The subsidy is determined by comparing the debt service (principal and interest) and mortgage insurance for the market rate of interest to the debt service (principal and interest) of a 1 percent mortgage. The owner of the project receives the difference as a rent subsidy.

TAX SHELTER SYNDICATIONS
Tax Shelter Concept

Individuals in high-income tax brackets are at an extreme disadvantage as to the investment alternatives which are available to them. Due to the large amount of earned income from salary or professional fees, the investment income of the individual may be taxed at a rate as high as 70 percent. For example, if Mr. X had earned income of

$150,000, investment income of $50,000, and tax deductions of $20,000, his investment income would be taxed at rates varying from 64 to 69 percent even though the earned income qualifies for a maximum income tax rate of 50 percent to the extent the earned income exceeds $52,000 (Sec. 1348).

The concept of a tax shelter is that an income tax loss generated by an investment will shelter other income from taxation. Assuming an income tax bracket of 50 percent, an income tax loss of $1.00 will result in an income tax saving of $.50. In the example mentioned above, if the individual was able to claim an income tax loss of $50,000 and therefore shelter the entire amount of investment income, his income tax liability would be reduced by $33,280. Therefore, for every dollar of income tax loss the investor would be able to save $.66 cents in income tax. The greater the income tax bracket, the greater the tax savings. Therefore, in the event an investor is in the 70 percent tax bracket, for every $1.00 of income tax loss, the individual will save $.70 in income tax.

Generally, an investment generating income tax losses will also generate cash flow (the cash receipts exceed the cash disbursements), which in essence means the investor will receive a distribution of the excess cash. Since the investment is generating an income tax loss, the cash flow received by the investor is tax free. As a result of said investment, the investor receives tax savings (the tax loss shelters other income and therefore reduces the income tax liability) and cash flow. In the area of tax shelter, the annual return on an investment is expressed in terms of cash generated, which is composed of the tax savings resulting from the loss sheltering other income and the cash flow received by the investor from the investment.

It is quite evident that cash generated by an apartment project is more desirable for a taxpayer in a high-income tax bracket than a good dividend paying stock. In the case of the dividend, 70 percent of the dividend could be paid as income taxes and therefore only $.30 out of every dollar would be available to the investor. The after-tax dollars of an investment are more important to a high-tax-bracket individual than the before-tax dollars. If an investor in the 50 percent tax bracket, receives income tax savings and cash flow in the amount of $20,000, a taxable investment must generate approximately $50,000 in order to have an equal amount of after-tax dollars.

Ownership Entities

Corporation   The corporate form of doing business has the benefit of limited liability for the investor. If a corporation is utilized, it is a taxpayer, and therefore pays tax on its income. Any subsequent distributions of the income (corporate after-tax dollars) from the corporation to the shareholder will also be subject to taxation. Therefore, the utilization of a corporation generally results in a double tax. The tax losses of the corporation are carried back or carried forward to offset income of the corporation in other years (Sec. 172(b)). The tax losses are not available to the shareholders.

Small Business Corporations (Sub-Chapter S Corporations)   A small business corporation is a corporation created under the laws of a particular state, but for income tax purposes it is treated as a partnership. The income of a small business corporation is taxed to the shareholders (with the exception of capital gains in certain situations) and the losses of the corporation are deductible by the shareholders (*Sec. 1373*). In order to elect to be taxed as a small business corporation, the corporation cannot have more than 10 shareholders and the nature of its income is restricted (*Sec. 1371(a)*). The corporation cannot have more than 20 percent of its gross receipts represented by a passive income (*Sec. 1372(e)*). The term *passive income* means gross receipts from royalties, rents, dividends, interest, annuities, and sales or exchanges of stocks or securities. Generally, an operating real estate company cannot qualify for Sub-Chapter S due to the passive nature of rents. In a few situations, revenue rulings have been issued by the Internal Revenue Service regarding Sub-Chapter S corporations owning shopping centers. The key factor was the amount of services performed by the corporation for the tenants of the shopping center. If a corporation does qualify for Sub-Chapter S status, the tax loss of the corporation is allocated to the stockholders and is deductible for income tax purposes by the stockholder. However, the amount of loss actually deductible by the stockholder is limited to the cost basis of his stock, plus loans to the corporation by the stockholder. If the loans are made to the corporation in order to increase the loss limitation, a future tax problem is created. The repayment of such loans will be taxable income and the rate of tax will depend on the existence of an underlying promissory note. The repayment of an open account loan (with a basis of zero) will generally be ordinary income, while the repayment of a promissory note will generally be capital gain.

Tenants in Common   Where a number of people own real estate as tenants in common, they each possess an undivided interest in the property. For income tax purposes they are considered to be joint owners of the property and in many cases such joint ownership is treated as a partnership (*Sec. 761(a)*). The sharing of the income and tax losses is determined by the ownership percentage interest in the property. Even though a partnership is not intended in many situations, the Internal Revenue Service treats it as a partnership in accordance with the provisions of the Internal Revenue Code (*Sec. 761(a)*). The sharing of the income and tax losses is determined by the ownership percentage interest in the property. Even though a partnership is not intended in many situations, the Internal Revenue Service treats it as a partnership in accordance with the provisions of the Internal Revenue Code (*Sec. 761(a)*).

Partnerships   A partnership is not a taxable entity but, instead, a conduit. The income of the partnership is taxed to the partners and the taxable losses of the partnership are deductible by the partners (*Sec. 702*). The partnership agreement determines the allocation of the taxable income and losses to the partners. A limited partnership is a partnership with two classes of partners, namely, the general partners and the limited partners. The limited partners, as such, are not liable for the obligations of the limited partnership.

   1   A limited partner is not liable to the creditors of the partnership unless, in addition to the exercise of his rights and powers as limited partner, he takes part in the control of the business.
   2   A general partner has all the rights, powers, and liabilities of a partner in a

partnership without limited partners, except that certain acts require written consent or ratification by all the limited partners.

3 A limited partner may not receive the return of any part of his contribution until all the liabilities of the partnership are paid, all the members of the partnership consent, and the Certificate of Limited Partnership is amended to set forth reduction of the capital contribution. However, a limited partner may demand return of his or her contribution upon the dissolution of the partnership.

4 A limited partner is liable to the partnership for the difference between actual contribution to the capital of the partnership in the amount stated in the Certificate of Limited Partnership and the actual amount contributed. A limited partner is also liable for any unpaid contribution which he or she agreed to make in the future, at the time and on the conditions stated in the certificate.

5 A limited partner's interest is assignable. A substituted limited partner is a person admitted to all the rights of a limited partner who has died or has assigned interest in the partnership. An assignee, who does not become a substituted limited partner, has no right to acquire any information or account of the partnership transactions, or to inspect the books of the partnership, but is only entitled to receive a share of the profits or other compensation by way of income or the return of contribution, to which the assignor would otherwise be entitled. An assignee shall have the right to become a substitute limited partner if all the members consent to the assignment.

6 The retirement, death, or insanity of a general partner dissolves the partnership, unless the partnership is continued by the remaining general partners.

7 On the death of a limited partner, an executor or administrator shall have all the rights of a limited partner for the purpose of settling the estate.

8 Upon dissolution of the partnership, a distribution of the assets may take the following priorities:
   a To the creditors.
   b To the limited partners with respect to their share of profits and other compensation.
   c To the limited partners with respect to the capital contributions.
   d To the general partners other than for capital and profits.
   e To the general partners with respect to profits.
   f To the general partners with respect to capital contributions.

9 In the limited partnership, all the liabilities are the responsibilities of the general partner. Some taxpayers have attempted to limit such liability by creating a corporation to be the general partner. In early 1972, the Internal Revenue Service issued a Revenue Procedure *(Rev. Proc. 72-13)* that established certain safe harbor rules. The purpose of the safe harbor rules was to establish a guideline for situations where the Internal Revenue Service is requested to issue an advance ruling regarding the status of a partnership being treated as a partnership rather than an association which is taxed as a corporation *(Sec. 7701(a)(3))*. The safe harbor rules set forth by the Internal Revenue Service are as follows:
   a Where the capital contributions to the partnership are $2,500,000 or less, the net worth of the corporate general partner must be equal to 15 percent of the total capital contributions to the partnership or $250,000, whichever is less.
   b Where the capital contributions to the partnership are in excess of $2,500,000, the net worth of the corporate general partner must be equal to at least 10 percent of the total capital contributions to the partnership.
   c Where a corporate general partner is a member of two or more partner-

ships, the tests for Sub-Chapter S corporations and for (**2**) above are based on the total capital contributions to all partnerships in which the corporate general partner is a member.

d The net worth of a guarantor of the corporate general partner's debt is not part of the corporate general partner's net worth.

e The limited partners must not own directly or indirectly more than 20 percent of the outstanding stock of the corporate general partner or a corporation that is affiliated with the corporate general partner (within the definition of affiliated groups Sec. 1504 of the Internal Revenue Code).

10 Partnership versus association taxable as a corporation. The following six major characteristics are ordinarily found in a corporation.

a Associates.

b An objective to carry on business and divide the gains therefrom.

c Continuity of life.

d Centralization of management.

e Liability for corporate debts limited to corporate property.

f Free transferability of interests.

The Internal Revenue Service applies the above six attributes to a partnership, and if a majority of the characteristics are found to exist in the partnership, it may be taxed as an association and, therefore, the tax losses would not pass through to the partners. The first two characteristics, namely, associates and objective to carry on business and divide the gains therefrom, are common to both the corporation and the partnership. Therefore, the first two items are ignored in the test. The remaining four characteristics are therefore applied to the partnership and if three of the characteristics are found to exist in the partnership, it will be treated as an association and taxed as a corporation.

11 In the event of termination of partnership for tax purposes, the Internal Revenue Code contains a provision which states that if more than 50 percent interest in the capital and profits and the losses of the partnership is sold within a 12-month period, the partnership will terminate for tax purposes and a new partnership will come into being (*Sec. 709(b)*).

Real Estate Investment Trust A real estate investment trust is a special-type entity and receives special tax treatment. Generally, a real estate investment trust is a business trust with more than 100 shareholders that meets certain income and asset tests set forth in the Internal Revenue Code (*Sec. 856*). In the event the trust distributes at least 90 percent of its taxable income, the real estate investment trust is not liable for tax on the amount distributed and the shareholders receiving the distribution are taxed on the distribution (*Sec. 857*). Tax losses do not, however, pass through to the shareholders. In the event that this 90 percent of taxable income is not distributed to shareholders, all income withheld is taxable under the Internal Revenue Code.

LIMITED PARTNERSHIP

General Information

The limited partnership is the most common ownership entity used for tax shelter syndications. By utilizing the partnership form, the double tax of the corporation is eliminated, the tax losses are deductible by the partners and the limited partners are not exposed to the liabilities of the partnership.

Registration of Securities

The general partners (developer, syndicator, or promoter) create the limited partnership and then solicit limited partners. The solicitation of limited partners constitutes the solicitation of investors for the purpose of selling a security. A share of beneficial interest in a limited partnership is a security and the sale is subject to federal regulation (Securities and Exchange Commission) and also state regulation (most states have a Securities Commission).

All limited partnerships offering shares for sale must file a registration statement with the SEC unless the transaction is exempt from registration. The following is a brief discussion of the two exemptions most commonly utilized to exempt the offering from registration with the SEC.

Private Placement   If the securities are sold to a small group of investors (not exceeding 35), the sale will generally qualify for an exemption from registration with the SEC.

Intrastate Offering   An offer of the securities to residents of one particular state will be exempt from federal registration (SEC). The proceeds of the offering must be invested within the state of the offer.

The state laws regulating the registration of securities generally contain an exemption for the offer of securities to a private group. Some states refer to the "sale" of securities to a private group rather than the "offer" of securities. The state statutes normally specify the actual number of offers or sales permitted. Generally, the private placement exemption also requires that a commission is not paid for the sale of the securities. In some states, a petition must be filed with the Secretary of State in order to utilize the exemption.

An intrastate offering (only offered to residents of a particular state) is exempt from federal registration; however, the offer must be registered with the state. Generally, the intrastate registration with the state of the offering is not as time-consuming or as expensive as a federal registration.

Generally, unless the person offering the security for sale is an officer or employee of the offering company (the limited partnership or an officer or employee of the corporate general partner), said person must be a licensed security salesman.

In an attempt to avoid the security registration, a number of developers syndicate a real estate investment by utilizing the tenant-in-common structure. Since the developer is selling an undivided interest in real estate, it would appear the offering is not within the scope of the securities law. However, in situations where the investors purchase an undivided interest in real estate along with a group of other investors and they all enter an agreement regarding resell, etc., in some cases the offering has been held to be the offer of a security (investment contract).

Deduction of Tax Losses

As explained earlier, the partners allocate the income tax loss of the partnership in accordance with the terms of the partnership agreement. The income tax loss allocated to a partner can be deducted by the partner and utilized to shelter taxable income from other sources.

Section 704(d) of the Internal Revenue Code limits a partner's distributive share of the partnership losses to the extent of the adjusted basis of such partner's interest in the partnership. The partner's basis for interest in the partnership is generally the property contributed to the partnership. The basis of interest in the partnership is increased by the sum of the distributive share, for the taxable year and prior taxable years, of the taxable income of the partnership. The basis of the partner's interest is reduced, but never below zero, by distributions of partnership property (including money). The basis of the partner's interest is also reduced by a share of partnership losses. Generally, the limited partner cannot deduct losses in excess of the amount of property or money contributed to the partnership. If a partner is liable for the partnership liabilities, the basis in the partnership is increased by the share of the partnership liabilities. In a limited partnership, however, the limited partners have no responsibility for the partnership liabilities. The general partner is the only person liable for partnership liabilities. Therefore, under this provision, the general partner would add the liabilities of the partnership to the basis of the partnership interest. In a situation where the partnership owns property subject to an indebtedness rather than the partnership being liable for the debt, the liability is considered to be a liability of all the partners, including the limited partners. The regulations (*Treas. Reg. 1.752(e)*) provide that the liability shall be allocated to all the partners in accordance with the profit ratio then in effect. Therefore, the limited partners increase their basis in the partnership interest by an amount equal to the indebtedness to which the property is subject multiplied by their profit ratio. This provision in the Internal Revenue Code (*Sec. 752*) and the regulations entitle the limited partners to deduct tax losses far in excess of their original cash contributions. If the general partner is liable for the mortgage amount or the partnership is directly liable for the mortgage amount, the entire mortgage is added to the basis of the general partner. This particular provision is the key to tax shelter investments. Generally, without the nonrecourse loan, an investment cannot be a true tax shelter investment, since the tax losses to be deducted by a partner would be limited to the capital contribution.

The limited partners receive the benefit of the nonrecourse mortgage and are allowed to deduct tax losses far in excess of their capital investment. Eventually, the day of reckoning comes and the excess losses become taxable income. When the real estate is sold for $1, it is actually sold for the mortgage balance plus $1, and when said amount is compared to the adjusted basis (cost less depreciation) of the asset, a large taxable gain is recognized. In essence, every dollar of tax loss and every dollar of cash flow received in excess of the equity invested will generally be taxable income upon sale of the asset by the partnership or the sale of the partnership interest by the partner. Depreciation recapture could result in a large portion of the taxable income being taxed at ordinary income rates.

Termination of Partnership for Tax Purposes

The Internal Revenue Code contains a provision which states that if more than 50 percent interest in the capital and profits of the partnership is sold within the 12-month period, the partnership will terminate for tax purposes and a new partnership will come into being (*Sec. 708(b)*). The termination will result in a new partnership owning used property, and, therefore, qualifying only for straight line or 125 percent declining balance depreciation. Because of this rule, it is extremely important that the limited partners are admitted to the partnership prior to the date the tenants occupy the premises. If the partnership is formed and substantially all the limited partners are brought in subsequent to occupancy, the Internal Revenue Service may attempt to claim that the admission of limited partners was in essence a sale of interest by the general partner and, therefore, more than 50 percent interest was sold and a new partnership came into existence. The regulations, by parenthetical language, specify that the rule will not apply to the expansion of an existing partnership. It would therefore appear that when a limited partnership is formed with a general partner and one initial limited partner, and subsequently (according to the intent specified in the partnership agreement) additional partners are admitted as limited partners, the termination rule should not apply.

Chapter 11

Construction Financing

Raymond A. Jensen

INTRODUCTION

This chapter pertains to construction financing as related to income-producing properties. Residential construction lending, whether on an individual or tract basis, as well
as other types of construction lending vis-à-vis FHA multifamily, nursing homes, and
other institutional structures, is intentionally outside the scope of this discussion.

The functional definition of a construction mortgage is a loan secured by proposed
(to be built) real property upon which the borrower (developer or owner) will build a
structure with the lender disbursing the loan proceeds as construction progresses. These
disbursed funds are allocated, obviously, to pay the costs of such construction. This
modest definition could be greatly expanded, but it will be more beneficial to examine
in some detail each of the many facets of construction lending philosophy and processes.

Some attention must be given to the source of the financing, since it may make a
difference in the nature of the documentation as in other related matters. Personal
guarantees during construction and the necessity for a permanent loan commitment that
will fund the construction loan upon completion are two high-priority items as the
construction loan is being considered. Until recent years, the mortgage banker did not
typically engage in construction lending on income property. This assertion is subject

to exception, since in certain areas of the country, particularly the Midwest, the mortgage banker has not infrequently been the construction lender. On the whole, however, the commercial banking system has historically supplied the bulk of credit needed for the construction of income properties. Generally speaking, both the commercial banks and the mortgage bankers who are engaged in such construction lending require a take-out commitment (permanent loan) from a responsible institutional investor to purchase the construction loan upon physical completion of the building.

Contrasted with this permanent take-out commitment requirement of mortgage banking and commercial banking, savings and loan associations are generally interested only in making construction loans if they also retain the long-term mortgage. In other words, they are typically permanent end lenders, who will make the construction loan only if necessary to obtain the permanent mortgage. A caveat as to the permanence of the foregoing statement should be entered here because of the fluid nature of all mortgage lending in the last few years.

The real estate investment trusts (REITs), the newest entry into the construction lending field, have become very large construction lenders. From the point of view of documentation, they occupy an intermediate position between the commercial banks and the mortgage bankers on the one hand, and the savings and loan associations on the other, since they frequently grant both a construction loan and an end loan even if the end loan is of relatively short duration, for example, three to 10 years.

While the construction lending activity on the part of insurance companies is minuscule, with the overwhelming majority doing no such lending, their effect on the required documentation is pervasive, since so much of the permanent lending on income property is done by these institutions.

On a national basis, construction lending on the part of the mutual savings bank industry is also negligible, although they do engage in such lending to some extent in their own state of domicile. Again, however, as with the insurance industry, these banks are very active as permanent end lenders, particularly in the FHA-multifamily project area.

CONSTRUCTION LENDING RISKS

In all probability the paucity of construction lenders until quite recently, even among those groups normally associated with this type of lending, has been due in no small measure to a perception that this type of lending is a high-risk business. This perception, however, has never really been buttressed by factual data relating to a failure rate. As a matter of fact, the few studies which have been done do not bear out the assumption that failure in this field is any greater than that in other lending areas. This does not mean that the lenders (and borrowers too) were wrong in their analysis, but merely that extra precautions taken by most lenders in this field have prevented and minimized those failures feared even by the experts.

In any evaluation of the nature and seriousness of risks confronting construction lenders, the type of lender involved must first be recognized. To a mortgage banker, with a limited amount of capital but with a substantial amount of credit, the failure of the borrower, for whatever reason, to meet the requirements of the permanent loan commitment is a disaster of the first magnitude. The seriousness of this situation lies in the borrower's inability, without special banking arrangements, to carry the loan until the problem can be resolved, even through refinancing if necessary. Any special arrangement frequently reduces both the banker's capital and the amount of credit the banking system is willing to continue to extend on other projects. The banker, therefore, views the risk of such lending as a potentially hazardous one.

On the other hand, although the commercial bank normally insists upon take-out commitments for all major construction projects it finances, a failure on the end loan does not normally produce the same trauma in a commercial banker as it does in the mortgage banker. Due to the greater flexibility and, usually, greater financial resources, the commercial bank has greater "holding power" with which to resolve the problem. It can afford to hold the building as an asset, pending a solution to the failure of an end loan commitment.

Physical Completion

Basically, the construction lender focuses intently on the physical completion of the building. All other potential risks remain merely secondary if the structure is not completed. The major reason for the concern of the lender, with respect to the physical aspects of completion is the difficulty the lender would have in finishing the structure if forced to take over the job of completion. Even large construction lenders are not builders and are not organized to perform construction work. Furthermore, even with an independent contractor on the job, the lender may be forced to pay extra costs to have the building completed. Invariably, the cessation of construction occurs because of the lack of sufficient funds or cost of overruns, both major problems for the take-over lender. Any number of physical factors may cause the stoppage of a large project: soil conditions, poor workmanship in general, inadequate plans and specifications are but a few such causes. Beyond these, complete stoppage often comes about because of labor strikes and/or material shortages.

A construction stoppage of any duration, however, may ultimately result in a shortage of sufficient funds to complete the structure, since the entrepreneur may have insufficient reserve funds to overcome the additional cost created by construction stoppage. For example, if the stoppage was caused by poor workmanship, which needs to be corrected, and if there are not sufficient funds in the construction loan, the only parties to supply the additional funds are the general contractor or the owner. In the event neither the contractor nor the owner is capable of supplying these additional funds, whether by means of secondary financing or from their own resources, the construction lender is the last resource. Frequently, it is in the lender's own self-interest to advance the necessary additional funds. To foreclose on a half-completed project, except in unusual circumstances, may be one of the greatest risks that a lender can face. This raises the issue of intervening liens, which are almost invariably present, when the contractor has insufficient funds and a stoppage of work has occurred. This, in turn, frequently makes it impossible for the construction lender to advance additional funds beyond the originally contemplated loan, because there is no way of satisfying the claims of all of the materials men and contractors. At this point, it should also be mentioned that in many states the construction lender does not have the benefit of any priority over mechanics' lien claims, regardless of how late in the stage of construction the claimant entered into a contract with either the prime contractor or the owner. In some states, of course, the construction lender does have a priority, and it is therefore easier to deal with the claims of the contractors. As a very general proposition, however, the intervening lien problem, at least in a project of any size in which the required additional equity funds are of a significant amount, will frequently force the mortgagee to adopt the foreclosure route despite a willingness to advance a reasonable amount of additional funds.

Failure of Permanent Mortgage Commitment

The ultimate category of construction risk, which has not had as much attention in the literature as the obviously dangerous nature of the risk requires, is the failure, for any reason, of the end loan to materialize. It would seem that, although on paper the requirements of the take-out commitment are very stringent and the risks of not meeting those requirements very great, most of the risks related to an end loan failure are not as significant as the character of the institutional investor that has committed to purchase the end loan. In addition, often the cause for failure of a permanent commitment is negotiable, whereas the fact that the entrepreneur has insufficient funds to complete the project is a fact of life that must be accepted.

One of the risks of end loan failure is that the plans and specifications as approved by the end lender were not followed to a substantial and acceptable degree. Under normal circumstances, if not of crucial magnitude, the investor may agree that the changes were not substantial, that they are acceptable, or that it will reduce the amount of the end loan accordingly. This, of course, forces either the construction lender or the entrepreneur to seek secondary financing for that amount of the construction loan which exceeds the end loan amount. This does happen, and it is a risk that construction lenders try very meticulously to protect themselves against.

A second risk of failure of the end loan arises because the time in which the permanent loan must be delivered to the end lender is insufficient. Reasons for this time shortage vary, ranging from bad weather to inefficient supervision, to failure of completion of documents by deadline. Such situations are frequent, and the end lender's response most frequently is dictated by its current need to invest funds. Should this need be strong, the permanent investor may agree to extend the delivery time either for a fee or at an increased interest rate. Investors often do extend delivery time without charge, however, if in fact they are particularly interested in the loan.

A third category of end loan failure is violation of zoning or building ordinances, or environmental rules and regulations. These problems are much more difficult to solve. Sometimes they are not soluble and, therefore, require the end lender to take that risk. The construction lender and the entrepreneur will attempt to resolve with the appropriate authorities some way for curing the alleged violation, either by an actual correction or by strategies such as zoning variations, by the redoing of impact statements, and by similar devices.

A fourth problem sometimes related to other risks occurs when the appraised value of the property—upon completion—does not equal the appraised value that the investor accepted in issuing its commitment arrived at on the basis of plans and specifications. This risk is greater in those cases where there are different appraisers at the beginning and at the end of the project. The problem, however, arises because of some major deviation from the plans and specifications or from some unanticipated neighborhood change. Usually, these problems are soluble by some additional work on the premises or some reconsideration by the appraiser as to whether the modification of the plans and specifications was really material in terms of valuation. Ultimately, the investor could reject the loan, but most frequently the problem resolves itself by a reduction in the valuation, which may or may not cause a reduction in the end loan amount.

A fifth risk factor is the possibility that a cost requirement in the investor's end loan commitment may not be met. Some investors require the cost of the construction, plus appropriate charges such as interest, insurance, taxes, and other soft costs, to exceed a certain amount or the loan will be reduced by some formula or by an amount determined by such a formula. Normally, the construction lender will determine as nearly as possible in advance of opening the loan whether or not the estimates received from the builder are sufficient to meet the cost requirement. This is also the kind of requirement that an investor will frequently eliminate from its commitment at the time the construction lender is ready to commence disbursement of the construction loan, provided the investor receives appropriate evidence from the entrepreneur as to costs. If these requirements are not met and are not satisfied in advance, the automatic formula becomes operative and reduces the end loan amount. An alternate method would be to withhold a larger percentage of the construction draw request.

A sixth risk factor concerns the possibility that special conditions in an investor's commitment, particularly physical conditions, that is, the meeting of certain sound-proofing standards, which have become very common in large commercial projects, may not be met. Again, this presents a risk which normally can be partially protected against prior to the opening of a construction loan by having the requisite tests made and obtaining the appropriate approval of the investor of the test results, as well as the testing laboratory, if such is required. An alternate method would be to require very exacting and inflexible plans and specifications.

A seventh possibility of not meeting the investor's end loan commitment exists when it requires that the initial applicant for the end loan mortgage remain the sponsor of the project at the time the end loan is delivered to the investor. The failure of the construction lender to police this by requiring, by means of appropriate documentation, that the sponsor remain the same from the inception of the construction loan to the completion can be very dangerous.

An eighth potential risk for the construction lender with respect to the end loan is the possibility of a casualty loss occurring during the construction, which is either not repaired or restored or, even more importantly, not adequately covered by insurance. The risk of its not being repaired if the funds are available is probably the type of risk that is assumed every day without too much thought. The only real risk is that there may be a question of time; generally speaking, end lenders would probably be willing to extend the time for delivery if a major casualty loss occurred. If there were a major casualty loss, the problem of insufficient loss proceeds is one that the construction lender has the power to prevent and is, therefore, a risk that must be taken.

Finally, the last risk for the construction lender is the end loan commitment which contains lease requirements that are not met by the entrepreneur by the expiration date of the end loan commitment. This type of problem is probably the most dangerous that can be imagined. The protection of the construction lender in this case really rests on an unwillingness to fund the gap between the minimum end loan amount and the greater amount available when the leasing requirements have been met. There are many substitutes for the construction lender's funding such gaps, namely, secondary financing, letters of credit, and other means. The risk is too large for the construction lender under normal circumstances. The entrepreneur under any proper system should put up the amount of money necessary for funding and collect the full loan at the end. However, this is not the way in which most construction loans work, and generally speaking, the construction lender ends up taking a significant part of the risk. Frequently, the construction lender receives additional compensation for this risk-taking function, but the leasing requirement of the end lender imposes a discipline upon the construction lender that is really not a construction risk; and the construction lender should recognize the difference in this function. Therefore, the construction lender should not, without appropriate compensation, take the risk of the gap.

CONSTRUCTION LOAN DOCUMENTATION

Application

Applications for a mortgage loan are as varied in terms of the information required as any documentation one can imagine. It is safe to say, however, that in the mortgage banking field the application signed by the prospective borrower is frequently also a request for a permanent mortgage and can additionally be a request for a construction loan. A caveat, however, must be entered, since the industry is still changing rapidly in the field of construction lending. Generally speaking, the kind of information required by any application will focus primarily on the potential entrepreneur's background, experience in building and real estate projects, credit standing, and the equity that will be supplied. In addition, the application will generally require, in outline form, the type of project, namely: whether it is commercial, industrial, apartment, or condominium; the number of units; and an estimate of the dates by which construction will begin and be completed. Furthermore, any additional information of significance as to leasing or prospective sale should be included.

One of the issues often discussed in the industry is whether or not an application should attempt to bind the applicant for a given period of time in order to allow the lender enough time to make a decision as to whether or not to undertake the project. This is less of a problem if only a construction loan is involved. A difference in the two situations arises if an end loan is requested because the mortgage banker must have sufficient time to attempt to place the permanent loan with one of the normal institutional investors. Since this ordinarily requires a significant amount of time for preparation, the mortgage banker wishes to be assured that during the necessary time period the entrepreneur does not ''shop'' the loan elsewhere. This is one of the basic problems of the mortgage banker, who in the end loan field is the equivalent of a wholesaler rather than the equivalent of the manufacturer. In contrast, when only the construction loan is at issue, the mortgage banker normally needs to ascertain only the financial position and perhaps consult a commercial banking source to ascertain whether to entertain the application. Even then sufficient time should be allowed to investigate the feasibility of the project. During this more limited time span, the application from the developer should be firm in order to conserve time for the mortgage banker.

Additional documentation, which will be either required at this stage or subsequently, but which ideally should be in hand at the time the lender makes the decisions as to the desirability of this loan from a construction viewpoint, will consist of at least the following:

1 Information of a detailed nature on the developer's "track record" in the construction field.

2 The decision as to whether a developer is going to use a general contractor or act as general contractor. If a general contractor is to be used, background credit information, as well as a listing of prior types of projects, is essential.

3 A preliminary set of plans and specifications.

4 The name and credentials of the architect or architects. For a very large project there generally will be a supervising architect as well as a design architect.

5 Next, and maybe of overriding significance, is the permanent loan commitment. All the details concerning it, including the name of the institutional investor, the amount, and the expiration dates should be supplied prior to the issuance of the construction commitment.

6 An appraisal of the land by the construction lender should be undertaken in order that any figures produced by the entrepreneur as to land value may be substantiated.

7 If a construction contract has been signed, a copy is essential for the construction lender. If one is not signed, some preliminary indication of what the amount might be is necessary.

8 A soil test at this stage is very desirable. Many times the entire project hinges on the ability of the subject land to support the projected building.

9 The issue of utilities in this energy-short society is now of even greater consequence than before. It is, therefore, important that the lender have a thorough idea as to the availability of water, sewer, electricity, and all other utilities, and that connection approvals can be secured. Certainly at this stage the entrepreneur should have checked all these items.

10 With current attitudes as to zoning, the zoning of the land in question must be known and confirmed in writing prior to the construction commitment.

11 In our consumer-oriented society, a new matter has arisen to make the life of construction lenders more complicated, namely, the requirement of environmental approvals from various local, regional, state, and federal authorities. Although all approvals may not be in hand at this time, the requirement that they be produced certainly must be brought to the attention of the developer, who may have overlooked some part of these requirements. Any good checklist would require exploration of this subject.

12 One of the most important items is the cost breakdown, which can be supplied in a number of forms, for example, a contractor's statement or a developer's estimated project cost analysis. Whatever the format used, it must show estimates for at least the following costs, separately stated:

a Wrecking costs.
b Construction costs (broken into broad categories such as electrical, plumbing, and other major trades).
c Estimated taxes during construction.
d Estimated insurance during construction.
e Architects' fees for design, supervision, and inspections.
f Legal fees.
g Overhead and profit if there is to be a general contractor.
h Contingencies to be covered. (An entrepreneur with a realistic view will want to include some amount for contingencies.)

Commitment

Assuming the construction lender has decided on the basis of the application and the preliminary documentation that it wishes to issue a commitment for a construction loan to this particular entrepreneur for this particular project, there are many different ways of doing it. The better view, however, is that a document as complete as possible within the bounds of practicality should be used. The mere acceptance of an application, which in the past was a thoroughly normal way of handling the situation, no longer suffices in this more complex era, at least not with respect to income-property projects. For any income-property project this is not an adequate approach and is unfair both to the lender and the borrower. It is, therefore, suggested that a printed form, which merely requires blanks to be filled in, be used by any construction lender who is in the business with any degree of regularity. This will allow the staff to be familiar with the kinds of questions that arise, and will familiarize developers who are repeat customers with the procedure of the organization. Overall, it will expedite to a very great degree the ability of the mortgage banker to respond quickly and to satisfy the needs of the construction borrower. Without reproducing a commitment form in full, it should suffice to outline in some detail the types of clauses that should be covered in any such commitment which pretends to completeness. The content would certainly include all of the following:

1   The identity of the party to whom the commitment is issued must be clearly specified. It would in all cases be desirable, if not essential, to have an *individual* principal identified and to have this principal sign the commitment. In those situations in which a corporation, and in some states a trust, neither of which has assets other than the land itself, is to be the mortgagor, it is most important that the personal responsibility for fulfilling the terms of the commitment be placed upon the principal *individual* borrower. It does not follow, though, that the individual must be personally liable on the mortgage. These are two entirely distinct problems, and the individual may be perfectly free from any liability on the note while remaining liable for compliance with the requirements of the commitment.

2   The date by which the project will be begun should be set out. One reason for this is to spur the entrepreneur to do all of the documentation necessary before that date. Otherwise, the developer typically wants the loan opened but has not supplied the necessary documentation. Such a clause also allows the lender to withdraw from the transaction should there be no progress by a reasonable date.

3   The amount of the loan should be set forth. If there is any gap financing necessary, it should be mentioned. It is desirable to indicate whether this gap is being supplied by the construction lender or by a third party. In addition, any peculiarities governing the amount of the loan, such as might arise from a formula established by the end loan commitment, should be clearly specified.

4   The interest rate should be established, whether it be on a formula basis—for example, so many percentage points over the prime rate on a fluctuation basis—or a nonfluctuating flat rate, or a split rate depending on how much is disbursed and at what stage of development. Whatever the method of determining the interest rate, the standard governing it should be clearly outlined so that there can be no subsequent dispute. If a fluctuating rate is tied to the prime, there should be a clear specification as to which prime is to govern and at what point in time the change is to take place.

5   The commitment must indicate the maturity date of the construction loan, and the date by which construction must be completed. The maturity date will not necessarily coincide with the maturity of the note or mortgage if the mortgage and note of the permanent lender are used, but the commitment must clearly specify that the construction loan itself matures. Naturally, this will also be specified in the construction loan agreement.

6   The security for the loan should be very clear. A legal description of the property is not necessary in the commitment, but certainly a common street address identifying the involved real estate is necessary. A brief description of the contemplated improvements would also be a part of the description of the security.

7   If a guarantee by all or any of the principals in the transaction is required, this too must be specified. There are any number of different types of guarantees which can be required, for example, a full guarantee of the principal amount, a guarantee of the top 10 or 20 percent of the principal amount, a guarantee of payment of the interest only. Although the guarantee need not be couched in legal form, it should be written without ambiguity. This is not an easy task, since such guarantees can present tricky and contradictory language problems.

8   The commitment should state the frequency with which the lender will disburse construction funds, giving some indication of the standard by which the amount will be determined. One of the excellent ways in which this issue can be met without making the commitment unduly complicated is to refer to the lender's customary construction loan agreement as governing this issue. The aware developer or lawyer will certainly want to review the construction loan agreement. This poses no problem, since that document, if properly written, will state in detail the basis on which disbursements will be made during the course of construction.

9   The commitment should also indicate the lender's requirements as to the construction contract, including any restrictions as to the identity of the contractor, that is, whether one general contractor is required or whether it is acceptable to the lender if the owner enters into a number of different prime contracts with different parties for different purposes.

10   The loan requirements of the end lender, as established by the commitment, should be incorporated into the construction loan commitment by reference. The commitment should indicate that all terms and conditions of the end lender's commitment that can be complied with prior to the opening of the construction loan must be complied with forthwith, and those that can only be complied with upon physical completion must be complied with prior to the delivery of the loan to the end lender. In addition, it should be clear that the construction lender has a right at any time to request the end lender to indicate affirmatively that certain conditions of the commitment have or have not been met.

11 If the construction lender has any special appraisal requirements, such as the requirement of an appraisal by a disinterested outside appraiser upon completion, or any other similar special appraisal requirements, it should be so stipulated in the commitment. Generally speaking, however, the construction lender would not at this time demand an appraisal, unless there is an appraisal requirement in the end loan commitment which must be satisfied. When the construction lender issues a construction loan commitment, it is assumed that any appraisal necessary for its protection has been made.

12 Timetable of approval of plans and specifications by the lender, along with number of sets required.

13 The fact that inspections will be made from time to time, only for the benefit of the lender, who will not incur any liability to the borrower for such inspections, must also be provided in the commitment.

14 The requirement for a soil test, if required, must be mentioned.

15 The requirement for a title insurance policy must be specified. Most lenders on income projects require an American Land Title Association (ALTA) lender's policy, along with various types of additional endorsements to cover matters ranging from usury to encroachments.

16 A plat of survey is also required. The requirement that it be updated from time to time and upon completion of the project should be clearly stated. Furthermore, the survey should meet specified standards. There are many different types of surveys and certain standards have been established by different organizations. In order to obtain the proper survey, it is important for the lender to be aware of the available variety. This is particularly true since most institutional lenders are particular with respect to the survey and most developers object to the payment of the fees charged by surveyors who comply with these standards.

17 Insurance during construction must also be covered in the commitment. Generally, casualty, workman's compensation, and liability insurance should be required. The required limits ought to be indicated at least in a general way. Obviously, the lender should be named as an additional insured or the appropriate mortgage clause should be attached, depending on the types of policies.

18 The question of bonding should be covered in the commitment. Many lenders have in the past required a performance and payment bond regardless of the project, the contractor, the developer, or the amount of funds involved. Other lenders, for economic reasons, have over the years dispensed with a bonding requirement and have instead accepted personal endorsements.

19 There should always be a clause in the commitment dealing with expenses. Obviously, all the expenses for insurance, surveys, soil tests, title insurance, appraisals, bonds, and all other lender requirements are costs to be borne by the applicant and are legitimate expenses to be paid out of the loan proceeds.

20 The question of the assignment of the commitment by the borrower should be covered. In most cases, the lender will not allow the commitment to be assigned, particularly without its consent. The question of keeping a responsible party in the transaction during the entire construction period is of crucial significance to most lenders. Sometimes at the beginning of a transaction it is known that the commitment will be assigned. If such is the case, and if the party to whom it is to be assigned is acceptable to the lender, the former can make an exception or can insert language in the commitment indicating that consent will not be unreasonably withheld.

21   The commitment should always provide for the lender's fee, usually stated as a percentage of the face amount of the loan. Very frequently the commitment provides for a refundable standby fee which will be forfeited in the event the loan is not opened, or if opened and the borrower subsequently defaults. Normally, this fee will be returned upon delivery of the project to the end lender or upon payment in full of the construction mortgage. Frequently, if the construction lender simultaneously issues a commitment for the end loan procured from one of its institutional investors, there will be a third type of fee passed through to the end lender in consideration of its issuance of the end loan commitment. This fee may or may not be refundable. All of the fees should be clearly distinguished, and it should be clear from the commitment what disposition will be made of each in the event of default.

22   The commitment should include a provision that should construction not proceed at a satisfactory pace in the determination of the lender, the lender has a right to assume the project and complete construction.

Note and Mortgage

Neither the note nor the mortgage need much elaboration, since they are both, with few exceptions, the standard forms used for any income-property mortgage loan. In the note, the interest may be established by a formula if the rate is geared to the prime rate. However, if the note is to be used as the permanent mortgage note, it may only contain the standard rate provision, leaving to the construction loan agreement the exact terms of the construction interest.

Frequently, a definite date, fixed at a certain number of months beyond the estimated completion date of the project and delivery date of the mortgage, is established for the commencement of amortization. At other times a more elaborate formula is set out by which to establish the beginning of amortization. As far as the mortgage itself is concerned, the usual mortgage form may be used, but the construction loan agreement should always be incorporated by reference. A self-executing method should be provided in the mortgage to allow the assignee of the mortgage, normally the permanent lender, to cut off all rights of the borrower under the construction loan agreement.

The Security Agreement

In order to preserve the priority of the construction loan over security interests in fixtures, the Uniform Commercial Code has been amended in a few states in accordance with the suggestion of the draftsmen of the Code. A construction loan will have priority over a security interest in goods that become fixtures before the completion of construction as long as the mortgage is recorded before the goods become fixtures. This priority will continue for a permanent loan if it is intended to refinance a construction mortgage. It is important that a provision be inserted in the construction loan document indicating that it is a construction mortgage within the code definition. As a consequence, it is no longer necessary in the states that have adopted this amendment to file a security agreement under the Uniform Commercial Code to make sure that certain types of items which may become fixtures are covered by the mortgage. In those states that have not yet adopted this modification of the Code, it may be neces-sary to prepare a security agreement and file it in the requisite office in the state where security agreements covering personal property must be filed. Normally, this is not a major problem if a form agreement is at hand so that only an enumeration of the personal property need be added.

Construction Loan Agreements

The preceding discussion focuses on many of the items that must be covered by a good construction loan agreement. There are many forms of construction loan agreements, but basically most of them contain the same requirements that are found in a good, detailed construction commitment, though in much greater detail. There are some things, however, of great consequence which would normally not be covered in a commitment that the construction loan agreement does cover. One of these items is the authority of the lender to establish reserves from the proceeds of the loan to pay for items such as interest during construction, real estate taxes, insurance premiums, title expense, bond premiums, and other such matters. What is more important, however, from the point of view of the lender, is for the agreement to establish a very clear mechanism requiring the loan proceeds to be in balance, and that there be at all times sufficient proceeds, after deducting reserves, to complete construction. This funds provision is based on the lender's estimate of the costs of the project as modified from time to time by new circumstances. Any deficiency that arises in keeping the loan in balance, either at the commencement of disbursement or during the course of construc-tion, must be deposited by the borrower upon the lender's demand. The balance concept is a difficult one for many entrepreneurs to understand or perhaps to accept. The requirement is, however, essential if the insufficiency of funds problem mentioned earlier is to be avoided. *The policing of funds is one of the major tasks, if not the major task, of a good construction loan department.*

The second major item that the construction loan agreement will cover, normally not found elsewhere in the documentation, is the contingency reserve. This reserve is created as part of the loan balancing mechanism. It is crucial for the protection of the construction lender. Most contractors have a 10 percent retainage or holdback provi-sion in their contracts with their subcontractors. Under this provision, pending satisfac-tory completion of work, 10 percent of the amount still due under the contract is not paid to the subcontractor. A similar type of provision is usually found in the contract between the entrepreneur and the general contractor. This retainage is often confused by lenders with the contingency reserve available to the lender for emergencies. This is not the case, since the retainage is merely a holdback of funds due the contractor under the contract when the work is completed. It should not, therefore, be used for cost overruns, extras, or other types of emergencies which frequently arise in construction lending. An additional justification for the contingency requirement lies in the fact that in the event of a default on the part of the entrepreneur's general contractor the lender or owner must obtain the services of a new general contractor. A general contractor will not take on the responsibility for a project that has default problems merely for the amount of the undisbursed funds left in the loan for payment to the general contractor. Therefore, a substantial reserve should be established to pay a newly hired contractor if necessary. This contingency fund will increase the amount of equity funds required from the entrepreneur, since the contingency reserve is added to the total estimated construction costs in ascertaining whether there are sufficient funds in the loan to complete construction.

Among other items that should be covered in the construction loan agreement is a default clause, specifying events of default and giving the lender several alternate remedies, including acceleration, foreclosure, and the right to complete the project.

Another item that should be carefully detailed is the authority of respective parties in the event of a casualty loss, and exactly how and in what amounts the insurance funds should be disbursed.

Of major significance is the prohibition of extras without written approval of the lender. Cost overruns can easily arise from extras or changes in the contract which are not authorized by the construction lender, and which may also violate the terms of the permanent take-out commitment.

Finally, the construction loan agreement is the place for all of the necessary detail relating to each disbursement, including the requirement for affidavits, lien waivers, architect certificates, and similar documentation. To a large extent, this particular clause will depend upon the state in which the construction loan agreement is to be used, though it is possible to write a generalized form of clause to establish the procedure the lender has determined to be the best for the purposes. Any changes necessitated by state law can be added by special riders.

Assignment of Existing Leases

It is important in a construction loan to take an assignment of major leases if there are any outstanding at the time the construction loan is recorded. During the course of construction, an assignment of all commercial leases as they are entered into should be taken. Finally, upon completion of construction, all leases to be taken as additional security for the mortgage should be assigned.

Guaranty

If a guaranty is required, the document itself should be prepared and signed prior to the opening of the construction loan. Any of the peculiarities of that document are to be carefully delineated.

DISBURSEMENT PROCEDURE

The major mechanical problem arising in a construction loan consists of the disbursement of funds in the form of progress payments. This is the essence of the construction loan, requiring the lender's personnel to be fully aware of the statutory mechanic's lien law of the state in which the disbursements are to be made. Since this is an area in which the state laws vary substantially, it is important for the mortgage banker who lends on a national basis to be constantly aware of any changes in the law of the state in which the property is located and to be knowledgeable about the customs of the construction trade in each particular area. Such customs can vary significantly even from one part of the state to another. There are, too, great differences between rural and metropolitan areas in the same state. Basically, however, a good disbursement procedure is substantially identical in the various states. There are rules to follow in the field of disbursement which would prevent most problems from arising, even though the procedure is not unaffected by the law of the state in which the disbursement is being made.

The construction lender has to make certain types of decisions with respect to the use of its own personnel versus the use of outside consultants or services. One issue which immediately arises is whether the mortgage banker should employ an outside organization to perform inspections. There are a number of such organizations which have engineers and architects as part of their team. They do the monthly inspections and examine the plans and specifications for the lender. Probably most mortgage bankers perform this service in their own offices without reference to any outside service.

Recently, there has been the development of construction loan disbursement services by title insurers, particularly by two of the major national title companies. This service actually guarantees completion. It is established as a construction escrow in which the funds are deposited periodically by the construction lender. All disbursements, collection of documentation, and inspections are performed by the title insurer in its escrow capacity. The issue of whether this is equivalent to a surety bond and therefore within the powers of a title company has been raised in some states. The answer seems to be that it is not the equivalent of a surety bond. The price charged for these services is generally the same as the price the mortgage banker would charge for the service if he performed it himself.

In some areas of the country, a service called *interim certification* is available from certain title insurers. This is an intermediate step between the guarantee of completion and the mere issuance of a title policy. Under this system the construction lender disburses the funds, but subsequent to disbursement, requests the title insurer to certify that up through the date of the last disbursement no mechanics' liens were recorded and, more importantly, that no mechanics' liens could arise except for ongoing work. In order to do this, the title insurer must examine the mechanics' lien waivers, affidavits, paid bills, and other documentation that the construction lender received at the time of disbursement. This certification is given monthly if the construction lender is disbursing monthly. As mentioned, not all title insurers supply this service and even those who do so do not necessarily supply it in all geographical areas. In those areas where it is available, the cost is less than a full construction disbursement escrow. It benefits the lender on a large project to the extent that it can be assured that up until a fairly recent date not only are there no outstanding mechanics' liens, but the documentation is sufficient to protect against the filing of any subsequent liens except for work that was in progress at the time of the disbursement. There are, however, traps for the unwary in this procedure, and unless the construction lender is extremely sophisticated with respect to the law of the state in which disbursement is made, it is probably not too wise to use this system.

It is important to emphasize at this point that a title insurer is always involved with the basic problems facing the construction lender. Upon completion, a title insurance policy insuring the lender is necessary in order to assign the mortgage to the permanent lender or in order to receive payment from the permanent lender who is making the loan. Consequently, title insurance is inextricably intertwined with construction disbursement. The legal requirements of the title insurer must be complied with and must be kept in mind from the beginning of disbursement. This varies substantially from state to state depending upon the mechanic's lien law of the state. One of the problems of construction lenders who operate in states with laws which stipulate that a construction mortgage must be recorded prior to any lien filed by a contractor is that the construction lender frequently thinks that this may be depended upon completely and progress payments need not be documented, other than to make sure that the work is in place for the payment being requested. This is a shortsighted view of the obligations of the construction lender, since too many problems can arise both legally and practically if proper documentation is not required for each disbursement.

This is the appropriate place to discuss the value of a construction payout expert in the mortgage banker's employment. There is no question that such a person is the crucial element in the success of a properly run construction loan operation, in the sense of disbursing the funds properly to prevent any default. It should be emphasized that a construction loan expert in the disbursement field need not be an architect, nor an engineer, nor an attorney. The attorney, for instance, can draw perfect documents to effectively regulate in the minutest detail the disbursement process, but unless the expert is there to handle the day-to-day problems, the documents become meaningless. What, then, are the actual functions of the construction disbursement department?

First, the analysis of the project prior to the commencement of disbursement and actually prior to the issuance of the commitment is of inestimable significance. The construction department should be able to take a project analysis offered by the developer and, by means of available figures, both as written data supplied by various organizations and as a matter of experience, determine if the developer's figures are reasonably calculated. To do this, it will be necessary for the construction department to have copies of all of the contracts drawn between the owner and the general contractor and between the general contractor and subcontractors and suppliers. In addition, the construction loan department will need estimates from the contractor as to the amount of the unlet contracts. The construction expert then matches these figures, which are generally supplied in the form of a listing called the contractor's statement or contractor's affidavit, with its data. On this basis, after analyzing the plans and specifications, the expert should be able to tell management that the project can or cannot be built at the construction cost figure used by the developer. The expert should be able to point out specifically those areas in which the costs of the contractor or the entrepreneur are overstated or understated. This function, in effect, is also a service supplied free to the entrepreneur, who may not be as expert in one field of construction as in others, or who may not have had recent construction experience in a particular type of project. In other words, a construction disbursement department must contain a cost breakdown expert, who knows current costs for all construction items. This will allow determination to be made that the available proceeds of the loan will suffice to complete the project. This is a fundamental aspect of construction lending.

The second major function of the construction expert is an ability to examine the project and to determine whether or not the requested progress disbursement is proper.

This is sometimes confused with the issue of quality. It is not the function of a construction lender to pass on the technical quality of construction unless the defect is patent. The inspection is a quantifying task and not an examination of quality. The expert must examine the work in place as of the date of the request for payment and determine that the bricks and mortar for which payment is being requested are there and that they are in conformity with the plans and specifications under which the building is being built. Most good construction lenders also require that the progress payment be certified by the owner, contractor, and architect. It is the supervising architect's function during the course of construction to certify that each payment is proper and in conformity with the requisite professional standards. However, the construction lender should not depend on these affidavits or certifications without making its own inspection to satisfy itself that the requested progress payment is proper. Often, contractors attempt to get out ahead of the disbursing agent to make sure they have no money in the project in terms of work except retainages. As a consequence, their requests for payments are not always totally in tune with the work in place.

The third major function of the construction loan expert is to examine with sufficient knowledge the documentation required by the state, the lender, or both. This requires an ability to analyze the progress payment documents and to spot their inconsistencies or inaccuracies. In certain states, mechanics' lien waivers are extremely important, legally as well as practically, and must conform in minute detail to certain requirements. In those states, the good construction loan expert becomes a quasi-legal expert in terms of an ability to analyze these documents.

RELATIONSHIP BETWEEN CONSTRUCTION
LOAN AND PERMANENT LOAN

The fact that an end loan or permanent mortgage has been mentioned previously does not preclude a discussion of the fact that the construction lender's responsibility and relationship with the end lender is to a substantial degree different, depending on what type of permanent loan the institutional investor is committing to purchase from the construction lender or to make directly to the borrower. It is important to mention that the permanent mortgagee may issue its commitment to make a loan on certain terms directly to the entrepreneur, who then contracts with the construction lender, who in turn uses the permanent take-out commitment as the basis for its construction loan. However, the mortgage banker normally procures from one of its institutional investors the commitment to make the end loan, which, generally speaking, runs directly to the mortgage banker. Frequently, however, the institutional investor will also insist on the developer, signing some documentation indicating its acceptance of the end loan commitment.

Types of End Loans

In most income-property loans the mortgage committed for by the permanent institutional investor is a regular mortgage loan, either on straight interest or with an incentive provision. No matter how complex the various clauses of the commitment may be, the security is generally a note signed by the entity controlled by the entrepreneur, which in turn is secured by a mortgage on the real estate. There are, however, several exceptions to this.

One very noticeable one in recent years has been the condominium project. It is rare for a permanent mortgagee to issue a commitment to the construction lender for the purchase of the construction loan upon completion. Instead, the end lender, which is usually a savings and loan association, a savings bank, or the Federal National Mortgage Association (FNMA), commits to make loans to the individual purchasers of the condominium units if they meet the credit standards of the end lender. The problem this raises for the construction lender is whether or not there will be sufficient sales of the units to allow for the release from the construction loan lien of those sold units on which the end lender is ready to make a mortgage. Most construction lenders require a minimum number of units to be sold prior to activating the release provisions under the construction loan. Many lenders insist on a minimum of 50 percent in number of units. Once the lender has partially released its construction loan, the condominium developer then has, in effect, only a mortgage covering individual condominium units and would not be able, if sales were to stop, to reconvert the project to an apartment building. This would pose insurmountable problems of foreclosure in the event of default by the condominium developer.

The gap commitment has been previously mentioned. It poses no problems for the construction lender, assuming the proper legal documentation. The issuance of a commitment by a third party, usually a second mortgage lender, to cover the difference in the value between the floor loan the first mortgage end lender has committed for and the top loan, which is usually predicated upon leasing of a certain number of residential or store units, allows the construction lender to use the proceeds of the second mortgage to bridge the gap. This, in turn, requires the phasing in of the gap loan with the requirements of the first mortgage end lender. It normally is much easier to expedite such a situation if both first and second end lenders allow the construction lender to use their approved documents as the construction loan documents. Advances are then made under the first mortgage until the proceeds are fully disbursed, at which time the second mortgage takes effect and advances are then made under it by the construction lender. Each mortgage, upon completion of the building, may merely be assigned to the respective end lender. If the construction lender advances the gap money, protection is sought by drawing a second mortgage and characterizing it as such, since it may be necessary to deliver the first mortgage to the end lender and hold the second mortgage until the terms of the first mortgagee's commitment are met. Frequently, the time within which the leasing requirements may be met extend far beyond the time necessary for the physical completion of the building. The same procedure is used when the gap lender is the construction lender as is used when a third party is involved. Another method of taking care of the gap is for the entrepreneur to give the construction lender an irrevocable letter of credit from a commercial bank. This is a subject in and of itself, but clearly the letter of credit should not be subject to any conditions and should expire at the same time as the permanent mortgage commitment. Without arranging in some manner for the gap to be taken care of, the chances of the construction lender opening its loan are minimal, because most entrepreneurs count on the funds being available from the gap financing. Normally, the amount of the gap is significant enough so that the developer will not be able to supply the deficiency out of personal funds.

A standby commitment is a somewhat different problem for the construction lender, though it is more nearly analogous to the regular end loan. The only difference insofar as the construction lender is concerned is found in the length of time that the commitment is outstanding. The "standby" is normally a commitment purchased by the entrepreneur to assure the construction lender that permanent financing will be available for some minimal period of time beyond completion of construction. If it is issued by a third party, the construction lender will frequently deliver the mortgage to the standby mortgagee just as if it were a regular mortgage. However, sometimes, it is possible that the construction lender will hold the loan after completion of construction on the theory that the issuer of the standby commitment will, just prior to the expiration of the standby commitment, purchase the loan on a permanent basis unless some other source has in the meantime issued a permanent commitment. The construction lender thus serves a warehousing function secured by the take-out commitment of the standby issuer.

Another type of transaction frequently discussed is the sale-leaseback in which the institutional investor purchases the fee simple interest in the land and then leases it back to the former owner, who is the developer. In this transaction, a commitment to make a mortgage on the leasehold interest leased back to the developer is sometimes given by the same lender. There are a number of variants of this transaction, but the construction lender is required to structure the construction loan to fit the needs of the institutional investor. Some investors do not wish to buy the land until such time as the buildings are completed. At that time they will purchase the land and enter into the leaseback transaction. Other investors insist on purchasing the land prior to the commencement of any construction and will then lease back the land simultaneously with the purchase. Often, there will be three parties to the transaction: the purchaser of the land, the institution making the leasehold mortgage, and the construction lender. Sometimes the institutional leasehold mortgagee insists on having the fee owner join in the mortgage to subject the ownership of the land to the lien of the mortgage even if there is no personal liability on the note. At other times the institutional investor will forego any such requirement and will merely make a leasehold mortgage without further comment. In all of these possible combinations, the construction lender is faced with the requirement that it must either get all of the institutional lenders to subordinate their rights to its outstanding construction loan or has to take certain risks. For example, if the construction lender is dealing with an institutional investor who insists on obtaining fee ownership prior to construction, it must in effect make a leasehold mortgage usually without any liability on the part of the institutional investor, who now owns the fee. If there is a takeout commitment for the leasehold mortgage, this may be a risk worth taking. It is also sometimes possible to work out with the institutional fee owner a side agreement under which, in the event of default in the construction mortgage, the construction lender may be able to buy back the fee from the institution at the price paid by the institutional fee owner. There are any number of situations that can arise, and each of them must be met by a tailor-made solution, since they do not fit into the normal category of construction lending.

Buy-Sell Agreements

Buy-sell agreements (or tripartite agreements) are entered into between the construction lender and the end lender. They serve several functions. The end lender frequently wants to tie the construction lender to its commitment to make sure that the construction lender does not sell the loan upon completion to anyone else. Between mortgage bankers and their normal institutional investors such agreements are frequently not used because of the history of dealing between correspondents and insurance companies, cemented by outstanding servicing agreements between the parties. However, many institutions feel they are necessary in any event and require the developer and mortgagor to join in such agreements. The main reason for this is to insure that the developer is contractually bound to perform and to execute whatever documents may be necessary to allow the construction lender to deliver the loan upon completion to the institutional investor. At times when the developer can obtain a lower interest rate upon completion of the project, because of a change in the market, some have insisted that they have a right to forfeit whatever good faith or standby deposit has been made. They then insist that the loan be delivered by the construction lender to an unrelated third party or that the construction lender accept payment in full. Therefore, the institutional investor who intends to purchase the permanent mortgage insists that both the construction lender and the borrower be bound contractually to deliver the mortgage to it. There certainly can be no objection to this on the part of the construction lender, who indeed benefits by this procedure.

These agreements usually provide that the construction lender will not accept any prepayment by the borrower or through the borrower, that it will give notice of any fault in its construction loan to the end lender, that the end lender, after a certain time period for consideration, has the right to purchase the loan in spite of any default, and finally, the end lender has the right to waive any default by the borrower with respect to the end loan commitment. Reciprocally, the construction lender has a right to be informed by the end lender of a default on the part of the borrower under the end commitment and should be given a chance to cure any such default. Another item that should be found in any good agreement of this type is the obligation on the part of the end lender to approve in writing any matters that the construction lender feels can be approved prior to completion of construction. Such items include approval of the plans and specifications, the legal documentation, and leases.

One of the most difficult problems for a construction lender is securing the end lender's approval of things that ultimately require such approval by the terms of the commitment. Many institutional lenders have not understood how important it is to good relationships with construction lenders to approve leases, legal documentation, plans and specifications, and other matters of the kind promptly, either prior to commencement of construction or as it proceeds. Since the loan may not be delivered to the end lender for 18 months to two years after the issuance of the commitment, many end lenders, until recently at least, have been unimpressed by the argument that they should approve such matters at this time. This is an incorrect position, because they have not taken into account the problems of the construction lender, from whose point of view it is necessary to proceed to obtain as many approvals as possible in order to obviate many of the risks involved in construction. There are sufficient risks of default without requiring the construction lender to take unnecesary ones. For example, in a shopping center situation, approval of the major leases by the end lender is indispensible in order to avoid serious and perhaps irreparable damage to the construction lender at a later time. It is impossible to understand this without having been in negotiations between major tenants and institutional investors, both of whom are really arguing from strength. To get into this middle, which the construction lender must, is not an enviable position. To take the risk that it will all be worked out can cause the construction lender to be left without a take-out commitment. It is therefore incumbent upon the construction lender to obtain the approval of all major leases and also, if possible, a form lease for small tenants. In connection with industrial properties the same situation occurs with fewer tenants. In apartment lending, there is, of course, no problem in this area.

PAYOFF OR DELIVERY OF CONSTRUCTION LOANS

The simplest problems, generally speaking, in connection with construction lending occur at the end of the transaction after the building is physically completed. The problems are simple only if the construction lender has been alert and has previously obtained the cooperation of the end lender. The simplest delivery problems arise in connection with those investors that will not purchase mortgages by assignment from the construction lender. There are a number of institutions that feel they must for various reasons have their own set of documents and therefore will not purchase loans by assignment. These are very simple transactions, because the mortgage documents during construction can be much simpler and do not need prior approval. However, the risk occurs when the time comes for the payment of the construction loan and the mortgagor refuses to cooperate and does not execute the required documents prepared by the end lender. This leaves the construction lender at the complete mercy of the mortgagor except for the right to accelerate the loan and finally to foreclose. These rights are not very helpful. Therefore, although the mechanics of a payment in full by the end lender are much simpler from the point of view of the construction lender, it is also a much riskier procedure. Many savings and loan associations insist on this method of doing business. A number of them also insist that the transaction be placed into an escrow with both the mortgage papers of the construction lender and their own mortgage documents being deposited. The escrow agent will then handle the transaction with respect to the terms of payment. These are, as stated above, very simple types of situations and very large loans can often be handled this way. The risk, however, is great and, from the point of view of the construction lender, is a critical point in the whole transaction.

The normal method of procedure, at least between mortgage bankers involved in construction lending and institutional investors, is for one integrated set of documents to be used. Frequently there are problems in the early stages of working out such a complex set of documents, but it can be done. Sometimes, the construction lender is able to convince the institutional investor to use the latter's own mortgage forms if they have been cleared in advance. Occasionally the construction lender uses the forms prepared by the institutional investor and adapts certain clauses for its own use as a construction lender. In any event, the documentation is approved in advance by the end lender and is therefore used for the construction disbursements subject, of course, to the construction loan agreement, which, as mentioned previously, is incorporated by reference in the mortgage. One of the advantages to this procedure, from the point of view of the institutional investor, is the fact that the priority of the construction lien inures to its benefit.

The actual delivery of the documents involves the following: (1) the assignment of the mortgage to be recorded; (2) the endorsement of the note to the institutional investor without recourse; (3) the assignment of any security agreement under the Uniform Commercial Code; (4) the assignment of leases if the property is commercial or industrial (this assumes the construction lender has taken an assignment of the outstanding leases from the owner and now in turn assigns its assignment to the institutional investor as an additional security); (5) a certificate of completion by the architect; (6) all occupancy permits, including any final zoning approval; (7) an updated appraisal, if such is required by the terms of the end loan commitment; (8) an estoppel certificate showing that the borrower claims no rights against the construction lender; (9) tenant acceptance letters, if there are commercial or industrial tenants, stating that rent has been paid no more than one month in advance and that there are no rental payment off-sets against the owner; (10) an ALTA lender's title insurance policy with all exceptions to title previously approved by the end lender; (11) a plat of survey that reflects completion, including all parking spaces, fences, and easements; (12) a certification from the construction lender or an estoppel certificate that there are no defenses to the loan and a statement of the amount due. With these items in hand, the normal payment for a mortgage takes place between the construction lender and the end lender. If the mortgage banker is servicing the loan for the end lender, there are numerous other internal documents that are necessary, but those normally follow subsequent to the payment for the loan.

SPECIAL PROBLEMS

One of the many special problems that has arisen with greater frequency in construction lending recently has been the problem of so-called "phased" loans. These are staged loans, generally for town house or garden apartments which have many amenities such as golf courses, swimming pools, sauna baths, and items of the kind. They are built over a period of years. Frequently, a commitment is issued by an end lender for one part or several parts of such a projected development, and then other institutional investors issue commitments for subsequent portions of the development. The construction lender is confronted with many problems, for example, legal descriptions are most complex since the land is frequently purchased in one large tract. The amenities to be offered by the developer pose a problem to the construction lender, since the end lender to whom the loan is to be delivered wants that portion of the project to have complete access, and this requires the provision of easements. Since there will be other phases of the project and since the tenants of the subsequent phases will also be entitled to the use of the amenities, various problems of staging the amenities and of establishing easements for the use of such amenities will exist. The complexity of the easements for ingress and egress and for use are very substantial and require expert legal advice both on the part of the owners and from the point of view of the construction lender and its take-out lender. Some of the problems that arise can also eventually raise a question of mechanics' liens, since a mechanics' lien on one phase may encumber another phase. All of these questions are of utmost importance to construction lenders and must be dealt with in any phased loan. Frequently, the attorneys representing the entrepreneurs have less experience in this area than the construction lender's attorneys and therefore they look to the construction lender for help.

Another problem that has arisen to bedevil the life of the construction lender relates to the potential liability of a construction lender to third parties for poor workmanship or other faults in construction. The issue was raised in a California case of some years ago which held a lender liable for cracked foundations. The trend of the law is to protect consumers; even individuals who buy a $40,000 or $50,000 house are considered consumers needing the protection of the law. The problem has become extremely complex and merely disclaiming liability in a construction loan agreement no longer seems to be adequate. A lender must remain completely separate from any entrepreneurial profit or may be held liable for any construction defects.

Chapter 12

Closing the Permanent Loan

Thomas J. Watt

Until recently, a loan closing was an event justifiably regarded with suspicion and disdain by most members of the real estate profession. To any observer, a closing presented a bizarre landscape populated by green-eye-shaded clerks, intimidating attorneys, and perpetual commitment extensions. Its atmosphere of lethargy was periodically disrupted by a flurry of excitement at the end of each calendar year, followed by a gradual return to a more placid and predictable norm accompanied by the soft soundings of gently rustling papers.

Fortunately, this scenario has undergone dramatic changes, primarily in response to the difficulties that buffeted real estate markets beginning in the late 1960s. Because of the unprecedented volatility of interest rates, for example, institutional cash flow planners began to demand precise and realistic closing forecasts in order to attune their cash revenues with their funding obligations. At many times and for many people, accurate cash flow planning was a prerequisite to continued economic existence.

At the same time, the emergence and proliferation of the REITs impacted on the closing business in various ways. First, they graphically demonstrated the effect of well-timed closings on the investor's earnings. During the boom days, an attractive spread existed between the price at which a REIT could borrow long or short and the rate at which it could lend those borrowed funds. By law, the REITs were also precluded from investing their cash in short-term securities; thus, if their cash was not invested in real estate deals, it was lying neglected.

Many REITs developed the capacity for instant closings; that is, they would actually send their closing representatives into field, literally armed with freshly minted loan commitments and satchels of money. Many more traditional investors, especially those that sponsored REITs, soon found parallel advantages in managing their non-REIT portfolios in a similar fashion. Others, in order to remain competitive, found it necessary to bring what historically had been back-office operations out into the mainstream of the business world.

During that period of growth and turmoil, closing a loan changed from an event into a process. This process begins at the time a deal has been formally approved and committed by an investor and ends when the money has changed hands and a completely documented loan transaction is entered in the investor's filing system.

If this process is handled improperly or is allowed to founder through inattention, it can easily develop into a distasteful, frustrating, time-consuming, and expensive chore for all of the parties, particularly the borrower. A bad closing experience can cost the lender and the mortgage banker repeat business. Alternatively, if the process is controlled in a constructive and professional manner, it can be an important distinguishing characteristic between you and your competition.

BEGINNING THE PROCESS: BASIC ASSUMPTIONS

Of all the axioms involved in the closing process, perhaps the most basic one to be aware of is: *A business person should be in charge at all times!* An important corollary might be: *Don't release your responsibilities to the attorneys*. An effective mortgage banker would not dream of turning over the role of banker in the loan origination process to an attorney or CPA; it is simply not good business. Yet time after time many experienced professionals jeopardize their important customer relationships by leaving them in the hands of "outsiders" with little or no feeling for the business sense of the deal, let alone the needs and the psychology of the customer.

In view of the manner in which most investors are organized, chances are high that the mortgage banker is going to have to be the prime mover in enforcing these principles. Unfortunately, most institutional investors, once a deal has been committed, turn the closing process over to their legal staff. This is done primarily in the name of safety and prudence, but well intentioned or not, it is guaranteed, if not controlled or guided, to be disruptive to customer relationships.

Knowing Your Investor   This concept is just as important in the closing process as it is in the making of new deals. Above all, understand how the investor's closing operation is organized. Never assume that any two investors function exactly the same way. Regardless of the investor's form of organization, the mortgage banker has an important strategic advantage that should never be overlooked: a natural alliance with the investor's underwriting staff. If this relationship is exploited with even moderate effort and skill, business control of the closing process can be insured.

Under no circumstance should attorneys be eliminated from the closing process; far from it. In fact, another important axiom is: *Have access to a competent, can-do attorney*. A good attorney is a critical cog in the machine, and can be absolutely essential in helping keep everyone out of all kinds of trouble, and making certain that all parties get the deal they bargained for. The attorney's input should be sought and weighed carefully when making decisions. However, it should not be overlooked that all decisions in the closing process are ultimately business decisions. The consequences of taking one course of action as opposed to another may well have legal consequences or risk, and these ought to be evaluated carefully and responsibly by a competent attorney.

Even if keeping the closing process under business control is successful, there will be no shortage of attorneys. Generally speaking, the borrower will have a personal legal adviser. Because of the nature of developing real estate, chances are high that the borrower's attorney is going to be an aggressive, results-oriented type and a tough negotiator. The investor will retain an attorney who, ideally, should have a similar style.

All too frequently, a geographically remote investor will select or retain local attorneys by consulting one of the major legal directories or rating services. Unfortunately, a high rating by no means guarantees excellent performance in the real estate field and often invites substantial legal fees. Every major city or region contains attorneys combining excellent professional abilities in real estate matters with constructive styles. Somehow, they rarely seem to be matched with investors. A mortgage banker attuned to the local scene will know who these attorneys are and identify them and expose their names to the investor. In time, a good match can be made.

Before leaving the subject of attorneys, legal fees should be treated. Borrowers who are pleased without hesitation to pay substantial sales or leasing commissions may still balk at the mention of attorneys' fees. The subject can become a real deal breaker. Like any other cost of doing business, attorneys' fees ought to be dealt with openly and forthrightly at the commitment stage of a transaction. Most attorneys will have no objection to providing a fee estimate before getting into a loan transaction. Since they are representing the investor, albeit at the expense of the borrower, the request for a fee estimate should emanate from the investor. Again, the mortgage banker will have to be the catalyst in developing in investors an awareness of the importance of this subject.

Another principle to keep in mind is: *Understand the basics of real estate law and loan documentation.* If you are going to manage the process, you have to be able to speak the languages of the various players. You are going to have to serve as an interpreter, a moderator, and a guide. Ways in which you might be able to acquire these skills might be:

1   Study a good basic textbook on the subject.

2   If you work for an established company, study a completed loan file and analyze its contents. What do the various documents accomplish? Better yet, ask an experienced co-worker to go through the process with you.

3   Form associations with attorneys or title company employees. Subject to the general caution that advice is often worth the price paid for it, ask your acquaintances in either occupation for some free advice. Most people like to talk to others about what they do and how they do it. The results may surprise you.

4   Involve yourself in a few closings as an observer.

5   Select an investor you feel is particularly professional and ask its staff for assistance. Better yet, try to combine this with a visit to the investor's home office.

6   Attend meetings or formal seminar sessions.

DESIGNING AND MAINTAINING
THE CRITICAL PATH

Assuming that one of your investors has issued a loan commitment to one of your clients and you want to get the closing process under way, what should you do? Like a construction project, the closing process has a sequential pattern of interdependent elements. To get the job done quickly and expeditiously some things have to be completed before others are begun. The first step should be to analyze the loan commitment and to identify a checklist of the various items that must be dealt with before the closing proceeds change hands. Next, the items must be arranged in order of desired accomplishment with a realistic time deadline assigned to each and, finally, responsibility for the preparation or solution of each must be assigned.

The person who establishes this list, parceling out responsibilities and setting deadlines, has laid a strong foundation for taking over management for the transaction. As a guide, let's take a straightforward, typical loan commitment and translate it into a closing checklist. As a word of caution, the commitment form used in this example is not necessarily recommended for anyone's usage. It is intended to be illustrative only. For the reader's convenience, the left-hand margin of the text is the commitment language. The right-hand margin isolates closing items required by the commitment language.

Thomas J. Watt, Inc.
RFD   1
Hartford, Connecticut 06115

Gentlemen:

Pursuant to your application, Burlington Insurance Company (hereinafter referred to as the "Lender") agrees to loan to Thomas J. Watt, Inc. (hereinafter referred to as the "Borrower") the sum of $2,350,000 for a term of 25 years, subject to the following conditions:

1.   *Interest and Repayment*

The note shall bear interest at the annual rate of 9¾%. It   *Note*
shall be repayable in monthly installments of $20,962 to be applied first to interest, then to principal. The full unpaid balance of the loan shall be due and payable at its maturity date.

2.   *Prepayment*

Borrower shall have no right to prepay the loan in whole or in part.

3. *Security*

The note evidencing the loan shall be secured by a first and valid mortgage lien upon Borrower's fee simple interest in the real estate fronting approximately 600 feet on Village Lane and containing approximately 350,000 square feet located in Bloomfield, Connecticut on which Borrower shall construct, prior to the closing of the loan, a 125-unit apartment complex with amenities, including 5 tennis courts, sauna, exercise and billiard rooms, covered parking for 125 cars and a swimming pool.   *Mortgage*

As additional security Lender is to have a first and valid lien on all personal property, whether presently on the real property or hereafter placed thereon, used in the management or operation of such real property (including, without limitation, all stoves, dishwashers, disposals, refrigerators, air conditioning units and maintenance equipment). All costs to accomplish this during the term are to be borne by the Borrower.   *Security Agreement* *Financing Statements* *Inventory*

4. *Title, Documents and Other Matters*

Title to all of the property to be mortgaged, the legal description of the mortgaged premises and all documents, agreements, instruments, legal arrangements and other matters relating in any way to the loan, or to the property to be mortgaged, shall be satisfactory to Lender. Borrower shall furnish to Lender a title insurance policy containing no exceptions other than those, if any, approved by Lender, issued by a company acceptable to Lender.   *Legal Description* *Approval of Title Company* *Title Binder* *Title Policy* *Copies of Exceptions*

Lender shall not be called upon to close the loan unless Lender shall have received from its counsel opinions of law confirming that all such matters are valid, enforceable and binding in accordance with their terms and do not violate any usury laws or other applicable laws or ordinances.   *Legal Opinions*

The loan documents shall provide that Borrower shall obtain and at all times keep in full force and effect such governmental and municipal approvals as may be necessary to comply with all environmental, ecological and other governmental requirements relating to the property to be mortgaged and to the occupancy thereof. Prior to the closing, Borrower shall submit to Lender proof reasonably satisfactory to Lender that Borrower has obtained all such approvals.   *Government Approvals*

5. *Survey*

Borrower at Borrower's expense shall furnish Lender an up-to-date engineer's survey of the premises to be mortgaged certified by a registered surveyor and showing no state of facts objectionable to Lender. Such survey shall   *Survey* show that all buildings are within lot and building lines and shall show all easements, improvements, appurtenances, utilities and rights of way whether above or below ground, which exist at the date of certification.

6. *Taxes*

Prior to the disbursement of the loan proceeds, any outstanding unpaid taxes, assessments and other governmental and municpal charges and liens shall be paid by Borrower.

Tax Bills

The loan documents will provide that Borrower will, within 30 days after the final date that taxes can be paid without penalty, furnish Lender with such evidence as it may require that all taxes have been paid in full.

7. *Insurance*

The loan documents shall provide for fire and extended coverage, rent insurance and for such other insurance coverage as Lender may require from time to time in amounts and with companies acceptable to Lender. All policies or certificates shall contain the proper mortgagee clause and shall be deposited with Lender throughout the life of the loan.

Approval of Insuror
Insurance Policies
Coverages
Amounts
Mortgagee Clause

8. *Construction Work*

Prior to the start of construction of the proposed improvements Borrower shall submit to Lender for Lender's approval final working plans and specifications which shall be in substantial agreement with the preliminary plans, specifications and descriptions accompanying the loan application.

Approval of
Specific Plans
and Specs

All construction work shall be completed prior to the disbursement of the loan proceeds in accordance with the final plans and specifications approved by Lender, and Borrower shall submit to Lender proof reasonably satisfactory to Lender that the improvements are ready for occupancy and comply with all ordinances, building codes, zoning requirements and other applicable government requirements. Inspections by designated representatives of Lender may be made at any and all times during the course of construction.

Certificates of Occupancy
Use Permits
Zoning Compliance

9. *Annual Reports*

The loan documents will provide that within 90 days after the end of each fiscal year of Borrower, Borrower will furnish to Lender a balance sheet of Borrower and statements of earnings from the mortgaged premises as at the end of and for such year and accompanied by the unqualified opinion of independent certified public accountants.

10. *Personal Liability*

    Borrower shall be personally liable for the payment of   *Guarantee*
the debt. Payment of the loan and of all other amounts
secured by the mortgage shall be guaranteed by Thomas J.
Watt.

11. *Rents and Leases*

    The loan documents shall provide a general assignment   *Assignment of Rents*
of rents to Lender to be operative in the event of default. All
leases shall be subordinate to Lender's lien unless otherwise
specified by Lender. Lender may require that specific leases
be made superior to Lender's lien at the expense of Bor-   *Superior Leases*
rower.   *Subordination Agreements*
    Lender is to be provided with a specific assignment of
such present and future leases as Lender may require. Lender shall be authorized to notify lessees of the existence of
such assignments, but Lender shall not exercise its right to   *Assignment of Leases*
collect rents until a default exists in any of the loan docu-
ments.
    Any standard lease forms to be used by Borrower shall   *Standard Lease Form*
be submitted to Lender for Lender's prior approval.
    Prior to the closing of the loan, Borrower shall furnish   *Specification of Leases*
to Lender lease ratification agreements executed by both   *Ratification Agreement*
landlord and tenant under all leases specified by Lender.   *Execution by Tenants*
Each agreement shall state that the tenant is in possession of
the demised premises, is paying the full lease rental, that no
rental payments have been made in advance, that all work
required to be performed by landord under the lease has
been completed and stating the commencement date of the
lease.

12. *Critical Dates*

    Lender will not be called upon to disburse loan funds   *Earliest Close*
prior to January 15, 1979.
    This commitment, except for the provisions relating to
costs and fees shall become null and void if the loan is not   *Must Close*
closed on or before March 31, 1979 unless such date is   *Extension?*
extended by Lender at its sole option.
    This commitment shall not become effective unless on
or before June 1, 1977, Borrower shall execute and deliver
to Lender a copy of this commitment, together with the fee
provided in Condition 13 hereof.

13. *Fees*

    The Lender shall receive from the Borrower, together
with Borrower's acceptance of this commitment, a fee of   *Fee Paid?*
$23,500 to be retained by Lender as consideration for the
execution and delivery of this commitment. This fee will
not be returned to Borrower.

14. *Agreement With Interim Lender*

Upon acceptance of this commitment, Borrower and Lender shall with reasonable promptness negotiate and execute a three-party agreement between themselves and the construction lender, providing for such of the following as may be appropriate:

a. Joint use of loan documents by lender and the construction lender;

b. Agreement by the construction lender that it will not accept payment from borrower or assign the loan documents to other than lender;

c. Transfer by assignment of the loan from the construction lender to Lender within 60 days after the fulfillment of the provisions of Lender's commitment by Borrower (except such provisions as Lender may waive);

d. Such other provisions as may be appropriate to facilitate the expeditious transfer of the loan from the construction lender to Lender, and to minimize costs to be incurred by Borrower.

In any event, the three party agreement shall provide that Lender shall not be required to accept a transfer of the loan if a default exists in the loan at the time of transfer.

15. *Costs*

Whether or not the transaction provided for in this commitment is completed, Borrower will pay all costs incidental to the transaction, including, but not limited to, title insurance charges, attorneys' fees, revenue stamps, recording fees, mortgage taxes, survey costs, and any and all other incidental expenses.

Very truly yours,

BURLINGTON INSURANCE COMPANY

By_____
    President

Our sample commitment contemplates a to-be-built project and a third-party construction lender. For purposes of this example, we should further assume that the construction loan has been underwritten on a real estate basis as opposed to a pure credit transaction. Given this set of circumstances, the construction lender will exert intense pressure upon the borrower to obtain approvals of most of the permanent lender's closing requirements before any construction loan disbursements. The primary objective, of course, is the elimination of every possible contingency that might eventually impede or prevent the repayment of the loan by way of the permanent loan closing.

The permanent lender (assuming it really is interested in closing the permanent loan as opposed to issuing a standby commitment for a fee) will be interested in locking up its future business. It should also be interested in providing its borrower with good service and the fewest possible headaches.

At the outset, the borrower will be eager to get construction under way and will display little patience with anything that will delay the development schedule, being interested, at the same time, in minimizing red tape and overall expenses. Above all, the borrower, if experienced, will not want to become involved with separate detailed closings of the construction loan and the permanent loan.

Upon close examination, the objectives of the three major parties are really quite similar. Moreover, because of the unique merger of pressures from both lenders, combined with the borrower's objective, the climate will never be better to get the closing process under way.

The ultimate goal should be one master closing prior to the commencement of construction. The transaction should be evidenced by a single set of loan documents that meet the needs and the commitment requirements of both the construction lender and the permanent lender (in the trade these are often referred to as "combination papers"). At the master closing an agreement usually called a *three-party* or *buy-sell* agreement should be signed by the three major parties restating the various conditions necessary to close the permanent loan, together with an acknowledgment of their approval by the permanent lender. There will be a number of requirements (such as completion) which cannot be approved; however, the agreement should set forth exactly what it will take for approval by the permanent lender to be granted. Finally, this agreement should provide for an orderly process of transferring the single set of loan documents from the construction lender to the permanent lender when construction has been completed.

The mortgage banker has a very real interest in getting a total transaction organized in this fashion. Since many permanent loan origination fees are payable only upon the closing of the permanent loan, the advantages should be fairly obvious.

How can you get this process under way? First, arrange the checklist items culled from an analysis of the permanent loan commitment into three general categories:

1 Those that must be dealt with immediately.
2 Those that must be dealt with periodically during the course of construction.
3 Those that must be handled at the time of the permanent loan funding.

Next, determine exactly who is to be responsible for the preparation or obtaining of each item. Generally speaking, try to persuade the construction lender to allow the permanent lender's attorney to prepare the combination loan documents by using the argument that the permanent lender has to live with the documents for a much longer period of time. Along with the assignments of responsibility, reasonable time frames to produce the items should be agreed upon.

Finally, make sure that you know how the approval process works for the construction lender, the permanent lender, and the borrower. Can binding decisions be made in the field or must each item be referred to a geographically remote and impersonal institutional home office? Who are the actual ultimate decision makers for each of the parties and how can they best be contacted?

After these basics have been accomplished, the mortgage banker should be prepared to act as the quarterback or catalyst of the process. This role will involve badgering the appropriate parties to meet agreed-upon deadlines, pushing for approvals, arranging meetings, and exerting leadership and diplomacy. If impasses seem to be occurring, try to identify them right away, distill their business essence and, if all else fails, be prepared to submit them to the appropriate ultimate decision makers for a practical solution. Lack of this type of leadership or management skill will almost always guarantee that the closing process will deteriorate into an endurance contest of lasting distaste for all parties.

Let us return now to the model commitment and categorize the items identified in the right-hand margin as suggested. Following each item is a short discussion of the problems that are typically encountered in relation to it in the context of a combination construction/permanent loan closing.

Category 1: Deal With Immediately

1 Note Outside of some mechanical difficulties relating to a clear description of the different terms of repayment required by the construction and permanent loans, the major area of controversy usually revolves around the concept of the lender giving written notices of default to the borrower and a subsequent period during which defaults can be cured prior to acceleration of the debt. Lenders prefer not to give any notices at all. They feel that the borrower ought to know whether or not the obligations are being performed. Furthermore, any kind of notice will impede the lender's ability to gain control of the property if the borrower is diverting funds for other purposes.

Borrowers maintain that notice is necessary because a default may occur due to an oversight or an error of omission, and they do not want to run the risk of losing their property or seeking a new loan "under the gun" to repay an accelerated debt.

The trend seems to be toward more and more notices. The issue may depend upon the nature of the borrower. A smaller owner-operator may not have the same notice needs as a national developer or a joint venture borrowing entity. Due to the volatility of the business, a construction lender has a more critical need to move quickly than a permanent lender. Perhaps the notice requirements could be tailored to the needs of each lender by requiring no notice during the construction loan and reasonable notice during the life of the permanent loan. The important concept is to isolate the practical and real needs of each party and recommend a solution responsive to them.

2 Mortgage The mortgage is the key document establishing the long-term ground rules for the loan transaction. It usually contains a lengthy series of affirmative covenants on the part of the borrower, such as keeping the property well maintained, paying taxes, keeping insurance in force, and complying with applicable laws and regulations. Although the sample commitment is relatively uncomplicated, many will contain restrictions as to a transfer of title or ownership. Others contain prohibitions against secondary financing or borrowing restrictions more customarily found in bond indentures or private placements. A breach of any of these covenants can lead to default, acceleration, and foreclosure. Borrowers again like to obtain formal written notices of default from the lender before any of such actions can be taken. Lenders tend to be more relaxed on the notice issue when nonmonetary defaults are involved. The borrower has a further problem in that frequently nonmonetary defaults cannot always be cured in 30 or even 60 days. Lenders recognize this and are often willing to accept the concept that, if the borrower is trying to cure the default with all due diligence, the lender will delay exercising its legal remedies.

Perhaps the most difficult issue to resolve satisfactorily is the disposition of fire insurance proceeds or condemnation awards. For many years lenders took the unshakeable position that they had complete control over these sums. At the lender's total discretion, the funds could be applied to restoration of the property or to repayment of the debt. Naturally, borrowers objected to this, especially when fire insurance proceeds were involved. In response to this, lenders would argue that they were really reasonable folks and their decisions would be based on what was truly best for the property.

Condemnation awards have a further confounding twist. No one can reasonably argue about the disposition of condemnation awards in the event of a total taking of the property. Since the lender's security is gone, it ought to be paid off prior to anything being paid to the borrower. On the other hand, what about a partial taking? To what extent is the economic potential of income property impaired by a partial condemnation? These and other related questions are not easily answered.

The overriding objective in determining the disposition of both types of proceeds is consistency. Complicated income property forms, such as large shopping centers, often have other parties extremely interested in the disposition of such proceeds. Most regional shopping centers, for example, involve some combination of diverse ownership. The mall portion and much of the parking areas are generally owned by the developer, while the department stores (or at least some of them) frequently own their own facilities and the underlying pads. In view of this divided ownership, agreements have to be reached by the various owners regarding access, the sharing of expenses, and operations. These agreements, often called Reciprocal Easement Agreements (REAs), contain provisions relating to casualty losses and condemnation. Many tenant leases do as well. Perhaps one can successfully convince the lender to agree to the REA or major lease provisions. The provisions will generally predate the mortgage and the practicality of renegotiating REAs or major leases is not great.

Virtually every lender has one or two areas of particular concern, yet no two may be alike. In all probability, the lender has suffered a loss by a particular problem in the past and is determined not to allow it to happen again. If you really know your investor well enough, you should be aware of what these issues are. Armed with this information, you can avoid unresolvable impasses by advising the borrower of the situation or, better yet, by advising the borrower to concede any objections in these areas in exchange for some concessions by the lender in other areas.

Finally, one of the great tools of compromise is the use of the concept of reasonableness. The mortgage will contain many provisions requiring the lender's consent, yet the borrower will regard them as obnoxious. If the lender will agree not to withhold his consent unreasonably, agreement can often be reached. While it is difficult to understand what this concept accomplishes from a theoretical sense, practically speaking, it works.

3 Security Agreement   This document deals with personal property in the same fashion that the mortgage deals with real estate; in fact, before the adoption of some version of the Uniform Commercial Code by most states, it was called a chattel mortgage. The issues of dispute will, therefore, be similar to those encountered while agreeing upon the form of mortgage. In some jurisdictions, the security agreement is often combined with the mortgage in a single document.

The importance of this document varies with the type of property being financed. Negotiations will be tougher in the case of a hotel or a furnished apartment complex than in the case of an industrial building or shopping center. The lender is interested in two basic things. First, in the event of foreclosure, it wants to acquire a property in operating condition without the necessity of investing additional money to make it so. Next, the lender may not want the borrower to add to the property's financial burden by carrying the debt service on personal property financing by lien or by lease. The borrower will want to retain as much flexibility as possible.

4 Financing Statements   These are usually preprinted business forms that are filed in the local record index and with the appropriate Secretary of State. They are designed to put the public on notice that the lender has a security interest in the project's personal property. No problems should arise in connection with them.

5 Inventory   To maximize the benefits of a security interest in personal property, the lender may require a detailed inventory of everything used in connection with the operation of the property. At the very least, the inventory should settle the issue of which specific items the lender is really interested in encumbering. The actual items will not be known until they are purchased or installed, and this may not occur until the project is nearly completed; thus, the inventory cannot be completed prior to the master closing. Future misunderstandings can be overcome if the three-party agreement contains a reference to the form of inventory the permanent lender will accept, and a copy of the form is attached to the agreement as an exhibit.

6 Legal Description   The legal description is simply a verbal recital of the numerical metes and bounds of the encumbered real property. Again, the major problems encountered are ones of consistency. The legal description will be contained in the mortgage, other miscellaneous loan documents, and the title insurance binder and policy. It also ought to be traceable on the survey of the property. Most closing attorneys try to alleviate the consistency problem by matching a legal description with the survey and then photocopying it, attaching individual copies to each document requiring a legal description as an "exhibit." Conservative lenders argue that exhibits have a way of disappearing, and, thus, descriptions should be manuscript typed into the body of instruments. If you meet up with this attitude, you will be in for a tedious siege of proofreading.

7 Approval of Title Company   Almost every lender has a method by which it rates the financial strength of title insurance companies. These formulas tend to be closely guarded secrets, and there is little consistency in the approaches that individual lenders take. In any event, the lender will have an "approved" list of title insurers and a set, maximum amount of title insurance it is willing to accept from a title company in any one transaction. You should be very careful that the company selected is both on the lender's approved list and can, in the lender's opinion, issue a policy in the amount of the loan. A lender's rejection of a title company can be a source of embarrassment, an avoidable cause of delay, and an unnecessary duplication of expenses.

Although title companies play varying roles in closing transactions in individual jurisdictions, good title company cooperation and service is a very valuable asset. You should be aware of which title companies have the best local offices in your town. Even if a particular company has an excellent national reputation, its local office may be having some short-term problems. There has been a significant turnover of qualified title company personnel in recent years, and the result of a loss of a key local manager can be chaotic.

A short time ago, individual title companies enjoyed virtual monopolies in certain markets. Today, this has been broken down significantly. The larger national companies have all gone through phases of rapid growth and expansion and have entered new markets for the first time. Often, a company entering a new market will bend over backward to gain new customers. Conversely, the established companies want to preserve their position. This type of healthy competition can be advantageous to you, and it ought to be exploited.

8 Title Binder A title binder can be compared to a commitment from the title company to issue a final policy with certain exceptions if certain conditions are complied with. It gives all of the parties to a transaction a look at the state of title and an early opportunity to deal with troublesome problems prior to the actual closing. A discussion of title problems would alone provide sufficient material for a textbook; however, suffice to say that, when a title problem occurs, a competent customer-oriented title company is your best friend.

At the master closing, the permanent lender should review the status of title. Moreover, the three-party agreement should acknowledge that the permanent lender has reviewed a specific title binder and it will consider the title condition of the permanent commitment satisfied if furnished with a title insurance policy as of the date of the permanent closing containing the exceptions (and only the exceptions) contained in the specified binder.

9 Copies of Exceptions Title policy or binder exceptions can be innocuous on the surface but extremely troublesome when carefully examined. When the binder is submitted to the various parties for review, make sure that copies of the exceptions go along with it. These can normally be obtained from the title company at a nominal cost, and valuable time can be squandered if this simple procedural step is forgotten.

10 Legal Opinions At the permanent loan closing, the permanent lender will normally require a detailed opinion from its local counsel that the transaction is enforceable and binding as documented. It is likely that the permanent lender will have checked out the legality of the transaction with its local counsel prior to issuing a commitment. Just to be on the safe side, you should check this point with the permanent lender's local counsel. It is also prudent to obtain the approval of the permanent lender to the form of the legal opinion and to have the three-party agreement witness the permanent lender's satisfaction with the legal opinion requirements of its commitment if its local counsel will execute such a form as of the date of the permanent closing. The form should be attached to the three-party agreement as an exhibit.

While laws will vary by state, the problem of usury should never be overlooked.

Permanent lenders are extremely sensitive to the dangers of usury, and this sensitivity is justified. At best, it is a very vague area of law, but a violation can lead to substantial fines, loss of interest and/or principal, and even criminal indictment. Over the years, many elaborate schemes have been developed to escape the consequences of usury laws, and some have been successful. It is equally true that, if the investment gets into trouble, a claim of usury by an aggrieved party is bound to be raised. Make sure that the permanent lender's local counsel has no problems with this point. This point should be double-checked directly with the permanent lender's home office. If the transaction has the faintest hint of usury, the permanent commitment will evaporate quickly.

11 Government Approvals Government approvals, particularly those relating to environmental issues, are a current source of extreme difficulty to the master closing concept. The field is full of overlapping jurisdictions and agencies. New laws and regulations are being promulgated daily, and it is unlikely this situation is going to change at any time in the foreseeable future. It is quite possible that a whole string of new regulations will be in effect at the time of the permanent closing that were not even remotely possible at the master closing. This problem seems to be one that the real estate profession will have to live with on a day-to-day basis. The best approach a lender can take is appraising the environmental climate of the area in which the property is located. Some areas or sections of the country seem to be more environmentally sensitive than others. Both the mortgage banker and the lender's local counsel can be important sources of information. In any event, you should be prepared to help the permanent lender to assess the probability of environmental problems.

12 Survey The permanent lender will not be able to approve a survey at the master closing, because that survey cannot possibly disclose the precise location of the completed buildings. It can, however, approve the legal description and the various courses and dimensions delineating the perimeter of the land. In the three-party agreement, the permanent lender should approve the perimeter survey and acknowledge that the survey conditions of its commitment will be met if the improvements and other matters affecting the property are sketched in by the surveyor on the final survey. Even so, the permanent lender will want to reserve judgment as to whether anything is objectionable until it has actually received the final survey.

13 Plans and Specifications Ideally, before construction gets under way and the master closing occurs, both lenders should approve a specific set of plans and specifications, detailed by page number and date. If the developer and the construction lender can deliver a project completed in accordancce with a specific set of plans and specifications within a finite time period, the permanent lender should have no basis to object that the improvements are not what it committed for.

Many construction lenders require an elaborate recitation of approved plans and specifications in the three-party agreement and that a definitive master set be deposited at a designated location as an objective point of reference should a dispute arise. This can be an extremely useful technique. They also prefer to obtain the agreement of the permanent lender that an independent engineer's certification that the improvements have been completed substantially in accordance with the definitive master plans will satisfy the completion requirements of the permanent commitment.

There are two major defects to these theories. First, it is a rare project that does not undergo significant changes during the construction period. Second, the more complicated a development is, the less likely it will be that all plans and specifications will be finalized when construction begins. The first problem we will deal with in a later section. The resolution of the second will necessitate some patient negotiating between the borrower and both lenders. The construction lender will have to be convinced that it is not exposing itself to a loss of its take-out or unanticipated construction cost overruns. If the borrower has reasonably strong credit and strong developmental experience, and if the permanent lender has a deserved reputation for closing on its commitment, you may be able to convince the construction lender to assume the risk. Beyond this, you should be aware of these problems, making sure they are surfaced before irretrievable decisions are made.

14   Guarantee   Since a guarantee is closely related to the note, similar problems will occur. The guarantor, particularly when it is someone other than the borrower, will demand notices of default and reasonable time in which to cure. A more substantive issue, however, is understanding what the permanent lender really means by a guarantee. For example, our sample commitment is to a corporate business unit; yet, there is a guarantee by an individual. Does this mean that the individual is personally liable for any deficiency remaining after a foreclosure sale or does it mean that the permanent lender can put the loan to the guarantor in the event of default prior to a foreclosure? Most real estate loan guarantees are thought of in the first sense, yet the scope of the guarantee and the form should be agreed to at the time of the master closing.

15   Assignment of Rents   Controlling the flow of rental payments is an extremely meaningful security tool for either lender. One way of doing this is to obtain the borrower's agreement that, in the event of a default, its tenants will make their required rental payments directly to the lender. This document is of greater theoretical utility than of practical benefit. Imagine yourself in the role of a tenant, and a lender with which you have no direct relationship tells you to start paying your rents to it instead of your landlord. Such requests are ordinarily not received with much enthusiasm. By recording this agreement, the lender can prevent the borrower from pledging the first claims on rentals to secure other debts. You will not encounter much difficulty in negotiating this document. Its lack of practical meaning is behind its noncontroversial nature.

16   Superior Leases   The priority of leases is another important concept, varying by state, which affects the lender's security and the borrower's ability to negotiate with potential lessees. A superior lease is a lease that will not be extinguished by a foreclosure of the mortgage. The permanent lender, because it may be the eventual landlord under these leases, will want to review them with a great deal of care. The developer will have a difficult time leasing space if prospective tenants cannot be assured that, as long as they pay their rentals, their economic continuity and the substantial investment made for tenant improvements are both secure. The trend toward all tenant leases occupying a "superior" status is running strong in all forms of income-property lending with the exception of apartments.

Oftentimes, this concept is referred to as "subordination with nondisturbance provisions" or some variation of this phrase. Some investors, particularly those domiciled in heavily regulated states, have taken the position that a superior lease jeopardizes a first and valid lien on the real estate. They, therefore, require all leases to be subordinate to the lien of the mortgage; however, they are willing to agree not to disturb the occupancy of the tenants, so long as the tenants comply with the terms of the leases. Practically speaking, it still means the leases survive a foreclosure.

Chances are that some leases will be in existence at the time of the master closing. If so, the permanent lender should make a written designation as to which are to survive a foreclosure, and this designation should be appended to the three-party agreement.

17 Subordination Agreements   These documents are used to set the priority of leases in relation to the mortgage. If a lease is executed prior to the master closing, it may be superior to the lien of the mortgage simply by chronological sequence. A lease executed subsequent to the closing will be subordinate, regardless of the intent of the parties. Since most leases will fall in the second category, it is a good idea to have the permanent lender pre-approve a form of agreement by which it subordinates its lien to a particular lease. If the lender prefers the *nondisturbance* agreement approach, its form should also be pre-approved. Either should be attached to the three-party agreement as an exhibit.

18 Assignment of Leases   This instrument is similar in intent to the assignment of rents, except that it goes one step further. Normally, it directs a specific tenant to pay rent to the lender in the event of default by the borrower/landlord. The names of specific tenants appear in the document; in fact, some lenders feel more comfortable in requiring an individual form for each tenant. Copies of the agreements are frequently sent to the tenants in the hope of putting such tenants upon actual notice of the assignments. They are recorded as well. Although the actual tenants may not be known until the final permanent closing, the form of the assignment of leases should be pre-approved by the permanent lender and attached to the three-party agreement as an exhibit.

19 Standard Lease Form   Since the sample transaction is an apartment complex, the only lease approval required is that of the standard form. If dealing with an office building or a shopping center, the standard lease form has considerable significance as well, although in those cases the permanent lender will require its approval of all or most of the individual leases. This issue will be dealt with in the leasing section of the final closing details category. If a standard lease form is to be utilized, it should be pre-approved by the permanent lender and attached to the three-party agreement as an exhibit.

20 Ratification Agreements   These documents, sometimes called *Estoppel Certificates*, are signed by the borrower/landlord and the tenants at the time of the permanent closing. They confirm that the lease is in full force and effect, that the tenant has accepted the premises, and there are no side deals, such as security deposits, prepayments of rent, or arrangements not set forth in the actual leases. The ratification agreement form should be pre-approved by the permanent lender and attached to the three-party agreement as an exhibit.

21 Fee Paid   Be sure that the commitment fee has been received before any substantial work toward the master closing has begun. Many times the fee deposited with the permanent lender will be refundable to the borrower if and when the transaction eventually closes. There is a great deal of controversy between developers and lenders as to whether or not refundable fees are "walking prices" collectible by lenders if a borrower chooses not to close the transaction. This issue assumes added significance in a market with falling interest rates. As one might expect, most borrowers agree with the theory, while the investors do not. Once the three-party agreement has been signed, assuming it has been drawn tightly, chances are great that the permanent loan will close even if the borrower would prefer to get out of it.

22   Three-Party Agreement   A well-constructed agreement is going to be fairly lengthy, with a large collection of exhibits. The comprehensiveness of this instrument will be dictated by the construction lender.

Two major issues that seem to recur in negotiating three-party agreements relate to the assignability of the permanent commitment and what happens in the event of a default. Going back to our example, suppose the borrowing business unit is about to file for bankruptcy mid-stream in construction. The construction lender is faced with a series of difficult choices. If it attempts to gain control of the property, with an objective of completing it on time and in accordance with the approved plans and specifications, the construction lender will definitely want assurances that the permanent loan proceeds will be there to reduce its exposure. To accomplish this, the construction lender will attempt to secure an assignment of the borrower's interest in the permanent loan commitment. Many permanent lenders resist this, arguing that their commitments are to specific individuals or groups uniquely qualified to successfully develop their projects. Moreover, with all due respect to the capabilities of construction lenders as developers, the collapse or disappearance of the original borrowers is sufficient grounds to cancel the permanent commitment. Many permanent loan commitments do contain this language.

The second issue concerns the rights of the two lenders in the event of a default in the construction loan. Suppose the project is not economically feasible when completed and the developers have run out of money. Through the late stages of the construction loan no money has been available to pay interest. The construction lender decides to waive interest in the hopes of keeping the project and the borrowers solvent until the funding of the permanent loan. While some interest may be lost, the permanent loan proceeds look more attractive than the risky future of a speculative real estate project. Does the permanent lender have to close its loan in these circumstances?

Neither of these questions has a predictable answer. Most assuredly they will come up and you should be prepared to deal with them. Construction and permanent lenders will probably have consistent postures on these points; yet, it is likely that they have done deals in the past. How did they resolve them before? Possibly, the difference in attitudes may be so irreconcilable that you should be prepared to recommend an alternate source of construction financing. Once again, the crucial point is knowing your investor.

23   Costs   We have already touched on the advisability of identifying estimated legal fees. The borrower should be confronted with all other estimated costs as well. It is better to deal with this unpleasant subject at the outset rather than being confronted with an unhappy client at the final closing. An unhappy ending is likely to cost you additional business.

Category 2: Deal With Periodically

Once the master closing has occurred and the construction loan has begun to be paid out, your chief tasks are to maintain the equilibrium established at the master closing and to begin working on the items that will be needed at the permanent closing. There are four or five good sources of information during the construction period with which one must keep current. The construction lender will probably retain a technical expert to review the progress of construction at least once a month. This will entail an on-site inspection by the expert followed by a written report to the construction lender. Try to accompany the inspector on an inspection tour or, at the very least, see if copies of reports can be made available to you on a regular basis.

Each time the construction lender makes a disbursement, a formal update of the title status will be made by the title insurer. You should arrange to receive copies of these reports. Meet with the construction lender's loan office on a regular basis and keep up to date on its view of the borrower and the project. Set up a regular meeting time with the borrower and keep abreast of the borrower's progress and concerns.

Going back to our original checklist, the following items should be addressed during this second phase of the closing process:

1 Plans and Specifications   Change orders are going to occur. It is not realistic to assume that they will be submitted to either lender for approval prior to their implementation. Your chief task should be the establishment of a system that identifies change orders when they occur and brings them to the immediate attention of the permanent lender for approval. Understand what the change orders are accomplishing and send them to the permanent lender with a businessman's recommendation for their approval. Change orders have a way of getting pigeonholed at investors' offices, yet their importance should be obvious. Despite the best of preparation at the master closing, inappropriate change orders can void the permanent commitment. Keep badgering the investor for approval.

2 Leases   During your regular meetings with the borrower, make sure that a review of the current status of leasing is on the agenda. Some successful mortgage bankers feel that leases are best submitted for approval to the permanent lender in single packages; others believe that sending them along as the deals are made is more efficient. How you do it is probably a function of your investor's style of operation. Either way, there is an excellent chance that leases submitted for approval may be filed under the change orders in the investor's office.

Keep pressing for approvals of these leases. Occasionally, an investor will agree that approval is automatic if it fails to respond with comments within a reasonable time frame. This is a very practical means of keeping the process moving.

When the leases are submitted for approval, the questions of assignment should be dealt with at the same time. As soon as a lease has been executed, the appropriate party should go to the forms attached to the three-party agreement and fill in the blanks as they pertain to the tenant in question.

If some of the tenants are able to take occupancy in advance of the final closing, you should do what you can to get the execution process for the lease ratification agreements under way with respect to them. Borrowers do not like the prospect of asking tenants to sign these agreements. They, quite accurately, point out that asking a tenant to sign a statement that everything is satisfactory is asking for trouble. Even with the best of preparations, it is likely that all of the necessary ratification agreements will not be in hand at the final closing. Nevertheless, periodic attention to this problem can lengthen your odds of getting them all.

3   Critical Dates: Earliest Close, Must Close, and Extensions   Timing the final loan closing has a number of dimensions. The three-party agreement will normally provide that the permanent loan is to close within 30 to 60 days of the borrower's compliance with the terms of the permanent investor's commitment, subject to an overall time limitation.

Our sample requires a permanent closing prior to March 31, 1979, or the commitment may expire. As you check the progress of the project with your sources, constantly test the expiration date. As soon as it appears that it is in danger, be prepared to obtain an extension of the expiration date. Many permanent lenders will include language in their commitment agreement to extend this crucial date for reasons of *force majeure*, yet not all of them will. Our sample commitment is written at least 24 months in advance, and much can happen to its attractiveness to the lender during that time. For example, 9¾ percent may be 100 basis points below the market rate for similar loans. Under those circumstances, an extension might only be given to a very steep cost. Permanent lenders, however, do not like to be bothered with extension requests month after month. Your request should be judicious; yet you should keep the investor closely informed of the progress of the project.

The relative cash flow positions of both lenders may also have an extreme impact on the critical dates at both ends. Notice that our sample states that the permanent loan cannot close before January 15, 1979. If the project is substantially completed prior to that date, it may be that the permanent lender wishes to meet a closing goal for the previous calendar year. The construction lender may be short of funds, and the borrower may be paying a construction loan interest rate in excess of the permanent constant. If you are attuned to each party's needs, a November or December permanent closing would definitely work to the advantage of each. It is equally possible to postulate circumstances that would lead you to conclude that, even given early completion, the permanent closing should be deferred to the expiration date.

4   Three-Party Agreement   An important ground rule inherent with the master closing approach is the need for both lenders to be consulted in the event of any changes or modifications in the permanent loan terms. If, for example, an extension of the permanent loan's expiration is obtained, the extension should be consented to by the interim lender as well.

Maintaining a cordial relationship between the two lenders should be an important objective during all phases of the closing process. Similarly, a borrower who has been subjected to the fallout resulting from the construction and permanent lenders doing battle with each other is likely to be so scarred from the experience that the borrower will not seek future business with either the investor or the mortgage banker.

Category 3: Deal With at Permanent Closing

If the process has been organized and maintained along the lines previously suggested, the final closing should be essentially a ceremonial event. There should be few, if any, surprises. Problems arising during construction have been identified, analyzed, and dealt with in a responsible and timely fashion. Final documentation should involve the preparation of a few assignment forms and the filling in of blanks on others that have been pre-approved by the permanent lender and attached as exhibits to the three-party agreement.

A month or so prior to the estimated closing date, an updated and complete closing checklist should be agreed upon with the permanent lender's closing representatives and attorneys. Although the list you develop should not differ materially from the checklist derived from your original commitment analysis, it is advisable to take this step as a precautionary measure. When the list has been prepared, you should reassert your role as the quarterback of the transaction, once again parcelling out responsibilities, establishing deadlines, and maintaining them through aggressive, but diplomatic, coordination.

Returning to the sample commitment once again, let us develop an updated completed checklist.

1   Note   Unless there has been a major modification of the deal, the note executed at the original master closing will be assigned by the construction lender to the permanent lender.

2   Mortgage   Identical to the note, in that no changes should be necessary. It will be assigned to the permanent lender by the construction lender.

3   Security Agreement   Same treatment as note and mortgage.

4   Financing Statements   New financing statements are generally executed at the permanent closing. Since these are preprinted forms in common usage in the jurisdiction in which the property is located, their preparation is a simple fill-in-the-blanks procedure.

5   Inventory   The only problem encountered here is having enough lead time to complete this laborious process. Since the form of inventory has been agreed upon and attached to the three-party agreement, the mechanical tasks of counting and describing the personal property are all that remain.

6   Legal Description   The description has been previously approved. Make sure, however, that the perimeter dimensions which appear on the final "as-built" survey conform with the legal descriptions in the various documents.

7   Title Policy   In spite of the best advance preparation, new title problems have a frustrating way of appearing at the very last minute. The title company will issue a binder to the permanent lender some weeks in advance of the final closing, normally plenty of time to deal with emerging title problems; however, a final check of title is made immediately before the recordation of final loan documents and the transfer of closing proceeds. It is this final title check that creates most of the frustrations. A new exception creates the precise situation you have so painstakingly worked to avoid.

An excellent local title company is your best friend in this situation. If you cannot seem to bring the matter to a satisfactory resolution, it might be advisable to turn to the permanent lender for help. If it has substantial lending portfolios, it is likely that it directly or indirectly accounts for the placement of millions of dollars of title insurance annually. National divisions of title companies are likely to respond to an emergency request from such an important source of premium income.

8   Legal Opinions   If you have done your homework in this area, the preparation of these opinions should be perfunctory.

9   Government Approvals   We have previously discussed the risks involved in this area. Immediately prior to the closing (ideally when the final checklist is being prepared), the permanent lender should agree to the precise identity of which government or environmental consents it is going to require. Possibly, this will be limited to a legal opinion. If permits or certifications from governmental agencies are required, get the acquisition process under way as soon as possible. Even if the appropriate agency is efficiently organized, it is likely, particularly if it relates to the environment, to be overworked, understaffed, and choked with a large backlog of unprocessed work.

10   Survey   The permanent lender will require a final as-built survey. This amounts to a visual representation of the completed improvements sketched in and certified as correct by a registered surveyor. Make sure that the surveyor has been instructed to delineate the location of all easements or encumbrances that show up as title binder exceptions. The permanent lender will want hard evidence that such items will not adversely affect the property. The chief difficulty is likely to be getting the survey completed on time.

11   Tax Bills   In the example, all the permanent lender is requiring is evidence that current taxes are paid. The stamped tax bills should be readily available. Occasionally, the borrower may be protesting an assessment, and may not want to pay the bills so as not to jeopardize the legal position with the assessor. In such a case, the lender will probably require a deposit equal to 125 percent or more of the contested assessment amount. If taxes are being protested, the circumstances should be exposed to the permanent lender as early in the process as possible to avoid last-minute controversy.

12   Insurance Policies   In order to bring casualty insurance matters to a satisfactory conclusion, a number of related items must be dealt with. To begin with, the identity of the carrier must be approved by the permanent lender. Unless the loan is a huge transaction, a casualty company enjoying a good rating by *Best's Insurance Reports* should be adequate. The permanent lender may, however, have a formula of its own for determining acceptability; thus, preliminary checking is in order.

Next, attempt to determine the amounts and coverages the permanent lender will require. The sample includes fire insurance with extended coverage and rent insurance. It also contains an elastic clause affording the permanent lender the opportunity to name other unspecified forms. The permanent lender should be willing to disclose its requirements upon request. As to amounts, different lenders approach this question in various ways. Some will be content to accept a policy in the amount of the original mortgage balance. Others will want to determine the insurable value of the improvements at the time of closing and require coverage amounts far in excess of the loan amount.

Creative and knowledgeable insurance experts have many suggested ways to save on insurance premiums through the use of deductibles, co-insurance factors and blanket insurance programs. The policy forms and techniques should be discussed with the permanent lender in advance of the closing. Finally, the permanent lender will require that its name be included on the insurance policy directly or by endorsement. This is another of those mechanical details which is noncontroversial in nature, but potentially troublesome if no attention is given to it ahead of time.

13 Completion If thoroughly drawn, the three-party agreement should define an objective standard of completion. Normally, this will consist of an engineer's certification and copies of certificates of occupancy or the appropriate form of local governmental consent. Zoning conformance and compliance with laws will generally be covered by one of the legal opinions. At one time, the title insurer might have been induced to issue title policy endorsements to cover these matters. Today, if such endorsements are available at all, they are prohibitively expensive. If the permanent lender requires a personal completion inspection, make sure that the timing arrangements are appropriate. At all times, remember that compliance with these conditions requires the cooperation of many inputs having no interest or involvement in the loan. Lead time and expert coordination will be crucial.

14 Guarantee In the example, the guarantee will be assigned, along with the note from the construction lender to the permanent lender. No further documentation should be necessary.

15 Assignment of Rents Generally, this document will also be assigned from one lender to another. No further documentation should be necessary.

16 Leases If the process has been well organized, the lender's designations of which leases are to be superior have been flowing to you and the borrower all along. The agreements fixing lease priority have been pre-approved as to form, and they should be circulating for signatures well in advance of the final closing. Obtaining tenant signatures takes time and patience even if the tenants are not in dispute with the borrower.

Assignments of specific leases should cause no problems, since the form has been pre-approved. We have covered lease ratifications and their problems in the previous sections.

In spite of the best preparation, it is quite likely that some ratification agreements will not have been executed by one or more of the tenants. In this event, you may be able to convince the permanent lender to accept a certification from the borrower that the leases are in full force and effect. The lender's willingness to accept this will probably be a function of the size of the lease and its relative importance to the transaction as a whole.

17 Three-Party Agreement (Assignment) One document, or a series of documents, will have to be drawn, accomplishing the transfer of the loan from the construction to the permanent lender. The borrower need not be involved in this item at all. It should not create any problems unless the lenders are disputing their obligations.

FINAL DETAILS

When all of these documents are in readiness, a closing meeting will be set, usually at an attorney's office or at the title company. Representatives of each party attend, and each item on the checklist is reviewed. The relevant documents are then executed and bundled for recording. The length and intensity of this meeting is inversely proportional to your advance preparations. The closing quarterback should always attend this meeting and must keep the proceedings moving in a constructive fashion. The quarterback's role may range from pacifying a nervous borrower to arbitrating last-minute crises.

If and when the checklist items are appropriately dealt with, the money is ready to change hands. There are a few simple guidelines to follow in setting up an efficient transfer of funds. Moving large sums of money through the banking system is not an easy thing to accomplish. Bank transfer departments are busy, and instructions get misplaced and lost. Some prominent financial institutions have been suspected for years of intentionally delaying transactions so as to enjoy the benefits of monetary float. Experience will teach you their names.

If the traditional bank wire system is going to be used, identifying a high-level contact at the originating bank and a specific individual at the recipient bank who is to be notified upon the receipt of the funds will prove essential. If delays are encountered, it is reassuring to know where individual inquiries may be directed. It can be extremely frustrating to contact the central switchboard of a large financial institution without an individual's name.

If the closing proceeds do not arrive on schedule, there are three distinct sources of potential delay. First, check with the permanent lender's office. The closing decision makers generally do not execute the authorization to the originating bank to start the transfer. Your transaction may be on the bottom of a pile of transfer orders in one of the permanent lender's accounting departments. If that source checks out, the next step is to direct an inquiry to your contact at the originating bank. It may be more effective if the permanent lender does this for you. When confronted, the originating bank should be able to provide you with the details of the transfer, including the exact time it was put on the wire.

The last source should be the recipient bank. Since it will probably be in your city, you will be in the best position to apply direct pressure to your contact there.

In spite of all of these precautions, never try to move money on a Friday, the day preceding a bank holiday, or on the last business day of a month. If you are forced to close on one of these adverse occasions, a clear understanding between the parties should be worked out in advance as to what happens if the money does not arrive and who pays the extra interest.

One variation of the bank wire that can be helpful is the account transfer technique. Very often, larger investors have considerable sums on deposit with one or more of the major local banks. If they have such an account in the recipient bank, they can authorize a transfer from their account to the account in the same bank of the title company, the closing attorney, or the mortgage banker.

Different investors have their own policies for moving money. Some will be flexible, while others will be very rigid. Once again, knowing the investor has another extremely important application.

When the money has finally been received, it is normally held in an escrow account. The title company or closing attorney makes a final check of the status of title, and, if nothing shows up, the documents can be delivered and recorded, and the payment of the loan is authorized.

The last event in the process is delivering a complete set of documents to the permanent lender. Using the final checklist as a guide and index, submit them in a single package as soon as you can. If you are in a jurisdiction where substantial delays are involved in getting documents returned from the recorder's office, send the lender an initial package, including executed copies of the recorded documents. The final recorded versions can be forwarded later. This final step, frequently overlooked, puts a recognized stamp of professionalism upon your involvement in the transaction. Only then is the closing process complete.

Chapter 13

Administering the Income-Property Loan

Ronald F. Poe

INTRODUCTION

The primary purpose of mortgage loan administration, whether in regard to income-property loans or residential loans, is to insure compliance with the provision of the investor's security documents. It is only through insuring this compliance that the loan administrator can properly fulfill a fiduciary responsibility to the investor and guarantee that all necessary steps have been taken to preserve the investor's security.

The administration of income-property loans, however, differs somewhat from the administration of single-family residential properties in that the very size and complexity of income-property loans make it essential that the approach to income-property loans be a very individual and personal one. The introduction of electronic data processing equipment has produced economies of scale in the loan administration segment of the real estate financing industry. It is only through the use of this equipment, and through the ability to process large numbers of loans, that loan administration is able to do the excellent job it has done in the past and continues to do today in regard to the servicing of single-family home loans.

Unfortunately, the only assured way to administer income-property loans successfully is to view each loan individually, have it assigned to a specific loan administrator, and have that loan administrator thoroughly understand each and every loan document, all of the aspects of the mortgaged property, and the responsibility to the investor.

The professional loan administrator, in reviewing the mortgage loan commitment or the mortgage loan documents prior to closing, must keep in mind at all times the five general areas in which proper functioning will be expected to and in which compliance will be required. These five general areas are:

1 Payments, collections, and foreclosures.
2 Insurance.
3 Property taxes.
4 Operating statements and the collection of contingent interest.
5 Property inspections.

PAYMENTS, COLLECTIONS, AND FORECLOSURES

It has long been said that "A loan well made is a loan half paid." While this is certainly true, the other half, the collection of monthly principal and interest payments from closing to maturity, is one of the loan administration department's most important functions.

Basically, income-property loans are divided into two categories: The first is those loans on which borrowers make prompt payments. The other category is, unfortunately, those loans where payments are not made promptly. While loans in the second category are in the minority in terms of both percentages and numbers, they constitute the biggest single problem faced by the experienced income-property loan administrator.

As in all other aspects of loan administration, the time to begin to eliminate problems is at the commitment stage. Nothing prompts a forgetful borrower like a substantial late charge. In jurisdictions where substantial late charges are permitted, it is common to have a penalty of 4 percent of the principal and interest payment represent the late charge or penalty for payments received after the tenth or fifteenth of the month in which due. Unrealistically small late-charge penalties only tend to make penalty clauses of this type an object of ridicule and create no incentive whatsoever for the borrower to pay promptly. Commitments should, whenever possible, contain provisions for substantial late-charge penalty clauses.

As more and more income properties are built and developed, it is not reasonable to assume that in all cases borrowers will be sophisticated. While the mortgage banking industry has taken great pains to insure that residential borrowers are properly informed and instructed as to the manner in which they are expected to maintain their loans, such is not always the case with income-property borrowers. As with residential borrowers, the income-property borrower should be given a letter of instruction at closing that clearly details the payment obligations, the date on which payment is expected, and the person in the loan administration department who should be contacted in case problems develop. Obviously, besides payment information, the letter of instruction should set forth the obligations the borrower has taken on in regard to the payment of taxes, insurance, contingent interest (if applicable), the forwarding of annual operating statements, and a host of other items set forth in the mortgage documents that may not have been brought to the borrower's attention either by his or her attorney or by the closing attorney. Bringing these obligations out in a clear, concise manner at the closing will eliminate many future problems.

Perhaps the mortgage provision most misunderstood by borrowers is the provision setting forth what the borrower considers to be a "fifteen-day grace period." This provision, when quickly scanned by the borrower, usually leads to the belief that payment need not be made until the fifteenth of the month and that it truly is a "grace period." It should be pointed out to the borrower that this fifteen-day period merely prohibits the mortgagee, during the first fifteen days of the month, from accelerating or calling the loan for nonpayment should the payment not be received on the first day of the month.

It is important that the mortgage loan administrator bear in mind at all times the essence of the loan being serviced; namely, that it is a loan on an income-producing property. As far as the matter of the monthly payment is concerned, this means that the funds to make the monthly principal and interest payment come from income generated by the property. It is not expected that funds to pay the first mortgage debt service will come from the borrower's own financial resources, but will come exclusively from the property. This means that if, in any month, the borrower does not generate sufficient income from the property, it will be virtually impossible to make the monthly payment. In residential loan servicing, a delinquent borrower can always work an extra job, take out a small installment loan, or raise funds in a variety of other ways to bring a mortgage loan current. These options are not available to the income-property borrower because of the very large amounts normally involved.

It can be seen from income-loan delinquency statistics that once a loan becomes delinquent for a period of 25 days, that loan will normally continue to be at least 25 days delinquent until the property is either sold, refinanced, or foreclosed. The reason for this is that when a loan is 25 days delinquent, the borrower will have diverted the income from the property to areas other than the payment of debt service. The borrower does this, fully expecting to deliver a check to the mortgage servicing agent for the monthly payment toward the end of the month, fully hoping to cover the check from the next month's rent collections. This is a reasonably common practice among borrowers who choose to divert funds from mortgaged income properties, and is the first sign of collection difficulty given to the mortgage loan administrator.

This situation points up the fact that payment due dates, in relation to income-property loans, should be carefully monitored. It is not sufficient for a computer print-out listing both income-property and residential delinquents to be turned over to a collector on the fifteenth of each month. Data processing equipment should be programmed in such a way that a daily listing of delinquent income-property loans is available not only to loan collectors, but also to senior loan administration management personnel. By making this information available on a daily basis, senior personnel are able to institute, on a timely and on-going basis, aggressive collection procedures to insure that funds are not diverted to other areas. It goes without saying that on the tenth of the month, each delinquent income-property borrower should be contacted either in person or by telephone and a reason determined for the delinquency. These delinquents should then be followed up on a day-to-day basis so that there will be no possibility whatsoever that the borrower will have the opportunity to divert one full month's income.

Most collection problems and, unfortunately, eventual foreclosures develop because the loan administrator did not follow the delinquency on a timely basis. A check received on the fifteenth or sixteenth of the month in which due, if subsequently returned by the bank for reason of insufficient funds, can by the time it is replaced easily allow the borrower sufficient time to divert one month's payment. Returned checks should be personally delivered to the borrower by a loan administration officer, and the loan administration officer should accompany the borrower to the bank, where a replacement certified check should be obtained. This assures the loan administration officer that the monthly payment is being paid with good, current monthly income funds, and that the delinquent situation will not continue.

On the subject of checks, an excellent way of determining future problems is to maintain records of banks on which income-property payment checks are drawn. The commercial banking system has been extremely aggressive in obtaining and maintaining good account relationships. When a borrower changes banks more than twice in a 12-month period it can, in many cases, be assumed that the borrower has been asked to terminate the account with the bank based on the fact that it was being handled improperly, or the borrower has been forced to move deposit relationships around in a futile search for additional bank credit. Also, when an income-property loan gets into trouble, an investigation will often reveal that within the past 24 months, checks were received from accounts drawn on a number of banks. While the maintenance of records of this type is clearly time-consuming, it provides an excellent early-warning mechanism, and enables loan administration personnel to place loans on a *watch-list* in advance of any problem actually developing.

The best defense against a delinquent situation is to continually anticipate it. While the method of recording the bank on which checks were drawn is an excellent early-warning device, the mortgage administration department should be organized in such a way that those responsible for the collection of payments are made aware of unfavorable inspection reports, deficits which may appear in annual operating statements, and a number of other warning signals. By having everyone aware of the fact that a number of problem indicators are beginning to manifest themselves, surprises in terms of delinquencies will be avoided and the loan administration department will be ready when the problem actually develops.

When all the signs begin to point toward a problem—returned checks, checks received after the fifteenth of the month, unfavorable inspection reports, and annual operating statements indicating a net operating deficit—the time has arrived for a conference of senior loan administration personnel to plan the steps to be taken when the problem becomes a reality.

The first thing senior management should consider when anticipating the course of action to be taken to cure a default in connection with a problem loan is whether or not it is an accidental default or a carefully planned default. Many income-property loans contain clauses prohibiting their prepayment for a minimum of 10 to 12 years from the date of closing. As a result, if economic conditions change, it may be in the borrower's best interest to attempt to find a way to negate this prepayment prohibition and refinance elsewhere to take advantage of more favorable conditions or more favorable interest rates. Some borrowers, in the past, have used the ruse of intentionally creating a default situation in an attempt to entice the lender into accelerating the loan, thereby effectively negating the closed option period of the loan and, of course, also waiving any right to a prepayment penalty if such is called for under the terms of the mortgage loan documents.

Next, the problem-loan review committee needs to determine whether or not the default is one caused by the borrower's actions or by actions beyond the control of the borrower. Let's first consider actions beyond the control of the borrower. The committee carefully reviews annual operating statements and current rent rolls, which of course should be in the file, and also carefully reviews recent inspection reports for the subject property. In addition, the original appraisal is reviewed and, if required, a study is done of comparable properties in the immediate vicinity of the subject. If the review indicates that the borrower is unable to make the monthly payment based on the fact that the property is not generating sufficient income to enable it to do so, and if the review further shows that other properties in the area are undergoing the same problem, then it is in the best interests of the lender and the borrower for the problem-loan committee to attempt to work out a forbearance situation with the existing borrower. In considering any type of action to take in a default situation, the problem-loan committee needs to ask itself only one question: "If we were able to take title to the subject property, could we do a better job of managing the property than the existing owner?"

If the answer to this question is "no," then it only makes sense to work with the existing borrower. The answer to the question should be reasonably easy to ascertain. If annual operating statements show that expenses are in line with or even less than other similar properties, if inspection reports show that the property is well maintained, and if vacancies are also in line with other similar properties, then it is reasonable to assume that the problem is caused by the overall market and economy, and the lender's agent managing the property probably couldn't do as good a job as the incumbent borrower.

If it is determined that the existing borrower is doing the best possible job, then various alternatives should be considered in regard to curing the default. Can the borrower be given some assistance in reducing the property tax assessment? Would a waiver or temporary postponement of principal for a year to 18 months give the borrower some relief? Does the borrower feel that the market for its property will turn around in the next 12 to 24 months, thereby enabling a reduction in vacancies? Has the bankruptcy of a major tenant severely hurt the borrower and does the borrower have a reasonable chance of obtaining a replacement in the coming year? These are all questions which must be asked and options which must be considered by the problem-loan committee. Once the committee is absolutely satisfied that the borrower is doing the best possible job, any option other than foreclosure which is satisfactory to both the borrower and the lender should be worked out, as foreclosure for the sake of foreclosure benefits neither of the parties.

On the other hand, if the answer to the question is a resounding "no, the borrower is not doing the best possible job," then the committee's course of action is clear. Again, the answer to this question is easy to ascertain. Has the borrower been uncooperative in providing information to the loan administrator? Does the property show signs of deferred maintenance? Have there been attempts, in the past, or even now to "milk" the property? Is the property overrented, with large families crowded into two-bedroom apartments and paying more than the market rent for two-bedroom apartments? Have taxes been allowed to go delinquent in the past? Does the borrower have a number of other problem properties which are receiving priority attention to the complete neglect of the subject?

If all indicators lead to the fact that the borrower is a negative factor in the operation of the property, rather than a positive one, then the obvious alternative is to pursue foreclosure.

Once it has been decided to pursue a foreclosure, the entire situation, including all documentation, should be reviewed by an attorney. The attorney's review should determine that all necessary papers are on hand and properly executed, and that all documentation necessary to proceed with the foreclosure is in proper form. Unfortunately, after the antagonism of the commencement of a foreclosure is generated, the lender often discovers that a critical document is either missing or was not obtained at the initial closing, and the fact that this document is missing may cause the lender to completely rethink its position in regard to going forward with a foreclosure. A comprehensive review by an attorney prior to the foreclosure is an excellent way of insuring that there will be no unpleasant judicial surprises during the course of the foreclosure.

Next, an architectural review should take place. Does the loan administrator have on hand a complete set of plans for the property, the electrical inspection certificate, the Certificate of Occupancy, and any other certificates or approvals from local governments which will be necessary for the operation of the property? Finally, does the loan administrator have on hand a list of suppliers, tradesmen, and others with whom to deal should the administrator take title to the property?

Once it has been determined that the loan administrator has a complete file with respect to legal matters and the operation of the property, then the foreclosure should be pursued with all due speed. A delay of a month or two, coupled with legal delays which a knowledgeable borrower can interpose, may permit the borrower to divert as much as four to five months' gross rent from the subject property, and this diversion may, in many cases, permit the borrower to recoup the entire equity in the property. It should be remembered that once the borrower knows a foreclosure is contemplated, an attempt will be made to maximize the diversion of funds from the property, which means paying no trade creditors or suppliers. While a foreclosure will wipe out the liens of the trade creditors and suppliers, many times, when the mortgagee takes over the operation of the property, it will be found that, in order to maintain good will in the community, these creditors will have to be paid—even those to whom there is no legal obligation.

While mortgagees may have foreclosed properties and then eventually sold them for substantial profits in days long gone by, that situation is no longer true. It only makes sense to assume that if a borrower is going to walk away from a property and permit it to be foreclosed, the borrower, the person closest to the property, has determined that the property has no value over and above the mortgage debt. By the time the mortgagee adds in the expenses of foreclosure, payments, etc., it can further be reasoned that there is little hope of substantial economic gain over and above the recoupment of the outstanding principal balance of the mortgage. It is, therefore, in the best interests of the mortgagee to attempt to sell a piece of foreclosed property as soon as possible. Bearing in mind that the first loss is often the smallest loss, the mortgagee should attempt to take a realistic view toward the sales price it hopes to realize from the foreclosed property. At this juncture in the mortgagee's decision-making process, the loan administrator plays a vitally important role. In order for the mortgagee to make an intelligent and informed decision as to the sales price which should be demanded for the property, it is necessary to receive from the loan administrator an accurate valuation of the property, which should take into consideration the cost of restoring the property and also any cash deficits which may be incurred during the operation of the property for the next 12 to 24 months, or until such time as it can be restored to complete economic strength.

All in all, foreclosure is the least desirable of all possible alternatives to solving a default situation. It can be assumed that in almost all cases, the lender, the borrower, and the mortgage servicing agent will lose money during the course of the foreclosure. This loss can be minimized, and the interests of the lender best protected, by being sure that all options are considered, that a complete file is maintained prior to the foreclosure, that a maximum amount of information is gathered in order to permit the lender to make the best possible decision in regard to the sale price for the property, and that the property be disposed of as swiftly as possible.

The main function of mortgage loan administration is to protect the investor's investment. The most important aspect of this protection is the prompt, monthly collection of principal and interest, which permits the investor to realize a return on investment and to reduce the outstanding principal balance, thereby reducing both investment and risk in the subject property.

INSURANCE

One of the most basic of the responsibilities of the loan administrator in either single-family residential or in income-property loan administration is the maintenance, at all times, of adequate hazard insurance coverage. In dealing with income-property lending, this responsibility for proper insurance coverage is expanded from hazard insurance into such areas as rental insurance, business interruption insurance, and, in some cases, liability insurance coverage. In recent years, losses sustained by property and casualty insurance companies have caused dramatic premium increases. They have also caused carriers to cease to insure certain types of properties on a nationwide basis, so that mass cancellations or nonrenewals of insurance coverage have become frequent. With this in mind, and further considering the tremendous loss that can be sustained by a mortgagee if proper insurance coverage is not maintained, it is important that the mortgage loan administrator responsible for income-property loans be completely familiar with all aspects of hazard insurance coverage.

Again, early involvement by the mortgage loan administrator in the underwriting and appraisal process in regard to insurance coverage is the first step to preventing future problems. All too often, commitments are issued with vague or general wording specifying that insurance coverage will be maintained "in types and in amounts as well as in insurance carriers acceptable to the investor."

At the time the loan is being underwritten and the commitment issued, it should be clearly explained to the prospective borrower exactly what insurance coverage will be required, the exact amounts required, and, finally, what the investor's guidelines are for determining acceptable insurance carriers. Rising insurance premiums have caused many borrowers to turn to cut-rate or discount insurance brokers, who often produce insurance policies in thinly capitalized and marginally reserved insurance carriers. By advising the borrower at the time the commitment is issued of the investor's insurance requirements, future conflict between the mortgage loan administrator and the borrower and the insurance agent can be avoided. During the decade of the sixties and the early seventies, before insurance premiums began to increase so rapidly, the practice with income-property loans of escrowing for insurance premiums gradually fell into disuse. The reason for ending this practice was that insurance premiums, in relation to the total income of the property, were not significant. However, as insurance premiums have continued to increase, they have become a material expense and should be escrowed monthly, along with taxes. All too often, the reason for a delinquent payment of principal and interest is the fact that the borrower has not properly provided funds to pay the insurance premium, and when it fell due, rather than risk a cancellation, monthly rental income was used to pay the insurance premium (instead of flowing to pay principal and interest), thereby creating a payment default under the terms of the mortgage loan.

The experienced mortgage loan administrator should meet with the borrower and/or the insurance agent at least two weeks prior to the loan closing to review all insurance coverage and verify that the coverage to be presented at the closing has been issued in accordance with the terms of the mortgage loan documents. All too often, much time is wasted at the closing discussing and negotiating insurance coverage, and frequently it is necessary to conduct insurance negotiations over the telephone with the borrower's agent or broker. This puts the mortgage loan administrator in the position of anxiously checking the mail each morning in the hope of finding a binder or endorsement confirming in writing what had been discussed on the phone with the insurance agent. All of this can be avoided by having proper insurance coverage presented for audit and review in sufficient time prior to the closing to permit the loan administrator to meet with the insurance agent and obtain any endorsements which may be needed to cause the coverage to conform to the investor's requirements.

As investors often have different ways of determining the amounts required for rental or business interruption insurance, it behooves the mortgage loan administrator to study the commitment well in advance and thoroughly understand its requirements. The face amount of rental insurance required is commonly determined by either an amount equal to one year's gross rent from the property or an amount equal to one year's debt service, operating expenses, and taxes. In addition, as investors have moved into equity positions and/or sale-leasebacks, it becomes incumbent on the mortgage loan administrator to insure that the equity-ownership position of the investor is properly protected. This means that the investor would need to have substantial amounts of liability insurance protecting its equity-ownership interest. It goes without saying that the protection of an investor with liability insurance is vitally important. Few entities make more tempting targets for liability lawsuits than does a multibillion dollar asset institutional investor.

As more and more income-property insurance policies are canceled or not renewed based on "unacceptable underwriting risks," it becomes necessary that the mortgage loan administrator continually review insurance coverage on all properties for which the administrator is responsible. Borrowers or their insurance agents should be contacted at least 60 days prior to the expiration date of the existing policy to determine that proper provisions are being made for replacement. Vague binders issued by insurance agents for multimillion dollar risks are situations which should be avoided. They can, in fact, be avoided by commencing to insure that a proper renewal policy will be delivered to the mortgage loan administrator prior to the time of expiration of the existing policy.

The cancellation of a policy for "underwriting risk unacceptability" during the term of the insurance policy creates a very substantial problem for the mortgage loan administrator. The standard 10-day mortgagee cancellation notice gives the mortgage loan administrator very little time to coordinate the borrower and its agent in an effort to obtain effective replacement coverage. The experienced mortgage loan administrator attempts to maintain close working relationships with a number of large insurance agents in order that, should an emergency situation develop, the administrator will be in a position of being able to obtain coverage which, at the very least, would protect the interest of the mortgagee.

Insurance policies, for a variety of reasons, generate a veritable blizzard of paper work. It seems that the average mortgage loan administrator's desk is always covered with insurance policy endorsements. All endorsements, however, which relate to income-producing properties should be carefully reviewed by knowledgeable personnel. It is not uncommon for borrowers to arbitrarily reduce insurance coverage, have deductibles increased to unacceptable amounts, or remove the mortgagee from the mortgagee clause of the insurance policy. Endorsements should be carefully examined to determine that they do not adversely affect the mortgagee's position.

In regard to the examination of insurance policy endorsements, careful review will provide the administrator with an excellent update on secondary financing which may be placed on properties in the portfolio. A second mortgagee is as anxious as the first mortgagee to provide that the former's interest is covered under the policy and, by mailing an endorsement of additional mortgagee interest to the holder of the original policy, namely, the first mortgagee, the holder of the first mortgage is kept current concerning junior financing.

One last word on the maintenance of insurance coverage. As mentioned above, it appears that insurance coverage generates a disproportionate amount of paper flow. All too often, the first mortgagee is provided with an official-looking document which often purports to be an insurance policy but which bears the legend "Memorandum Only—this document is for information purposes only and conveys no rights whatsoever." Obviously, only an original policy or a certified copy with an endorsement indicating that the holder of the certified copy has all rights as if holding the original policy is acceptable to the first mortgagee. Constant vigilance must be exercised by the loan administrator to insure that the policy held is an original or certified copy which conveys all rights to the mortgagee as if holding the original policy.

PROPERTY TAXES

Next to debt service, property taxes normally constitute the greatest charge against gross income experienced by an income-producing property. Property taxes are also unique in that they are outside the area of control of both the borrower and the lender, and constitute a prior lien on the property, senior to the lien of the first mortgagee. In many areas, rapidly rising property taxes and/or increased assessments have caused some properties to become uneconomical to own and operate and, in some extreme cases, have caused owners to abandon their properties. Cash flow problems experienced by many municipalities have recently caused them to readjust their tax collection structure. This has placed a tremendous burden on the individual property owner, who suddenly faces the problem of a tax payment schedule which benefits the cash flow of the municipality but substantially disrupts the borrower's cash flow.

With these items in mind then, especially mindful of the fact that taxes constitute a prior lien against the property, the income-property loan administrator will find it important to understand thoroughly all the implications property taxes have on income-producing properties. The loan administrator must also be fully knowledgeable of the steps that must be taken to insure that taxes are paid when due and, if so provided in the mortgage, that sufficient funds are accrued to pay taxes as they become due in properly maintained escrow accounts. Finally, the loan administrator must be sure that taxes are properly checked on a frequent basis to insure that, at all times, the mortgagee maintains the absolute priority of its mortgage lien.

The time for proper property tax administration begins during the underwriting and appraisal process. Up-to-date and accurate tax records which show assessments, rates of increase, and patterns of assessment and rate changes can be valuable to the underwriter and appraiser. Rather than searching public records, the records maintained by the mortgage banker's loan administration department can provide the underwriter and the appraiser with a wealth of accurate information in regard to taxes and assessments. Most important, though, is an accurate view of the tax rate increases which can reasonably be expected to occur from the time an appraisal is prepared on a to-be-built property to the time the loan actually closes and the loan administrator begins to accept the responsibility for the payment of taxes from an escrow account. In some cases, it would not be unreasonable to assume that over a two- to three-year period, taxes may increase by as much as 25 percent, thereby seriously affecting the success of the project.

Early involvement by a loan administrator familiar with taxes and assessments in the underwriting process will assure both the investor and the underwriter that a realistic and knowledgeable approach is being taken in regard to the property tax expense section of the appraisal.

The key to a successful closing in regard to property taxes is to plan well in advance. The loan administrator should meet with the tax assessor to determine if the property has been fully assessed. If the property has not been fully assessed, as is the case in many properties where the mortgage loan is being closed at the time of completion, then the administrator must determine when the property will be fully assessed and the amount of the assessment. At the closing, as the administrator attempts to establish a tax escrow reserve, it would not be unreasonable to assume that the borrower may hope to base the projected monthly escrow deposit and the reserve deposit on a partial assessment. Obviously, this is a situation which cannot be permitted, as funds are usually escrowed for the payment of future taxes, and the future taxes will normally be based on a full assessment.

Advising the borrower well in advance of the tax escrow deposit and reserve requirements needed at the closing is an important step to assuring that these funds will be available. Frequently, unexpected expenses arise at income-property closings, and it is often the case that when compromises need to be made due to the borrower's shortage of funds, the compromise sometimes will take the form of a reduced escrow reserve. By providing the borrower with sufficient time to have the necessary funds available, this obstacle can be overcome.

Obviously, it is vital that accurate tax information be obtained that clearly sets forth the tax description of the subject property, the tax assessment of the subject property, and the tax rate. This is especially true in the case of income-producing properties which, because of their size and complexity, may lie in different tax jurisdictions, have extremely complex tax descriptions, and in many cases involve properties which may or may not be contiguous. The trend toward larger income-producing properties in suburban and rural areas which may not have the sophistication of city tax descriptions further complicates the matter. In cases where tax descriptions in rural areas may be somewhat vague or general, it is necessary that the loan administrator do whatever is necessary to insure the receipt of an accurate tax description of the property.

Once the loan has been closed, and especially in those cases where the mortgage documents contain a provision for the maintenance of a tax escrow account, it becomes the responsibility of the loan administrator for the life of the loan to provide that sufficient funds are accrued on a monthly basis to pay taxes as they become due. Assessment changes during the life of the mortgage loan, as well as annual or semiannual tax rate increases, can create a situation in which the borrower is suddenly faced with a deficit in the escrow account and cannot fund it. This situation can, in many cases, be eliminated by the alertness of the loan administrator. Careful attention to assessment change dates and tax rate increase dates can normally give the loan administrator a three- to four-month advance warning of impending deficits. This deficit, if discussed early, should give the borrower sufficient time to accumulate the necessary funds to fund the deficit. While this approach is frequently resisted by the borrower, many municipalities have placed heavy penalties and interest on unpaid taxes. Normally, pointing out to the borrower the substantial penalties and interest that will be incurred by the late payment of taxes will serve as an incentive to encourage the accrual of funds in advance to pay tax increases. As many tax authorities will not accept partial payments, the argument becomes even stronger for the borrower to make every effort to pay the tax increases promptly, due to the fact that penalties and interest will not only be assessed against the tax increase amount but against the entire amount of the tax, even though the majority of the funds to pay the taxes may be on hand in the borrower's escrow account.

Unfortunately, once the borrower has allowed a tax to become delinquent and accepts the inevitability of penalties and interest, and if the borrower is in a cash flow deficit position, the normal assumption will be that penalties and interest are merely the "cost of doing business" and the taxes will be allowed to run delinquent. This is obviously a serious situation, which must be dealt with firmly by the loan administrator. A typical response of the delinquent tax escrow borrower will be, "I'll pay the taxes right before the lien sale date and in the meantime my loan is current as I have promptly paid the principal and interest." Accordingly, most mortgage documents are written in such a way that all funds received flow first to the payment of taxes, and then to interest, and finally to principal. This is a strong collection tool for the loan administrator, in that applying funds first to tax escrow deficits will normally cause a material default under the mortgage loan and permit the loan administrator to threaten foreclosure should the deficit not be paid.

While the practice in recent years has been relatively rare, mortgage loan documents occasionally provide that the borrower need not maintain an escrow account. In these cases, it is vital that the mortgage loan administrator develop a mechanism for the prompt verification of the fact that the taxes are paid when due. What the documents may say in terms of the borrower promptly forwarding tax receipts after payment and what may actually take place in the loan administration department are, unfortunately, two different things. The loan administrator needs to be sure that a prudent tickler and verification system is maintained to insure that taxes have been paid. It is not enough to merely accept a receipted tax bill, since the possibility exists that the tax may have been paid with a check which was subsequently returned unpaid. Consequently, the tax, while showing paid on the loan administrator's records, would show open on the tax collector's record and would constitute a prior lien, which could be foreclosed at some point in the future. Bearing these problems in mind, it behooves the loan administrator to arrange to personally check the municipal tax records frequently during the course of the year to verify that all non-escrow account, income-producing property taxes have been paid.

A rather nonstimulating task, and one that is frequently turned over to outside services, is the task of annual tax checking. While this may be a practical approach in single-family residential lending, in income-property loan administration, due to the size and complexity of both the properties and the amounts involved, it is prudent for the loan administrator to check taxes personally or directly through staff members. Improper tax receiver postings, improper tax descriptions, erroneous billings, and a host of other problems may be difficult for an outsider to detect, but if tax records are inspected at least twice a year by a loan administrator familiar with all of the details of the subject property, the loan administrator and the investor can be assured that any inaccuracies, omissions, or discrepencies will be detected.

It is, of course, not reasonable to assume that each and every borrower will always pay taxes when due, or will always be in a position to deposit sufficient funds in a tax escrow account to insure that funds are available to pay taxes as they become due.

Frequently, the loan administrator will be faced with workout situations in regard to the payment of tax deficiencies or tax delinquencies. While each situation must be handled on a case basis, the proper solution to the problem lies in aggressive administration and attempting to never let the deficiency or delinquency grow so great that the borrower, if threatened with foreclosure, would be unable to fund the deficit or delinquency. In the same vein, the delinquency or deficiency should never be permitted to grow so great that it would cause the property to be uneconomical for the investor to foreclose if it were necessary to pay the tax deficiency or delinquency in order to perfect the mortgage lien at foreclosure.

In an age of rapidly rising processing and clerical costs, there is an increasing trend toward automation. Unfortunately, the proper handling of property taxes in regard to income-producing properties does not lend itself to the automated approach. Personal knowledge, frequent personal review by experienced personnel, and the acceptance of frequent, serious, and often harried meetings with borrowers to face difficult situations before they become problems, or to engage in workouts which may require tedious amounts of special payment handling, all contribute greatly to professional loan administration in regard to property taxes for income-producing properties.

OPERATING STATEMENTS AND THE COLLECTION OF CONTINGENT INTEREST

It is the policy of most mortgage investors to require annual operating statements. These are necessary to determine amounts on which contingent interest will be based in those cases where contingent interest is a mortgage loan requirement. Further, the collection and proper analysis of operating statements is a valuable early-warning device in detecting potential problems. Operating statements which show dramatic increases in operating costs, large increases in rates of vacancies, and negative cash flows certainly point to potential problems. Operating statements also function as a valuable method of verifying the accuracy of appraisals prepared in connection with loan underwritings. Lastly, a comprehensive file of annual operating statements provides a valuable source of material for loan underwriters in preparing future submissions. There are, however, many problems associated with obtaining, on a timely basis, annual operating statements.

The experienced mortgage loan administrator will attempt, as soon as possible, to become involved in the manner in which annual operating statements will be prepared and collected.

Early involvement by the mortgage loan administrator in the annual operating statement collection process begins at the time the loan is underwritten. The first question to be addressed at the time the commitment is being prepared is whether or not the annual operating statement will be prepared by a certified public accountant in accordance with generally accepted accounting principles. It is rather naive to expect a borrower with a 60-unit apartment project on which a $700,000 mortgage has been placed to pay upwards of $3,000 to obtain a fully audited and certified statement. The cost of this statement could well exceed the borrower's annual return on investment. On the other hand, large, national real estate corporations normally prepare only one consolidated audited and certified statement, and excessive expenses would be incurred if their accounting firms were to prepare individual certified and audited statements for each individual property. With this in mind, when considering statement requirements, thought should be given to accepting statements, on a nonaudited basis, certified to by an officer of the borrowing corporation or by the borrower and supported by a copy of the borrower's federal income tax return. A small amount of spot checking and analysis by a seasoned mortgage loan administrator or underwriter can determine discrepancies in statements prepared on this basis, and should they not be accurately prepared, a more detailed investigation could be conducted. It only seems logical to face the problem of the unavailability, in general, of audited and certified statements on smaller projects at the time the loan is being underwritten, rather than go through the process of continually waiving this requirement each year.

Thought and participation by the loan administrator should also take place at the time contingent interest provisions are being considered. It would seem that what the mortgage lending world needs most is an easy-to-understand, easy-to-collect *kicker*. With the problems brought about by being unable to reach a mutually acceptable definition of the term *net*, most contingent interest participations are based on a percentage of gross rents. When the term *gross rents* is defined as all income from a property, inherent in this definition is also those monies collected for tax escalations, operating escalations, etc. Borrowers, obviously, are quite reluctant to pay a contingent interest on funds merely passing through their hands, such as tax and operating escalation funds, and normally actively resist payment of any contingent interest on these funds, even though this may be written into the documents. The mortgage loan administrator should make every effort, at the time the commitment is being prepared, to advise the mortgage loan underwriter that the absence of a mechanism for removing from gross rents items of escalation will only create future problems and make the contingent interest difficult to collect and, in some instances, the object of a lawsuit.

At the mortgage loan closing, the mortgage loan administrator should clearly call to the borrower's attention the annual operating statement provision of the mortgage loan document and, if applicable, the contingent interest provision. To stress the borrower's obligation, it may be practical to obtain, at the closing, the name of the borrower's accountant, the fiscal year of the borrowing entity, and perhaps a letter of authorization executed by the borrower to authorize the mortgage loan administrator to write directly to the borrower's accountant and request the operating statement. While this letter would not legally obligate the accountant to forward the statement, it certainly reinforces the borrower's obligation to provide the statement.

Discussion of the method in which the contingent interest, if applicable, will be collected should also take place at the closing. This is the time to discuss with the borrower the fact that the contingent interest, as an example, is written into the papers to coincide with the loan year. Does the borrower understand this and is the borrower able to comply with it? Should the papers be modified at this time to change the contingent interest period from the loan year to either the borrower's fiscal year or the calendar year? These are all questions which will, if discussed and satisfactorily resolved at the closing, eliminate a great deal of trouble and litigation.

Clearly, the experienced mortgage loan administrator maintains accurate tickler files to call attention to the exact date annual operating statements are due. Soon after the close of the borrower's fiscal year, a personal letter should go out to the borrower concerning the obligation to provide an annual operating statement. This letter should be followed up, within 30 days, with a personal telephone call asking for a status report as to when the statement can be expected. At this time, it is an excellent idea, if a previous authorization has not been received, to ask the borrower for permission to contact the borrower's accountant directly to discuss the status of the annual operating statement. Should the statement not be received within a period of 30 days after its due date, and no reasonable explanation for the delay be forthcoming, it is practical for the mortgage loan administrator to pay a personal visit to the borrower and discuss the obligation to provide a statement and attempt to obtain either a statement or a reason for the lack of cooperation.

Once the statement has been received, it should be reviewed in terms of format and then properly analyzed. The statement can be analyzed either by a mortgage loan administrator or by a mortgage loan underwriter, but in any case, all statements, prior to being sent on to the investor, should be reviewed by an officer to insure that any major discrepancies between the statement and the original loan underwriting are properly explained. A decision should also be made as to the continued economic potential of the subject property and whether or not it should be placed on a watch-list as a potential problem. At the time the statement is transmitted to the investor, it should certainly be accompanied by a detailed letter setting forth an explanation of discrepancies between the statement and the original loan submission.

The same procedures mentioned in connection with the collection of annual operating statements should be applied to the collection of contingent interest. The borrower should be advised immediately after the close of the fiscal year of the contingent interest obligation, and continuous follow-ups by letter, telephone, and personal visit should be made until such time as the contingent interest payment is satisfactorily resolved. It is, unfortunately, a rather rare situation in which the mortgage loan administrator receives a certified and audited statement, setting forth gross rents, accompanied by a check equal to the contingent interest as interpreted by the mortgage loan administrator in accordance with a reading of the mortgage loan documents. Checks and statements are frequently received accompanied by the borrower's letter setting forth rather unique interpretations of the mortgage loan documents or, in many cases, appeals for relief from the contingent interest provision. While many appeals for relief are without merit, many do have merit and should be seriously considered by the mortgage loan administrator. If so, the entire loan should be reviewed and, if justified, a recommendation made to the investor for relief from, or an adjustment of, the contingent interest provision.

Collection of annual operating statements and, where applicable, contingent interest is an area fraught with problems. There is little that can be done when a borrower absolutely refuses to deliver a certified statement if there is no contingent interest provision. Courts have consistently shown a reluctance to permit a mortgagee to use foreclosure as a weapon to cure other than substantial monetary default. The most effective method for obtaining operating statements from reluctant borrowers is to always be aware of the exact number of statements the borrower has not delivered. If the mortgage loan administrator waits long enough, sooner or later the borrower will come forth with a request of some type. The request may be something as simple as the endorsement of an insurance loss payment draft, but, nonetheless, it is a request that the borrower is making of the loan administrator. At this time, perhaps some gentle arm-twisting can force the reluctant borrower on a *quid pro quo* basis to deliver the statements. The collection of contingent interest from a reluctant borrower is an entirely different matter. Here, as money is involved, the courts have not been reluctant to allow mortgagees to foreclose in order to obtain contingent interest rightfully due them. The mortgage loan administrator should review the collection of contingent interest from a reluctant borrower in exactly the same way as the collection of delinquent interest from a borrower in default.

One final word on contingent interest. As can be seen from the preceding paragraph, the collection of contingent interest is a difficult, sophisticated, and time-consuming procedure. It is rare that a proper fee is paid by the investor to the correspondent for the collection of this interest. Mortgage loan administrators, at the time commitments are issued, should be sure that they enter into meaningful negotiations with the potential investor to insure that they receive, for the collection of contingent interest, a fee commensurate with the work, time, and responsibility involved.

PROPERTY INSPECTIONS

In mortgage loan administration, probably next to the checking of taxes, the least stimulating assignment is property inspection. All too often, this responsibility falls to the junior member of the administrator's team, who views it as a training exercise instituted by the loan administrator to give the trainee some field experience. Nonetheless, no internal early-warning system can ever replace the property inspection as an effective tool for spotting real or potential problems long before they develop. It is difficult to imagine a problem property which did not display, in some way or other, some early signs of deferred maintenance, improper rental, poor tenancy, or any of a host of other indications which clearly point to a problem. The loan administrator who arranges to inspect income properties in a timely and professional manner will rarely, if ever, be surprised by a "problem property."

As with all other aspects of income-property loan administration, the time for the loan administrator to become involved is during the appraisal and underwriting process. The loan administrator should insure that copies of plans and specifications are maintained in the loan servicer's permanent files. Further, wherever possible, copies of construction contracts, lists of subcontractors and trade suppliers, copies of warranties, and all of the other important documents generated in connection with the construction of a project should be maintained. Not only do these documents enable the mortgage loan administrator to thoroughly understand the physical properties of the real estate, but further, in case of foreclosure, complete plans, specifications, and warranties provide a valuable asset. A review of the file containing plans, specifications, etc., before starting out on a property inspection, gives the property inspector a head start in knowing any potential weaknesses in design which should be given particular attention during inspection.

There is only one way to inspect an income property, and that is to start at the top and work your way all the way to the bottom. Major roof and boiler repairs have caused many borrowers to throw up their hands hopelessly and conclude they must abandon their property because they could never generate sufficient capital dollars to repair either of these two items. While starting at the top, the property inspector should pay particular attention to the roof. The inspector need not be an experienced roofer to determine if it is sound. Simple observation will determine if the roof is undergoing any deterioration, and visits to three or four of the top-floor tenants will instantly determine whether or not any roof leakage is taking place. The same is true of the boiler and other mechanical plants. Interviews with tenants will indicate whether or not the heating and air conditioning systems have been malfunctioning, whether or not sufficient hot water has been available, and whether or not the elevators have been operating properly.

In making inspections of income-producing properties, timing is essential. A visit to an apartment project should normally be done in the middle to late afternoon, at the time children would normally be home from school. An overabundance of children in the playgrounds, parking lots, and lobbies indicates that, perhaps, the borrower is overrenting the project with hopes of maximizing cash flow and then quickly selling it at a profit or abandoning it, leaving the mortgagee with the rather unpleasant task of evicting large families from small apartments.

The inspection of a shopping center at noon on Wednesday does absolutely no good to either the property inspector or the investor for whom the inspection is being made. Visits on Saturday afternoon or Thursday night will clearly point out that the center does not have adequate parking, that the parking lot is not full at times when it should be, that there is difficulty in obtaining access to the center, that the center may be poorly policed or overrun with marauding gangs, that the merchants have put out less than attractive displays, and a host of other items which will indicate potential problems.

In inspecting office buildings, more so than with any other type of property, great care should be given to reviewing the quality of the tenants. Frequently, borrowers, in an attempt to comply with the rental achievement portion of a commitment, will quickly fill up an office building with marginal office tenants or, in many cases, will merely fill out the building directory with a list of names that is nothing more than a listing of all the subsidiary corporations that the borrower may operate. Attention should be given to mechanical plants, especially the elevator, and halls should be very carefully surveyed for signs of damage caused by movers. Hallways showing signs of substantial wear and tear caused by movers is clearly an indication that the building tenancy is not a stable one. As greater and greater emphasis is placed on safety, especially in regard to fire safety, during an inspection the inspector should note, if possible, the potential effects on the subject property of the many and varied safety regulations which are currently being enacted by many municipalities to protect workers in office buildings from the dangers of fire. Obviously, the economics of an investment could be severely affected if a great cost were to be incurred by the developer or builder in causing an office building to comply with local safety fire regulations.

While surprise inspections may be proper for cash auditors, they are hardly proper for inspections of real estate. The borrower should be notified well in advance of the inspector's arrival, and arrangements should be made for inspection to be guided by the borrower and the building superintendent. There is precious little that the borrower or building superintendent can correct prior to the arrival of the inspector which would have any meaningful bearing on the inspector's overall evaluation of the property. By having a tour conducted, access can be gained to boiler rooms, storage rooms, the roof, and vacant apartments, and introductions can be made to tenants. Further, the building superintendent is in a position to discuss problems with the building in terms of maintenance, quality of tenants, problems with local authorities, and many other items which affect the project.

A complete review of the plans and specifications of the project, as well as a review of the project's operating statement prior to the inspection is a must for the professional property inspector. Each property inspection should be followed up with a letter to the borrower, giving thanks for the courtesy in conducting the tour, and also mentioning any deficiencies, and where appropriate, of course, paying a compliment on an excellent operation. Deficiencies should be subsequently followed up to impress upon the borrower the obligation to continually keep the property in first-class operating condition.

Perhaps the one element which makes property inspections frustrating is the fact that it is extremely difficult to foreclose or commence court action under the *waste provision* of the mortgage loan document. Essentially, this provision provides that a default occurs under the terms of the mortgage loan if the owner does not keep the property properly maintained.

CONCLUSION

Income-property lending has come to represent a significant factor in the overall picture of the real estate financing industry. Each day, this financing becomes more and more complex, and as the complexities increase, so also does the investor's risk. This risk can be greatly reduced by efficient, effective, and professional mortgage loan administration. The professional loan administrator can contribute significantly to the reduction of the investor's risk by fully understanding the primary responsibility, namely, insuring strict compliance with the terms of the security documents. By keeping in mind, at all times, the following five key areas of loan administration and security document compliance, the loan administrator will be able to properly fulfill all fiduciary responsibilities to the investor:

1   Payments, collections, and foreclosures.
2   Insurance.
3   Property taxes.
4   Operating statements and the collection of contingent interest.
5   Property inspections.

Chapter 14

Land and Land Development Loans

W. Richard Blagdon

Nothing is more basic to real estate lending and investing than land. This, in fact, is the basic real estate commodity. To the uninitiated, a land loan or land development loan might appear to be a relatively simple transaction, but, in reality, this type of lending requires the most thorough analysis and consideration of any type of real estate lending.

First, let us define our subject. As the words imply, a land loan is simply a loan to one or more individuals or a business entity of one form or another for which the security is primarily the land itself. The security will be in the form of a note and mortgage (or deed of trust) on the land with the note generally endorsed by the business entity, the individuals, or both. The mortgage is usually a first mortgage, although it is conceivable that the buyer could have arranged for advantageous financing from the seller in the form of a purchase money mortgage, and, if the land has appreciated in value significantly enough, it may be that a second mortgage could be prudently placed, because the convenient terms of the first mortgage might make it to the lender's and borrower's best interests not to disturb that financing. An example of this would be where the developer has negotiated the purchase of the land with a relatively small down payment, with the balance to be paid in prescribed installments over a long period of time at low interest or released for construction financing on the basis of a pro-rata paydown of principal per acre. Further, the developer might obtain an immediate release of certain acreage for development without additional principal paydown. This situation must, of course, be approached with extreme caution, because the second lender would have to cure or retire the first mortgagee's position to protect its own interests in the event of default.

There are several reasons for a borrower to want land financing. Most obvious is that it allows for the acquisition of a parcel of land on which to develop a particular project. This project might consist of a single structure of one type or another, or might encompass many types of real estate, including industrial, residential, commercial, and special-purpose facilities. Zoning is most often the key to the land developer's success. Because spot zoning has resulted in many inharmonious adjacent uses in the past and has tended to detract from the overall community, many zoning authorities are tending toward the Planned Unit Development (PUD). This involves the approval of an overall plan for a large tract of acreage within the community and gives that community a greater measure of control over the total environment to be created. The developer might be a builder familiar with only one type of property who will go into the PUD, nevertheless, to acquire the parcel, obtain the zoning, and continue through development, with the intent of selling to others at a profit, land not wanted, thereby retaining only that land which is zoned for the type of project planned. One typical requirement in a PUD is to leave specified areas unimproved as green belts. This creates a more aesthetically pleasing development and provides land to be used for parks and recreational facilities for the community. This also works to the advantage of the developer in that the green belt areas can be included in the calculations of the land-use density and, therefore, results in substantially lower development costs. Sites for new schools are very often donated to the local school board, to the benefit of the citizenry. It serves to help reduce their ever-rising costs of education, but the net effect of all of this is that the developer is not just selling or renting to the public, but offering them a way of life. This would require development financing as well. This type of financing would presume development of the land and the buildings at an early date. If the intended use for a particular parcel of land is to build a single project, such as an apartment complex or office building, it generally does not require a land loan but rather a construction loan, the first advance of which would be for all or part of the cost of the land, with the borrower contributing the difference. In this case, the developer who does not own the land will option it, arrange financing for the entire project, and then at closing have the land funds disbursed, or perhaps use personal funds, or obtain a short-term loan just for the acquisition of the property.

Another purpose for land financing can be merely to hold the land after acquisition for a period of time with the intent of future development or perhaps pure speculation in the hope the land will appreciate in value and can be sold at a profit. While financing of this kind can be handled prudently, the lender would be well advised to use a very conservative loan-to-value ratio even after the most careful consideration of all of the factors involved in the underwriting. One requirement in this type of financing that will vastly improve the security of the lender's position is to insist the borrower use some personal funds in the acquisition of the property and pay the carrying cost out of his own pocket. Still another reason for the borrower to seek land financing would be to obtain capital on land which has been held for some period of time and which has appreciated considerably in value. This is perhaps the riskiest of all types of land financing, since the borrower most likely will have realized more cash from the loan than has been invested in the land with the intent of using this cash in other ventures. Consequently, the borrower's motivation to develop the particular parcel may be somewhat abated and could lead to a troubled loan. Many land lenders by policy will not do this type of financing. If they do consider it, it must certainly be done on a very conservative basis and only with a few select borrowers.

For the purpose of this chapter, let us concern ourselves with a typical case of land and development financing where the developer wants to acquire a significant parcel of land with the thought of improving it for construction of more than one building. In the case of a Planned Unit Development, this might range from single-family homes through a large regional shopping center and possibly include office and industrial facilities as well. Financing in this case would typically be an acquisition and development loan. The funds for the development of the property would be used for the installation of utilities and streets and, perhaps, other amenities such as lakes and recreational facilities. The loan, in fact, might be calculated to cover all of the acquisition and development costs, including the carrying costs (primarily interest on the loan) through to the successful completion.

Let us assume that the developer has located a parcel of land that is felt to be ready for development, and is convinced the price at which it can be acquired makes it economically feasible. The developer now comes to us, the lender, with a plan for development, including not only the improvements to the land itself, but what is intended to be done with it when improved. The developer may plan to sell part of it or keep it all for development. Now begins the underwriting process. The paramount consideration in real estate lending should be whom we are lending to—that is, people. Is the developer a person of proven ability and integrity? Does the developer have experience with this type of land development and the end product planned thereon? Does the developer have the time and staff capable of handling another project of this magnitude? Does the developer have the financial staying power to carry on through unforeseen delays or cost overruns? In the case of the last question, the lender should be honest and realize that where significant additional funds are required, the developer will seldom be able to cover these personally and, therefore, the lender is almost forced to advance them for the protection of the rest of the principal. The underwriting analysis should lead to the conclusion that there is enough margin in the amount of funds anticipated to be received from proceeds of sale or construction and permanent financing to cover such contingencies and to repay the lender in full. If the developer is known to the lender, the decision of whether or not to do business is an easier one, since it is based on past experience and a history of performance. If the developer is not known to the lender, a thorough investigation should be made before deciding to proceed. This would include such things as a good credit report, an analysis and confirmation of financial statements, an inspection of previous projects done, and, most importantly, conversations with a variety of people with whom the developer has done business, including bankers, mortgage bankers, other lenders, and even material men, subcontractors, and perhaps fellow developers. The lender is also well advised to determine the competency and loyalty of the developer's key personnel, since much of the success of the project will rest on their shoulders, especially with a large tract of land that requires a varied number of architectural, engineering, marketing and financing skills.

Now that we have determined that we want to do business with the developer, let's look at the real estate. First of all, what is the zoning? Very often the parcel will not be zoned entirely for the proposed development, and even if it is logical to assume that the developer can obtain proper zoning, the loan must be analyzed on the basis that it can be profitably developed for whatever it is zoned. For example, if it is zoned for just single-family residences on large lots, would the market absorb this many in a reasonable period of time at sufficient profit motive for the builder to have the incentive to proceed and repay the loan on schedule? The key to this is sufficient profit incentive to the developer, because this is the lender's best assurance of being repaid.

To determine whether or not the developer has made a good buy on the land, there is no better way than looking at sales of comparable parcels; and here the important element is to be certain they are, in fact, comparable. Among the items of comparability to be concerned with are location, relative sizes of the parcels, zoning, availability of utilities, date and conditions of sale, topography, access, soil conditions, etc.

Assuming that the appraisal evidences a beneficial purchase, let us begin to study the developer's specific plans for the improvement of the real estate. First of all, is there a need for types of real estate for which the project is or will be zoned? To know something about the city itself, especially if we are not familiar with the city on a current basis, a comprehensive study should be undertaken to establish the growth rate, the stability of the economy, and any other factors that could have a bearing on the success of the project. Obviously, the location now becomes of paramount importance in relation to the particular city. Is the land on the side of town where people want to live most? Is the absorption rate for the city and particularly this section of the city sufficient to support a development of this kind in a reasonable period of time? The reasonable period of time is extremely important in that the cost to carry a project based on interest alone tends to increase the investment at a very rapid rate, and if overly optimistic projections are relied upon and not met, the project may run into trouble for this reason alone. Another important determination that bears heavily on the success of a given project is what is going to happen to the other vacant land around it. This should be analyzed from the standpoint of what zoning it now has, who owns it, and what are their plans for it and when. Obviously, everything could look good for our subject parcel, but if four comparable projects were started around it at about the same time, they would probably all suffer and be troublesome cases.

If an analysis of these factors results in favorable conclusions, we should continue our in-depth underwriting. The topography of the land is, of course, important, since it will determine the overall relative costs of the improvements. Assuming a terrain that is reasonable to work with and that will afford proper drainage, etc., it is just as important to determine as best as possible what the subsoil conditions are. Soil tests are important but cannot be completely relied upon, because it would be impossible to take an adequate number of soil tests on a large parcel of land to tell you everything that you need to know. Sometimes, one of the most expeditious methods is merely a reliance upon what subsoil conditions are like in the general area as a whole. This can be found out by discussions with a number of people in the community who have been in the building business and an analysis of other projects in the general vicinity. Soil tests can be most meaningful to determine if rock conditions exist that would make the installation of improvements and foundations too costly to be economically feasible. Having passed these tests, the land might appear very attractive. It would, however, be relatively useless without the benefit of utilities, including water, electricity, natural gas, sewers, and storm sewers. It must be determined that they are available at the property, that they can be tapped into at reasonable costs, and that they are in adequate supply. This is especially important with the current emphasis on energy shortages of one kind or another, and absolute assurance of their availability and adequacy must be obtained before proceeding. This assurance must come from the utility companies themselves and from the governmental authorities, and as much assurance as possible must be obtained to be certain that such things as sewer tap-in charges will not be significantly increased in the foreseeable future, because this can obviously affect the economics of building. Very often a parcel will require a private sewer plant or water system. In either case, we must be certain that permits for construction and operation of same are obtainable.

Having satisfied ourselves that governmental authorities will be friendly to the project and that permits and approvals either have been or will be readily available, there is one more external influence which in recent years has become a critical factor in the development of large parcels of land. Various environmental protection agencies, whether of the federal government or the particular state in which the property is located, have become critical observers of all such developments. Starting without the approval of whichever authority has jurisdiction can be foolhardy, since delays can be economically disastrous. Even with these approvals, there are still certain risks, because various environmentalist groups can bring suit and try to obtain an injunction to prevent work from going forward until the suit is tried. While suits of this kind can never be totally anticipated, it is wise to know the social and political climates of the given area and to have all of the proper backing and know that the chances of winning are quite good in the event a suit is filed. Again, to anticipate this type of thing, one must be as intimately familiar as possible with a given area and with the approach and philosophies of the environmental groups in the area.

Another external influence we should always look at is the possibility of new roads being built that could perhaps have significant influence on our subject parcel. This, again, can be determined by contact with government authorities. Most interstate highway routes are reasonably well determined today even if construction has not begun, and this should be analyzed in light of its influence on the project. Obviously, one of the first things we look at in the case of our subject is to determine that it has good access to transportation and that it also has good visibility, which can be extremely helpful in the marketing aspect.

While we have been investigating the various factors referred to above, a preliminary title report should have been prepared by a competent title company and analyzed by the underwriter and an attorney for all factors affecting title of the property. The first question to ask is, "Does the title report show that all rights and benefits of ownership are available or are there liens or encumbrances of any kind?" These could include, in addition to mortgages, such items as mineral rights, easements for utilities or road-ways, easements or restrictions for height limitations, or various other limitations on the use of the property which could affect its value. The title report should be accompanied by a survey from a registered surveyor clearly defining any such easements or limitations that are a matter of record. This is not to suggest that all easements are detrimental. For example, an easement over the subject parcel might be tied in to one over a contiguous parcel which, in fact, benefits the property for reasons of access, utilities, or other favorable influences. Conditions such as these can be specific to certain areas and the lender must be familiar with them. A good example of this is water rights in certain states, the inclusion or exclusion of which can render a property either valuable or worthless.

In addition to having a developer we want to work with, a well-located parcel at the right price with the benefit of utilities and no adverse factors affecting title, and with no external influences that might be anticipated to cause a delay or change in the plans, we are now on the verge of committing to make this loan and had better reinforce our opinion of the economic feasibility of the proposed plan. We mentioned earlier the appraisal process in determining the land value and our concern with the absorption rate of the proposed developments, whether done by the developer or by the eventual purchasers of portions of the parcel. In this regard, we must determine that the proposed buildings can not only be absorbed in the projected period of time, but that they will be at market rentals or sale prices appealing to the typical users and that they can be built at costs justified by such rentals or sales. Again, we must look at what is happening in the particular market we are addressing ourselves to and benefit ourselves with the best knowledge available of what is happening in that marketplace today and what might happen in the future. Automatic wage increases for construction workers, pending unionization, or other such factors which might affect the cost of proposed improvements can be critical. Because most lenders are not in the building business, pinning down costs can be a difficult thing. One safeguard, if available, can be the requirement of completion bonds if, in fact, the developer or his subcontractors or general contractor, as the case may be, are bondable. It is also wise to obtain counsel from independent engineers as to the adequacy of the plans for the proposed under-ground and surface improvements, particularly in view of the specific requirements of the governmental jurisdictions in which the property is located. Experience has proven that it is best to have someone who is intimately familiar with the given locale and who works on a regular basis on similar kinds of projects.

At this juncture it would be well to reflect on many of the factors affecting the decision-making process which we have discussed. We have repeatedly mentioned the influences affecting a particular area and given parcel. It is virtually impossible for the typical lender to have all of the knowledge necessary to make this decision in the various locations in the country and, therefore, we get back to the major premise set forth earlier in the chapter, namely, dealing with the right people. Admittedly, any sophisticated lender with the proper staff could develop all the data necessary to make the prudent decisions; but while we all know that time is money to the developer, it is just as true for the lender. There is, therefore, no better way to rapidly but prudently arrive at the proper decision than with the aid of a good intermediary or, more specifically, a professional mortgage banker whose integrity and judgment can be relied upon by the lender. It is not to say that the mortgage banker should be relied upon without recourse; always welcome a lender's questioning and requirement of proof of certain salient factors. This is the ingredient which benefits both the developer and the lender and more than justifies the fee charged by the mortgage banker because of the savings in time and possible errors in judgment.

At this point in our consideration of the loan, perhaps we should ask ourselves, weighing all of the pitfalls and negatives which have been discussed, why we should consider this type of loan. From the standpoint of the developer, who typically could not handle such a development without borrowed funds, the decision is simple. From the mortgage banker's standpoint, the fee earned may not be worth all of the time and responsibility required to see the project through to a successful conclusion. But it is important to recognize that the mortgage banker has provided the developer with the basic ingredient, namely, the funds necessary to get the project off the ground. The mortgage banker, when doing the job right, will be primarily responsible for all of the financing required for the parcel which will go into many, many millions of dollars beyond just the development financing, and will prove valuable to the developer over and over again. This brings us to why the lender should undertake this type of financing. One consideration has to be the yield. Obviously, because of the additional risks, the yield should be commensurate. Unquestionably, the lender should be rewarded according to the risk being taken. If the borrower has a sound financial condition pledged to the loan and, in addition to that, is infusing a number of dollars into the project, the risk is minimized and the rate should not be significantly different from that of a construction loan with a take-out commitment. Very often, however, the lender is putting up the majority of dollars, if not all, and the yield should be significantly higher than almost any other kind of real estate financing. The yield to the lender does not necessarily have to be expressed totally in the base rate or coupon rate of the loan. If the lender is totally convinced of the feasibility and profitability of the project, it is just as well advised to wait and receive a higher yield in the future than it might obtain from the base rate negotiated at this time. To burden a project with an inordinately high initial return could prove detrimental rather than advantageous to both lender and borrower. Therefore, the lender could obtain a better overall yield through the means of contingent interest or "kickers," by sharing in the proceeds of sale as the project becomes mature. Depending on the lender, this can be in the form of gross proceeds or net proceeds—that is, a share in the profitability of the project.

This leads us to a consideration of this type of financing. Some lenders by law are precluded from doing this type of financing and others by their corporate makeup or personality are not good sources. Financial institutions in various states, as well as some of the national institutions, will have specific legislation which include or exclude them from this type of financing. Depending upon the type of project, it could be appealing to a bank, savings and loan, a credit corporation subsidiary of a major company, or a life insurance company. Regardless of who the lender might be, one of the advantages to the lender is not just the present yield and possible contingent income but the built-in source of future income. Depending on the lending philosophy of the given lender, it might be well to have an option or at least a first right of refusal on future business derived from a given project, such as the construction financing, permanent financing, or, in the case of an equity-minded institution, the right to purchase at least some of the completed structures on a predetermined basis.

Setting aside the future benefits of this type of lending, one thing that the lender must be concerned with is when funds will be prepaid from the project. It would certainly be unwise for the lender to wait until the project is totally sold out to get all funds back, since it is taking a primary risk by putting up the majority or all of the funds. Therefore, in the negotiation stages it should be determined that with each sale the lender will be repaid more than pro rata for the amount of funds it has committed to that specific amount of acreage. This has to be related to each parcel sold or developed, depending on whether it is residential, commercial, etc., so that at any time the remaining indebtedness is presumably less than the value assigned to the acreage under the zoning rather than controlling that specific usage for the acreage remaining. As a general rule, it is well to determine in advance that a lender will have received repayment of principal and interest in full when the project is 70 to 80 percent completed. For the lender to be paid out at an earlier date is generally not economically feasible, and payment at a later date tends to put the lender in too insecure a position. It is in the best interest of both lender and borrower to retire the acquisition and development loan as soon as possible; therefore, both should consider delaying the receipt of their maximum profits until a future date. In this regard, the lender can defer payment of equity participations of one form or another until the project is proven, at which time it can share in a greater proportion. By the same rationale the borrower should not be permitted to take substantial profits out of the project until that same point in time.

In structuring the loan, two other conditions should be embodied in the agreement to the fullest extent possible. In analyzing this type of financing, it has become eminently apparent that the time required for development is a most significant factor and everything possible should be done to encourage the development as rapidly as is feasible. This can perhaps be best accomplished by requiring the developer to keep significant amounts of personal funds in the project, including all or parts of the cost to carry until development is under way and certain achievement points have been met within a specific time frame. This leads us to the next point in this regard, which involves the staging of development. This covenant requires that in order for the borrower to qualify for the advancement of funds for a successive stage, the preceding stage should have achieved an agreed-upon degree of success, again within a specified time period.

Once a loan of this nature has been committed and funds advanced, it is imperative that the lender's staff and agent or agents follow the project closely to see that all the terms of the loan agreement are being abided by and that work is progressing on schedule and in accordance with the cost estimates. Regardless of the thoroughness of the analysis and documenation preceding funding, it is inevitable that a number of changes and variances will be required from time to time as the project progresses. These frequent judgment decisions can only be properly rendered if lender, borrower, and mortgage banker have particular individuals who follow the progress of the development and remain intimately familiar with it throughout its life. From the lender's standpoint, all of the safeguards preceding any advance of funds should be inherent in the terms of the loan agreement. These are discussed in more detail in the chapter concerning construction financing. To them should be added any peculiarities specific to a given acquisition and development loan.

In summary, let us touch on the highlights of a typical case. The mortgage banker brings to the lender a request for an acquisition and/or development loan on a specific parcel of land with a given developer. A good mortgage banker will have prenegotiated with the developer the majority of the terms and conditions which will be a requirement of commitment and funding of the loan. After careful underwriting and evaluation, the lender will determine that the borrower, the real estate, and the proposed development plan and objectives indicate every chance for the success of the project. The basic purpose for this financing will be to provide a current yield plus possible future benefits to the lender, current fee income plus future business to the mortgage banker, and potential profits to the developer/builder. Also, an important determinant for each of the parties involved is the inventory of potential future business, not only from the specific loan under consideration but from other developments in which they might work together. Beyond this there are many important benefits to the community and to companies involved with the development of the land and the buildings to be created thereon. Additionally, this makes possible the creation of structures for better housing, commerce, and industry to the community involved. Thus, if we have collectively done our job properly, the yield to society will be even greater than the economic yield to those immediately concerned.

Chapter 15

The Function of the Constant

Jay J. Strauss

The *constant* (K) is the basis of the concept of financial *leverage*. As most commonly used, the constant is a factor multiplied by the loan amount (L) to determine the annual payments (debt service or D/S) necessary to amortize the loan in a desired term and pay interest at the coupon rate on the unpaid balance. For example: $L \times K = D/S$. A $120,000 loan at a $10K$ has annual payments of $12,000 or $1,000 per month. Convenient tables are available which save the bother of calculating constants.

The constant is a combination of interest *on* the loan and repayment *of* the loan so that many combinations of interest rate and term will result in the same constant; a 6% loan for 15 years and 4 months; a 7½% loan for 18 years and 7 months; and a 9% loan for 25 years and 9 months all result in a $10K$: all would produce monthly payments of $1,000 for principal and interest on a $120,000 loan. The following chart shows the first loan year relationship of interest and principal (amortization) for the various interest rates at a $10K$:

Interest	Principal	K	Term
6%	4%	10%	15 yrs. 4 mos.
7%	3%	10%	17 yrs. 3 mos.
7½%	2½%	10%	18 yrs. 7 mos.
8%	2%	10%	20 yrs. 3 mos.
9%	1%	10%	25 yrs. 9 mos.

All these rates and terms will result in the same payment. As the interest rate and term increase, the principal repayment decreases so that a greater proportion of the payment goes to interest and a lesser amount to repay the loan. This is because interest is being paid on only the remaining principal balance of the loan.

This relationship of equal constants for varying rates and terms is important in the analysis of income properties for leverage. Financial leverage is the ability to borrow capital at a lower constant than the property produces on a free and clear basis:

Example: An apartment building costs $1,000,000 and has a net income of $110,000. Its all cash constant is 110,000 ÷ 1,000,000 or 11%. If one could borrow at a constant below 11%, positive leverage exists and the return on equity will increase; that is, a loan of $750,000 at a 10$K$ will require debt service of $75,000. The cash flow will be $35,000 (110,000 − 75,000) on an equity of $250,000 (1,000,000 − 750,000) or a return of 14% (35,000 ÷ 250,000).

Conversely, if a property produces a lesser all cash return than is available on borrowed capital, it is said to have *negative leverage*.

Example: An apartment building costs $1,000,000 and has a net income of $90,000. Its all-cash constant is 90,000 ÷ 1,000,000 or 9%. The same loan as above, that is, $750,000 at a 10$K$ will leave a cash flow of only $15,000 (90,000 − 75,000), which means a return of 6% on the $250,000 equity.

The prudent income-property lending officer can take a quick look at a loan proposal and determine if positive leverage exists. If not, probably no time should be spent on the loan, since there is no way to satisfy the typical borrower's need—a high debt-to-equity ratio.

The constant is also used in the risk-analysis technique of income-property lending. Since a basic economic theory is that as risk increases, return should increase, one readily sees this to be true with the constant. Certainly a lender's risk increases as the loan term increases. This is due to the lender's exposure of higher loan balances for longer periods of time. Using the same constant and increasing the term increases the rate of interest (return) to the lender.

The other factor in risk analysis of income-property lending is the coverage factor (C). This represents the amount of net income (NI) that is to be used for debt service. It is a function of the quality and reliability of the income stream. Obviously, a long-term net lease from a prime credit tenant is a higher quality and more reliable income stream than is the net income from an apartment building where tenant turnover creates loss of income while operating expenses and taxes tend to increase. It is, therefore, obvious that one could use a higher percentage of the income from the net lease than from the apartment building. Debt service coverage is expressed as a ratio. It can range from a low of 1:1 to a high of 2:1 or higher.

In utilizing the constant and coverage concepts in loan underwriting, the calculations are rather simple. The net income is divided by the coverage factor with the result being the net income available for debt service ($NI \div C = DS$). Rewriting the first formula in the chapter ($L \times K = DS$) to read $DS \div K = L$ gives us the loan amount fitting the underwriting criteria we have established.

> *Example:* $110,000 net income from the U.S. Government or a similar quality tenant for 25 years might require a coverage factor of 1.05:1. This means that we would consider using $104,761.90 for debt service at the same $10K$. The available loan would be $1,047,619 or, say, $1,050,000. This is a loan of $300,000 more than the apartment building used in our first example with the same net income. This is because the quality and reliability of the income stream have reduced the risk and therefore increased the amount we can invest.

Another factor which affects the debt service coverage is the rate of return that the two sources of funds (debt and equity) demand. In each real estate transaction, a certain portion of the capital comes from borrowed funds (debt) and a certain portion comes from the owner's capital (equity). Each of these sources of funds requires both a return on their investment (interest) and a return of their investment (principal). This combination results in constants (K) for both debt and equity. If we are making a loan equal to 75 percent of appraised value and the constant required on debt exceeds the constant required on equity, the debt service coverage will be less than 1.33:1. If the constant required on debt is less than the constant required on equity, then the debt service coverage will be above 1.33:1. If the constants required for both debt and equity are the same, the debt service coverage will be 1.33:1.

Similarly, the coverage will be affected by loans which are more or less than 75 percent of the value of the property. A loan of more than 75 percent of value may have a coverage factor below 1.33:1 and a loan of less than 75 percent of value may have a coverage factor of more than 1.33:1.

In establishing the coverage factor, we must, therefore, consider three facts:

1 The quality and reliability of the income stream.
2 The relative costs of debt and equity funds (in constants).
3 The loan-to-value ratio.

The last and perhaps the most unusual fact about the constant is that it really is not constant. Each time the borrower makes a payment of principal and reduces the loan balance, the effective constant changes.

> *Example:* A loan of 6% for 20 years has an $8.6K$. On a $1,000,000 loan the payments are $86,000 per year. In 10 years, the unpaid balance of that loan is $645,000. Utilizing our formula, $L \times K = DS$, and solving it for K, we see that $K = DS \div L$ or, in this case, $86,000 \div 645,000$, giving us a constant (K) of 13.33% ten years after the original loan was made, instead of the original 8.6%.

What has happened? In the first loan year of the $86,000 of debt service, approximately $60,000 (6% on 1,000,000) went for interest and $26,000 went for principal. As the payments continue and principal is reduced, less of the payment goes to interest and more to principal until the tenth loan year where $38,700 goes to interest (6% on $645,000) and $47,300 goes to principal. This represents a return of 7.33% of the $645,000 (47,000 ÷ 645,000). Since we said that the constant (K) consists of return on investment (interest) and return of investment (principal), the constant in the tenth year of the loan is 13.33% (6% × 7.33%).

As the effective constant changes each year, the lender's risk is being reduced as the loan principal reduces due to amortization. This can be offset by the increased risk inherent in an older property. Again the risk-reward concept comes into play. Some properties mature with age and become more stable and valuable. These properties should be refinanced when the constant on the existing unpaid balance exceeds the then prevailing constants in the marketplace.

A common method of utilization of the constant by real estate developers is the purchase financing and resale of net leased properties for immediate profit. This is referred to in the trade as a "scalp" transaction. Let us assume that a company desires to sell and lease back a facility which it owns or is building. The company will usually offer the property to several bidders, each of whom will calculate the minimum rental they are willing to accept for the purchase price. Each developer must, in his or her own mind, establish the amount of equity capital available for the property, how much debt can be placed thereon, and what constant each source of money demands. If we assume that the cost of the facility is $1 million, various developers might look at the project as follows:

Developer A   Equity of $100,000 at a constant of 10% and debt of $900,000 at a 10.5% constant, for a total rental of $104,500, or an overall constant of 10.45%.

Developer B   Equity of $300,000 at a constant of 9% and debt of $700,000 at an 11% constant, for a total rental of $104,000, or an overall constant of 10.4%.

The above two developers are very close to each other in rental, and if we assume that Developer A is in the deal for a "scalp" the rental could be reduced to $103,500, the deal closed, and restructured as follows:

If the lender were willing to make a 90 percent loan at 10.5% constant, it is reasonable to assume that if the loan is reduced to $750,000 the constant could probably be reduced by 20 basis points to 10.3%. This would require $77,250 of debt service and $26,250 for a 10.5% constant on equity of $250,000. If a higher tax bracket individual could be found to purchase this facility at 8% constant on the cash flow in excess of debt service, the equity portion would raise an additional $328,125. This would mean that $1,078,125 would be available on an original cost of $1,000,000 or turn-around profit, or a scalp of $78,125.

Obviously, the key to this type of business is the ability to have both the equity and debt sources of funds available to you. Each deal must be individually structured based upon the positive and negative aspects inherent therein so as to decide the appropriate amount of debt and equity necessary to give the optimum return to the developer.

In summary, the constant is a vehicle of many uses. First, it tells the annual debt service required for various loans. Second, it helps to make a quick decision on a loan proposal by determining if positive leverage exists. Third, it is used in the risk analysis of income property loans. Last, but not least, it helps in locating loans that are in need of refinancing.

The income property loan officer, with either a mortgage banker or a lender, must be conversant with the constant factor and its applications. It is the one tool available that plays a multitude of roles in the day-to-day drama of our profession.

Chapter 16

Unusual Financing Techniques

Benjamin B. Cohen

To discuss a topic such as "Unusual Financing Techniques" is like riding a horse around a ring—there is no beginning and no end. The methods of financing real estate are only subject to the limits of creativity and imagination on the part of the income property lender.

This chapter is not designed to give answers, but rather to stimulate the thought processes. Some of the more classic methods of less conventional financing will be discussed. They include the land sale-leaseback, wraparound loan, the sale and installment repurchase, and others. The concept of *leverage* which applies in these techniques can be used to conceive other methods of utilizing borrowed capital to increase equity returns.

In deciding how to approach a financing transaction, it is important to understand the motivation of both the borrower and lender. Some common motivations of the borrower and lender are listed below:

Borrower Motivations	**Lender Motivations**
Cash flow	Safety
Maximum loan	Yield
Tax benefits	Minimum amortization
Limited liability	Diversity of portfolio

Matching the motivations of borrower and lender in a particular transaction dictates the type of financing ''package'' the loan officer should recommend. It will also dictate which of the mortgage banker's lenders should be offered the loan, since motivations vary from institution to institution. A borrower who is interested in cash flow should probably be matched with a lender who is primarily interested in safety, while a borrower interested in a maximum loan should probably be matched with a lender primarily interested in yield, that is, one willing to take larger risks. Once motivations are determined, the loan officer plunges forward into the sea of financing seeking the best course to the journey.

WRAPAROUND LOAN

The most maligned and misunderstood financing vehicle is the wraparound loan. In its simplest form, a wraparound is the writing of a new first mortgage loan without paying off the existing first mortgage loan, with the new lender and borrower taking advantage of the spread in interest rates between the two. The most important factor, which is most often overlooked, is that the constant on the new loan must be no less than the constant on the unpaid balance of the old loan. If this is not the case, the new lender must continually add more principal to the loan, thereby reducing the yield.

In order to truly calculate the average yield on a wraparound loan, the internal rate of return formula is used as follows:

The following formula calculates the effective rate on new money (capital letters = new loan; small letters = old loan) $P(p)$ = loan amount (balance); T (t) = loan term or maturity (remaining term); $R(r)$ = interest rate:

$$\frac{(P \times T \times R)}{(P \times T)} - \frac{(p < t \times r)}{(p \times t)} = \text{estimated effective rate on new money}$$

Example:

		Loan amount	Term or Maturity	Rate	Closing or Funding date
New Loan	(P)	$ 1,800,000	20 yr. term	7 ¾% (New)	7-1-74
Old Loan	(p)	653,700	(bal. 7-1-74) 12.91 yrs. left	5.875% (Old)	
New Money		$ 1,146,300			
then:		$ 1,800,000	× 20 × .0775	=	$ 2,790,000
		$ 653,700	× 12.91 × .05875	=	$ 495,807
		$ 1,800,000	× 20	=	$36,000,000
		$ 653,700	× 12.91	=	$ 8,439,267 effective
or:		$ 2,790,000	− $ 495,807	= 8.234%	=rate on
		$36,000,000	− $8,439,267		new money

1. Calculations of effective rate the first year only shows a new money yield of 8.72% as follows:

$$
\begin{array}{rll}
\$1,800,000 \times 7\ 3/4\% & = \$139,000 \\
\underline{653,700} \times 5\ 7/8\% & = \underline{\ \ \ 38,500} \\
\$1,146,300 \times \quad x & = \$100,500 \\
x & = 8.72\%
\end{array}
$$

2. Over the proposed new 20-year term, the total cumulative *additional* loan exposure will be \$27,560,733 for which lender will be paid \$2,294,193 in *additional* interest.

3. With 15-year term (or call privilege), effective rate will increase to 8.6% (.08602).

The formula can be worked in reverse starting with the necessary rate on the new money to determine the rate on the new loan as well as its term. A simple way of calculating this using the same figures as the above example is as follows: The old loan's balance of $653,700 was from an original loan of say, $800,000, which had annual payments of $60,214. This makes the constant on the existing unpaid balance 9.21 ($60,214 ÷ $653,700). If we assume the lender wants approximately 8¼% interest on new money and is willing to take a 20-year term, that is the equivalent of a 10.23 constant on the new portion of the loan, or an annual payment on the new money ($1,146,300) of $117,266. Adding that payment to the old payment of $60,214 ($177,480) divided by the total amount of the loan ($1,800,000) gives a constant of 9.86. This is the equivalent of a yield on the total indebtedness of 7¾% for the 20-year term. This use of comparative constants makes the calculation of yield on a wraparound loan quick and simple. The exact yield is then recalculated using the internal-rate-of-return formula.

As can readily be seen, a wraparound loan is only prudent when the constant available in the marketplace exceeds the constant on the unpaid balance of the original indebtedness. This normally occurs in the early years of a loan. To the wraparound lender the loan is nothing more than a second mortgage with the appropriate risk. However, the leverage gained by the spread in interest rates makes it an appealing transaction, and the fact that the wraparound lender collects a full payment for both the first and second mortgages gives greater control than might ordinarily be accomplished.

LAND SALE-LEASEBACK

The second technique mentioned above is the land sale-leaseback, which has been used for many years. This constitutes the separation of the land from the improvements, with the land being sold to an institutional investor either prior to or subordinate to first mortgage financing.

If the land is sold first with leasehold financing occurring afterwards and subject to the ground lease, the ground rent is usually at a rate commensurate with a credit transaction, since the ground lessor has the satisfaction of knowing that another institutional investor is lending money secured by the leasehold estate. This puts the ground lessor in a senior position, since a default in the ground rent can eliminate the lien of the leasehold mortgagee. It is prudent to sell land prior to arranging leasehold financing when the land represents a higher percentage of the total asset. This practice is most common in urban areas, particularly in the commercial center of a community where land values range upwards from $100 per square foot. Terms of the ground leases are generally long, giving the owner of the leasehold estate at least lifetime residual benefits. Principal purchasers of land include insurance companies, colleges, and other eleemosynary institutions who have perpetuity and can afford to accept fixed yields on their investments and wait for the residual value inherent in the land.

In financing properties on this basis, the borrower in essence finances 100 percent of the value of the land through its sale and 75 percent of the value of the improvements through a leasehold loan. This will create more dollars than the borrower would be able to achieve through conventional financing.

If the land is a lesser portion of the total asset, it is then prudent to finance both the land and the improvements on a conventional basis and sell the land while leasing it back subject to the first mortgage financing encumbering the fee estate. Obviously, ground rent on this type of lease will be higher, since the ground lease is junior to the first mortgage. Lenders doing this type of financing should be compensated accordingly. It is not unusual to offer the purchaser of the land in such a transaction an inflationary hedge in the form of additional ground rent based upon the income stream of the property. This is a true form of equity financing, since the borrower first finances 75 percent of the land and buildings and then finances 100 percent of the land through the land sale technique. Investors who purchase land on a subordinate basis include insurance companies and other institutions who are adept in real estate financing and are willing to accept the risks for proper compensation. This type of financing is, in concept, a joint venture, although the equity during the term of the ground lease is solely in the hands of the developer, while the residual value of the property reverts to the investor purchasing the land. Ground leases on this type of financing are generally shorter in term so that the residual value of the property is transferred to the ground lessor within the economic life of the property.

The decision as to whether land should be sold prior to or subordinate to financing is determined by the type of property, the variations in yield in the current market, and the percentage of the asset invested in the land. A good rule of thumb is that if land is 30 percent or more of the total asset, then the land sale should probably be accomplished prior to the leasehold, and if it is less than 30 percent, it should be done subordinate to the financing.

SALE AND INSTALLMENT REPURCHASE

Another method is the sale and installment repurchase technique used rather sparingly in the past), which has merit in certain types of transactions. This entails the sale of the real estate to an institutional investor by the developer for cost (or its value) and the repurchase through an installment sales contract of the property by the developer from the institutional investor. The advantages to the developer are 100 percent financing, since the sale is accomplished at the value, while the benefits to the lender are the ease of obtaining title in the event of default, since a deed to the property is not conveyed to the installment purchaser until a substantial amount of the payments have been made. The payments in such a transaction are calculated at the constant in the same manner as are the payments under the conventional first mortgage. The lender can book the transaction as real estate owned rather than as a mortgage and, in doing so, perhaps qualify the transaction as a legal investment. This type of financing is most generally accomplished on single-tenant properties occupied under long-term leases.

STANDBY LOAN

Another technique utilized by innovative mortgage bankers has been the use of standby financing. The standby loan is most commonly used where the borrower feels that rents, which will be achieved upon completion of the development, will be above current supportable rents and where there is a likelihood that interest rates will decline during the development period. A standby loan is nothing more than the use of the credit of the lender to allow an interim source of funds to lend money to the developer until permanent financing is accomplished. The standby lender charges a fee for the use of credit if the loan is funded.

One could logically ask, "Why should a borrower seek a standby loan rather than permanent financing?"

This question can be best answered by the following example:

An apartment building is to be constructed at a cost of $1,000,000. Present gross rental income is projected at $192,500. Assuming a 5 percent vacancy, the effective gross income would be $182,875. If we assume that operating expenses, real estate taxes, and replacement reserve would be 40 percent or $73,150, the effective gross income would be $109,725. If we assume a 1.33 debt service coverage and an 11% constant on the loan, the maximum loan would be $750,000 or 75 percent of the cost. Over the two-year development period, however, if rentals increased at an annual rate of 7 percent, the gross income at the end of the two-year period would be $220,400. The vacancy allowance would be $11,020, giving an effective gross income of $109,380. Expenses of 40 percent would be $83,750, for a net income available for debt service of $125,630. Assuming interest rates had fallen, and a loan constant of 10.5 was now available with the same debt service coverage, a $900,000 loan would be available (or an increase of 20 percent over the $750,000 figure). The borrower would achieve 90 percent financing rather than 75 percent on his cost of $1,000,000.

Typical costs of standby loans are between 1½ percent and 2 percent of the loan amount per year, so that at worst the standby commitment would cost the borrower $30,000, giving him a net increase in proceeds of $120,000. A word of caution, however: One should not utilize the standby technique unless the developer has both a probable increase in rentals and possible betterment of financing terms going for him. This method can be quick, convenient, and give flexibility to the borrower, who can choose the appropriate time to finance, gain the benefits of financing a successfully completed project, and still finance, as the holder of a bankable takeout, the construction and development period at favorable interim rates.

The advantages to the standby lender are immediate earnings in the form of fee increases and the building up of inventory for permanent financing on a successfully completed project.

The previous chapter on the constant indicates that, as a loan is amortized, the constant increases and more of the loan goes to principal and less to interest. Very often, particularly in net leased industrial properties, the appropriate time to refinance is in the later years of a medium-term lease (15 years). The unfortunate problem is that the rental is based upon a market 12 years past, and the borrower desires a loan based upon present value. A concept which has been utilized successfully in this type of transaction is to provide an interest-only period utilizing all of the cost of the property until the old lease runs out, at which time the borrower would release the property and the lender, for granting the interest-only provision, would participate in the additional rental achieved from the property. As an example: A one-story industrial building constructed 16 years ago contained 25,000 square feet of building, of which approximately 10 percent was office, on 75,000 square feet of land in an excellent industrial area. At the time the building was constructed, the rental was $34,078 per year ($1.36 per square foot) for a 20-year term with one 5-year renewal option at the same rental. If we assume the original loan was $300,000 at an 8.6 constant (6% for 20 years), that loan would be paid down to approximately $90,000, but would have payments of $25,800 per year, or a 28.67 constant. If we assume interest rates have increased to 10% and the tenant has nine years remaining on his lease, including options, the typical lender would probably want a mortgage term no longer than 20 years at current rates on an 11.59 constant. Assuming a 1.33 debt service coverage, this would allow for a loan of $220,000. Current market rentals for this property could be supported at $2.00 per square foot, or $50,000 per year, but the property is saddled with nine remaining years at this 16-year-old rental. If the lender were willing to take almost all of the existing rental at interest only for nine years, then amortize the loan over 20 additional years, and in consideration thereof was to receive 20 percent of the cash flow, that is, net income in excess of debt service during the last 20 years of the loan, the refinancing could be accomplished. A loan of $325,000 would require $32,500 of debt service for the first nine years, leaving a cash flow of $1,578 to the borrower. All of the debt service would be interest, which would be totally deductible by the borrower from income tax. At the end of nine years (where the property was leased for $50,000), the debt service would increase to $37,667, leaving a cash flow of $12,333. The lender would receive 20 percent of this or $2,467, which represents ¾ of 1% of additional interest yield on his $325,000 loan.

The borrower has achieved a loan commensurate with current market rentals, since if the building were leased initially at $50,000, the loan at a 1.33 coverage and an 11.59 constant would be $325,000. The borrower has converted a loan with heavy amortization to one of interest only, thereby favorably affecting his after-tax income, and the lender has put out money at the market rate with a substantial kicker coming to him when the property is released. Once again the innovative mortgage banker has satisfied borrower and lender motivations and earned a well-deserved fee.

These methods are several of the more commonly used "unusual financing techniques" and are not to be construed as being all-encompassing, nor are they meant to give the reader the impression that they fit every transaction. As previously stated, the number of financing methods is limited only by the creative minds of the individual loan officer and the willingness of the lender to accept new concepts which give the necessary rewards for the risks involved. The successful income-property loan officer and lender are constantly striving to find new methods to service both the borrower's needs and the needs of the lender to compete for a share of the investment dollar.

Chapter 17

Leasehold Financing

John H. Holler

The demand for leasehold mortgage financing has substantially increased in the past decade. This has been the result of a variety of circumstances, and the complete mortgage banker must be able to fully comprehend the intricacies of this form of financing. Considerable mystique and ignorance have surrounded leasehold financing over the years, whereas, actually, it is a simple device which may enable undeveloped land to be properly developed and create two streams of income to satisfy two divergent interests. Further, it can allow for the separation of a developed parcel of real estate to again create two forms of income for two owners (owner of the fee and owner of the leasehold).

Leasehold financing is necessary when a property has been separated into two distinct entities, the leased fee estate and the leasehold estate. The former is the land and the holder of this position is the lessor. The latter has the exclusive right to the use of the property and is the lessee. This separation is accomplished by a ground lease by which the lessor, in return for a contract rent and the right to regain the exclusive use of the property at the termination of the lease, gives to the lessee the exclusive use of the land for the term of the lease.

The separation of a parcel of real estate into two distinct entities may develop for a variety of reasons. An owner of land may have neither the desire nor the capability to develop the property, perhaps seeking only a steady stream of income (virtually an annuity) from the property via the ground rent, but this can only be obtained by the development of the property. An owner of a parcel of land that has appreciated considerably during ownership may be practically restricted from the outright sale of the property due to personal tax considerations. Also, through a ground lease, the fee owner enjoys not only a steady stream of income for the term of the lease, but obtains the residual value of any improvements placed on the leasehold at the expiration of the lease.

There are attractive considerations for the lessee-developer for entering into a long-term ground lease rather than the outright purchase of the specific parcel. First, the land may be high-priced, thereby requiring a considerable capital outlay by the developer. By leasing the property, the developer eliminates the need for the large capital outlay for the land alone.

Second, land is not a depreciable asset to the developer, while the improvements developed are subject to depreciation and the resultant tax advantages. The greatest disadvantage to the lessee-developer for many years was the problem of obtaining adequate mortgage financing for the leasehold estate. Many institutional lenders either refused to make leasehold mortgages or underwrote them on a very conservative loan amount basis. This situation has seen considerable change during the past 10 to 15 years due, to a large extent, to the rapidly rising values of commercial land both in the cities and surrounding suburbs and the resultant creation of many leasehold estates by astute land owners and developers.

Subordination

While this chapter is on leasehold financing, it should be noted that a developer, in initial negotiations to lease a parcel of land, will in most cases request that as a part of the ground lease the lessor agree to subordinate the land to any mortgage on the proposed leasehold improvements. When this is accomplished, the fee and leasehold are, in fact, two separate entities. From the lender's underwriting viewpoint, however, they are not separated. The lender, in the event of a foreclosure, would obtain title to both the land and leasehold improvements, thereby extinguishing the separation. A fee owner may consider subordination of the fee in return for a higher annual lease rental. This reflects the risk and compensates the fee owner for that risk by subordinating the fee. Further, the fee owner may restrict the amount of financing allowed as well as the term of financing in order to partially protect the position taken by making the fee and contract rent subordinate to the mortgage. Therefore, if the ground lease calls for subordination or requires the fee owner to ''join in'' the mortgage for lending purposes, it is a first mortgage fee loan for the lender. The ground rent is not deducted as an expense to the property, because the owner of the fee has, in essence, become part of the mortgagor entity by joining in the execution of the mortgage and pledging the fee and the ground rent subordinate to the mortgage. When the ground lease calls for subordination, the lender values both the fee and leasehold interests in arriving at the loan amount rather than just the value of the improvements.

The importance of a thorough review of the ground lease involved in the financing of a leasehold mortgage loan cannot be too highly stressed. Recognizing that the rights and the restrictions of the leasehold estate are fully covered within this document, the mortgage banker should review this instrument closely before seeking leasehold financing for the client. Without this personal review, the mortgage banker may have done considerable work for nothing, due to restrictions within the ground lease as to the rights granted to the lessee. Some of the major items to check and review in relation to the financing requested are as follows.

Term of Lease

There is nothing magical about the term; it is nothing more than a negotiated item between lessor and lessee. In most cases, the lessee will seek as long a term as can be obtained, say, 99 years. However, an astute lessor will possibly seek a shorter term in the hopes of obtaining, upon the lease expiration, the use of the improvements placed on the leasehold by the lessee while they still have some economic value. However, if the lessor is leasing land to a financially strong lessee and is seeking a long-term stream of income, then the lessor may readily agree to a long-term lease.

The lessee is most concerned with the term of the lease, not only to be able to enjoy rights during the full economic life of the proposed improvements, but also to have a term long enough to obtain leasehold financing of an adequate term. Most major lenders require that any leasehold loan be fully amortized within 80 percent of the firm ground lease term. Thus, if a developer is about to enter into a ground lease on a parcel expecting to erect a 10-story office building there, and cannot negotiate a lease longer than 30 years, the developer has possibly taken an uncompetitive market position. Assuming that the mortgage market for competitive buildings dictates a 30-year amortization term, but the subject leasehold developer is limited to a 24-year term due to the lender's 80 percent payout requirement, then the debt service would be more than ½ of 1% or 50 basis points above that of competitors. The difference would have to be reflected either in rents charged for office space or, if that were not possible, in a lower return to the developer.

The initial or firm term of the ground lease is all that lenders will recognize in calculating the term of their financing. Too often, a developer will represent to a mortgage banker possession of a 60-year ground lease, but when reviewed, it will be seen to be a 40-year lease with two 10-year renewals. Further, these renewals at the developer's option to exercise will have a ground rent to be determined at that future date based upon the then appraised value of the land at a rate based on the existing rate multiplied by some government index, for example, cost of living. Obviously, this means that only the initial term of the lease (40 years) can be recognized by the lender, since the lender has no idea what the amount of ground rent might be at that future date and, therefore, how much ground rent may be ahead of the mortgage at a future date.

One way in which renewal or extension options can be made acceptable to a lender is for the lessee to exercise the options prior to the placement of financing. This is satisfactory to most lenders so long as the ground rent is fixed. However, if the future ground rent is based on unknown factors involving future reappraisals, as previously discussed, this fails to accomplish the purpose intended.

Another acceptable manner of making a leasehold loan more attractive to the lender is for the lessee to deposit with the lender in an escrow account funds adequate to pay the ground rent during the term of the loan.

Lenders have also on occasion requested the direct assignment to them of any renewal options in the ground lease, thereby insuring that the leasehold will not terminate due to failure of the lessee to exercise renewals at the proper time.

Rental

Ground lease rentals in virtually all instances are net to the lessor. Specifically, this indicates that all real estate taxes and any special land assessments are the responsibility of the lessee.

The lease rental most preferable to the lessee will be a fixed amount during the initial term. If the lease has been recently negotiated, this contract rent should reflect the current market or economic rent for comparable land. However, if the lease is a few years old and there has been appreciation to the land during that period of time, then there would exist what is known as "excess value in the fee attributable to the leasehold estate" or a "leasehold interest in the fee." Therefore, when appraising the leasehold for mortgage financing purposes, this excess value is added to the value of the leasehold physical improvements to arrive at the total value of the leasehold. An example of this leasehold interest in fee would be as follows:

Ten-acre parcel with a value of $50,000 per acre = $500,000

Current economic rent indicates a 9 percent return or $45,000

Contract rent established by existing ground lease is $25,000
Therefore, the difference between the Economic Rent ($45,000) and the Contract Rent established by the ground lease ($25,000) is = $20,000

This difference of $20,000 is attributable to the leasehold because it is a benefit to the owner of the leasehold. This $20,000 is then capitalized into value at the appropriate rate and added to the value of the leasehold improvements to arrive at the total value of the leasehold.

Other forms of ground rent could be any or a combination of the following:

1 *Graduated or stepped-up rental:* At prescribed intervals during the lease, the rent is automatically increased.

2 *Reevaluation:* At specific times within the lease, the lessor has the right to call for a reevaluation appraisal of the fee. Thus, the rental could be adjusted upwards to reflect an increased value in the fee. Naturally, the lessee has the right to obtain an appraisal and a provision is made for arbitration if the two parties cannot agree—which is often the case. As can be seen, this could be a very risky situation for the lessee if a reappraisal could be required by the lessor early in the lease.

3 *Index adjustment:* On certain anniversary dates set forth in the lease, the rental is automatically increased or decreased based upon the application of a recognized cost index such as the Government's Cost of Living Index.

4 *Percentage:* A percentage ground lease is one where the lessor sets the ground rent based upon the income produced by the improvements of the leasehold estate. For example, a discount center or other retail operation is specified as the improvement in the lease and the ground rental is a percentage of the gross sales of the operation. Naturally, this can and probably will produce a widely varying ground rent over a number of years and, therefore, it would be virtually impossible for the lender to predetermine with any accuracy the risk in lending on this type of leasehold situation.

Condemnation

The condemnation clause in a ground lease often creates the most serious problems to the mortgagee of the leasehold. Most lenders require the lessor to recognize and allow that the leasehold mortgagee be entitled to the first proceeds of an award. Further, the ground lease must provide that in the event of partial condemnation, the lease may not be cancelled unless the leasehold mortgage has been fully satisfied, or in a partial taking, any award should be required to be applied to the restoration of the leasehold improvements. The obvious worry to the leasehold mortgagee is that the lessor of the fee in a superior position would obtain some part of the award and thereby leave either an insufficient balance of an award to restore the improvements or to fully satisfy the existing mortgage.

Right to Mortgage Leasehold

A ground lease should be reviewed carefully as to any restrictions the lessor may impose upon the lessee regarding the right to place financing on the leasehold. Despite the fact that the lessor's position is superior to the proposed leasehold mortgage, nevertheless, the lessor may place certain restrictive clauses in the ground lease for self-protection, which may adversely affect the lessee's ability to obtain proper financing.

Examples of these restrictions are as follows:

1 *Type of improvement:* The lessor may list in detail what physical improvements the lessee is allowed to build on the leasehold estate.

2 *Cost of improvement:* The lessee may be required to improve the property with an improvement at a stipulated minimum cost.

3 *Amount of financing:* The lessor may limit the total dollars of financing permissible. This most probably would be related to the costs of the proposed improvement.

4 *Sources of financing:* The lessor could recite the types of financing sources that would be acceptable and thereby limit the lessee as to where funds may be obtained.

Right of Lender to Cure Default

A provision giving leasehold lenders reasonable time to cure any possible default in the ground lease created by the lessee-mortgagor is mandatory. The lender must be assured of receiving notice of any default by the lessee and be given adequate time to cure the default.

Fire Insurance Award

Similar in nature to the problems of condemnation, the leasehold mortgagee's main concern is that any proceeds are used either to restore the leasehold improvements or to fully satisfy the then outstanding mortgage debt prior to any payment to the ground lessor.

Right to Assign or Sublet

A mortgagee will demand that the ground lessor allow the leasehold to be assigned or sublet, so that in the event that the lessee-mortgagor defaults, the mortgagee will be able to take over the leasehold estate and then assign or sell it without disturbing the then existing ground lease.

Subordination of Any Fee Mortgage

The ground lease should be unequivocal regarding the rights of the fee owner to mortgage the fee position. Also, that any fee mortgage is subordinate to the leasehold financing. Otherwise, the holder of the leasehold financing who is in a secondary position has the added risk of a third party (the fee mortgagee) stepping in through a default in the fee mortgage and terminating the leasehold mortgage. To avoid this conflict, if subordination of the fee mortgage is not agreeable, many leasehold lenders will accept a nondisturbance agreement from the fee mortgagee which recognizes the leasehold mortgagee's position and rights.

Purchase Option

This can be an option beneficial to lessee and leasehold mortgagee. The ground lease stipulates that at some future date or dates the lessee may purchase the fee position at a predetermined price. There are many ramifications to this covenant, but it is one that is often found in a ground lease.

Leasehold financing is actually secondary mortgage financing, since the ground lessor is entitled to ground rent prior to the payment of the leasehold debt service. Therefore, not only must the mortgage banker be fully aware of the terms of the ground lease when requesting a leasehold mortgage, but should be equally conversant of the market for leasehold mortgages. The mortgage banker is offering a lender a higher risk loan than that of a fee or first mortgage. Historically, a leasehold loan has commanded between ¼ and ½ percent more in interest rate than a comparable fee mortgage. Nevertheless, virtually all major lenders are willing to make leasehold loans, and the complete mortgage banker should be capable of understanding, analyzing, and placing leasehold loans.

Chapter 18

Sale-Purchase Leasebacks

Henry Rasmussen, Jr.

The sale of real property, with the buyer extending a leaseback to the seller, is becoming more commonplace than ever before. With time, the process becomes more and more sophisticated. New innovations are limited only by the creativity of the parties involved.

Generally speaking, the sale itself is not complicated. However, the terms of the leaseback challenge the investor. Some of the more common types of leases include:

1 Level rental, either long-term or month to month.
2 Graduated rental, increasing or decreasing in subsequent years of the lease.
3 Level rental for fixed periods of time with reappraisal at specified periods during the term of the lease, with rental being adjusted accordingly.
4 Straight percentage of sales volume.
5 Percentage of sales against a minimum rental provision.
6 Level rental adjusted periodically to a specific cost of living index.
7 Net lease, wherein lessee pays all expenses, including taxes, etc., or some modification as to payment of expenses.
8 Leaseback with earn-out provision.
9 Lease subordinated to financing.
10 Lease with repurchase option on a formularized basis.
11 Ground lease with provision for lessee to sublease improvements.
12 Sandwich lease.

13   Purchase of partial interest with leaseback provisions.
14   Land purchase-leaseback via second trust deed conversion.

Perhaps the best way to understand the sale-leaseback concept is by way of illustration. Therefore, the following examples will further demonstrate some of the various sale-leaseback concepts being used in the industry.

SIMPLE SALE-LEASEBACK ON LEVEL RENTAL BASIS

National oil firm (seller) sells property to an individual (buyer) and leases it back on a net basis for 20 years with two 5-year renewal options. Rent is usually determined by required return on investment by the buyer.

Modifications possible include:

1   Lease can be subordinated to loan.
2   Oil firm pays percentage of sales or so much per gallon against minimum rental.
3   Lessor pays taxes, but with ceiling. Oil company pays anything above.
4   Many other possibilities, but above represents the most common provisions.

GRADUATED OR STEP-UP LEASEBACK IN CONNECTION WITH A SALE

In this type of leaseback, the rent would be increased each year by, say, 2 percent (or an agreed-upon amount) per year for a given period of time, at which time the rent would be reviewed as it relates to value and perhaps adjusted accordingly, up or down. This method, by and large, has been replaced by the percentage lease or by an adjustment to the cost of living index. Often, both the "cost of living index" adjustment clause and the "percentage lease" clause provide for controls such as: The increased rental is not to exceed 2 percent per year or some specified amount per year.

SALE-LEASEBACK WITH REAPPRAISAL AT SPECIFIC TIME PERIODS

This form usually involves a long-term ground lease wherein the property is reappraised every 5, 10, 15, or 20 years and an adjusted rent based on the new value (either up or down). Practically speaking, the minimum rent is never below the original rental agreed upon. Arranging financing on a nonsubordinated ground lease of this type is difficult, as the lender is concerned with the rent obligation increasing indefinitely during the term of its loan. One way of getting around this provision is to have the lessor subordinate the entire lease or at least the increased rental provision in the event the lender acquires the property through foreclosure.

SALE-LEASEBACK WITH A STRAIGHT PERCENTAGE OF SALES VOLUME

Jenny's Department Store sells a property to an investor and leases it back for a fixed term (with options for renewal) and agrees to pay a given percentage of sales to lessor as rent (with no minimum rental provision).

SALE-LEASEBACK WITH PERCENTAGE OF SALES VOLUME AGAINST A FIXED MINIMUM RENT

Magic Foods sells property to an investor for $500,000 and leases it back for a fixed term with options for renewal and agrees to pay a minimum net rental of $48,000 per annum against 1½ percent of sales in excess of $3,200,000 up to $4,000,000 and 1 percent of all sales over $4,000,000.

Modifications include:

1 Lease could be subordinated to financing.
2 Any increase in property taxes over base year to be applied against excess percentage rent.
3 Right to repurchase after, say, 10 years, with the price being determined by capitalizing income including overages at an agreed upon rate.

SALE-LEASEBACK WITH LEVEL RENTAL PERIODICALLY ADJUSTED TO COST OF LIVING INDEX (OR SOME OTHER COMPARABLE INDEX)

A group of doctors sells its medical building for $725,000 to an investor and leases it back on a net basis for 20 years with a cost of living adjustment every five years. The level rental was based on a 9 percent net return to equity plus the loan payments. Every five years, this rental will be adjusted up or down in accordance with the Consumer Price Index. Normally, however, the original rent will be the floor and the rent will never decrease below this amount.

SALE-LEASEBACK ON A MODIFIED NET BASIS

The above examples all could have been on a net basis or a modified net basis such as the following:

Taxes:

1 Paid by lessor.
2 Paid by lessee.
3 Paid by lessor, however, with tax-stop. In the event taxes increase over the base year, the tax increase would be adjusted against percentage rents, excess rents via cost of living adjustment, or paid by the lessee.

Common area maintenance in the case of shopping centers:

1 Paid by lessee or lessees.
2 After first year of operation, dollar amount for common area established and any increase over this amount adjusted against percentage rent or excess rent.

Other expenses could be handled in a similar manner.

SALE-LEASEBACK WITH EARN-OUT PRIVILEGE

If the seller of a mobile home park and a buyer (investor) cannot agree on a price, the seller sells the property at a lower figure (buyer's offer) and leases it back from the buyer for a specified term with the provision that within this term, the seller could select, for example, any two consecutive years to establish the income and expenses. However, these two years would have to be selected no more than 90 days following the two-year period selected. In other words, the seller could not wait out the entire term of the lease and then go back to the two best years to establish the value. The average net income on equity for the two years would then be capitalized at some agreed-upon rate to establish value (probably the "going in" rate). The seller would then receive the difference between the original equity and the "now" established equity (if greater) within, say, 120 days. If the value is lower, generally no adjustment is made.

SALE-LEASEBACK WITH SALE BEING SUBORDINATED TO FINANCING (NEW OR EXISTING)

An apartment owner wants to sell the land underlying an existing project to a trust. The trust purchases the land and leases it back to the apartment owner for a specified period of time. In so doing, it automatically subordinates its position to the deed of trust or mortgage on the property. Although the ownership of the land is in a junior position to the existing financing, the return on the investment by way of lease payments with a kicker such as a percentage of the rents when they exceed the gross scheduled rents at the time the deal is consummated, plus the residual value of the improvements at the lease expiration, are considerations given when making such a purchase.

SALE-LEASEBACK WITH REPURCHASE OPTION

The example given above in Magic Foods' sale-leaseback with option to repurchase is one method used. Basically, the repurchase option is based on some predetermined formula. There are cases in which each party selects an appraiser and these appraisers select a third to arrive at a current fair market value at the time the option is exercised. These options can be at various specified times, such as the anniversary of the tenth, fifteenth, twentieth year, etc.

SALE-LEASEBACK WITH PROVISION TO SUBLEASE

As an example, a developer sells the land under a proposed large shopping center to an insurance company and leases it back for 99 years with the provision to sublet to tenants approved by the insurance company on condition that as additional rent, the insurance company would receive, for instance, 30 percent of the excess rents.

SANDWICH LEASE

Similar to the above case, an entrepreneur leases a large parcel of land with a view to developing a shopping center. After securing several key tenants and then subleasing the land and the business position to a developer at a much higher rental figure, the entrepreneur pockets the difference in rent each month with little or no invested capital. This position is known as the sandwich lessee-lessor, and the vehicle is known as a sandwich lease.

PURCHASE OF A PARTIAL INTEREST WITH A LEASEBACK PROVISION

An apartment owner wants to sell a project, but the price is higher than an investor wants to pay. Selling, for example, 50 percent of the project at the desired price and taking back a lease for a given period of time with a preferential cash flow of an agreed-upon percentage to equity, say, 10 percent to the purchaser of the 50 percent interest, accomplishes the desired purpose. The next, say, 12 percent would go to the seller and any income over that would be shared 50–50, or whatever basis is agreed upon. There could be many variations of this method of sale-leaseback. This preferential cash flow is particularly interesting to institutional or publicly held investors.

Example

1 Seller offers an apartment project for sale at a price of $2,000,000 with $500,000 cash down to a $1,500,000 loan. Seller further states that cash flow is $50,000 per year.

2 Buyer thinks price is high, so offers to buy 50 percent of the deal by paying $250,000 cash down for half interest providing 10 percent preferential cash flow on equity is received.

3 The seller agrees to the deal provided the next 12 percent of cash flow on the 50 percent interest (this assumes that in the future, rents will increase at a greater rate than expenses) is received. Any cash flow after $55,000 ($25,000 to buyer = 10 percent; $30,000 to seller = 12 percent) would be split 50–50.

4 The buyer of the 50 percent interest would receive 10 percent cash flow, even if the property developed only a 5 percent return on the assumed $500,000 equity.

CONVERTIBLE TRUST DEED

There is another innovation of financing which, while not new, has come to the fore with the advent of the REIT—the convertible second deed of trust or mortgage. In this case, the investor agrees to lend a specified amount of money, usually the discounted value of the land, for a short period of time, perhaps five years. The borrower has the right to pay this secondary financing prior to the five-year term on some agreed-upon basis. However, if it is not paid at the end of the term, the second is converted to a sale of the land with a leaseback provision for a predetermined period of time. There are many variations of this form of financing.

The preceding are samples of sale-leaseback situations found in the marketplace. We can be certain that as times change, so will the terms of sale-leasebacks. For any deal to be sound and lasting, it has to be fair both to the seller-lessee and to the buyer-lessor.

Chapter 19

Fee-Purchase-Leaseback Leasehold Loan

Glenn W. Justice

The subordinated land leaseback leasehold mortgage was developed and became popular two decades ago when segmental financing theory clearly demonstrated that each aspect of a real estate project has different values to differing parties, each with unique investment needs and goals. This theory, combined with the acceptance of the subordinated land leaseback by both the owner developer and institutional investor, resulted in a new and highly leverageable financing technique. While this hybrid is of recent vintage, it is based on the ground lease, whose origin in English law dates back to William the Conqueror. The ground lease is a long-term lease of a parcel of land with or without improvements that grants to the ground lessee a series of rights permitting him almost all the advantages of fee ownership. The lessee's rights in a ground lease are known as the leasehold estate, thus the name of this financial technique evolved.

The sale and leaseback form of real estate financing is the most innovative form of creative finance in the business to date. The sale and leaseback of commercial property allows a borrower to attain the full amount of dollars needed to make a project successful. The standard procedure used in a sale and leaseback transaction is for a lending institution to purchase property upon which is situated an existing or proposed income project such as an apartment complex, shopping center, office building, industrial park, or motel. The price that the financing entity pays for the land is determined by the actual cost paid, or an appraised value, and/or economic factor that has been placed on the land. Once the land has been purchased, the purchaser then leases the land back to the seller on a ground rent basis. This ground rent is determined by a percentage of the sale price. The following examples will show how the dollars are arranged and the economic valuation is derived.

The financing proposal would be similar to the following examples:

EXAMPLE 1:

Loan Summary
Purchase and Leaseback of Land

Proposal:	To purchase, upon completion of the proposed improvements, approximately 145,000 sq. ft. of land fronting on Z Avenue west between X & Y Streets.
Purchase price:	$725,000 or $5.00/sq. ft.
Fixed ground rent:	$72,500 per annum (10%) payable monthly.

Leasehold Loan on Improvements

Amount:	$3,065,000
Interest rate:	9%
Repayment:	$308,952/yr.
Term:	25 years
Constant:	10.08%

Now that we have all the salient facts, we can turn to the first example and see how our leasehold value is determined when only one lender does both the leasehold loan on the improvements, purchases the land, and leases it back to the borrower. We shall also see how the borrower's profit and loss statement is affected in the first year of operation of the project.

Economic Evaluation to Determine the Leasehold Loan Value

Source of income	
Rental income from office building	$850,000
Less: (5% vacancy & adjustment)	(42,500)
Effective Gross income	$807,500
Less: (40% of the effective gross income for operating expenses, reserves & real estate taxes)	(323,000)
Net income before reduction of annual ground rent, depreciation, debt service & personal taxes	$484,500
Less: Annual ground rent of 10%/yr. or	(72,500)
Net income before depreciation, debt service & personal taxes	$412,000

Underwriting Procedure

(A) Net income before depreciation, debt service, and personal taxes ÷ .1008 constant = economic value.
(B) Economic value × 75% = maximum leasehold loan
    Ex. 1: (A) $412,000 ÷ .1008 = $4,087,301
          (B) $4,087,301 × 75% = $3,065,000 (rounded) = Maximum Loan
    Debt service = $308,952 or $3,065,000 × .1008

Borrower's Profit & Loss Statement

Basic assumptions:

(1) The borrower is in 50% tax bracket and has no tax shelter other than that provided by this project.
(2) The net income before depreciation, debt service, and personal taxes remains the same in all examples used.
(3) The method of depreciation will be straight line with a 50-year life on the project, and the project's value shall always be the amount of the leasehold loan.

Profit & Loss Statement

Net income before depreciation, debt service & personal taxes	$412,000
Less: Annual debt service	(308,952)
Net income before depreciation & personal taxes	$103,048
Less: Depreciation ($3,065,000 ÷ 50)	(61,300)
Net income before personal taxes & ground rent write-off for tax purposes	$ 41,748
Less: Annual ground rent write-off	(72,500)
Net income or *Loss* before personal taxes	$(30,752)
No personal taxes due to loss in first year	-0-
Net profit or *Loss* shown on books	.$(30,752)
Add back: Depreciation	+61,300
and ground rent	+72,500
Actual net cash flow to borrower	$103,048

Summary

The borrower gains an additional $30,752 tax shelter the first year due to the use of the land sale and leaseback technique of financing. The borrower has received $3,790,000 from the leasehold loan and land sale and also receives $103,048 per year totally sheltered.

The second example will demonstrate the standard technique of arriving at a loan value without the use of a land sale and leaseback technique. We shall also see the result of this procedure in the borrower's profit and loss statement.

EXAMPLE 2:

Loan Summary

Proposal:	To make a first mortgage permanent loan on the proposed improvement, located at Z Avenue west between X & Y Streets.
Loan amount:	$3,600,000
Interest rate	9%
Repayment:	$362,880/yr.
Term:	25 years
Constant:	10.08%

Ecomonic Evaluation to Determine the Leasehold Loan

Source of income:	
Rental income from office building	$850,000
Less: (5% vacancy & adjustment)	(42,500)
Effective gross income	$807,500
Less: (40% of the effective gross income for operating expenses, reserve & real estate taxes)	323,000
Net income before depreciation, debt service & personal taxes	$484,500

Underwriting Procedure

(A) Net Income before depreciation, debt service & personal taxes ÷ .1008 constant = economic value
(B) Economic value × 75% = maximum loan
    Ex. 2: (A²) $484,500 ÷ .1008 constant = $4,806,547
            (B²) $4,806,547 × 75% = $3,600,000 (rounded) = maximum loan
    Debt service = $362,880 or $3,600,000 × .1008

Borrower's Profit & Loss Statement

Basic Assumptions:
Will remain the same as those listed in Example 1.

Profit & Loss Statement

	Year 1
Net income before depreciation, debt service & personal taxes	$484,500
Less: Annual debt service	(362,880)
Net income before depreciation & personal taxes	$121,620
Less: Depreciation ($3,600,000 ÷ 50)	(72,000)
Net income before personal taxes	$ 49,620
Less: Personal taxes (50% of taxable income)	(24,810)
Net profit or loss as shown on books	$ 24,810
Add back: Depreciation	+ 72,000
Actual net cash flow to borrower	$ 96,810

Summary

The borrower receives a $3,600,000 loan and a cash flow of $96,810, which is fully sheltered. However, the borrower had to pay the government a total of $24,810 for income from the project which was not sheltered and has received no additional shelter from the project.

EXAMPLE 3

The third example of the use of a land sale and leaseback form of financing deals with two different lending institutions being involved in the same deal. Contrary to Example 1, where the same lending institution bought the land and made the leasehold loan on the improvements, this example will illustrate the use of two different lenders, one making a leasehold loan and the other purchasing the land and then subordinating their lien to the leasehold loan. By subordinating the land loan, it is not necessary to deduct the annual ground rent from the net income before figuring a leasehold loan value, as is necessary when the same lender does the leasehold loan and purchases the land.

The major reason for this is that a lender doing both transactions must adjust income before determining a leasehold loan value, due to the fact that the land purchase ground rent drains from the income because the lender actually holds a superior lien on both the land and the improvements. If the project fails, the lender must have the loan adjusted down to reflect the total value of the project and thus be able to recover both loans out of the project.

If, as in Example 3, the land purchase is subordinated to the leasehold loan, the leasehold lender can use the entire net income on which to base the loan amount, because, if the project fails, this lien is superior to the land lien and the lender can collect all of the principal before the land purchaser can file a claim to recover equity. If the land purchase is not subordinated to the leasehold loan, the same procedure would be used to determine the leasehold loan amount as was used in Example 1.

Loan Summary
Purchase and Leaseback of Land

Proposal:	To purchase upon completion of the proposed improvement, approximately 145,000 sq. ft. of land fronting on Z Avenue west between X & Y Streets and to subordinate this land purchase to a leasehold loan on the improvements.
Purchase Price:	$725,000 or $5.00/sq. ft.
Fixed Ground Rent:	$72,500 per annum (10%) payable monthly.

Leasehold Loan on Improvements

Amount:	$3,600,000
Interest rate:	9%
Repayment:	$362,880/yr.
Term:	25 years
Constant:	10.08%

Economic Evaluation to Determine the Leasehold Loan Value

Source of income:	
Rental income from office building	$850,000
Less: (5% vacancy & adjustment)	(42,500)
Effective gross income	$807,500
Less (40% of effective gross income for operating expenses, reserves & real estate taxes)	(323,000)
Net income before *subordinated* ground rent deduction, depreciation, debt service & personal taxes	$484,500
Less: Annual Ground Rent 10%/yr. or	(72,500)
Net income before depreciation, debt service & personal taxes	$412,000

Underwriting Procedure

(A) Net income before subordinated ground rent deduction, depreciation, debt service and personal taxes ÷ .1008 constant = economic value.
(B) Economic value × 75% = maximum leasehold loan
    Ex. 3 (A) $484,500 ÷ .1008 = $4,806,547
        (B) $4,806,547 × 75% = $3,600,000 (rounded) = maximum loan
    Debt service = $362,880 or $3,600,000 × .1008

In this underwriting procedure, we were able to use net income without first deducting the annual ground rent because the land purchase was *subordinated* to the leasehold loan.

Borrower's Profit & Loss Statement

Basic Assumptions:
Will remain the same as those listed in Example 1.

Profit & Loss Statement

	Year 1
Net income before depreciation, debt service & personal taxes	$412,000
Less: Annual debt service	(362,880)
Net income before depreciation & personal taxes	$ 49,120
Less: Depreciation ($3,600,000 ÷ 50)	(72,000)
Net income before personal taxes & ground rent write-off for tax purposes	$(22,880)
Less: Annual ground rent write-off	$(72,500)
Net income or *Loss* before personal taxes	$(95,380)
Less: Personal taxes (no taxes due to loss)	-0-
Net income or loss	$(95,380)
Add back: Depreciation	+ 72,000
Annual ground rent	+ 72,500
Actual net cash flow to borrower	$ 49,120

Summary

The borrower receives a $3,600,000 leasehold loan, plus $725,000 for the land, making a total of $4,325,000 in loan and land sale funds, and also receives $49,120 cash flow completely sheltered. In addition to this shelter, the borrower receives $95,380 in tax shelter for other income.

In summary, it can be seen by the three examples the advantages of using a land sale and leaseback method of financing.

Example 1   The total funds to the borrower using the land sale and leaseback technique with only one lender doing loans totaled $3,893,048, including loan, land sale, and profit from the first year's operation, and also receives $30,752 of excess tax shelter.

Example 2   The total funds to the borrower not using the land sale and leaseback technique totaled $3,696,810, including loan and profit from the first year's operation. However, the borrower received no additional tax shelter, and had to pay $24,810 in taxes because of the lack of sufficient shelter to cover the income from the project.

Example 3   The total funds to the borrower using the land sale and leaseback technique with two separate lenders, one making the leasehold loan and the other purchasing the land totaled $4,374,120, including loan, land sale, and profit from the first year's operation. The borrower also receives $95,380 in excess tax shelter. Looking at the land sale and leaseback technique from the view of cost of the project to the borrower, we can depict other advantages. For example, the land sale technique may allow the borrower to attain the additional funds necessary to make the deal work.

These examples illustrate how the land sale and leaseback method of financing can open more doors of opportunity for both the borrower and lender.

Although some of the following may be repetitious, it is important to emphasize the tax advantages to both the "seller-lessee" and the "purchaser-lessor."

In real estate transactions, the selling price is usually geared to the value of the property with the rental payments arranged so that the lessee pays an amount sufficient to return the lessor's investment over the term of the lease together with interest on the investment. The interest factor in this type of leaseback is higher than in other conventional types of financing. Upon expiration of the original lease term, and after the purchaser has recouped his cost, the lease may be renewed at a reduced rental.

The sale-leaseback may be utilized in many situations as a practical device for the operation of real property. In addition to the economic and financial benefits to be derived from its use are the tax advantages it affords both the seller and the purchaser. It has also been successfully used as a means of splitting income by selling the property to related parties and immediately leasing back the property. But before entering upon such a transaction, the taxpayer would be well advised to be sure that there is an economic as well as a tax motivation.

It is the purpose of the following section to present some of these tax advantages while pointing out the many pitfalls and shortcomings of which the tax advisor must be cognizant.

TAX CONSIDERATION FOR SELLER

Before entering into a sale-leaseback of real property, the seller should compare the tax liability as owner of the fee with a projection of the tax due on operating the property as lessee. This computation should include the tax consequences of the sale itself as well as a comparison of the deduction for depreciation and interest with the deductions for rental payments.

Treatment of Gain or Loss on Sale

Where the property is sold to an unrelated party at its fair market value, the seller will be able to obtain tax advantages and still retain the use of the property on the leaseback. If the property has been held for more than six months, the gain will be treated as gain from the sale of a capital asset. If there is a loss on the sale, the loss would be deductible as an ordinary loss. The benefits to the seller are apparent where the tax basis of the asset is higher than its fair market value. The deduction of the loss may reduce the income tax liability or, in some situations, permit a refund of the prior year's taxes. This reduction or refund of taxes will add to the funds available from the proceeds of the sale. Where the selling price of the property is greater than its tax basis, funds will be obtained at favorable capital gain rates.

However, the benefits of capital gain and ordinary loss treatment, with the continued use of the property as a result of the leaseback, may not be available under various situations. Special tax problems may arise in the following circumstances, which should be considered.

1 Leaseback is for a period of thirty years or more.
2 Sale is to related parties.
3 Selling price is less than full value of property.
4 Lessee has option to repurchase property.
5 Sale-leaseback is not (as determined by tax authorities) a *bona fide* transaction.

Rental Payments vs. Depreciation and Interest Deductions

Upon the leaseback of the property, the seller, in computing taxable income, will be substituting a deduction for rental payments for depreciation and mortgage interest. A comparison should therefore be made to determine which results in greater allowances for tax purposes.

The rental payments, which are fully deductible, in effect include interest and a return of capital to the purchaser-lessor. By comparison, the property owner may deduct only the interest portion of the cost of carrying a mortgage, not the amounts paid for amortization. However, the owner is allowed a deduction for depreciation of the property. Where the depreciation is less than the amortization, a fee owner will be paying out funds without comparable tax benefits. By the use of the sale-leaseback, all of the rental payments become deductible.

Low Depreciation

Rental payments under a leaseback should indicate tax savings when compared to the low depreciation allowances available to a fee owner under certain circumstances. For example, where assets are almost fully depreciated, there obviously is little cost basis to depreciate in future years.

Where the ratio of land value to building value is high, depreciation will be relatively limited, as the land is not depreciable. On the other hand, rental payments are geared to the entire value of the property, including the land. Thus, by utilizing the sale-leaseback, the vendor-lessee obtains a deduction for the cost of using the land as well as the building.

Where the tax basis of real property is substantially less than its fair market value, a fee owner does not have the advantage of a depreciation allowance based on actual values. By disposing of the property, the fee owner not only realizes cash equal to the value of the property, but also obtains, on the leaseback, a deduction for rental payments related to the full value of the property.

Accelerated Depreciation

It may be advisable, in some cases, to purchase property and utilize one of the methods of accelerated depreciation. After maximum advantage has been taken of the depreciation deduction, consideration might then be given to the sale and leaseback of the property. The selling price at full value would result in capital gain, and rental payments based upon full value would be substituted for the reduced depreciation that would have been allowable had the property not been sold.

"Group Accounting" for Depreciation

It may often be possible to obtain higher depreciation in the early years by the use of group accounting for depreciable property. Under this method, assets similar in kind with approximately the same useful lives may be grouped together and depreciated separately from the building. For example, in depreciating real property it may be advisable to segregate assets with shorter lives such as asphalt parking areas, air conditioning, elevators, or other equipment. This group accounting method ordinarily results in a greater allowance for depreciation in the earlier years than the composite account method. Under the latter method, depreciation is computed annually on the average useful life of the entire building without segregating the assets which have shorter lives.

The use of the group accounting method combined with accelerated depreciation methods may result in very substantial depreciation allowances in the early years following acquisition or construction of the property. After these rapid methods have been exhausted, consideration might be given to a sale and leaseback of the property.

Interest on Mortgage

As previously noted, leaseback rental payments actually represent a return of investment coupled with an interest factor. In comparing the tax benefits, it must therefore be remembered that only the interest portion of mortgage carrying charges is deductible, whereas the entire rental payment under a leaseback represents a tax deduction. This becomes significant in view of the fact that most mortgages provide for constant payments, as a result of which the interest deduction is greatest in the early years. As the mortgage balance declines, the interest portion decreases and the amortization increases.

Therefore, after property has been held for a number of years, the sale-leaseback offers even greater advantages, because, at that time, the deductions from income for both depreciation and interest are substantially less than in the earlier years.

Type of Rental Payments

While depreciation allowances are spelled out in the tax law and regulations and interest deductions are measured by the terms of the mortgage, it may be possible to formulate various types of rental arrangements in a leaseback that will provide substantial tax benefits to the lessee.

The normal arrangement is one under which rent is paid equally over the period of the lease. However, it is possible to arrange a lease where the payments are larger in the early years and smaller in later years. Where the rental is reasonable in amount and the lease does not contain a clause permitting the lessee to repurchase the property, the rental payments should be deductible when paid.

However, if the payments are unreasonably high in the early years of the lease and drop sharply thereafter, a portion of the early rental, if considered to be excessive, might be regarded as the cost of acquiring a leasehold. If these payments were so treated, they would have to be capitalized and amortized over the life of the lease.

Another type of lease which may be attractive to a lessee is one that is geared to its sales or profits. This will permit rental payments geared to income and allow greater deductions in years in which the lessee is in higher tax brackets.

The sale-leaseback is beneficial to the buyer in that it offers a passive investment similar to a mortgage investment but yielding a higher rate of return. The typical sale-leaseback is a *net lease* arrangement which does not require the purchaser to operate the property. All expenses, including repairs and maintenance, are usually paid by the lessee. In addition, the purchase of real estate is a hedge against inflation, since property values have increased over the years as the value of the dollar declined. Even in the case of a long-term lease which has a fixed annual return, this inflationary hedge is significant. While the improvements on the property may be worthless at the expiration of the lease term, the land would still constitute a valuable asset at that time. On the other hand, a mortgage investment is in no way secure against decline in value due to inflationary pressures. Furthermore, the rate of interest is fixed for the long-term period of the mortgage.

The tax advantages of real estate investments lie in the fact that part of the return may be partially tax exempt. Usually, the depreciation allowance, especially in the early years, will be greater than the mortgage amortization. This will result in an annual cash return greater than the income subject to tax.

Tax-exempt Organizations

This sale-leaseback has been a particularly attractive investment for tax-exempt organizations, such as charitable organizations and pension and profit-sharing trusts.

Where the purchase is entirely for cash, all of the income is tax exempt. However, where the property is purchased subject to indebtedness, a portion of the income will be taxable. Generally, the portion of rents included in taxable income of the tax-exempt organization is the percentage of total rents received from business leases which is equal to the ratio of business lease indebtedness at the close of the taxable year to the adjusted basis of the property.

Where property is irrevocably conveyed to an independent purchaser in a bona fide arm's length sale and, as a part of the sales agreement, the seller retains the right to lease back the property for a period of less than 30 years upon payment of a reasonable rental, the loss on the sale is deductible. Inasmuch as the real property subject to the sale-leaseback is ordinarily used in the trade or business of the seller, the loss on the sale would be deductible against ordinary income.

Leasebacks for 30 Years or More

Various tax regulations provide that no loss is recognized where a taxpayer exchanges property used in trade or business, together with cash, for other property of like kind for the same use. It is further stated that for this purpose "a leasehold of a fee with 30 years or more to run" and "real estate" are property of like kind. Therefore, according to the regulations, if real estate is sold for less than its basis and, as part of the same transaction, leased back for a period of 30 years or more, the leasehold is an asset of "like kind," received by the seller, so that the loss on the sale is not recognized.

What is the effect of renewal options on leases with initial terms of less than 30 years which, if exercised, will bring the total life to more than 30 years? Under these circumstances, unless the lease has been renewed or the facts indicate with reasonable certainty that the lease will be renewed, the renewal periods should not be taken into account in determining whether the lease is for a term of 30 years or more. It is usually difficult to determine, at the time the property is sold and leased back, that the lease will be renewed with reasonable certainty at the expiration of a long-term lease such as 25 years. However, an example of such a situation might be a lease with an initial term of 25 years, with a renewal option for five years or more at greatly reduced rentals. This type of renewal clause might indicate that the tenant intended with reasonable certainty to renew the lease, thereby bringing the entire term of the lease to at least 30 years.

A loss on a sale between certain related parties is not deductible, even though the selling price is at full value, the property is leased back at a reasonable rental, and the sale is in every respect a bona fide transaction.

Treatment of Disallowed Loss

Where the loss is disallowed on a sale to a related party, the loss is not capitalized and amortized as in the case of an unrecognized loss in a "like kind" exchange. The loss under these circumstances may not be utilized until the property is subsequently sold. At that time the loss may be offset against gains realized on the disposition of the property only to the extent that the gain exceeds the loss. Thus, the loss may never result in an ordinary deduction but may only offset capital gains in later years when the property is sold.

Loss on Bargain Sale

As previously noted, if property is sold to an independent purchaser in an arm's length transaction, the loss will be recognized, providing there is no 30-year leaseback issue involved. If the selling price is less than the fair market value, will the loss be recognized? Where the seller does not have any option to repurchase the property, the sale is a completed transaction and the loss should therefore be deductible. However, where the property is sold for an amount substantially less than its full value and the seller may repossess the property either during the lease term or at the expiration of the lease, it may not qualify as a bona fide sale. Under these circumstances, the loss would not be deductible.

Under tax regulations, where property is sold by a corporation to its controlling stockholder, the loss on the sale will be disallowed as a sale between related parties. What is the effect, however, of such a sale on the stockholder? Where the property is sold at full value, there will be no dividend consequences to the stockholders, even though the property is simultaneously leased back to the corporation.

However, a sale by a corporation to its stockholders for less than full value would have the effect of a dividend distribution.

TREATMENT OF GAIN ON SALE

Where real property held for business purposes for more than six months is sold to an independent purchaser, any gain realized on the sale is taxable as a capital gain. Generally, the gain is the difference between the selling price and the basis of the property to the seller.

Gain on Sales with Long-term Leasebacks

Long-term leases often have a definite market value. This is especially true where the purchaser pays less than full value for the property and the rents payable under the lease are less than prevailing rates for leasing similar property. The seller, having disposed of the tangible real property, has received in return a valuable intangible asset in the leasehold. Therefore, gain to the seller might be measured not only by the cash received, but the consideration for the sale of the property would include the value of the leasehold. This leasehold value would then be amortized over the term of the lease.

The effect of this with respect to taxes is that the seller would report an immediate capital gain on the value of the leasehold even though its equivalent in cash at the time of sale was not received. This, however, would be offset by the saving of reduced rentals in future years. Thus, over the full term of the lease, the seller would be substituting deductions on leasehold amortization and low rentals for the higher rentals that would have to be paid had the rentals been at full value.

Measure of Gain

It is highly unlikely that an owner of real estate would sell property to an independent purchaser for a low price and lease it back under a short-term lease, even at a low rental. However, such an arrangement might occur under a long-term lease.

Where the leasehold is for 30 years or more, the gain on the exchange, according to tax regulations, would be limited to the cash received. This is based on the provision in the regulations that a leasehold of 30 years or more and real estate are property of "like kind," and therefore there was not a sale but an exchange of "like kind" property . The cash would be treated as premium received on the exchange.

To illustrate: Real property is sold for its basis of $75,000 and leased back for $7,000 per annum for a period of 99 years. A reasonable rental is determined to be substantially higher than $7,000, and it is established that the leasehold has a fair value of $100,000.

If the leasehold had no value, the seller would have no gain or loss on the sale, ($75,000 basis less $75,000 cash received). However, under the regulations, the seller has a taxable gain of $75,000, computed as follows:

Value of leasehold received by tenant	$100,000
Cash received	75,000
Total	$175,000
Less: Basis of property transferred	75,000
Gain	$100,000
Gain recognized to extent of cash received	$ 75,000

The $75,000 would be the basis of the leasehold acquired and could be amortized over the term of the lease. Under ordinary circumstances this would not be advantageous, since the seller would be required to pay an immediate capital gain tax on $75,000 after having received only the basis for the real estate. To some extent this would be offset by the amortization of the leasehold over the 99-year term.

There are circumstances, however, where it might be advantageous to establish that the leasehold received was a valuable asset and therefore the leasehold plus cash was exchanged for real estate. For example, the seller may have an unused capital loss carryover which otherwise might not be utilized. By setting up the leasehold as part consideration for the sale, a gain could be created which would not result in any tax because of the capital loss carryover. However, in subsequent years, the lessee could deduct leasehold amortization against ordinary income.

Under a principle established by the *Jordan Marsh Company* case, the treatment of gain on the sale as illustrated above would not apply if the property is sold for full value and leased back under a long-term lease at a fair and reasonable rental. The sale would be considered a completed transaction and the leaseback would have no value. An acquisition of a lease with an assumption of a long-term lease obligation at a fair rental could not be considered an asset.

Gains on Sales of Depreciable Property Between Certain Related Parties

Where depreciable property is the subject of a sale and leaseback between certain related parties, any gain on the sale is taxable as ordinary income under Section 1239 of the Code. Sales between the following parties are affected: husband and wife; a corporation and an individual, where the individual, his spouse, minor children or grandchildren own 80 percent of the stock of the corporation; a partnership and an 80 percent partner; or, two partnerships controlled by persons owning 80 percent of both partnerships.

A literal interpretation of the statute would indicate that this provision would not apply to the sale by a partnership to a corporation whose stock is owned by the partners, where the partners are not related in the manner indicated above. Therefore, though there has been no legal opinion issued, it would appear that a partnership of two brothers could sell property to a corporation owned by the two brothers, as neither brother, nor brother's wife or minor lineal descendant would own 80 percent of the stock of the corporation. However, the Internal Revenue Service has yet to rule on this point.

DEDUCTIBILITY OF RENTAL PAYMENTS

The Code provides that rentals or other payments made for the continued use or possession of property used in the taxpayer's trade or business are deductible for tax purposes providing there is no equity in the property. There is no provision in the Code limiting the deductions to a reasonable allowance as in the case of salary or compensation payments. However, special problems do arise in the case of sale-leasebacks, as the Commissioner may contest the rental payments as representing something other than rent.

Where the leaseback arrangement contains a clause which permits the lessee to repurchase the property by paying a small amount at the expiration of the lease term, the purchase may be considered a mortgage loan and the rentals considered interest or interest and amortization. In a case dealing with a sale-leaseback, the Supreme Court held that the administrators of taxation are concerned with "substance and realities." Here the property was conveyed to a bank, as trustee, with the seller having the option to repurchase the property. The Court held that the deed was, in effect, security for a loan on the property. The rent stipulated in the leaseback was intended to be interest and the depreciation was intended to be an amortization fund designed to pay off the loan within a fixed period. The Court concluded that there was no sale of the property but rather a mortgage loan.

It is essential, if rental payments are to be deductible as such, that the lease arrangement not appear to create any equity in the property for the tenant. As previously indicated, rentals are deductible only if the taxpayer has no equity in the property. Thus, a lease arrangement may be held to be no more than an installment purchase of property. This would be indicated if the lessee is permitted to repurchase the property for a nominal consideration upon expiration of the lease, or if the repurchase option permits all or a portion of the rentals to be specifically applied to the selling price of the property. Abnormally large rentals would similarly indicate that the payments are not for the current use of property, and create the presumption that portions of such rentals are really partial payments under the repurchase plan.

If rental payments are to be deductible where there is a recapture clause, it is necessary to establish that the rentals are fair and reasonable; that the repurchase price is at full value at the time of resale; that the rentals are not to be applied against the repurchase price; that the original sale is a bona fide sale; and that the rentals paid are not in effect payments for interest and amortization.

Where property is sold to an employee's pension or profit-sharing trust at a price less than its fair market value, the difference between the selling price and the fair market value is a deductible contribution. The Tax Court has held that such a sale, even though coupled with a leaseback and an option to repurchase, was a transfer of an asset which was immediately and irrevocably beneficial to the trust. The sale at less than full value was a contribution of property, which represented a payment in kind rather than cash. The transaction thus was within the intent of the Code.

Similarly, property sold to a charitable organization at less than fair market value accompanied by a donative intent gives rise to a charitable deduction. However, it is necessary to prove both donative intent and the fact that the fair market value actually exceeds the sale price.

This may be especially helpful where the tax-exempt organization does not have sufficient cash to purchase the property. If it borrows the funds or purchases the property with a purchase money mortgage, its income would be subject to the tax on unrelated business income.

Another example is a property owner who may be required to make a contribution to a pension or profit-sharing trust or wish to make a contribution to a charitable foundation, but does not have adequate funds. The sale at less than full value will accomplish the objectives of providing liquid funds to the seller to the extent of the cash received and give rise to a tax deduction for the difference between the selling price and the fair market value. This in turn will provide additional funds resulting from the tax saved by the deduction. The subsequent leaseback will permit tax deductions for the rental payments, which in turn will be tax exempt to the lessor.

Grounds for Denial of Tax Exemption

Care should be exercised on sales to a tax-exempt organization lest the organization lose its tax-exempt status. If a creator, member, or substantial contributor of a tax-exempt organization sells property to the organization for more than its fair market value or rents property from the organization for an unreasonably low rental, these acts would be considered prohibited transactions. Any such transaction could permit the tax authorities to deny the organization exemption from taxes. It is therefore essential in dealing with a controlled tax-exempt organization to sell the property at a price not more than the fair market value and rent back the property at a reasonable rental.

CONCLUSION

The sale-leaseback is an effective and recognized method of supplying liquid funds to owners of real property and yet permit them to retain the continued use of the property. Whether to use it in lieu of conventional mortgage financing must be determined in each situation. While there are many tax benefits to be derived from the use of the sale-leaseback, the tax advisor must be aware of the various pitfalls and drawbacks for property tax planning.

Chapter 20

Secondary Financing

Claude E. Pope

Secondary real estate financing continues to assume an expanding role in the realm of income-property finance. Junior mortgages have long been a source of funds to income-property owners and other forms of secondary finance have more recently gained popularity. Real estate lenders and equity investors have shown an increasing interest in financing techniques such as piggyback mortgage loans, wraparound loans, and land sale-leasebacks, all of which have one significant feature in common: the lender's (or in the case of the land sale-leaseback, the purchaser's) claim against the security is subordinated to the claim of some other lender. As a consequence of this distinctive feature, secondary financing techniques must be given special attention.

This chapter explores the principles of secondary real estate finance. The first of three sections identifies the various situations which are generally suited for the use of secondary finance methods. Various sources of funds in the secondary finance market are discussed in the following section, and the chapter is concluded with an analysis of each of the more frequently used secondary finance techniques.

THE USE OF SECONDARY FINANCING TECHNIQUES

In the interest of providing background for the following discussions of secondary real estate finance, this section identifies in general the various situations suited to the use of secondary financing methods. Such situations are as follows:

1   Secondary financing is probably most often used as a means of reducing the equity requirement associated with real estate investment. The high potential yields associated with leveraging, the natural aversion to exposing equity capital, and, in some cases, a shortage of equity capital motivate real estate investors to attempt to minimize their equity investment by the use of secondary financing methods.

2   For some of the reasons mentioned above, secondary financing is common in land acquisitions. Developers and investors typically finance raw land acquisitions by means of purchase money mortgages so that frequently traded parcels may ultimately be financed by two or more mortgages of varying priorities. In financing the acquisition of land for a proposed development, a developer might, on the other hand, structure a sale-leaseback of the fee interest with subordination of the fee to subsequent development and construction financing. This device is particularly attractive to developers for various reasons discussed in the following section.

3   In situations where existing first mortgages carry high prepayment penalties, or prohibit prepayment, junior mortgages provide a means by which the investments may be partially refinanced without disturbing the first mortgage. Similarly, where it is desirable to retain an existing first mortgage because of its favorable interest rate or other terms, junior mortgages may be utilized to partially refinance a project while maintaining the favorable first mortgage.

4   Where permanent loan commitments for proposed projects provide for a partial holdback of funding until a specified rent roll is achieved or some other condition is satisfied, construction lenders will usually require that the potential gap created by the holdback provision be covered by a commitment for a second mortgage. This is done so that in the event the permanent lender's rent roll or other requirement is not satisfied, the funding of the second mortgage in combination with the reduced permanent loan funding will be sufficient to repay the construction loan. The second mortgage commitment in this case is frequently called a *gap commitment*.

5   Secondary financing is also useful as a means of funding capital improvements to income property or extracting cash from an investment for other purposes. Increasing property values in an inflationary economy and amortization of existing first mortgages facilitate the structuring of second mortgages for these purposes.

SOURCES OF FUNDS FOR SECONDARY FINANCING

As a consequence of the inherent inferiority of a junior lien position, the volume of funds committed on junior liens is substantially less than first mortgage loan volume. Virtually all institutional mortgage lenders are restricted in the volume of their junior lien investment activity by either internal policy or by federal and/or state regulations. This section identifies the various participants in the market for secondary financing and the extent to which each is involved.

During the early 1970s, mortgage investment trusts were probably the most active participants in the field of secondary financing of income property. The high yields and relatively short terms associated with secondary income-property financing induced many of the trusts to make extensive commitments in secondary financings. The extent to which mortgage investment trusts will participate in secondary financing in the future is dependent upon the ability of that industry to recover from the problems experienced in the mid-1970s and the ability and willingness of the trusts to renew their participation in secondary financings.

Life insurance companies provide an additional source of funds for secondary real estate finance, although state regulations limit their activity in this area. The life companies, for the most part, are limited to first lien investments, but are able to devote a certain percentage of total assets to riskier, higher yielding investments through *basket* provisions. Investments secured by subordinated fee interests and other junior real estate interests constitute a substantial proportion of all life company basket investments.

Mutual savings banks and commercial banks are, for all practical purposes, inactive in secondary real estate financing. Both of these institutional lenders are prohibited from making junior lien investments except under two specific circumstances. Mutual savings banks and commercial banks are permitted to make second mortgage loans on properties for which they also hold the first mortgage, provided there is no intervening lien and the aggregate of the amounts due on the two mortgages does not exceed 90 percent of the property value.

In addition, banks may lend funds on second liens by the *incidental collateral provision*, which stipulates that a bank may take *any* real estate lien as incidental collateral to additional authorized securities.

Individual real estate investors provide a substantial source of funds for secondary financing by way of purchase money mortgages and land sale-leaseback transactions as discussed previously.

SECONDARY FINANCING TECHNIQUES

Junior Mortgages

Junior mortgages are probably the most common method of secondary financing. The junior mortgage is a device which allows a borrower to raise capital in addition to first mortgage funds by pledging a subordinate mortgage lien as security for the additional funds. The priority of mortgage liens on a specific property is generally established by the date on which the liens are recorded, such that the first lien recorded has first priority, the second lien recorded has second priority, etc. This order of priority may be reversed for any two liens by an appropriate *subordination clause* added to the superior lien.

No matter how a borrower may employ the proceeds from junior mortgages, these mortgages inevitably have the effect of increasing the amount of *leverage* on a given real estate project. Lenders therefore tend to view junior mortgages with caution. To begin with, the lender on a junior mortgage assumes a greater risk of capital loss than any senior mortgagee as a consequence of the subordinate lien position. In addition, the use of a junior mortgage increases the total debt service obligation of the project, and the subsequent decrease in the margin by which total debt service is covered by project cash flows results in an increased possibility of default.

Lenders recognize these inherent risks of second mortgage financing and have taken various precautionary steps to minimize the risk associated with second mortgages. For example, lenders tend to limit the terms of second mortgages on income properties to 15 years or less in order to limit the duration of their risk exposure.

Furthermore, it is a common practice for lenders on subordinated mortgage liens to retain some control over future refinancing of the first position that would weaken the position of the second mortgage.

Even when refinancing of the first position is permitted, the subordination clause typically stipulates that the sum of the new first mortgage loan amount and the balance on the second mortgage may not exceed a specified amount—usually 80 to 90 percent of the property value. A similar requirement may be included to limit the amount of debt service payable on a refinanced first mortgage. The object of these provisions, of course, is to protect the second mortgagee from the risk of potential overfinancing on the first mortgage.

In addition to the above provisions, second mortgagees generally stipulate that the mortgagor may alter neither the terms and conditions of the first mortgage nor the terms and conditions of leases without the permission of the junior mortgagee.

All second mortgage agreements should provide that default on the first mortgage constitutes default on the second as well. This clause together with a provision for the second mortgagee's right to cure defaults on the first mortgage gives the second mortgagee greater flexibility in coping with a default situation.

Wraparound Loans

Wraparound loans are actually junior mortgages, but due to the special nature of the wraparound loan, it is discussed separately.

By definition, a wraparound loan is a junior mortgage loan, the principal amount of which is the sum of the outstanding balance on the prior mortgage(s) plus the amount actually disbursed on the wraparound loan. The wraparound concept is best explained by an example.

Suppose an investor owns an apartment property financed by a 6% first mortgage loan with a current balance of $100,000 and a remaining term of 10 years. He needs additional financing without disturbing favorable first mortgage terms. To accomplish this, he might obtain $50,000 additional financing by arranging a $150,000 wraparound loan on a 15-year term. Note that the stated amount of the wraparound loan is the sum of the outstanding balance of the first and the initial loan amount of the second. The second mortgage, in effect, wraps around the first.

The mechanics of a wraparound loan entail some unusual features. For instance, the wraparound lender collects the debt service due on the wraparound loan and, from the proceeds, remits to the first mortgagee the debt service due on the first mortgage. The remainder of the debt service is retained by the wraparound lender. Again, consider the above example with the additional provision that the rate on the wraparound loan is 9%. The debt service due on the first mortgage is $13,587 per year and the wraparound loan debt service is $18,609. The wraparound lender collects $18,609 annually from the borrower and forwards $13,587 to the first mortgagee, retaining the remainder of $5,022. The table on the following page illustrates the method of accounting used in the example.

Columns 1–4 represent the amortization table for the first mortgage as it is paid out over the last 10 years of its term. Column 5 indicates the net investment of the wraparound lender, initially $50,000 (the actual cash disbursement under the

Illustration of Wraparound Loan Accounting

| | First Mortgage | | | | Wraparound Mortgage | | | | | | | | |
| | (1) | (2) | (3) | (4) | (5) | (6) | (7) | (8) | (9) | (10) | (11) | (12) | (13) |
End of year	Out-standing balance	Annual debt service	Interest earned	Amortiza-tion payment	Net in-vestment (5)+(11)	Total out-standing balance	Total debt service	Total interest	Interest earned (8)−(3)	Debt service retained (7)−(2)	Deferred interest (9)−(10)	Amortiza-tion payment	Yield (9)÷(5)
1	$100,000	$13,587	$6,000	$ 7,587	$50,000	$150,000	$18,609	$13,500	$7,500	$ 5,022	$2,478	…	$15.00%
2	92,413	13,587	5,545	8,042	52,478	144,891	18,609	13,041	7,495	5,022	2,474	…	14.28%
3	84,371	13,587	5,062	8,525	54,952	139,323	18,609	12,539	7,477	5,022	3,455	…	13.61%
4	75,846	13,587	4,551	9,036	57,407	133,253	18,609	11,993	7,442	5,022	3,422	…	12.96%
5	66,810	13,587	4,009	9,578	59,828	126,638	18,609	11,398	7,389	5,022	2,367	…	12.35%
6	57,232	13,587	3,434	10,153	62,195	119,427	18,609	10,748	7,314	5,022	2,292	…	11.76%
7	47,079	13,587	2,825	10,762	64,487	111,566	18,609	10,042	7,217	5,022	3,195	…	11.19%
8	36,317	13,587	2,179	11,408	66,682	102,999	18,609	9,270	7,091	5,022	3,069	…	10.64%
9	24,909	13,587	1,495	12,092	68,751	93,660	18,609	8,429	6,934	5,022	1,912	…	10.09%
10	12,816	13,587	771	12,816	70,663	83,479	18,609	7,513	6,742	5,022	1,720	…	9.54%
11			…	…	72,383	72,383	18,609	6,514	6,514	18,609	…	12,095	9.00%
12			…	…	60,288	60,288	18,609	5,426	5,426	18,609		13,183	9.00%
13			…	…	47,106	47,106	18,609	4,240	4,240	18,609		14,369	9.00%
14			…	…	32,736	32,736	18,609	2,946	2,946	18,609		15,663	9.00%
15			…	…	17,073	17,073	18,609	1,536	1,635	18,609		17,073	9.00%

wraparound loan). The balance of the principal outstanding during year 1 is $150,000, as shown on Column 6. Column 7 illustrates the annual debt service due on the wraparound loan, while Column 8 shows the amount of interest due on the balance of the wraparound (Column 6).

Column 9 indicates the amount of interest earned by the wraparound lender. This amount is simply the difference between the interest due on the wraparound balance and the interest due on the first mortgage (Column 3). In year 1, the wraparound lender earns $7,500 in interest ($13,500−$6,000). However, as indicated in Column 10, the wraparound lender retains only $5,022 per year for the duration of the first mortgage. Thus, at the end of the first year, the wraparound lender can only retain $5,022 in interest and must defer the remaining portion of the interest due ($2,478 as shown in Column 11) by adding that amount to his net investment in the loan (Column 5).

As a result of the deferment of part of the first year's interest payment, the wraparound lender's net investment in the second year is $52,478 ($50,000 initial disbursement plus $2,478 interest earned but deferred the previous year). Each year of the 10-year duration of the first mortgage the amount of interest earned exceeds the amount of debt service retained, resulting in an annual deferment of interest and a continual increase in the wraparound lender's net investment.

At the end of the tenth year the first mortgage is completely paid off. Consequently, the wraparound lender retains the full $18,609 annual debt service payable on the wraparound loan. This annual debt service is sufficient to completely pay off the wraparound lender's current $72,379 net investment, with interest at 9% over the remaining five years of the loan term.

It is critical to note that although the stated interest rate on the wraparound loan is 9% in the example, the wraparound lender's yield is substantially higher than 9 percent. In year 1 he earns $7,500 in interest on a net investment of $50,000, for a yield of 15 percent. This yield differential is the result of the effective leverage position of the wraparound lender. He collects 9% on the entire wraparound loan balance while he remits to the first mortgagee only 6% interest on the balance of the first mortgage. In essence, the wraparound lender in the example earns 9% on his net investment plus 3% (9%−6%) on the balance of the first mortgage. It follows that the greater the balance outstanding on the first mortgage, the greater will be the wraparound lender's yield (the 3% differential will be applied to a larger base). Column 13 in the table illustrates this concept in that the wraparound lender's yield (interest earned/net investment) decreases as the first mortgage balance decreases. In years 11–15, the leverage position is lost and the face rate becomes synonymous to the wraparound lender's yield. However, over the 15-year term, the unweighted arithmetic mean rate of return to the wraparound lender is 11.09 percent, significantly above the face rate of the wraparound loan. Because the rate of return is higher early in the life of the loan, the actual yield on a discounted cash flow basis should be even greater than 11.09 percent.

In the preceding example, the term of the wraparound loan exceeds the remaining term of the first mortgage. In such cases, debt service based upon the constant for the wraparound loan terms will allow for the repayment of both the first mortgage and wraparound loan over their respective terms. On the other hand, if the wraparound loan term should be less than the remaining term of the first mortgage, use of the constant for the wraparound loan terms will result in early repayment of the wraparound loan. In such cases, the periodic debt service to repay both loans on schedule must be determined without the benefit of mortgage constant tables.

Wraparound loans may be used in any situation suitable for junior mortgage financing. As discussed in the preceding section, such situations might include the acquisition of additional capital in the initial financing package or at some later stage in the life of a project. Wraparounds, as other junior mortgages, allow the borrower to refinance the investment without disturbing the existing financial structure.

Despite the considerable amount of publicity devoted to wraparound financing, the wraparound loan, as compared to ordinary junior mortgage financing, offers little or no net advantage over conventional second mortgage financing to either the borrower or the lender. The one aspect of wraparound loans that might prove advantageous to the lender is the control exercised by the wraparound lender over the remittance of debt service to the first mortgagee. The wraparound lender might gain additional flexibility in the event of default through his closer contact with the borrower and first mortgagee.

Piggyback Loans

The piggyback loan is another income-property financing technique. In essence, it is a combination first and second mortgage loan, secured by a single mortgage lien. By agreement evidenced in the mortgage documents, the first mortgage lender is given first claim on the security, while the second lender takes a subordinate claim.

The distinguishing feature of piggyback loans is that the second mortgagee receives the amortization payments on the full loan amount until the principal is completely amortized. From that point forward in the life of the loan, only the first mortgagee remains and, of course, retains the full periodic debt service to amortize its position. The following example illustrates how the piggyback concept might be employed.

Suppose a life insurance company is presented with a request for a mortgage loan at a 90 percent loan-to-value ratio. Since life companies are generally prohibited from lending in excess of 75 percent of property value, the lender may be forced to reject the loan request. However, assuming the loan security is satisfactory, the life company may use the piggyback loan conception in conjunction with another lender in order to make the loan.

Let's assume the property is valued at $1,000,000 and the requested loan amount is $900,000 for a 10-year term at 9% interest. It follows that the life company's participation in the financing package is $750,000 (75 percent of value) and the second lender's participation is $150,000. The table on the following page illustrates the payment schedule of the loan.

Notice that the second lender's interest is completely paid off by the end of the third year, at which time the first lender begins to amortize its position. Both lenders receive a yield of 9 percent on the outstanding balance of their respective investments.

In the above example, the interest earned on both the first and second positions is 9 percent. It is by no means a necessary feature of piggyback loans that both lenders earn the same rate of interest. In fact, due to the subordinate position of the second lender, it is likely that most piggyback loans will carry a higher interest rate on the second position than on the first.

Illustration of Piggyback Loan Accounting

End of year	Piggyback Loan				Second position			First position		
	Outstanding balance	Interest earned	Debt service	Amortization payment	Outstanding balance	Interest earned	Amortization payment	Outstanding balance	Interest earned	Amortization payment
1	$900,000	$81,000	$140,220	$ 59,220	$150,000	$13,500	$59,220	$750,000	$67,500	...
2	840,780	75,670	140,220	64,550	90,780	8,170	64,550	750,000	67,500	...
3	776,230	69,860	140,220	70,360	26,230	2,360	26,230	750,000	67,500	44,130
4	705,870	63,528	140,220	76,692	...	...	...	705,870	63,528	76,692
5	629,178	56,626	140,220	83,594	...	...	...	629,178	56,626	83,594
6	545,584	49,102	140,220	91,117	...	...	...	545,584	49,102	91,117
7	454,466	40,902	140,220	99,318	...	...	...	454,466	40,902	99,318
8	355,148	31,963	140,220	108,257	...	...	...	355,148	31,963	108,257
9	246,891	22,220	140,220	118,000	...	...	...	246,891	22,220	118,000
10	128,891	11,600	140,220	128,890	...	...	...	128,891	11,600	128,891

Like the wraparound loan, the piggyback loan offers little advantage over an ordinary first and second mortgage combination. Identical terms and yields may be structured by either financing technique. The only possible advantage attributable to the piggyback arrangement is that the single lien concept might prevent legal snarls in the event of default and foreclosure on the loan. On the other hand, it should be noted that a poorly written piggyback loan may well create additional legal problems in such a situation.

Land Sale-Leasebacks

The final secondary financing technique to be explored is the land sale-leaseback. It is important to note at the outset that this financing device involves a fee interest—actual ownership—rather than a creditor interest as with the previously discussed financing methods.

Land sale-leasebacks involve the concept of *split fee* financing, whereby the fee title to property is split between land and improvements. This concept has gained wide popularity in recent years by virtue of its ability to provide real estate developers with relatively high yields and to accommodate lower equity requirements than traditional mortgage financing.

In typical land sale-leasebacks, the financing institution purchases the land for a proposed commercial development and then leases the land back to the developer. The developer/lessee retains the right to use the land and build upon it, and does so without tying up capital purchasing the land. With the land sale-leaseback, the developer obtains 100 percent financing of the land rather than the usual 75 percent available through mortgaging the land.

Note that the developer may retain title to all improvements to the land. Thus, the developer may retain the benefit of all depreciation write-offs on the improvements and enjoy the benefit of any appreciation in the value of the improvements. In addition, the developer enjoys the privilege of deducting the full land rent expense from taxable income.

Giving up ownership of the land in no way impairs the ability of the developer to finance improvements to the land as long as the land fee is subordinated to the financing for the improvements. Subordination of the land fee in effect gives the mortgagee on the leasehold first claim against the total project, including land and improvements. In like manner, subordination of the land fee places the land owner/lessor in a position much like a second mortgagee. In the event of default on the leasehold mortgage, the land owner/lessor has only a subordinate claim upon the land and consequently must be prepared to pay off the leasehold mortgagee or take some other measure to protect its investment.

Compensation for the subordinated fee purchaser/lessor is typically computed in terms of a percentage yield on the purchase price of the land. In recent years, this fixed yield has generally been supplemented by a participation in income generated by the improvements. Such participation provides the lessor with a built-in inflation hedge and gives the added benefit from the future success of the overall development. As a condition in some land purchase-leasebacks, the lessor is given the additional benefit of taking a share of refinancing proceeds and/or eventual resale of the improvements.

Chapter 21

Contingent Interest

David H. Buchanan, Jr.

Contingent interest is any increase in return to the lender over the fixed interest rate called for in the mortgage documents. This type of increased return to the lender is most often contingent upon changes in the income of the project being financed. Lenders feel this technique protects them from being ''locked in'' to an artificially low interest rate in inflationary times. Furthermore, this technique provides lenders with an opportunity to share in increasing income from a project to which they provide the bulk of the financing and, therefore, have the greatest exposure in absolute dollar amounts while receiving a low, fixed return at the same time. On the other hand, borrowers feel that their equity contribution limits the vulnerability of the lender's position and, therefore, the lender is not entitled to contingent interest. This emphasizes the fact that contingent interest provisions create a quasi-equity benefit for the debt position. For competitive reasons, most lenders are unable to obtain contingent interest agreements during periods of plentiful money supply. The cyclical nature of our economy dictates periodic shortages of long-term capital funds. However, there are, at times, certain indications that in the long run our economy will be lacking in long-term capital funds. Such a shortage would dictate increasing use of the contingent interest techniques. The use of subordinated financing and higher debt-to-equity ratios often requires the use of contingent interest techniques. Mortgage bankers find it imperative to familiarize themselves with the techniques that can be used to attract investor funds which might not otherwise be available.

The concept of sharing in the income from a property is by no means a new one. It undoubtedly dates back to Biblical times, when landlords shared in the crops produced on their land by tenant farmers. In the modern sense, lenders sharing in income from property became common in the 1950s, when the percentage lease in shopping centers came into vogue and insurance company lenders would share in a part of the overage rents. Recently, a developer in the northeastern United States used a contingent interest technique upon selling a building. The building was to be used as a funeral home and, in this instance, in addition to a fixed rate of interest, the purchase money mortgage provided for additional interest calculated as a portion of the gross income from any funeral over a set monthly number. This is just one unusual example of the many factors upon which additional interest may be contingent. Only the most common, general types of contingent techniques will be discussed here in the hope that an understanding of these techniques will permit the handling of unusual situations as they arise.

Gross income is frequently used as the basis for contingent interest. Gross income is relatively easy to quantify and, therefore, is a convenient basis. A lender may require additional interest at a fixed percentage of the entire gross income from a property, say 2 or 3 percent. An alternative technique would be to require additional interest at a percentage of the gross income above a fixed level, say 10 to 15 percent. The level at which additional interest payments begin can be fixed anywhere, but two common levels are the break-even point and the stabilized gross upon which the loan is predicated. The break-even point is that predetermined point at which gross income equals the stabilized operating expenses, taxes and fixed debt service. The percentage of lender participation in the gross income above the break-even point would generally be less than the percentage of lender participation in the increase of gross income above the stabilized gross income. The decision to base contingent interest on either full gross income, gross income above the break-even point, or on increases in gross income above the stabilized level can have a great deal of impact on future earnings for the lender and costs for the borrower.

A case in point might be a loan of $750,000 on a property where the stabilized gross income was estimated at $100,000 when the loan was underwritten. The mortgage is self-liquidating in 25 years, 9 months, and bears a fixed interest rate of 9% with a constant of 10%. A contingent interest provision is to be written into the loan based on either 3 percent of the gross income or 15 percent of any gross income above $100,000. The lender believes that the gross income will attain an average increase of $5,000 per annum. The table and graph below illustrate how contingent interest payments differ depending on which basis of calculation is chosen.

The impact of the contingent interest of annual yield to the lender is also significant. Due to reductions in the outstanding loan balance, the contingent interest based on 3 percent of the gross would be 0.5, 0.7, and 1 percent of yield in the fifth, tenth, and fifteenth years of the loan, while on a basis of 15 percent of the increases in the gross income, the contingent interest would equate to 0.4, 1.1, and 2 percent of yield for the same years. The present value of these future returns should be considered in making the decision as to which basis to choose.

Using gross income as a basis for calculating contingent interest can create a situation in which the borrower pays more and more contingent interest to the lender as

| Year | Gross income | Contingent Interest | |
		3% of gross	15% of increase
1	$100,000	$3,000	$ -0-
2	105,000	3,150	750
3	110,000	3,300	1,500
4	115,000	3,450	2,250
5	120,000	3,600	3,000
6	125,000	3,750	3,750
7	130,000	3,900	4,500
8	135,000	4,050	5,250
9	140,000	4,200	6,000
10	145,000	4,350	6,750
11	150,000	4,500	7,500
12	155,000	4,650	8,250
13	160,000	4,800	9,000
14	165,000	4,950	9,750
15	170,000	5,100	10,500

the gross income rises while, at the same time, receiving a decreasing cash equity return. This would occur because the gross income must increase by not only the amount of increased expenses, but also by the amount required to pay the additional contingent interest if the borrower is to at least maintain cash flow. The situation can easily become critical in inflationary times on a highly leveraged property when gross income-based contingent interest provisions can overburden a property.

Net income is an alternative to gross income as a basis for calculating contingent interest. In this instance, a lender may require additional interest at a rate of 10 to 20 percent of the net income from the property. But what is the net income? The success of any net income-based contingent interest provision depends on the parties involved being able to reach agreement as to the amount of net income. There are always debates on which items and what amounts can be deducted from gross income to reach net income. Therefore, many contingent interest provisions of this type use *defined net income* as a basis for calculations. Definitions of net income are tailor-made for each project. The greatest problems arise in defining which deductions for operating expenses are to be allowed. Once the gross income has been determined, the amount to be deducted for real estate taxes and debt service is easily established. It is possible to allow a fixed percentage of the gross income for the operating expense deduction as opposed to itemizing these expenses. Because reaching agreement on the net income can be so difficult, sometimes only a few deductions from the gross income are allowed, and the result is a combination situation where the basis for contingent interest calculations is somewhere between the gross income and the actual net income. In many cases, only deductions are taken for real estate taxes or increases in real estate taxes, or increases in certain operating costs that can be accurately determined. The result is a hybrid combination of gross income and net income, which is useful in special cases, as it eliminates some of the difficulties that arise in using either one of these bases alone.

Overage rents can also be used as a basis for calculating contingent interest. This use is generally confined to retail properties where the owner may have leases calling for additional rents above a fixed rent when the lessee's net or gross business receipts exceed a certain level. There is some parallelism between the lessor/lessee and mortgagee/mortagor relationships, and frequently the mortgagee wishes to participate in the mortagor's increasing income. In this instance, the lender takes a percentage of the overage rents, say 10 to 25 percent. For example, a tenant agrees to pay overage rents in the amount of 7 percent of gross sales above $1,000,000 and experiences sales of $1,327,000 in a year. The landlord would receive $22,890 in overage rents. However, the landlord has agreed to pay 15 percent of overage rent receipts to the lender as contingent interest. The lender would receive $3,433.50 of the overage rents and the landlord (mortgagor) would retain $19,456.50 of these rents. This technique can become extremely complicated when one encounters situations where offsets against overage rents are allowed for increased real estate taxes or common area charges paid by tenants. At best, it is difficult for a lender to closely audit such a situation. The lender may have to verify the tenant's records in order to insure the accuracy of the overage rents collected. The accuracy of tenant records and the process of verification are probably easier when a large tenant with fixed record systems is involved. A small, local tenant with sketchy records may be almost impossible to control. When offsets against the overage rents are allowed for such items as increased real estate taxes or common area charges, the cross-correlation necessary can become quite difficult.

A *sale or refinance* of a property may prompt contingent interest in some situations. In order to induce a lender to make a mortgage, it may be appropriate to offer

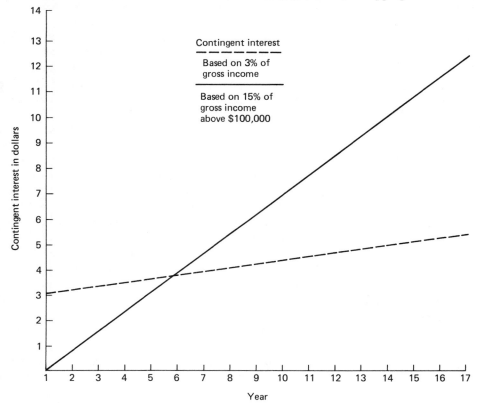

participation in the net proceeds from a refinance or a sale of the property. This technique does not involve continuing payments, as it is frequently a once-and-done provision. For example, suppose a situation in which a lender makes a $1,000,000 mortgage on an apartment complex and requires, in addition to a fixed interest rate, a 20 percent participation in the net proceeds of a refinance and a 20 percent participation in any first sale proceeds above the original mortgage amount. If the mortgage were paid down to about $947,480 in six years, and the project was refinanced with a mortgage of $1,200,000, the lender would be entitled to 20 percent of the net proceeds of $252,520, or $50,504. The same lender, if refinancing and negotiating the same type of contingent interest provision, would be entitled to 20 percent of the sale proceeds above $1,200,000. A property is relatively difficult to market with this type of provision in the mortgage and it is generally appropriate to provide for termination of this provision when a bona fide sale occurs. A contingent interest provision based on sale or refinance proceeds is relatively easy to monitor, because it does not call for periodic documentation.

Contingent interest can be a useful tool in certain money market conditions. The technique used can be custom-tailored to the needs of the project within the framework of borrower/lender negotiations. However, contingent interest techniques must be fully analyzed before they are employed as they are often a cause of dissent between borrower and lender. Often, contingent interest payments begin in loose money markets and borrowers resent paying this charge, even though it was mutually agreeable when the mortgage was negotiated in a tight money market. At any time, there is a great likelihood that the lender and the borrower will not agree on the amount payable, because they will calculate the basis differently. Disagreements on gross income, net income, overage rents, and all other bases are the rule, not the exception. Therefore, contingent interest provisions must go into great detail in specifying how such interest is to be calculated. Extra servicing time and expense involved in contingent interest collections is significant. One must provide for audits of the borrower's records in connection with contingent interest in the loan documents. Such audits are frequently necessary and, at times, may even involve an examination of a tenant's records when overage rents are involved.

Usury will affect contingent interest in certain localities. Frequently, high interest rates are encountered on loans that require contingent interest payments. If usury limits apply, there exists the possibility that the combination of fixed interest and contingent interest may exceed that limit. Structuring a transaction with a subordinated land sale-leaseback or a sandwich lease position may avoid usury implications in some states because, in such situations, contingent interest is not provided under the mortgage but additional rent is required under the lease provisions. The additional rent is structured in the same manner as contingent interest. Subordinated land sale-leasebacks and sandwich lease situations are most commonly encountered in high-leverage financing situations where contingent interest is most often appropriate.

Contingent interest techniques generally apply to the investment of long-term funds. Interest rates in the short and intermediate sector are commonly tied to the cost of funds to the lender. For instance, the interest rate charged the borrower will be so many points above the prime lending rate charged by commercial banks or the rate necessary to sell short-term commercial paper. As mortgage investment trusts increase their long-term mortgages, it is conceivable that contingent interest provisions will relate to such short-term borrowing rates. Another contingent interest technique which may be seen in the future will involve coupling contingent interest requirements with the cost of living or consumer price index. This is foreshadowed by the increasingly common use of long-term retail and office leases calling for rent increases based on cost of living or consumer price indexes.

Contingent interest is difficult to predict, police, and analyze. It can be an obstacle in negotiating a mortgage and an abrasive in borrower/lender relationships after the closing. Nevertheless, contingent interest is a function of the money market and can be pressed into service when supply and demand of lendable funds dictates. Since the mortgage market competes for funds with alternative forms of investments, any method which will offer a hedge against inflation and an opportunity for increasing yield on a long-term mortgage provides a competitive advantage. Contingent interest provides such an advantage and, therefore, requires attention from the investment community.

Chapter 22

Joint Ventures

John C. Opperman

A joint venture is loosely defined as an association of two or more entities to carry out a business enterprise for profit. In real estate, a joint venture may be considered as a "marriage" between the real estate knowhow and experience of the developer and capital of the financial partner.

Until the mid-1960s, joint ventures between developers and institutional investors were uncommon. Projects were relatively small, and favorable economics allowed loans that were a high percentage of cost. Equity requirements above the mortgage were modest and were provided by the entrepreneur's own funds or from a small group of friends. Then came the era of syndication, during which equity pools were raised from a number of investors in search of a tax shelter. For the larger developer, the stock market provided financing as more builders went public. Banks furnished liberal lines of credit to assist development.

Economic conditions then began to change and a number of factors developed conducive to making the joint venture an adequate and successful means of providing real estate finance. Projects became larger, more complex, and required more equity. As equity sources previously available began to dry up when the syndication bubble burst, the stock market was less enthusiastic about real estate companies and bank lines became more restrictive. Increased costs narrowed the spread between actual cost and economic value. This precluded "financing out" (borrowing 100 percent of total development costs).

As money became tighter, the institutional investor sought and the market allowed a greater return for equity funds. Meanwhile, usury limitations of many states necessitated a vehicle for higher returns than normally permitted via mortgage lending. As financing techniques became more complex (land and gap loans, standbys, sale-leasebacks, etc.) the developer found it less cumbersome to deal with one large sophisticated institutional partner rather than a myriad of small investors. Thus, the joint venture evolved—a financial mechanism structured to satisfy the objective of both the financial institution and the developer. The financial partner, who also received an inflation hedge with an interest in a hopefully growing income stream and, ultimately, a capital gain, was able to obtain opportunities for increased yields that were greater than those with straight mortgages. Through depreciation, it provided a tax shelter not found in mortgage investments. It gave the financial partner real estate ownership without management responsibilities and a low profile without divulging an identity to the public. It was also a vehicle for investing in certain desirable states otherwise precluded by usury laws.

The objectives of the developer were likewise met with the ability to become involved in larger projects. It meant relative ease of dealing with one knowledgeable investor who had greater financial strength in an adverse economy.

A joint venture, as such, is not generally recognized as a legal entity in most states. The form utilized is usually that of a corporation, a general partnership, or limited partnership.

The corporation form is rarely used, although it has certain advantages. These include the continuity of existence, limitation of liability, flexibility of various classes of stock, and immunity from usury statutes in some states. There is, however, a major disadvantage in this structure of a joint venture which generally precludes its use, namely that it is a separate taxable entity.

The general partnership is most often used when both the developer and the financial partner associate as general partners. This form of joint venture permits a flow-through of tax benefits to the partners. A general partnership also allows a voice in management by both partners. One disadvantage is that the financial partner is subject to liability, which in most cases is undesirable because of the extensive assets of such a partner.

A limited partnership is the most common form of joint venture for real estate development. Typically, the developer is the general partner and is responsible for the day-to-day management, while the financial partner fills the more passive role of limited partner with liability limited to the amount of its investment.

As joint ventures have evolved, the financial partner has become less content with passivity for the sake of limited liability, and today most joint ventures are structured as follows: The developer and a subsidiary of the financial partner serve as general partners (the latter to give the financial institution a voice in management), and the financial partner serves as limited partner. Generally, this form of ownership is made up as follows:

General partners, developer 50 percent and subsidiary of financial partner 1 percent.

Limited partner, financial partner 49 percent.

Although most joint ventures are complex and large in scope, a simple example will be used to demonstrate the major areas of negotiation.

A developer/builder with an excellent track record in the garden office building field has an option on a well-located suburban site and approaches a mortgage banker asking him to finance the development. The costs are as follows:

Land	$150,000
Improvements	$700,000
Total cost	$850,000

After a careful analysis of the plans, comparable rents, absorption rates, and expenses, the mortgage banker estimates the economic value as follows:

Gross income	$170,000
Vacancy allowance (5%)	8,500
Effective gross income	$161,500

Expenses:		
Taxes	$25,000	
Operating		
Expenses	$36,500	$61,500
Net income		$100,000
Capitalized at 10%		$1,000,000

Although feasibility of the project is favorable in that economic valuation is substantially greater than cost, a standard 75 percent loan would be only $750,000, or $100,000 short of total cost. It is proposed that the financial institution commit to the loan of $750,000 at, say, 9½% for a term of 30 years (a loan constant of about 10) and provide an equity contribution of $100,000 from which the lender will earn a preferred 10 percent return.

It is proposed that ownership be split 50-50. Cash flow from the property would be divided as follows:

Net income	$100,000
Debt service ($750,000–9½%–30	75,000
Net to equity	$ 25,000
Return on equity (10% on $100,000)	$ 10,000
Net to partnership	$ 15,000
50% to developer	$ 7,500
50% to financial partner	$ 7,500

The developer has received a normal builder's overhead and profit, and an equity return of $7,500 with no investment. The financial partner gets 17.5 percent return on a $100,000 equity investment (10 percent return and $7,500 share of profit). In future years, the partners benefit from equity build-up as the loan is paid down and greater profits if the net income should increase.

The basic document in a joint venture is the limited (or general) partnership agreement. It contains a variety of nuances not reflected in the preceding example, which result from hours of intensive negotiations. Before the joint venture is drawn, it is essential that the basic elements are agreed upon, that the parties are compatible, the real estate is desirable and the yield is mutually acceptable. Although there is no standard format for a joint venture, the major areas to be considered would include:

1 *The objective of all parties.* What is the specific purpose of the venture? For example, is it to acquire, develop, lease, or sell land? Is it the intention of the venture to develop, to sell, or to hold?

2 *What are the contributions?* There should be a complete understanding between the parties as to their obligations and responsibilities. The percentages of ownership are determined by the relative contribution of the partners, and can vary depending on the agreement between the parties. Arrangements may vary from all financial contributions by the institutional financial partner (with entrepreneurial skills by developer) to an ''equal dollars from each party'' concept. Frequently, equities are matched—*hard* dollars from the financial partner and *soft* dollars from the developer. Soft dollars are noncash items such as the difference between the developer's cost of land and fair market value, the equivalent of developer's profit, leasing commissions contributed by the developer, etc. If ownership is 50-50, in the concept of ''matching equities,'' the party with the larger net cash contribution receives a preferred return on the differential before profits are split. In many ventures, cash equity receives a preferred return and soft dollar equity receives a subordinate return before profits are split. In any event, it is considered desirable for both parties to have an equity contribution (hard or soft dollar) so that each has a vested interest in the venture's success.

3 *How will profits be distributed?* After operating expenses and debt service for the first mortgage are paid, there are various plans for allocating the remaining cash flow. If equities are considered matching, then the cash flow distribution is split in proportion to each partner's percentage of ownership. However, if they are not matching, there are several alternatives. The first would be to have all cash flow to the financial partner until equity is recaptured with interest. After recapture, cash flow is then split according to percentage of ownership. Another method might be to consider equity as a second mortgage amortized over a period of 10 to 20 years, with interest prior to the split of cash flow. A third alternative would be for the financial partner's cash equity to receive a preferred return (cumulative or noncumulative) and the balance of the cash flow split in accordance with ownership interest. This is considered by many to be the most equitable method whereby equity contribution is treated as such and not as ''debt.'' It also allows for cash flow to the developer, which is a better incentive and also provides funds to pay taxes that may be due on the developer's ownership interest.

Joint ventures usually have the same formula for sharing profits and losses; however, losses payable by the limited partner do not exceed the original investment.

When the property is refinanced or sold, the remaining equity of the partners is returned and the balance of the proceeds divided as per ownership interests.

4 *What will be the use of leverage?* There are several approaches to the structuring of debt in a joint venture. Often, the financial partner initially commits to a first mortgage, usually at terms competitive in the current market. Some lenders require mandatory delivery of the loan. However, some financial partners require just the opposite—that the loan be obtained from outside sources. A third method would be for a financial partner to issue a "bankable standby-commitment" in the amount of the total cost of the project in order to facilitate construction financing from a bank. After the project is completed and leased, the most advantageous mortgage is obtained and the remainder is considered to be an equity contribution from the financial partner. A similar concept and one growing in acceptance is the issuance of a commitment at current terms with the understanding that if a better loan can be obtained upon completion of the development, that it is to the best interests of the venture to accept it.

If the financial partner provides a commitment for long-term financing, it rarely contains a leasing requirement, inasmuch as it would tend to impede construction financing.

In a joint venture, first mortgage financing is typically exculpated (without personal liability).

It is typical that a right of first refusal is granted to the mortgage banker (or to the financial partner) for permanent financing.

   5 *How will cost control be handled?*   Undoubtedly, the greatest problem area in joint venture developments is in cost overruns. It is essential that the agreement be specific regarding the responsibility of the partners relative to costs.

Inasmuch as the joint venture is often negotiated before working drawings are completed and bid, it is good business practice to reassess the feasibility of the project when actual costs are finalized. If costs are higher than first estimated, yields should be recalculated and if not then acceptable, the development perhaps should be aborted. There are many cases in which the developer guaranteed a contract from preliminary plans, risking financial jeopardy. A venture with complete plans and specifications, properly bid out and the contract price guaranteed by the builder-developer is off to a good start. It is important that the developer's overhead and profit are precisely specified. If there are cost savings, they usually inure to the benefit of the venture.

What if there are cost overruns? Generally, the cause and type of the overrun determines which partner is responsible for providing the additional capital required. If there is a construction cost overrun, then the increase in construction cost is usually the responsibility of the developer under guarantee. Exceptions are *force majeure* items such as strikes, fire, material shortages, etc., which are usually the responsibility of the venture.

Interest overruns are usually attributed to four basic causes. They are: protracted incubation period before construction starts; delays in construction; slow rent-up period; and an increase in short-term interest rates affecting a construction loan which floats above the bank prime rate. This type of cost overrun is usually the responsibility of the venture. It is important to allow a liberal interest contingency in the construction budget.

Although joint ventures vary widely as to how cost overruns are funded, there are several basic methods. Usually, the financial partner funds the overrun but is given priority return on and of funds advanced. Alternatively, the overruns may be funded pro rata as to the partners' ownership interests. There is sometimes a combination of the above wherein the financial partner funds overruns up to a dollar limit with a priority return, then up to a certain limit both partners contribute equally, and after a certain total is reached, the developer funds the balance. In some extreme cases, the financial partner funds the overrun and takes a larger percentage of ownership.

   6 *Who is responsible for management?*   The area of decision-making control is an important and sensitive one. Early joint ventures placed the financial partner in a relatively passive role in order to protect limited liability status and because the de-

veloper was the expert. It is now more typical for the partner to have a voice in management through a subsidiary which serves as general partner with the developer. The general partner must agree on the initial concept of development, plans and specifications, financing, rental schedules, construction contracts, sale of the property, etc. The developer usually acts alone as the managing partner in charge of the day-to-day management decisions during and after completion. Expenditures authorized have a certain dollar limit.

The developer frequently signs a management contract specifying management duties and compensation. The contract may be either cancellable "for cause" or at the sole discretion of the financial partner. Compensation generally commences when the property reaches the break-even point.

The joint venture agreement may, but typically does not, specify noncompetition by either party on a geographic basis.

7 *How will depreciation be handled?* Typically, the partners agree on a method of depreciation and receive depreciation benefits in proportion to their percentage of ownership. The benefits of tax shelter to the partners is a function of their relative income tax brackets and of their preferences. Usually, depreciation is of more value to the developer. The financial partner, typically a publicly held company, suffers in reported earnings on a financial statement by taking depreciation deductions from income. Therefore, tax benefits are often shifted to the developer (possibly in exchange for increased yield to the investor). To allow all depreciation to be shifted to the developer, it may be advantageous to split ownership of the project so that the financial partner owns the land and the developer owns the building, that is, land sale-leaseback and leasehold loans.

Important questions to be answered in the structure of the joint venture are: (a) Will tax benefits match cash flow? (b) Will either party pay tax on money they don't get? or (c) Will either party get tax benefits they can't use? Cash flow should be adjusted with this in mind or alternatively, tax benefits may be "sold" to third parties.

As real estate accounting procedures come closer to conventional corporate accounting procedures, depreciation may become less valuable as a tax shelter and more emphasis will be placed on financial performance.

8 *Will there be partnership buy-sell (or put-call) agreements?* It is generally accepted as good business practice to make provision for one partner to precipitate an ending of the venture (usually after construction is completed). The simplest form of buy-sell agreement provides that either party may offer to buy the interest of the other party for "X" dollars. However, this offer entitles the other party to buy the interest of the initiating party on the same basis. Another condition provides that a partner, before selling an interest to a third party, must give the joint venture partner first refusal to match the offer. The venture agreement may also specify that if it is agreed that one party sell to a partner, the price be based on fair market value. Many agreements allow the limited partner to sell an interest without consent of the general partner.

9 *What provisions are made for dissolution?* In addition to the provision for a buy-sell agreement, dissolution of the joint venture may be caused by such things as the default of a performance standard, bankruptcy of a general partner, death of a general partner, sale of the asset and distribution of proceeds, end of term of the venture, or by the aborting of the project and agreement to dissolve.

10 *Will there be any land banking?* If the joint venture contemplates the development of more than one parcel of land, special provision should be made for carrying the additional land until it is developed. Of course, if the original seller of the land agrees to retain title and release parcels as needed, the venture is not faced with the problem. If, however, the venture must acquire the land, financing can be structured by the financial partner making a land loan to the venture, or by the financial partner contributing capital to the venture to buy the land (with or without outside financing), or by the financial partner buying the land and leasing it to the venture.

Carrying costs of the land once acquired can be accrued by the venture, funded by the financial partner, or shared by the partners. Occcasionally, the developer is required to pay all land-carrying expenses. If the venture decides not to continue with further development, the developer may have the option to repurchase the land plus carrying charge, or the developer may have the obligation to repurchase, or the joint venture sells the land and distributes proceeds as specified in the agreement.

It should be stressed that a joint venture agreement is an extremely complex document which is the product of a careful synthesis of real estate and legal expertise tailored to provide the most workable vehicle for a successful real estate development.

Although a joint venture is by nature complex, there are certain fundamental elements requisite to success.

1   Selection of sound real estate.
2   Matching of compatible, knowledgeable partners.
3   Mutuality of objectives of partners.
4   The venture must be satisfactory to both partners, or it is good for neither.
5   Complete disclosure by both parties should be implicit.
6   Adequate contingencies should be included—guard against overoptimism—conservatively assess feasibility.
7   Realization that high risk is a concomitant of high yields.

Many institutional investors prefer the mortgage banker to be an active member of the joint venture team, often with a financial interest. To warrant such position, the mortgage banker, whose expertise is sought in feasibility analysis and in assisting in the evolution and evaluation of the design concept and plans, must become actively involved. The mortgage banker may be asked to arrange financing of land, construction, gap, standby, and permanent loans and to monitor construction and cost control. Continuing interest would be the surveillance of management when the project is an operating entity.

As a result of recent credit stringencies, there have been numerous failures in the joint venture field. Many institutional investors have become disenchanted with this investment vehicle. Economic conditions, however, are only partially responsible for the lack of success of joint ventures. Many were victims of improper underwriting, selection of a weak or inexperienced partner, faulty management, lack of flexibility, inadequate control, and investor avarice.

However, a joint venture that is properly structured can satisfy the investment objective of the financial partner in an inflationary era and compatibly offer the skilled, entrepreneurial developer the stability of financial resources necessary for a successful development. It is likely that joint ventures will constitute a major vehicle for the creation of major real estate projects in the future.

Chapter 23

Financing—The Developer's Viewpoint

Gordon E. Emerson, Jr.

The real estate developer is a manufacturer just as much as the widget manufacturer, whose products, while not widgets or automobiles or bakery products, are the result of manufacturing. The difference is that the developer's products are real estate values or appreciation of real estate values. The successful developer is also a value creator, thus performing an economically useful and socially desirable function. This discussion will be concerned with the effect of financing on real estate values, which are the product of the developer. Financing will then be examined from the point of view of timing, matching the risk and reward equation of the lender, with special consideration of financing techniques to maximize financing.

In this chapter, we will discuss real estate development in a generic sense and not qualify each statement as to whether it is more or less applicable to residential developers or a shopping center developer. As the developer does not have an auction system, such as the stock exchange or the commodity markets to price efforts, the valuation of the product is not easily established. Nor does the developer's output typically have an established marketplace. This is in part the result of the fact that no property is the same. The developer produces the product by translating ideas and concepts into realities by combining land, utilities, bricks, and mortar into a functional piece of real estate. Not only is value established by the combination of demand, land, and labor and materials, but by the introduction of financial contracts and obligations in the form of mortgages, leases, and fee instruments into a feasible real estate project. The nature of these financial instruments affects value in a direct way.

There are a number of appraisal techniques which are employed by professionals in the field. The most meaningful appraisal techniques for the developer are not those that contemplate the property free and clear of financing, but those which include either completed or contemplated financing. Financing is an encumbrance, the same as a lease, and either enhances or diminishes value. An acceptable method of real estate valuation is the composite method, the procedure whereby net income after operating expenses and debt service is capitalized, with the result added to the mortgage debt to arrive at an estimate. This estimate is modified by a further factor to reflect the imminence of changes in the actual income stream, the quality of that income stream, the availability of a revised debt service by reason of changing values, and the existence or nonexistence of prepayment privileges. This modification process should not be considered a minor step, because it is here that appraisals move from the area of science to that of art. An economic valuation without reference to physical value or replacement cost is totally unrealistic, and the same is true of financing. For example, a property with a 6% interest, 8% constant mortgage with a balloon due in two years in a mortgage market of 8% interest, 10% constant has a value different from one with a 15-year maturity.

TIMING

The developer, when preparing to finance a project, must consider, in addition to the mortgage amounts, the term of the interest rate, the constant restrictions on partial and full prepayment, and many other factors—some of which are related to time:

1 Is financing the project being done prior to an increase in values? If an important restatement of values can be foreseen, short-term borrowing and postponing long-term financing must be seriously considered. Short-term loans might involve credit loans from commercial banks, secured real estate loans from commercial banks, or interest-only short-term permanent loans from real estate investment trusts, with terms of three to five years.

2 Can establishing new and higher levels of occupancy rents than comparables now indicate be anticipated? If so, the developer may wish to consider a floor-to-ceiling loan based upon rates above the comparables to achieve the gap to be realized. A loan holdback (or gap) may be preferable to being locked into a mortgage which recognized too low rental rates. Gaps should only be sought by developers when they are confident that they can establish a new plateau of rental rates or the possibility of a new location.

3 A developer, while seeking significant jumps in value, may wish to consider a long-term loan, and, if so, should seek out those institutions who will premit early prepayment with only a small prepayment penalty. Inasmuch as one of the major motivations of a real estate owner is the ability to refinance property when circumstances warrant, the rights to prepay in full should be looked at more carefully than many other items. Many regard that the ability to receive tax-free proceeds of new borrowing is one of the fundamental benefits of real estate ownership. Many developers would be willing to pay a stiff penalty or front-end fee to receive this right. A

permanent mortgagee should be protected against voluntary prepayments during periods of relatively low interest rates, but should be willing to consider the equivalency of this higher interest rate in the form of a prepayment penalty or premium.

A knowledgeable and financially sophisticated developer will maximize the value of property by close attention to the timing of each step in the financing process and by matching financing with the particular needs of a lender. As an illustration, the following five-step procedure could be used by a developer of industrial parks:

1 Industrial parks have a life cycle which involves land acquisition and assembly, zoning, the introduction of roads and utilities and restrictive covenants, the creation of buildings, and, finally, the management of a group of buildings. With this cycle in mind, a developer could maximize values by furnishing a commercial bank with an opportunity to invest an amount equal to, say, 50 percent of the acquisition cost of the land and 100 percent of the cost of roads and utilities. Since this would be a conservative loan, with a short-term duration, say, of 18 to 36 months, the interest rate should be a reflection of the modesty of the risk. This sort of loan often matches the need of the commercial banker.

2 The second step in financing this hypothetical industrial park could involve the financing of the balance of the acquisition cost plus the debt service on both loans through some form of junior instrument. If the project has merit, a rate-conscious real estate investment trust (REIT), for example, might find the financing opportunity attractive, especially if the developer is willing to pledge a personal or corporate guarantee for all or some part of the loan. The maturity would match the commercial loan. The interest rate to the REIT would be at a higher level floating above prime, but the blend of the two loans would be lower than that which would have prevailed had only one lender been utilized. This procedure also avoids the need for equity, either by cash from the developer, a participation by a long-term lender, or through the sale of limited participation.

This procedure permits the developer to fully finance the acquisition and early development expenses on a temporary basis and to postpone the permanent loan until an increase in values has occurred by reason of the assembly process, the zoning changes, the imposition of restrictive covenants, and the introduction of roads and utilities. Later, the developer can substitute imputed or created equity for the guarantee.

3 The next step could be one which would be available to a developer who has an association with a general contractor, either on a permanent basis or on a case basis. The contractor, on the strength of personal credit, would borrow from a commercial bank on a relatively short-term basis—six to nine months—the costs of the construction of the industrial building or buildings to be created. The use of the general contractor's line borrowing eliminates the need of removing the land from the lien of the commercial bank and the REIT and all the attendant paper work and expense. The cost would be no more than a conventional construction loan, and may even be less. If the industrial park is of any size, several buildings would probably be under construction at the same time, some being created on a "build to suit" basis for a known tenant, or some as speculative or inventory buildings.

4 The fourth step would involve the packaging of several individual buildings as the security for a single secured loan. As previously stated, some of the buildings could be under lease and others available for lease. The loan amount would equal the amount due the contractor, to allow repayment of the commercial bank loan and the sum of the two release prices paid to the first two lenders, that is, commercial bank and REIT. A REIT might again be a reasonable candidate for this loan opportunity. The term of the loan might be for three years or thereabouts, with a right to release pieces of the security from time to time. I might state, parenthetically, that a well-conceived industrial park would experience a second increase in land valuations once a number of leases had been secured and the industrial park has a history of some degree of success, either in land sales or leases. At this point, lenders would be prepared to shift valuations from wholesale to discounted retail.

5   When the second increase in valuations has occurred is the time when permanent financing, the fifth and final step, may be appropriate. The developer would, undoubtedly, delay such action until the second increase in valuation, the fact that the inventory buildings had been leased, and that an upward movement in occupancy rental rates had been clearly demonstrated. With the existence of the prior package loan, the developer could ''spin off'' the particular properties which match the interest and appetite of certain permanent lenders such as savings and loan associations, mutual savings banks, or insurance companies, in each instance matching the need of the lender for credit or rate.

There is no hard and fast rule concerning the use of mortgage bankers or mortgage brokers as opposed to the use of in-house capabilities to obtain mortgage financing. Many developers believe in arranging their own mortgage financing, or having someone within their organization arrange financing on the theory that they know their product best and are better able to describe to a lender the special features that need to be considered. Many developers are of the opinion that lenders would prefer to deal with a principal rather than through an intermediary. Further consideration is the cost of the service to the developer for the use of an intermediary. If a developer is constantly entering the financing market, a staff employee might be less expensive. The argument is often raised that a single individual, whether the developer or an associate, cannot understand the entire spectrum of the marketplace and may fail to maximize some element of the mortgage financing. This latter point would seem to support the contention that a brokerage organization with nationwide operations, including relationships with most of the principal lenders, is a desirable approach. Many developers object to this on the basis that the service they receive through these operations offers little individualized attention. The use of a mortgage correspondent by a developer, out of choice rather than out of a response to the requirements of a lender, involves a judgment on the part of the developer that the constancy of the relationship between the lender and correspondent and the correspondent and developer/client establishes rapports that cannot be otherwise duplicated. No matter what type of service is used, there is a strong need for professional, quality service, a service that includes keeping both the lender and the developer appraised for developments subsequent to the lender's commitment concerning the project and the lender's attitude. The intermediary should relieve, to the greatest degree possible, the developer from the red tape that is generally implicit in the matter of the preparation of closings.

While it may appear that large or long-established developers have some special advantage in the marketplace on mortgage financing, this is not necessarily so, as there are no special advantages in real estate development of scale. The advantages of one developer over another are integrity, creditworthiness, ability, and skill. The large developer has the special problem of avoiding remoteness and slowness of decision making and redundant support functions. Lenders generally, and rightly so, regard the project and not necessarily its sponsor.

Leverage is often called the ''name of the game'' in real estate, but leverage, as many have found, is a two-edged device. It is hard to resist too much financing when ''enough'' is available. ''Enough'' should meet out-of-pocket costs and leave a margin of postdebt service cash flow. Unless true value or appreciation has occurred, the developer, who has not fulfilled a role as a ''manufacturer'' is not entitled to ''enough.''

An active developer often wants more accounting tax losses than needed to shelter cash flows. Provided the obligations created by a syndication of limited partnerships does not totally remove the margin of safety after conventional debt service, the sale of partnership interests may be the least expensive form of financing and promote the use of an important asset of the business of development—excess depreciation.

There are many financial tools and approaches available to the sophisticated developer, but in the final analysis, there is no substitute for solid real estate property values.

Chapter 24

Financing Condominiums, Cooperatives, Planned Unit Developments, and New Towns

W. Dean Goodman

Why are these types of real estate developments included in an income-property finance text? Are condominiums, cooperatives, and planned unit developments merely residential developments? Many may have the mistaken belief that condominiums and cooperatives pertain only to residential dwelling units, since our experience and exposure primarily has involved residential properties, What about condominium and cooperative professional office buildings, shopping centers, mobile home parks, hotels, office warehouse and industrial properties? Large planned unit developments in new-town communities include large commercial developments within the project. Residential condominiums and cooperatives are actually multiunit apartment buildings that have complex and intricate legal ramifications in the divisions of ownership interests for each individual unit. It is one thing to underwrite a specific commercial loan, but in a condomonium or cooperative, there are additional aspects to consider.

It is extremely important to have your most experienced commercial mortgage lenders involved in the analysis and underwriting of mortgage loans on these types of properties. Planned unit developments and new-town communities are generally large, complex real estate projects that demand and require the most knowledgeable and experienced type of mortgage personnel.

The following facts and information must be obtained and properly analyzed in underwriting these types of loans:

What is the market?
What sizes of units are needed?
Is the location compatible with the market?
Who are the buyers?
What is the availability of existing units?
What is the developing inventory?
What is the absorption rate?
Should the development be constructed in phases?
What should be constructed first?
Will front-end costs be too high for the economic success of the development?
Is the overall plan and design correct for the intended market and the particular location?
Are the amenities sufficient?
Is it an apartment designed for use as a rental unit or is it designed for ownership?
Does the design fit the particular geographic area?
Is there adequate parking and are garages, carports, or open spaces required?
Should the interior streets be public or private driveways?
Do the designs and specifications require large maintenance costs in the operation of the property?
Is the design compatible with the soil, drainage, and other engineering reports?
If a land lease is created for the leasing of the land and/or common facilities, is the lease properly written with both developer and the lessee properly protected?
What are the projected operating expenses for the property?
What is the cash-flow analysis (what is the break-even point and how and when do we get paid back)?
Are the legal documents properly drawn and complete?
Do the documents properly provide for the establishment of a homeowners association, and is there proper, competent, professional management?

A total evaluation of the sales program is required. Without a proper sales program, we cannot expect to have a sound economic investment. It is obvious that only an experienced mortgage loan underwriter can properly evaluate, analyze, and underwrite this type of investment.

The concept of condominiums and cooperatives is not new. The Romans used a form of condominium, and in the mid-1800s cooperatives were formed in Europe, particularly in Scandinavia. Cooperatives make up 20 to 33 percent of all housing starts in Europe. Cooperatives were first developed in the United States primarily along the Eastern seaboard. In 1961, Congress enacted Section 234 under the National Housing Act, which recognized and permitted the condominium concept of ownership: Hawaii enacted a condominium statute within 10 days of the enactment of Section 234 and all other states soon followed with condominium statutes. In recent years, there has been spectacular growth in condominiums, cooperatives, and planned unit developments.

REASONS FOR THE CONDOMINIUM, COOPERATIVE, AND PLANNED UNIT DEVELOPMENT TREND

Owner Reasons

The change in life styles with more carefree living is a reason for condominium living. In comparison with single-family dwellings, many condominiums have more amenities, with an emphasis on recreational aspects such as health clubs, swimming, tennis, golf, racketball, etc. Many single-family dwelling owners are tired of weekend work in maintaining the yard and the exterior of the property, and many "empty nesters" would prefer maintenance-free condominiums. The purchase price of a condominium or cooperative is generally less than for a single-family dwelling and, due to the energy problem, many people may desire to live closer to the central business district where they work.

Developer Reasons

Large inflationary cost overruns, increased operating expenses (especially utility costs), overbuilding of rental units, and "rent lag" (needed rental increases lagging behind the cost of construction for an economic investment) have created a reverse equity position known as *negative equity*. In constructing condominiums, developers today can obtain a profit rather than a potential negative cash flow from rental units. There still are some developers who, from unrealistic motivation, will continue to build negative equity rental units. With proper planning, a developer will be able to construct a better product with more extras that will be paid for in the purchase of a condominium and will have an opportunity to create equity by continuing to own the individual units that would be free and clear after the construction loan has been paid off through the sales of the individual units.

COOPERATIVE

A cooperative is a business that is owned by its customers. There are many types of cooperatives throughout the country, but this discussion will involve only housing cooperatives. The title to the property is generally held in a corporation, which has articles of incorporation and by-laws which control the use and management of the property. Each individual who desires space in the building purchases stock in the corporation, with each stockholder having the right to occupy space in the property. The corporation functions as a typical corporation with a Board of Directors that controls and manages the property. The Board hires professional management and establishes necessary committees for the operation and management of the property. Usually, one mortgage loan is made to the corporation without any individual personal liability. Each stockholder is obligated to pay his pro-rata share of the mortgage payments, taxes, and operating expenses.

A disadvantage of the cooperative is the inflexibility of financing. The financial status and needs of stockholders vary; however, in a cooperative all stockholders assume a pro-rata expense of the debt service. Each tenant cannot choose how much equity to pay down and how large a mortgage to have on his or her individual unit. Another financial disadvantage to the stockholder is the fact that if there are vacant units or stockholders who have defaulted on their pro-rata payments, it is the obligation of the other stockholders to pay the required payments for the vacant or defaulted units. In many cases, cooperatives make the individual tenant return his or her unit to the cooperative corporation at the price paid or at a price that is agreed upon at the time of sale.

It is an advantage not to have personal liability on the mortgage; however, the tenant has less control of the unit. It should be noted that some lenders prefer cooperative loans rather than condominium loans, since the loan is large, and when some of the units are vacant or in default, the other unit owners pay the defaulted unit payments and the lender does not have a delinquent loan.

CONDOMINIUM

Each state has enacted a *horizontal property act* or condominium statute that provides for legal descriptions of each condominium unit, whether it be located on the ground or in the air. Consequently, each individual unit owner can convey title in fee simple. Further, the taxing authorities can recognize each fee simple ownership and tax each individual unit rather than assessing the total property. A definition of condominium ownership could be stated as follows: A form of ownership of real property characterized by title (created by statute) to a unit in a project together with an undivided real estate interest in the common areas which are a part of said project in accordance with state enabling law. The common areas generally are maintained by, but not owned by, the owners association. The common areas typically include, among other things, the land, roofs, lobbies, and community space and facilities.

From a resident's point of view, the advantages of condominiums over cooperatives are:

1 There is not the possibility that one owner will experience a loss due to the unwillingness or inability of another owner to pay real estate taxes or to service the mortgage. This is because such charges are liens only on the individual dwellings. A similar default on the part of a shareholder in a cooperative could result in the assessment of the delinquent charges among the other shareholders. A foreclosure on the cooperative's mortgage precipitated by a substantial number of defaults or vacancies could erase the equity of nondefaulting members.

2 More importantly, the condominium owner has the same financing alternatives available as does the owner of a detached single-family subdivision home. There is a particular advantage on resale where an owner hopes to recover increased equity as a result of mortgage amortization and appreciation in value. On the resale of a cooperative, in those states where individual mortgages are not available, the seller must find a buyer who is willing to pay cash above the seller's share of the blanket mortgage.

The *master deed* is the basic document used in the creation of a condominium. It is sometimes called the declaration of horizontal property regime, enabling declaration, or deed of constitution. The recorded master deed indicates that the property is submitted to a condominium regime and describes the division of the project into units and common areas. The master deed indicates the covenants, conditions, and restrictions for the condominium regime and ordinarily contains provisions dealing with:

1 Legal description of the land.
2 Legal description of each unit.

3 Legal description of common areas.

4 The establishment of an owners management association.

5 A method for sharing common expenses.

6 Means of collecting assessments for the operation of the property through foreclosing on a unit of a delinquent owner.

7 The unit of the ownership of each specific unit and its related common portions of the building or buildings. (Each condominium unit and its supporting, adjoining, and necessary common elements are to be separated as to ownership through conveyancing or mortgaging.)

8 How the total property making up the development is going to be managed.

9 Restrictions on the individual owner's rights to partition his property interest.

10 A limiting of the use of units by owners to its intended purpose.

11 Restricting the occupant's ability to alter the exterior of the structure.

12 Limitations in keeping animals on the premises as pets.

13 Prohibiting the blocking or hindering of occupant ingress or egress over the common areas.

14 Granting the governing board of the development the power to adopt and enforce reasonable rules controlling the conduct of people on the premises.

15 Limiting the personal liability of governing board members for their actions so long as they act in good faith.

16 Rebuilding a destroyed structure.

17 The method whereby the covenants, conditions, and restrictions can be amended by the owner/occupants.

In addition to the master deed, by-laws are established which set forth the rules applicable to the operation of the owners association. These by-laws will commonly provide for:

1 Organization membership requirements.

2 Raising and collecting funds to operate the association.

3 The meetings of the association.

4 Methods of membership voting.

5 Officers and directors of the association.

6 Methods of selecting officers and directors.

7 Functions and powers of officers and directors.

8 Rules by which the directors shall convene and conduct meetings.

9 Filling the offices of directors and officers if they become vacant before terms of office have expired.

10 Methods to be used in carrying out the financial administration of the association.

11 Procedures in amending the by-laws.

Another important document is the condominium plat, a detailed survey of the entire property showing graphically the relative location, configuration, and dimensions of each condominium unit which shows the floors, ceilings, etc. This survey plat is the basis for legally describing each unit in the condominium subdivision. The condominium plat should be certified by a registered engineer, and since this plat is the basis for the legal descriptions, it is important that the survey be absolutely accurate in all respects.

PLANNED UNIT DEVELOPMENT

The definition or connotation of a planned unit development (PUD) can vary tremendously. There is planned unit development zoning in various metropolitan areas that gives tremendous control to the governmental authorities, and there are small and large planned unit developments such as new town communities. Large planned unit developments consist of all types of residential, commercial, and industrial developments. While small planned unit developments generally consist of a single type of use of property, the Federal National Mortgage Association (FNMA) defines planned unit development in their Conventional Selling Contract Supplement as follows: A real estate development which consists of separately owned lots with contiguous or noncontiguous areas or facilities usually owned by an owners association in which the owners of the lots have a stock or membership interest.

Title to the real estate under the dwelling units is held by the individual lot owners and not by the association. The association usually has title to and administers the common areas, and levies monthly charges against the lot owners for common-area expenses. Membership in the owners association cannot be served from the ownership of an individual unit. This type of development is similar to row-house development, modern town house development, or cluster housing. It is similar to a condominium development; however, the land underneath each unit is conveyed in fee simple title. The owners association is a nonprofit corporation or association having management responsibility to the project as a whole and actually holds title to the common areas. The shares in such corporation, or membership in such association, are transferred with the transfer of title to the individual units. In the case of a condominium, the owners association is a nonprofit corporation authorized by law composed of the individual owners of units in a condominium project which manages but has no ownership interest in the common areas.

Planned unit developments generally provide for better land use through cluster housing, thus providing for more green belts and amenities and in general creating a better environment. The developer can usually zone a particular parcel of land more easily by trading off green belts and open spaces for higher densities and showing a well-blended use of land.

Generally, lenders, developers, and purchasers have been too casual and naive in developing and purchasing condominiums, cooperatives, and planned unit developments. It is a complex type of development, and it is imperative that the developers, lawyers, and lenders involved do their homework and educate themselves about the proper procedures in order to obtain a properly underwritten and economically successful development. Many have been lucky, but there is no excuse for incompetence in creating real estate properties. In the past, many lenders did not require market studies, and the vast majority did not obtain sufficient information and data to successfully evaluate, analyze, and underwrite a development. The majority didn't even know what information and data to obtain, let alone have the knowledge to analyze such data.

The construction lender may feel secure with a take-out commitment for the end loans, but if the project is not compatible with the market and, consequently, there are no sales, what good is an end loan take-out? Almost all permanent end loan commitments are conditional, containing requirements for a certain number of sales (generally a certain percentage of sales of the entire project must be sold before closing the first sale), satisfactory credit of the individual borrowers and other various "outs." It is easy for a lender to issue a conditional commitment, collect the fee, and only fund if there are sufficient sales under the correct circumstances when it is evident that the project is successful.

Construction lenders should have competent staffs to review information and require that certain safeguards be present for a successful development. Now that we have seen many unsuccessful ventures, perhaps the experience of improper underwriting judgment will create better underwriting in future lending.

The Federal Housing Administration (FHA), Veterans Administration (VA), FNMA, and the Federal Home Loan Mortgage Corporation (FHLMC) have all inaugurated condominium programs to stabilize the end loan money market. You may not want to use their programs, but you should educate yourself and take advantage of the free information available. Their program requirements provide an excellent check list for insuring a successful mortgage loan.

How Should We Underwrite?

First, the location of the site, the design, and the market must be analyzed thoroughly before proceeding further. Completely answer these questions:

Is the general location proper for the intended development?
Does the site have engineering and topography problems, and is the site compatible with the general location?
Are the design and plan correct?
What size should the units be?
Should it be a high-rise or a low-rise development?
Are the specifications satisfactory for owner appeal?
Is the parking adequate?
What type of parking is required?
Are the recreational facilities properly located?
Are there sufficient amenities?
Is the overall layout satisfactory?
What is the existing competition?
How many unsold units are in the market area?
What is the developing inventory?
What market groups are purchasing, that is, empty nesters, families, older persons, singles, etc?
What are the absorption rates?
What would the expected absorption rate be for the intended development?
Are the unit prices competitive?

Second, the developer, the sales program, the financial analysis, and the legal documentation must be evaluated.

The developer obviously should have proper financial strength and experience to oversee the construction of the intended development, and preferably, should have a track record in the development of these types of properties. A vital ingredient necessary for success is the business ability of the developer—in managing the organization, in having or being able to hire or create an adequate sales staff, in understanding financing needs, and in getting the job done.

Even though we have the correct location with the right design and a good market with an experienced, financially capable developer, the project will fail if we do not have the proper sales program with a good sales team. All the numbers, cash-flow analysis, etc., mean nothing if we have no sales. If sales are slow, or there is too much front-end investment, the only way to be repaid is through higher prices on the individual units or an accelerated sales program. Is there an adequate budget for advertising? Is the advertising media correct for the market? Will the sales personnel present the honest and realistic expenses and obligations of each unit owner? Any sales effort can be destroyed with unscrupulous practices and incorrect information. Are the units priced in accordance with their particular location within the development?

Take the case where a high-rise was constructed adjacent to a lake. The unit price increased from floor to floor, and the sales were fantastic, but what happened? The sales staff did not say that only the lake-front units were selling— result, the prices on units without a view of the lake had to be reduced to create sales, and the lender barely escaped. The lake-view units should have been priced higher with lower prices for the non-lake-view units so that the combined prices easily paid back the lender and left a nice profit for the developer. Ask yourself, does a unit have a view, is the unit conveniently located, which units would be the most difficult to sell? I am sure that all concerned will see that a proper sales effort is vital.

Now that we have a satisfactory location with the proper design, the proper market, an experienced developer, and an adequate sales team, we can at long last analyze the financial aspects. We now have knowledge of the total development. We know the time for construction, we know when the sales staff should begin selling, and we have projected the absorption rates. We now can establish a cash-flow analysis and project the construction disbursements and the sales expenses on a month-to-month basis. We then analyze the sales closings with a range of conservative and optimistic numbers to determine the approximate time of payout to finally arrive at a decision whether or not the financing request has merit.

Let's say that 1000 condominium units are planned in and around an elaborate golf course with many other recreational facilities and the estimated operating expenses are acceptable for each unit owner in our underwriting. What happens if only one-half of these units sell? Who pays? The developer, the unit owner, or the lender? We know the answer. Always evaluate fully the total property, and consider all contingency problems.

Once there are sales, who closes the long-term permanent end loans? Is there a conditional commitment from a savings and loan, FHA, VA, FNMA, or FHLMC? Perhaps a short-term construction lender will want the long-term loan. It is certainly advisable to require a written conditional commitment so that when you do have sales on the units, your lender has an obligation to close the loan.

It appears that we may now have an economically successful development. Let's record the legal documentation and close the interim loan. Someone from the mortgage banker's staff should read the declaration (master deed) and the by-laws. The underwriting procedure as indicated in this chapter has been on a chronological basis to minimize time in our production departments, but the legal documentation is the foundation of the entire project. Remember, condomoniums are a part of our lives solely by the enactment of laws through each state legislature. Without a proper legal framework, the proposed development will undoubtedly fail.

One should be aware that many states have totally inadequate condominium statutes. In some states, the statute is one and one-half pages in length, hardly sufficient to deal with the many types of condominiums. Since these laws vary from state to state and are vague and provide insufficient safeguards, it is important to employ experienced legal counsel in establishing the framework for the condominium development. It would be helpful if all states reevaluated these laws. Use your own lawyer and not the developer's lawyer (*you* are lending the money). Perhaps the developer's lawyer can draft the documents, but your lawyer should review, redraft, or amend the documents in a valiant attempt to have proper safeguards in the underwriting of the intended project.

Why do we use the word "safeguard"? Let me illustrate: We are constructing a residential condominium, and the declaration reads that there are not to be any commercial uses in the property. The property is then fully developed, sales are great, and purchasers are moving into their units. What could possibly go wrong? Well, it seems that the unit owners immediately clash with the developer in the owners association meetings, and one owner happens to notice that there are to be no commercial uses. The owners immediately notify the developer to take down its commercial signs and close its commercial sales office. Yes, a residential condominium property with no on-site sales programs!

Consider another actual case. A developer completed 25 units of a 50-unit project, sold 20, and then had trouble moving the remaining five because of an unexpectedly soft market. He decided not to build out the rest of the land. But, since this situation was not covered in his declaration, he couldn't sell the unused acreage. It no longer belonged to him, it was a common area owned by the condominium association. If something terrible is going to happen in a condominium project, it will probably be because of an oversight in the master deed: It is quite important that the lawyer have a practical viewpoint and be certain to know and understand all aspects of the proposed development. The lawyer should carefully review all purchase contracts, the plat, and all important documents. It is also suggested that a title company lawyer review the legal documentation. In some states, condominium offerings have to be registered with state agencies and certain types of condominium sales require SEC registration. These are generally second-home or resort-type condominiums that indicate an investment, or where a management firm is renting the individual units, generally in a rental pool arrangement.

The casualty insurance coverage should be carefully considered. Unfortunately, the states and the insurance companies have not given sufficient thought to losses on these types of property. Generally, each building should be insured under a master policy with each unit owner receiving a certificate of insurance. It is required that in the event of a loss the unit or units be rebuilt, after all, what happens to values if an individual and/or a lender should choose not to rebuild and pockets the money?

Some developers have chosen to retain ownership of the land and/or the recreational amenities and lease the land and amenities to each individual unit owner. The developer hopes, if the property can be mortgaged out and ownership of these income-producing assets still be retained, to retire and live happily thereafter. Extreme caution is advised when the developer proposes to retain ownership of a portion of the property. Many lease abuses have occurred which have given the concept a questionable reputation. The developer may have complete control and charge exorbitant rent. What happens to unit value if the recreational facilities are foreclosed by the developer's lender? This is not to say that leases should be prohibited. Some end-loan lenders will not permit leases, probably because of their inability to properly evaluate the lease ramifications. There are, indeed, many well-structured economic leases that have considered the developer, the unit owner, and the lender. The lease can be a good earning asset for the developer, the unit owner can pay less for the property, and the end-loan lender can have a safe investment, providing all parties and possible problems are considered.

End-loan lenders probably will want all common recreational facilities either completed or the money escrowed for the construction of these amenities. The appraisal is based on the amenities, and the total value purchase should be assured. In large developments, it may be necessary to establish separate condominium regimes for each phase so as to phase the recreational amenities and satisfy any sales requirements imposed by the end-loan conditional commitment.

Homeowners Association

The developer and the lender should retain control of the property as long as possible, but at some point in time there is a transaction of giving control to the homeowners association. The developer should employ an independent professional management company to manage the property, with the managing company being retained by the homeowners association to minimize any problems and to give continuity during this transition period. The developer should assist in the early formative homeowners' meetings to acquaint the homeowner with the property, to set forth the organizational chart and the duties of the Board of Directors and its officers, and to establish policies and procedures necessary for a well-managed association. It should be evident that this type of communication and assistance by the developer is required for a good sales program and a successful investment by the interim lender and the end-loan lender. In underwriting apartment loans, we carefully analyze the management aspect, and the same careful scrutiny should be experienced in underwriting these types of properties. The master deed states the monthly assessment is to be paid by each owner. Monthly cost estimates should be verified by outside professionals lest at some future date the homeowners association decides to sue the developer (and the lender) for fraudulent presentation of cost estimates. Sometimes the developer creates a long-term "sweetheart management contract" that is onerous for the unit owner. This practice should be eliminated.

It is suggested that the homeowners association apply for a nonprofit status, since the Internal Revenue Service has indicated that excess cash receipts over cash disbursements are considered taxable income. Additional Internal Revenue Service rulings on this aspect can be anticipated.

Real estate properties require management. Take the case of an 18-unit condominium that appealed to senior citizens. An elderly gentleman in his seventies called the lender one day to state that ambulances or hearses were continually coming to and going from the property, and all that was left was one senile person and old widows. He was the youngest owner, at 74 years, and he was trying to manage the property. He went on to say that the reason he purchased the condominium unit was to rid himself of the worries of home ownership, and he was not about to continue to manage the complex. "Please help, Mr. Lender, please take over the management."

His problem illustrates the fact that a small property probably should not be a condominium unless professional management is hired. Professional management should be required in all condominium and cooperative properties. One of the most common complaints of homeowners is having to spend time on Board of Directors or on Board-appointed committees, while finding that the maintenance and overall management of the development are unsatisfactory. If the Board would hire a competent management firm, many grievances and problems would disappear, and a good management company can provide a qualified, professional executive vice-president of the organization to assist and counsel in management decisions.

The Department of Housing and Urban Development (HUD) recently completed a condominium and cooperative housing study that concluded that maintenance is one of the greatest condominium problems. The greatest potential problem related to the long-run success of the condominium form of ownership is the ability of the association to operate and maintain their commonly owned properties. Failure to maintain such properties will directly affect the value of the individual units. Failure and dissolution of the association will seriously affect the owners in the neighborhood in which the project is located. Maintenance work must be well organized and properly done for a property to keep its value.

Resort Condominiums

Resort condominiums have been well received by the public. Many people have more leisure time to enjoy weekend condominiums or long winter vacations, and to some, owning a condominium gives status in our affluent society. A person can purchase a resort condominium and include the unit in the management rental pool and, if lucky, receive income to offset some of the operating expenses; perhaps the unit will not cost any additional money after the equity money is paid. Usually, the individual unit will cost additional money, but many owners have realized substantial appreciation in value on the second home investment. The construction cost usually is much higher and the design is more informal with multiuse rooms which reduce the size of the units. Be careful that the architect has properly designed the buildings for the area and the climate conditions. Some ski condominium properties suggest that the architect has never seen a snowflake. Generally, the second home condominium is sold with decorating and furniture options available or included in the purchase price.

What is a condotel? Several hotels have been established as condominiums, with each unit owner providing individual financing, which is an excellent way to obtain a high sales price for a hotel or motel. Usually the unit owner has the right to use the unit for a preestablished number of days, with the remaining time being utilized by transients as a typical hotel operation. The majority of the condotels are located in resort areas, but there is no reason that an investment (syndication) hotel couldn't be established in any metropolitan area.

The Marriott Corporation, for example, owns a luxury hotel facing Central Park in New York City. They converted the upper 23 floors of this 41-floor hotel into condominiums, leaving the lower 18 floors for commercial, revenue-producing facilities. Of the 448 condominium units in the upper 23 floors, 200 were sold to individuals who could choose from among all 448 units in order to obtain a desired size and location. The remaining 248 units (57 percent) were retained by Marriott for hotel purposes. Ownership of the commercial and hotel facilities, such as the restaurant, ballroom, and lobby area, remained with the sponsor. The total condominium sales price was in an amount sufficient to return the sponsor's investment, or a large part thereof, while the sponsor retained a long-term, income-producing property.

Because of the structure of this condominium concept, the annual charges imposed on residential owners is split into two portions—a share of the total common charge, and a share of the total service charge.

The common charge includes all the expenses of operating the condominium property, including maintenance, repair, and replacement. Excepted from these common charges are the expenses incurred solely for the benefit of the hotel units and those that apply solely to the operation of the commercial unit, since the profit from the commercial unit is received by the sponsor, the one exception being that the commercial unit includes the hotel facilities to which individual unit owners have an easement of use. Consequently, the maintenance expenses of the hotel facilities are treated as a common charge, of which unit owners must pay a share.

The service charge expenses in connection with hotel services are allocated differently from the common charges (which are allocated in proportion to the fair value of each unit). Essentially, the allocation of service charges is based on some measure of use by each unit, for example, housekeeping expenses are allocated on the basis of square-footage-rate fair value.

This condominium concept permits a substantial return on the initial capital investment while generating a continual rental or management fee income. The concept should prove to be very attractive to the industry.

Marriott also owns a 408-room resort condotel in Scottsdale, Arizona, where the purchaser of a unit is entitled to use it only four weeks a year. For the remainder of the year, Marriott treats the unit as an ordinary hotel suite and rents it to the general public. The owners receive a share of the income derived from the hotel. Eventually, the Marriott Corporation hopes to develop a worldwide string of condominium hotels and perhaps offer an exchange option that would allow owners to exchange vacation time in their condominium for time in another location.

Time Sharing?

What is this type of resort sales program? From the condotel concept sprang the time-sharing approach, where the developer sells a number of different buyers the right to use the same unit, generally for time segments of one week, with most buyers purchasing two or three time segments, or two or three weeks. The term "time sharing" is borrowed from the computer industry. Because the expense of owning and operating a second home is split among various users, the price of each can be as low as $1,000 to $2,000, putting second homes within the reach of a much broader market than in the past. Time sharing can be structured in several ways: As an outright sale so that the buyer acquires fee simple title to a particular unit for a particular time segment, or as a lease, a vacation license, a club membership, or a limited partnership arrangement. Time sharing ownership has two general types: (1) tenancy in common, or (2) estates-for-years, revolving successfully among the various owners with a vested remainder interest. A co-owner can go to a judge and say, "I want out," and the judge could partition the property unless there is a waiver of partition among the tenants in common. A tax lien against one of the owners could be another problem. To solve these problems, the estate-for-years concept evolved whereby the title and the right to occupy coexist and are created simultaneously by the same deed. All the interval owners own the fee together, but they are not tenants in common. Each owns an estate-for-years, and these estates succeed each other for a period of 99 years. However, this form of ownership may be construed as a lease and be subject to landlord-tenant regulations. The individual states should pass statutes validating these types of ownership.

In a lease, a buyer purchases a lease for a specific unit and, in essence, prepays rent for the term of the lease, which is generally 40 to 60 years, or the economic life of the property. The prepaid lease is paid either in cash or, generally, within five years. When a buyer wants to use the unit, he or she simply makes a reservation with the managing company. A buyer has three choices in disposing of the lease; ask for the money back, as is usually provided for in the lease; sell the lease, especially if the lease value has appreciated; or ask the managing company to sell the lease and pay a commission. A developer may choose to sell licenses, which function as use permits for specific units at specific times.

In some instances where the developer and managing agent have several resort properties, the time-share owner may choose a vacation at any one of the resort properties. This concept is also used by condominium owners by trading vacation times with other condominium owners, with some condominium exchange companies being established as a clearing house for trading vacation times. The condominium exchange companies charge a commission for their services.

What are the reasons for this time-sharing trend? Obviously a broad, untapped market is a prime reason. Each purchaser can buy only the time desired instead of taking on the liability of owning an entire unit. A purchaser can buy future vacations at today's prices and avoid inflationary increases. A time share with a company which has several resort properties gives vacation flexibility and enables the purchaser to avoid being tied to one unit in one location. Tax benefits are usually available to the time-share owner. For a resort community, the selling of off-season times creates a year-round resort. Resorts often strive to attract off-season conventions to enable them to operate all year, and time-sharing tends to offset the need for pursuing convention business.

It has been stated that time sharing may be the best way to sell resort condominiums. There are some crucial aspects to time sharing which will require you to learn some new marketing rules. Remember that you are selling vacations and not shelter. With this in mind, the property and the location must be considered as a vacation site. Many time-shared properties are successful because they are sufficiently close to population centers for weekend use.

Time-sharing marketing is quite similar to land sales. The unit should be professionally decorated with high-quality furniture for all the sizzle, pop, and sex appeal possible. The buyers are not people who can afford a second home, they only want to spend a week or two on vacation; so your competition is not the second-home project, it's the resort hotel down the road. As a result of these factors, the advertising media and the market approach must cater to your purchasing market.

As mentioned previously, land sales marketing concepts have been the most successful. It should be noted that large numbers of purchasers are required; for example, a 30-unit condominium with 52 one-week time segments may require 1560 purchasers. Since time-sharing is new, many lenders are wary of getting involved. As mentioned previously, there are some legal ambiguities regarding ownership, but these problems should be corrected in the near future. The values of time shares may be difficult to verify. Marketing expenses sometimes range upwards to 40 percent, and with other more costly merchandising specifications and items required, the typical one-owner condominium price of, say, $50,000 may have to be increased to $75,000 or even $100,000. The lenders will want to limit their exposure on a ratio based on the $50,000 price. A developer may obtain individual loans on each condominium unit and then sell contracts for deeds, licenses, leases, etc., but what happens if the developer defaults and you wish to foreclose? Statistics show that 75 percent of the purchases are cash sales, and only 25 percent of the sales require financing; however, how does a construction lender determine the loan amount? Many time-share leases have been financed through commercial paper and there are other developer bank financing relationships which may be explored.

Conversions

With the advent of the popularity of the condominium, many apartment properties have been converted to cooperatives or condominium regimes. The well-located conversion property with the well-organized sales program can be a profitable venture. The profit motive in obtaining a maximum sales price for an apartment property is the prime reason for conversion. There have been many unsuccessful conversions due to the lack of sufficient analysis. What important factors should be considered in potential conversion? Many novices may think that all apartments can be profitably converted, but only a small percentage of apartments are suitable for conversion, since the buildings and units were designed for rental and not for sale. The majority of apartments are constructed for the younger person, while the largest single market for condominiums is the empty nester.

The physical property should be given a thorough inspection and analysis. The "mix" of units should be compatible with the market. The buildings should be well constructed with above-average soundproofing, and there should be adequate amenities to generate sales appeal. In every conversion it is a necessity to renovate, change some of the small features for ownership, properly decorate the common areas and units, and generally prepare the units for sale. In addition, the building codes and zoning codes should be carefully checked, and the governing authority asked to approve the intended conversion. If each unit does not pay its own utilities, considerable thought should be given for the equitable solution of paying these.

After approving the property, a thorough, in-depth market study should be undertaken with emphasis on comparables, existing inventory, developing inventory, absorption rates, profile of purchaser, etc. Simply stated, a successful conversion offers a product comparable to those selling in the market at a lower price than competitors are asking.

Some lenders will not want to finance a conversion due to their lack of knowledge or to their desire to obtain a quick pay-off on a low-interest loan. The existing mortgagee usually should agree to a partial release program, assuming that a certain number of sales are required before the conversion is triggered. Another reason for complete and thorough underwriting analysis is to prove to the existing lender the merit of the conversion. The existing mortgagee may or may not desire the end loans on the individual units. If the existing lender will not agree to a partial release program, then a *bridge loan* is required. A new lender must underwrite a temporary bridge loan while the sales program is in effect and the property is converted. Some developers may obtain a high condominium appraisal and expect a 75% loan-to-value ratio, which would probably be 100 percent of the apartment cost. A typical apartment ratio loan, with proper relief clauses, should be considered. If an individual lender is unavailable, a standby loan commitment and bank financing may be the solution. If the existing mortgagee does not agree to a conversion, the developer could structure contracts for deeds, leases, etc., and not pay off the lender, but there is severe danger for both the developer and the lender, since it would be difficult to foreclose on the various interests.

It should be illuminating to analyze the primary abuses (complaints) that indicate a degree of failure of condominiums, cooperatives, and planned unit developments.

Design and Layout

1   High density (too crowded).
2   Lack of privacy (poor soundproofing).
3   Inadequate parking.
4   Poor layout—building and units are poorly oriented for a view, whether it be a view of someone's garbage pail or aesthetic view of surrounding area. Parking is poorly positioned to the units and the narrow streets and traffic plan are totally inadequate.

Developer

1   Bad construction and a lackadaisical attitude toward post-construction repair work and warranty items.
2   Misleading sales tactics.

3 Incorrect estimate of maintenance fees.
4 No professional management team.
5 Some common facilities and amenities never constructed as promised.
6 Long-term ''sweetheart'' management contracts.
7 Onerous land lease and/or recreational facility lease.

Resident Owners

1 Mismanagement of homeowner associations.
2 Poor maintenance.
3 Noisy neighbors.
4 Improper pet control.
5 Rentals—developer or unit owner is renting the units, creating bad harmony and problems for the owners.

The issues arising from distressed condominium defaults, recreational leases, fraud, and other problems are being seen on court calendars. A February 16, 1976, newspaper financial section heading reads, ''Condominium Craze Subject of Study.'' This is the first Congressional investigation of the condominium industry to determine if legislation is necessary to protect consumers interested in buying condominiums.

Business Condominiums

Business condominiums have been well received and are commonplace in Puerto Rico, South America, and other countries. In this country, in addition to condotels and apartments, there have been relatively few business condominiums. Through a business condominium, a company or individual has the opportunity to participate in prime locations, such as downtown, by buying a floor or an office where one normally could not acquire an entire building. Nonspace users also have the opportunity to purchase property in prime locations and lease the space to a user. A limited partnership may purchase a large building where you as a small investor can participate, but you are controlled by the partnership agreement, which may have too many restrictions for your needs and desires. While a condominium will permit flexibility by permitting you to do what you want with the space, and as a passive investor, you may vary the rent as you want and personally control your investment.

Reasons for the business condominium regime are as follows:

1 Investment opportunity—receive part of the action.
2 Purchase space in a prime location and need for a specific location.
3 Share common facility costs with other owners, for example, library and medical laboratory.
4 Stop inflationary rental increases.
5 Convenience in operating from supporting facilities.
6 Independence of space—do what you want with your space and manage your own investment, and not be bothered with landlord-tenant lease problems, for example, eliminate percentage leases.
7 Limit loan liability to individual condominium unit.

Legal, medical, and professional research office buildings have been the most popular business condominiums. The unit owners can enjoy the advantages mentioned above, but more particularly, they share the cost of a large law library, a medical laboratory, or a research library and/or computer facilities or other necessary equipment that may be needed in their professional business. Another factor is the elimination of joint and several personal liability on a large mortgage loan involving a doctor- or lawyer-owned property.

Office warehouse and industrial parks have received condominium market interest. Several designs have a recreational package that includes such items as a golf course, tennis courts, racket courts, and a health spa that are appealing to and desired by the individual owners. In some industrial parks, the owners can establish central machinery for waste disposal, air and water processing, and other procedures to which most companies will be forced to turn.

There have been some condominium shopping centers. However, shopping center developers have elected not to emphasize the condominium design even though the broader sales market might be quite appealing.

More widespread use of the business condominium concept has been delayed because of the reluctance of lenders providing long-term loans for the unit owners, since many lenders prefer larger loans rather than several smaller loans. The future of business condominiums may be appealing and interesting to our industry, as the market accepts this type of usage.

An illustration of a multiuse business condominium shows the flexibility and need for the condominium concept. A 52-story residential and commercial condominium in midtown Manhattan, for example, has 31 upper floors with 230 residential units and the lower 21 floors with office and retail space. It is sponsored by a partnership and is owned by a trust.

The various interests in the land and building making up this building offer an example of the ''pineapple technique'' of slicing up a real estate property to satisfy different user and investment participants.

The management of the condominium, consisting of the residential units and the commercial unit, is run by a 19-member board of managers elected by the unit owners. The board of managers, however, has authority only over the residential units and the common elements. The commercial unit is separately operated by its owner, and none of its expenses are borne by the residential owners.

The sponsor was to have voting control of the board of managers until titles to all the residential units were conveyed, or two years after the date the declaration of condominium was filed, whichever occurred first. Even beyond this date the sponsor continued to have voting control so long as more than 50 percent of the interests in the common elements were held.

The handling of the common elements of the condominium, that is, those portions of the building and the land that are used by all of the unit owners, is similar to the procedure followed in many single-use condominiums. Certain common elements are shared by all the resident unit owners (the residential limited common elements), and some are used only by the commercial unit owner (the commercial limited common elements).

Multi-use condominiums are likely to become the next major trend within the condominium field. In essence they permit a developer to retain as income property a portion of the structure that can be devoted to commercial or office use, while at the same time recouping most or all of the equity investment by the profit on the sale of the residential units. At the same time residential owners may benefit because a large portion of the maintenance costs of the building are being borne by the commercial unit owner, which may lend an additional element of stability to the structure's financing in times of economic distress should vacancies occur in the residential units.

NEW TOWN COMMUNITIES

New towns can consist of extremely-high-density developments near the core of the downtown area, large planned unit developments having various land uses as a part of the metropolitan area, or completely new towns that are created contiguous to or separate from a particular city, with Columbia, Maryland, and Reston, Virginia, being the most publicized.

Population growth, city problems, and expanding expectations for a better life and environment have focused national attention on new communities as a potentially superior form of urban development.

New Town Community Objectives, Goals, and Success Requirements

The objectives may be stated simply as follows:

1 Rationalizing urban growth.
2 Reducing environmental pollution.
3 Improving urban design.
4 Conserving land and natural resources.

The goals of the new town of Reston, Virginia, are as follows:

1 Widest choice of opportunities for leisure and use of time.
2 Environment flexible enough for residents to remain in a neighborhood for their entire lives.
3 Planning for the improvement and dignity of the individual.
4 Chance to live and work in the same community.
5 Availability of cultural, recreational, and commercial facilities from the outset.
6 Preservation and encouragement of beauty.
7 Profitability to the developer.

What Should a New Town Possess?

Any large-scale development should have a strong employment base. If possible, the new town should be located near an existing plant or industrial park having several employers. The actual plan of the new town shold permit a broad range of employment opportunities within the community itself.

There must be a variety of housing types and styles, that is, single-family dwellings, rental housing, condominiums, town houses, etc. It should be remembered that these housing units are in competition with other choices that a purchaser may have available within the given market area. It is fine to have a proper master plan, but you must have the correct merchandise for sale.

There must be a good internal transportation system as well as a system which provides quick, easy access to other communities within the urban region. New towns should be well located near transportation facilities for access throughout the metropolitan district and access to employment centers.

New towns must have proper community facilities, services, and amenities. Almost all new towns have developed an abundance of these facilities which are necessary for meeting the total community concept, which generates sales activity.

An effective local government must be established for the proper control and direction of the new community. This aspect may be easily overlooked by the developer. However, effective local government can make the difference between success or failure.

Important Considerations in Developing New Communities

With the objectives, goals, and needs of a new community in mind, let's analyze the important considerations in new town community development. The economic law that land, labor, capital, and management are the ingredients necessary for economic success is certainly true in the development of new communities. These large developments require sizable land parcels, tremendous sums of capital investment, expert management, and a lot of hard work.

The availability of land and the location of the land is the first and most important aspect of successful new communities. The developer is attempting to create a new town community by developing property for sale and for use. The location and market demand must be correctly analyzed. The following site information should be obtained: drainage capability, topography, portable water supply, types of soil and soil test, existing water and sewer facilities, gas, electric, telephone service capabilities, existing road systems, etc.

These questions should be answered:

Is employment easily accessible?
Can new employers be attracted to this location?
Will industrial users require rail facilities?
Can new freeways be built for easy access to this location and will the freeways permit quick access to all portions of the region?
What public transportation facilities will be needed and available?
Are the local and state governments receptive to this new development?
Will they permit the required zoning and give assistance toward utility problems and perhaps assist in the financing of the needed development costs?

It should be noted that large cities generally will fight new town development, since they believe that the core city may die as development intensifies in the suburban areas.

Unless the land is owned by one owner, it is extremely difficult to assemble the required tract needed for the development. Also, it is necessary to have certain easements and rights-of-way in conjunction with the intended development. It is for these reasons that the power of eminent domain is extremely important. If we are to develop new communities, it is believed that a new community authority should be established which would be similar in function to an urban renewal authority. This authority would have the right to purchase and assemble land and to sell to the proper developer. Further, the authority would be able to guarantee the underwriting of bonded indebtedness and other necessary debt instruments incidental to the development of the new community. This right of eminent domain is an extremely important tool that should be made available to new town developers.

Low-cost land is important, since the land will be held for a long period of time and the carrying costs can be enormous, not to mention the profit factor potential in lower-cost land. In fact, a series of land options (rolling options) should be obtained from the seller, and this structure would be ideal to minimize the investment and the interest carrying costs. Perhaps the seller of the land could be given a participation in the profits for permitting rolling options, or the developer might pay a lower cost for the land and give the seller a future participation in profits. The developer might also agree to permit the seller to continue owning some land peripheral to the new town development, thus giving the seller increased land value as the new community is developed. As mentioned previously, if the right of eminent domain is available, the new community authority can subsidize the purchase of the land. It should also be noted that the development should proceed as rapidly as the market permits to further minimize the carrying costs of the land.

Planning and Engineering

Employ the best realistic planners, engineers, and lawyers. After the site meets the necessary requirements for a successful development, a practical master plan must be developed with all aspects carefully considered. Certain aspects should be carefully analyzed. For example, what are the specific markets, what are the housing absorption rates in the market area, what housing units should be constructed and how many, when should the commercial development be started (the search for new industry to locate in the new development should be started immediately), where are the existing utilities, and must a totally new utility system be developed? In conjunction with the utility development, where should the first construction begin, is there proper access to the first development? What necessary community and public buildings should be initially constructed for marketability? It is easy to complete a master plan, but is the plan realistic and practical for the market area? This is a crucial part of the development process in that the planners and designers may be too innovative and totally incompatible with reality.

Probably the most important aspect in the modern development of new towns and new communities is the proper, realistic approach to the development of these new communities. This particular aspect of practicality has probably been the primary reason for the failure of modern new towns. It is easy to dream and think of pie-in-the-sky versus reality. Perhaps this analogy could be drawn: success versus failure—reality versus dream.

In general, land use in the communities is planned so that land use schemes and circulation patterns encourage interaction of people and uses and assure accessibility to services and facilities. Open-space areas serve a dual purpose as recreational areas and as buffers between incompatible land uses. The open space consists of lakes, golf courses, parks, streams, valleys, marinas, riding trails, walkways, etc. The traffic circulation system attempts to maximize mobility and reduce dependence on the automobile via provision of complementary systems and promotion of safety and convenience for pedestrian and vehicular traffic. Environmental quality must be specifically considered in the overall planning of the new community. An abundance of public and community facilities is generally planned and well located throughout the new development. Educational facilities, health services, and cultural facilities are also strongly considered and provided for in the development. While commercial development facilities will generally be located primarily in the town center of each of the new communities, daily convenience services are generally programmed for distribution throughout the neighborhood and village centers of the new communities. The development of the large regional shopping centers and the industrial areas of the new community development are excellent opportunities for the developers to receive tremendous land-price increases, to construct the facilities themselves and sell these properties, or build and hold the property for investment.

In several new community developments, it took approximately three years for the total planning and local government approval. Increased legislation on environmental protection may further tend to complicate the timing problem, and as these new laws are passed, additional bureaucratic delays may be expected. The developer's technical staff must be well prepared to convince local government that the development is good for the area and that there will be no financial burden borne by the present utility districts or the people themselves.

The New Community Developer

Since new community development involves the development of large parcels of land, with many developments taking from 10 to 20 years, it is obvious that the developer should have the proper management team and the proper philosophy before undertaking such a development. The financial strength of the developer or the partner/lender is extremely important. There have been various private entrepreneurial developers; however, the majority of the developers have been large corporations who generally have not been in the development business.

Economics of New Community Development

The basic economic objective of a new town development is to acquire land at a relatively low price, add basic services and amenities, and then sell it at a price that covers cost and provides a reasonable net profit. Large-scale, new community developments have three economic advantages over smaller-scale developments. First, they have the potential for capturing virtually all the land value increment resulting from the external or "spillover" benefits of major public and private improvements. The improvements increase the value of the surrounding land and, likewise, certain developments such as junkyards, service stations, rendering plants, etc., which can have a negative effect on land values, can be eliminated in the new community. Second, new community projects afford the opportunity to create a superior living and working environment, which is more desirable than the environment produced in smaller-scale developments. Third, they have a capability for more efficient development through economies of scale, improved management, and coordination of different phases of development.

The simplicity of the economic rationale mentioned above belies the complexities, risks, and difficulties intrinsic to the actual development of such projects. These risks include:

1   Extremely large carrying costs over a long period of time.
2   Uncertainty with regard to the change in the external economy and governmental relations.
3   Heavy overhead and start-up costs.
4   Management of land development, community facilities, and citizen participation.
5   Economic failures which may not become apparent until the last several years of development.
6   Scale of investment and the timing of the cash returns is much different from a typical land development project.

Financing

The financing of new town developments can be complex and requires a tremendous capital investment.

After the location of the land meets the necessary requirements, and the market appears to be correct for the development, and the local government authorities appear to be receptive, we can then begin to analyze the financing aspects. Since it generally requires up to three years of planning before construction commences, the initial carrying costs of the land become crucial in the early stages of development. Obviously, it would be preferred, as stated before, that a new community authority were established so that the authority would subsidize the purchase of the land as well as the interest rate on the loan required to purchase. An attempt should be made to reduce these initial costs via rolling options or joint-venture concepts with the land owner/ seller or any other structure of purchase that reduces the land cost.

Development costs are the next large investment problem. Generally, entirely new utility developments must be constructed. Federal grants may be sought for the development of these utility facilities. In states where the law permits, the county or the city may assist in underwriting revenue bonds for the construction of these utility developments. This reduces the interest rate on this portion of the investment and a portion of these costs would be refundable to the developer. Ideally, some of the original community facilities could be included in the bonding of the land development.

In summary, there are numerous complex problems which must be resolved by a developer of a new community. It should be reiterated that in addition to the low-cost land, the market study must prove an adequate demand and the cooperation of local governments must be gained.

Construction of housing, shopping centers, and conventional-type development can easily obtain conventional financing at market rates. This is not a difficult problem, since the holding period is not particularly long.

Always, the initial investment is quite large. In the following illustration, the cost of the land is $10,000,000 with the initial start-up development costs totalling $18,754,000, which is a fairly quick investment of $28,754,000. It would be several years before the developer and the lender could expect to have this money returned from sales of the property.

The HUD assistance program under Title VII should be thoroughly analyzed to determine if this program can be of financial assistance in the development of a new community. The major drawback of utilizing a federal program is the bureaucracy involved and the time required to complete the process of approval.

The proper underwriting of a proposed new community is of the utmost importance. A realistic economic model should be developed that gives a critical path for the entire development. Economic success is dependent upon the delicate balance of cash outlay, and the development facilities that should be constructed and the market demand that exists should be closely correlated with one another in establishing the cash-flow analysis. It should be obvious to the developer and lender that they both need a deep pocket with plenty of "patient" money.

Let's examine some of the capital investment required in new communities. The development of one typical new town was a joint venture between a large institutional investor and a mortgage banker. Originally, the investor loaned $23,500,000 to purchase the land. Later a $50,000,000 loan was obtained to repay that investor and to provide additional money for development. Then a $19,000,000 land expansion was required for a major industrial corporation and the capital investment was increased to $76,000,000. Within a few months, the mortgage banker arranged for another $30,000,000 from the original investor and a new investor.

In another similar development, a large life insurance company committed a $20,000,000 leasehold loan and a major corporation invested $15,000,000. Even with that type of investment, financial troubles developed and the industrial corporation took over the new town community. In spite of the early financial problems, it appears that this new town will be a financial success, since land that cost $1,900 an acre in 1961 was later being sold at approximately 20 times its original cost.

Perhaps it would be helpful for us to analyze the reasons for failure and success in the development of new towns.

Reasons for Failure of New Towns

Poor location.
High cost of land.
Poor access.

Improper market analysis.
Lack of local government cooperation.
Bureaucracy.
Lack of practicality.
Inordinate amount of carrying costs.
Lack of federal incentives.
Poor management and organization.
Underfinancing.
Lack of proper legislation (state and local).

Reasons for Success

Good location.
Low-cost land.
Good access to employment.
Continuous development.
Minimum carrying costs.
Standardization of living units.
Variety of units through proper grouping.
Low interest rates.
Receptive local government.

New Town Community Trends

Due to the size of new towns, the massive amount of money required, the length of time to develop, the volatile changes in the market, and recent environmental controls which delay and increase the cost of the development, there is a trend to develop smaller communities. With smaller developments, the chances for success are greatly improved. Nonetheless, large new multiuse developments are being constructed within our cities where the market demand is more assured and transportation and employment needs are no longer a problem.

Smaller 600- to 1500-acre developments are normally located where regional shopping centers with office building demands are present. The housing units are developed and, more importantly, the commercial development is constructed, thereby weighing the financial success of the development toward the commercial development.

Bringing the suburbs downtown into new town/in-town developments is another definite trend. Examples of new town/in-town developments are Crown Center in Kansas City; Renaissance Center in Detroit; Century City, California; and the Houston Center. Obviously, downtown locations have employment demand as well as commercial development demand. If new, well-designed, and desirable communities can be properly developed where the population will not have to commute, the traffic congestion will be greatly reduced and we will have less pollution in our environment. This concept should be a challenge to the large cities and to the large corporate developers.

How Should New Town Communities Be Developed?

Since national attention has been focused on our environment, our natural resources, our social problems, and our increasing population, how should we plan and construct our urban growth to create a better community? Beginning in the mid-1930s, the federal government attempted to become a new town developer. Obviously, the plan was not a success, due to the tremendous governmental bureaucracy problems. It has been said that perhaps the government should purchase the land, create the master plan, and then sell the land to the various developers as the market dictates the need for specific uses. This idea is also fraught with the lack of practicality, not to mention the bureaucracy problem. It is generally and correctly believed that if private enterprise can be given the proper tools, new town communities will be properly developed.

Our continuing task is to provide for the increasing population through better planning and orderly growth, the conservation of our natural resources, the creation of a better environment, and the creation of a sense of community and well-being.

URBAN RENEWAL

Urban renewal, as generally understood in the United States, denotes an attempt to solve the pervasive problems of older areas in our cities through a carefully planned combination of redevelopment, rehabilitation, and conservation. As the twentieth century moved toward its second half, it became increasingly obvious to concerned observers that our major cities were heading for serious trouble, stemming from the rapidly advancing economic, functional, and physical obsolescence of the older, central portions of our cities. The scale of these problems necessitated major federal involvement in the attempt to solve them. In fact, the history of urban renewal in the United States is essentially the history of federal programs.

The first major federal legislation in the field of urban renewal was Title I of the Housing Act of 1949. This law provided for up to $1 billion in federal loans and $500 million in federal grants over a period of five years, to be made available to local public agencies for their use in specified, preapproved redevelopment plans. A major provision of this legislation was its emphasis upon residential redevelopment. The Act limited federally supported projects to those which were "predominantly residential in character" or which were to be "developed or redeveloped for predominantly residential uses."

Until 1974, all major urban renewal legislation was added to the basic skeleton of the 1949 Act, with the general modifications designed to expand the program so as to involve the private sector to a greater degree, and to modify the original residential character of the program so as to emphasize redevelopment of inner-city commercial areas.

The ongoing modification and expansion of Title I finally resulted in a labyrinthian combination of categorical grant programs for urban physical development which a former HUD Secretary once described as "a team of 22-legged jackasses hitched up backwards by a blind man." The aptness of this description was eventually recognized by Congress, with the result that a complete revision of federal urban renewal programs was effected by the Housing and Community Development Act of 1974. This Act abolished nearly all of HUD's categorical grant programs for urban physical development and replaced them with a consolidated federal assistance program which has increased the amount of federal monies available to communities and greatly expanded the power of local officials over the use of these federal funds. Rather than requesting categorical grants for closely defined specific uses, cities may now ask for monies to be placed into a general account from which they may approach such problems as urban renewal, model cities programs, water and sewer grants, urban beautification, and historic preservation as they see fit.

The allocation of funds under the Housing and Community Development Act of 1974 is based upon a formula which considers the population, the amount of over-crowded housing, and the number of persons living at or below the poverty level in a given city. The general objectives for which these federal monies are to be used include the elimination of slums and of blighted neighborhoods; the conservation and expansion of the existing housing stock, especially for families of low and moderate income; the extension of community services; the more rational utilization of land; the reduction of the now-prevalent isolation of income groups within narrow geographical areas; and the preservation and restoration of historically, architecturally, and aesthetically significant buildings.

It can readily be seen that the present Act, through its broadened objectives and its increased emphasis upon local discretion in the use of funds, has made it much more difficult to write with precision regarding the present state of urban renewal in the United States. Early experience under the Act indicates a pronounced tendency on the part of recipient cities to use such funds to finance the expansion of municipal services at the relative expense of other programs. It can be expected that urban renewal activities across the nation will continue their growth from the early, specific housing emphasis to a much wider community-development approach.

Concomitant with the growing community-development approach to urban renewal has been an increasing realization that the answer to urban blight does not lie in a simple process of tearing down old buildings and replacing them with new ones.

Chapter 25

Financing Leisure Facilities

Laurence H. Cleland

Leisure facilities are generally considered to be those which people turn to for diversion once the basic necessities such as food, shelter and clothing are met. At that stage of development, the basic unit, whether individual or family, can broaden its horizon for personal satisfaction, diversion, or for minimizing boredom.

Necessity

The need for such diversion, to a greater or lesser extent, is constantly called to our attention by the medical fraternity as an important ingredient in helping us operate at our optimum. Although this is the antithesis of the Puritan ethic, it can be established with utter medical and psychiatric certainty that if leisure time were not actively cultivated by people in high-stress positions, physical and emotional disaster would follow.

Challenge

Financing leisure facilities is one of the most challenging experiences facing the mortgage banking industry. In times when mortgage money is not readily available, leisure financing is generally difficult to arrange, and since these facilities are not primary necessities, lenders feel that users can cut down on or cut out patronizing or using such facilities. And so, the user, they think, may let interest and principal go unpaid, with the resulting high risk factor.

When mortgage funds in general are scarce, it takes the utmost ingenuity to arrange for such financing.

We are yet too close to the recently experienced fuel shortage to know how long and to what extent it will affect us. Nevertheless, in the short run, this is having a very negative effect on travel-oriented facilities. This points to the fact that even if the fuel crisis lessens quickly, lenders will be more and more suspicious that such a fuel crisis may reappear and again negatively affect the remote leisure developments.

Each type of leisure facility has its own unique consideration. However, there is a common thread running through all income properties, including those which are leisure-oriented.

1 The ability and experience of the developer—in other words, the track record.
2 Cost.
3 Location and concept of the project.
4 Feasibility.
5 The financial strength of the developer.
6 The management ability and depth of the developer.
7 Value "as is" upon completion.
8 Alternate use for property.
9 Loan-to-value ratio.
10 Interest rate and amortization bracket.

TYPES AND CLASSIFICATION OF LEISURE FACILITIES

Leisure facilities have been classified into two categories: close-by facilities and travel-oriented developments. Close-by recreation or diversionary activities are generally found in the local community. It is recognized that certain communities are in or adjacent to oceans, mountains, etc. For this discussion we are including these special locations in travel-oriented facilities. Close-by leisure facilities include:

1 Boating facilities and marinas.
2 Bowling facilities.
3 Golf courses.
4 Tennis clubs.
5 Movie (indoor/outdoor) theatres.

A camping facility is an example of a remote, travel-oriented facility. There follows a brief treatment of each facility mentioned, and the following aspects are discussed for each type of property.

1 General description.
2 Location and feasibility.
3 Optimum size.
4 Value approach.
5 Rules of thumb for financing, including the loan-to-value ratio.
6 Most likely lenders (insurance and savings and loan associations).
7 Special aspects.
8 Pitfalls.

Boating Facilities and Marinas

General Description   Such installations usually consist of many types of real estate and personal property including waterfront land, retail store building, restaurant, bar, bait and waterfront facilities, boat renting and storage, launching ramp, trailer, storage, camping and maintenance (gas, oil, ice, boats and snowmobile).

Location   Such locations are obviously safe, attractive waterfront properties accessible to as many users as possible.

Optimum Size   The size of the installation is directly relative to the number of users, both from the local community and from distant areas.

Value Approach   Replacement cost less depreciation plus land is usually the best value approach. Raw cost plus an entrepreneurial profit is a good check. Sales of comparable properties are helpful, if available. There is usually a scarcity of locations.

Rules of Thumb   In this category, the rule of thumb is best related to the loan-to-value ratio. Most lenders will go from two-thirds to three-quarters of basic real estate value (cost) plus some special requirement for personal property.

Most Likely Lenders   Local banks and savings and loan associations.

Special Aspects   In addition to the basic real estate, much personal property is involved. This is usually financed by a bank and may require collateral.

Bowling Facilities

General Description   A bowling facility is a recreation complex occupying a special building devoted primarily to the game of bowling. In addition to this activity, the modern complex may include a cocktail lounge, restaurant, banquet room, billiard room, pro shop, locker rental, and various coin-operated machines.

Location and Feasibility   As in all economic ventures, location and management are two of the most important factors. Most equipment manufacturers have resource staffs that advise as to location.

Optimum Size   Here again the manufacturers can be most helpful. One rule of thumb is one lane for each 1500 or 2000 people in the location's primary area.

Value Approach   The replacement cost less depreciation plus land is usually the best approach to value. An economic approach can be used if an appraiser can accurately estimate income and operating expenses. Also, sales of comparable facilities are helpful. Some items that go into a cost approach are:

Land		$_____
Building		
_____ square feet @ $_____	$_____	
Driveway and parking	_____	
Parking lot lgtg.	_____	
Landscape, walks, etc.	_____	
Total building	$_____	$_____
Total land and building		_____
Interest legal, etc.		_____
Bowling equipment		_____
Total		$_____

Rules of Thumb   Yardsticks as to loan-per-lane have a broad range, depending on the section of the country, and who owns the equipment, etc. Rules currently applying in most areas are $15,000 per lane. The loan-to-value ratio falls between 66⅔ to 75 percent.

Most Likely Lenders   Banks, savings and loan associations and real estate investment trusts. Where the national manufacturers guarantee the obligation, it becomes a credit loan.

Golf Courses

General Description   The two chief types of golf courses are the regulation and short courses. Regulation courses may be either nine holes (about 3200 yards with a par-35 rating) or eighteen holes (about 6500 yards long with a par-70 rating). Some nine-hole courses have two sets of tees which vary in length, and each hole is played twice for an 18-hole round. Equipment storage and shop buildings of 6000 square feet for 18-hole courses, including 300 square feet for an office and employee lockers, etc., are an essential part of the total facility. Regulation courses are of three types:

1   Private—restricted to members and guests.
2   Semiprivate—some members; nonmembers pay greens fees.
3   Municipal courses—mainly nonmembership; daily greens fees.

Short courses (pitch and putt, par-3 or executive) have become popular with golfers with limited time or energy. These courses originated after World War II and have somewhat relieved crowding on regulation-sized courses.

Location and Feasibility   Nearly half the new courses are part of real estate developments where the developer sells parcels fronting on courses. These may be purchased as single-family homes, apartments, retirement homes, and even industrial property. Proper soil is of primary importance in selecting a site.

Optimum Size   The best size is determined entirely by the characteristics of the surrounding development. Nine-hole courses range from 50 to 90 acres, and 18-hole courses from 110 to 180 acres.

Value Approach   Development costs average $20,000 per hole and range from $10,000 to $40,000 per hole. This amount varies depending on the support facilities needed, such as a clubhouse and storage facility.

Rules of Thumb for Financing   Two-thirds to three-quarters of value.

Most Likely Lenders   Banks, insurance companies, and savings and loan associations.

Tennis Clubs

General Description   A complete indoor tennis facility usually includes lockers, sauna, nursery, etc., in addition to the courts.

Location and Feasibility   Since an alternate use is important, a good location is one close to potential users either in or near to an industrial park or warehouse locale. It should certainly be close or accessible to a clientele which will play tennis.

Optimum Size   There is not enough research available to indicate what an optimum size is. Most have six to 14 courts. It currently takes 150 to 200 members per court to produce an adequate cash flow.

Value Approach Usually, estimated replacement cost plus land. A good plan is to build the structure for industrial or warehouse use and then to add those facilities which are needed for tennis activities. Also, estimated net rents can be ascribed to the building as industrial, with this being capitalized into value using a capitalization rate close to the financing constant.

Rules of Thumb Per court: $70,000, or loan per court: $50,000 to $70,000, say, $10 per square foot of building. For most cases the loan is 75 percent of value.

Most Likely Lenders Local savings and loan associations, insurance companies, real estate investment trusts, etc. In most cases, guarantors will be needed.

Movie Theatres

General Description Many new theatres are located in or near existing shopping centers when there is unused land for the theatre building and for parking. Such theatres can contain one, two, or more auditoriums. Many of these units are leased to national or regional theatre operators with medium to good credit. The landlord is pleased with the additional rent and the operator is pleased that he does not have to buy the land.

Location As indicated above, in or near an existing shopping center or any site of adequate size and zoning not too close to competition.

Optimum Size Typical land needed is three-and-a-half to four acres. Building sizes in larter metropolitan areas range from 11,000 square feet to 18,000 square feet. The 11,000 square feet building contains from 900 to 1000 seats while the larger buildings contain up to 2000 seats.

Value Approach In appraising a theatre, all three approaches to value are applicable. However, most informed appraisers lean to the income approach to value. In this event, the estimated income of the property is capitalized at a rate appropriate to arrive at the value of the property. If the property is owner-operated, the appraiser must obtain accurate figures on income from admission and concession sales, as well as the expenses of operation during the last five years in weighing the assembled data. After all expenses and operating costs are paid there should be a profit before income taxes of about 5 percent of gross admission receipts.

Land leased from a shopping center usually ranges $10,000 to $15,000 net, with net rent on the building, if rented, ranging from 10 to 12 percent of net. A recent deal involved a 68' × 180' building containing 1100 seats at a cost of $375,000. The projection equipment, carpets, seats, etc., are typically furnished by the operator. Land and building rent in that area totalled $55,000. Typical leases range from 15 to 25 years and may contain options for renewal.

The economic approach to value in this case would involve capitalizing the net rent of $55,000 at a rate consistent with the strength of the tenants, such as 10 to 12 percent.

Rules of Thumb on Financing Loans on such installations range from two-thirds to three-fourths of the final value as arrived at by balancing the cost, economic and comparative sales approaches.

Most Likely Lenders   In situations where the theatre is placed in an existing center, the original lender is usually the best source for such financing by way of a second mortgage.

Camping Facilities

General Description   Chain or franchise-operated campsites consist of installations along main roads, particularly in the vicinity of main road junctions. These usually include a park with electricity, water, and sewer hookups. There is usually a central lodge with showers and food, including a facility for food concessions. Many of these camping facilities are franchises and are usually financed with the aid of the parent company.

Location   Generally within a few hours' driving time of large metropolitan areas.

Optimum Size   These are really so new there is no pattern as to size. One camping area, though certainly not typical, consists of 460 acres of land and 850 campsites.

Value Approach   Replacement cost less depreciation plus land is usually the best approach. The market value of the individual units has to be tested on a comparable basis. One such project sells units at $3,600 per owner with up to four owners per unit. These owners share the park on 25%-of-the-time per year basis. Units are generally sold with 10 percent down with bank financing.

Financing Rules of Thumb   Financing of the original development is usually arranged with a joint venture financial partner, such as a real estate investment trust, bank or insurance company. The end loans are arranged much as in the case of a mobile home park.

Most Likely Lenders   Financial institutions for the development proper, and end loans by savings and loan associations, mortgage bankers and commercial banks.

Obviously, for purposes of example, only a few of the potential leisure-type properties have been discussed. The varieties are endless. Nonetheless, they are limited only by developer/lender intuitiveness and ability to dream.

Chapter 26

Franchise Financing

Ira C. Prouty

INTRODUCTION

Franchising is a method for distribution of products and services—but, in essence, it is leverage and promotion, and limited-purpose real estate is usually added. It is monopolistic, because without controls it could not exist. It has business and legal dilemmas, environmental problems, and energy shortages. All together, it is difficult to mend franchise financing into the traditional concept of institutional financing of income-producing real estate.

Yet, most all franchised distribution systems require the use of real estate, either as owner or lessee. This real estate is usually well-located and is income-producing. With proper underwriting, it does constitute acceptable investment security.

Franchise financing of income-producing real estate presents the challenge to determine the risk consistent with sound real estate and investment underwriting. Managers of real estate and analysts of real estate investments, such as mortgage bankers and institutional finance officers, are particularly well qualified, by training and experience, to meet this challenge. The client who may be involved in the use of real estate for the specialized field of franchised distribution may use, profitably, the services of such skilled underwriters.

It serves no purpose to suggest here any new creative financing methods or equity sources for the franchise industry. The role of public security and private placement markets as sources of funds will be disregarded. The objective here will be to suggest adherence to the traditional concept of institutional real estate financing with basic appraisal techniques and underwriting practices normally relied upon to make such decisions. There will be little difference in procedure other than for the additional impact that a franchise agreement may or may not have on the situation.

A point of beginning will be the time that a financially responsible franchised owner or occupant of real estate seeks the assistance of the investor and mortgage banker who is knowledgeable in the concept of franchised distribution.

DEFINITION OF FRANCHISING

Franchising is difficult to concisely define, as there appears to be some ambiguity and diverse opinion about what is and what is not franchising. To quote the United States Department of Commerce:

> Franchising is the form of licensing by which the owner (the franchiser) of a product, service or method obtains distribution at the retail level through affiliated dealers (the fanchisees). The holder of the right is often given exclusive access to a defined geographical area. The product, method or service being marketed is identified by a brand name and the franchiser maintains control over the marketing methods employed.

Many manufacturing and service firms develop, as alternative methods of distribution, various relationships and techniques for selling, through other parties, their products or services to the ultimate consumer situated in many different locations. These methods of distribution will be identified here as "franchised distribution," or simply as "franchising."

CONCEPT OF FRANCHISED DISTRIBUTION

This concept is a modern marketing phenomenon. It contemplates that franchisers shall have the objective of retailing their products or services to the ultimate consumer by creating and maintaining the capability of supporting all distributive operations of their affiliated dealers in many different localities. It has been better stated that:

> In effect, the company is designing every element of a model business, which must then be reproduced and sustained in large numbers in many different areas. The total of these elements—including the product and the way it is distributed—is often referred to as the company's "franchise concept."

HISTORICAL BACKGROUND

In 1898, franchising in the modern sense was introduced in the United States by General Motors, followed by Rexall Drugs in 1902. Thereafter, other companies in the automotive industry and firms in the petroleum, soft-drink bottling and variety store fields formed the traditional sectors of franchised distribution. After World War II, newer methods of franchised distribution of goods and services proliferated, among others, in retailing, fast foods, and hotel and motel enterprises.

The traditional sector now seems quite stable, with sales increasing steadily at a moderate pace from establishments declining somewhat in number. Generally, in all sectors of franchising, there seems to be a continuing trend toward the concentration of establishments to fewer but larger and more responsible franchisers.

It should be concluded that the industry has reached a stage of maturity and more orderly growth. For example, in a survey and report prepared as far back as September, 1971, by the U.S. Department of Commerce, *Franchising in the Economy, 1969-1971*, it was stated that:

> In 1969, 384,000 establishments were engaged in all kinds of franchising; in 1971, the number of such establishments is estimated to total 407,000—an increase of 6 percent. Sales of all kinds of franchising establishments are estimated at over $131.6 billion in 1971—a 10.1 percent increase from $119.5 billion in 1969.

This survey concludes that:

> Except in construction and remodeling and in recreation, entertainment and travel, large franchisors with more than 500 establishments predominate in the newer methods of franchising. In 1971, 54 franchisors will account for about three-quarters of franchise sales and establishments; 90 percent of the sales will be made in 87 percent of the outlets of only 137 companies. The other 471 franchisors will account for only 10 percent of the sales and 13 percent of the establishments. In the traditional sector of franchising—auto and truck dealerships, service stations and soft-drink bottlers—there is similar concentration.

Further, that:

> While franchisor-owned outlets in the newer areas of franchising will account for 21 percent of the establishments, they will make 51 percent of the sales in 1971. Retail franchisors, which own 15 percent of the establishments, will account for 72 percent of total retail franchising sales. In rental services, franchisors owning 15 percent of the establishments will account for 61 percent of the sales. In the fast food area, 24 percent of the sales will be made by 17 percent of franchisor-owned establishments.

The International Franchise Association, a trade group representing more than 150 of the nation's major franchising companies, predicted early in 1973:

> A growth in franchising sales of between $10 and $15 billion during 1973.
> Some 15,000 new franchised outlets will be opened during the next 12 months.
> Franchising now accounts for more than 25 percent of all retail sales and 13 percent of the gross national product.

These expectations of growth in the "franchising" technique did indeed materialize as predicted.

KINDS OF FRANCHISED BUSINESS

From additional data presented in the 1971 report of the Commerce Department, we have computed that the number of establishments and total sales volume of all kinds of franchised goods and services, expressed as a percentage of all franchising, generally appear to have relative importance as follows:

Kinds	Establishments	Sales
Total—all franchising	100%	100%
Gasoline service stations	53.8%	19.9%
Automobile and truck dealers	9.1%	52.4%
Fast foods	8.7%	4.1%
Retailing	7.7%	10.9%
Automotive products and services	5.1%	1.5%
Business aids and services	3.1%	.6%
Rental services	3.1%	1.0%
Convenience grocery	2.5%	1.5%
Educational products and services	1.4%	*
Miscellaneous	1.4%	.2%
Laundry and dry cleaning	1.1%	.1%
Hotels and motels	.9%	3.0%
Recreation, entertainment, travel	.8%	.1%
Soft-drink bottlers (see note)	.7%	3.6%†
Vending	.4%	*
Construction and remodeling	.2%	*

*Less than .1%.

†Includes soft drinks, fruit drinks, and ades; syrups, flavoring agents and bases.

Note: Establishment and sales data do not include figures for independent private label and contract-filler bottling companies which accounted for 16.4 percent in 1969, 11.5 percent in 1970, and 10 percent in 1971 of total industry.

The franchised business continues to be dominated by the traditional sectors, as the following summary indicates:

Kinds	Establishments	Sales
Traditional sector, including gasoline service stations, automobile and truck dealers, and soft-drink bottlers.	63.6%	75.9%
Newer sector, including retailing, fast foods, hotel-motel enterprises and all others.	36.4%	24.1%

These kinds of franchises are designated as traditional and newer sectors of franchising, as indicated by a Commerce Department survey. The franchised-distribution concept is too complex and varied to characterize neatly into two absolute types. However, for simplicity, we shall take the liberty herein of using the words "franchiser" to generally indicate traditional-sector franchisers employing straight product distribution agreements, and "franchisor" for newer-sector franchisors employing product license franchises.

TYPES OF FRANCHISED DISTRIBUTION SYSTEMS

Franchising involves different types of contractual distribution systems depending generally on the class of franchiser. Franchisers are divided into three classes, as follows:

First: the franchisers who are product oriented—that is, primarily concerned with distribution of the franchiser's product.

Second: the franchisers who are manufacturing oriented—that is, primarily concerned with establishing manufacturing or processing plants.

Third: the franchisors who are service oriented—that is, primarily concerned with licensing of a trademark, trade name, method and format of doing business.

The franchisees of the franchisers in each of these classes are faced with different financial requirements and different financing needs although there are many considerations that are common to all of the classes.

Straight Product Distribution Franchises

Franchisers who are product-oriented and franchisers who are manufacturing-oriented employ straight product distribution arrangements. Under this system, a manufacturer may grant an exclusive distributorship to his authorized retail dealer. Such a dealer undertakes to purchase, sell, and service the manufacturer's trademarked product by providing an outlet within his designated market area convenient to the consumer. Under this system, the dealer generally has little or no opportunity to alter the mix or influence the characteristics of the product of the manufacturer.

Straight product distribution arrangements are the most common of all and involve most of the traditional sectors of franchising. Retail marketing of products such as food, liquor, beer, variety stores, and others may regularly use this type of franchised distribution. Often, the soft drink and beer industries franchise wholesale distributorships who, in turn, service retail outlets.

Product-License Franchises

Franchisors who are service-oriented employ product-license distribution arrangements. This involves the licensing of a trademark product or service associated with the planned franchising concept of an entire business. The trademark franchisor does not manufacture the product or render the service. However, control of the business practices of franchisees is essential. To enhance the value of the trademark, the franchisor is vitally interested in the merchandising of product or service. The success of a well-defined and publicly accepted image rests, first, with the franchisor to provide a high degree of brand identity. Then, to provide a control method for quality and uniformity in manufacturing and dispensing the products or service to the consumer.

Finally, to supply the organizational and technical skills required to maintain a profitable and growing business.

The product-license franchisee enters into a business operation obviously subject to various controls imposed by the franchisor—depending on the nature of the products and services franchised. In return, the system offers entrepreneurial opportunities for the small businessman to compete effectively with larger distribution organizations. It provides a small, financially limited business with a means of rapid entry into the franchised distribution field without the large-scale capital and personnel requirements demanded otherwise.

Restaurants, motels, laundry and dry-cleaning, and particularly fast-food establishments often fall into this category of product-license franchises.

Operational Variations

Straight-product and product-license methods of franchised distribution may diverge further into many specialties and operational variations. Such variables involving income-producing real estate may be briefly described and identified as:

Operating Franchise   This is the most common and is the single outlet franchise for one retail store or service facility as part of a franchise chain.

Multiple-unit Franchise   This covers more than one outlet franchise for retail store or service facilities located within a specified geographical territory.

Operating Franchise with Sub-licensing   This is a multiple-unit franchise additionally permitting sub-licensing and supervising other independent franchisees to operate consistent with the franchise standards.

RATING FRANCHISE OPERATIONS

Consideration of credit, franchise agreements, property improvement, and location are all involved in the analysis of financing real estate used for franchising. To make a final determination, it may be desirable to rate (on a 0–100 scale) the franchiser, the franchisee, the franchise agreement, and the real estate security—as their respective interests may appear. A study of the pertinent information prevailing in a given situation may result in assigning a relative weight to each interest.

For example, it might be assumed that the rating on an absolute net bond-type lease signed by the United States of America would obviously be 100. This would mean that no weight need be given (to the extent the net rental covered the debt payments through to the point of debt extinguishment) to the property or the borrower, other than for purposes of meeting the legal investment requirements, if any, of the investor. On the other hand, but perhaps not so readily accepted, one might assume that, on land unquestionably accepted as the "100% location," no weight need be given to the credit or property improvement if the financing required was equal to, or less than, the value of such land. Between these extremes (in shopping centers and retail properties, and in all sorts of one-tenant realty) one will find that such properties are best when they are most monopolistic in character and give the most exclusive control over the product or service being offered in a given market by the property. Thus, a relative weighing of the various factors is always involved in determining the highest and best franchise value of the property.

Evaluating Traditional Sector Franchisers

As has been noted above, the traditional sectors of franchising are the most common and involve the greatest number of franchisees whose franchisers include many of America's highest-rated companies. Some franchisors in the newer sector of product-license franchising have attained similar high credit ratings. The credits of these companies are frequently available to their franchise operators directly or through guarantees in various meaningful ways. Such credit, when passed through directly or by assignment to the real estate investor, constitutes excellent additional collateral security.

In most cases, there is a lease executed by the "blue chip" credit franchiser. This lease should be in an acceptable legal form to assure that there is little or no cause for cancellation for reasons beyond the control of the investor so long as the debt remains unpaid. More frequently, it will provide for lessor's obligations being limited to payment of exterior and structural maintenance, insurance, and taxes—with meaningful escalation provisions. In such event, the franchiser/lessee, under separate lender's agreement, may be induced to guarantee payment of maintenance and taxes, with no offsets against rentals. Sometimes, direct obligation for payment of the debt by the franchiser/owner may be obtained.

All of the "blue chip" franchise companies enjoy high credit ratings assigned by such services as Moody's Investment Service and Standard & Poor's. Depending on such assigned ratings, the analyst might rely on the credit being offered on relative rating interpretations suggested as follows:

85 or above	equal to Aaa
80	equal to Aa
75	equal to A
70	equal to Baa

With such credit, together with valuable land, both being pledged as security, an investor/analyst might not need to lean much on the physical improvement or capability of the franchisee.

Evaluating Newer Sector Franchisors

The rating of the franchisor who may be acceptable but less than manual rated (that is, less than Baa) presents a challenging problem for real estate financing by investors and financial officers. The process requires considerable investigative inquiry and observation and examination of the facts.

A responsible franchisor should be willing to demonstrate that contributions to the franchisor-franchisee relationship may be recognized as highly accountable and answerable. There are many aspects of the franchise concept and method of operation on which the franchisor may advise and counsel the real estate analyst, including, but not limited to, the following subjects:

Type of operation.
Number of franchised and company-operated units.
Capital requirements of franchisees.
Training available to franchisees.
Longevity in business.
Increasing profits each year.
Products and services provided franchisees.
Market research.
Financing assistance for the franchisee.
National and local promotion and advertising.
Merchandising help to franchisees.
Continuing supervisory support for franchisees.
Volume per unit.
Source of franchisor's profits and how reinvested.
Source of franchisor's new capital funds and how used.

Time will be well spent in visiting more than one operating franchisee of the company being considered to check their experience with the franchisor. One should observe the business, the customers, the volume of sales, and the acceptability of the product or service. The franchisee should consider the franchisor to be fair in providing the promised training and services at the profits expected. In other words, one should check out the franchisor as though one was a serious franchisee prospect.

In addition to being satisfied on these matters, the real estate analyst should be favorably impressed with a Dun and Bradstreet credit report, data sheets of Standard & Poor's, and others, if the franchisor is a listed company. Reports from the Better Business Bureau and your local banker are highly recommended. The franchisor's comparative balance sheet and profit and loss statement, preferably for at least five years, should be examined and the usual significance of the figures determined. This financial statement and credit analysis should show the franchisor to be financially sound and generally acceptable to the analyst.

A relative weight should be given to certain categories of development and growth of the franchisor. This rating must be considered complementary to the rating to be given the franchisee owner/operator. Some categories that may be considered are suggested as follows:

Designation	Relative weight
1. Sales:	
(a) Growth is steady and geographically consistent (that is, not dependent on a limited area and thus subject to premature saturation).	0–4
(b) Volume per unit is increasing regardless of the number of new locations opened each year.	0–4
(c) Growth is being sustained without conglomerate addition of unrelated products or services.	0–4

Designation	**Relative weight**

1. Sales: *(cont)*
   (d) There is a reasonable mix of franchise-operated and company-operated units (insufficency of the former may indicate a weak franchising program; absence of the latter may indicate inadequate or weak central management; both may simply be a signal to the analyst that the financing inquiry is premature). 0–4
2. Profits:
   (a) Increase has been relatively independent of economic cycles (successful franchise operations have not been inordinately affected by minor recessions). 0–4
   (b) They are primarily a result of revenues and not franchise fees (any company that derives less than 65 percent of its profits from operations should be rejected). 0–4
   (c) They are substantially reinvested (beware of the "fast buck" artist). 0–4
3. Marketing:
   An increasing percentage of sales are diverted to promotion and advertising—and the franchisees participate. 0–6
4. Capital formation:
   The company has gone to the "public trough" at least once and most (preferably all) of the funds have been for the benefit of the company. 0–6

The final relative weight may be determined by weighing each of these categories as suggested with an aggregate perfect score being set at 40 and, possibly, 25 as the minimum for favorable consideration of the financing inquiry. While this proposed theoretical rating is somewhat of a gimmick, the examination of the suggested areas in the operation of the franchisor should be considered as a means of quickly rejecting weak situations.

EVALUATING THE FRANCHISE AGREEMENT

As in a mortgage that is drawn up by the mortgagor (or a lease drafted by the lessor) the franchise (or license) agreement tends to be explicit in defining the franchisee's responsibilities but rather vague about the specific contractual obligations of the franchisor. Unfortunately, there appears to be a shortage of professionals skilled in the negotiation of franchise agreements, which works to the detriment of many new franchisees. At any rate, the contract should not be executed until the franchisee has consulted a lawyer and an accountant.

The investment analyst should examine and approve the franchise agreement as part of the required legal documentation, and should be assured that the franchisee/applicant has a legal and contractual relationship that binds the franchisor and franchisee together. The document should clearly define the obligations and duties of each party. The analyst should know that it is not generally inconsistent in form and content with other required terms and conditions upon which the decision to finance the franchisee may be based. In a lease, the obligations of the franchisee must be determined by the investor/underwriter to enable the reaching of a decision as to the actual pro forma cash requirements expected of the franchisee by the franchisor. If the franchise agreement is to be assigned as additional collateral security, the investor may wish to reserve the right to cure defaults and assume the obligations of the franchisee without cancellation by the franchisor. The analyst may wish to have the benefit (at the borrower's expense) of advice and opinion from an outside counsel and accountant to further determine all of the essential facts. At the same time, an examination of the agreement provides additional opportunity to judge the intentions and reliability of the franchisor.

With the franchise agreement being accepted favorably as to form and content, the analyst might then proceed to assign a higher overall weight to the entire inquiry than would otherwise be justified. In fact, without such legal and accounting approval of the franchise concept proposed, there would be little reason for proceeding further in the matter.

Evaluating the Franchisee

Ownership of franchised business premises appear to be about evenly divided between:

1 Ownership by franchisee.
2 Ownership by third party and leased to franchisee.
3 Ownership by franchisor, or ownership by third party and leased to franchisor.

Premise ownership by franchisees seems to be most common in the retail automotive sector, followed in order by those engaged in fast-food and beverage, gasoline service stations; and least prevalent among personal services and nonfood retailers who generally lease their office space or store facility.

An operating franchisee/owner, when applying for real estate credit, becomes subject to the generally accepted underwriting procedure deemed prudent by the investor. The franchisee should show that he or she is qualified to own and operate the real estate acquired under a franchise distribution concept, and must emerge as a prudent businessperson with personal, financial, and general background demonstrating a capability of profitably owning and operating a franchised business. The franchisee should be encouraged to have as much equity invested as possible to insure best efforts and continued interest, and should have ready access to additional cash resources to cover the period until the operation reaches the break-even point. This will include an allowance for family living expenses during this period.

The knowledgeable franchisee will have available, from the beginning, typical pro forma balance sheets and profit/loss presentations prepared by the franchisor. The franchisee's own accountant will have favorably commented on the venture by furnishing a realistic projection of the cash requirements, plus contingencies, for a specified future period. These projections should be checked, if possible, against certified figures furnished by the franchisor, indicating capital requirements and net profits for more than one existing operating franchisee, preferably on nearby similar operations.

Underwriting the ability and credit of an operating franchisee/owner, who is the key factor in the franchise distribution concept to the investor/analyst, requires care and rigid requirements. Given an above-average rated franchisor, an acceptable franchise agreement, adequate physical improvement in which to conduct a business, and above-average location, the importance of the franchisee/owner may be considerable and controlling.

Therefore, in the sector of product-license franchising the analyst might rely on the franchisor and franchisee being offered on combined relative rating interpretation suggested as follows:

63 to 50—Equal to acceptable given adequate physical improvements and above-average location.
Less than 50—Reject.

FRANCHISED BUILDING AND OTHER IMPROVEMENTS

Franchising depends for much of its success on the unique construction and design of its buildings. Generally, such improvements have characteristic design, frequently tailored to some major brand identification. Most of these specialized buildings are built at a high cost per square foot of ground floor area due to special area construction and on-site improvement requirements. Such improvements are subject to rapid depreciation, through both physical and economic obsolescence. As it is impossible to lease these buildings economically for other uses, overpriced specialized buildings, combined with a weak tenant, have presented serious situations for too many investors.

For this reason, the real estate investor and analyst may be well advised to recognize that separation of the business value from the real estate value is necessary, but often difficult to do. Otherwise, in the absence of "blue chip" credit available in the traditional franchise sector previously discussed, the investor may not be adequately compensated for the risk taken if it develops that this is more of a business venture than a real estate investment.

Practically, of course, the ratio of investment to value will be determined by negotiation on amount and terms between franchisee and investor. It is suggested that this negotiation should be on the basic element of physical value—being land cost plus the adjusted cost of the building and other improvements, less above average depreciation, if any.

Cost of construction of the building and other improvements should be certified in (1) an itemized contractor's affidavit or (2) a unit-in-place breakdown by a qualified appraiser or building contractor. From such cost breakdowns it may be found that the franchise operation requires extensive special construction. This total cost may be a rather substantial portion of the total amount, possibly 15 to 30 percent in some instances. At the very least, this cost separation is useful to determine the full insurable value of the building for depreciation purposes. Certain other costs should be isolated, such as items for the fixtures and equipment necessary for the intended franchise operation. These may include, but not be limited to, such items as counters, cabinets, tables, stoves, refrigerators, processing equipment and machinery, fans, special heating and air conditioning, grills, countertops, storage tanks, pumps, etc. As accurately as possible, the cost of the shell building should be determined. To this may be added reasonable site improvement expenses plus usual indirect items—possibly expressed as an arbitrary fixed percentage (5–10 percent) of building and other improvement costs.

Obviously, it is being suggested that all costs as may be properly assigned to the expense of doing business should be borne by the franchise owner/operator and identified as an equity contribution. As little relative weight as practical should be assigned to the building because of its special-purpose nature.

LAND USED FOR FRANCHISING

In many instances, the franchiser will determine the location for the franchisee. How and with what skill this is accomplished is always a critical matter. It may be assumed that the franchiser must generally be capable of choosing good sites to the best of its ability, knowledge, and experience, if the intention is to maintain and expand the franchise distribution concept and image in a responsible manner. There are a variety of options used by senior management in strategic planning for determining site location and territorial design for establishing franchises. Most franchise companies take into account the combination of geography and population in their site selection practices. Then, generally, the responsibility for choosing individual local sites for their outlets is delegated to a regional manager and staff specialists. This group acquires expertise in evaluating and selecting possible sites. They become proficient in developing an analysis and technique to aid them in making such decisions for their company. It appears that the principal problems encountered, among others, are the high cost of making acquisitions, zoning and environmental control difficulties, and the possible harmful effects of competitive "clustering."

These procedures and problems are well known to the real estate investment analyst, who, with knowledge and experience is well qualified to recognize and sense how well the choice of location has been accomplished by the franchise personnel. The analyst should determine for himself an opinion of the value of the site based upon a comparison with similar land recently sold or currently offered for sale. The price of a good site for a franchise operation frequently constitutes 25 to 60 percent of the total cost of the project. This may indicate that a relative weight up to 80 might be assigned to the land in "75% loan-to-value" investment situations.

SUMMARY OF RATING INTERPRETATIONS

	Traditional sector straight product franchises	Newer sector product-license franchises
Franchiser	70 to 85 or above	Included under "Franchisee"
Franchisee	Minimize	50 to 65
Buildings	Minimize	Included under "Land"
Land	25 to 60 or above	25 to 60 or above

DETERMINATION OF "FRANCHISE" VALUE OF THE PROPERTY

Value may normally be best established and evidenced by an appraisal from a qualified real estate appraiser, who should apply all three approaches to value to arrive at a final opinion of market value. Within the investor's legal requirements and investment controls, the amount of each investment probably will be some percentage of the fair market value of the real estate. Given the basic appraisal and other factual data, underwriting guides may be devised to determine the extent of interest the mortgage banker or financial officer may have in the offering being made. From this date, the analyst may want to make a determination of the "franchise value" of the property. Suggested methods are presented, as follows:

I. Product-license franchises

Establishments	Fast foods, retailing, etc.
Approach to value	Primary —Cost
	Secondary —Income and market
Property: Land	"Franchisee" holds title in fee simple.
improvements	Buildings and other improvements required to provide the facilities for the subject product-license franchise distribution concept.

Primary cost valuation example:

Establishment   Average of 44 similar fast-food facilities constructed and occupied during 1972–1973.

Land—actual cost	$109,000	(41%)
Site improvements		
Averaged 31 percent of contractor's sworn statement	44,000	(17%)
Building improvements—contractors sworn		
statement	98,000	(37%)
Trade fixtures and equipment		
Cost to franchisee as equity contribution	none	(0%)
Total	$251,000	(95%)

Indirect Costs

Itemized or arbitrary fixed percentage, say		
9 percent of site and building improvement cost or		
5 percent of total (including land)	12,700	(5%)
	$263,700	
Total "franchise" value of the property, say	$264,000	(100%)

Analysis:

The investment may be 79 percent (or less) of this valuation if the rating interpretation is accepted as follows:

Apportioned to:	Valuation	Indicated maximum investment	Rating adjustment	Within rating range
Land	$109,000 ×100%=	$109,000	$ 73,400 (35%)	Yes
Franchisee–Franchisor	155,000 × 65%=	100,750	136,350 (65%)	Yes
Total	$264,000 × 79%=	$209,750	$209,750 (100%)	*

*Subject to individual investment policy.

II Service-license franchises

Establishments	Hotel-motel enterprises and all others.
Approach to value	Primary —Cost, income and market
Property: Land	"Franchisee" holds title in fee simple.
Improvements	Buildings and other improvements required to provide the facilities for the subject service-license franchise distribution concept.

Primary valuation example:

Establishment—Any hotel-motel or other classification of commercial income-producing property.

Total "Franchise" value of the property is assumed to be evidenced by a MAI type of appraisal from a qualified real estate appraiser who should apply all three approaches to value to arrive at a final opinion of market value. As an example, we use the following for illustration (this is a hypothetical case):

Land valuation	$ 400,000
Building and other improvements	2,000,000
Final opinion of fair market value	$2,400,000

Analysis:

The investment may be 58 percent (or less) of this valuation if the rating interpretation is accepted as follows:

Apportioned to:	Valuation	Indicated maximum investment	Rating adjustment	Within rating range
Land	$ 400,000 ×100%=	$ 400,000	$ 400,000 (28%)	Yes
Franchisee–franchisor	2,000,000 × 50%=	1,000,000	1,000,000 (72%)	No
Total			$1,400,000 (100%)	*

*Subject to individual investment policy.

III Straight product distribution franchises

Establishments	Gasoline service stations, etc.
Approach to value	Primary —Income
	Secondary —Cost and market
Property: Land	"Franchisee" or "third party" hold title in fee simple.
Improvements	Buildings and other improvements to provide the facilities for the subject straight product franchise distribution concept.

Primary income valuation example:

Establishment—gasoline service station (this is a hypothetical case).

Land—cost or comparative market value	$100,000
Land improvements—cost (included in building cost)	$ -0-
Building improvements—cost	$ 50,000
Trade fixtures and equipment—cost	$ none
Total cost approach	$150,000

Lease Data

Leased to "Franchiser" (highly rated company).

Term: As may be negotiated, but at least long enough to create sufficient economic value to support financing as may be required.

Rental: Usually a minimum guaranteed "accommodation" amount equal to the amortization of land cost and reasonable building improvement costs during the lease term at a current interest rate—all as may be determined by the franchiser.

Renewal (and repurchase) option: as may be negotiated.

Lessor's obligations: none or all, as may be negotiated.

Lessee's obligations: if none, "franchiser," under separate lender's agreement, may guarantee payment of all real estate taxes, and maintenance, with no offsets against rentals.

Remarks: this lease would be assigned to the investor as additional collateral secruity.

Sublease Data

The franchiser may simultaneously sublet the entire leasehold to the franchisee usually on the same terms and conditions in the primary lease. This leaseback may include other related documents, such as a product agreement (franchise license) and a management agreement. The franchisee acts as owner/operator of the complete facility and as exclusive distributor will realize all retail profits from the sale of the trademarked products of the franchiser who, in turn, achieves the establishment of an outlet for the distribution of its franchised products. Until such time as this project will have been in existence long enough to be considered on the merits of its records of operation, the value of this sublease by an income approach would be unreliable and, therefore, may be ignored.

Appraisal approach

Gross annual rental, during prime lease term			$ 15,600
Less: Estimated annual expenses (if any)			
Taxes	)	$ _____	
Insurance	) Net Lease*	$ _____	
Maintenance	)	$ _____	
Other	)	$ _____	$ None

*If Lessor pays all real estate taxes, maintenance, and insurance, deduct estimated expense and increase margin (see below).

Net annual income	$ 15,600

Capitalization of net income:

$15,600 for 15 Years @ 8%* (8.559)†	$133,520

*This interest rate may be (by reason of lease vs. senior debt) somewhat above the rate that the subject "franchiser's" senior securities, if recently issued, might be quoted. If unavailable, a comparable rate might be obtained from current quotations from recent issues of similarly rated industrial corporate senior securities. This information is easily obtainable from a number of sources, such as *The Wall Street Journal* and Moody's or Standard and Poor's average bond yield indexes.

†Inwood Coefficient—"Present Worth of One Dollar Per Annum—Compound Interest Valuation Premise for Computing Lessor's Interest or Lessee's Profit."

Add: Reversionary value:			
Land—cost		$100,000	
Building—cost	$50,000		
Less depreciation 15 years			
@ 5%* per annum	$37,500	$112,500	
$112,500 after 15 years @ 8%† (.3152)‡			$ 35,460
		Total	$168,980
Total franchise value of the property		Say	$169,000

*Depending on type of improvements—4 to 6 percent—"Such improvements are subject to rapid depreciation, both physical and economic obsolescence."

†This rate may reflect the analyst's opinion as to the relative desirability of the subject location—and quality and type of the improvements remaining at the end of the prime lease term.

‡See "Present Worth of One Dollar—Compound Interest Valuation Premise for Computing the Value of a Reversion."

CALCULATIONS FOR MAXIMUM LOAN

Sample Case

Lease—15 years @ $1300 per month

Lessee pays all taxes, insurance, and maintenance

Reported cost—	Land		$100,000.00
	Building		50,000.00
		Total	$150,000.00
Estimated expense—	Real estate taxes	)	$ —
	Insurance	) Net Lease*	$ —
	Maintenance	)	$ —
		Total	$ None
Income—	Annual rental ($1300 × 12)		$15,600.00
	Less: Estimated expense*		—
	Net income		$15,600.00
	Less: Margin* (7% of $15,600) say		
	Balance to amortize loan		$14,500.00

Maximum loan—	($14,500 + $118.†) 15 years @ 8½%	$122,000.00
Monthly payment—	($9.85 × $122.)	$ 1,201.70
Annual payment—	($1,201.70 × 12)	$ 14,420.40

*If Lessor pays all real estate taxes, maintenance, and insurance, deduct estimated expense and increase margin to, say, 15%.

†Amount per year to amortize $1,000—15 years @ 8½% $9.85 × 12 = $118.20, say $118.

Analysis:

The investment may be 92 percent (more or less) of this valuation if the rating interpretation is accepted as follows:

Apportioned to:	Valuation	Indicated maximum investment	Rating adjustment	Within rating range
Land	$100,000 × 100%=	$100,000	$ 31,040 (20%)	Minimize
Franchiser	69,000 × 80%=	55,200	124,160 (80%)	Yes
Total			$155,200 (100%)*	

*Subject to individual investment policy and calculations for maximum loan (see above).

CONCLUSION

For the subject covered by this chapter, we have attempted to show that investments involving high credits are easier to underwrite than investments involving real estate. Whether the investor feels more secure with strong credit at a lower rate of return than with lesser security at a higher rate of return must be evaluated in this era of rising inflation.

By generalizing the users of real estate devoted to franchise distribution into two proposals (high credit or real estate), we conclude that mortgage bankers and institutional finance officers will continue to find that:

1 Straight product distribution franchises in the traditional sector (being in the majority) are more easily acceptable as situations for franchise financing.

2 Service-license franchises used by the remaining sector comprising the newer franchisors present real estate situations that are considerably more difficult to underwrite and accept.

But then, having accepted that there is a franchise value to the property, as respects the investment amount, the rate of interest to be charged, and any other terms or restrictions to be imposed, each of us (within the respective investment policy and practices existing from time to time), will use judgment as to the extent of interest in franchise financing of income-producing real estate.

Chapter 27

Real Estate Investment Trusts

Cornelius C. Rose, Jr.

Real estate investment trusts (REITs) are one of the most recent and most controversial financial intermediaries serving the mortgage market. The controversy surrounding the REIT industry has tended to obscure its economic role and significance. The purpose of this chapter is to provide a systematic analysis of the history, nature, and prospects of the trusts.

HISTORY AND RECENT DEVELOPMENTS

While the business trust is an ancient form of business organization, REITs as we know them trace their origins to the passage of a 1960 amendment to the Internal Revenue Code. The amendment provided that trusts meeting certain statutory prescriptions with respect to the composition of their assets and the sources of their income would not be taxed on income distributed to shareholders if at least 90 percent of taxable income was distributed. The key statutory provision stipulates that 75 percent of a REIT's assets must consist of mortgages and real estate equities and that 75 percent of its income must be derived from these two sources. Recently, many REITs have given up this tax status to become public real estate companies.

The principle undergirding the enabling legislation is much like that which inspired the creation of mutual funds. Essentially, Congress sought to give small investors the opportunity to participate in a professionally selected and managed portfolio of real estate equities and mortgage loans. Since mutual funds and trusts are similarly premised, it is not surprising that they have a number of common characteristics. Both were essentially conceived as passive repositories for investments. The real estate supporting a particular REIT investment and the companies whose shares are owned by mutual funds are operated by persons unrelated to the investor. Neither trusts nor mutual funds play an active role in the management or disposition of the underlying assets.

As a consequence of this essentially passive role, trusts have tended to have small operating staffs and usually, as in mutual funds, the day-to-day operations of a REIT are managed by an independent investment advisor. The advisor usually operates under a contract which provides that it is responsible for originating, underwriting, and servicing investments which fall within the investment guidelines prescribed by the trust's Board of Trustees. The advisor is compensated by a fee which is usually based on the dollar value of the assets managed. This fee will typically range between 0.5 and 1.25 percent of assets and will be subject to the limitation that total operating expenses of the trust may not exceed the greater of 25 percent of the trust's net income before extraordinary losses and the fee itself or 1.5 percent of the trust's net assets. In addition, there are frequently incentive compensation provisions designed to reward the advisor for superior performance.

Notwithstanding the major role played by the trust's advisor, the ultimate responsibility for conducting the REIT's affairs resides with its Board of Trustees. The Board, which usually contains a majority unaffiliated with the advisor, is responsible for formulating the trust's asset and liability management policies and for supervising their implementation. While trustees are frequently compared to corporate directors, it is probably fair to say that their responsibilities, powers, and liability exceed those of directors.

In the eight years immediately following the passage of the enabling legislation in 1960, the REIT industry grew slowly. At the end of this period, total REIT assets were less than $1 billion. During these years the investment emphasis of most trusts was on real estate equities. These equity trusts typically purchased and operated existing income-producing properties. For the most part, their investable funds were provided by shareholders' equity and conventional mortgage financing, with very little coming from long-term unsecured debt and even less from short-term bank line or commercial paper usage.

Despite the early dominance of equity trusts, the REITs experiencing the best operating results from 1961 to 1968 were a handful of mortgage trusts. These trusts initially invested the bulk of their funds in long-term government-insured and -guaranteed mortgages. Later, they became more venturesome and began to place a portion of their funds in short-term loans, particularly construction and development loans. These loans not only provided substantially higher yields than long-term loans, but they also enabled the trust to fund its assets with short-term bank and commercial paper borrowings. As the result of higher returns and the profitable employment of greater leverage, these REITs produced a growing stream of dividends and higher per-share prices for their shareholders. This, is turn, enabled them to sell new shares at premiums over the book value of outstanding shares, thereby further leveraging earnings, book value, and market value per share. In addition, the superior market performance of these trusts enabled them to issue straight and convertible longer-term debt, which also served to increase leverage and profitability.

It was inevitable that the success of these trusts would eventually attract imitators. This tendency to imitate was strongly reinforced by the credit crunch of 1966. That unhappy experience suggested that the traditional sources of mortgage money could not be counted upon in periods of severe credit stringency. In 1966, disintermediation, coupled with policy loan pressures, effectively precluded thrift institutions and insurance companies from playing their accustomed role in mortgage financing. The resulting distress in the real estate market convinced most commentators that new sources of mortgage money were crtically needed. The remarkable success of the early mortgage trusts seemed to provide an answer.

Thus, beginning in late 1968, the trust industry began an astonishing six-year period of expansion. The period began in a climate of euphoria and closed in an atmosphere of despair. During these six years, total REIT assets grew from less than $1 billion to over $22 billion. Construction and development loan trusts, which had been an insignificant factor in a market dominated by commercial banks, had captured, by the third quarter of 1973, over 23 percent of this rapidly expanding market. In addition, although the industry's position in the permanent mortgage market did not rival its role in the short-term sector, REIT holdings of long-term loans increased tenfold from 1968 to 1974.

Since the rapid proliferation and growth of trusts was largely predicated on the excellent performance of the early short-term trusts, it is not surprising that the initial phase of the expansion was dominated by new trusts seeking to emulate that successful formula. Thus, from mid-1968 to mid-1970 several dozen new trusts devoted to the construction and development loan market were created.

The timing appeared to be most felicitous. Early in 1969, the prime rate began to rise rapidly. By mid-year it had risen 175 basis points to 8.5%, where it remained through March of 1970. As rates rose, many traditional lenders withdrew from the mortgage market because of sharply curtailed cash flows. As a result, the new trusts had little competition and were able to invest their funds at very attractive rates. However, tight money precluded them from leveraging as extensively as they had hoped. This proved to be a boon of sorts in that they were under no pressure to put large sums to work and were able to invest very selectively.

The credit stringency of the 1969–1970 period also fostered the creation of a number of trusts devoted to long-term lending. This development was most pronounced in 1970, when it became apparent that the most serious shortage of mortgage funds was in the long-term sector. Thrift institutions and life insurance companies suffered massive cash hemorrhages, which, in many instances, forced them to withdraw from the market. Indeed a number of these institutions undertook to sponsor and advise long-term REITs in an effort to keep their staffs of mortgage specialists profitably occupied. The emergence of these institutionally sponsored trusts was further encouraged by the development of bank and insurance holding companies which found the fee income generated by trust sponsorship very attractive.

Late in 1970 conditions in the money markets began to ease, prompting a major, but at the time little perceived, change in the fortunes and direction of mortgage REITs. From mid-1970 through mid-1972, a dramatic increase in the growth of the money supply, coupled with a business slump, brought about a sharp improvement in the availability of credit and a dramatic reduction of its cost. From November of 1970 to January of 1972, the prime rate declined from 7.50% to 4.75%. As a result, REITs, particularly construction and development loan trusts, began to grow dramatically. Most of this growth was funded by expanding short-term bank and commercial paper borrowings. From the first quarter of 1971 through the first quarter of 1972, REIT holdings of C and D loans grew from $3.3 billion to $12.8 billion. Debt-to-equity ratios, which for most trusts had been limited to two to one, expanded in this period to four, five and, in a few instances, ten to one.

At the same time REITs were expanding their portfolios, other lenders, most notably commercial banks, were also adding mortgage loans at startling rates. The inevitable result of this rapid, undisciplined growth was overbuilding, an easing of underwriting standards, and a significant deterioration in the quality of real estate credit.

Real estate is a cyclical business in which periods of overbuilding are normally followed by corrective contractions in which bloated inventories are worked off. These contractions, while predictable, usually entail a significant amount of economic distress. The reversal which followed the 1972–1973 boom was especially severe. The severity of the correction was due in large measure to an unusual and largely unanticipated set of extrinsic forces.

RECENT PROBLEMS

First, an explosive world-wide inflation combined with shortages occasioned by the energy crisis to increase construction costs dramatically. As a result, cost overruns of 30 percent or more became commonplace. Second, there was a sharp constriction in the money market, resulting in record-high interest rates. This served to further increase cost overruns and to diminish the availability of long-term mortgage money. Moreover, the combination of higher equity yield requirements resulting from higher interest rates, and lower profits tracing to higher energy costs, caused a sharp decline in realty values. This decline, together with cost overruns, eroded, and in many instances wiped out, the borrowers' equity, which has traditionally protected mortgage lenders.

The impact of these setbacks to the real estate market fell more heavily on REITs than on other lenders for several reasons. First, REITs were more highly leveraged and therefore more vulnerable to a turn in the economic cycle. Higher leverage and the consequent pressure for repayment also resulted in a diminished capacity to hold real estate for the period necessary for depressed realty values to be restored. The leverage pressures were exacerbated by the fact that 80 percent of REIT leverage consisted of bank lines and commercial paper where rates rose most rapidly and where lender demands for repayment were most insistent. A significant corollary of the reliance on high-cost, short-term debt was the need to make riskier loans in order to maintain adequate profit margins. Thus, REITs tended to have a relatively high proportion of their assets in land loans and other high-yielding loans which are more vulnerable to a downturn in realty values.

Second, the problems of REITs are more visible and more publicized than those of other lenders. This is because the trusts are publicly owned and devoted almost entirely to real estate investments. Therefore, many mortgage problems which would be unnoticed in privately held portfolios, or immaterial and therefore not disclosed by other public lenders, must be publicly disclosed by REITs. The public attention thereby focused on trusts exacerbates their problems with their lenders and inhibits their ability to tap alternative sources of capital. The problem of public disclosure and adverse publicity is further aggravated by the fact that REITs are generally subject to more stringent accounting standards than are most other lenders. Consequently, the same problem may appear more serious if reported by a trust than it would if reported by another lender.

As a result of the very real problems confronting many trusts, and particularly as a result of the notoriety which has attended the disclosure of these problems, many commentators have questioned the potential of the REIT industry and the importance of its future role as a financial intermediary. These questions are worthy of serious discussion.

To begin with, it should be noted that the kinds of problems afflicting trusts are not unprecedented in American business or even unique in real estate. Other industries have sprung up in response to a genuine economic need, expanded too rapidly, and then suffered through protracted periods of distress and contraction as the overexpansion is redressed. However, almost invariably if the economic need which prompted the emergency of the industry is real and persists, the industry survives, albeit frequently in a significantly modified form. Thus, if the generally held assumption that the long-term demand for mortgages is likely to exceed the presently visible supply is valid, then the REITs should survive. The operative question is: "What changes in the form, emphasis, and direction of trusts may be expected?" Based on the experiences of the last 15 years and the anticipated exigencies of the years immediately ahead, several likely changes may be identified.

CHANGES TO COME IN REITs

First, it seems clear that there are too many trusts and that a significant amount of consolidation is inevitable. The groundwork for consolidation should be laid as some trusts emerge from their present difficulties having managed their problems professionally and well, while others emerge having done less well. Under these circumstances, it is likely that the per-share market prices of those who have done well will be higher in relation to book value than those who have done poorly. This should facilitate acquisitions of the latter by the former through a favorable exchange of shares. The inducement to a less successful trust to merge should grow as its inability to attract new capital because of poor performance makes it difficult to retain competent personnel and to attain profitable levels of advisory fees. In addition, the strain and disenchantment which have accompanied the current contraction may cause some trusts to withdraw from the business either through merger or liquidation.

A second change in REIT operations which may be expected is the reduced use of leverage and, particularly, less reliance on short-term variable-cost debt. As noted above, the extensive use of bank lines and commercial paper contributed importantly to the problems of many REITs. Not only were the trusts more vulnerable to liquidity pressures as a consequence of employing this type of leverage, but also they tended to make riskier, higher-yielding loans in order to justify the higher cost of these funds. As a result of this experience, it appears that the banks will be less willing to lend, and the trusts will be less likely to borrow, short-term funds. REITs will undoubtedly seek to replace bank debt with longer-term issues. However, while some trusts may be successful in concluding private placements of debt and equity with knowledgeable investors, it is probable that the erosion of short-term debt will more than offset any possible gains from this new source. In short, debt-to-equity ratios will probably recede from the present four or five to one to something approaching two or three to one.

A corollary of the reduced reliance on bank debt should be an increased interest in long-term loans and equities and a diminished appetite for the more speculative, higher-yielding types of short-term loans. This does not mean, however, that the REITs will eschew innovative financing techniques. The trusts, because they are essentially free of arbitrary lending restrictions, are better able than other lenders to consider and implement new financing ideas. Indeed it is this capacity to innovate which constitutes the REITs' principal contribution to mortgage lending.

A final change in the operations of trusts which may be expected is a modification of the basis on which advisory fees are computed. Fees which are based on the volume of assets managed do not create an identity of interest between the advisor and the shareholders. The advisor has a theoretical economic inducement to increase total assets through the use of leverage whether or not the proceeds can be employed profitably or prudently. As a result, in some instances, trust managements may expand assets too rapidly at the expense of quality and, ultimately, to the detriment of the shareholders. To rectify this potential problem, fees in the future may be based on net income, the effective net yield on the portfolio, or some other basis related to profitability and the return to shareholders.

In conclusion, while REITs will undoubtedly bear the scars of their present difficulties for many years, and while the industry may emerge from this period radically transfigured, there is a high probability that the trusts will continue to play a vital and growing role in mortgage lending. This is so because REITs have the capacity to tap new sources of capital and to employ innovative techniques free of statutory encumbrances. If there is to be an expanding need for real estate capital and imaginative financing, this industry, because of the unique qualities it brings to its task, will survive and prosper.

Chapter 28

Mathematics of
Real Estate Finance

Stephen A. Pyhrr

INTRODUCTION

The objectives of this chapter will be to acquaint the reader with the economics and mathematics associated with income-property financing. Specifically to:

Establish an analytical framework for evaluating income-property loans.

Expand the basic framework to include the analysis of equity investments and joint venture positions from the viewpoint of both lender and equity investors.

Review the basic financial and mathematical concepts, principles, and techniques associated with income-property financing.

Consider the most sophisticated capital budgeting techniques and methods available, including consideration of time value of money, discounted cash-flow analysis, present value, internal rate of return, and sensitivity and risk analysis.

In approaching the subject of income-property financing, we first need to make some basic assumptions about the economic motivation of the investor participants, be they lenders or equity investors. Let us assume that both are (or attempt to be) rational economic decision-makers. That is to say that their primary financial goal is to maximize financial wealth. To maximize financial wealth means to make capital investments that offer some optimum or desirable combination of returns and risks that satisfies the investor's preferences. Generally, investors want the rates of return to be relatively high, and they usually prefer more of it to less of it. Simultaneously, they prefer their rates of return to be stable, thus not subject to high risks; they prefer less to more risk, other things being equal. There is perhaps a group of people in the world who ignore risk, who refuse to contemplate it, evidently hoping that it will go away if its existence is not admitted. We could call this group risk-ignorers, but for our purposes, we will ignore them. Finally, in trying to maximize wealth, the investor should try to obtain the highest rate of return at some acceptable risk level, the lowest risk at some acceptable rate of return level, or some other optimum combination of risks and returns.

Given this underlying set of assumptions, let us proceed to develop the concepts, principles, and techniques which logically follow. First, we will develop a basic framework and model for evaluating income property.

OVERVIEW OF THE REAL ESTATE FINANCING PROCESS

Real estate financing can be described as the process of creating a financial package for an income-producing real estate investment that satisfies the objectives of the lenders and equity investors. As shown in Exhibit 1, the financing process involves the following four steps:

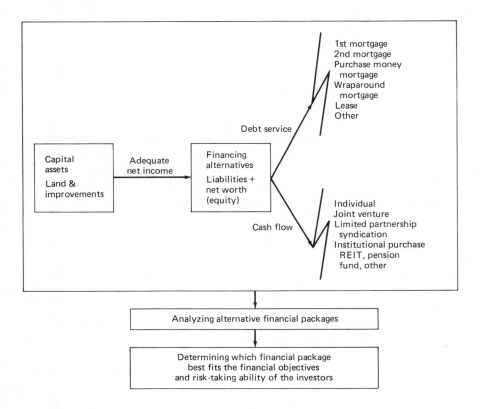

1 *Finding a real estate project that is economically sound*—a set of capital assets that produces an adequate net income, before consideration of the financing techniques employed. This is generally the toughest job in the financing process.

2 *Determining what the financing alternatives are*—looking at both debt and equity sources of financing. With regard to debt alternatives, we are concerned with the methods of leverage financing to be employed, the amounts and terms of the loan(s), and the types of financial institutions to deal with. On the equity side, we are interested in the sources of equity to be employed, the amounts of equity to be raised, the rate of return, and other objectives sought by equity investors.

3 *Analyzing the alternative financial packages*—analyzing the impact of the various financing alternatives on the investor's rate-of-return and risk parameters. Each financial alternative will have a different impact on the ratios and underwriting criteria used by the investor.

4 *Determining which financial package best fits the financial objectives and risk-taking ability of the investors*—an acceptable solution should consider the financial position of both lender(s) and equity investor(s) in the transaction.

In working through this financing process, we must be proficient in the basic mathematics involved in the financing process. We must know how to prepare an accurate cash-flow statement, the basis of all financing; we must know how to work with a mortgage-constant table, and debt-coverage ratios; we must know how to compute rates of return on investment; and finally, we must understand and master the concepts of positive leverage, negative leverage, and risk. These important concepts, principles, and techniques are discussed in the following sections.

IMPORTANT CONCEPTS, PRINCIPLES, AND TECHNIQUES

The Cash-flow Statement

Consider an existing 84-unit apartment complex in a strong rental market in Houston, Texas. The mix consists of 64 one-bedroom and 20 two-bedroom units; one-bedroom units average 600 square feet; two-bedroom units average 850 square feet. The complex is five years old, and the asking price is $1,000,000. The investors are seeking to refinance with an $800,000 loan at $9\frac{1}{4}\%$ for 28 years; the mortgage constant (K) is 10 percent; required equity is $200,000. Based on past performance, the cash flow is estimated as follows:

Cash Flow Pro Forma

Gross possible rental income		$163,800
Plus:	Other Income (vending machines, parking, etc.)	2,868
	Gross possible income	$166,980
Less:	Vacancy & collection losses (5%)	8,349
	Gross effective income	$158,631
Less:	Operating expenses (40% × gross possible)	66,792
	Net income	$ 91,839
Less:	Debt service (.10 × $800,000)	80,000
	Cash Flow	$ 11,839

Note that the cash-flow statement does not consider tax-shelter factors, equity buildup through loan amortization, or property appreciation. These items would be added in a more sophisticated analysis, as we shall see later. Note also that the cash-flow statement is a one-year statement, where we estimate the "most likely" outcome. In a more sophisticated analysis, we would attempt to measure cash flows for each year over the expected holding period of the investment, or over some assumed long-analysis period. Also, we may want to vary our assumptions to simulate a pessimistic and optimistic set of outcomes as we shall see later when the subject of risk analysis is discussed.

Despite all its shortcomings, a one-year cash-flow pro forma, as shown, is currently the most widely used method of investment analysis by lenders, brokers, and investors throughout the nation.

Working with Mortgage Constants and Debt-Coverage Ratios: The Lender's Viewpoint

The *mortgage constant* is defined as the amount of annual debt service, stated as a percent, necessary to pay interest at some stated rate and the entire principal over the amortization period. The mortgage constant (K) is used to compute the annual debt service (principal plus interest) on a loan, as shown by the following formula:

Annual debt service = (Loan amount) × (Mortgage constant)

In our previous example, the loan amount was $800,000 and $K = .10$, resulting in debt service of $80,000. We found K by reference to a mortgage-constant chart ("Constant Annual Percent Charts," Table 1). Going down the left side of the chart to 9¼% and across to 28 years, resulted in a K of 10.01%, or roughly 10%.

Now, suppose the interest rate rises to 9½% and the lender will only allow a 25-year term. What happens? The mortgage constant increases to 10.49%. Debt service increases from $80,000 to $83,920:

Annual debt service = (Loan amount) × (Mortgage constant)
$83,920 = ($800,000) × (.1049)

As a result, the cash flow decreases by $3,920 and the value of the property will decrease by a multiple factor, as we will see later.

In summary, the mortgage constant, determined by the mortgage term and interest rate granted by the lender, is used to compute the debt service on a loan, and thus impacts on the cash flow generated by the project. For each dollar increase in debt service, cash flow decreases by one dollar, and the value of the project declines. An equity investor, attempting to maximize cash flow, and thus the investment value of property, would logically bargain with the lender for the longest term and lowest interest rate possible, thus keeping K to a minimum.

Two other formulas which are useful are the following:

Table 1

Monthly Payments

Table of Constant Annual Percent needed to amortize a principal amount, calculated on a monthly basis. Divide by 12 to determine monthly payment.

Interest Rate	16 YEARS	17 YEARS	18 YEARS	19 YEARS	20 YEARS	21 YEARS	22 YEARS
7	10.41	10.08	9.79	9.54	9.31	9.11	8.93
¼	10.58	10.25	9.97	9.71	9.49	9.29	9.11
½	10.75	10.43	10.14	9.89	9.67	9.47	9.30
¾	10.93	10.61	10.32	10.08	9.86	9.66	9.49
8	11.10	10.78	10.50	10.26	10.04	9.85	9.68
⅛	11.19	10.87	10.59	10.35	10.14	9.94	9.78
¼	11.28	10.96	10.69	10.45	10.23	10.04	9.87
⅜	11.37	11.05	10.78	10.54	10.32	10.14	9.97
½	11.46	11.14	10.87	10.64	10.42	10.23	10.07
⅝	11.55	11.24	10.96	10.73	10.51	10.33	10.16
¾	11.64	11.33	11.06	10.82	10.61	10.43	10.26
⅞	11.73	11.42	11.15	10.91	10.71	10.52	10.36
9	11.82	11.51	11.24	11.01	10.80	10.62	10.46
⅛	11.91	11.60	11.34	11.10	10.90	10.72	10.56
¼	12.00	11.70	11.43	11.20	11.00	10.82	10.66
⅜	12.09	11.79	11.53	11.29	11.09	10.92	10.76
½	12.18	11.88	11.62	11.39	11.19	11.01	10.86
⅝	12.28	11.98	11.72	11.49	11.29	11.11	10.96
¾	12.37	12.07	11.81	11.58	11.39	11.21	11.06
⅞	12.46	12.16	11.91	11.68	11.49	11.31	11.16
10	12.56	12.26	12.00	11.78	11.59	11.41	11.26
⅛	12.65	12.35	12.10	11.88	11.68	11.52	11.37
¼	12.74	12.45	12.20	11.98	11.78	11.62	11.47
⅜	12.84	12.55	12.29	12.08	11.88	11.72	11.57
½	12.93	12.64	12.39	12.17	11.99	11.82	11.68
⅝	13.03	12.74	12.49	12.27	12.09	11.92	11.78
¾	13.12	12.84	12.59	12.37	12.19	12.03	11.88
⅞	13.22	12.93	12.69	12.47	12.29	12.13	11.99
11	13.31	13.03	12.79	12.57	12.39	12.23	12.09
⅛	13.41	13.13	12.88	12.68	12.49	12.34	12.20
¼	13.51	13.23	12.98	12.78	12.60	12.44	12.30
⅜	13.60	13.32	13.08	12.88	12.70	12.54	12.41
½	13.70	13.42	13.18	12.98	12.80	12.65	12.51
⅝	13.80	13.52	13.29	13.08	12.91	12.75	12.62
¾	13.89	13.62	13.39	13.18	13.01	12.86	12.73
⅞	13.99	13.72	13.49	13.29	13.11	12.96	12.83
12	14.09	13.82	13.59	13.39	13.22	13.07	12.94
¼	14.29	14.02	13.79	13.60	13.43	13.28	13.16
½	14.49	14.22	14.00	13.80	13.64	13.50	13.37
¾	14.68	14.42	14.20	14.01	13.85	13.71	13.59
13	14.88	14.63	14.41	14.22	14.06	13.93	13.81
¼	15.09	14.83	14.62	14.44	14.28	14.14	14.03
½	15.29	15.04	14.83	14.65	14.49	14.36	14.25
¾	15.49	15.25	15.04	14.86	14.71	14.58	14.47
14	15.70	15.45	15.25	15.08	14.93	14.80	14.69
¼	15.90	15.66	15.46	15.29	15.15	15.02	14.92
½	16.11	15.87	15.68	15.51	15.36	15.24	15.14
¾	16.32	16.09	15.89	15.72	15.59	15.47	15.37
15	16.53	16.30	16.11	15.94	15.81	15.69	15.59

Monthly Payments

Table of Constant Annual Percent needed to amortize a principal amount, calculated on a monthly basis. Divide by 12 to determine monthly payment.

Interest Rate	23 YEARS	24 YEARS	25 YEARS	26 YEARS	27 YEARS	28 YEARS	29 YEARS
7	8.76	8.62	8.49	8.37	8.26	8.16	8.07
¼	8.95	8.81	8.68	8.56	8.46	8.36	8.27
½	9.14	9.00	8.88	8.76	8.65	8.56	8.47
¾	9.33	9.19	9.07	8.96	8.85	8.76	8.68
8	9.53	9.39	9.27	9.16	9.06	8.97	8.88
⅛	9.62	9.49	9.37	9.26	9.16	9.07	8.99
¼	9.72	9.59	9.47	9.36	9.26	9.17	9.09
⅜	9.82	9.69	9.57	9.46	9.36	9.27	9.20
½	9.92	9.79	9.67	9.56	9.47	9.38	9.30
⅝	10.02	9.89	9.77	9.67	9.57	9.48	9.41
¾	10.12	9.99	9.87	9.77	9.67	9.59	9.51
⅞	10.22	10.09	9.97	9.87	9.78	9.69	9.62
9	10.32	10.19	10.08	9.97	9.88	9.80	9.73
⅛	10.42	10.29	10.18	10.08	9.99	9.91	9.83
¼	10.52	10.39	10.28	10.18	10.09	10.01	9.94
⅜	10.62	10.50	10.39	10.29	10.20	10.12	10.05
½	10.72	10.60	10.49	10.39	10.31	10.23	10.15
⅝	10.82	10.70	10.59	10.50	10.41	10.34	10.27
¾	10.93	10.81	10.70	10.60	10.52	10.44	10.38
⅞	11.03	10.91	10.80	10.71	10.63	10.55	10.48
10	11.13	11.01	10.91	10.82	10.73	10.66	10.59
⅛	11.23	11.12	11.02	10.92	10.84	10.77	10.70
¼	11.34	11.22	11.12	11.03	10.95	10.88	10.82
⅜	11.44	11.33	11.23	11.14	11.06	10.99	10.93
½	11.55	11.43	11.34	11.25	11.17	11.10	11.04
⅝	11.65	11.54	11.44	11.36	11.28	11.21	11.15
¾	11.76	11.65	11.55	11.46	11.39	11.32	11.26
⅞	11.86	11.75	11.66	11.57	11.50	11.43	11.37
11	11.97	11.86	11.77	11.68	11.61	11.54	11.48
⅛	12.08	11.97	11.87	11.79	11.72	11.65	11.60
¼	12.18	12.08	11.98	11.90	11.83	11.76	11.71
⅜	12.29	12.18	12.09	12.01	11.94	11.88	11.82
½	12.40	12.29	12.20	12.12	12.05	11.99	11.94
⅝	12.50	12.40	12.31	12.23	12.16	12.10	12.05
¾	12.61	12.51	12.42	12.35	12.28	12.22	12.16
⅞	12.72	12.62	12.53	12.46	12.39	12.33	12.28
12	12.83	12.73	12.64	12.57	12.50	12.44	12.39
¼	13.05	12.95	12.87	12.79	12.72	12.67	12.62
½	13.26	13.17	13.09	13.02	12.96	12.90	12.85
¾	13.48	13.39	13.31	13.24	13.18	13.13	13.09
13	13.71	13.62	13.54	13.47	13.41	13.36	13.32
¼	13.93	13.84	13.77	13.70	13.64	13.59	13.55
½	14.15	14.07	13.99	13.93	13.87	13.83	13.79
¾	14.37	14.29	14.22	14.16	14.11	14.06	14.02
14	14.60	14.52	14.45	14.39	14.34	14.30	14.26
¼	14.82	14.75	14.68	14.62	14.57	14.53	14.49
½	15.05	14.98	14.91	14.86	14.81	14.77	14.73
¾	15.28	15.21	15.15	15.09	15.05	15.01	14.97
15	15.51	15.44	15.37	15.32	15.28	15.24	15.21

Reprinted from Financial Constant Percent Amortization Tables, Publication no. 287, computed by Financial Publishing Company, Boston, Massachusetts.

$$\text{Loan amount} = \frac{\text{annual debt service}}{\text{mortgage constant}}$$

$$\text{Mortgage constant} = \frac{\text{annual debt service}}{\text{loan amount}}$$

The first formula is used to determine the amount of a loan that a lender can grant when the amount of debt service the project can support is known. The second formula is used to compute the debt service on an outstanding loan where the debt service and loan amount are known.

Note that the mortgage constant will increase each year as a loan is amortized, since the denominator of the mortgage-constant formula (loan amount) is decreasing as loan amortization occurs. From the equity investor's viewpoint, a rising constant means an increase in the effective cost of borrowed money each year, and explains why investors periodically seek to refinance their properties, thereby raising the loan amount and term to a more desirable level.

Debt-coverage Ratio   Most large institutional lenders now favor the debt-coverage ratio as the primary financial underwriting criterion for granting loans. The debt-coverage ratio is defined as follows:

$$\text{Debt-coverage ratio} = \frac{\text{net income}}{\text{debt service}}$$

Many institutional lenders have developed minimum acceptable coverage ratios for different property types. For example, a lender may require a minimum coverage ratio of 1.3 for an apartment project and a coverage ratio of 1.5 for a motel property (which is usually considered more risky). As the perceived risks associated with the property increase, the lender demands compensation in the form of a higher coverage ratio, and perhaps a higher interest rate and mortgage constant. Thus the lender wants a cushion, a buffer, in case net income in any year should drop due to a rise in vacancies, expenses, etc., and wants this cushion to increase as the risk increases.

To illustrate, take the 84-unit apartment where the expected net income was $91,839, with an equity investor seeking a loan of $800,000 for 28 years at 9¼%. The resulting mortgage constant (K) was 10% and debt service was $80,000. The lender does not make loans that result in a coverage ratio less than 1.3. Can the loan be granted? Obviously not, because the resulting coverage ratio is less than 1.3, and such a loan would be too risky:

$$\text{Coverage ratio} = \frac{\text{net income}}{\text{debt service}} = \frac{\$91,839}{\$80,000} = 1.15$$

In order to raise the coverage ratio, and thus make the loan acceptable, the lender can do one of three things:

1 Reduce the mortgage constant and debt service by increasing the amortization term of the loan.

2 Reduce the mortgage constant by lowering the interest rate (which is generally the least desirable alternative for the lender).

3 Reduce the amount of the loan.

A fourth possibility for raising the coverage ratio would be to raise the net income estimated by finding some realistic method of raising rental income, or reducing vacancies or expenses. For example, utilization of a professional property management company with a proven record may convince a lender that better-than-market operating results are consistently possible and such inputs should be reflected in the net income estimate.

Maximum-loan Formula   Once the loan terms are established, the lender can use the following formula to determine the maximum loan that can be gained while maintaining the desired coverage ratio:

$$\text{Maximum loan} = \frac{\left[\dfrac{\text{net income}}{\text{desired coverage ratio}}\right]}{\text{mortgage constant}}$$

$$= \frac{\left[\dfrac{\$91,839}{1.3}\right]}{.10}$$

$$= \$706,454$$

In our example, the lender can grant a loan no greater than \$706,454 if a coverage ratio of 1.3 is desired. The loan request was for \$800,000.

The numerator of the formula above (\$91,839/1.3) tells the lender what the maximum amount of debt service can be so as to achieve a 1.3 coverage ratio. The maximum amount of debt service is simply the net income divided by the desired coverage ratio, and is derived from the formula: Coverage ratio = net income/debt service. The loan amount is then computed by our previous formula, which states: Loan amount = annual debt service/mortgage constant. In summary, the maximum-loan formula is derived by combining and manipulating the previous described coverage ratio and loan-amount formulas.

Consider the effects of a reduced mortgage constant on the maximum loan. Assume K falls from 10% to 9.3%. (What loan terms will produce this result?) The result is that the lender can make a loan of approximately \$759,600.

$$\text{Maximum loan} = \frac{\left[\dfrac{\$91,839}{1.3}\right]}{.093} = \$759,628$$

If the lender will reduce his desired coverage ratio to 1.25, he can further increase the loan to approximately $790,000, which is near the amount requested:

$$\text{Maximum loan} = \frac{\left[\dfrac{\$91,839}{1.25}\right]}{.093} = \$790,012$$

In summary, we can use the maximum loan formula to compute how much of a loan a lender should be willing to grant if we know the desired coverage ratio, the constant that will be accepted (and this is to some degree negotiable), and the net income figure that will be accepted.

Risk and the Debt-coverage Ratio   While other financial ratios may also be used (for example, break-even ratios, loan per square feet, etc.) the coverage ratio tends to be the primary financial criterion used by most institutional lenders, and is therefore the key to creating acceptable financial packages.

Risk is explicitly considered by the lender when establishing the minimum acceptable coverage ratio and mortgage constant. If a lender feels that a project is relatively risky, but wishes to make the loan, it can compensate by raising the desired coverage ratio and mortgage constant. As a result, the amount of the loan offered will decrease. Conversely, anything the borrower can do to convince the lender that the risks are less should result in a more favorable loan for the borrower. For example, lease insurance or longer-term leases, proof of a successful record, strong anchor tenants with substantial preleasing, and a good feasibility study and mortgage submission are factors which will decrease the perceived risks for the lender and increase the maximum loan amount.

Break-even Ratio (Default Point)   Another ratio that many lenders look at when evaluating a loan proposal is the break-even ratio:

$$\text{Break-even ratio} = \frac{\text{operating expenses + debt service}}{\text{gross possible income}}$$

In our original example, where a loan of $800,000 was requested, the break-even ratio is:

$$\frac{\$66,792 + \$80,000}{\$166,980} = 87.9\%$$

In the restructured case, which resulted in a mortgage loan of $706,454, the break-even ratio falls as a result of reduced debt service:

$$\frac{\$66,792 + \$70,645}{\$166,980} = 82.3\%$$

A break-even ratio of 82 percent means that a project can have up to an 18% vacancy rate before the net income from the project fails to cover the debt-service payments. Thus, there is an 18% cushion for the lender before possible default occurs. Alternatively, the project must be 82% occupied in order to break even. After break-even is reached, a positive cash flow will occur.

As with the coverage ratio, the break-even point can be used as an underwriting ratio by the lender. For example, many lenders will not make a loan on a general-use income property where the resulting break-even ratio is greater than 82 percent.

Computing Rates of Return on Investment

Two important rate-of-return measures are important for evaluating the debt and equity structure of a project. The first is the *rate of return on total capital*, and is sometimes referred to as the *free and clear return* or the *overall rate*.

$$\text{Rate of return on total capital (ROR)} = \frac{\text{net income}}{\text{total capital investment}}$$

This rate-of-return measure focuses on the productivity of the total capital invested, including both debt and equity capital. The second important rate-of-return measure is the *rate of return on equity*, and is sometimes referred to as the *cash-on-cash return* or the *equity dividend return*.

$$\text{Rate of return on equity (ROE)} = \frac{\text{cash flow}}{\text{equity investment}}$$

The ROE is probably the most frequently used rate-of-return measure by equity investors to evaluate proposed income-property investments.

Using our original example, where net income is $91,839 and cash flow is $11,839, the total capital investment (asking price) is $1,000,000 and equity investment is $200,000, ROR and ROE can be computed as follows:

$$\text{ROR} = \frac{\$91,839}{\$1,000,000} = 9.18\%$$

$$\text{ROE} = \frac{\$11,839}{\$200,000} = 5.92\%$$

Clearly, the above situation is undesirable for the equity investor. Previously, we noted that the situation was also unfavorable for the lender because the resulting coverage ratio was only 1.15. The basic problem here is negative leverage.

Positive and Negative Leverage

Leverage exists whenever debt exists in the capital structure. Simply stated, leverage means the use of debt financing. The greater the use of debt financing relative to equity financing, the greater the leverage.

The situation described above is unfavorable because the return on equity (ROE) is only 5.92% while the total assets (ROR) are earning at a rate of 9.18%. The problem is that $K = 10\%$. The equity investor can only earn 9.18% on the assets, but he must pay 10% to the lender. There is only 5.92% left for the equity investor. In this case, leverage works against the investor. Thus, we have negative (or reverse) leverage.

Negative leverage exists whenever the ROR is less than K (ROR $< K$). In contrast, whenever ROR is greater than K (ROR $> K$), leverage works for the equity investor. Thus, we have *positive leverage*. In plain English, the rate of productivity on the total money invested in a project must be greater than the cost of debt financing in order to create a favorable leverage position for the equity investor. A lender should beware of any financing situation which is expected to create a negative leverage situation for the borrower.

In summary, comparing K with ROR tells us whether we have positive or negative leverage. Remember, whatever net income is earned by the project can only be given to the lenders or the equity investors. If too much is given to the lenders (ROR $< K$), then there will be little left for the equity investors (ROE $< K$). As we saw in our example:

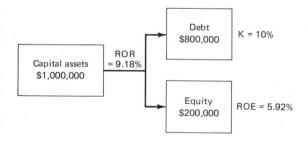

This situation is *not* acceptable! What we need to do is to raise ROR and/or lower K in order to achieve positive leverage. The desired result can best be achieved using a basic financial feasibility model. The basic financial feasibility model incorporates all the concepts discussed to this point and allows us to program in a positive leverage advantage for the equity investor and a desirable coverage ratio for the lender.

BASIC FINANCIAL FEASIBILITY MODEL FOR STRUCTURING THE DEAL

The model presented in Exhibit 2 allows us to manipulate the numbers in order to structure the economics of a project so that we can simultaneously achieve the financial objectives of both the lender and equity investors.

The final outputs of the model are estimates of (1) the maximum loan amount; (2) the maximum equity investment; and (3) the maximum project value or purchase price.

The inputs in the model which we are required to provide are (1) estimates of rents, vacancies, and expenses; (2) the debt-coverage ratio and mortgage constant desired by the lender; and (3) the desired rate of equity return (ROE) sought by the equity investor.

Illustration of the Model

To illustrate the use of the basic financial feasibility model, consider again the 84-unit apartment building and the following information:

Total leasable area in the buildings is approximately 55,400 square feet. The income per net leasable square foot is 25.1¢ per month or $3.01 annually.

Vacancy and operating expenses are 45 percent of gross possible income.

Required debt coverage ratio is 1.3 and the mortgage constant (K) is 10% (9¼% for approximately 28 years). The investors are seeking a loan of $800,000.

The equity investors require a 12% return (ROE). In the proposed sale of the property, a $200,000 equity price is asked.

The feasibility model (Exhibit 2) indicates that the project is worth approximately $883,000, not $1,000,000. In order to maintain a coverage ratio of 1.3, annual debt service cannot exceed $70,645, and a loan greater than $706,450 is not acceptable. In regard to the equity value, the investor cannot pay more than $176,617 if he wishes to achieve a 12% return and thus maintain a positive leverage position in the project. Using this model, the investor dictates the required ROE necessary to make the investment, then capitalizes the cash flow to determine equity value.

Restructuring the Financial Package

The value of a project to both the lender and equity investor is highly sensitive to the terms of the financial package, including the required debt-coverage ratio, and the required K and ROE. This model allows us to play with the numbers and restructure the deal in order to achieve a more desirable solution.

Let us assume that the financial package and solution shown in Exhibit 2 is not acceptable to either an institutional lender or to the seller. The seller is insistent on a $1,000,000 selling price and current interest rates for apartment buildings have risen to 10%. Is a solution possible that is acceptable to the seller, buyer, and lender?

Clearly, with interest rates of 10% or greater, conventional refinancing through an institutional lender is not feasible. However, in many cases with existing properties, seller financing can be provided in tandem with the assumption of existing notes to achieve a solution. For example, assume that four mortgage notes exist on the 84 units (which are completed in two phases). Two of the notes are from institutional lenders and two are from a previous owner. The interest rates range between 6 and 7¼%, but have relatively short maturities (18–23 years). The balance on the four notes totals approximately $650,000.

We can arrive at an acceptable solution if we can wrap around the existing notes and capture the low interest rates. At the same time, we wish to negotiate a relatively

Basic financial feasibility model

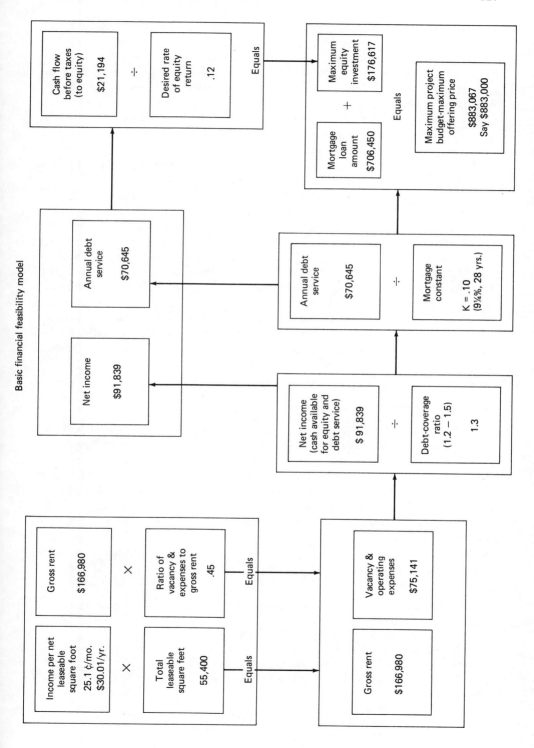

long mortgage term on the wraparound note so as to reduce the debt-service payments, thus increasing the cash flow and value of the project to the equity investors.

Assume that we negotiate the following solution: The seller takes a note for $825,000 on the property, 7½% for 28 years, and this note wraps around the four existing liens. A third-party trustee receives debt-service payments on the $825,000 note, pays the debt service on the four underlying mortgage notes, then pays the seller what is left over. In effect, the seller provides $175,000 of debt financing to the buyer ($825,000 − $650,000), and receives 7½% on the entire $825,000 note while the underlying notes bear interest rates of 6½ to 7¼%. Clearly, the seller's effective yield on the $175,000 financing provided is significnatly greater than 7½%; in addition the seller qualifies for installment sales treatment for tax purposes.

In order to maintain the desired risk profile for both the lender and equity investor, the debt-coverage ratio was kept at 1.3 and the equity investor maintained his ROE at 12%. Exhibit 3 shows the new solution, which produces a purchase price in excess of $1,000,000, satisfies the explicit financial objectives of the buyer and seller, and shifts the burden of financing to the seller. Instead of receiving a fee for arranging a new loan from a financial institution, the mortgage banker receives a fee for arranging the wraparound financing and acts as the servicing agent (trustee) on the wraparound loan.

This example illustrates the pronounced effect of changes in the mortgage interest rate on the investment value of a project. Additional changes in the financial package, such as a change in the loan term or the desired ROE or debt-coverage ratio will also make a significant impact on the project valuation. It is not uncommon to use the basic financial feasibility model 20 or 30 times in analyzing and restructuring the project to achieve a solution acceptable to all the parties involved.

Shortcomings of the Basic Financial Model

Substantial criticism can be levied against the use of the basic financial feasibility model for project evaluation. It utilizes a single net-income and cash-flow figure which purports to represent the productivity of the property for each year in the future over the useful life of the property. Appraisers have contended that real estate works on this normalized or stabilized net-income statement, and have successfully convinced most lenders, brokers, and syndicators to adopt these measures of return.

This stabilized-income measure skillfully ignores the complexities of real estate investments and thus ignores many important variables which affect investment value and loan quality. Specifically, the basic financial feasibility model does not explicitly consider seven variables:

   1   Inflation of rents, expenses, and property value, which cause the income and cash flow to change each year.
   2   Equity buildup over time through loan amortization.
   3   The expected holding period of the investment (from the lender's viewpoint, the expected period that the loan will be outstanding).
   4   The borrower's income and capital gains tax position, and investor logic and motivation.
   5   Start-up and acquisition costs.

Basic financial feasibility model

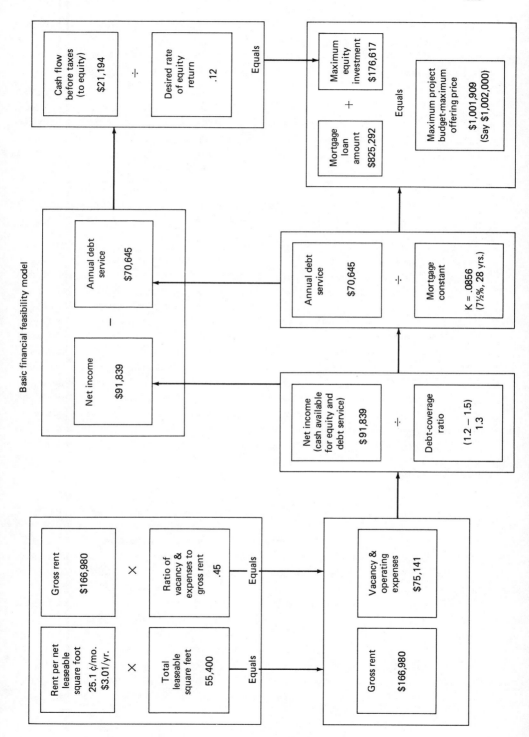

6 The uneven and erratic nature of the net income stream from year to year, thus the riskiness of the investment.

7 The time value of money (the fact that a dollar promised in the future is worth less than a dollar today).

These shortcomings can be overcome with the use of discounted cash-flow models and the application of modern capital budgeting techniques. While the basic feasibility model can be used effectively during the initial stages of project analysis and financial structuring, the more sophisticated capital budgeting techniques should be employed before the final investment or loan decision is made.

MODERN CAPITAL BUDGETING TECHNIQUES— DISCOUNTED CASH FLOW AND RISK ANALYSIS

The essence of modern capital budgeting techniques is the incorporation of the time-value-of-money concept, which in turn has led to the use of discounted cash-flow (DCF) methods of analyzing projects. The two DCF methods which have developed are known as the *internal-rate-of-return* method and the *present-value* method. Both methods are widely utilized by industrial corporations throughout the United States for evaluating capital expenditures, and are slowly being integrated into use by firms in the real estate industry.

In the following sections, we will first review the mathematics and economics of discounted cash-flow methods. Second, we will develop a full-scale after-tax cash-flow analysis model using the DCF methods and analyze a project over a projected holding period. Third, we will review various types of annual financial ratios which can be utilized for evaluating lender/equity investor positions. Finally, we will develop the concept of sensitivity and risk analysis, and show how a computer-simulation model can be utilized to evaluate the risk/return tradeoff in a real estate investment.

Time Value of Money

We have all heard the expression, "A bird in the hand is worth two in the bush." This refers to the time value of birds, but the principle involved is equally applicable to money. If offered a choice between a dollar today and a dollar a year from now, most of us would choose a dollar today. Clearly, a dollar a year from now is less valuable than a dollar today. Why is this so? As individuals, we may reply that the dollar today will give us immediate pleasure in the form of a dinner or a movie. Immediate pleasure is preferable to postponed pleasure.

However, we must look at this problem from the point of view of the real estate investor, who prefers the dollar today not because of the immediate pleasure that will be gained, but because the dollar can be put to work and earn some return. Should the investor choose to receive the dollar a year from now, it will mean foregoing the money that might be earned over the course of the year on the present dollar. In the words of the economist, there is an "opportunity cost" involved in passing up the cash flow that could be obtained by using the present dollar in an income property over the year.

We can agree that we would not ordinarily relinquish today's dollar in exchange for a promise that it will be returned a year from now. We will want our dollar back plus some payment for its use. If we think that we should receive 20% for the intended use of our money, today's dollar should be returned a year from now with an additional 20¢. Thus, $1.00 invested at 20% today would be worth $1.20 a year from now. To put it another way, the present value of $1.20 a year from now, discounted at 20%, is $1.00. This is a bit awkward, however. We are seldom going to be called upon to give the present value of $1.20 a year from now; we are much more likely to be faced with the problem of calculating the present value of $1.00 received a year from now, or some multiple of $1.00. Thus, we would like to know what amount invested at 20% will cumulate to $1.00 a year from now. As it turns out, $.833 invested at 20% will be worth a $1.00 a year from now ($.833 + 20% × $.833 = $1.00). In other words, the present value of $1.00 a year from now, discounted at 20%, is $.833.

If today's dollar is worth $1.20 a year from now, it would be worth even more two years from now. Today, we invest a dollar at 20%; at the end of the first year we reinvest $1.20 at 20%. Consequently at a rate of 20%, compounded annually, a dollar today is worth $1.44 at the end of the second year. Alternatively, we could say that $1.00 two years from now has a present value of $.694; that is, if $.694 were invested at an annual compound interest rate of 20%, it would amount to $1.00 at the end of the second year. This is proved below:

	Amount invested first of year	Interest earned at 20% on amount invested	Amount available at end of year
1st year	$.694 × 20% =	$.139	$ .833
2nd year	.833 × 20% =	.167	1.00

Thus we can construct a small table showing the present value of $1.00 received one year from now and two years from now, in each case assuming an interest rate of 20%.

Years hence	Present value at 20% of $1 received at end of the year
0	$1.00
1	.833
2	.694

Fortunately, we need struggle no longer to develop our own table; the necessary tables are readily available. A portion of a present-value table is shown in Table 2.

If the present value of $1.00 received a year from now is $.833, and the present value of another $1.00 received two years from now is $.694, what is the present value of a stream of cash benefits of $1.00 at the end of year 1 and year 2 discounted at 20%? Clearly, the present value of a dollar a year for the next two years is $.833 + $.694, or $1.527. (Because of differences due to rounding, it is actually $1.528.) There will be occasions when we will wish to evaluate a steady stream of income. For this purpose

Table 2

PRESENT VALUE OF $1

Years Hence	1%	2%	4%	6%	8%	10%	12%	14%	15%	16%	18%	20%	22%	24%	25%	26%	28%	30%
1	0.990	0.980	0.962	0.943	0.926	0.909	0.893	0.877	0.870	0.852	0.847	0.833	0.820	0.806	0.800	0.794	0.781	0.769
2	0.980	0.961	0.925	0.890	0.857	0.826	0.797	0.769	0.756	0.743	0.718	0.694	0.672	0.650	0.640	0.630	0.610	0.592
3	0.971	0.942	0.889	0.840	0.794	0.751	0.712	0.675	0.658	0.641	0.609	0.579	0.551	0.524	0.512	0.500	0.477	0.455
4	0.961	0.924	0.855	0.792	0.735	0.683	0.636	0.592	0.572	0.552	0.516	0.482	0.451	0.423	0.410	0.397	0.373	0.350
5	0.951	0.906	0.822	0.747	0.681	0.621	0.567	0.519	0.497	0.476	0.437	0.402	0.370	0.341	0.328	0.315	0.291	0.269
6	0.942	0.888	0.790	0.705	0.630	0.564	0.507	0.456	0.432	0.410	0.370	0.335	0.303	0.275	0.262	0.250	0.227	0.207
7	0.933	0.871	0.760	0.665	0.583	0.513	0.452	0.400	0.376	0.354	0.314	0.279	0.249	0.222	0.210	0.198	0.178	0.159
8	0.923	0.853	0.731	0.627	0.540	0.467	0.404	0.351	0.327	0.305	0.266	0.233	0.204	0.179	0.168	0.157	0.139	0.123
9	0.914	0.837	0.703	0.592	0.500	0.424	0.361	0.308	0.284	0.263	0.225	0.194	0.167	0.144	0.134	0.125	0.108	0.094
10	0.905	0.820	0.676	0.558	0.463	0.386	0.322	0.270	0.247	0.227	0.191	0.162	0.137	0.116	0.107	0.099	0.085	0.073
11	0.896	0.804	0.650	0.527	0.429	0.350	0.287	0.237	0.215	0.195	0.162	0.135	0.112	0.094	0.086	0.079	0.066	0.056
12	0.887	0.788	0.625	0.497	0.397	0.319	0.257	0.208	0.187	0.168	0.137	0.112	0.092	0.076	0.069	0.062	0.052	0.043
13	0.879	0.773	0.601	0.469	0.368	0.290	0.229	0.182	0.163	0.145	0.116	0.093	0.075	0.061	0.055	0.050	0.040	0.033
14	0.870	0.758	0.577	0.442	0.340	0.263	0.205	0.160	0.141	0.125	0.099	0.078	0.062	0.049	0.044	0.039	0.032	0.025
15	0.861	0.743	0.555	0.417	0.315	0.239	0.183	0.140	0.123	0.108	0.084	0.065	0.051	0.040	0.035	0.031	0.025	0.020
16	0.853	0.728	0.534	0.394	0.292	0.218	0.163	0.123	0.107	0.093	0.071	0.054	0.042	0.032	0.028	0.025	0.019	0.015
17	0.844	0.714	0.513	0.371	0.270	0.198	0.146	0.108	0.093	0.080	0.060	0.045	0.034	0.026	0.023	0.020	0.015	0.012
18	0.836	0.700	0.494	0.350	0.250	0.180	0.130	0.095	0.081	0.069	0.051	0.038	0.028	0.021	0.018	0.016	0.012	0.009
19	0.828	0.686	0.475	0.331	0.232	0.164	0.116	0.083	0.070	0.060	0.043	0.031	0.023	0.017	0.014	0.012	0.009	0.007
20	0.820	0.673	0.456	0.312	0.215	0.149	0.104	0.073	0.061	0.051	0.037	0.026	0.019	0.014	0.012	0.010	0.007	0.005
21	0.811	0.660	0.439	0.294	0.199	0.135	0.093	0.064	0.053	0.044	0.031	0.022	0.015	0.011	0.009	0.008	0.006	0.004
22	0.803	0.647	0.422	0.278	0.184	0.123	0.083	0.056	0.046	0.038	0.026	0.018	0.013	0.009	0.007	0.006	0.004	0.003
23	0.795	0.634	0.406	0.262	0.170	0.112	0.074	0.049	0.040	0.033	0.022	0.015	0.010	0.007	0.006	0.005	0.003	0.002
24	0.788	0.622	0.390	0.247	0.158	0.102	0.066	0.043	0.035	0.028	0.019	0.013	0.008	0.006	0.005	0.004	0.003	0.002
25	0.780	0.610	0.375	0.233	0.146	0.092	0.059	0.038	0.030	0.024	0.016	0.010	0.007	0.005	0.004	0.003	0.002	0.001
26	0.772	0.598	0.361	0.220	0.135	0.084	0.053	0.033	0.026	0.021	0.014	0.009	0.006	0.004	0.003	0.002	0.002	0.001
27	0.764	0.586	0.347	0.207	0.125	0.076	0.047	0.029	0.023	0.018	0.011	0.007	0.005	0.003	0.002	0.002	0.001	0.001
28	0.757	0.574	0.333	0.196	0.116	0.069	0.042	0.026	0.020	0.016	0.010	0.006	0.004	0.002	0.002	0.002	0.001	0.001
29	0.749	0.563	0.321	0.185	0.107	0.063	0.037	0.022	0.017	0.014	0.008	0.005	0.003	0.002	0.002	0.001	0.001	0.001
30	0.742	0.552	0.308	0.174	0.099	0.057	0.033	0.020	0.015	0.012	0.007	0.004	0.003	0.002	0.001	0.001	0.001	0.001

Table 3

PRESENT VALUE OF $1 RECEIVED ANNUALLY FOR N YEARS

Years (N)	1%	2%	4%	6%	8%	10%	12%	14%	15%	16%	18%	20%	22%	24%	25%	26%	28%	30%
1	0.990	0.980	0.962	0.943	0.926	0.909	0.893	0.877	0.870	0.862	0.847	0.833	0.820	0.806	0.800	0.794	0.781	0.769
2	1.970	1.942	1.886	1.833	1.783	1.736	1.690	1.647	1.626	1.605	1.566	1.528	1.492	1.457	1.440	1.424	1.392	1.361
3	2.941	2.884	2.775	2.673	2.577	2.487	2.402	2.322	2.283	2.246	2.174	2.106	2.042	1.981	1.952	1.923	1.868	1.816
4	3.902	3.808	3.630	3.465	3.312	3.170	3.037	2.914	2.855	2.798	2.690	2.589	2.494	2.404	2.362	2.320	2.241	2.166
5	4.853	4.713	4.452	4.212	3.993	3.791	3.605	3.433	3.352	3.274	3.127	2.991	2.864	2.745	2.689	2.635	2.532	2.436
6	5.795	5.601	5.242	4.917	4.623	4.355	4.111	3.889	3.784	3.685	3.498	3.326	3.167	3.020	2.951	2.885	2.759	2.643
7	6.728	6.472	6.002	5.582	5.206	4.868	4.564	4.288	4.160	4.039	3.812	3.605	3.416	3.242	3.161	3.083	2.937	2.802
8	7.652	7.325	6.733	6.210	5.747	5.335	4.968	4.639	4.487	4.344	4.078	3.837	3.619	3.421	3.329	3.241	3.076	2.925
9	8.566	8.162	7.435	6.802	6.247	5.759	5.328	4.946	4.772	4.607	4.303	4.031	3.786	3.566	3.463	3.366	3.184	3.019
10	9.471	8.983	8.111	7.360	6.710	6.145	5.650	5.216	5.019	4.833	4.494	4.192	3.923	3.682	3.571	3.465	3.269	3.092
11	10.368	9.787	8.760	7.837	7.139	6.495	5.988	5.453	5.234	5.029	4.656	4.327	4.035	3.776	3.656	3.544	3.335	3.147
12	11.255	10.575	9.385	8.384	7.536	6.814	6.194	5.660	5.421	5.197	4.793	4.439	4.127	3.851	3.725	3.606	3.387	3.190
13	12.134	11.343	9.986	8.853	7.904	7.103	6.424	5.842	5.583	5.342	4.910	4.533	4.203	3.912	3.780	3.656	3.427	3.223
14	13.004	12.106	10.563	9.295	8.244	7.367	6.628	6.002	5.724	5.468	5.008	4.611	4.265	3.962	3.824	3.695	3.459	3.249
15	13.865	12.849	11.118	9.712	8.559	7.606	6.811	6.142	5.847	5.575	5.092	4.675	4.315	4.001	3.859	3.726	3.483	3.268
16	14.718	13.578	11.652	10.106	8.851	7.824	6.974	6.265	5.954	5.669	5.162	4.730	4.357	4.033	3.887	3.751	3.503	3.283
17	15.562	14.292	12.166	10.477	9.122	8.022	7.120	6.373	6.047	5.749	5.222	4.775	4.391	4.059	3.910	3.771	3.518	3.295
18	16.398	14.992	12.659	10.828	9.372	8.201	7.250	6.467	6.128	5.818	5.273	4.812	4.419	4.080	3.928	3.786	3.529	3.304
19	17.226	15.678	13.134	11.158	9.604	8.365	7.366	6.550	6.198	5.877	5.316	4.844	4.442	4.097	3.942	3.799	3.539	3.311
20	18.046	16.351	13.590	11.470	9.818	8.514	7.469	6.623	6.259	5.929	5.353	4.870	4.460	4.110	3.954	3.808	3.546	3.316
21	18.857	17.011	14.029	11.764	10.017	8.649	7.562	6.687	6.312	5.973	5.384	4.891	4.476	4.121	3.963	3.816	3.551	3.320
22	19.660	17.658	14.451	12.042	10.201	8.772	7.645	6.743	6.359	6.011	5.410	4.909	4.488	4.130	3.970	3.822	3.556	3.323
23	20.456	18.292	14.857	12.303	10.371	8.883	7.718	6.792	6.399	6.044	5.432	4.925	4.499	4.137	3.976	3.827	3.559	3.325
24	21.243	18.914	15.247	12.550	10.529	8.985	7.784	6.835	6.434	6.073	5.451	4.937	4.507	4.143	3.981	3.831	3.562	3.327
25	22.023	19.523	15.622	12.783	10.675	9.077	7.843	6.873	6.464	6.097	5.467	4.948	4.514	4.147	3.985	3.834	3.564	3.329
26	22.795	20.121	15.983	13.003	10.810	9.161	7.896	6.906	6.491	6.118	5.480	4.956	4.520	4.151	3.988	3.837	3.566	3.330
27	23.560	20.707	16.330	13.211	10.935	9.237	7.943	6.935	6.514	6.136	5.492	4.964	4.524	4.154	3.990	3.839	3.567	3.331
28	24.316	21.281	16.663	13.406	11.051	9.307	7.984	6.961	6.534	6.152	5.502	4.970	4.528	4.157	3.992	3.840	3.568	3.331
29	25.066	21.844	16.984	13.591	11.158	9.370	8.022	6.983	6.551	6.166	5.510	4.975	4.531	4.159	3.994	3.841	3.569	3.332
30	25.808	22.396	17.292	13.765	11.258	9.427	8.055	7.003	6.566	6.177	5.517	4.979	4.534	4.160	3.995	3.842	3.569	3.332

we will use Table 3, which shows the present value of $1.00 received annually for a specified number of years.

Both Table 2 and 3 assume that the cash benefits are received at the end of each period of time. Other tables are available that assume that the cash benefits are available continuously throughout the year. Moreover, Tables 2 and 3 could be used to evaluate income streams received monthly or semi-annually. Instead of the time periods being years, they can be considered as months of half-years. Rates of return would then be monthly or semi-annual rates, but could readily be converted to or from annual rates.

With the concept of the time value of money in mind, let us view the problem of evaluating an investment requiring equity cash of $10,000, in return for which we expect to receive an annual cash-flow benefit of $4,500 in each of the three following years. Later, we will expand the concepts discussed here and apply them in some actual projects.

Internal Rate of Return

The internal-rate-of-return method of evaluating proposed real estate investments is used to indicate the expected annual rate of return to be gained from an investment. In more precise terms, rate of return may be defined as the interest rate equivalent to the cash flows which the investment will yield in addition to returning the original expenditure. We can then compare this yield with our required rate of return. We will seriously question the desirability of committing funds to an investment whose yield is less than the required rate of return.

Calculation of Internal Rate of Return   Let us return to Table 3. Assume we are told that if we will invest $2.106 in some venture, we will receive a total of $3.00—a return of our original investment plus compounded annual interest. What is the interest rate? This is a little different from the problem that we have faced before. In our earlier discussion, we knew the interest rate, or yield, and were trying to calculate the present value of a known future stream of dollars at that known discount rate. Now we know the future stream of cash flows and the investment required to achieve the cash flows, but we would like to know the yield. The answer lies somewhere in the "3-year" line of Table 3. As we move along this line, we find that the rate that equates an annual return of $1.00 a year for three years is 20%.

Let us apply this technique to determine the rate of return on our $10,000 investment. We can estimate the rate of return, or yield, by a series of successive approximations; that is, by making guesses at its value. We wish to find the one rate that will equate the stream of $4,500 cash flows for three years wtih the present required investment of $10,000. Let us see if a rate of 16% works. From Table 3 we see that the present value of $4,500 received annually after three years and discounted at 16% is $10,107:

$$2.246 \times \$4,500 = \$10,107$$

This tells us that if we were to invest $10,107 in return for $4,500 a year for three years, the annual rate of return would be 16%. However we do not need to invest this much money; our investment is only $10,000. Therefore, the true rate of return we will receive must be more than 16%. Let us try 18%. Using Table 3, again, we find that the present value of $4,500 received annually for three years and discounted at 18% is $9,783:

$$2.174 \times \$4,500 = \$9,783$$

This calculation tells us if we were to invest $9,783 in return for the specified cash flows, the rate of return would be 18%. Because we actually must invest more than $9,783, the rate to be gained must be less than 18%, but more than 16%. Moreover, it must be closer to 16%, because the actual required investment of $10,000 is closer to $10,107 than to $9,783. We can approximate the actual rate by interpolation:

	Difference in rate	Difference in calculated present values	Difference in calculated present value and required investment
	16%	$10,107	$10,107
	18%	9,783	10,000
Difference	2%	$ 324	$ 107

$$\frac{\$107}{\$324} \times 2\% = 0.7\% \quad 16\% + .7\% = 16.7\%$$

Observe that the calculated rate is, as we expected, closer to 16% than to 18%. In other words, a net cash inflow of $4,500 at the end of each year for three years is equivalent to a rate of return of about 16.7% compounded annually on an initial investment of $10,000. We can easily check the validity of this figure, as shown below. To obtain great accuracy, we shall use a rate of 16.66%, rather than the rate rounded off to one decimal point.

	Amount invested first of year		Interest at 16.66% earned on amount invested		Amount available at end of year	Amount withdrawn at end of year
1st year	$10,000	+	$1,666	=	$11,666	$4,500
2nd year	7,166	+	1,194	=	8,360	4,500
3rd year	3,860	+	634	=	4,503	4,500

The difference between $4,503 and $4,500 is small considering the amounts involved. If the true rate had been used, no difference would have resulted.

Another way of viewing this problem would be to consider that we have deposited $10,000 with a rather generous banker who has agreed to pay almost 16.7%, compounded annually, on all deposits. At the end of each year, we withdraw $4,500 after the bank has calculated the interest on our account. Our last withdrawal of $4,500 at the end of the third year empties the account.

Internal rate of return can also be applied in situations in which the cash flow is not the same in each year. This is usually the case in real estate. If the proposed investment is estimated to have some reversion value at the end of the third year, this cash flow should be added to the cash flow of that year. In addition, inflation factors and a strengthening market demand may cause increasing cash-flow returns in future years. For example, this might have been the case with the proposed investment of $10,000, which in three successive years would produce net cash flows of $2,500, $4,500, and $6,500, respectively. The proposal to invest $10,000 to obtain annual cash flows of $4,500 for three years offers a higher rate of return, however. Even though the total dollar return is the same in both cases, the yield on the capital investment is about 16.7% for the level cash flows as compared to slightly over 14% for the project with the delayed cash flows. To obtain the latter rate, we must have successive approximations from Table 2 and then interpolate if necessary. We find the 14% rate is very close to the true rate:

$$
\begin{array}{l}
\textbf{14\% rate} \\
.877 \times \$2,500 = \$ \ 2,193 \\
.769 \times \ \ 4,500 = \ \ \ 3,461 \\
.675 \times \ \ 6,500 = \ \ \underline{\ \ 4,388} \\
 \$10,042
\end{array}
$$

Thus, if these were competing proposals, we would rank the project with the yield of 16.7% above the project offering a return of only 14%.

Comparison of Internal Rate of Return with Required Rate of Return   If we knew our required rate of return, we would now be in a position to determine whether or not the proposed investment of $10,000 is worthwhile from a monetary point of view. Let us assume that we have a required rate of return (RROR) of 10%. In this case, the difference between the internal rate of return (16.7%) and the required rate (10%) suggests that it would be worthwhile to purchase the investment.

Present Value

A second acceptable method of evaluating capital expenditure proposals is to calculate the present value of the cash flows discounted at our required rate of return. If we calculate the present value in this manner, we can describe the present value of an investment as the maximum amount an investor would pay for the opportunity of making the investment without being financially worse off. This present value is then compared to the cost of the investment. If the calculated present value is more than the investment cost, it must mean that the internal rate of return is greater than the required rate of return. Therefore, there are net monetary benefits to be gained by undertaking the investment. In contrast, if the calculated present value is less than the investment cost, the internal rate of return must be less than the required rate of return, and we cannot undertake the investment without suffering a financial loss.

Let us illustrate the process. Assume again that our required rate of return is 10%. The cash benefits of a $10,000 investment have been estimated at $4,500 per year for three years. Using Table 3, we find that the present value of this stream of cash flows discounted at 10% is $11,192.

2.487 × $4,500 = $11,192

Exactly the same process is sometimes presented as summing the present values of the outlays on the investment and the present value of the cash proceeds expected from the investment. If this sum is greater than zero, a net gain will be realized from the investment. Thus we have:

Present value of outlays	$−10,000
Present value of proceeds	+11,192
Net present value	$ 1,192

This particular approach may be useful when we find it necessary to make investment outlays during the first few years of the life of the project. This would be typical if we were building a large apartment complex in phases. We would then have to calculate the present value of the outlays, as well as the present value of the proceeds from the investment. In all of our illustrations, we have assumed that the required cash outlays occur in the first period.

Because it is difficult to evaluate or rank projects on the basis of net present value, it is customary to calculate a *profitability index* or *desirability index*; that is, the present value of cash flows divided by the present value of cash outlays required. For example, the profitability index for the $10,000 investment would be 1.12:

$$\frac{\text{Present value of cash flows}}{\text{Present value of investment outlays}} = \frac{\$11,192}{\$10,000} = 1.12$$

By computing profitability indexes for other projects, we can rank them in order of desirability, as shown below. A project with an index of profitability of less than 1.00 would be undesirable; that is, its internal rate of return would be less than the required rate of return.

	Present value of required investment	Present value of proceeds	Net present value	Profitability index
Project C	$4,000	$6,400	$2,400	1.6
Project A	1,000	1,500	500	1.5
Project B	5,000	6,500	1,500	1.3

Present-value and internal-rate-of-return methods are adaptable to almost all income-property situations. They can be utilized to evaluate cash flows on a before- or after-tax basis. They can be used to evaluate mortgage investments as well as equity investments, and they produce values which allow comparisons between projects and other forms of investments.

The internal-rate-of-return approach seems to be preferred by real estate practitioners because the concept of "yield" is well ingrained and widely utilized, and because project comparisons are easily made using this approach. In contrast, the present-value approach presents greater conceptual problems to most real estate practitioners.

In the following sections, we will see both approaches applied to income-property analysis.

Tax Shelters from Financial Leverage

As we noted previously, investors can be divided into two groups—mortgage lenders and equity investors. The mortgage lender, who is exposed to less risk from market flucutations and future improvements to maintain the investment project, is willing to accept a level, often somewhat lower return on investment than the equity investor. The lender has the first claim to income from the property and to the property itself in the event the equity investor defaults. A greater rate of return is anticipated by the equity investor to balance the additional risk assumed for the residual claim on the benefits of the investment.

The value of an investor's equity increases whenever the amount of principal amortization exceeds any losses in property value during the ownership term, or whenever total property value increases. Generally, real estate investments are financed with level-payment mortgage contracts, each payment including a certain portion allocated to interest and another portion allocated to debt reduction. Over time the proportions shift; that is, the first payments are mostly interest payments and reduce debt very little, whereas later payments reduce debt considerably and involve little interest.

This level-payment amortization method can significantly affect the equity investor's income tax payments, and thus his after-tax cash flow. Interest expense is a deductible item for income tax calculations—repayment of debt principal is not. As the interest portion of the amortization payment decreases over time, other factors remaining constant, the amount of income tax payable will increase and the amount of cash flow sheltered by the investment will decrease. Thus, the investor's debt-service payment remains constant while his total income tax liability increases and his tax shelter decreases.

After holding property for four to 12 years, many real estate investors refinance their investment. Two of the most common reasons for this strategy are to get cash out of the project, and increase the tax effect by increasing interest deductions. The equity investor obtains a new mortgage based on the market value of the property, using part of the money to repay the first mortgage lender. Because market values have typically risen in the past and the debt balance on the old loan has been decreased through amortization payments, the equity investor receives the difference as a tax-free cash flow. Plus, the investor starts the interest cycle over once again on the new loan, thereby raising the level of tax shelter.

Tax Shelters from Depreciation

For tax purposes, the Internal Revenue Code allows a taxpayer to recover investments in certain assets by depreciating them over time. Assets in this category include property used in a trade or business and property held for rent. Land is not subject to depreciation because it is not considered a wasting asset; that is, it is not considered to deteriorate over time. Because no cash payment is involved but taxable income is reduced, depreciation is called a non-cash-flow expense.

A tax shelter results from depreciation when the depreciation expense for tax purposes exceeds the actual decline in value of the assets being depreciated. In most of the post-war period, the market value of the majority of buildings has increased rather than depreciated as they aged because of inflation and relative shortages. This fact has allowed real estate investors a deduction from income for income tax calculations when no expense has in fact been incurred.

Accelerated Depreciation In calculating depreciation expense, the current Internal Revenue Code allows a real estate investor the privilege of using an accelerated method for certain situations. He gains an advantage by using one of these methods because (1) more depreciation (as a percent of total depreciation) can be charged during the holding period than would have been possible had the straight-line method been used, since typical holding periods will be less than the remaining economic life of the depreciable asset; (2) although the investor's total tax liability will often be the same by the end of the holding period, his payment of a portion of these taxes has been postponed to a later period, enabling earlier use of money and for a longer period of time; and (3) the total actual cash inflows accruing to the investor may be increased because, although an expense which requires a cash outlay has not been incurred, the investor is allowed a deduction depreciating the entire capital asset to arrive at taxable income.

Allowable Depreciation Methods Taxpayers are not allowed to select any depreciation method they desire. Maximum levels have been established dependent on classification of the real estate unit being considered. Exhibit 4 shows the depreciation method limitations applicable to fixed assets acquired after July 24, 1969. The current Internal Revenue Code rules state that the investor cannot claim a depreciation deduction that would be larger in amount than one determined according to the method indicated in Exhibit 4. In most cases, a taxpayer is free to switch from any rapid-depreciation method to the straight-line method when it becomes advantageous. In addition, for qualified, low-income housing rehabilitation projects, the tax rules authorize depreciation over a 60-month period without reference to any of the usual rules. An investor will find competent tax advice helpful in selecting a depreciation method.

Reversion and the Capital Gains Tax Reversion, as applied to real estate, refers to the transfer of property from one individual to another. This transfer could occur when property is sold, when it is exchanged for another piece of property, or when it passes through the estate of an individual. A transfer of property can also take place when ownership reverts to a former owner, either through default or under the terms of the original agreement. The tax consequences relating to any of these situations are complex and require competent tax advice. Only tax factors relating to the sale of real estate will be considered here.

As the tax laws are currently structured, certain types of gains are preferable to others. For instance, if a dealer in real estate sells property held for resale at a gain,

Exhibit 4

**Depreciation Method Limitations Applicable to Fixed Assets
Acquired After July 24, 1969**

Type of property	Maximum depreciation method authorized
Depreciable, tangible property other than buildings	
If the property is new	200% declining balance
If the property is used	150% declining balance
Depreciable buildings	
If residential rental property	
Acquired new	200% declining balance or sum-of-the-years digits
Acquired used with an estimated remaining life of 20 years or more	125% declining balance
Acquired used with an estimated remaining life of less than 20 years	Straight line
If other than residential property	
Acquired new	150% declining balance
Acquired used	Straight line
All intangible property	Straight line

income will be taxed as ordinary income at rates from 14 to 70%. The sale of the same property by an investor could be taxed as a capital gain, and provided the property had been held for six months or longer, the income could be taxed at a maximum rate of 35%. Clearly, capital gains tax treatment is preferred. A real estate investor must plan transactions wisely to minimize taxes.

Recapture   The amount of gain recognized on the sale of real estate is equal to the difference between the depreciated basis of the property and the selling price of the property. If the owner has used the straight-line method of depreciation and the property qualifies for capital-gains tax treatment, this difference will be taxed as a capital gain. However, if rapid depreciation was claimed, part or all of the difference between accelerated and straight-line depreciation (called excess depreciation) may be taxed as ordinary income.

Depreciation recapture converts to and treats as an ordinary gain a certain amount of the dollars that would normally be recognized as capital gain. The amount of recapture is a function of time and the classification of the property involved. The effect on the investor is to increase the amount of tax that must be paid when the investor has used the accelerated-depreciation method. The Tax Reform Act of 1969 has established the current depreciation recapture rules.

The recapture rules favor residential properties. On a residential property, if the holding period is less than 100 months (8⅓ years), all excess depreciation is recaptured as ordinary income. For each month thereafter, a 1% credit is given toward capital gains treatment. After 200 months (16⅔ years), all excess depreciation has been converted to capital gain income. However, for commercial properties (that is, non-residential) there is no "phase-out" rule. All excess depreciation is recaptured as ordinary income and taxed at the ordinary rate regardless of the holding period.

Exhibit 5 depicts the tax situation for residential investment property for a 20-year period. The graph is based on property with an estimated useful life of 40 years, purchased for $100,000, which appreciates in market value at the rate of 1% (noncompounded) per year; that is, at the end of 20 years the property has a market value of $120,000. Line A shows the annual market value of the property. Line B shows the annual basis for the property assuming the investor used straight-line depreciation. The amount of gain represented by the distance between lines A and B will be taxed as a capital gain. Line C shows the annual basis for the property, assuming the investor uses double-declining-balance depreciation. The amount of gain represented by the distance between lines B-D and C is the portion subject to recapture and will be taxed as ordinary income. The percentage of the difference between straight-line depreciation and the accelerated method (which is subject to recapture as ordinary income) declines until, after 16 years and eight months, the entire gain is taxed at the investor's capital gains tax rate.

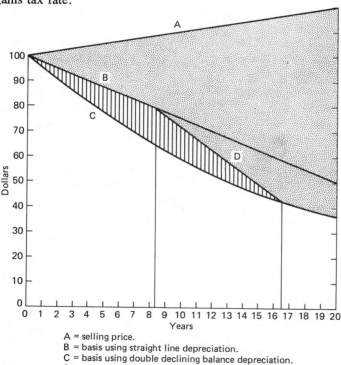

A = selling price.
B = basis using straight line depreciation.
C = basis using double declining balance depreciation.
D = recapture line.
|||||| Ordinary income   Capital gain

Example of Discounted Cash Flow After-Tax Analysis

Discounted cash flow analysis focuses on the valuation of cash flows expected over some holding period of the investment. We generally focus on three primary sources of after-tax cash flows when performing our analysis of:

    1   Annual cash flow from operations (as measured previously).

    2   Annual cash flow from tax savings (or taxes paid). Whenever taxable income is negative, a tax savings is produced by sheltering outside income. When taxable income is positive, income taxes must be paid.

    3   Cash flow from the sale of property after debts and capital gains taxes (reversion).

A fourth source of cash flow (cash proceeds from refinancing the property) is possible also but not generally considered in most cash-flow projections. For the present, we will ignore refinancing proceeds.

    Assumptions Used for the Analysis   The following real estate analysis focuses on the previously described 84-unit (used) apartment complex. We are interested now in adding to our analysis the factors of increasing rentals and expenses, loan amortization, accelerated depreciation, investor tax considerations, price appreciation, transaction costs, and time value of money. We are interested in analyzing the effects these factors will have on the property's total investment (or loan) value and rate of return. The property analysis incorporates the following assumptions:

    1   First-year gross possible income of $166,980 increases by 4% annually (compounded). There are 84 units, the average unit brings in $165.65 of gross income monthly (including "other income"), and contains approximately 659 square feet.

    2   Vacancy and credit loss allowance is expected to be 5 per cent of gross income.

    3   Total operating expenses are estimated to be 40 percent of gross possible income during the first year of operations, or $66,792. Thereafter, expenses increase at 7% per year (compounded).

    4   The total cost of the project is $1,000,000. Land is valued at $100,000 and the improvements at $900,000. Since there are 55,356 leasable square feet in the building (659 sq. ft. per unit × 84 units), the square foot cost of the improvements is approximately $16.26.

    5   Mortgage debt of $825,000 was negotiated at 7½% for 28 years. This results in annual amortization payments (debt service) of $70,574 and a mortgage constant of 8.55%.

    6   The improvements will be depreciated at the 125% declining-balance rate, and the remaining economic life of the improvements is 22 years. This economic life is an estimate of the average useful life of the building components, which have in fact been separated and individually depreciated by the tax accountant.

    7   The project value is expected to grow at 3%, based on the original $1,000,000 cost of the project. A selling expense (brokerage commissions and closing costs) of 5% is anticipated.

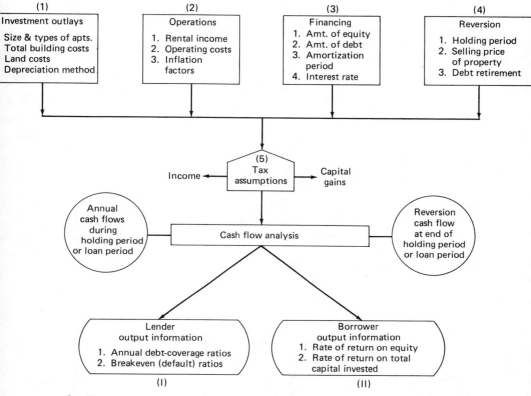

(1)	(2)	(3)	(4)
Investment outlays	**Operations**	**Financing**	**Reversion**
Size & types of apts. Total building costs Land costs Depreciation method	1. Rental income 2. Operating costs 3. Inflation factors	1. Amt. of equity 2. Amt. of debt 3. Amortization period 4. Interest rate	1. Holding period 2. Selling price of property 3. Debt retirement

(5) Tax assumptions

Income ← → Capital gains

Annual cash flows during holding period or loan period

Cash flow analysis

Reversion cash flow at end of holding period or loan period

Lender output information
1. Annual debt-coverage ratios
2. Breakeven (default) ratios
(I)

Borrower output information
1. Rate of return on equity
2. Rate of return on total capital invested
(II)

8 The investor's marginal income is taxed at 50%, and capital gains on the sale of the property are taxed at 25%.

9 An after-tax (internal) rate of equity investment of 18% is sought. This is the required rate of return necessary to induce the investor to commit equity funds.

This analysis will provide information on the most likely consequences of the investment and will be analyzed from both lender and equity investor viewpoints. As illustrated above and in Exhibit 6, our cash-flow model incorporates five sets of input variables: investment outlays, operations, financing, reversion, and tax assumptions. The output of the analysis includes cash-flow projections annually, discounted cash-flow information, and various types of financial ratios. The calculation of these is explained in the following sections.

Calculation of Financial Data   Our cash-flow analysis is illustrated in Exhibit 7, and has been generated for us by a computer program. The first section is simply a recap of the data already given.

Section 2 provides property information and shows our balance sheet as of the purchase date. Also calculated is the leverage ratio as of the date of purchase, which is simply the total debt ($825,000) divided by the total property cost ($1,000,000). The project has a debt ratio of 82.5%. The equity investment of $175,000 therefore represents 17.5 percent of the total purchase cost.

EXHIBIT 7

COMPUTER ANALYSIS: OUTPUT DATA
PROJECT NAME: 84 UNIT APARTMENT
DATE:

. . . .
OUTPUT DATA RUN NUMBER 1
. . . .

1. RECAPITULATION OF INPUT DATA
   *1.   TYPE PROPERTY (0. = RESIDENTIAL. 1. = COMMERCIAL) = 0
   *2.   NUMBER OF UNITS IN PROJECT =   84
   *3.   AVERAGE SQUARE FOOTAGE PER UNIT =   659.00
   *4.   AVERAGE MONTHLY RENTAL PER UNIT =   165.6547
   *5.   EXPECTED OCCUPANCY = .9500
   *6.   ANNUAL GROWTH RATE OF RENTAL INCOME OVER THE HOLD PERIOD = .0400
   *7.   TOTAL LAND COST =   100000.0000
   *   SQUARE FOOT COST OF ALL IMPROVEMENTS =   16.2584
   *9.   REQUIRED RATE OF RETURN ON EQUITY = .1800
   *10.   OPERATING COST AS A PERCENT OF TOTAL RENTAL INCOME = .4000
   *11.   ANNUAL GROWTH RATE OF OPERATING COST OVER HOLDING PERIOD = .0700
   *12.   DEPRECIABLE LIFE OF IMPROVEMENTS = 22
   *13   DEPRECIATION METHOD =1.250
            1. = STRAIGHT LINE
            1.25 = 125 PERCENT
            1.5 = 150 PERCENT
            2.0 = DOUBLE DECLINING
   *14.   ORDINARY INCOME TAX RATE = .5000
   *15.   CAPITAL GAINS TAX RATE = .2500
   *16.   HOLDING PERIOD OF THE INVESTMENT = 7.0
   *17.   ANNUAL GROWTH RATE OF PROPERTY VALUE = .0300
   *18.   SELLING EXPENSE (PERCENT) = .0500
   *19.   INVESTORS SHORT TERM BORROWING RATE = 0.0000
   *20.   AMOUNT OF LOAN 1 = 825000.0000
   *21.   EFFECTIVE INTEREST RATE ON LOAN 1 = .075000
   *22.   AMORTIZATION TERM OF LOAN 1 = 28.00
   *23.   DOES THIS PROJECT INVOLVE SECONDARY FINANCING = NO

   * — INDICATES DATA CHANGED FOR THIS RUN

2. PROPERTY INFORMATION
   TOTAL SQUARE FEET OF IMPROVEMENTS   55356

   TOTAL PROPERTY COST   1000000

ASSETS		LIABILITIES AND NET WORTH	
LAND	100000	TOTAL DEBT	825000
BUILDING	900000	EQUITY INVESTED	175000
TOTAL	1000000	TOTAL	1000000

   LEVERAGE POSITION (DEBT/PROPERTY COST) = .825

3. DEPRECIATION INFORMATION

YEAR	BEGINNING BASIS	DEPRECIATION CLAIMED	UN-DEPRECIATED BALANCE	STRAIGHT LINE BASIS	EXCESS DEPRECIATION
1	900000	51136	848864	859091	10227
2	848864	48231	800633	818182	17549
3	800633	45490	755142	777273	22130
4	755142	42906	712236	736364	24127
5	712236	40468	671768	695455	23686
*6	671768	39516	632253	654545	22293
7	632253	39516	592737	613636	20899

*NOTE — STRAIGHT LINE DEPRECIATION AMOUNT EXCEEDS
        ACCELERATED DEPRECIATION AMOUNT, SWITCHED
        TO STRAIGHT LINE DEPRECIATION

4. LOAN INFORMATION

LOAN 1 INFORMATION
                     AMOUNT =   825000
                     RATE =   .0750
                     TERM =   28.00
                     MORTGAGE CONSTANT =   .0855

EXHIBIT 7 continued

YEAR	AMORTIZATION PAYMENT	INTEREST EXPENSE	AMORTIZATION OF PRINCIPAL	REMAINING PRINCIPAL	EFFECTIVE MORTGAGE CONSTANT
1	70574	61570	9004	815996	.08649
2	70574	60871	9703	806293	.08753
3	70574	60117	10457	795836	.08868
4	70574	59306	11268	784568	.08995
5	70574	58431	12143	772425	.09137
6	70574	57488	13086	759339	.09294
7	70574	56472	14102	745237	.09470

5. CASH FLOW ANALYSIS

YEAR	A GROSS POSSIBLE INCOME	B VACANCY ALLOWANCE	C GROSS EFFECTIVE INCOME (A-B)	D OPERATING EXPENSES	E NET INCOME BEFORE TAX AND AMORTIZATION (C-D)
1	166980	8349	158631	66792	91839
2	173659	8683	164976	71467	93509
3	180606	9030	171575	76470	95105
4	187830	9391	178438	81823	96615
5	195343	9767	185576	87551	98025
6	203157	10158	192999	93679	99320
7	211283	10564	200719	100237	100482

YEAR	F INTEREST EXPENSE	G DEPRECIATION EXPENSE	H TAXABLE INCOME (E-F-G)	I EQUITY CASH FLOW (BEFORE TAX) (E-AMOR. PAY)	J EQUITY CASH FLOW (AFTER TAX) (I-(TAX RATE X H))
1	61570	51136	−20867	21265	31699
2	60871	48231	−15593	22935	30731
3	60117	45490	−10503	24531	29783
4	59306	42906	−5596	26041	28839
5	58431	40468	−874	27451	27888
6	57488	39516	2316	28746	27588
7	56472	39516	4494	29908	27661

YEAR	K CASH FLOW TO TOTAL CAPITAL (AFTER TAX)	L CUMULATIVE CASH FLOW (BEFORE TAX)	N M CUMULATIVE CASH FLOW (AFTER TAX)	PROPERTY VALUE AT END OF EACH YEAR
1	71488	21265	31699	1030000
2	70870	44200	62430	1060900
3	70298	68731	92212	1092727
4	69761	94773	121052	1125509
5	69247	122224	148940	1159274
6	69418	150970	176528	1194052
7	69999	180878	204189	1229874

6. CALCULATION OF NET PROCEEDS FROM SALE OF PROPERTY

SELLING PRICE OF PROPERTY AT END OF HOLDING PERIOD	1229874
LESS SELLING EXPENSE	61494
LESS REMAINING DEBT PRINCIPAL	745237
NET PROCEEDS FROM SALE OF PROPERTY (BEFORE TAX)	423143
LESS TAX ON SALE OF PROPERTY AT END OF HOLDING PERIOD	124136
NET PROCEEDS FROM SALE OF PROPERTY (AFTER TAX)	299007

7. INTERNAL RATE OF RETURN — PRESENT VALUE ANALYSIS

TOTAL PRESENT VALUE OF EQUITY INVESTMENT =	206895
PLUS ORIGINAL MORTGAGE BALANCE =	825000
TOTAL PROJECT VALUE =	1031895

INTERNAL RATE OF RETURN
ON TOTAL CAPITAL INVESTED = .0820
ON INITIAL OWNERS EQUITY = .2214

EXHIBIT 7 continued

8. FINANCIAL RATIO ANALYSIS

YEAR	O NET INCOME TO TOTAL PROPERTY COST	P NET INCOME TO PROPERTY VALUE	Q CASH FLOW (PRETAX) TO INITIAL EQUITY	R CASH FLOW (AT) TO INITIAL EQUITY
1	.092	.089	.122	.181
2	.094	.088	.131	.176
3	.095	.087	.140	.170
4	.097	.086	.149	.165
5	.098	.085	.157	.159
6	.099	.083	.164	.158
7	.100	.082	.171	.158

YEAR	S CASH FLOW (AT) PLUS EQUITY BUILDUP TO INITIAL EQUITY	T CASH FLOW (AT) PLUS EQUITY BUILDUP PLUS APPRECIATION TO INITIAL EQUITY	U LOAN BALANCE (END OF YEAR) AS A PERCENT OF ORIGINAL COST	U LOAN BALANCE (END OF YEAR) AS A PERCENT OF PROPERTY VALUE
1	.233	.404	.816	.792
2	.231	.408	.806	.760
3	.230	.412	.796	.728
4	.229	.417	.785	.697
5	.229	.422	.772	.666
6	.232	.431	.759	.636
7	.239	.443	.745	.606

YEAR	V DEBT COVERAGE RATIO	W BREAKEVEN POINT	X OPERATING EXPENSE RATIO GROSS POSSIBLE	X OPERATING EXPENSE RATIO GROSS EFFECTIVE	Y GROSS RENT MULTIPLIER
1	1.301	.823	.400	.421	6.168
2	1.325	.818	.412	.433	6.109
3	1.348	.814	.423	.446	6.050
4	1.369	.811	.436	.459	5.992
5	1.389	.809	.448	.472	5.935
6	1.407	.809	.461	.485	5.877
7	1.424	.808	.474	.499	5.821

Section 3 provides depreciation information. The depreciation coefficient used to calculate annual depreciation expense is the following:

$$\text{Depreciation coefficient} \; = \; \frac{1}{\text{useful life}} \; \times \; (\text{Depreciation method})$$

$$.056818 \; = \; \frac{1}{22} \; \times \; 1.25$$

Depreciation for each year is calculated by multiplying the depreciation coefficient by the *basis* at the beginning of the year (for example, $900,000 \times .056818 = $51,136$). The beginning basis is $900,000 and declines each year by the amount of depreciation claimed the previous year. The *undepreciated balance* at the end of the year is found by deducting *depreciation claimed* from the *beginning basis* (for example, $900,000 − $51,136 = $848,864$). Note that each year the depreciation declines until it becomes advantageous to switch to straight-line depreciation, which occurs in year 6.

The straight-line-basis calculation is made to determine the amount of excess depreciation which is subject to recapture at ordinary income tax rates. The straight-line basis is calculated by taking 1/22 of the original basis ($900,000), then reducing this result from the original basis; each year the basis declines by $1/22 \times $900,000 = $40,909$. For example, the straight-line basis at the end of year 1 is $900,000 − $40,909 = $859,901$, and at the end of year 2 is $859,091 − $40,909 = $818,182$.

The excess depreciation is simply the difference between the straight-line basis and the undepreciated balance. For a clarification of the concepts involved, refer back to Exhibit 5 and the discussion on depreciation.

Section 4 of Exhibit 7 provides the loan information and calculations. The amortization payment of $70,574 is calculated by multiplying the mortgage constant (8.55%) by the loan amount ($825,000). Allocations are made each year to interest and principal. The remaining principal is calculated by taking the amount of principal at the beginning of the year and deducting the amount amortized during the year (for example, $825,000 − $9,004 = $815,996$).

The effective mortgage constant is calculated by the following formula:

$$\text{Effective mortgage constant} = \frac{\text{amortization payment}}{\text{remaining principal}}$$

While the mortgage constant is originally 8.55% (70,574 ÷ 825,000), it increases to 9.47% (70,574 ÷ 745,237) in year 7 as the loan is paid down from $825,000 to $745,327. Thus, the effective cost of borrowing rises for the equity investor as equity buildup (loan amortization) takes place.

Note that interest deductions (like depreciation) decrease as the loan is paid down, and this as well as declining depreciation deductions result in loss of tax-shelter benefits.

Section 5 provides cash-flow projections and calculations. The calculation of net income, columns A through E, are self-explanatory.

Observe the changes in net income over the projection period. Net income increases each year, despite the fact that operating expenses are increasing a 7% each year while income is increasing at only 4%. This is a somewhat surprising result to most individuals, and the result is not intuitively obvious. However, the explanation is quite simple: 7 percent of the operating expenses (a relatively low dollar amount) is less than 4 percent of gross possible income (a relatively high dollar amount) throughout the projection period so that increases in income outweigh increases in expenses. However, the rate of increase of net income is decreasing each year. Eventually, as the expense ratio rises above a certain point, 7% increases in expenses will be greater than 4% increases in gross income, and net income will begin to decrease. This is expected as a property gets older, and will usually occur until a property renovation is undertaken.

Taxable income (Column H) is calculated by deducting depreciation expense and interest expense from the net income estimate each year. In this case we can generate tax losses for five years; thus we can shelter other income earned by the equity investor. In addition, all cash flows generated by the project itself are being sheltered as long as tax losses occur.

Equity cash flow before tax (Column I) is computed by deducting the amortization payment from the net income estimate each year (for example, $91,839 - $70,574 = $21,265; $93,509 - $70,574 = $22,935).

Equity cash flow after tax (Column J) is different than the before-tax cash flow by the amount of tax saving or taxes paid. During the first five years in our example, tax losses generate a tax saving equal to the tax rate times the amount of tax losses. For example, in year 1 the tax savings is 50% × $20,867 = $10,434. Added to the $21,265 cash flow from operations, the after-tax cash flow is $31,699. In year 2 the tax loss declines to $15,593 and the before-tax cash flow rises to $22,935 as a result of rising net income, but the net result is a decrease in the cash flow after tax to $30,731 ($30,731 = $22,935 + (.50 × $15,593)).

Of course the underlying assumption in computing tax savings in this manner is that the investor has a substantial amount of taxable income from other sources to shelter and that these "artificial" accounting losses can be applied against this other income. Tax revisions are currently being proposed in Congress which would severely restrict this tax-saving benefit, and the investor should be aware of this possibility.

After year 5, the taxable-income figure turns positive and the investor must pay taxes instead of receiving a tax saving. From this year on, unless the project is restructured so as to increase the tax shelter, the equity cash flow after tax will be less than the cash flow before tax. In the example shown, the decline in tax shelter outweighs the increase in net income from increasing rentals each year, so that the final result on the "bottom line" is a declining cash-flow figure. After-tax cash flow declines from $31,699 in year 1 to $27,661 in year 7.

The cash flow to total capital after-tax is computed in exactly the same way as the equity cash flow after-tax is computed, but the former calculation eliminates all leverage factors. If the project were 100% equity financed, the equity cash flow after-tax

(Column J) would be identical to the cash flow to total capital after tax (Column K). The reason for computing this cash-flow figure is to show the unlevered after-tax return on the total capital investment. In the internal-rate-of-return analysis, it will be used to calculate the unlevered internal rate of return on the $1,000,000 total capital investment. This is useful for comparison purposes, and certainly would be an important rate-of-return figure to institutions which buy unlevered properties.

The cumulative cash flow before- and after-tax calculations (Columns L and M) are calculated by adding the annual cash-flow figures in Columns I and J for the number of years specified. These estimates are useful for determining when the equity investor receives "payback." On a before-tax basis, we will get our original $175,000 back during the sixth year. On an after-tax basis, our payback is before the end of year 5. Some investors use this measure as one criterion for evaluating the investment. For example, some investors reject a project if it has a payback greater than five years.

Section 6 in Exhibit 7 shows the calculation of net proceeds from the sale of the property, otherwise known as the *reversion*. The selling expense is calculated at 55 percent of the selling price. The property value is assumed to have increased at 3% annually (Column N) and the property is sold at the end of year 7 for $1,229,874. The remaining debt principal at this time is $745,237 and the taxes on the sale of the property are $124,136. The tax on the sale of the property is computed by adding the capital gains tax to the ordinary income tax on excess depreciation, as shown below:

Gross selling price	$1,229,874	
Less: Selling expenses	61,494	
Net selling price	1,168,580	Difference =
Original basis	1,000,000	capital gains income
Straight-line basis	713,637	Difference =
Undepreciated balance (accelerated basis)	692,737	excess depreciation
Capital gains tax = (1,168,380 − 713,637) × .25 =	113,686	
Ordinary income tax = (713,637 − 692,737) × .50 =	10,450	
Total tax on sale of property	$124,136	

In this case, the phase-out rule has not come into effect, so that the entire amount of excess depreciation is taxed at the ordinary rate. The capital gains rate (25%) is applied to the difference between the net selling price and the straight-line basis, while the ordinary rate (50%) is applied to the difference between the straight-line basis and the accelerated basis.

The cash flow which remains in the investor's pocket after all is said and done is $299,007. We assume that it is received at the end of year 7 (in its entirety) when the property is sold. This cash flow will be used in computing the internal rate of return and present value of the owner's equity, and is indeed the largest cash flow received during the holding period. Consequently, revision cash flow is the single, most important factor that affects the internal rate of return and present value of the project.

Internal Rate of Return and Present Value Analysis

So far, our equity investor expects to receive a total of eight cash flows during the seven-year holding period (Columns, J & K, Section 5, Exhibit 7).

Year	Equity ($175,000) after-tax cash flow	Total capital ($1,000,000) after-tax cash flow
1	$ 31,699	$ 71,488
2	30,731	70,870
3	29,783	70,298
4	28,839	69,761
5	27,888	69,247
6	27,588	69,418
7	27,661	69,999
7	299,007	1,044,244*

*The reversion in this case simply eliminates the debt principal repayment of $745,237. Tax liability is not affected by eliminating leverage factors. Consequently, this cash flow can be calculated by taking the selling price, then deducting selling expenses and taxes ($1,044,244 = $1,229,874 − $61,494 − $124,136).

To find the present value of equity investment, shown in Section 7 of Exhibit 7, we take the equity cash flows shown above, multiply them by the present value coefficients for each year at 18% (described previously), then add the resulting present value figures. The sum will be $206,895.

The mathematical formula (with RROR = required rate of return) for determining the same result is the following:

$$\text{Present value of equity} = \frac{\text{cash flow}}{(1 + \text{RROR})^1} + \frac{\text{cash flow}}{(1 + \text{RROR})^2} + \frac{\text{cash flow}}{(1 + \text{RROR})^n}$$

$$= \frac{31,699}{(1 + .18)^1} + \frac{30,731}{(1 + .18)^2} + \frac{29,783}{(1 + .18)^3} + \frac{28,838}{(1 + .18)^4}$$

$$+ \frac{27,888}{(1 + .18)^5} + \frac{27,588}{(1 + .18)^6} + \frac{27,661}{(1 + .18)^7} + \frac{299,007}{(1 + .18)^7}$$

$$= \$206,895$$

Next, if we add the original mortgage balance (which already is a present-value figure) to the present value of the equity, we arrive at an estimate of the total project value. The total project value is therefore $206,895 + $825,000 = $1,031,895.

The project is acceptable, using the present-value criterion, because its value ($1,031,895) is greater than its cost ($1,000,000). Likewise, the equity value ($206,895) is greater than the equity cost ($195,000). Whether comparing equity value and cost, or total project value and cost, the resulting net present value is positive and the profitability index is greater than 1. The investor will achieve his criteria of an 18% return by investing in this project.

It is important to review the meaning of total project value and present value of equity investment. The present-value analysis shows us that if we invest exactly $175,000 in the equity, and acquire the project for $1,031,895 (and assume a mortgage of $825,000), we will receive an interval rate of return of exactly 18 percent on our equity investment. Thus, the 18% required rate-of-return figure that we use in the analysis is an internal-rate-of-return figure, and we have used this rate as your capitalization rate for valuing the project.

Now, since the project cost is less than the project value, we know that the actual internal rate of return (IRR) is greater than 18%. To compute it we must use the trial-and-error process described previously and the equity cash flows after tax given above. If we did so, we would find the IRR to be about 22%. The computer computed the IRR more accurately, using the same trial-and-error process, to 22.14%. At 22.14%, the present value of the equity cash flows just equal the cost to acquire the equity ($175,000).

If we performed an internal-rate-of-return calculation on the total capital invested ($1,000,000) using the cash flows shown previously, we would find that rate to be 8.2%. Thus the free-and-clear return after tax is substantially below the levered equity return, which is 22%. Said differently, the effect of using leverage here is to raise the after-tax return from 8% to 22%. Assuming we actually receive the cash flows projected, this rate is equivalent to putting money in a savings and loan association or bank and earning 44%, compounded annually, then paying the federal government taxes equal to 50% of this return.

Mathematically speaking, the internal-rate-of-return formula is identical to the present-value formula presented. The only difference is the dependent variable. In the present-value approach, we are given the capitalization rate (required rate of return) and the cash-flow estimates, and we must find the present value on the left-hand side of the equation. In the internal-rate-of-return approach, we are given the value (cost of project) on the left-hand side of the equation and we must find the rate (RROR) on the right-hand side of the equation (by trial and error). In effect, we try a different RROR until the resulting present value equals the cost to acquire the project.

To illustrate, consider the computation of the IRR on the total capital contributed. Through trial and error, the rate was found to be 8.2%:

$$1,000,000 = \frac{71,488}{(1 + .082)^1} + \frac{70,870}{(1 + .082)^2} + \frac{70,298}{(1 + .082)^3} + \frac{69,761}{(1 + .082)^4}$$
$$+ \frac{69,247}{(1 + .082)^5} + \frac{69,418}{(1 + .082)^6} + \frac{69,999}{(1 + .082)^7} + \frac{1,044,244}{(1 + .082)^7}$$

The 8.2% rate is the only rate that results in a present value of $1,000,000; thus we have by definition found the IRR on total capital invested.

Financial Ratio Analysis

In Section 7 of our DCF analysis, we calculate data for 13 financial ratios. These are simple accounting ratios which are calculated annually, and no consideration is given to the time value of money when they are calculated.

We are interested in using financial ratios for four purposes. First, they will tell us more about the nature of the profitability of the project; that is, how much of the return, relatively speaking, is from the cash flow from operations, tax saving, equity buildup, and appreciation. Second, they give us primary information about the riskiness (or risk profile) of the project. Third, they help us to analyze our leverage *position* each year and indicate when refinancing may be advantageous to the investor. Fourth, financial ratios are used to test the underlying assumptions we used in the analysis, and to suggest when we have used assumptions which are inconsistent with the marketplace.

The following sections discuss each of the ratios, show how they are calculated each year, and illustrate how each can be used to accomplish the purposes described above.

Net Income to Total Property Cost   This ratio is the same as the ROR profitability measure described earlier, but is calculated at the end of each year. As discussed earlier, whenever this ratio is less than the ROE (therefore greater than the mortgage constant, K), a *positive leverage* situation exists, and vice versa.

Year 1   91,839/1,000,000 = .092
Year 2   93,509/1,000,000 = .094
   .   .   .   .
   .   .   .   .
   .   .   .   .
Year 7   100,842/1,000,000 = .100

Our analysis here shows the ROR rising from 9.2% to 10% in year 7. The basic productivity of the property is rising each year relative to the total capital investment. Because the mortgage constant is 8.55%, a positive leverage situation exists in each year.

Net Income to Property Value   This ratio is used to test the underlying assumptions used in the analysis, and is better known to students of appraisal as the *overall capitalization rate*. Specifically, this ratio tests our assumption on increasing property values over time.

Year 1   91,839/1,030,000 = .089
Year 2   93,509/1,060,900 = .088
   .
   .
   .
Year 7   100,482/1,229,874 = .082

Our analysis shows the capitalization rate falling from 8.9% to 8.2% in year 7. This might be a realistic assumption in a period of falling interest rates, but is highly suspect in a period of high inflation when capitalization rates are, in fact, rising. We probably have property value rising too fast relative to net income. If this is true, then we have overestimated the IRR on equity, total capital, and any other return measure which includes capital appreciation. We might try another analysis with a more conservative property-value assumption, or we might want to reassess our assumptions that affect the net income increases each year.

Cash Flow (Pretax) to Initial Equity   This ratio is identical to the ROE profitability measure described earlier. The cash-flow return increases each year, and rises to 17.1% in year 7, indicating a very profitable situation for the equity investor.

Year 1   21,265/175,000 = .122
Year 2   22,935/175,000 = .131

.

.

.

Year 7   29,908/175,000 = .171

Cash Flow (After tax) to Initial Equity   This profitability ratio takes the pretax cash flow, then adds the amount of tax savings (or deducts the amount of taxes paid), then compares the result to the initial equity invested.

Year 1   31,699/175,000 = .181
Year 2   30,731/175,000 = .176

.

.

.

Year 7   27,661/175,000 = .158

Our analysis shows the after-tax cash-flow return is decreasing each year due to declining tax shelter, which is outweighing the effects of increasing cash flow from operations. The before-tax cash-flow return increases from 12.2% to 17.1% in year 7, while the after-tax cash-flow return decreases from 18.1% to 15.8% in year 7. After year 5, the investor must pay taxes (instead of receiving a tax saving) and the after-tax returns fall below the before-tax returns.

This ratio helps the investor to understand the net impact of tax-shelter items on the tax return and might be used to indicate when a sale or refinancing of property to achieve tax-shelter objectives should be considered. For example, some equity investors should consider selling after year 5, when artificial accounting losses are lost. Other investors would want to consider what else is happening to the property, as measured by the following ratios.

Cash Flow (After-Tax) Plus Equity Buildup to Initial Equity   This ratio adds to the ratio above the impact of equity buildup (loan amortization). While the after-tax cash flow is decreasing each year, the equity buildup is increasing because each year a larger part of each amortization payment represents amortization of principal. What is the net effect?

Year 1   (31,699 + 9004)/175,000 = .233
Year 2   (30,731 + 9703)/175,000 = .231

.

.

.

Year 7   (27,661 + 14,102)/175,000 = .239

The net effect is that profitability, measured this way, decreases for four years, then levels off and starts increasing. Obviously, the effect of declining tax shelter is greater than the effect of increasing equity buildup in the early years. Then the situation reverses. For all practical purposes, we might say that profitability remains fairly stable at 23% during the holding period.

It is important to recognize that, while the equity buildup adds to the investor's return, it is an unrealized gain until the time of sale or refinancing. Consequently, the time value of money is ignored in its measurement. The next ratio discussed can be criticized for the same reason. Nevertheless, the ratio does help us to understand the relative impact of tax shelter and equity buildup on the investor's rate of return.

Cash Flow (After-tax) Plus Equity Buildup Plus Appreciation to Initial Equity   This ratio adds to the above ratio the impact of property value appreciation (or depreciation) which occurs each year. Property-value appreciation is calculated as the difference between the property value at the end of the year less the value at the beginning of the year, as shown in column N in the cash-flow analysis (Exhibit 7, Section 5).

Year 1   (31,699 + 9004 + (1,030,000 − 1,000,000))/175,000 = .404
Year 2   (30,731 + 9703 + (1,060,900 − 1,030,000))/175,000 = .408

.
.   .
Year 7   (27,661 + 14,102 + (1,229,874 − 1,194,052))/175,000 = .443

Measured in this fashion, the total return rises from 40.4 to 44.3% in year 7, as contrasted with a 23% return before this factor is included. This illustrates the importance of property-value increases in the investor's return; property-value increases add 7–10% to the investor's rate of return and further offset the effect of declining tax shelters.

We should note that this return measure makes no deductions for taxes and selling expenses resulting from the sale of the property. If, however, we would deduct these expenses, then apply the time value of money discount, we would arrive back at our internal rate of return on equity of 22%. Surprisingly, our 44% accounting rate of return at year 7 falls to a 22% "true yield" when we add these important economic variables.

Loan Balance as a Percent of Original Cost and Property Value   These two leverage ratios allow us to measure the impact of a declining loan balance, relative to our original cost and property value.

Year 1   815,996/1,000,000 = .816
Year 2   806,293/1,000,000 = .806

.
.
Year 7   745,237/1,000,000 = .745

Year 1   815,996/1,030,000 = .792
Year 2   806,293/1,060,900 = .760

.

.

.

Year 7   745,237/1,229,874 = .606

On a cost basis, our leverage ratio declines to about 75% in year 7, and on a value basis to about 61%. To the extent that the loan is a decreasing percentage of either cost or value, we might argue that the riskiness of the investment tends to decrease over time. In addition, the potential benefits of refinancing with conventional financing after the property has been held for a number of years is readily apparent from the ratios.

Debt-coverage Ratio   An analysis of the debt-coverage ratio each year indicated decreasing risk and increasing project liquidity. Each year, net income is increasing, while debt service remains constant.

Year 1   91,839/70,574 = 1.301
Year 2   93,509/70,574 = 1.325

.

.

.

Year 7   100,482/70,574 = 1.424

Break-even Point   Like the debt-coverage ratio, the break-even point is a measure used to analyze the risk and liquidity profile of a project. Since it decreases somewhat over the seven-year projection period, the liquidity of the project is said to increase as the risk decreases. Each year, a lower occupancy level is necessary to pay operating expenses and service the debt.

Year 1   (66,792 + 70,574)/166,980 = .823
Year 2   (71,467 + 70,574)/173,659 = .818

.

.

.

Year 7   (100,237 + 70,574)/211,283 = .808

Operating-expense Ratio   Two operating-expense ratios are calculated, one based on gross possible income, the other based on gross effective income. Primarily, these ratios are used for comparative analyses and for testing the underlying assumptions used. As a project ages, the expense ratio usually increases, and the ratio which results should be consistent with experience results kept by the operators of comparable properties and statistical reports published by the Experience Exchange Commmittee of the Institute of Real Estate Management.

Year 1   66,792/166,980 = .400
Year 2   71,467/173,659 = .412

.

.

.

.

Year 7   100,237/211,283 = .474

Year 1   66,792/158,631 = .421
Year 2   71,467/164,976 = .433

.

.

.

.

Year 7   100,237/200,719 = .499

Gross-rent Multiplier   Like the expense ratios, the primary purpose of the gross-rent multiplier is to test the underlying assumptions of the analysis. The ratio is calculated by dividing the property value at the end of each year by the gross possible income for the corresponding year.

Year 1   1,030,000/166,980 = 6.168
Year 2   1,060,000/173.659 = 6.109

.

.

.

.

Year 7   1,229,874/211,283 = 5.821

Generally, we expect this ratio to decline over time as a structure is getting older and becoming more expensive to maintain. A more important variable, however, is the geographic location of the property and that the properties in the equation are truly comparable. An investor should be willing to pay more to acquire a dollar of rent from a new structure than from an older structure, all factors remaining the same. Since most experienced income-property appraisers keep extensive data on gross-rent multipliers, comparisons are easily made to see if the estimate used is realistic. In the analysis presented, we have already questioned the validity of our property-value appreciation assumption. In fact, comparative sales data studied in the area of the subject property suggests that a 5.5 to 5.7 gross-rent multiplier might be more appropriate.

The assumption on property-value increases has a very substantial impact on the equity investor's internal rate of return, but in comparison, a very nominal (or no direct) effect on the ratios a lender is most concerned with, such as the coverage or break-even ratios. Consequently, the equity investor is vitally concerned with this input assumption. A property value increase of 4% instead of 2.5% may increase the IRR on equity from 22% to 29%. Therefore, the investor should worry a lot about this assumption and expend much research effort to ascertain the most likely input value, one which is logically and internally consistent with the other input data and most likely market conditions.

Sensitivity and Risk Analysis

As we can readily see, cash-flow analysis provides valuable information not provided by traditional investment- and mortgage-analysis techniques. The model considers the impact of inflation factors over time, the time value of money, transaction (brokerage) costs, and the borrower's tax position and investment goals. All of these should be important to the lender and equity investor, since each affects the value of the property and the investor's ability to pay debt service each year.

The important variable not explicitly and directly measured by the DCF model is risk—the probability that the expected net income and cash flows will not be received. While financial ratios (such as the coverage ratio and break-even point) provide some information on the risk profile of a project, they do not provide information on the probable deviations from the most likely or expected values used in the analysis. A thorough risk analysis should provide information on (1) the magnitude of possible deviations in cash flows which can occur under varying market and economic conditions, and (2) the probability associated with each of these projections. None of the ratios presented provide this information adequately. In the following sections, two techniques are presented which attempt to better harness the risk dimension and provide the investor with information about the possible consequences of risk and uncertainty. These techniques are known as (1) sensitivity analysis, and (2) Monte Carlo risk simulation.

Sensitivity Analysis   This is a technique which attempts to test the impact of uncertainties on the investment decision. We can perform a sensitivity analysis by varying values of input variables in the DCF model that we believe are uncertain and see how they affect the IRR, debt-coverage ratios, break-even ratios, or other relevant output data which is important in arriving at a decision.

If it is discovered through sensitivity analysis that certain variables have values which are uncertain but do not have a significant impact on rates of return, debt-coverage ratios, or other outcomes, the investor can stop worrying about these uncertainties. He should not waste his time worrying about variables that don't count. Often, lenders and equity investors are surprised to discover which uncertain variables are important and which ones are not. This is because it is difficult to predict the results of the interaction of many complex economic and market interrelationships.

Exhibit 8   Summary Table of Sensitivity-analysis Calculations
287-unit Apartment Complex

(Loan $2.6 mil., 9% rate, 30-year term)*

Run:	I Optimistic	II Most probable	III Pessimistic
A. Input variable assumptions			
1. Growth rate in rental income	5 %	3 %	1%
2. Growth rate in operating			
expense ratio	3 %	4.5%	6%
3. Growth rate in selling price			
(reversion)	5.5%	3 %	0%
4. Vacancy & bad debt allowance	4 %	7 %	13%
B. Yields on equity investment			
1. Year 3	31.64%	21.24%	5.75%
2. Year 7	31.24%	22.63%	7.67%
3. Year 10	30.10%	22.05%	6.94%
C. Internal rate of return on total investment			
1. Year 3	11.46%	9.07%	6 %
2. Year 7	11.69%	8.96%	5.54%
3. Year 10	11.89%	8.95%	5.23%
D. Net income (earnings before taxes and debt service)			
1. Year 3	$426,577	$369,336	$293,389
2. Year 7	544,742	395,583	236,800
3. Year 10	651,901	414,931	181,332
E. Break-even point			
1. Year 3	.728	.768	.812
2. Year 7	.639	.754	.893
3. Year 10	.581	.747	.967
F. Debt coverage ratio			
1. Year 3	1.686	1.459	1.159
2. Year 7	2.152	1.563	.936
3. Year 10	2.576	1.640	.717

*Prepared by Steven Topletz, Research Analyst, Department of Finance, The University of Texas.

To illustrate the use of sensitivity analysis, Exhibit 8 shows the results of a sensitivity analysis performed by a lender on a 287-unit apartment property. Through a sensitivity analysis, it was discovered that the three most important determinants of the lender's coverage ratio over the seven-year period analyzed were: (1) the growth rate (inflation) in gross rents over time; (2) the growth rate (inflation) in expenses over time; and (3) the occupancy level. In addition, increases in property value had an important effect on the equity investor's return and equity build-up, thus the lender's ultimate security in the event of default. Exhibit 8 shows the effect of changes in the values of these four variables on: (1) debt-coverage ratio; (2) break-even point (default ratio); (3) net income; (4) internal rate of return on total investment; and (5) yield on owner's equity. Three different holding periods are tested to show the effect of the time period chosen on the desired output variables.

Under sensitivity analysis, it is advisable to conclude the analysis by preparing input forecasts under optimistic, most likely, and pessimistic assumptions as shown in Exhibit 8. This gives the lender (or equity investor) data that represent the possible range of results that can reasonably be expected, if the inputs have been measured accurately. Clearly, the most crucial aspect of this whole process is performing the necessary market research to generate accurate input information.

In the example presented, the coverage-ratio range is probably acceptable to the lender, with the most probable coverage ratio being 1.46–1.64. Only in the most pessimistic case for seven- and ten-year holding periods does the coverage ratio drop below 1.0, where project revenues are insufficient to meet all expenses. If the loan was perceived to be too risky under existing conditions, the lender could change the loan amount and terms and generate a revised—and perhaps more acceptable—set of numbers.

Monte Carlo Risk-simulation Model   Sensitivity analysis is not a true form of risk analysis. While the sensitivity analysis performed in the last section provides the lender with ranges of possible coverage ratios, it does not tell what the probabilities are that the different coverage ratios will actually occur. The risk-analysis model that attempts to overcome this problem is pictured in Exhibit 9. It measures the probability that a certain coverage ratio will be achieved if we can measure the probability distributions for uncertain variables. Similar models are available for measuring the equity investor's position that also generate probability distributions for the IRR on equity and other cash-flow variables.

The first step in using the risk-simulation model is to designate which variables are control variables (single-value estimates) and which are uncertain variables (probability distribution estimates). In the example (Exhibit 9) six variables are considered control variables: (1) the square foot dimensions of the property; (2) the equity contribution; (3) the depreciation method employed and the depreciable life of the property; (4) the existing tax structure; (5) the holding period of the investment (effective load period); and (6) the loan amount and the terms of the loan which the lender wants to test.

The remaining variables in the model are assigned probability distributions by the analyst. A number of methods for estimating or assessing these probability distributions have been developed and used extensively in the field. Some of these methods require that the real estate forecaster understand probability concepts; some do not. Some allow the forecaster to estimate probability distributions; others employ interview techniques. While there is not space to discuss these methods in depth, it is important to recognize that recent experiences with probability estimation are encouraging and reinforce the credibility of its use as a technique to quantify risk. Experience has shown that decision-makers and experts can realistically estimate probability distributions for variables and, after some practice, become comfortable with the concept and process involved.

Given the values of the control variables and the probability distributions for the uncertain variables, the Monte Carlo simulation procedure is used to generate rents, expenses, net income, coverage ratios and other desired statistics. As shown in Step 3

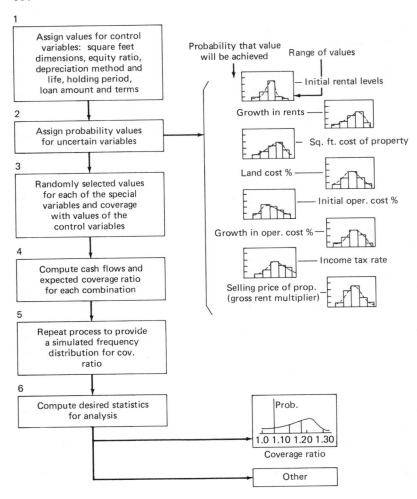

(Exhibit 9), a value for each of the eight uncertain variables is randomly chosen from its respective probability distribution and combined with the value of control variables. Then, in Step 4, annual cash flows and coverage ratios are compared for that particular combination of input values.

This process is repeated a large number of times at electronic speeds. A count is kept of the number of times that various coverage ratios are computed, and when the computer runs are completed, the probability that various coverage ratios will occur can be calculated and plotted as shown at the bottom of Exhibit 9. Other data and statistics can also be computed according to the wishes of the lender.

The result is a clear picture of the risk characteristics of the project which can be used in the lender's decision process. If the lender thinks the resulting risk is too great for the amount of yield demanded (as evidenced by a substantial probability that the coverage ratio will be less than "1" in numerous years, resulting in cash deficits), the lender has a number of choices as previously discussed—refuse to make the loan, reduce the amount of the loan, raise the yield to compensate for the risk, etc.

Benefits of Using Sensitivity and Risk Analysis   Sensitivity and risk analysis are very useful techniques and a notable improvement over conventional risk-analysis methods employed by lenders. Lenders can use the techniques as in-house tools to evaluate their load decisions and perhaps avoid some unwise investments. The use of these techniques forces the lender to generate more data than were previously collected, thus providing more and better information for analysis. It also forces the lender to ask many important questions about the market, costs, inflation trends, probabilities, etc., which otherwise would not be closely scrutinized. The result, of course, should be better investment decisions and fewer loan defaults. It was also noted that sensitivity analysis shows which variables are important and which variables the lender should focus on when evaluating the project.

The mortgage banker and lender should not overlook sensitivity and risk-analysis techniques as counseling aids. It is becoming increasingly more incumbent on the lender and mortgage banker to give sound financial advice to the equity investors, since it is evident that equity investors tend to rely on such advice. Unfortunately, a good project from the point of view of the lender is not always a good project for the equity investors. Because the model simultaneously analyzes the lender's and equity investor's financial positions, the lender or mortgage banker can use the model to create financial packages that simultaneously satisfy the objectives and constraints of both parties.

Chapter 29

The Prevention and Cure of Distress Real Estate

Daniel S. Berman

When confronted with problem real estate loans, the best solution is to have none. Unfortunately, that is no longer possible. Even institutions with very healthy property-loan portfolios are affected by distress real estate. It is difficult to visualize a healthy office building, shopping center, or apartment house being unaffected by a distressed neighboring property, yet distress spreads rapidly. Distress real estate begins by cutting rents, attracting undesirable tenants to the area, and squeezing neighboring properties by affecting rental renewals and by reducing market value rents all across the board.

ORGANIZING FOR PROBLEM LOANS

Most lenders wish the problem would go away by itself and, therefore, many are not sufficiently organized to cope with it. To begin with, problem property loans need specialized treatment and full-time watching. Therefore, the first thing to do about problem loans is to assign personnel to watch them. It is not possible to delegate this work to an inexperienced bookkeeper who merely makes notations on ledger cards that taxes are in arrears and payments are not coming in.

In many cases, when the problem arises, the file is sent back to the original underwriter on the theory that he or she knows the property best. Also, when a property gets into trouble, it may be because it was unwisely underwritten in the first place, and the last person who will be able to admit that mistake is the original underwriter.

The Need for New Faces

The problem property loan-workout person should add a new fact to the package—not to the old one. If nothing else, the new person is able to start afresh, to admit that the loan may have been ill-conceived in the first place, and to reject any implied personal commitments to the owner or the developer that have come out of past relationships.

A problem loan starts out by needing a long, hard, fresh look to answer the question, "Why is it a problem, and what are we going to do about it?"

Adequate Staffing Indispensable

We mentioned before that you should be adequately staffed for problem loans. Many more hours are going to be needed to "work out" troubled loans than to supervise clean ones. Your workout officer, if given 25 or 30 files, can only give each file a few minutes. If you have assigned as many as 100 files, you might as well not have given any.

The problem loan officers should report to an experienced workout executive and should have access to legal counsel familiar with real estate problems. Since problem real estate loans involve both business and legal decisions, the loan workout officer needs to be able to tap both kinds of knowledge.

CONSTRUCTION LOANS—SPOTTING PROBLEMS IN THE FIELD

The sooner a problem loan is recognized, the more we are able to cut our losses, and the faster we are able to turn the property around. This is true whether we are dealing wtih a construction loan or a permanent loan, but an early-warning system is especially important in an incomplete construction loan. If you find out your developer or contractors are "stealing from the job," the sooner you find out, the less money will be wasted. If honest cost overruns are involved, and if this is detected early in the construction loan, the wisest decision might be to abandon the job entirely. Abandoning a 20 percent advanced construction loan may be cheaper than completing the job.

Symptoms of cost overruns, overdrawn jobs, dissatisfied tradespeople, poor workmanship and a failure to monitor the project become apparent long before the project becomes hopeless. In troubled times, you should be constantly updating construction progress in the field, comparing loan balances with the projected cost to complete, and making certain that sufficient reserves are available to build the job with the balance of the loan. If you cannot keep the job in balance, you may be able to cut your losses or decide to reconsider where you are going before you get fully advanced. In some cases, your architectural inspectors will be able to help, and their job should be newly defined to spot today's troubles. In other cases, you may want to get a look at the owner's books and records before continuing the advance, and you may need some accounting assistance in reviewing the borrower's financial statements.

Getting Financial Information

As far as financial information is concerned, you should try to find out what the developer's current total cash flow is. We are talking about his overall cash-flow budget and position—not just the cash flow on your job. Thus, you should get a list of all the other jobs your developer is involved in and check with other lenders, commercial banking sources, and accountants as to whether the developer is in trouble anywhere else.

If either the developer or the job is in trouble, you must ask yourself, "What is the size and cause of the trouble, and what are the possible solutions?" This question may seem too general in nature, but there are no rules for distress property loans except to get all the information possible and as up-to-date as possible. When all the information is at hand, the solution normally becomes apparent. Without hard facts, all you deal with are such clichés as, "*It is best to stop the job as soon as possible*," or "*The best loss is the first loss*," which, of course, run contrary to other clichés like "*It's best to get the job finished, no matter what the cost.*" None of the clichés do you any good, but up-to-date information makes the answers come out crystal clear.

FIND THE REAL CAUSE OF THE TROUBLE

The question of why the job is in trouble must be answered before any solution can be suggested. If the job is in trouble because the developer does not know how to control costs or timing schedules, the controls can be built in to get the job back on the track. If the trouble is inattention or understaffing, the solution is obvious. If the trouble is stealing, the answer becomes apparent. But you must be in the field to spot this. You cannot determine the trouble from a file in your office. The sooner someone goes out on the job and walks into the job shack and visits with local suppliers and commercial banking sources, the faster you will be able to decide what to do.

Sometimes just asking questions on the job site is an eye-opener. Before that it may be desirable to audit the developer's books. That simple request can uncover the fact that the developer has no books, no controls, and hasn't the foggiest idea of where the job is going and how it will come out at the end.

Marketplace Changes

Often, the problem is not the developer but the marketplace. Have conditions changed since the original underwriting? To continue to advance on a condominium construction loan in an overbuilt area and ignore the huge overhang of unsold units would have been just as disastrous as if the job had come in over budget.

Once again, your local representative should be alerting you to problem market areas as well as problem developers. Up-to-date information on changing conditions is indispensable. In some cases, you still have time to change the marketing concept when the job is 75 percent complete. So, condominiums could be converted into rental apartments, full floor office space into subdivided units, or jobs may be slowed down to await better timing or boarded up rather than being fully equipped or outfitted.

Once marketing problems are spotted, up-to-date comparables should be sought, today's rental and sales prices compiled, and the entire underwriting concept rethought. If you have enough information, the answer will be obvious. You will then be in a position to decide whether to complete, who is to complete, and what will happen when the job is completed. You can then decide whether to take a loss right then and there, approximately what the loss will be, or you may decide to hold the property through rent-up to try for third-party financing. You might want to sell the property subject to liberal financing that you yourself may supply, thus deferring realization of your loss to a later period.

You must know what is going on in the field. Someone from your shop must visit the job as regularly as possible. If you are a national lender, you should insist that your mortgage banker or correspondent or your field staff do this work. If you are a local lender, make sure someone from headquarters is going out and looking at the job regularly. Is it moving along according to schedule? Does it look as if it is going forward in a workmanlike manner? What do local renting agents, suppliers, commercial lenders, subcontractors, and materials men think about the job?

What to Look for

What is the developer's current reputation in the community? Do colleagues think the developer is experienced and knowledgeable, or do they feel that the job is running away with itself? How is our developer doing on other jobs? Is the developer tied up and in trouble on other jobs, or are labor and materials men refusing to make deliveries because of arrearages on other jobs?

Make sure that someone is assembling this field information for you on all loans so that you are constantly monitoring progress, quality, and the outside marketplace. If you have your own field personnel, they should be doing it. If not, you had better make sure that your mortgage banker or correspondent is doing it. Field information on a current basis is indispensable in preventing problems. All sources of information should be tapped on a regular basis. A sick construction loan does not die at once. It starts to get sick slowly, and if you are out in the field you will see it happening, day by day.

PERMANENT LOANS—SPOTTING PROBLEMS IN THE FIELD

The best way to spot problems in advance is to go out into the field and visit the property. What is the condition of the property? Does it appear to be rundown? Is the property fully rented or is it partly vacant? Are the tenants satisfied? Would they renew their leases today, and at what rentals? Poor maintenance and vacancies are an indication of trouble to come. Real estate taxes should be up-to-date. Try to get income and expense statements on the property, and see that they are up-to-date. An analysis of those statements can tell you if there is a sufficient cash-flow cushion to keep the property safe or if it is about to slip into trouble.

Someone from your home office should be inspecting the property and assembling the other information referred to.

Of course, no request for deferral of loan interest or amortization should be considered without two or three years of the latest income and expense figures, together with a projection of the forthcoming year. You should also have an up-to-date leasing and rental schedule and an idea about what is going on in competing properties and whether the current rentals shown are at market, too low, or too high compared to the competition.

Financial Trend of the Property

If you have been getting financial reports on the project, look to see what the trends are. Reevaluate the project based on today's numbers and on next year's projections before making any decision about deferring interest or amortization. Do not waive interest or amortization unless you have thought the entire problem through, because you may get the debtor deeper and deeper into trouble, unless you have. If the equity is already gone as a result of current conditions, and unless you visualize how the debtor is going to work you out of trouble and rebuild equity, any deferral is only going to permit the property to slip further into trouble.

If you give a deferral of interest or amortization, what are you trying to accomplish? What should happen during the breathing period? What should the owner be doing while you defer payment? How will you measure his performance, so that you are buying something for your deferral?

Get a Written Understanding

Whatever understanding you come to should be written up and result in some sort of mortgage modification. Perhaps you will want to make sure that during the rest period you collect all the rents and you make all the payments through an agent of yours, rather than entrusting the funds to the hands of a desperate borrower who may collect rents, pay nothing to you, nothing toward real estate taxes or suppliers, and give the property back to you with large arrearages. If there are junior lien holders, make sure they, too, defer collections during troubled periods.

Usual workout agreements may provide for interest or principal deferrals for short or long periods, for interest rate reductions, for smaller amortization payments and a longer maturity, or, on some occasions, additional funding may be supplied by the lender for specific purposes.

If you are going to defer interest and amortization, lengthen the mortgage term, or add money of your own, you should get something back. Perhaps it will be collecting the rents yourself and making the disbursements. Perhaps there should be monthly payments of real estate taxes, or monthly or quarterly financial reporting. In some cases, you may get personal guarantees of the new loan or new real estate as security. Before giving something, review your entire file to make sure that you have thought through what you are going to get in exchange. Don't just hope that time by itself will help you. Experience has shown that time, without a plan, only results in further deterioration.

Protecting the Permanent Loan Take-Out

If you are a construction lender and if there is a commitment to make a permanent loan, you want to make sure that you protect that commitment. One of the first things you would look at in a problem construction loan file is a way to protect the permanent take-out. That may be the best way out, even with a small loss of principal.

The commitment letter should be carefully read to see if it is possible to fulfill. If extensions of time are required, getting them is too important a job to leave to the developer, and you should make sure that someone from your team is also pursuing it. The strength of the permanent lender should also be considered, as well as the permanent lender's capacity to deliver the permanent loan.

It is easy to pay an additional fee to extend the loan commitment, but you should make sure that you know what you are buying before putting any more money into commitment fees. Obviously, if the construction loan is in trouble, the only source of funds for further commitment fees is you, so make sure you are buying something of value for your money.

CONSTRUCTION LOAN PROBLEMS

If you are a construction lender, you have some problems a permanent lender does not have. Your decision must be to "lock everything up" to prevent its getting stolen and think the entire problem through before getting in deeper. Here is how that is done: You should plan to take control as soon as possible, making sure that onsite materials do not get "reclaimed" by unhappy subcontractors and that neighbors do not help themselves to the refrigerators, washing machines, and other readily portable building supplies. A reputable guard service is often required. You may also have to take precautions to prevent damage due to inclement weather.

At the same time, someone should be putting together a cost-to-complete analysis. Make sure that the building permits are being kept current and that they are transferred or transferable. You do not have to do this by yourself, but make sure someone is doing it for you. The existing subcontracts should be reviewed, together with a cost-to-complete analysis. Punch lists should be prepared for all complete work. If there has been unauthorized substitution or downgrading of materials, try to find out who was responsible and what can be done about it.

Checking Subcontracts and Cost-to-Complete

Check the validity of existing subcontracts and the credit standing of your subcontractors. If problems exist, don't be afraid to consider alternate contractors and subcontractors. However, in many cases your options will be limited. You must face the realities of subcontractors' strength in the union hall and their knowledge of what must still be done and where the connections can be found. Still, alternatives must be considered, at least for trading purposes.

The cost-to-complete should be reviewed with a new, hard-nosed look. Shall we abandon unstarted buildings and reduce the total number of units? Can we cut the amenity package? Perhaps we should trade up, or trade away something, to produce a better market value. A new cash-flow budget should be prepared on a trade-by-trade basis and on a month-by-month basis. A detailed plan and budget should be laid out, and the job should be continued on a piecemeal basis until someone understands what the total cost is going to be and whether the additional funding is going to make the project more successful.

Remember the basic plan: "Lock it up and think it through." "Lock it up" means control—not necessarily stopping the job. It means taking inventory to be sure you don't get charged twice for materials that disappear or for work that has or has not actually been done.

In some cases, you will want to speed things up to meet a permanent mortgage commitment. In other cases, you may want to slow down construction to recognize the realities of an oversaturated market.

Bargaining with Trade Creditors

If the plan involves getting trade creditors to take less than 100 cents on the dollar, you need to know two things:

1   Who is going to take the public relations burden of being the ''bad guy''? It is best to have the original developer do this, if you can; but the negotiating job should not be left to the developer alone, who may have an ax to grind. Your local attorney or field representative should also be present to protect your interests.

2   How should you control the future payments to this distress job? You might want to disburse through another corporation you own, through a title company, through the old developer, or through the new contractor. You may want to make sure that your inspection procedures are changed so that you don't repeat the mistakes you were making before.

SOME INTERIM REMEDIES—WITHOUT FORECLOSING

Foreclosure is the standard that all interim procedures are measured against, and the cost and time needed to obtain good title must be considered. Accepting a deed in lieu of foreclosure should be considered because of the speed. But, ask yourself, if you accept a deed, what will you have to give up for it? A deed in lieu of foreclosure does not cut off mechanic's liens and possible third-party creditors. If they must be wiped out, you may have to go back to the longer, more expensive foreclosure proceedings. Also, you may have to release the borrower from any guarantees or liabilities in exchange for the deed. Are those guarantees and liabilities worth anything?

Also, you need to consider the effect of having your own developer step in to finish the job and the effect of extending the time of performance, etc., on the liabilities of third parties. In other words, by making a new deal with the developer, the contractor or the subcontractors, are you wiping out your rights against the bonding company, the title insurer, or third-party guarantors?

Getting Up-to-the-Minute Facts

In making these decisions, you must look at the facts realistically. Even clean title may not give you what you need. A fully insured, bonded job may not help you finish in time to meet your take-out commitment. What can be done must be measured against your real objective, which is to save as much of your principal as possible.

In planning what to do next, the construction lender should consider the additional funding that may be available from third parties. The lender is not the only one with a checkbook. Limited partners may be prepared to add fresh money to avoid the tax impact of a foreclosure.

Contributions can come from bonding companies, title companies, and general contractors. Also, trade creditors may subordinate their mechanics' liens, make cash contributions themselves, or reduce their contract price to salvage their junior positions.

Prospective tenants or contract buyers are sometimes sources of funds. A tenant who needs to open a store at a particular time may help bail out the project. A warehouse tenant or prospective owner of an industrial plant that needs the facility by a particular date may also be willing to put some more money into the project.

Junior lenders, construction loan participants, and permanent lenders may all invest funds to rescue a distressed property, but you must understand what your leverage is and why they made their commitments in the first place. Other potential contributors may be the inspecting and supervising architects or the developer's commercial banker, who prefer to see the project successful rather than face liability and bankruptcy risks.

Importance of Timing

Of course, first comes the need to meet the date of the permanent commitment. Other key dates are the completion dates called for by leases to major tenants, by contracts to sell the property, by building and sewer permit expirations, and by market timing. Completing a condominium project in time to hit the sales or rental season may be important, and so may weather conditions.

Before planning to make further advances, make sure those new advances are protected as first liens. Also, before making additional advances, check your rights against the bonding company and any defenses the bonding company may have.

Get Rights to Assign

If you are going to step into the middle of a construction job, you must consider whether construction contracts, the building and sewer permits, the permanent loan, and the contracts to sell condominium units are assignable.

Reexamine the file now, with a jaundiced eye, and make sure the completed structure will comply with building codes, zoning requirements, title insurance, survey restrictions, and condominium registration requirements. Be sure the property has the required access roads and utilities. Also, looking at the project when it is in trouble often discloses sloppy paper work on the initial closing and, before advancing further funds, make sure that the building you expect to complete will be able to get certificates of occupancy, title insurance, etc.

Consider Alternate Plans

With all the facts in front of you, consider your alternatives. How will you control the project during the workout period? If you find the developer or contractor honest but incompetent, you may let them remain in possession, but you will exercise more careful payment control. If you don't want to exercise payment control directly, you may bring in another general contractor to watch the job in your behalf and act as the controlling joint venturer with the defaulted borrower.

If your developer is in trouble but not fully under water, you may ask for additional equity, too. Sometimes you may decide to go to court to ask for an appointment of a receiver and start foreclosure. Consider both the cost of the receivership and the kind of receiver you will get. Will you get a political hack who will dissipate the proceeds of the job or someone who will try to earn the fee? Consider selling the mortgage to a third party at a discount and let the third party do the workout. You may have to commit to supply permanent financing when the job is finished, but that may be cheaper than finishing the job yourself. Perhaps the title company or the bonding company will take over the job and build it out.

Using Nominees

If you are going to take title, consider having a nominee hold title, rather than putting your institution on the line. This may avoid the local tax problem of "doing business" in the area during the workout period. Perhaps additional funds can come from the permanent lender, who might advance them in exchange for a higher interest charge, or for some kind of sale-leaseback guarantee by you. Perhaps additional funds can be raised by selling the tax-loss position to a new syndicate.

Mortgagee in Possession

If you plan to be a mortgagee in possession, or take a deed from the developer, or foreclose, consider:

1   The impact of a takeover on your balance sheet, your loss reserves, and your future earnings. Will you have to amortize your own property? What rights of redemption does the present owner have, and how will these rights hold up the resale of the property? Would you rather have title and foreclose, or do you want to try to collect from the developer on the note or guarantee? Can you do both? What effect will the bankruptcy laws have on obtaining title?
2   If you are a Real Estate Investment Trust, is your charter broad enough to permit active management of the project? What will the federal income tax impact be if you engage in active property management? Are there any other regulatory problems?

Perfect solutions may not be obtainable. You may have to weigh your need to meet timing deadlines, your desire to cut off the rights of inferior lienholders, the availability of a deed in lieu of foreclosure, and the impact of accepting your solution on proposed deficiency judgments, rights against guarantors, bonding companies and title insurers.

Remember the cardinal rule: Once you get all the facts in front of you, the answer will become apparent. Without facts you are just digging a bigger hole for yourself. Don't get yourself out of one pack of troubles and into a new one. Your new general contractor or job supervisor must have the responsibility of completing the project. That will include the responsibility for getting a certificate of occupancy, for forwarding to you detailed reports showing where your funds are going, and the responsibility of getting "clean" mechanics' lien waivers.

Be prepared to pay a good price for this. You will probably have to work out a cost-plus contract with substantial fees for the new contractor/developer. While it is expensive, remember the need for 24-hour guards on the premises to prevent mysterious disappearances, to protect your builder's risk and casualty insurance, and to make sure that everything is accounted for.

If new documents are prepared and if you have junior loan participants, make sure that all of them give written approval for the proposed course of action. In summary, "Lock it up and think it through."

TAX ASPECTS OF DISTRESS REAL ESTATE

There are three reasons why you must understand the tax aspects of distress properties:

1 Much of the distress real estate now on the market was originally owned by limited partnerships. Most of them were organized for tax write-offs. So, the fact that this property is now losing money is not necessarily a detriment. The limited partner investors may be a source of additional funds which they can put into the deal as long as write-offs continue. Understanding their position will help you raise money for the project.

2 Even if there were no limited partners in the project initially, depreciation write-offs are still worth money to investors. A group of new investors packaged with an enterprising management team can add the new funds and skills needed to turn the property around.

3 If there are already limited partner investors in the project, a mortgage foreclosure is a tax disaster. Understanding the ramifications of this disaster can give you bargaining leverage in negotiating with the existing limited partners. They, too, can be persuaded to invest new funds.

Perhaps the best way to see the tax consequences of distress real estate is to look at some actual numbers. Below, in approximate numbers, are the tax consequences of operating a distress property, and the tax consequences of a foreclosure, so that you can understand the thinking of the limited partner investors.

The Assumptions

Let us assume the investors originally put up $300,000 of equity above a $2,000,000 construction loan. Let's assume that the $2,000,000 construction loan bore interest at 12%, and that during the two-year construction period the average loan balance was $1,000,000, but the first year gave rise to only $20,000 of interest with $100,000 of interest during the second year, or a total of $120,000 of construction interest on the average balance of $1,000,000.

In addition to the 12% interest rate, let's assume there was a $100,000 charge for the $2,000,000 construction loan, including discounts, loan commitment fees, and other construction loan charges.

Assume the equity investors were in the 60% tax bracket (city, state and federal combined); that the property had a 33⅓-year useful life (which would give rise to a 3% straight-line depreciation rate, or a 6% rate at the 200% double-declining-balance method of depreciation); and that there was a permanent loan available at a 9% interest rate, or $2,000,000. Here is what happens during operations:

Tax Consequences of Operations

	Total	Year 1	Year 2	Year 3	Year 4
Construction Loan					
Discount and fees	$100,000	$100,000			
Interest at 12%	120,000	20,000	$100,000		
Permanent loan interest	360,000	—	—	$180,000	$180,000
Depreciation at 200% of 3% or	318,000	—	108,000	106,000	104,000
6% on $1.8 million of structure					
No net income in any year	—	—	—	—	—
Tax losses	898,000	120,000	208,000	286,000	284,000
Worth, at 60% tax bracket	538,000	72,000	124,800	171,600	170,400
Return on $300,000 of equity	179%	24%	41.6%	57.2%	56.9%

Tax Consequences of Foreclosure

Tax recapture of depreciation write-offs at ordinary income rates of 60% on $318,000 of depreciation =	$191,000
Capital gains taxes at rates of 35% on interest ($220,000 + $360,000) =	203,000
Income tax impact of foreclosure	$394,000

But Note These Important Conclusions

In the event of foreclosure, the equity investor would have to invest $394,000 as additional equity in the project, but continue to have a $170,400 return in tax savings each year (see Column 4—Operations) assuming that the depreciation does not decline too rapidly. Thus, equity investor will make 43% per annum on an additional $394,000 investment ($170,000 on $394,000 of new money). A new investor would probably not be able to take more than 125% declining-balance depreciation instead of 200%. This would give him a 3.75% rate on $1,800,000 or $67,500 of depreciation plus the $180,000 interest for a $247,500 loss. At the 60% tax bracket, the new investor would get $148,500 a year (60% of $247,500) or a 37.6% return on an investment of $394,000, which is a pretty good return.

TAX LOSS DEALS CAN YIELD GOLD

There is much negotiating gold in the tax aspects of distress real estate. Old investors can be induced to put more money into the project to protect themselves against the tax aspects of foreclosure. Also, if the real estate is any good, their money continues to produce a return out of tax losses, even though there is no other cash flow out of the project. If the real estate actually turns around, it can be an even bigger bonanza.

If there was no old investment group and the property must go into foreclosure, new investors may find substantial tax shelter in the project.

So, before the old investors are squeezed out by foreclosure, make sure they understand the tax impact. Point out that any sum they invest with you to keep the project alive is preferable to paying a large income tax on the foreclosure, since there is always hope that the property will turn around, and cash-on-cash returns out of current income tax savings can be enticing.

THE PROBLEMS

One of the largest problems in dealing with limited partner investors is locating them. Often, the general partner developer no longer has any interest in the job, having diverted all the funds possible and perhaps even having gone broke because of mismanagement, greed, or overextension. Unfortunately, the fact that the property is about to be foreclosed rolls off the back of the general partner, who can't lose anything, nor see how to make a buck out of the project any longer.

Also, the general partner finds it difficult to deal with limited partner investors. They are already dissatisfied, since the general partner has not fulfilled promises or fulfilled their dreams. Without attempting to assess blame, once a project gets into trouble, the relationship between the general partner and limited partner investors becomes extremely strained. To expect the general partner to convince limited partners to invest more with the mortgage lender to protect themselves against a large income tax is unreal.

It is up to you (or your local counsel) to find the limited partners (through the recorded limited partnership certificate), to see that they are represented by their own lawyer, and to negotiate with them. But, you must first find them and recognize that the interests of the limited partners are different from those of the general partners. You must find them before the foreclosure. They can be a source of new funds, of local know-how, and management.

EFFECT OF THE BANKRUPTCY LAWS ON
MORTGAGE LENDERS

The bankruptcy and reorganization laws are complex and are constantly changing. Congress got the right to pass federal bankruptcy laws in the Constitution and passed the first federal statute before 1800. But mortgage lenders were not affected by the bankruptcy laws until recently. As secured lenders, even in the 1930s, there were not many real estate reorganizations. Projects were smaller and more localized. In the past, limited partnerships were rare and public real estate corporations were few.

But the pattern of the last ten years, with its larger number of real estate syndications and many limited partners, together with the coming of the public Real Estate Investment Trusts, have given the bankruptcy courts a new interest in the field. Until now, most secured mortgage lenders felt that they were not affected by real estate bankruptcies, since they believe the courts could not set aside their secured mortgage liens.

But important changes are occurring in the field. We must get a realistic look at current bankruptcy patterns by understanding the ins and outs of bankruptcy and reorganization. In doing so, you will get a more realistic fix on your own position and be able to react with knowledge instead of fear.

Recent reorganizations illustrate the increasing interest of the bankruptcy courts in protecting the rights of equity investors. The courts try to balance the rights of secured mortgage lenders with their efforts to salvage something for the small equity investor.

WHAT TO DO ABOUT BIAS AGAINST SECURED LENDERS

Currently, many lenders feel that there is a bias against them in the bankruptcy courts in favor of the small equity investor. Institutional lenders are made to feel like Scrooge foreclosing a mortgage at Christmas time.

It is the job of the mortgage lender's local attorney to convince the bankruptcy court that the owner, or developer, and not the lender is the villain. The court must be shown by skilled trial counsel that the lender represents hundreds of small depositors and/or policyholders, whereas the developer is a young opportunist who invested not one nickel in the project, but mismanaged the project, pocketed all of the funds, failed to properly supervise, took kickbacks from subconctractors, and went broke on another job. Also, the villain misled poor tradespeople into working on the job and never told them the truth. Such a person should not be protected by the bankruptcy courts, because such protection would encourage questionable operators to perpetrate similar frauds. If the poor policyholders are not protected on their mortgage loans, their money will be forced into the bond market and local industry will wither.

Also, the developer/borrower has no equity in the project. The job cannot be finished unless the lender forbears or adds additional funds of its own, and the lender cannot do so while the bad-boy developer hangs over the project and continues to divert funds improperly.

Finally, it is unconstitutional to deprive the lender of a secured lien and, in most cases, the bankruptcy court has no right to interfere with that lien, but it can delay foreclosure and make sure the lien does not exceed fair market value.

WHAT THE COURT CAN DO TO SECURED LENDERS

In other words, the bankruptcy count can hurt the secured lender by delaying foreclosure, while the bankruptcy court takes a look around to see if some equity can be salvaged for the limited partners. Also, while the bankruptcy court is "supervising" the property, it may slide downhill through lack of management and direction. But, if the court can be convinced that, ultimately, there will be little or nothing for the equity investors, it can permit the lender to get on with its foreclosure, and sell the property.

In all likelihood, the bankruptcy court can delay foreclosure during the period of reorganization (and that period may be a long one), but, ultimately, the mortgage lender should prevail.

The ideal approach to bankruptcy and reorganization proceedings is to demonstrate, as early as possible, that there is no equity for the owners and that a continued delay harms everyone. Generally, you must come up with some kind of plan of your own which may yield something in return for a faster sale, and you should be represented by the best local bankruptcy counsel you can find. That lawyer must be committed in advance to vigorously pursue your rights through the courts and must be prepared to fight instead of to compromise.

WHAT KIND OF LAWYERS DO YOU NEED TO REPRESENT YOU LOCALLY?

The capable mortgage loan closing attorney who represented you at the initial loan closing may not be the person to represent you in a foreclosure proceeding or in squeezing out mechanics' lien holders. Temperamentally, the person who draws careful mortgage papers is not the kind of person to represent you in the courts, or to prove that the developer is a thief, or an incompetent, or unworthy of the court's consideration.

Local counsel must be a tough, aggressive litigator, and bankruptcy counsel representing the secured lender must understand that the job is to act vigorously, and not just complacently settle down to await the outcome. There is a tendency on the part of many local bankruptcy counsel not to rock the boat, and it is the job of the lender (and lender's general counsel) to rock that boat as often as possible, so that the loan can be protected and the asset not dissipated through neglect or mismanagement.

Most local bankruptcy counsel are not accustomed to representing secured mortgage lenders. Furthermore, there is an occasional tendency on the part of bankruptcy counsel to cooperate with the debtor's counsel, since all bankruptcy lawyers meet each other in the courts more often than they will meet you. So, you must insist on vigorous representation from your local bankruptcy person if you are to get protection.

At the present time, bankruptcy lawyers are outrageously overworked. They are in a boom business. There is a natural tendency to oil the wheel that squeaks the loudest and to let things take their natural course so that the workload can be smoothed out. But, you want action—immediate action—and you want every protective order you can get from the court to prevent the rents from going into the debtor's pocket or being used to pay administration expenses. You must insist that the rents be used to maintain your property and that real estate taxes be paid.

Furthermore, you want to try to get good property management. Therefore, your attorney and your workout man must not take the bankruptcy proceedings lying down. You must pursue your rights aggressively.

With that in mind, let's go through some of the more common provisions of the bankruptcy laws which affect real estate mortgage loans.

HOW THE BANKRUPTCY AND REORGANIZATION LAWS AFFECT MORTGAGES

Chapters I through VII of the Bankruptcy Act relate to straight bankruptcy. We will not deal with them much, because they seek sale and liquidation of the bankrupt property and the distribution of the proceeds to creditors. In straight bankruptcy, the secured creditors get paid first and general creditors get paid second. In most cases, straight bankruptcy (including the sale and liquidation of the property) is not what the borrower wants at all. If there were really any equity in the property, the borrower would not now be in bankruptcy and probably would not be in arrears on the mortgage.

So, we will deal mainly with the reorganization sections in which the debtor seeks rehabilitation and to salvage something for the equity investors and general creditors. How secured creditors and mortgage lenders are involved will be discussed below. The main reorganization chapters are X, XI, and XII.

CHAPTERS X, XI, AND XII

Chapter X (Sections 101 through 276 of the Bankruptcy Act) covers the reorganization of corporations in which the public has a substantial interest. Chapter X proceedings usually involve publicly held corporations or the holders of public debt securities (such as subordinated debentures). The SEC takes an active part, and Chapter X reorganizations take as much as five or six years because of their complexity.

Chapter XI (Sections 301 through 399 of the Bankruptcy Act) covers not only corporations but partnerships and individuals as well. Theoretically, at least, the rights of secured creditors (mortgage lenders) cannot be affected by Chapter XI proceedings; only the debtor and unsecured creditors are involved.

If Chapter XI cannot interfere with secured mortgage debt, why be concerned? Because Chapter XI can defer foreclosure, so that the debtor's equity is not wiped out until the court has had a closer look at the situation, and deferral of foreclosure can have a substantial economic impact on the property.

Chapter XII (Sections 401 through 526 of the Bankruptcy Act) deals with real property reorganizations of individuals and partnerships. Chapter XII is not available to corporations which would use Chapters X or XI, but Chapter XII can help individuals and partnerships with the restructuring of their secured and unsecured debt, which includes mortgage debt. Chapters X and XII are the only reorganization sections that specifically deal with secured mortgage creditors.

A LOOK AT SOME OF THE BANKRUPTCY AND REORGANIZATION LAWS

Let's look at the bankruptcy laws through the eyes of the secured mortgage lender. Always bear in mind as you go through these sections that:

1   The holder of a real property mortgage, if it is a valid lien, is unaffected by the filing of a bankruptcy petition. But the bankrupt can try to get the liens set aside (such as an ineffective preference, a failure to comply with local law, a failure of consideration, etc.).

2   Theoretically, the reorganization and bankruptcy courts cannot destroy the preferred rights of a lien holder. But the secured lender's mortgage is limited to the current value of the property held as security. In other words, the lien cannot be used to wipe out the rights of equity holders if they hold an equity above the value of the mortgage property.

Then, how do the bankruptcy laws affect the rights of secured property lien holders? The procedural rights (the rights to foreclose) of a mortgage holder may be limited, controlled, or otherwise modified or altered by the bankruptcy court. Since the right to postpone foreclosure while the property is managed by a court-appointed receiver or trustee can undermine the property's value, the court's power to stay foreclosure and sale can seriously affect the rights of the mortgage holder. But, it is important to note that the courts must operate within the law, and that there are appellate procedures and constitutional guarantees to secured mortgage holders who find themselves threatened with indefinite delay.

CONTROL BY THE BANKRUPTCY COURT

Once the bankruptcy court takes over, it has exclusive jurisdiction to determine the validity, amount, and priority of liens upon the property. The court has the exclusive jurisdiction to authorize the sale of the property free and clear of the liens, with the lien to attach to the proceeds up to the amount of the lien if the court decides that there is some equity in the property above the mortgage.

The bankruptcy court can require nonbankruptcy receivers and trustees (foreclosure receivers) to turn the property over to the custody of the bankruptcy court, provided the receiver took possession within four months prior to the bankruptcy. But the bankruptcy court cannot generally interfere with a receiver who has been appointed more than four months prior to the filing of the petition. And the bankruptcy court does have jurisdiction to stay and prevent foreclosure proceedings and receiverships commenced within four months of the filing of the bankruptcy petition.

One of the first things the court looks into is whether the alleged secured lien is actually a perfected lien. Often, the first efforts of the court are to find a technical ground for setting aside the mortgage. If the court is successful in setting aside your mortgage, you had better hope you have sufficient title insurance or that your closing lawyer has adequate malpractice insurance.

Let's examine the specific kinds of reorganization you are likely to run into.

Chapter X

Chapter X is available only to corporations, but also covers Real Estate Investment Trusts. Chapter X proceedings may be voluntary or involuntary, and once a Chapter X petition is filed in court, the bankruptcy court has exclusive jurisdiction over the debtor and its property, wherever located. In other words, if Chicago is the appropriate place to file the bankruptcy petition, the Chicago Federal Bankruptcy Court will have jurisdiction over all the debtor's property, even though some of it may be located in New York or Los Angeles. The filing of a petition operates as a stay of prior-pending-mortgage or equity-receivership proceedings. This means the Chapter X petition prevents continuation of a state foreclosure *unless* application is made to the bankruptcy court and cause is shown why the foreclosure should take place. An attempt to remove specific property from the court's protective umbrella by showing why foreclosure should take place would be the secured lender's first attack. At the very least, protective orders should be sought to impound rents and apply them to the property.

Chapter X contemplates a reorganization in which *both* ''secured and unsecured debt and the interests of stockholders may be adjusted, modified or otherwise dealt with by the court.''

WHICH CHAPTER APPLIES?

When is Chapter X used? Generally, where there is ''a substantial public interest or the necessity to adjust the rights of public debt holders.'' Chapter X involves the possibility of a successful reorganization in the hope that the debtor may be rehabilitated so that there will be some equity left for the stockholders.

In Chapter X, the debtor alone retains little or no control over the administration of the property. The reorganization court appoints an independent trustee, who takes over management. There is no ''debtor in possession'' in Chapter X which could permit the current management to continue running the property. The trustee must be disinterested, but occasionally the court may appoint part of the current management to help run the business in coordination with the independent trustee. Also, the independent trustee may hire some of the former employees of the debtor to continue running the business under court control.

Under Chapter X (and Chapter X is different from ordinary bankruptcy and Chapter XI in this respect), the court may stay any state proceedings, including the foreclosure proceedings commenced prior to the four-month bankruptcy period. Under Chapter X, the date of the commencement of a state foreclosure action is irrelevant.

The secured mortgage creditor has rights under Chapter X and should pursue them vigorously after understanding what they are. The secured mortgage lender may ask for foreclosure or sale of the property if:

1   There is no equity above the mortgage and the value of the property is not sufficient to pay the full amount of the secured creditor's mortgage.

2   There is no likelihood that the debtor will be able to come up with a reorganization plan (since the debtor is hopelessly insolvent, and the total secured debt far exceeds asset values).

3   Your particular secured parcel is not needed to accomplish the reorganization.

Damages incurred by a secured mortgage caused by improper continuation of the foreclosure stay can result in a claim against the bankrupt estate. The claim may even get a ''priority.'' A special provision permits FHA-insured mortgages to be foreclosed even though the debtor is in bankruptcy. The bankrupt's leases may be rejected by the court, although the landlord is permitted to file a damage claim, which is generally limited to three years' rent. But actual damages must be proven before the rent claim will be allowed. These may include loss of rent, leasing commissions, new tenant improvements needed to re-lease the premises, etc.

The leases, which may be canceled by the bankruptcy court, usually involve the bankrupt as a tenant, if the lease is a burden. Where the bankrupt is the landlord, the tenant may not be deprived of the right to continue the lease by having the court cancel it. The court has the same power to set aside liens and transfers that the bankrupt had. If the lien is defective, the court can act to set it aside.

CHAPTER X REORGANIZATIONS

Now, what about the actual plan of reorganization under Chapter X? The responsibility for preparing a plan lies with the trustee who has been appointed by the court. In Chapter X, the Securities and Exchange Commission takes the role of representing the public. Various creditors' committees also have the right to make reorganization suggestions. The plan may alter or modify the rights of both secured and unsecured creditors, but each secured creditor with a claim to a specific property is placed in a separate class. This means each separate mortgage holder controls the vote on its separate mortgage. But if groups of creditors have liens against the same property (mechanics' lien claimants), the creditors may be bulked together in a single group for voting purposes.

We said that the court had the right to alter or modify the rights of secured creditors. What does that mean? Chapter X requires acceptance of the plan by two-thirds of the secured creditors in each class. A plan can be confirmed without the consent of secured creditors only if the court finds that they have adequate protection to realize the value of their security. Thus, for example, if the court orders the property sold at auction with the proceeds going first to pay off the lien, the secured creditors can have no objection. If the court leaves the lien unimpaired and only sells the equity subject to the mortgage, the secured creditors will have no complaint.

Some of the dilemmas facing the secured mortgage lender under Chapter X are that the court may disregard secured claims where it finds security valueless, or where the property is worth less than the amount of the secured loan. The rule is that mere court appraisals of secured loan values cannot be used to divert benefits to unsecured creditors. But, it is left to the court to give "fair and equitable protection" to the various classes of creditors. Therein lies much bitter contention.

The *de facto* operating techniques of balancing the actual equity in the property and deciding whether it is substantially less than the value of the mortgage is left to the courts. There are no hard-and-fast rules to apply. Thus, the ability of the courts to threaten that the secured creditor will get less than 100 cents on the dollar is occasionally referred to as the "cram down" provision of Chapters X and XII. The only way to beat "cram down" is to make sure that your side of the case is aggressively presented to the court by competent bankruptcy counsel. Self-serving appraisals should be attacked in court and appeals taken where necessary.

SEC's ROLE

Because of the SEC's intervention in Chapter X, because of the interests of public stockholders, and because the independent trustee wants to review the prefiling conduct of the debtor, Chapter X cases are more complex, more time-consuming, and more expensive than either Chapter XI or Chapter XII cases. Many Chapter X cases have run five years or more. Your specific parcel may not be tied up for five years, but the entire proceedings may last that long. Your job is to shake your property loose before neglect and mismanagement destroy its value to you and to the equity owners.

Chapter XI

Chapter XI is available to any person, individual, partnership, or corporation. Chapter XI can only be voluntary. Chapter XI generally permits the present management to continue to operate as "debtor in possession." The theory is that the debtor in possession will come up with a plan to reorganize the property so that equity may be developed for the debtor and the general creditors.

An automatic stay of foreclosure takes place under Chapter XI, unless you make a successful application to modify or lift the stay. Even though your application for foreclosure may be unsuccessful, you may be able to impose useful conditions on its continuance. You can have the court order that the rents from your property be used to pay taxes, to maintain your specific property, and avoid having the funds pooled with the other assets of the debtor. You may also seek a provision that, unless a plan of reorganization evolves within a certain amount of time, the property will, in fact, go to foreclosure. Vigorous court representation by the mortgage lender is the only way to protect the lien.

From the debtor's standpoint, the important advantage of Chapter XI over Chapter X is that the debtor is left in possession of the property and an independent trustee is not appointed. A Chapter XI petition can be converted into a Chapter X by the debtor, a group of stockholders, or the SEC. Chapter XI does not include any "cram down" provisions and cannot directly modify the rights of secured lien holders.

Chapter XII

Chapter XII can be utilized by individuals and partnerships and not by corporations. Corporations would use Chapters X or XI. Chapter XII provides for rehabilitation of a debtor who needs relief from both secured and unsecured creditors. The plan should include a modification of the rights of one or more real estate lien holders. The debtor generally retains property control in Chapter XII, as in Chapter XI, but court-appointed trustees are used in various cases and in certain federal district courts, while trustees are not used in other districts. Local practices are important in Chapter XII cases.

The filing of a petition acts as a stay of any foreclosure proceedings under XII (as it does under Chapters X and XI). Unwise executory contracts and leases can be rejected by the court under Chapter XII in the same manner as they would be under Chapter XI.

The reorganization plan sections under XII are similar to Chapter XI; that is, the debtor files the plan. But under XII, the plan must seek to modify the rights of secured creditors and require acceptance by two-thirds in amount of the debts of each class of creditors. Dissenting secured creditors must be compensated, but, as in the case with Chapter X (where there is insufficient value in the secured real property to cover all the liens), "cram down" provisions apply. The court is left with the job of balancing the interests and making sure everybody is completely compensated. Problems of proof and appellate rights are available to dissatisfied secured creditors, but the threat of the "cram down" must be realistically assessed before accepting dilution or compromise of your lien.

SUMMARY AND CONCLUSIONS

To begin with, the job responsibility for watching distress property loans should be assigned today, even if you have no properties in trouble. Someone should start thinking about how to spot problem loans as early as possible. If you already have problem loans, adequate staffing must be supplied.

Speed is most important. While it is easier to procrastinate than to bite the bullet, no problem loan will get better by itself. Time only makes it get worse. Therefore, you must assemble an up-to-date file on the problem loan as quickly as possible, so that you have all the facts in front of you.

While you are assembling the facts, you should make arrangements to get your hands on any rentals that are coming in, or at least make sure they are applied to the property while negotiations are pending. If you are still disbursing under a construction loan, as soon as you spot a problem, you must start controlling your disbursements carefully, to make sure they are going into the job.

As soon as possible, evaluate the legal and business problems in connection with taking over immediately, versus those which will occur if you delay. Anticipate the intervention of the bankruptcy courts and ask yourself what you can do to put yourself in the best possible position.

If you are a construction lender with a permanent take-out on which you rely, make sure you meet the terms of the commitment for the permanent.

All distress real estate deals should be reviewed in the light of the tax laws. Evaluate the threat to current owners of a foreclosure (the tax cost) and the value to them of future tax losses.

The following is a checklist for loan workout officers. It covers many practical and legal problems of distress loans. Almost every item in the checklist (except those which are self-explanatory) is discussed in this article. We hope the checklist gathers together for you in one place the essential information, so that you may distribute it among your staff. Use it to make sure you are not overlooking anything!

CHECKLIST FOR WORKOUT OFFICERS*

I   Legal and practical problems of income-property loans in trouble
     A   Preparing for distress loan management
         1   Staffing up for adequate supervision
         2   Updating the budgets to "today's realities"
         3   Personal inspection of the site and marketplace
         4   Problem property or problem people?
     B   Control
         1   Who has it?
         2   Is it transferable?
         3   Respective rights and obligations of:
            a   Owner
            b   Developer

---

*This checklist was designed by Daniel S. Berman, a New York attorney and member of the firm of Fink, Weinberger, Fredman & Charney, p.c., of New York City and White Plains. Mr. Berman is a lecturer for Association and university graduate courses, and is the author of several books on the subjects of real estate and tax law.

        c   Construction lender
        d   Permanent lender
        e   Mechanics and other lien holders
        f   Fee owner
        g   Long-term and space tenants
        h   Unsecured creditors
        i   Receivers
        j   Bankruptcy trustees
        k   Limited and general partners
        l   Brokers and managers

II   Legal problems: Construction and development loans
   A   Is there default?
   B   Rights, duties, and liabilities of a mortgagee in possession
   C   Acceleration provisions
   D   Self-help?
   E   Protecting the job
       1   Guards
       2   Subcontract rights
       3   Books and records
   F   Appoint a receiver?
   G   Lease and rent assignments
   H   Protecting the buy and sell agreement
   I   Protecting rights against a bonding company, personal guarantors of completion and payment
   J   Particular problems on leasehold mortgages
   K   Protecting credit leases
   L   Deed in lieu of foreclosure
   M   Other nonjudicial remedies
   N   Protecting disbursement procedures
   O   Obtaining lien waivers

III Cost to complete
   A   Timing and urgency (weather)
   B   Cost to complete
       1   How firm?
       2   Who guarantees cost and quality?
   C   Hidden liabilities in existing partnership or other title holding entry?
   D   Creditors' rights, torts, tax and securities law problems, assignability of leases, mortgages, and subcontracts
   E   Status of title, income tax status, permits, and ecological problems
   F   Cost of guard service

IV Interim losses and sources of funds
   A   Budget to completion, including:
       1   Rent-up
       2   Sales costs
       3   Promotion
       4   Interim operating cash deficits
   B   Source of funds?
       1 New investors
       2 Tax shelter buyers

      3 Old limited partners
      4 Developer
      5 General contractor
      6 Subcontractors
      7 Bonding company
      8 Title company
      9 Insurers
      10 Borrowers
      11 Commercial bankers
   C Effect of transfer or timing on liability to fund any of the above commitments (can they walk?)
   D Are existing leases an asset or a liability?

V What have you got after completion?
   A Rethinking feasibility under "today's" circumstances
   B Competition from existing and from other distress deals
   C Current rental trends and projections
   D Income tax projections and tax risks during and after rent-up
   E Computation of recapture risk
   F Interim and permanent financing, rates, terms, and timing
   G Compare return on investment and risk-reward ratios with other real estate offerings, other types of investment

VI Permanent loan problems
   A Early warning signs
   B Current financial statements
   C Inspection and tax search
   D Lease modification
   E Rent-impairing activities
   F Tenancy or neighborhood changes
   G Defer interest or amortization?
   H Forbearance?
   I Documentation
   J *Quid pro quo*
   K Nonjudicial remedies

VII Bankruptcy and reorganization laws
   A Consulting specialized counsel
   B Real estate vs. bankruptcy counsel
   C Role of house counsel
   D Powers of bankruptcy courts
   E Restraining orders
   F Preferences
   G Turn-over proceedings
   H Relief from stay
   I Representation on creditors' committees
   J Voidable preferences
   K Liens
   L Venue
   M Fraudulent conveyances
   N Rights of secured creditors
   O Chapters X, XI, and XII

P Estimating bankruptcy costs and legal fees

VIII Legal problems of workouts
  A Foreclosure or not foreclosure?
  B "Good" vs. "bad" creditor jurisdictions
  C Nonjudicial remedies
  D Receivership
  E Mortgagee in possession
  F Defenses and delay
  G Counterclaims
  H Lien priority of advancing additional funds
  I Mechanics' lien waivers
  J Rights to continue guarantee, bonding, and other contractual obligations
  K Anticipating bankruptcy and preference problems
  L Collecting rents
  M Extending leases and buy and sell provisions

IX Legal problems of partnership entities
  A Default provisions
  B Rights and duties of general vs. limited partners
  C Tax aspects of:
    1 Modifying
    2 Liquidating
    3 Foreclosing
    4 Entity modification
  D Resolving conflicts among partnership and contracting groups at various levels
  E Protecting first user and construction loss status
  F Securities law problems

X Legal risks of new investment group
  A Check:
    1 Real estate
    2 Lien
    3 Trust
    4 Tax
    5 Securities
    6 Bankruptcy
    7 Debtor and creditor
    8 Corporate
    9 Partnership
    10 Usury laws
  B Is long-term tenant really a tenant whose lease can be canceled or a mortgagor with an equity of redemption to which bankruptcy trustee may have rights?
  C Responsibility to third parties or tax authorities for antecedent debts, torts, or acts
  D Legal and "practical" obligations to:
    1 Creditors
    2 Tenants
    3 Contractors
    4 Employees

       5 Managers
       6 Developers
       7 Unions
       8 Receivers
       9 Assignees of rents
      10 Trustees in bankruptcy
      11 Junior mortgagees
      12 Other lien holders
E Effect on new investor group of:
       1 New general partner
       2 New limited partner
       3 Partnership entity
F Cash flow and tax priorities and obligations of new vs. old group

G Effect of bankruptcy laws on:
       1 General partner
       2 Partnership entity
       3 Multiproperty partnership
       4 Permanent and construction lenders

Chapter 30

Organizing the Income-Property Team

Felice A. Rocca, Jr.

We find, as a result of uncontrollable external pressures, that former, well-established profit lines either no longer exist or are extremely volatile. This has occurred in a time frame during which the emphasis of most of our investor sources has changed to fewer loans, larger dollar amounts, high yield requirements, and loans either not restricted or more liberal in terms of usury. Hence, the volume of activity in the commercial loan sector had demonstrated the investment thrust and appetite of these capital sources.

The mortgage banker's commercial loan market position has been steadily eroding during the past 20 to 25 years. Traditional mortgage bankers are now originating less than 20 percent of the total long-term, income-property mortgage loan business, even though dollar totals are increasing.

Books and published literature on mortgage banking have either not discussed income-property financing at all or have merely given it a few passive lines with their main emphasis directed at the other areas of operation within the company such as the residential department, the construction loan department, and the servicing and legal departments.

This subject, insofar as the mortgage banking industry is concerned, is something that has received little attention from an organization and department structure point of view. One reason this condition exists is that many companies organized their income-property departments by utilizing personnel who only had experience in residential lending.

Frequently, as can be imagined, this practice does not produce a "best fit" organization which is most responsive to the markets in which we deal. It does not promote a method of operation where opportunity can be projected, a criterion for selecting capable people, or a program for the accomplishment of specific goals. Since our industry is subject to a wide number of external factors, all producing changes beyond the control of any single organization or even its professional organization, it is incumbent upon us to revise, edit, and recast our efforts in those specific areas that are in keeping with these changes.

STRUCTURE OF THE DEPARTMENT

The ideal department is structured toward the objective of fulfilling its investor/developer obligations in terms of satisfying their requirements for type of property, desired yield, and dollar amounts obtained on loans sought. It should make maximum use of all its personnel, have no duplication of effort, operate within reasonable budget limitations, and be capable of being expanded to meet increasing demand for its services. Numbers of people are, of course, a function of the size of the operation. However, the arrangement where there is a department manager who oversees the activities of the production team can achieve the desired operating efficiency.

The manager's job is a complex one. He or she must be able to set objectives, organize work, motivate members of the work force, evaluate their performance, and develop other people to eventually assume management responsibilities.

The department structure will cover all activities of operation, including long-term loans on commercial, industrial, and multifamily properties. Interim loan activity will include land acquisition loans, condominium conversion activity, construction lending, gap loans, standbys, wraparound loans, and all other forms of real estate lending activity, whether funded by using in-house lines (with or without participation) or on a brokered basis.

A primary objective is to develop a group of income-loan specialists with a technical and diversified background where skills from a number of areas can be brought together to meet objectives. The actual form the department structure will take should, in all likelihood, consist of a manager or vice president of the company, responsible for loan origination, processing, submission, sales, and supervision of underwriting personnel, backed up by appraisal expertise and whatever secretarial assistance is required to meet its workload. The smooth operation of this team, which, in effect, tends to shape the department, is the main objective.

PERSONNEL CHARACTERISTICS

The manager, having the responsibility for production and profit, should also have the necessary ability to select people to work in the department. Skills sought should normally require college training or equivalent experience. In many cases, undergraduate courses with emphasis in law, finance, economics, and real estate provide an excellent background. The aggressive graduate who lacks formal training can supplement education by taking advantage of the numerous courses being offered by colleges, universities, and professional organizations.

Proper personnel selection will assist the manager in reaching goals and, as in all other facets of mortgage banking, the combination of the individual parts working in concert with all the other parts of the department make an indivisible contribution to these objectives. Therefore, acquiring personnel with character, resourcefulness, initiative, ability, and tenacity are the keys to success.

Since a basic force inherent in most people is a desire for personal worth and importance, the manager's work should be geared toward developing programs in which the employee can fulfill these desires.

By definition, the originator's responsibility is to produce mortgage loan commitments. This must be followed by good service to the involved parties. Delivery must benefit all parties if the originator is to be successful, because the markets we serve are small and the continued good reputation of the individual is the best stock in trade.

The following job description illustrates the general duties, qualifications, and requirements for this type of work:

Position

Title: Loan originator
Department: Income loans

DESCRIPTION

General Responsibilities

Under the supervision of the department head, the loan originator is responsible for the origination of real estate opportunities, including field contact with borrowers, loan screening, preliminary structuring, packaging of submission, investor contact for loan placement, and delivery of an acceptable and clean loan commitment.

Regular Duties

1 Maintains day-to-day contact with borrowers with major emphasis on builder/developer-type borrowers. Keeps records of such contacts posted to card record system indicating other types of projects completed and contemplated by sponsor.

2 Seeks to develop select lending opportunities by reviewing sponsor-originated data when available, and in many cases, assists in the accumulation of data essential to formulating a conclusion about the efficacy of the proposal.

3 Upon concluding that a proposal has merit, originator then procures authorization and deposit in order that there is no misunderstanding as to employment arrangements and objectives of said employment.

4 Works with borrower in accumulating the information required for loan-offering package, and also does whatever additional field work may be required. An example of the kinds of data would be:

a Financial statements and résumés from borrower, sponsor, guarantors, and general contractors; signed, dated, and not less than 90 days old.

b Experience of sponsors, ownership portfolio, particularly as to specific property type in question; photographs of other jobs.

c Bank and business references (at least three each); (get name of bank, address, loan officer, phone number); identify supplier or furnisher of services.

d Management team and/or marketing plan; copy of contract outlining responsibilities, property type involved; ability to maintain tenant relations.

e Description of area; county and surrounding data, population, growth, roads, etc.

f Description of town; map of city locating property, aerial photograph, road patterns, main shopping area, distances, satellite shopping facilities, transportation, types, routes, schedule, main road arteries, distance to subject, major industries, types, stability, wages, tax base millage breakdown, public facilities, schools, churches, etc.

g Description of neighborhood; map of area, strip map (uses on both sides and across street from subject), age, type, condition of adjoining properties, trend in neighborhood, type of residents, etc., demolitions, transition of use.

h Plot plan showing existing and finished grades, easements, if any exist or are contemplated; building orientation.

i Narrative or physical description of site; discuss prominence, visibility, size, orientation, topography, ease of ingress-egress, transportation, amenities, parking, future expansion, tree, shrub and brush growth, other site improvements, use and regulations.

j Zoning; evidence that use or proposed use is in conformity with currently applicable regulations.

k Utilities and letters from respective suppliers indicating their availability; water, sewer, rail, gas and electric, source, amounts available, adequacy for proposed project's relative costs.

l Competitive locations.

m Plans and specifications (four sets); can be preliminary if best data available.

n Brochures and photographs (if existing property); ground-level photos showing subject and four directions; aerial photo, if possible.

o Itemization of hard and soft costs, signed and dated; have borrower source of costs, for example, bid, architect's estimate, etc.

p Breakdown of maintenance costs.

q Services to be provided to each owner.

r Income and expenses (pro forma, if proposed); if existing, three years previously operating expenses.

s Tax basis and analysis showing support for projected taxes; where no comparables are available, try to obtain letter from town assessor or data on other income-producing properties to support projected taxes for subject.

t Demand for this facility (performance of comparable/competitive properties); also helps establish reasonableness of: gross income, vacancy, operating expenses, net income, cap rate, value, etc.

u Land comparables.

v Rental comparables.

5 Supervises and is directly responsible for the expeditious completion of the loan-offering package. This assumes the coordination of any ancillary services essential to its completion.

6 Either directly or with other staff personnel introduces loan offering to loan committee (for in-house funding) or to outside source for placement. Is responsible for any formal presentation that may be required and any follow-up that is necessary.

7 Negotiates all reactions and interaction in connection with loan offering aimed toward the production of an acceptable commitment.

8 Upon receipt of commitment, makes formal delivery to borrower indicating that upon acceptance, subject to any contingencies that might be a part of the commitment, employment contract has been fulfilled, and fee is earned. Turns fee over to department head for forwarding to accounting section.

9 Coordinates any other activity which may be essential to produce a clean commitment, such as appraisal reports, feasibility studies, plans, and specifications.

10 Where loan is placed with principal and is to close at a distant point in time, originator is required to keep lender advised of status of progress on a regularly scheduled basis, in order to insure that delivery will be made as called for in the commitment.

11 Surveys competition as to types of loans being originated. Seeks to learn of any specific terms and conditions that are pertinent and reports this information to the department head.

12 Surveys markets as to numbers and types of real estate ventures being developed in order to determine areas where market has depth or is soft.

Periodic or Occasional Duties

1 In connection with the last two items above, may be required to make management reports on a periodic basis for specific areas of coverage or interest.

2 Attends home builders' meetings, conferences, seminars, or other functions as may be required by the department head.

3 Entertains customers and clients as the need may arise.

Contacts in the Office

Department head, staff assistants, loan committee (as the need presents itself), all other loan originators.

Contacts Away from the Office

Borrowers, lenders, resource people essential to the purpose of the position.

Equipment Used

Automobile, dictating unit, and calculator.

Number of Persons Supervised

None, unless volume requires assistance.

Major Responsibility of Persons Supervised

Assistant loan originator—assists originator with various duties while learning and developing into a loan originator.

Job Condition

Agreeable—works under pressure.

REQUIREMENTS

Minimum Education

College preferred, but high school with sufficient specialized experience is also acceptable.

Specialized Job Knowledge and Abilities

Knowledge of the financial aspects of real estate, including lending market activity, borrower and lender motivations, desires and methods. Valuation, management, construction, sales and lending experience are required.

Experience

At least two years in any of the above capacities or combinations thereof.

Personal Requirements

Above-average neatness and appearance, pleasant manner, aggressiveness, initiative, good judgment, leadership ability, and intellectual honesty.

The fulfillment of the department's objectives is dependent on people skilled in real estate. The specific skills, while best developed through experience, can frequently be supplemented by training, and the alert manager should be aware of the resources available. The need for training is universal and is a continuing responsibility of all parties. Even the accomplished originator who is a proven success needs training on new procedures, changing markets, changing concepts, and company policies. It is even more essential to the new person, who has little or only a minimum of production experience. It is a basic human characteristic for employees to amplify their areas of experience and to tend to cover up shortcomings.

The manager can learn of specific areas of difficulty by learning of those areas where personnel are encountering the most difficulty. If, for example, a number of applications are executed none of which produce an acceptable commitment, this then provides the ideal basis to attempt to discover those areas of weakness or difficulty. In

this analysis, the manager attempts to isolate the effort into its component parts beginning with the producer, then reviewing the load offering for reasonableness, packaging, and presentation.

MEETING NEW CHALLENGES

Mortgage banking has experienced great and rapid changes in recent years which have
presented us with numerous challenges. The opening statement of this chapter indicates
change is in order. In some cases, entire companies have made, while others are
considering, a reorientation of their basic corporate structures, and the reestablishment
of policies that will cause far-reaching changes from production to management points
of view. This kind of corporate change frequently requires the recruitment of trained
and experienced personnel and the education and retraining of some existing personnel.
In other cases, the change has created new areas of lending opportunity where the
redirection of a department might become essential to meet either previously established production goals or newly created ones.

When this occurs, the change should be planned and it can, for purposes of this
chapter, be defined as a program that results in a change of the attitudes or perspec-
tives. At this point, we will presuppose that the change has occurred or is about to
occur and the objective is to meet this transition as smoothly and as productively as
possible. By dividing the department into four component parts such as its task,
structure, area of activity, and personnel, and examining each part separately, we will
be in a position to understand how new challenges can best be met.

The basic task of the department is mortgage banking; hence, this can be assumed
and any change program would not be directed to change or alter a department task.
The other parts may then be considered, and if we relate structure in terms of systems
of authority, work flow and responsibilities, areas of activity in terms of what was for
the main part a correspondent-investor relationship with servicing only, which is now
being expanded to include interim lending opportunities, short-term financing positions, or a modification of the kinds and types of lending opportunities that are to be
encouraged, then strategies can be developed toward the modification of personnel
within the department.

How to best accomplish this challenge is dependent on the individual manager,
since whatever the method, it must fit the existing or modified constraints of structure,
be responsive to areas of activity, and be implemented by people.

IMPLEMENTATION OF CHANGE

Let's examine the mechanics for bringing about this desired change so that we improve
the human factors in the organization and create a better working environment. Since
meeting the new challenge is paramount from management's position, it should be
accomplished through genuinely sincere personal relationships, mutual trust, and in an
atmosphere where the objective of solving whatever problems may arise as a result of
the new challenge can be approached in a problem-solving environment.

The first step would be to establish a well-defined purpose that supports or provides the basis for the change.

An example might be a mortgage banking company that did no construction lending and is interested in using its existing income-loan personnel to develop this area of business. The thrust of this new activity will impact on loan originators in various ways.

Implementation can be accomplished by way of change, replacement, or supplementation of certain key individuals, which is a change in the structure of the department. It can also be effected by including the income-loan personnel in the decisions essential to the objectives and in this way develop within the personnel a sense of identification with the methods of achieving these goals. Another method would be to embark on an comprehensive training program as discussed earlier. In any case, some direct, overt effort must be made in order to maintain morale and confidence.

GOAL SETTING

An individual's performance is usually better if the activity is guided by standards and goals. It also follows that goals must be realistic and attainable; otherwise, they carry little value. These serve as a tool enabling the manager to more effectively guide and direct the activities of the loan originators. In addition, goals establish a basis for letting the originator know what is expected for measuring actual results and identifying strengths and weaknesses. As an example, the originator who constantly develops multifamily opportunities may be missing other opportunities simply because of feeling less comfortable in them. Also, goal setting can play a significant part in the originator's compensation plan, whereby incentive programs can be implemented upon the attainment of reasonably established quotas. Goals in mortgage banking can only be established on one basis, and that is based on production of department income. Of course, this takes into account all forms of activity whether placed with a correspondent or funded with in-house dollars on an interim basis. The question of allowing originators to set their own goals is of interest and this allows the originator to make certain judgments. Opposing points of view are valid and should also be considered. For example, there is some question as to whether the originator has the time and training to establish realistic goals. Also, experience seems to indicate that loan originators may be too optimistic, especially in connection with their negotiating prowess. If the result is that the goal is unattainable, the effect can develop into a morale problem.

Typically, the department manager, who is more acutely aware of the multitude of internal and external factors that will govern the productiveness of the originator, should set the individual goals. In setting goals, the manager should be reminded of some basic characteristics inherent in a good plan and also some weaknesses that might occur. As mentioned previously, goals must be realistic and attainable. They should be based on an objective forecast of market activity, and since external market conditions are beyond the control of the originator, they should be responsive to these forces.

The setting of goals is more than merely establishing quotas. The effective manager not only sets the goals, but develops the planning methodology needed for their attainment and then evaluates individual performances. This indicates that the problem is a far-reaching one, since the responsibility involves the required motivation for the originator to perform to the best level of ability without day-to-day supervision. The manager must be assured that each originator has a clear picture of the organization, the investor, loan policies, underwriting and yield requirements, in order to pursue these goals in the field.

COMPENSATION

The range of compensation plans is unlimited, and since we have previously reviewed the personal and motivational characteristics of our production team, it can be seen why incentive compensation is almost a must in order to attract and retain high-volume producers. Obviously, the plan should be designed to reward the producer. Compensation plans should be competitive, fair, and attractive both to the producer and to management. A well-thought-out program can achieve this balance.

Base Salary

Base salaries are essential to any compensation plan and this can range from a low or minimal base with greater production incentives to a greater than average base with lower or no incentive compensation. Experience, training, and past performance are essential considerations to be given weight in establishing the base. Also, some firms may wish to differentiate between in-house funding producers and those individuals who operate on brokerage production.

The base salary should be in an amount sufficient to make the producer feel like a recognized contributor to the corporate effort. By being providing a satisfactory wage level, the individual can react and respond to lending opportunities with a sense of confidence and a feeling of security about basic financial obligations.

Incentive Programs

Like percentage leases, incentive programs can be geared to apply when minimum production objectives have been met. The incentive is applied as a percentage of volume production where in-house dollars are used for funding or as a percentage of fee income where loans are placed or brokered with correspondents. Normal company fringes, expenses for travel and entertainment, and an automobile allowance or equipment are usually offered in addition to salary and incentive plans.

INTEGRATION INTO THE TOTAL CORPORATE EFFORT

The responsibilities, duties, and product of the individual producer generate extensive implications to management from a legal, portfolio-management, and profit point of view. The producer can work with the staff engineer in reviewing plans, making progress inspections, and understanding loan-disbursement schedules, field changes, methods under which funds are drawn, and a variety of day-to-day problems that must be responded to as construction progresses.

Portfolio management is another area where the producer gains keen insight into the total responsibility of the company. In some cases, loans get into trouble and the resolution of problems essential to its workout gives the individual a better feel for the work done, why it is done, and how it is done. Further, the insight gained by the exposure of having to manage property under distress conditions evokes an awareness to people, buildings, and circumstances that cannot be duplicated.

In summary, it can be seen that income-property lending is extremely vital to many mortgage banking companies. A high-level, specialized kind of expertise can only be achieved when a direct and concerted effort has been made to attract people who are educated, trained, and qualified to respond to the challenge. We have met the challenge, it is ever changing and so are our people. We must continue to grow to meet these dynamics.

Part Two

Case Studies

Following are case studies on eleven different types of income-producing properties. No single case is the same and all vary in length and content. This can be said of all real estate, where no two properties are exactly alike. They also vary in the amount of analysis required to underwrite their potential.

Some are rather long and written in a narrative manner, while others are short and concise and completed on standard forms provided by the investor. The purpose of the cases which follow is not so much to present a "perfect" case as it is to challenge the reader's analytical processes. Some are intended to be only narrative commentary on the loan's history and negotiations, with some appraisal and loan data included.

These case studies are not meant to minimize in any way the role of the appraiser in developing a sound estimate of value in order to structure the loan amount. It is assumed the mortgage banker will have fee or staff appraisers available who are familiar with proper appraisal reports. It is recommended that appraisal competence be a part of mortgage banker/correspondent capabilities.

A brief analysis, written by an experienced underwriter other than the author of the case study, can be found at the conclusion of each case to follow. Do not refer to this analysis, however, until the case has been independently studied.

Case Study 1

Garden Apartments

Lawrence J. Melody

<u>REFINANCING PROPOSAL</u>

<u>SILVERFLOW APARTMENTS</u>

Edina, Minnesota

Submitted By:

Northland Mortgage Company
6600 France Avenue South
Edina, Minnesota 55435

SILVERFLOW APARTMENTS

REFINANCING PROPOSAL

TABLE OF CONTENTS

<u>REFINANCING PROPOSAL - SILVERFLOW APARTMENTS</u>

<u>PROPOSAL SUMMARY</u>

INTRODUCTION

The proposal contained herein calls for a commitment to refinance the
Silverflow Apartments, a five year old, 360 unit garden apartment complex
that is located in Edina, Minnesota. At the present time, there is no
secondary financing on the project. The original loan placed on the property
by Moral Life on January 15, 1971, remains in effect. To date, Moral Life
has had an excellent relationship with the borrower, Knugget Investment
Company, which developed the project. Robert A. Knugget continues to be the
sole stockholder of the company which owns and manages the Silverflow
Apartments.

Since its initial opening, Silverflow Apartments have been recognized as
a landmark garden apartment project. In 1971, the project won several local
and national landscape and building awards. Complete rent-up of the project
occurred within less than six months after it became available to the public.
During its entire operating history, the complex has consistently been
occupied in excess of 95%; and, since the original first mortgage was placed
on the property, it has experienced a significant increase in rental income.
Maintained to meet the highest management standards and located in one of the
wealthiest communities in the United States, it continues to be one of the
most prestigious and successful apartment complexes in the Minneapolis-
St. Paul Metropolitan Area. It is an excellent example of the incorporation
of first class sponsorship, location and design, the basic elements of sound
development.

LOAN PROPOSAL

In view of the extraordinary quality, condition, location and operating history
of the subject and in consideration of the attractive new money yield and
participation feature of the loan, the following refinancing is recommended:

Loan Amount	$5,775,000.00
Interest Rate	9.50%
Amortization	30 Years
Annual Constant	10.10%
Annual Payment	$ 583,275.00
Monthly Payment	$ 48,606.25
Maturity	20 Years
Funding Date	7/1/75
Maturity Date	7/2/95
Prepayment Option	Closed 10 years, then at 105 declining 1/2 to 0.
Gross Income Participation	As additional interest, 10% of annual gross rents in excess of 1975 base of $1,288,500

Principal Balances:

After	5 years	$5,555,550
	10 years	5,269,050
	15 years	4,648,875
	20 years	3,753,750

BORROWER

Knuggett Investment Company (Inc.)

Robert A. Knugget, age 47, is the sole stockholder of Knugget Investment Company. His personal net worth, as shown in the attached financial statement (Exhibit I) dated December 31, 1974, is $15,170,000.

Robert A. Knugget has over 20 years' experience in apartment development, management and ownership. He currently owns and manages over 1000 units in the Minneapolis-St. Paul Metro Area. Each of his projects incorporates attractive design, site planning, quality construction and finishing, and aggressive management and maintenance. Mr. Knugget is the 1975 president of the National Apartment Association. He has served as an advisor to HUD on various housing and financing programs. He enjoys an excellent business reputation, has made moderate use of his financial credit and is considered an excellent business risk.

LOCATION

The Minneapolis-St. Paul Metropolitan Area is the largest market between Chicago and the West Coast north of St. Louis. Its population is currently in excess of 2 million people. Based on national studies and surveys, it has consistently been ranked as one of the top metro areas based on a composite "quality of life" index. Its economy is diversified and expanding and its unemployment rate is one of the lowest in the nation. It is served by a broad spectrum of cultural and recreational facilities and outlets and is considered to be an educational and medical center. The area's business environment has attracted many major industries who are civically active in many local programs and causes. Minneapolis-St. Paul is an area noted for its steady growth and economic stability.

The subject is located in the City of Edina which is a first ring suburb located eight miles southwest of the Minneapolis downtown central business district. Edina has a population of 44,000 and is recognized as one of the wealthiest suburbs in the United States. Average effective household income exceeds $25,000.

The project is served by Southdale Shopping Center, one of the most successful regional centers in the country, Southdale-Fairview Hospital and the Southdale Medical Clinic in addition to many other high grade satellite stores and facilities. It is convenient to three major office and industrial parks and within walking distance of two golf courses and tennis clubs.

Edina has a favorable and stable tax base and is administered by a very capable government. The city comprises an area of 16 square miles, the whole of which is occupied by a large percentage of the doctors, professional people and corporate managers who work in the Metro Area.

SITE DESCRIPTION

The subject site is located in the northwest quadrant of Interstate 494 and State Highway 100 fronting on Melody Lake Road between the Indian Hills Golf Course and Cahill Road. The site contains 21.68 acres or 944,380 square feet or 16.6 units per acre. The land site contains a lake and a significant amount of open area. The topography is gently rolling and slopes down to the lake at the southeast corner of the site. The land is heavily wooded, crossed by streams and dotted with pools and waterfalls. The natural setting has greatly enhanced the value of the project and is partly responsible for the strong demand that has and does exist for the rental units.

IMPROVEMENTS DESCRIPTION

The project consists of six 3 story apartment buildings, each having its
own underground parking. Each building contains 60 units and 60 parking
spaces. There is also a recreation building which houses a pool and
recreation facilities. In addition to the underground parking, there are 325
surface parking spaces which give the complex a 1.9 parking ratio. The
apartment mix is as follows:

1 Bedroom Units	216
2 Bedroom Units	144
Total	360

The amenity package for each unit is varied and includes one to two ceramic
tile baths, patios, balconies, carpeting and all kitchen appliances. Each
building has an automatic elevator serving all floors and laundry and storage
facilities on each floor. The individual unit sizes range from 830 square feet
for the one bedrooms up to 1,125 square feet for the largest two bedroom.

Construction is concrete and frame with a brick and stucco exterior. The units
are well insulated and soundproofed. Electric garage doors serve the underground parking areas. The buildings are heated with a hot water baseboard
system that is very efficient. The improvements are well designed and have
attractive layouts and individual room sizes.

VALUATION

Land Value:

Based on comparable data, the land value has been established at $1,800 per unit
which is a conservative estimate considering the location and natural setting
of the site.

Land Value	$ 648,000

Reproduction Cost:

Based on recently bid contracts for similar construction in the Minneapolis-
St. Paul Metro Area, the effective depreciated reproduction cost of the
five year old improvements has been established at $20,162 per unit.

Improvements	$7,258,327
Land	648,000
Total	7,906,327
Reproduction Value . . . . (Rounded)	$7,900,000

Market Data Approach to Value:

Based on recent sales of comparable apartment projects in the Edina area,
a conservative market data estimate of 6 times gross income was applied to
the project's stabilized gross income of $1,288,500.

Market Value . . . . (Rounded)	$7,700,000

Economic Value

Based on an analysis of the project's historical income and expense which
was compared to similar projects, a stabilized pro forma operating statement
was constructed as follows:

Gross Income	$1,288,500
Vacancy Factor	51,540
Total Expenses	459,340
Net Operating Income	777,620

An overall capitalization rate of 10.15% (Exhibit H) was constructed
using the Ellwood Mortgage/Equity Method and the net income was capitalized
as follows:

$777,620 ÷ .1015 . . . . $7,661,281
Economic Value . . . . . . (Rounded) $7,700,000

Value Correlation:

Insofar as the Economic Value is generally felt to be the most meaningful,
and since it correlated with the lower conservative indicated value, for
mortgage purposes the property was appraised in fee simple title as follows:

Final Indicated Value $7,700,000

ANALYSIS

Property Data:

Land Area (21.68 acres)	944,380 SF
Gross Building Area (including garages)	567,036 SF
Gross Building Area (excluding garages)	426,552 SF
Net Rentable Area (apartments only)	332,460 SF
Total Cubic Feet (including garages)	5,627,118 CF
Total Cubic Feet (excluding garages)	4,292,520 CF
Total Units	360
Total Rooms	1,404
Total Underground Parking Spaces	360
Total Surface Parking Spaces	325
Land Coverage Ratio	1.66
Apartment Units per Acre	16.6
Parking Space Ratio per Unit	1.9
Average Rooms per Unit	3.9
Average Square Feet per Unit	923.5 SF

Stabilized Income and Expense Analysis:

Gross Income	$1,288,500
Vacancy Factor	51,540
Total Operating Expenses and Taxes	459,340
Net Operating Income	777,620

Gross Income is equal to:

(332,460 SF NRA)	$0.32/SF/Month
(332,460 SF NRA)	$3.88/SF/Year
(1,404 Rooms)	$76.47/Room/Month
(360 Units)	$3,579/Unit/Year

The Vacancy Factor is equal to:

. . . .	4% of Gross Income
. . . .	14.4 Vacant Units/Year

Total Expenses are equal to:

. . . .	37% of Effective Gross Inco
. . . .	$1,275/Unit/Year
. . . .	$27.26/Room/Month

Net Operating Income is equal to:

. . . . 60% of Gross Income
. . . . $180/Unit/Month

Indicated Value Analysis:

A Value of $7,700,000 is equal to:

. . . . $21,389/Unit
. . . . $ 5,484/Room
. . . . 6 x Gross Income
. . . . 9.85 x Net Income
. . . . $13.58/SF of GBA
. . . . $1.37/C.F. of GBA

Loan Analysis:

1. A loan of $5,775,000 is equal to:

($7,700,000) . . . . 75% of Value
(360 Units) $16,042/Unit
(1,404 Rooms) . . . . $ 4,113/Room
($1,288,500) . . . . 4.48 x Gross Income
(567,036 SF) . . . . $10.18/SF of GBA
(332,460 SF) . . . . $17.37/SF of Apt. NRA

2. The default point is as follows:

Annual Debt Service . . . . $ 583,275
Operating Expense and Taxes   459,340
    Total $1,042,615

which is equal to:

    81% of Gross Income
    $2,896/Unit/Year
    $61.88/Room/Month

3. The debt service coverage is:

$$\frac{\text{Net Operating Income} \quad \$777,620}{\text{Annual Debt Service} \quad \$583,275} = \underline{1.33}$$

SUMMARY (See Exhibits J and K)

1. The proposed refinancing represents a $1,573,216 increase (37.44%) in Moral Life's existing loan exposure of $4,201,784 (balance 7/1/75).

2. Moral Life's existing loan exposure is equal to 54.56% of the present indicated property value of $7,700,000.

3. By increasing Moral Life's current interest rate by 1.5% on the existing financing, and providing for a 20 year maturity on the new loan, the effective yield on the increased loan is nearly 14%.

4. The present financing ratios (See Loan Analysis) reflect a nearly identical exposure when compared to Moral Life's original loan. But, the project is now a proven success rather than proposed construction; consequently, it is believed that the new position is better secured than the original financing.

5. Refinancing of the existing loan as indicated will provide Moral Life
    with positive leverage on its present investment insofar as the
    constant on the new money exceeds that of the existing loan.

6. Notwithstanding the added security provided by Silverflow's now seasoned
    operation and the attractive new money yield available via refinancing
    the existing loan, the interest income "kicker" provided in the form
    of a 10% participation in increases in the project's 1975 stabilized
    gross income base of $1,288,500, will increase the overall yield of the
    loan over its 20 year life. The participation feature has been neg-
    otiated to insure Moral Life of an inflationary hedge. An estimate of
    probable increases in gross income receipts supported by our
    assumptions is shown on Exhibit J.

In conclusion, based on our review, and analysis of the project, coupled with
our past experience with the borrower, we strongly recommend this loan as an
excellent addition to Moral Life's investment portfolio.

NORTHLAND MORTGAGE COMPANY

Date: March 1, 1975

               REFINANCING PROPOSAL - SILVERFLOW APARTMENTS

                         PROPERTY LOCATION

METROPOLITAN AREA

The Twin Cities Metropolitan Area has grown to be the largest market between
Chicago and the West Coast north of St. Louis. The U. S. Census of 1970
set the population of the 5 county Standard Metropolitan Statistical Area
(SMSA) at 1,813,647. This represents a 22.4% growth rate for the metropolitan area in the last decade. According to the 1970 census, the Twin Cities
SMSA ranks 15th in population among the nation's metropolitan areas and
third among these 15 largest areas in percentage growth. SMSA population
projections by the Twin Cities Metropolitan Planning Commission predict
nearly two million Twin City residents by 1980 and three million by the year
2,000. The most recent population figure for the Metro Area was in excess of
2,000,000.

In a 1970 report prepared by the Washington D.C. based Urban Institute
entitled "A Study in Comparative Urban Indicators: Conditions in Eighteen
Large Metropolitan Areas", twelve indicators or quality of life were identified
Among these indicators were: Employment, Income, Housing, Health, Public Order
Citizen Participation, Educational Attainment and Transportation. According
to this report, the Twin Cities ranked no lower than 6th in three quarters
of the indicators and was first in two: Health and Citizen Participation. If
each indicator is given equal weight, a composite ranking places the Twin
Cities first among the eighteen metropolitan areas studied.

The economy of the Twin Cities is continuing to expand at a faster rate than the nation's as a whole. As of December, 1974, the seasonally adjusted unemployment rate was 3.2%, with non-agricultural employment at nearly 835,800 persons. If past trends continue, by 1980 over 1,100,000 people will be employed in nonagricultural activities. It is anticipated that most of these new jobs will come from expansion and development of new products by firms or individuals already operating in the Twin City area such as Minnesota Mining and Manufacturing (3M), Honeywell, Pillsbury, General Mills, Cargill, Control Data, Hamm's Brewing, West Publishing, American Hoist and Derrick, Munsingwear, Land-O-Lakes, Investors Diversified Services and others. Employment is dominated by no major company or product classification.

Excellent recreational facilities serve the area. Within an hour's drive are ski resorts, fishing and boating lakes, hunting and camping. Major sports are represented by teams in the largest nationwide leagues of baseball, football, basketball and hockey.

In summary, the nature and size of the Twin Cities area economic activity is strongly influenced by its location relative to the distributional pattern of human and natural resources. The advantageous location factors are: 1) A position athwart the westward trend of national population and industrial growth; 2) A location at the juncture of the industrial East, the agricultural Great Plains and the northern forest, which enables the Twin Cities to draw on a wide variety of resources; 3) An attractive natural environment with abundant nearby opportunities for recreation; 4) A regional population with high standards of health, education, and behavior; and 5) Favorable labor costs. The Minneapolis-St. Paul area is noted for its steady growth and economic stability.

CITY OF EDINA

The subject property is located within the City of Edina. Edina is a first ring suburb approximately eight miles southwest of the Minneapolis CBD. According to the 1970 census, the population of Edina was approximately 44,000; this represents an increase of approximately 13,500 since 1960 or a percentage increase of over 44%. It is anticipated that by 1985 the population of Edina will increase to approximately 65,000.

Edina is the wealthiest and most prestigious suburb in the Twin City Metropolitan Area and, with its excellent school system, its athletic and recreational programs, its broad tax base, its conscientious government and its dedicated citizens, has become a model community. Sales Management and Marketing Magazine describes Edina as having "gilt edge buying power" exceeding $370 million annually, of which $135 million is in retail sales. Eighty-two per cent of Edina households have income in excess of $10,000 and the average effective buying income per household exceeds $25,000. Edina ranks first in average household income among all cities or municipalities in the United States of comparable or larger size.

Edina is a planned community with one of the lowest tax bases in the Metro Area. The Edina Area comprises sixteen square miles of major retail, office, medical and educational facilities which peacefully coexist with parks, golf courses, wildlife and unregimented homes.

NEIGHBORHOOD

The subject is located in Edina's newest and most prestigious commercial-residential area. The areas to the north and east are virtually 100% developed.

The areas to the south and west are approximately 80% developed, principally
with attractive custom built homes, open space, wildlife areas, golf courses,
elementary through senior high schools and recreational facilities.

The subject is situated in a wooded, gently rolling area on an 18.3 acre
parcel which slopes down to a landscaped lake which serves as a catch basin
for the streams and waterfalls which run through the property. The site
fronts on the south side of Melody Lake Road approximately one mile east of
County Road 18, a four lane, divided thoroughfare running from Interstate 494
on the south to Interstate 94 on the north. The area bounding the subject is
also bordered by Crosstown Freeway 62 two miles north, State Highway 100 one
mile east and Interstate 494 one mile south.

Commercial developments in the general area east of the subject include the
Edina Interchange Center Industrial Park, Norman Center Office Park, Pentagon
Office Park, Normandale Industrial Park, Southgate Office Center, Southdale
Regional Shopping Center, and the Radisson South Hotel to highlight only a
few landmarks within a three mile radius. There are also two golf courses
within walking distance of the subject along with many famous restaurants and
several tennis clubs. The area surrounding the subject is the Metro Area's
prime growth sector. In fact, the intersection of Interstate 494 and State
Highway 100 is an area considered to be the third major business district of
the Minneapolis-St. Paul Metropolitan Area.

Driving time to the Minneapolis CBD is roughly 20 minutes; to St. Paul's CBD,
roughly 30 minutes. Twin Cities International Airport, the Metropolitan
Sports Complex, Fairview-Southdale Hospital, and all work, entertainment
and shopping centers can be reached inside of 10-15 minutes. All parts of
the Metro Area are accessible without inconvenience.

COMPETITION AND DEVELOPMENT TREND

Edina is noted for the excellence of its land use plan which was laid out in
the late 1950's. Careful attention was given to density factors, architectural
aesthetics and screening, land patterns and type such that a very homogenous
mix of land use types exist today within a quality transportation and utility
network.

Land still remains available for development in selected areas of Edina, none
which, however, passes any competitive threat to Silverflow. For the most
part, apartment development is complete in the area. As a result of the
strong demand for residential single family land, only one other apartment
complex exists within a three-quarter mile radius of the subject. The
majority of the apartments built in Edina are concentrated south of the
Southdale Shopping Center two miles away. Because of its superior design
and location, Silverflow has tended to lead the rental market. It can generally be said that because of the shortage and high cost of housing, a
lack of further apartment development in the general area and the essential
lack of competition, Silverflow will continue to be a successful apartment
complex.

SUMMARY

The subject is ideally located in a diversified, stable and growing Metro
Area; in the City of Edina, which offers one of the highest standards of
living in the United States; and, in a neighborhood which has been meticulously
planned to offer its residents the finest services and amenities. The status
of and general trend for housing and apartment development can only serve to
improve and secure Silverflow's dominance in the rental market.

REFINANCING PROPOSAL - SILVERFLOW APARTMENTS

PROPERTY DESCRIPTION

SITE

The subject site is located in the northwest quadrant of Interstate 494 and State Highway 100. It fronts specifically on Melody Lake Road between the Indian Hills public golf course and Cahill Road. It has a frontage on the north of 1,489.29 feet. The eastern boundary measures 1,288.41 feet, the southern boundary measures 917.81 feet and the westerly boundary measures 382.39 feet.

The total site contains approximately 944,380 square feet or 21.68 acres. Three hundred sixty apartment units exist on the site in addition to the recreation building. This is equivalent to 16.6 units per acre. Open areas are, therefore, very generous.

The land within the confines of the site and the land adjoining the site has a pleasant rolling terrain and is heavily wooded. The overall topography slopes down to a lake at the southeast corner of the site. The natural aspects of the site have been heavily integrated into the project plan. Streams, ponds and collecting pools and waterfalls empty into the lake and are maintained in a natural setting. The overall effect creates an external setting such as those developed in some of the southwestern and far western areas of the United States.

IMPROVEMENTS

The project consists of six 3 story apartment buildings, each having its own underground heated garage parking. Each building contains 60 apartment units and 60 parking spaces. The apartment mixes are as follows:

	Per Building	Total Complex
1 Bedroom Apartments		
1 Bedroom	16	96
1 Bedroom with Patio	12	72
1 Bedroom with Balcony	8	48
	36	216
2 Bedroom with 2 Baths		
2 Bedroom	4	24
2 Bedroom with Patio	4	24
2 Bedroom with Balcony	4	24
	12	72
2 Bedroom with 1¼ Baths		
2 Bedroom	6	36
2 Bedroom with Patio	2	12
2 Bedroom with Balcony	4	24
	12	72
TOTAL	60	360

The total project contains 360 underground parking spaces and 325 surface parking spaces.

Parking ratio per unit 1.9

Each building has an automatic elevator serving all floors including the garage level. All entryways and hallways are carpeted. Each floor has a laundry and storage area located in the central core near the elevator.

Each unit has a recessed entryway, decorated with various wall treatments to create an individual identity for each resident. The units are very well laid out and provide good traffic patterns, large room sizes and good closet areas. Each unit has either a private balcony or patio. The buildings are centrally heated and the corridors and public areas centrally air conditioned. The apartments have individual air conditioning units and hot water baseboard heat. Amenities include carpeting, good grade plumbing fixtures, stove, hood and fan, refrigerator, disposal and dishwasher.

Unit Breakdown

Type	Number	Rooms	Baths	Area
One Bedroom	216	3½	1	830 SF
Two Bedroom				
A	36	4½	1	985 SF
B	36	4½	1	1,020 SF
C	72	4½	2	1,125 SF

Construction of the improvement is frame with the exception of the ground floor garage facility which is concrete. The exterior finish is brick and stucco. Paneling is used in the balcony areas. The roof is asphalt and gravel 20 year bond type over a 1½" rigid insulation. Interior walls are 5/8" gypsum board with styrofoam sound insulation. Ceilings are ½" Super X one hour rated gypsum board. Special care was taken in insulating and sound-proofing the buildings. The final floor covering is carpet. Bathroom floors and walls are of ceramic tile. Wood doors and trim are used throughout.

The basement area is given over entirely to parking. Service doors are opened by electric door openers. The use of knock-out panels eliminated the need for sprinklering. The garage is properly lighted, heated and ventilated.

The separate recreation building offers an enclosed swimming pool, whirlpools, men's and women's sauna facilities, as well as party and exercise rooms available for the tenants. There are also walk paths, outdoor barbeque facilities and patios.

SUMMARY

The site planning and amenities are far superior to the typical projects built in this metropolitan area. The improvements are extremely well planned, offering an attractive design, excellent layouts and room sizes, and exceptional convenience and recreational amenities.

REFINANCING PROPOSAL - SILVERFLOW APARTMENTS

PROPERTY VALUATION

LAND VALUE (See Exhibit A)

The subject land was purchased in June, 1969 at a price of $417,600 which included certain special assessments against the property. At the time of purchase, this cost was equivalent to $0.44 per square foot or $1,160 per unit. After the property was purchased, we know that certain additional costs were incurred to bring in the sewer and water loops, dredge the lake area and clear the land of trees. The actual additional costs are not known.

In our approach to land value, we gathered data on apartment land sales which occurred between February of 1972 and November of 1974. The parcels involved a wide range of dwelling units in different municipalities. The sale prices on a per square foot basis had a range of from $0.48 to $0.69 per square foot or $1,063 to $1,775 per unit. As was expected, land costs in Edina were higher than in other municipalities. A time and location adjustment was made to attempt to correlate the data.

The land value for the subject was determined on the basis of (a) a time adjustment of 10% per year increase in the subject's value since the original purchase date, (b) a recent sale (comparable #9) which indicated that a land parcel in Edina permitting 200 units sold within the last six months for $1,775 per unit, and (c) an existing ground lease (comparable #8) which indicated a capitalized (10%) minimum and percentage rent income value of $1,800 per unit.

The subject site is highly desirable land with an advantageous location. Measuring the value of the subject by other known land values, the subject is conservatively valued at:

Land Value: 360 Units @ $1,800/Unit $648,000

REPRODUCTION COST APPROACH (See Exhibit B)

The estimate for the current cost of construction is based upon the known costs of recently bid and/or completed apartment properties. As a check, nationally published building costs were reviewed. However, due to the inflationary spiral occurring over the last three years, coupled with the recent downturn in construction activity, the national averages on costs were found to be too imprecise. We, therefore, relied upon actual signed contracts for similar type construction to determine realistic present cost.

A base figure of $12.25 per square foot was found to be the most representative for frame and brick construction containing underground parking and hot water baseboard heating.

Assuming a 40 year life (2.5% per year) and the current actual age of the project (5 years), the accumulated depreciation amounted to 12.5%. However, a physical inspection of the project clearly indicates that the effective depreciation of the project is considerably less than this amount. There is really no evidence of physical, functional or economic obsolescence.

The tenants in the project tend to be well educated, upper middle class residents in the over 30 age group. Significant leasehold improvements are made by the residents in the form of decorating, etc. Management has also taken extraordinary care to maintain and repair the complex with a view to preventative maintenance. As such, minimum depreciation (1/3 of the accumulated economic) amounting to 4% or $277,847 was deducted.

Additional costs pertaining to paving and landscaping, appliances and equipment and the pool and its equipment were determined and applied at their current depreciated costs.

Exclusive of land, the total depreciated cost for the improvements was $7,258,327. Our final figure for reproduction of the project is as follows:

Reproduction Cost Approach to Value:

```
    Improvements . . . . . . . . . . . . . . . . . . .    $7,258,327
    Land     . . . . . . . . . . . . . . . . . . . . .       648,000
    Valuation   . . . . . . . Total . . . . . . . . . .     7,906,327
                              (Rounded)  . . . . . . . .    $7,900,000
```

MARKET DATA APPROACH (See Exhibit C)

Information on five recent sales of apartment properties were obtained and correlated with the subject. All of the sales occurred between February, 1972 and October, 1974. The sale prices ranged from 5.78 to 6.79 times the annual gross income with the gross income multiplier tending to decrease with the increase in property age and increase with the property's size and quality.

In view of the size, quality and age of the subject, and based on the income multipliers reflected in the sale of other similar properties in the same general area, a gross income multiplier of 6-6.25 times was felt to be realistic To be on the conservative side, however, the lower multiple was chosen. Gross income multipliers can be good indicators of a value range, but fail to include and reflect underlying financing arrangements which affect value. The case is particularly true during the last five years with the increases in rental income followed by higher yield and debt financing requirements.

Market Data Approach to Value:

```
    Valuation:
        $1,288,500 Gross Income x 6 . . . . . . . . . .    $7,731,000
                          (Rounded) . . . . . . . . .      $7,700,000
```

ECONOMIC APPROACH (See Exhibits D, E and F)

Rental Income:

In arriving at a fair market rental, the audited income statements were analyzed and compared with rent comparables on similar one and two bedroom units that possess a comparable amenity package. The rent schedule currently in effect at Silverflow is in part determined by view and location in the building as follows:

Type	#	Rooms	Baths	Rentable Area	Monthly Rent	Per Room Per Month	Per S.F. Per Year	Per S.F. Per Month
One Bedroom	36	4½	1	985 SF	$295.00	$65.55	$3.59	$0.30
	36	4½	1	1,020 SF	315.00	70.00	3.70	0.308
	24	4½	2	1,125 SF	335.00	74.44	3.57	0.297
	48	4½	2	1,125 SF	345.00	76.67	3.68	0.307
Two Bedroom	24	3½	1	830 SF	210.00	60.00	3.03	0.252
	72	3½	1	830 SF	230.00	65.71	3.32	0.277
	120	3½	1	830 SF	255.00	72.86	3.69	0.307

Garages   360 spaces @ $20.00/Month
                 (Minimum: One space per tenant required by lease)

Silverflow was opened in 1971. Since that time rental income from this
and similar type property has increased significantly. A review of the
rent comparables will show that while not unrealistic, the current rent
schedule is in the upper range. This is only because demand for the units
has allowed the rents to rise to this level. Factors such as a location
in a wooded, rustic setting; appealing design of the buildings; underground
parking to blunt the effect of winter weather; generous equipment and
recreational facilities, have attracted many people. In addition to its
location in the City of Edina, the convenience to all family and business
oriented facilities has created a strong long term market for the units.
There is no threat of competition and while deluxe, the building is not of a
luxury class which reaches into the upper limits of the rental range. It
is unlikely that any of these facts will change or that Edina will lose its
prestigious character. The gross annual rental income can, therefore, be
stabilized per the schedule as follows:

Total Annual Income:

Apartments	$1,185,120
Underground Parking	86,400
Washer/Dryer/Vending	17,000
(3 year average)	
Total	$1,288,520
(Rounded)	$1,288,500

Vacancy Allowance:

The subject has had a very successful occupancy history since coming on the
market. Even through the very soft market period which the Metro Area
experienced in 1973, rents continued to rise and vacancies were below average.
The subject has had a high of 4% in vacancy and a low of 1.5%. No units were
vacant as of December, 1974. This low can partially be attributed to the
fact that few people choose the months of December-January to relocate.
Natural turnover will occur as the warmer months come up. A typical vacancy
allowance would be 5% of gross income. We have used a 4% allowance, however,
because of the property's previous occupancy history; the fact that management maintains an above average operation; and the fact that Silverflow
attracts a quality tenant who has proven to invest in leasehold improvements
thereby indicating an intent to remain in occupancy longer than is usually
experienced in similar type properties.

Gross Income of $1,288,500 @ 4% . . . . $ 51,540

REAL ESTATE TAXES (See Exhibit G)

The actual real estate taxes due in 1975 are $259,960 which is 5% over those
due in 1974. The taxes due in 1975 on six other apartment projects in Edina
were obtained and show a range of from $167-$245 per room and from $622-$858
per unit. Real estate taxes for the subject amount to $185 per room, $722
per unit and 21% of effective gross income, which is realistic. There are
no due or pending special assessments against the subject.

Real Estate Taxes . . . . $ 259,960

PROPERTY INSURANCE

The insurance premium of $13,150 is based on the actual contract which runs
for an additional two years. The amount is in line with other projects and
amounts to $9.37 per room.

1,404 Rooms x $9.37/Room . . . . $ 13,150

OPERATING EXPENSES

Management Fee:

Professional management for this type of project is typically 4% of collected annual income. Present management operates under this same fee
schedule.

Effective Gross Income: $1,236,960 x .04 . . . . . . $49,480
                                                       (Rounded)

Fuel:

Each building has its own heating plant on a hot water baseboard system
which is fired by a gas interruptible oil heating plant, providing for
a very efficient system. While heating costs have been rising generally,
the project's cost experience is in line with similar operations. To
offset any possible increases in costs, we have chosen to indicate a
slightly higher charge for 1975 as follows:

1404 Rooms @ $15.00/Room $21,100
                                                      (Rounded)

Electric and Gas:

As is typical for this area, the tenant pays for electricity for his
lights, air conditioning and other appliances and the landlord pays
for the lighting of the common areas of the buildings and the grounds.
Based on the owner's experience and that of other similar projects,
an estimate for electricity and gas for the subject property of $6 per
room is more than adequate. We have checked this estimate with Northern
States Power Company and they believe that the estimate is ample. Therefore, this item of expense has been calculated as follows:

1404 Rooms @ $6.00/Room . . . . $ 8,400
                                                      (Rounded)

<u>Water</u>:

The water for the subject property is used principally for domestic purposes. Lawn sprinkling and water for the meandering streams are provided for by private wells. Based on the experience of many other apartment projects, an allowance for water of $25 per unit per year will be adequate. The water expense, therefore, is estimated as follows:

360 Units @ $25.00 . . . . $ 9,000

<u>Janitor</u>:

For apartment projects of over 100 units, the standard management arrangement in the Minneapolis area is for the managing agent to provide a resident manager as a part of the management fee. Therefore, the duties of the janitors for the subject property are limited to custodial and caretaking matters. The compensation of janitors in this area rarely exceeds $60 per unit per year. In view of the large size of the subject project, there is more than one janitor and, therefore, the caretaking duties are relatively less than if there were only one janitor. An allowance of $60 per unit per year for the janitor is more than adequate. Therefore, the estimated janitor expense is as follows:

360 Units @ $60.00 . . . . $21,600

<u>Painting and Decorating</u>:

In a complex the size of the subject property, expenditures for painting and decorating can be scheduled and performed on a continuing basis which effects a substantial reduction in cost. Based on the project's experience, the painting and decorating of tenant areas can easily be accomplished for $9 per room per year. The painting and decorating of public areas will be adequately covered by an allowance of $3 per room per year. Estimates for future painting and decorating have therefore been calculated as follows:

Tenant Areas:	1,404 rooms @ $10.00 =	$14,000 (Rounded)
Other Areas:	1,404 rooms @ 4.00 =	5,600 (Rounded)
T .al:	1,404 rooms @ $14.00 =	$19,600 (Rounded)

<u>General Repair</u>:

The materials and equipment used in the subject property are of a high quality and therefore result in an expense for general repairs of less than typical allowances. An allowance of $6 per room per year is typically ample for this category of expense. However, because of the quality of the subject property and the necessity of superior maintenance, we have used an allowance for general repairs of $7 per room per year, which should be adequate for the subject property. Therefore, the estimate for general repairs is as follows:

1,404 Rooms @ $7.00/Room . . . . $ 9,800
                                                        (Rounded)

Elevators:

The subject property has six elevators, each having four stops for a
total of 24 stops in the project. Elevator service contracts in other
projects having only one elevator range from $7 to $9 per stop per month.
Therefore, we have used an allowance of $8 per stop per month, and
estimate as follows:

24 Stops @ $8.00 x 12 Months . . . . $ 2,300
                                                     (Rounded)

Replacement Reserves: (See Exhibit B-2)

The schedule of appliances and equipment and carpeting is a summary of
the equipment and carpeting costs and the annual reserves for the subject
property. Because of the large size of the subject property and the
fact that the builder buys appliances in carload lots, the appliance
costs will be minimal; the unit prices used are the prices at which the
appliances for this project can be purchased. The total cost of
appliances per unit is in excess of $600, which reflects the quality
of the equipment to be used. We have projected a useful life of 15 years
for the ranges, refrigerators and disposals, 12 years for the air conditioning units and 10 years for the dishwashers; we believe these
allowances to be realistic for this area.

In estimating the reserve for carpeting, we have calculated that the total
carpeting required will be approximately 30,600 yards. The carpeting
will be of a $10 per square yard quality but, because of the large
quantity of carpeting being used on this project as well as the bulk
purchasing by the builder, the actual cost of the carpeting for the subject
property will be reduced to $7 per yard. Through regular cleaning and
rotation, the life of this grade carpet can conservatively be estimated
at 10 years.

Therefore, allowances for replacement reserves are as follows:

Equipment	$17,600	@	$ 49.00 per unit
Carpeting	21,400	@	59.50 per unit
Total	$39,000	@	$108.50 per unit

Miscellaneous:

The expense of snow removal, garbage collection, pool maintenance is
based on actual contracts. Additional costs for supplies, fees, etc.
must be considered. An allowance of $13.50 per unit is adequate.

Therefore, the allowance for miscellaneous expense is as follows:

360 Units @ $12.50/Unit . . . . $ 4,500

PRO FORMA OPERATING STATEMENT

Gross Income $1,288,500
    Vacancy @ 4%   51,540
Effective Gross Income   1,236,960

Expenses:

Real Estate Taxes	$259,960
Property Insurance	13,150
Management Fee	49,480
Fuel	21,100
Electric and Gas	8,400
Water	9,000
Janitor	21,600
Painting and Decorating	19,600
General Repair	9,800
Elevators	2,300
Supplies	1,450
Replacement Reserves	39,000
Miscellaneous	4,500

Total Expenses   459,340

Net Operating Income . . . . $ 777,620

CAPITALIZATION (See Exhibit H)

The Ellwood Method has been used to determine the capitalization rate. In our opinion, the assumptions used are completely valid in reflecting current equity yields and mortgage rates available for this type of property which is owned in fee simple title. The rate established by the Ellwood Method is 10.15%. The net operating income capitalized at 10.15% is as follows:

Economic Approach to Value:

Valuation: $777,620 ÷ .1015 . . . . $7,661,281
                                 (Rounded). $7,700,000

CORRELATION OF VALUE

The present value of the subject property has been estimated according to three approaches as follows:

Physical Value $7,900,000

Market Value $7,700,000

Economic Value $7,700,000

For mortgage loan purposes, it is generally determined that Economic Approach is the most meaningful, and since in this case it also correlates with the lower value indicated by the three methods, a conservative posture will be taken by using the Economic Value. Therefore, the value of the subject is established as:

Indicated Value $7,700,000

LAND SALE COMPARABLES

(EXHIBIT A)

LOCATION	MUNICIPILITY	SALE DATE	PRICE	S.F. AREA	UNITS ALLOWED	PRICE PER S.F.	PRICE PER UNIT	LOCATION ADJUSTMENT	TIME (1) ADJUSTMENT	ADJUSTED PRICE/UNIT
S. W. Corner of Hwy. 7 & 18	Hopkins	2-72	$345,475	707,850	325	$0.488	$1,063	+20%	+30%	$1,595
York Avenue & Byerly Road	Edina	6-73	64,800	128,118	50	$0.505	$1,296	+10%	+15%	$1,620 (2)
Dance Avenue & Tracy Road	Edina	5-72	168,000	320,295	125	$0.524	$1,344	+ 5%	+25%	$1,747
Blake Road & Excelsior Blvd.	Hopkins	12-73	175,000	322,324	148	$0.542	$1,182	+20%	+10%	$1,537
N.E. Corner Hwy. 62 & 18	Edina	8-74	136,890	230,612	90	$0.593	$1,521	+10%	--	$1,673
Shady Lake Road & Hwy. 62	Minnetonka	3-73	732,600	1,187,999	600	$0.616	$1,221	+15%	+20%	$1,648
West 78th Street & Normandale	Bloomington	4-72	145,700	271,039	112	$0.537	$1,300	+10%	+25%	$1,755
Cahill Road - West 70th St.	Edina	10-72	Ground Lease		180	Minimum	+ % Rent ÷ 10% Cap Rate		=	$1,800
Wind Avenue & Wood Lake	Edina	11-74	355,000	512,471	200	$0.692	$1,775	--	--	$1,775
SUBJECT	Edina	6-69	417,600	944,380	360	$0.442	$1,160	--	+55%	$1,800

Notes:

(1) Time adjustment equals 10% per year.

(2) Site had soil problems.

LAND COMPARABLES

1. Southwest Corner of Highway #7 and 18

    Hopkins municipality. Sold February, 1972 for $325,000 plus $20,475
    in special assessments or a total consideration of $345,475. The
    site contained 707,850 square feet and permitted 325 apartment units
    (20 units per acre). Total consideration was equal to $0.488 per
    square foot or $1,063 per unit. Property is located in an older area
    which does not have good access to shopping and the freeway system;
    + 20% location adjustment.

2. York Avenue and Byerly Road

    Edina municipality. Sold June, 1973 for $64,800. The site contained
    128,118 square feet and was permitted 50 units (17 units per acre).
    Total consideration was equal to $0.505 per square foot or $1,296 per
    unit. Property is located in well kept, older area of Edina which
    does not have proximity to shopping, etc.; +10% location adjustment.
    Site had soil problems which cost $5,000 to cure. This adjustment
    ($100/unit), if added to the indicated adjusted price, would bring the
    final figure to $1,720/unit.

3. Dance Avenue and Tracy Road

    Edina municipality. Sold May, 1972 for $168,000. The site contained
    320,295 square feet and permitted 125 units (17 units per acre). Total
    consideration was equal to $0.524 per square foot or $1,344 per unit.
    Property is located in excellent residential setting, but lacks same
    access to recreational public and private facilities afforded subject;
    + 5% location adjustment.

4. Blake Road and Excelsior Boulevard

    Hopkins municipality. Sold December, 1973 for $175,000. The site contained
    322,324 square feet and permitted 148 apartment units (20 units per acre).
    Total consideration was equal to $0.542 per square foot or $1,182 per
    unit. Property is located adjacent to shopping, railway and heavily
    traveled artery; + 20% location adjustment.

5. Northeast Corner of Highway 62 and 18

    Edina municipality. Sold August, 1974 for $135,000 plus $1,890 in
    special assessments or a total consideration of $136,890. The site
    contained 230,612 square feet and was permitted 90 units (17 units per
    acre). Total consideration was equal to $0.593 per square foot or $1,521
    per unit. The property is located in a newer area of Edina which is not
    as heavily wooded and rolling as the subject site and generally lacks
    the subject's access to offices, shopping, etc.; + 10% location adjustment.

6. Shady Lake Road and Highway 62

    Minnetonka municipality. Sold March, 1973 for $732,600. The site
    contained 1,187,999 square feet and was permitted 600 units (22 units
    per acre). Total consideration was equal to $0.616 per square foot or
    $1,221 per unit. The property has a generally central location per-
    taining to shopping facilities and freeway access, but lacks the subject's
    proximity to work locations; + 15% location adjustment.

7. <u>West 78th Street and Normandale</u>

   Bloomington municipality. Sold April, 1972 for $145,700. The site
   contained 271,039 square feet and was permitted 112 units (18 units per
   acre). Total consideration was equal to $0.537 per square foot or
   $1,300 per unit. The property is located within a commercial area that
   lacks the residential character and conveniences of the subject; + 10%
   location adjustment.

8. <u>Cahill Road and West 70th Street</u>

   Edina municipality. The land was leased in October of 1972 for a
   minimum rent of $17,000 per year and percent rent equal to 10% of
   the net income receipts or approximately 15,400 in 1974. The total
   lease income of $32,400 capitalized at 10% equals $324,000. The site
   allowed 180 units (17 units per acre) which indicates a present land
   value of $1,800 per unit. The site is within a mile of the subject
   and requires no location adjustment.

9. <u>Wind Avenue and Wood Lane</u>

   Edina municipality. The site was sold November, 1974 for $355,000. It
   contains 512,471 square feet and is permitted 200 units (17 units per
   acre). Total consideration is equal to $0.692 per square foot or
   $1,775 per unit. The site is within a mile of the subject and requires
   no location adjustment.

PHYSICAL VALUE

(EXHIBIT B)

<u>IMPROVEMENTS</u>

   Total Building Area:

       567,036 SF @ $12.25/SF $6,946,191

   Less Accumulated Effective Depreciation:

       2.5%/Year x 5 Years x 33% = 4% 277,847

       Subtotal: Buildings 6,668,344

   Paving and Landscaping:

654,416 SF @ $0.30/SF	$196,325	
Less Effective Depreciation @ 4% . . .	7,853	
Balance		188,472

   Appliances and Equipment:

See Schedule	$221,256	
Carpeting:		
See Schedule	214,200	
Total	435,456	
Less Effective Depreciation @ 10% . .	43,545	
Balance		391,911

```
          Pool and Equipment . . . . . . . . . .  $ 10,000
          Less Effective Depreciation @ 4% . . .       400
          Balance . . . . . . . . . . . . . . . . . .            9,600
```

```
   Total Improvements . . . . . . . . . . . . . . . .  $7,258,327
```

LAND

```
   360 Units @ $1,800/Unit . . . . . . . . . . . . . .  $  648,000
```

```
Total Physical Value  . . . . . . . . . . . . . . . .  $7,906,327
```

```
                           (Rounded)  . . . . . . .    $7,900,000
```

Building Dimensions

(Exhibit B-1)

A. **Gross Apartment Area**

Typical Floor

```
        129' x 68'      =     8,772 sq. ft.
      + 30' x 73.17'    =     2,195 sq. ft.
      +  8.5' x 37'     =       315 sq. ft.
```

Gross Area per Side	11,282 sq. ft.	
Times 2 Sides	x 2	
Gross Area both Sides	22,564 sq. ft.	

Core

```
      12.5' x 68' x 1/2 x 2   =            850 sq. ft.
```

Gross Area per Floor	23,414 sq. ft.	
Times 3 Apartment Floors	x 3	
Gross Apartment Area per Building		70,242 sq. ft.
Times 6 Buildings		x 6
Total Gross Apartment Area		421,452 sq. ft.

B. **Gross Area of Parking Garage**

Gross Area per Floor (As above)	23,414 sq. ft.
Times 6 Buildings	x 6
Total Gross Area of Parking Garage	140,484 sq. ft.

C.   Gross Area of Recreation Building

     Pool Building - 60' x 50'   =   3,000 sq. ft.

     Party Building - 50' x 42'   =   2,100 sq. ft.

     Gross Area   5,100 sq. ft.

D.   Cubic Content of Apartment Areas

     Ground Floor Area per Building   23,414 sq. ft.

        Times 6 Buildings   x 6

     Total Ground Floor Area   140,484 sq. ft.

     Above Ground Building Height   30 feet

     Total Cubic Content of Apartment Areas   4,214,520 Cu. Ft.

E.   Cubic Content of Parking Garage

     Total Gross Parking Garage   140,484 sq. ft.

     Garage Height   9.5 feet

     Total Cubic Content of Parking Garage   1,334,598 Cu. Ft.

F.   Cubic Content of Recreation Building

     Pool Building . . . .   3,000 sq. ft.

     Average Height . . . .   19 feet

     Cubage . . . .   57,000 Cu. Ft.

     Party Building . . . .   2,100 sq. ft.

     Average Height . . . .   10 feet

                                         21,000 Cu. Ft.

     Total Cubic Content of Recreational Building   78,000 Cu. Ft.

G.   Recapitulation

	Gross Area	Cubic Content
Apartment Areas	421,452 Sq. Ft.	4,214,520 Cu. Ft.
Parking Garage	140,484 Sq. Ft.	1,334,598 Cu. Ft.
Recreation Building	5,100 Sq. Ft.	78,000 Cu. Ft.
Total	567,036 Sq. Ft.	5,627,118 Cu. Ft.

SCHEDULE OF APPLIANCES AND EQUIPMENT

(Exhibit B-2)

	Unit Price	Number	Total Cost	Life	Reserve per Year
Ranges	$115.00	360	$ 41,400	15	$ 2,760
Refrigerators	136.00	360	48,960	15	3,264
Disposals	22.00	360	7,920	15	528
Air Conditioning	144.00	504	72,576	12	6,048
Dishwashers	140.00	360	50,400	10	5,040
Total			$221,256		$17,640
			$641.60 per unit		$49.00 per unit

Carpeting

Type Unit	Number of Each	Yards Carpet Each	Total Yards
A	36	82.2	2,959.2
B	36	75.3	2,710.8
C	72	89.5	6,444.0
D	216	68.4	14,774.4
Halls	18	206.0	3,708.0
Total Carpeting			30,596.4 yards
		Called	30,600 yards

Total . . . . @ $7.00 per yard $214,200

Annual Reserve: (10 year life) . . . . $ 21,420

APARTMENT SALE COMPARABLES
(EXHIBIT C)

	Year Built	Sale Date	Sale Price	Gross Income	# Units	# Rooms	Price per Unit	Price per Room
1 7450 Xerxes Avenue	1967	3-73	$ 4,525,000	782,872	215	699	$ 21,046	$ 6,473
2 4715 W. Blake Road	1973	10-74	1,275,000	187,776	55	165	23,182	7,727
3 2800 E. Diamond Lake	1972	8-72	2,950,000	479,675	135	506	21,851	5,830
4 5100 Brookside	1968	9-73	2,000,000	344,828	96	331	20,833	6,042
5 6720 France	1971	2-74	6,000,000	978,420	300	1,110	20,000	5,405
Subject	1970	-	7,731,000	1,288,500	360	1,404	21,475	5,506

REAL ESTATE SALES COMPARABLES
(APARTMENTS)

Address   7450 Xerxes Avenue   City Bloomington   State   Minn.

Year Built   1967   No. of Units 215   No. of Rooms   699

PHOTOGRAPH

(March)
DATE OF SALE - 19 73 .   SALE PRICE - $ 4,525,000

GROSS INCOME (time of sale) $ 782,872

Gross Income Multiplier   5.78

Price paid per Unit $ 21,046

Price paid per Room $ 6,473

COMMENTS: Three story brick veneer, outside pool, detached garages.

Comp. # 2

REAL ESTATE SALES COMPARABLES
(APARTMENTS)

Address 4715 W. Blake Road   City   Hopkins   State   Minnesota

Year Built   1973   No. of Units 55   No. of Rooms   165

PHOTOGRAPH

(October)
DATE OF SALE - 19 74 .   SALE PRICE - $ 1,275,000

GROSS INCOME (time of sale) $ 187,776

Gross Income Multiplier		6.79
Price paid per Unit	$	23,182
Price paid per Room	$	7,727

COMMENTS: Four story and ground floor luxury masonry building. Year round
          pool, sauna, central air, underground parking, elevatored.

Comp. # ___3___

REAL ESTATE SALES COMPARABLES
(APARTMENTS)

Address __2800 E. Diamond Lake__   City __Minneapolis__   State __Minn.__

Year Built ___1972___   No. of Units __135__   No. of Rooms __506__

PHOTOGRAPH

(February)
DATE OF SALE – 19_72___.   SALE PRICE – $ _2,950,000___

GROSS INCOME (time of sale) $ __479,675_____

      Gross Income Multiplier   6.15

      Price paid per Unit   21,851

      Price paid per Room   5,830

COMMENTS: Four buildings, 2½ story walk-up. No elevator, outside pool, detached garages.

Comp. #   4

REAL ESTATE SALES COMPARABLES
(APARTMENTS)

Address   5100 Brookside   City   Edina   State   Minnesota

Year Built   1968   No. of Units   96   No. of Rooms   331

PHOTOGRAPH

                                    (September)
DATE OF SALE - 19 73 .   SALE PRICE - $ 2,000,000

GROSS INCOME (time of sale) $ 344,828

          Gross Income Multiplier   5.80

          Price paid per Unit   20,833

          Price paid per Room   6,042

COMMENTS: 3 Story, detached garages. Outside pool, sauna and exercise room.

Comp. #   5

REAL ESTATE SALES COMPARABLES
(APARTMENTS)

Address 6720 France   City   Edina   State   Minn.

Year Built   1971   No. of Units   300   No. of Rooms   1,110

PHOTOGRAPH

(February)
DATE OF SALE - 19 74 .   SALE PRICE - $ 6,000,000

GROSS INCOME (time of sale) $ 978,420

            Gross Income Multiplier   6.13

            Price paid per Unit   20,000

            Price paid per Room   5,405

COMMENTS: Four buildings, 3 story, basement garage, no elevator, no pool.

YEARS ENDED DECEMBER 31, 1971-1974

(Exhibit D)

	1971	1972	1973	1974
Income:				
Apartment & Garage	$ 989,489	$1,047,752	$1,156,770	$1,268,280
Washer, Dryer, Vending	10,800	15,300	17,700	18,050
Total Income	$1,000,289	$1,063,052	$1,174,470	$1,286,330
Expense:				
Real Estate Tax	$ 112,750	$ 202,918	$ 234,650	$ 247,000
Property Insurance	10,700	10,700	13,150	13,150
Management Fee	40,011	42,522	46,979	51,453
Fuel	16,940	17,670	19,450	20,300
Electric & Gas	6,177	6,259	7,543	7,865
Water	8,598	8,755	8,700	8,850
Janitor	18,356	19,475	19,500	20,245
Painting & Decorating	8,751	12,430	17,780	18,400
General Repair	5,150	8,275	9,151	9,455
Elevators	1,950	1,975	2,033	2,150
Supplies	1,176	1,150	1,239	1,275
Replacement Reserve	34,000	34,000	34,000	34,000
Miscellaenous	3,599	3,650	3,874	4,122
Total Expense	$ 268,138	$ 369,059	$ 418,049	$ 438,265
NET INCOME	$ 732,151	$ 693,993	$ 756,421	$ 848,065

SUMMARY OF APARTMENT RENT

2/28/75

(Exhibit E)

Building Address	Income Per Month	Income Per Year
10101 Melody Lake Road	$ 17,645	$ 211,740
10201 Melody Lake Road	17,470	209,640
10301 Melody Lake Road	17,445	209,340
10111 Melody Lake Road	17,710	212,520
10211 Melody Lake Road	17,710	212,520
10311 Melody Lake Road	17,710	212,520
Actual Income – Apartments & Garages	$105,690	$1,268,280
Scheduled Income	107,377	1,288,520
Deficit	$ 1,687	$ 20,240
Current Vacancy Factor		1.57%

SILVERFLOW APARTMENTS
10101 MELODY LAKE ROAD

EDINA, MINNESOTA

APT. NO.		
101	2BR	$ 335.00
102	2BR	315.00
103	2BR	365.00
104	2BR	365.00
105	1BR	270.00
106	1BR	270.00
107	1BR	270.00
108	1BR	270.00
109	1BR	270.00
110	1BR	270.00
111	1BR	270.00
112	1BR	270.00
113	1BR	275.00
114	1BR	270.00
115	1BR	270.00
116	1BR	270.00
117	2BR	365.00
118	2BR	365.00
119	2BR	335.00
120	2BR	315.00
201	2BR	335.00
202	2BR	315.00
203	2BR	365.00
204	2BR	355.00
205	1BR	250.00
206	1BR	270.00
207	1BR	250.00
208	1BR	270.00
209	1BR	250.00
210	1BR	250.00
211	1BR	250.00
212	1BR	250.00
213	1BR	250.00
214	1BR	270.00
215	1BR	250.00
216	1BR	270.00
217	2BR	365.00
218	2BR	355.00
219	2BR	335.00
220	2BR	315.00

APT. NO.		
301	2BR	$ 335.00
302	2BR	315.00
303	2BR	365.00
304	2BR	355.00
305	1BR	250.00
306	1BR	270.00
307	1BR	250.00
308	1BR	270.00
309	1BR	250.00
310	1BR	250.00
311	1BR	250.00
312	1BR	250.00
313	1BR	250.00
314	1BR	270.00
315	1BR	250.00
316	1BR	270.00
317	2BR	365.00
318	2BR	355.00
319	2BR	335.00
320	2BR	315.00

TOTAL RENTS $17,645.00

SILVERFLOW APARTMENTS
10201 MELODY LAKE ROAD

EDINA, MINNESOTA

APT. NO.				APT. NO		
101	2BR	$	335.00	301	2BR	$	335.00
102	2BR		315.00	302	2BR		315.00
103	2BR		365.00	303	2BR		365.00
104	2BR		365.00	304	2BR		355.00
105	1BR		270.00	305	1BR		230.00
106	1BR		275.00	306	1BR		275.00
107	1BR		270.00	307	1BR		230.00
108	1BR		275.00	308	1BR		275.00
109	1BR		270.00	309	1BR		230.00
110	1BR		275.00	310	1BR		250.00
111	1BR		270.00	311	1BR		230.00
112	1BR		275.00	312	1BR		250.00
113	1BR		270.00	313	1BR		230.00
114	1BR		275.00	314	1BR		275.00
115	1BR		270.00	315	1RR		230.00
116	1BR		275.00	316	1BR		275.00
117	2BR		365.00	317	2BR		365.00
118	2BR		365.00	318	2BR		355.00
119	2BR		335.00	319	2BR		335.00
120	2BR		315.00	320	2BR		315.00

TOTAL RENTS $ 17,470.00

201	2BR	335.00
202	2BR	315.00
203	2BR	365.00
204	2BR	355.00
205	1BR	230.00
206	1BR	275.00
207	1BR	230.00
208	1BR	275.00
209	1BR	230.00
210	1BR	250.00
211	1BR	230.00
212	1BR	250.00
213	1BR	230.00
214	1BR	275.00
215	1BR	230.00
216	1BR	275.00
217	2BR	365.00
218	2BR	355.00
219	2BR	335.00
220	2BR	315.00

SILVERFLOW APARTMENTS
10301 MELODY LAKE ROAD

EDINA, MINNESOTA

APT. NO.				APT. NO.			
101	2BR	$	335.00	301	2BR	$	335.00
102	2BR		315.00	302	2BR		315.00
103	2BR		365.00	303	2BR		365.00
104	2BR		365.00	304	2BR		355.00
105	1BR		270.00	305	1BR		230.00
106	1BR		275.00	306	1BR		275.00
107	1BR		270.00	307	1BR		230.00
108	1BR		275.00	308	1BR		275.00
109	1BR		270.00	309	1BR		230.00
110	1BR		275.00	310	1BR		250.00
111	1BR		270.00	311	1BR		230.00
112	1BR		275.00	312	1BR		250.00
113	1BR		270.00	313	1BR		230.00
114	1BR		275.00	314	1BR		275.00
115	1BR		270.00	315	1BR		230.00
116	1BR		275.00	316	1BR		275.00
117	2BR		365.00	317	2BR		365.00
118	2BR		365.00	318	2BR		355.00
119	2BR		335.00	319	2BR		335.00
120	2BR		315.00	320	2BR		315.00

201	2BR		335.00				
202	2BR		315.00	TOTAL RENTS		$17,445.00	
203	2BR		365.00				
204	2BR		355.00				
205	1BR		230.00				
206	1BR		275.00				
207	1BR		230.00				
208	1BR		275.00				
209	1BR		230.00				
210	1BR		250.00				
211	1BR		230.00				
212	1BR		250.00				
213	1BR		230.00				
214	1BR		250.00				
215	1BR		230.00				
216	1BR		275.00				
217	2BR		365.00				
218	2BR		355.00				
219	2BR		335.00				
220	2BR		315.00				

SILVERFLOW APARTMENTS
10111 MELODY LAKE ROAD

EDINA, MINNESOTA

APT. NO.			APT. NO.		
101	2BR	$ 335.00	301	2BR	$ 335.00
102	2BR	315.00	302	2BR	315.00
103	2BR	365.00	303	2BR	365.00
104	2BR	365.00	304	2BR	355.00
105	1BR	270.00	305	1BR	250.00
106	1BR	275.00	306	1BR	275.00
107	1BR	270.00	307	1BR	250.00
108	1BR	275.00	308	1BR	275.00
109	1BR	270.00	309	1BR	250.00
110	1BR	275.00	310	1BR	250.00
111	1BR	270.00	311	1BR	250.00
112	1BR	275.00	312	1BR	250.00
113	1BR	270.00	313	1BR	250.00
114	1BR	275.00	314	1BR	275.00
115	1BR	270.00	315	1BR	250.00
116	1BR	275.00	316	1BR	275.00
117	2BR	365.00	317	2BR	365.00
118	2BR	365.00	318	2BR	355.00
119	2BR	335.00	319	2BR	335.00
120	2BR	315.00	320	2BR	315.00

201	2BR	335.00			
202	2BR	315.00	TOTAL RENTS		$17,710.00
203	2BR	365.00			
204	2BR	355.00			
205	1BR	250.00			
206	1BR	275.00			
207	1BR	250.00			
208	1BR	275.00			
209	1BR	250.00			
210	1BR	250.00			
211	1BR	250.00			
212	1BR	250.00			
213	1BR	250.00			
214	1BR	275.00			
215	1BR	250.00			
216	1BR	275.00			
217	2BR	365.00			
218	2BR	355.00			
219	2BR	335.00			
220	2BR	315.00			

SILVERFLOW APARTMENTS
10211 MELODY LAKE ROAD

EDINA, MINNESOTA

APT. NO			APT. NO.		
101	2BR	$ 335.00	301	2BR	$ 335.00
102	2BR	315.00	302	2BR	315.00
103	2BR	365.00	303	2BR	365.00
104	2BR	365.00	304	2BR	355.00
105	1BR	275.00	305	1BR	250.00
106	1BR	275.00	306	1BR	275.00
107	1BR	275.00	307	1BR	250.00
108	1BR	275.00	308	1BR	275.00
109	1BR	275.00	309	1BR	250.00
110	1BR	275.00	310	1BR	250.00
111	1BR	275.00	311	1BR	250.00
112	1BR	275.00	312	1BR	250.00
113	1BR	275.00	313	1BR	250.00
114	1BR	275.00	314	1BR	275.00
115	1BR	275.00	315	1BR	250.00
116	1BR	275.00	316	1BR	275.00
117	2BR	365.00	317	2BR	365.00
118	2BR	365.00	318	2BR	355.00
119	2BR	335.00	319	2BR	335.00
120	2BR	315.00	320	2BR	315.00

201	2BR	335.00	TOTAL RENTS		$17,710.00
202	2BR	315.00			
203	2BR	365.00			
204	2BR	355.00			
205	1BR	250.00			
206	1BR	275.00			
207	1BR	250.00			
208	1BR	275.00			
209	1BR	250.00			
210	1BR	250.00			
211	1BR	250.00			
212	1BR	250.00			
213	1BR	250.00			
214	1BR	275.00			
215	1BR	250.00			
216	1BR	275.00			
217	2BR	365.00			
218	2BR	355.00			
219	2BR	335.00			
220	2BR	315.00			

SILVERFLOW APARTMENTS
10311 MELODY LAKE ROAD

EDINA, MINNESOTA

APT. NO.				APT. NO.			
101	2BR	$	335.00	301	2BR	$	335.00
102	2BR		315.00	302	2BR		315.00
103	2BR		365.00	303	2BR		365.00
104	2BR		365.00	304	2BR		355.00
105	1BR		270.00	305	1BR		250.00
106	1BR		275.00	306	1BR		275.00
107	1BR		270.00	307	1BR		250.00
108	1BR		275.00	308	1BR		275.00
109	1BR		270.00	309	1BR		250.00
110	1BR		275.00	310	1BR		250.00
111	1BR		270.00	311	1BR		250.00
112	1BR		275.00	312	1BR		250.00
113	1BR		270.00	313	1BR		250.00
114	1BR		275.00	314	1BR		275.00
115	1BR		270.00	315	1BR		250.00
116	1BR		275.00	316	1BR		275.00
117	2BR		365.00	317	2BR		365.00
118	2BR		365.00	318	2BR		355.00
119	2BR		335.00	319	2BR		335.00
120	2BR		315.00	320	2BR		315.00

201	2BR		335.00	TOTAL RENTS		$17,710.00	
202	2BR		315.00				
203	2BR		365.00				
204	2BR		355.00				
205	1BR		250.00				
206	1BR		275.00				
207	1BR		250.00				
208	1BR		275.00				
209	1BR		250.00				
210	1BR		250.00				
211	1BR		250.00				
212	1BR		250.00				
213	1BR		250.00				
214	1BR		275.00				
215	1BR		250.00				
216	1BR		275.00				
217	2BR		365.00				
218	2BR		355.00				
219	2BR		335.00				
220	2BR		315.00				

SCHEDULED RENT – UNIT/INCOME BREAKDOWN
1/1/75

(EXHIBIT F)

TYPE	NUMBER	BATHS	ROOMS	S/F RENTABLE AREA	MONTHLY RENT	PER ROOM PER MONTH	PER S/F PER YEAR	PER S/F PER MONTH
TWO BEDROOM								
A	36	1	4½	985	$ 295.00	$65.55	$3.59	$0.30
B	36	1	4½	1,020	315.00	70.00	3.70	0.308
C	24	2	4½	1,125	335.00	74.44	3.57	0.297
C	48	2	4½	1,125	345.00	76.67	3.68	0.307
Sub Total	144	216	648	153,180				
ONE BEDROOM								
D–1	24	1	3½	830	210.00	60.00	3.03	0.252
D–2	72	1	3½	830	230.00	65.71	3.32	0.277
D–3	120	1	3½	830	255.00	72.86	3.69	0.307
Sub Total	216	216	756	179,280				
TOTAL UNITS	360	432	1,404	332,460	98,760.00	$70.34	$3.56	$0.297

Underground Parking 360 Spaces @ $20.00/Month   7,200.00

Total Monthly Income $ 105,960.00

Total Annual Income $1,271,520.00

Washer – Dryer-Vending Income (3 year Average)   17,000.00

ANNUAL SCHEDULED GROSS INCOME $1,288,520.00

CORRELATION OF RENT COMPARABLES
ADJUSTMENTS
(EXHIBIT F-1)

Type Unit

SUBJECT
1 BR UNITS

Comparable #	Actual Rent	Appeal	Location	Size of Unit	Construction	Carpeting	Balcony	Sec.System	Extra Bath	Lobby	Elevator	Rec. Area	Other	Air Cond.	Dishwashers	Disposals	Swim. Pool	Saunas	Party Room	Lake,Streams, Walk Paths	Lndscp.; etc.	Total Adjustments	Adjusted Rents
1. 5290 Runna Way	$205/225	E	E	+10	E	E	E	E	E	E	E	E		E	E	E	E	E	E	E		+10	$215/235
2. 4100 Luxem Blvd.	200	+10	E	+5	+5	E	E	E	E	E	E	+15		E	E	E	+5	E	E	+10		+45	245
3. 4360 Hookside	195/215	E	E	+5	E	E	E	E	E	E	E	+5		E	E	E	+5	E	E	+10		+25	220/240
4. 6750 Mork Ave.	215.50 AV	E	E	E	E	E	E	E	E	E	E	+10		E	E	E	+5	E	E	+10		+25	240/250
5. 5100 Chateau Blvd.	242/257	E	-5	-5	E	E	E	E	E	E	E	+10		E	E	E	+5	+2	E	+10		+17	259/274
6. 2100 Parklawn Dr.	210/230	E	E	+5	E	E	E	E	E	E	E	+10		E	E	E	+5	E	E	+10		+30	240/270
7. 7350 Gallagher Blvd.	205/250	E	E	+5	E	E	E	E	E	E	E	E		E	E	E	E	E	E	+10		+15	215/265
8. 6300 Bell Ave.	195/205	E	E	+2	E	E	E	E	E	E	E	+10		E	E	E	+5	+2	+2	+10		+31	226/236
SUBJECT	210/255																						210/265

CORRELATION OF RENT COMPARABLES ADJUSTMENTS
(EXHIBIT F-2)

Type Unit

SUBJECT
2 BR UNITS

Comparable #	Actual Rent	Appeal	Location	Size of Unit	Construction	Carpeting	Balcony	Sec.System	Extra Bath	Lobby	Elevator	Rec. Area	Other	Air Cond.	Dishwashers	Disposals	Swim. Pool	Saunas	Party Room	Lake, Streams, Walk Paths, Landscp.; etc.	Total Adjustments	Adjusted Rents
			General						Building Amenities						Appliances			Recreation Facilities				
1. 5290 Runna Way	$300/325	E	E	+ 5	E	E	E	E	E	E	E	E		E	E	E		E	E	E	+ 5	$305/330
2. * 4100 Luxem Blvd.	247.50 AV	+10	E	+15	+ 5	E	E	E	E	E	E	+15		E	E	E	+ 5	E	E	+10	+60	307.50
3. 4360 Hookside	320 AV	E	E	+ 5	E	E	E	E	E	E	E	+ 5		E	E	E	+ 5	E	E	+10	+25	345
4. 6750 Mork Ave.	317.50 AV	E	E	E	E	E	E	E	E	E	E	+10		E	E	E	+ 5	E	E	+10	+25	342.50
5. 5100 Chateau Blvd.	340 AV	E	- 5	- 5	E	E	E	E	E	E	E	+10		E	E	E	+ 5	+ 2	E	+10	+17	357
6. 2100 Parklawn Dr.	297.50 AV	E	E	+ 5	E	E	E	E	E	E	E	+10		E	E	E	+ 5	E	E	+10	+30	327.50
7. 7350 Gallagher Blvd.	270/320	E	E	+ 5	E	E	E	E	E	E	E	E		E	E	E	E	E	E	+10	+15	285/335
8. 6300 Bell Ave.	240/255	E	E	+10	E	E	E	E	E	E	E	+10			E	E	+ 5	+ 2	+ 2	+10	+39	279/294
SUBJECT	295/345																					295/345

*Also have a deluxe 1,170 sq. ft. unit which rents for $370

Address _5290 Runna Way_   **City** _Edina_

Built _1969_   **Units** _165_   **Name** _COMPARABLE #1_

3 story & basement - frame - brick veneer - elevator

PHOTOGRAPH

Rent Schedule:		Size		Analysis	
		Sq. Ft.	Rooms	Per Sq.Ft.	Per Room
1 BR	$ 205/225	752	3	3.27-3.60	68.33-75.00
2 BR	$ 300/325	1,046	4	3.44-3.73	75.00-81.25
3 BR	$ 500	1,536	5	3.90	100.00
	$				
	$				

COMMENTS: Variance in 1 BR and 2 BR units depends on whether it is poolside or not. Six 2 BR units having 922 sq. ft. and 1 bath rent for $275.00.

Garage Rent:
·Detached $
Basement $ 20.00

Features:	Yes	No		Appliances:	Yes	No
Refrigerator	X			Air Cond.-Central		X
Stove & Oven	X			Air Cond.-Unit	X	
Hood Fan	X			Dishwasher	X	
Carpeting	X			Disposal	X	
Balcony	X					
Sec. System	X			Recreational:		
Extra B. (Full)	X	(in 2 & 3 BR)		Pool-Inside	X	
Lobby	X			Pool-Outside		X
Elevator	X			Sauna	X	
				Party Room	X	
				Other Rec. Area		

Comp. to Sub.	Superior	Inferior		Vacancy:	
Location	E			No. of Eff.	
Site	E			No. of 1 BR	
Gen. Const.	E			No. of 2 BR	2
Appeal (Inside)	E			No. of 3 BR	
Appeal (Outside)	E			Total Vacancy	2
				% to Total Units	1.2%

Address 4100 Luxem Blvd.   City   Edina

Built 1970   Units 62   Name   COMPARABLE #2

3 story & basement - masonry construction - elevator - 231 rooms

PHOTOGRAPH

Rent Schedule:		Size		Analysis	
		Sq. Ft.	Rooms	Per Sq.Ft.	Per Room
1 BR	$ 200.00	650	3	3.69	66.66
2 BR	$ 242.50	913	4	3.19	60.62
2 BR	$ 252.50	996	4	3.04	63.12
2 BR	$ 370.00	1,170	4	3.79	92.50
	$				

Garage Rent:
Detached $
Basement $ 20.00
   " Indoor   15.00

Features:	Yes	No		Appliances:	Yes	No
Refrigerator	X			Air Cond.-Central		X
Stove & Oven	X			Air Cond.-Unit	X	
Hood Fan	X			Dishwasher	X	
Carpeting	X			Disposal	X	
Balcony	X					
Sec. System	X			Recreational:		
Extra B. (½)	X	(in 2 BR units)		Pool-Inside		X
Lobby	X			Pool-Outside	X	
Elevator	X			Sauna	X	
Extra Full Bath	X	(in 2 BR deluxe)		Party Room	X	
				Other Rec. Area		

Comp. to Sub.	Superior	Inferior		Vacancy:	
Location	E			No. of Eff.	
Size		X		No. of 1 BR	
Gen. Const.	X			No. of 2 BR	1
Appeal (Inside)	E			No. of 3 BR	
Appeal (Outside)	E			Total Vacancy	1
				% to Total Units	1.6%

Address 4360 Hookside Ave.   **City** Edina

Built 1969   **Units** 189   **Name** COMPARABLE #3

3 buildings, 3 story, elevator, frame & brick veneer

PHOTOGRAPH

Rent Schedule:

1 BR	$	195/215
2 BR	$	310/330
3 BR	$	525/550
	$	
	$	

Garage Rent:
Detached $
Basement $ 20.00

Size			Analysis	
Sq. Ft.	Rooms		Per Sq.Ft.	Per Room
775	3		3.02-3.33	65.00-71.66
1,070	4		3.48-3.70	77.00-82.50
1,751	5		3.60-3.77	105.00-110.00

COMMENTS: A larger type 1 BR unit (1,018 sq. ft.) rents from $240/255, and with a fireplace for $270. 3 BR units all have fireplaces. Rents vary because of size and location of units in buildings.

Features:	Yes	No
Refrigerator	X	
Stove & Oven	X	
Hood Fan	X	
Carpeting	X	
Balcony	X	
Sec. System	X	
Extra B. (Full)	X	(in 2 & 3 BR)
Lobby	X	
Elevator	X	

Appliances:	Yes	No
Air Cond.-Central		X
Air Cond.-Unit	X	
Dishwasher	X	
Disposal	X	
Recreational:		
Pool-Inside	X	
Pool-Outside		X
Sauna	X	
Party Room	X	
Other Rec. Area	X	

Comp. to Sub.	Superior	Inferior
Location	E	
Site		X
Gen. Const.	E	
Appeal (Inside)	E	
Appeal (Outside)	E	

Vacancy:	
No. of Eff.	
No. of 1 BR	
No. of 2 BR	1
No. of 3 BR	
Total Vacancy	1
% to Total Units	.05%

Address   6750 Mork Avenue   **City**   Edina

Built   1967   **Units**   81   **Name**   COMPARABLE #4

4 story & ground floor - masonry construction - 2 elevators

PHOTOGRAPH

Rent Schedule:

			Size		Analysis	
			Sq. Ft.	Rooms	Per Sq.Ft.	Per Room
1 BR	$	185/246	790	3	2.81-3.74	61.66-82.00
2 BR	$	350/366	1,050	4	4.00-4.18	87.50-91.50
2 BR	$	345/351	1,115	4	3.71-3.78	86.25-87.75
2 BR & Den	$	420/426	1,380	5	3.65-3.70	84.00-85.20
	$					

COMMENTS: Rents increase $5.00 per floor. Second floor is first rental floor.

Garage Rent:
·Detached $
Basement $ 25.00

Features:	Yes	No		Appliances:	Yes	No
Refrigerator	X			Air Cond.-Central	X	
Stove & Oven	X			Air Cond.-Unit		X
Hood Fan	X			Dishwasher	X	
Carpeting	X			Disposal	X	
Balcony	X					
Sec. System	X			Recreational:		
Extra B. (Full)	X	(lge. 2 BR &		Pool-Inside	X	
Lobby	X	2BR w/Den)		Pool-Outside		X
Elevator	X			Sauna	X	
				Party Room	X	
				Other Rec. Area		

Comp. to Sub.	Superior	Inferior		Vacancy:		
Location	X			No. of Eff.		
Site		X		No. of 1 BR		3
Gen. Const.	Part	Part		No. of 2 BR		
Appeal (Inside)		X		No. of 3 BR		
Appeal (Outside)		X		Total Vacancy		3
				% to Total Units	3.7%	

Address   5100 Chateau Blvd.   **City**   Edina

Built   1968-1969   **Units** 44   **Name** COMPARABLE #5

```
┌─────────────────────────────────────────────┐
│                                             │
│                                             │
│                                             │
│                 PHOTOGRAPH                  │
│                 ──────────                  │
│                                             │
│                                             │
│                                             │
└─────────────────────────────────────────────┘
```

		Size		Analysis	
Rent Schedule:		Sq. Ft.	Rooms	Per Sq.Ft.	Per Room
Studios	$ 185	607	2	3.66	92.50
1 BR	$ 242/257	954	3	3.04-3.23	80.67-85.67
2 BR	$ 335/345	1,246 &			
	$	1,252	4	3.23-3.31	83.75-86.25
	$				

Garage Rent:
Detached $
Basement $ Included

Features:	Yes	No		Appliances:	Yes	No
Refrigerator	X			Air Cond.-Central	X	
Stove & Oven	X			Air Cond.-Unit		X
Hood Fan	X			Dishwasher	X	
Carpeting	X			Disposal	X	
Balcony	X					
Sec. System	X			Recreational:		
Extra B. (½-Full)	X	(2 BR)		Pool-Inside	X	
Lobby	X			Pool-Outside		X
Elevator	X			Sauna		X
				Party Room	X	
				Other Rec. Area		

Comp. to Sub.	Superior	Inferior		Vacancy:	
Location	X			No. of Eff.	
Site		X		No. of 1 BR	
Gen. Const.	E			No. of 2 BR	
Appeal (Inside)	E			No. of 3 BR	
Appeal (Outside)	E			Total Vacancy	0
				% to Total Units	

Address ___2100 Parklawn Drive___   **City** ___Edina___

Built ___1973___   **Units** ___105___   **Name** ___COMPARABLE #6___

3 story & basement garage - brick veneer - 2 elevators

PHOTOGRAPH

Rent Schedule:		Size		Analysis	
		Sq. Ft.	Rooms	Per Sq.Ft.	Per Room
1 BR - 1 Bath	$ 210/230	760	3	3.63	76.67
2 BR - 2 Bath	$ 290/305	1,080	4	3.39	76.25
2 BR - 2 Bath-fpl.	$ 325/350	1,120	4	3.75	87.50
	$				
	$				

Garage Rent:
Detached $
Basement $ 25.00

Features:	Yes	No		Appliances:	Yes	No
Refrigerator	X			Air Cond.-Central	X	
Stove & Oven	X			Air Cond.-Unit		X
Hood Fan	X			Dishwasher	X	
Carpeting	X			Disposal	X	
Balcony	X					
Sec. System	X			Recreational:		
Extra B. (Full)	X	(2 BR units)		Pool-Inside		X
Lobby (2)	X			Pool-Outside	X	
Elevator (2)	X			Sauna	X	
				Party Room	X	
				Other Rec. Area	X	

Comp. to Sub.	Superior	Inferior		Vacancy:	
Location	E			No. of Eff.	
Site		X		No. of 1 BR	
Gen. Const.	E			No. of 2 BR	
Appeal (Inside)	E			No. of 3 BR	
Appeal (Outside)	E			Total Vacancy	
				% to Total Units	

Address   7350 Gallagher Blvd.   **City**   Edina

Built   1972   **Units**   300   **Name**   COMPARABLE #7

PHOTOGRAPH

Rent Schedule:

		Size		Analysis	
		Sq. Ft.	Rooms	Per Sq.Ft.	Per Room
1BR	$ 205/225	752/768	3	3.23-3.55	68.33-75.00
1BR	$ 220/225/230	787	3	3.35-3.43-3.51	73.33-75.00-
	$				76.67
1BR	$ 250	843	3	3.56	83.33
2BR	$ 270/290	943	4	3.44-3.69	67.50-72.50
2BR	$ 280/290	957	4	3.51-3.66	70.00-72.50
2BR	$ 300/320	1,032	4	3.49-3.72	75.00-81.25

ARAGE   ·Detached $
ENT: Basement $ Included

Features:	Yes	No		Appliances:	Yes	No
Refrigerator	X			Air Cond.-Central		X
Stove & Oven	X			Air Cond.-Unit	X	
Hood Fan	X			Dishwasher	X	
Carpeting	X			Disposal	X	
Balcony	X					
Sec. System	X			Recreational:		
Extra B. (½-Full)	X	(2 BR)		Pool-Inside	X	
Lobby	X			Pool-Outside	X	
Elevator	X			Sauna	X	
				Party Room	X	
				Other Rec. Area		

Comp. to Sub.	Superior	Inferior		Vacancy:	
Location	E			No. of Eff.	
Site		X		No. of 1 BR	
Gen. Const.	E			No. of 2 BR	
Appeal (Inside)	E			No. of 3 BR	
Appeal (Outside)	E			Total Vacancy	
				% to Total Units	

Address ___6300 Bell Avenue_____   City___Edina_____

Built ___1969_____ Units__44___   Name___COMPARABLE #8_____

PHOTOGRAPH

	Size		Analysis	
Rent Schedule:	Sq. Ft.	Rooms	Per Sq.Ft.	Per Room
1BR $ 195/205	800	3	2.93-3.08	65.00-68.33
2BR $ 240/255	1,000	4	2.88-3.06	60.00-63.75
$
$
$

Garage Rent:
Detached $ 20.00
Basement $

Features:	Yes	No
Refrigerator	X	
Stove & Oven	X	
Hood Fan	X	
Carpeting	X	
Balcony	X	
Sec. System	X	
Extra B. (½-Full)	X	(1-3/4 2 BR)
Lobby	X	
Elevator		X

Appliances:	Yes	No
Air Cond.-Central		X
Air Cond.-Unit	X	
Dishwasher	X	
Disposal		X
Recreational:		
Pool-Inside		X
Pool-Outside	X	
Sauna		X
Party Room		X
Other Rec. Area		

Comp. to Sub.	Superior	Inferior
Location	E	
Site		X
Gen. Const.	E	
Appeal (Inside)	E	
Appeal (Outside)	E	

Vacancy:	
No. of Eff.	
No. of 1 BR	
No. of 2 BR	
No. of 3 BR	
Total Vacancy	1
% to Total Units	

REAL ESTATE TAX COMPARABLES

EDINA, MINNESOTA

(EXHIBIT G)

	LOCATION	Amount of Tax Due 1975	Number of Units	Number of Rooms	Tax per Unit	Tax per Room	Remarks
1.	6750 Mork Avenue	$ 69,509.70	81	283	$858.00	$245.61	To be paid under protest.
2.	5290 Runna Way	$118,401.48	165	590	$717.58	$200.67	
3.	4360 Hookside	$130,632.00	189	660	$691.17	$198.00	
4.	4100 Luxem Blvd.	$ 38,613.81	62	231	$622.80	$167.15	
5.	6005 Prairie Road	$ 12,813.65	19	64	$674.40	$200.20	
6.	5300 Lois Cane	$ 75,246.31	118	432	$637.68	$174.16	
	SUBJECT	$259,960.00	360	1,404	$722.00	$185.00	

Comp. #   1

REAL ESTATE TAX COMPARABLES
(APARTMENTS)

Address   6750 Mork Avenue South   City   Edina   State   Minnesota

Year Built   1967   No. of Units 81   No. of Rooms   283

PHOTOGRAPH

4 Story and Ground Floor Masonry Apartment Building. Year around
pool, saunas, party room, heated parking, central air conditioning,
elevatored.

AMOUNT OF R. E. TAX FOR YEAR 19 75 (excluding special assessments) $ 69,509.70

Tax per unit   (81 Units) = $ 858.00

Tax per room   (283 Rooms) = $ 245.61

Comp. #   2

REAL ESTATE TAX COMPARABLES
(APARTMENTS)

Address   5290 Runna Way   City   Edina   State   Minnesota

Year Built   1969   No. of Units   165   No. of Rooms   590

PHOTOGRAPH

3 Story and Basement Garage. Frame superstructure, year around
pool, saunas, party room, elevatored.

AMOUNT OF R. E. TAX FOR YEAR 19 75 (excluding special assessments) $ 118,401.48

      Tax per unit   (165   Units) = $ 717.58

      Tax per room   (590   Rooms) = $ 200.67

Comp. # _____3_____

REAL ESTATE TAX COMPARABLES
(APARTMENTS)

Address _____4360 Hookside_____ City _____Edina_____ State _____Minnesota_____

Year Built _____1969_____ No. of Units _____189_____ No. of Rooms _____660_____

PHOTOGRAPH

3 Buildings – 2 Story and Basement Garage. Frame superstructure,
party rooms, saunas, inside pools, elevatored.

AMOUNT OF R. E. TAX FOR YEAR 1975_ (excluding special assessments) $__130,632.00_

      Tax per unit   (__189__ Units) = $_691.17_____

      Tax per room   (__660__ Rooms) = $_198.00_____

Comp. #   4

REAL ESTATE TAX COMPARABLES
(APARTMENTS)

Address   4100 Luxem Boulevard   City   Edina   State   Minnesota

Year Built   1970   No. of Units   62   No. of Rooms   231

PHOTOGRAPH

3 Story and Basement Parking.   Outside pool, party room, saunas,
elevatored.

AMOUNT OF R. E. TAX FOR YEAR 19 75   (excluding special assessments) $ 38,613.81

        Tax per unit   (62   Units) = $ 622.80

        Tax per room   (231   Rooms) = $ 167.15

Comp. #   5

<u>REAL ESTATE TAX COMPARABLES</u>
(APARTMENTS)

Address   6005 Prairie Road   City   Edina   State   Minnesota

Year Built   1972   No. of Units   19   No. of Rooms   64

<u>PHOTOGRAPH</u>

2 Story and Basement Garage. Frame superstructure, elevatored.

AMOUNT OF R. E. TAX FOR YEAR 1971 (excluding special asses. ents) $ 12,813.65

Tax per unit   (19   Units) = $ 674.40

Tax per room   (64   Rooms) = $ 200.20

Comp. #   6

REAL ESTATE TAX COMPARABLES
(APARTMENTS)

Address   5300 Lois Lane   City   Edina   State   Minnesota

Year Built   1971   No. of Units   118   No. of Rooms   432

PHOTOGRAPH

3 Story - Basement parking. Frame superstructure; elevatored.

AMOUNT OF R. E. TAX FOR YEAR 19 75 (excluding special assessments) $ 75,246.31

      Tax per unit   (118 Units) = $ 637.68

      Tax per room   (432 Rooms) = $ 174.16

CAPITALIZATION RATE FORMULA

ELLWOOD TABLES

(Exhibit H)

Assumptions:

```
Projection Period . . . . . . . . . . . . . . .10 Years
Depreciation. . . . . . . . . . . . . . . . . . . None
Appreciation. . . . . . . . . . . . . . . . . . . None
Mortgage Percentage . . . . . . . . . . . . . . . 75%
Mortgage Term . . . . . . . . . . . . . . . . .30 Years
Equity Yield. . . . . . . . . . . . . . . . . . . 12%
Interest. . . . . . . . . . . . . . . . . . . . 9.50%
```

Formula:

$R = Y - MC$

R = Capitalization Rate
Y = Equity Yield 12%
M = Mortgage Percentage 75%
C = Mortgage Coefficient

Mortgage Coefficient: .024676 *

* 3rd Edition, Page 225   10 year projection

By substituting in formula thus:

$R = .12 (.75 - .024676)$

$R = .12 - .018507$

$R = .101493$

$R = 10.15\%$

ROBERT A. KNUGGET

WAYZATA, MINNESOTA

BALANCE SHEET
As of December 31, 1974

(Exhibit I)

ASSETS:

Cash:
Checking Account . . . . $	35,000
Savings Account.	250,000
Life Insurance Cash Value.	1,000,000
Listed Securities.	3,175,000
Knugget Investment Company	5,000,000
Knugget Apartment Enterprises.	15,500,000
Residence.	500,000
Lake Home.	350,000
Contracts for Deed	975,000
Undeveloped Land	310,000
Personal Property.	200,000
Condominium.	125,000
Automobiles.	25,000
Boat	55,000
Plane.	80,000
TOTAL ASSETS.	$27,580,000

LIABILITIES:

Long Term Mortgages.	$12,300,000
Land Contract.	110,000
TOTAL LIABILITIES.	12,410,000
Net Worth.	15,170,000
TOTAL LIABILITIES AND NET WORTH	$27,580,000

1ST MORTGAGE GROSS INCOME PARTICIPATION

10 YEAR YIELD PROJECTION

(EXHIBIT J)

YEAR ENDING 12/31		1975	1976	1977	1978	1979	1980	1981	1982	1983
1. GROSS INCOME	(1)	1,288,500	1,352,925	1,420,571	1,491,600	1,566,180	1,644,488	1,726,713	1,813,048	1,903,700
BASE		1,288,500	1,288,500	1,288,500	1,288,500	1,288,500	1,288,500	1,288,500	1,288,500	1,288,500
INCREASE	(2)	-0-	64,425	132,071	203,100	277,680	355,988	438,213	524,548	615,200
2. PARTICIPATION: .10%		-0-	6,442	13,207	20,310	27,768	35,598	43,821	52,454	61,520
3. INTEREST PAID	(3)	274,313	546,979	543,531	539,755	535,575	531,044	526,082	520,649	514,699
TOTAL (2+3) INTEREST		274,313	553,421	556,738	560,065	563,343	566,642	569,903	573,103	576,219
4. LOAN BALANCE	(4)	5,757,675	5,721,379	5,681,635	5,637,635	5,589,935	5,537,704	5,480,511	5,417,885	5,349,309
PERCENTAGE YIELD		4.76%	9.67%	9.79%	9.93%	10.07%	10.23%	10.39%	10.57%	10.77%
ANNUALIZED	(5)	9.52%								

Notes to Projection: Lender to receive 10% of any increases in gross income over the base for 1975 as additional interest.

1. Proforma stabalized gross income for 1975 is $1,288,500.00

2. A 5% per year increase in gross income is projected.

3. Interest on the new first mortgage is 9.5% per year, 10.1% payment constant.

4. Original principal balance on the new first mortgage is $5,775,000.

5. New loan closes 7/1/75.

REFINANCING: EFFECTIVE INTEREST RATE CALCULATION

(Exhibit K)

ORIGINAL LOAN

Loan Amount	$4,500,000
Funding Date	1/5/71
Interest Rate	8.00%
Amortization	25 Years
Maturity	25 Years
Original Payment Constant	9.27%
Annual Payment	$ 417,500
Monthly Payment	$ 34,791.66
Loan Balance (7/1/75)	$4,201,784
Loan Age	4.5 Years
Current Payment Constant	9.93%

NEW LOAN (REFINANCED)

Loan Amount	$5,775,000
Funding Date	7/1/75
Interest Rate	9.50%
Amortization	30 Years
Maturity	20 Years
Payment Constant	10.10%
Annual Payment	$ 583,275
Monthly Payment	$ 48,606
Additional Interest	10% Participation

Formula: $\dfrac{(P \times T \times R) - (p \times t \times r)}{(P \times T) - (p \times t)}$ = Approximate effective rate on new money

Amount	P
Term (Years)	T
Interest Rate	R
New Loan	Capital Letters
Original Loan	Small Letters

Formula Substitution:

	Loan Amount	Term or Maturity	Rate	Funding Date
New Loan:	$5,775,000	20 Years	9.50%	7/1/75
Old Loan:	$4,201,784	20.5 Years	8.00%	1/5/71
New Money:	$1,573,216			

Then: 5,775,000 x 20 x .0950 = 10,972,500
4,201,784 x 20.5 x .0800 =   6,890,926
5,775,000 x 20   = 115,500,000
4,201,784 x 20.5   = 86,136,572

$$\frac{10,972,500 - 6,890,926}{115,500,000 - 86,136,572} = \frac{4,081,574}{29,363,428} = .13900$$

Effective New Money Interest Rate 13.9%

LEVERAGE CALCULATION

	Principal Balance	Annual Debt Service		Constant
New Loan:	$5,775,000	$583,275	=	.1010
Old Loan:	4,201,784	417,500	=	.0993
New Money:	$1,573,216	$165,775	=	.10537

ANALYSIS: CASE STUDY 1—GARDEN APARTMENTS

The security being offered in this case is very close to "perfect" in terms of the quality of the real estate. It has the advantages of being a successful project, well designed and well located, and offers a borrower with whom the lender has had excellent servicing experience.

This lender is operating in a tight money market, with apparently limited funds to invest, even though there are many opportunities, and is faced with the dilemma of refusing to increase the present loan and being "locked in" with a low-rate, long-term mortgage or parting with some of limited lendable dollars.

The mortgage banker is trying to point out to the lender the fine qualities of this solid real estate to be measured against a return of 14% on new money invested, plus an almost certain higher yield based on a further participation in the increasing income stream.

This case study is very complete and can be used as an excellent and well-detailed format for a loan submission on any kind of income-producing property.

Two-Story
Highway Motel

S. Douglas Arnott

This is the study of an actual mortgate loan submission involving a major life insurance company and a highly successful motel in a large metropolitan center. The story· is spread over a five-year period and can be broken up into three separate financing stages.

STAGE I

At the time the insurance company was introduced to the security by a prominent and knowledgeable mortgage banker, the motel had been operating for about one year, and was already highly successful.

It is important to know that the insurance company had been involved in financing many similar properties on a national scale and was considered to be a leader in this type of financing. Also, the mortgage banker had a fair amount of experience in appraising and arranging financing for motels in its own market. So, both companies felt confidence in their own, and in each other's, abilities and judgment.

The following facts were brought out in the appraisal or during the analytical period.

458

1   The structure consisted of a two-story, 108-room motel with dining room, coffee shop, a bar, and banquet facilities. The public areas were considerably larger than would normally be required for 108 rooms, but they had been designed to handle future expansion. Land area was about 12 acres, which provided more than adequate parking. The grounds were nicely landscaped, and the motel had an outdoor pool, including a pool for small children.

2   The property is located in the suburbs of a major city in an area where major growth is in the early stages. It is on a major freeway which has just been completed, and the metropolitan airport is about two miles away. Within walking distance is located the city's new outdoor sports stadium, the home of professional baseball and football. In a radius of three or four miles are located many local and national industries. A large amount of single-family and apartment construction was occurring in the general area. The concept of suburban highway motels serving the businessman as opposed to the tourist was fairly new. The trend to airport motel locations was just beginning. The location might have been viewed as speculative by some investors.

3   At the time, very little competition existed. One mile away was a 76-unit "Ma and Pa" operation. Six miles further was a 106-unit Howard Johnson motel. Both of these properties were reported to be operating at near capacity.

4   The property was owned by a corporation, which had about 20 shareholders. Many of these were prominent and well-to-do local citizens. Although several had a construction or real estate background, none were experienced in managing a large income-producing real estate property. It appeared that several of the owners took a hand in management of the facility, with a former contractor, Mr. Smith, devoting full time to the operation.

5   A review of the motel's operating statements, covering a period of just under one year, revealed that room occupancy had averaged about 89%. Also, gross income from food and beverage operations was very high and well above normal for the industry. A substantial profit was earned during the period.

At this point, the insurance company had satisfied itself on the nature of the security, on its location, on competition, and on the operating report to date. Some concern was felt over the question of management, in terms of experience and depth, but it was difficult to quarrel with the venture's success to date.

The purpose of the mortgage request was to consolidate a series of existing debts and to finance a proposed addition to the property.

1   It appeared that construction costs had run well over the original budget, and the combination of a relatively small first mortgage, chattel financing, and other short-term obligations was choking the operation.

2   The addition was to consist of 48 rooms, making a total of 156 rooms.

The application was for $1,800,000, and the appraisal indicated a physical value of $2,805,000 and an economic value of $2,810,000. Thus, the loan requested was 64 percent of value. This worked out to more than $11,500 per room, and at that time, this was considered to be on the high side. However, the mortgage was approved on the following terms:

Amount	$1,800,000
Rate	6¼%
Term	20 years
Amortization	$1,500,000 amortized over 20 years concurrently with $300,000 over 10 years. The purpose of this acceleration was to reduce the loan quickly during the early years when high profits seemed assured, which recognized what appeared to be a full loan. On this repayment plan the mortgage was about $975,000 in 10 years.
Prepayment option	The privilege of prepaying in the 6th year with a bonus of 6¼%, said bonus declining 1% annually to 2¼% in the 10th and ensuing years.

The approval also required the usual title insurance in the amount of the mortgage, a survey, an assignment of rents, a refundable deposit of $18,000, a chattel mortgage, and other usual provisions.

Two other interesting features were:

1   Further property expansion was contemplated. Because the lender had the borrower locked in for five years, any attempt to finance an addition elsewhere would prove very difficult. Therefore, the lender was granted the right of first refusal to finance any proposed addition. But, if the lender was unwilling or unable to do so at market terms, the borrower had the privilege to prepay the mortgage in full during the third to fifth years inclusive with a one-year interest bonus.

2   Secondly, the mortgage contained a participation clause. To digress for a moment, the concept of participation was, at that time, quite new. It had developed because occasionally lenders provided more than the normal mortgage amount, or in other words, provided what would usually be equity funds. In recognition of this, the lender was entitled to an equity return in the event the property was successful. The lender should receive a share of the profits, but since the funds were actually being loaned, and therefore preferably would be repaid with interest, the lender had some lesser risk than a true equity partner.

Motels make an ideal vehicle for participation-type financing, because the potential profit is very great. Unlike apartments and office buildings where the overall return on cost will move in a fairly narrow range, motels may earn as much as 20 percent or more on cost.

It makes no sense to burden a property with a debt or obligation that it cannot carry, but motels offer the potential for high returns to the lender if the participation is properly structured.

In the case under discussion, the lender made the following analysis of the potential earnings of the property.

Economic Projections

	Underwriting 156 rooms
Occupancy	80%
Average daily rate	$12.00
Total Sales & Income	
Total room sales	$ 546,600
Food sales	750,000
Beverage sales	375,000
Telephone revenue	18,000
Other dept. profits	10,000
Other income	20,000
Total	$1,719,600
Wages & Expenses	
Rooms	147,600
Food & Beverage	922,500
Telephone	21,000
Total	1,091,100
Gross operating margin	$ 628,500
Deduction from Income	
Administration & general	111,200
Adv't.—promotion	40,000
Heat, light & power	46,800
Repairs & maintenance	39,000
Total	237,000
House profit	391,500
Add—Store rentals	4,000
Operating profit	395,500
Insurance & R.E. taxes	52,000
Net before other capital charges	343,500
Debt charges	
1,500,000.—6¼%—20 yrs.)	172,000
300,000.—6¼%—10 yrs.)	
Cushion	171,500

It should be noted here that the hotel-motel industry has developed its own system of accounting and reporting. The above table is a rough approximation of standard hotel accounting. The lender and mortgage banker should become familiar with the various methods used in reporting hotel results. Two or three C.P.A. firms have made a specialty of this field, and excellent annual studies are available.

Coming back to the above table, the lender had assumed an average occupancy of 80 percent at a daily rate of $12.00. In fact, the motel was experiencing close to 90% occupancy, and was recently averaging over $12.00 per occupied room. Thus, the lender was fairly conservative in this analysis. The proposed participation was. . .

The lender is to participate in the gross annual sales during the currency of the loan. Participation is based on:

5% gross annual room sales in excess of $400,000
1% gross annual food sales in excess of $500,000
2% gross annual beverage sales in excess of $300,000

The effect of this participation based on the underwriting projections would be:

5% of $146,600 = $ 7,330
1% of   250,000 =   2,500
2% of   75,000 =   1,500
Total participation   = $11,330

The yield to the lender in the first year of operation would be approximately 6.8%.

This meant also that if the motel did in fact produce a net income of $171,500, deducting $11,330 would leave the owners $160,000, or a return on the equity (based on the appraisal) of 16%.

Another way to look at the lender's position is this: the lender felt that a mortgage of $1,500,000 was normal, and the extra $300,000 was a contribution of equity-type funds. Relating the participation of $11,330 to $300,000 gave a first-year extra yield of 3.75%, on top of the mortgage interest of 6.25%, or, say, 10% on equity.

These terms were acceptable to all parties, and the mortgage was eventually made.

STAGE II

About three years later, the owners of the motel were ready to proceed with an expansion program. During this three-year period, several building plans had been considered. One involved an ambitious 7-story addition of about 210 rooms. This plan was rejected as being too large for the market, and was finally shelved because the lender was unwilling or unable to come up with the funds. The owners elected not to use the escape clause in the first mortgage which would have permitted them to finance elsewhere.

Another plan seriously considered would have involved an additional boiler, a freight elevator, expanded kitchen and storage, and similar improvements. This actually reached the commitment stage, by way of a second mortgage of $325,000 at 7%, but the owners changed their minds. It finally became apparent that there was a conflict between the active owner/manager, Mr. Smith, and the other shareholders, as to whether any expansion should take place, and if so, how extensive it should be.

Mr. Smith approached the lender with a proposal whereby the company's capital structure would be reorganized to provide for more effective management, with a reduced number of shareholders.

Specifically the request was for $1,150,000, which would:

1   Retire all the preferred shares and debentures held by the shareholders.
2   Purchase all the common shares of all the shareholders except Mr. Smith, thus giving him complete control.
3   Provide funds for 25 additional rooms and an enclosed swimming pool.

This request was also approved by the lender, as a second mortgage of $1,150,000 for 20 years at 7%. Again, Mr. Smith changed his mind, deciding to add 40 rooms instead of 25, and a new approval was granted for $1,400,000 for 20 years at 7¼%.

What analysis led to the decision to proceed with this second mortgage, which together with the balance on the first mortgage of $1,650,000 gave a total outstanding balance of $3,050,000 for 196 rooms?

First, the area had experienced substantial growth during the previous three years. There was a high degree of industrial expansion, the sports facility in the area was doing very well and had been enlarged, population was growing rapidly, and the airport was solidly entrenched.

Second, no new competition had developed, and it was hoped that the subject's leading position in the market could be maintained by adding new rooms and the pool.

Third, concern still existed over management. No effort was being made to create a back-up for Mr. Smith, who was one of those 15-hours-a-day-every-day managers.

Fourth, and very important to the analysis, was the actual operating results of the property. They were nothing short of spectacular. The tale is told in the following chart.

	Actual Year 1	Actual Year 2
Occupancy	86.8%	90.4%
Average daily rate	$13.73	$14.12
Total Sales & Income		
Total room sales	$ 653,000	$ 748,000
Food sales	760,000	780,000
Beverage sales	464,000	444,000
Telephone revenue	30,000	30,000
Other	14,000	18,000
Total	$1,921,000	$2,020,000
Wages & Expenses		
Rooms	225,000	230,000
Food & beverage	891,000	921,000
Telephone	38,000	38,000
Total	1,154,000	1,189,000
Gross operating margin	767,000	831,000
Deduction from Income		
Administration & general	113,000	129,000
Adv't.—Promotion	40,000	54,000
Heat, light & power	47,000	49,000
Repairs & maintenance	45,000	45,000
Total	245,000	277,000
House profit	$ 522,000	$ 554,000
Add—Store rentals	—	—
Operating profit	522,000	554,000
Insurance & R. E. taxes	64,000	74,000
Net before other capital charges	458,000	480,000
Debt charges	172,000	172,000
Cushion	286,000	308,000

Observe that the occupancy had again passed the 90% level. Room rates were increasing. Net income before mortgage payments was $480,000 in the most recent year compared to the earlier underwriting estimate of $343,500. Based on the earlier value of $2,800,000, the yield was over 17%.

Participation during the first three years was roughly $11,700, $21,300 and $25,000, a handsome extra return on the mortgage. During the previous year, based on an equity value of $1,000,000, yield to the owners was $283,000 or 28.3% after paying participation. Neither the owner nor the insurance company had any cause to complain about these results.

A new appraisal was submitted, showing a value of $4,200,000. The combined first and second mortgages at $3,050,000 were 72 percent of value.

The underwriting department made a new economic projection, based on 196 rooms.

Occupancy		85%
Average daily rate		$15.37
Total Sales & Income		
Total room sales		$ 935,000
Food sales		982,000
Beverage sales		542,000
Telephone revenue		40,000
Other		10,000
Total		$2,515,000
Wages & Expenses		
Rooms		299,000
Food & beverage		1,143,000
Telephone		50,000
Total		1,492,000
Gross Operating margin		$1,023,000
Deduction from Income		
Administration & general		159,000
Adv't.—Promotion		65,000
Heat, light & power		61,000
Repairs & maintenance		57,000
Total		342,000
House profit		$ 681,000
Add—Store rentals		3,000
Operating profit		684,000
Insurance & R. E. taxes		81,000
Net before other capital charges		603,000
Debt charges		
First mortgage	$ 172,000	
Second mortgage	156,000	328,000
Cushion		275,000

Using a value of $4,200,000, overall yield would be 14.3%. On an equity value of $1,150,000, yield would be 23.9%, before calculating participation. The loan per room was now about $15,500, but net earnings per room were projected at over $3,000 per year. Many motels did not achieve this much gross income per room per year.

Repayment on the second mortgage was on the basis of monthly interest payments for two years, then a combined monthly payment which would amortize $700,000 over 12 years concurrently with $700,000 over 18 years. The purpose was to give some relief during the construction period, and then to achieve rapid principal recapture during the profitable years to follow.

Several special clauses were inserted in the new mortgage.

1 Recognizing that the property was doing well and that the participation clause was paying off handsomely, the lender agreed to amend the basis of participation. The lender wished to maintain the participation already being received, but was willing to accept a lower share of future gross income above current levels.

The new participation schedule was:

5% of gross annual room sales in excess of $400,000

2½% of gross annual room sales in excess of $750,000

1% of gross annual food sales in excess of $500,000

2% of gross annual beverage sales in excess of $800,000

1% of gross annual beverage sales in excess of $450,000

Based on this schedule, the lender anticipated annual participation of $30,865. On a total investment of $3,050,000 the yield would be increased about 1 percent in the first year and would grow thereafter on a declining mortgage balance.

2 Concern over the one-man nature of the operation was still very strong. As a partial solution the lender required that the borrowing corporation purchase a large amount of life insurance on the life of Mr. Smith. The borrower was the beneficiary, but the policy was assigned to the lender, and in the event of the death of Mr. Smith, the proceeds would be applied to reduce the mortgage.

3 The lender also acquired a stock option. The manner in which this would be achieved was through the exchange of its participation rights for a 25% share of the borrowing corporation's common stock. The privilege was open for 10 years. Whether or not this option would be exercised would depend largely on the tax implications of the lender.

4 The right of first refusal in regard to financing any future improvements was extended to the new mortgage.

STAGE III

Another year went by, during which the 40 rooms and the indoor pool were built, and the corporate changes were achieved. Mr. Smith proceeded with planning to construct a seven-story tower to create 138 new rental rooms, plus expanded public facilities. Adjacent land was purchased to handle anticipated parking needs. Over $140,000 had been spent on plans for the addition and changes to the existing structure.

This was the beginning of the "tight" money era, and Mr. Smith felt that money was too expensive. After arranging through the insurance company to borrow a further $3,500,000 to finance the addition, at 9¼%, Mr. Smith changed his mind and decided to wait for cheaper financing. However, he had invested a substantial amount in the new land and the plans, so a smaller third mortgage was arranged. The terms of this mortgage were $400,000 at 9% for 5 years, with no principal repayment until maturity.

No special conditions were attached to the mortgage, which was open for prepayment without penalty at any time.

During the years following the arranging of the second mortgage, operations continued to be very successful. Participation amounted to over $30,000 the first year and over $35,000 the next. Occupancy ran close to 90 percent. Although competition developed fairly extensively, the subject property more than held its own.

ANALYSIS: CASE STUDY 2—TWO-STORY HIGHWAY MOTEL

This is a dramatic success story. The lender kept in close touch with the property and showed a great deal of flexibility in structuring the financing to suit the needs of the motel as it developed. The staggered repayment plan, the participation clause, the three mortgages which went ahead (plus several which did not), the life insurance protection, and many other features were all designed to aid in the growth and the success of the property. They took time and effort on the part of the mortgage banker and the lender.

Because of the quality of the property, and also because substantial sums were borrowed which did not go to improve the real estate, the total debt reached about $3,337,000, or $17,000 per room, which was very high based on cost and the point in time. There was a great deal of inefficiency in the manner in which the owners planned the future.

The lender adopted the position that since it was putting up all the capital requirements, if the property was successful it was entitled to a share in the profits. This was achieved through the participation agreement.

An imaginative approach to financing plus hard work helped to make this a successful venture.

Regional Shopping Center

Robert E. Raymond

INTRODUCTION

The purpose of this case study is to increase the reader's ability to analyze and underwrite the financing of a regional shopping center. Two related subjects will be discussed: the loan submission and the financing proposal itself. The comments on the loan submission will refer to the types of information received rather than show voluminous examples, with the hope of making relevant points by reference rather than with more space-consuming material. The financial proposal will be outlined and a loan "brief," the actual case study, will contain in summary fashion the basic information contained in the submission about the property itself and the proposal. The remaining information will be comments about the analysis of the submission and the proposed transaction.

THE REQUEST

Financing of $9,200,000 to provide long-term financing for a proposed regional shopping center containing two department stores (313,000 sq. ft.—total) and an enclosed mall containing 280,000 sq. ft. of gross leasable area. The financing of $9,200,000 would not cover the two department stores, which are owned and financed separately.

THE SUBMISSION

A submission package containing the following information was prepared for the proposed lender by its local mortgage and real estate correspondent:

1   A transmittal letter containing a list of exhibits, comments about the form of the transaction, the correspondent's recommendation that the financing be approved and a summary of reasons for recommending the transaction.

2   Information regarding the general location including a map of the city, a detailed area map, and aerial photographs showing the surrounding area in all four directions.

3   Information regarding the specific site including its size, shape, street frontage, drainage, utilities and visual exposure.

4   Information regarding access, including comments on major highways nearby and a traffic-capacity analysis for adjacent streets.

5   Information regarding population, including past growth data, projected growth, and relevant comments, income levels, source of employment, and other factors affecting the area's future.

6   Information regarding retail sales and trends including a five-year-old retail market analysis for the area and recent updating of the report commenting on both the accuracy of the earlier report (somewhat conservative!) and the current outlook.

7   Information regarding competitive retail facilities, both downtown and suburban, including competing facilities' sizes, tenants, and known sales volumes.

8   Detailed plans and specifications, including a careful measurement to determine the gross area of the center and its gross leasable area.

9   An occupancy analysis showing the details of signed leases, leases under negotiation and an estimate for unleased space. For each tenant, information was given regarding its area, minimum rent, percentage rent, contributions for operating expenses and taxes, length of lease and any renewal options, and the sales volume point at which percentage rent would be payable.

10   Comments on the character and the mix of the tenants describing their individual and collective impact on the local competitive retail picture.

11   An economic appraisal, including a breakdown of income derived from the above-mentioned occupancy schedule, and detailed operating expenses and taxes. The operating expense and tax data were supported by comparisons with other similar properties and careful analysis of local real estate assessments and tax rates.

12   A detailed physical appraisal including comparables to support land value and supporting information regarding the cost of all site and building improvements.

13   Information regarding the lease forms to be used in leasing the mall stores and the operating agreements between the owner of the mall stores and the owners of the department stores.

14   Information regarding the owner, including background data, other real estate interests, experience in the planning, building, leasing, and management of retail property and financial information.

15   Information regarding other people involved in the project, including the market analyst, traffic engineer, architect, and builder.

THE BRIEF

All of the information referred to above was analyzed and distilled onto a loan brief (attached). The brief contains all the pertinent information regarding both the shopping center and the terms of the transaction. Attached to the brief is a record of leases showing the key elements of each tenant's lease.

COMMENTS

The quality of the real estate was determined by an analysis of the information contained in the submission about the location, area growth, competition, access, construction, etc.

The quality of the ownership was determined by an analysis of the information regarding the developer's experience and financial strength.

The quality of the appraisal was determined by an analysis of the appraisal data furnished by the correspondent and the reviewers' opinions of the correspondent's judgment.

The quality of the transaction being proposed was determined by an analysis of the total initial exposure believed to be involved, the rate at which the exposure would be amortized, and the amount of compensation to be received.

The quality of the compensation was determined by an analysis of the interest to be received on the leasehold loan plus the minimum and percentage income to be received from the rental of the land.

Midwest _____ Shopping Center

Loan Summary

$7,700,000 - Leasehold Loan
1,500,000 - Fee Purchase (See Below)
$9,200,000 - Total Investment

Amount	
Loan Term	25 Years 9 Months (10% Constant)
Interest Rate	9% Gross 8.93% Net
Method of Repayment	$64,167 monthly, interest and principle to fully amortize during the term. ADS = $770,000.

(Incl. ownership of land)

Balances:
5 yrs. $8,715,000 $33.60/Sq. Ft. GLA
10 yrs. 7,960,000 30.65/Sq. Ft. GLA
15 yrs. 6,775,000 26.00/Sq. Ft. GLA
20 yrs. 4,911,000 18.90/Sq. Ft. GLA
25 yrs. 2,008,000 7.75/Sq. Ft. GLA

Prepayment Option: None for 12 yrs. Open in the 13th year at 107, declining 1% per year to 101 in the 25th year.

Purpose: To provide approximately 82% of the cost of land and improvements.

Economic Valuation

Major Tenants Min. Rent	$ 497,600	$4.80	/Sq. Ft. GLA
Minor Tenants Min. Rent	919,400	5.88	/Sq. Ft. GLA
Total Min. Rents	$1,417,000	5.45	/Sq. Ft. GLA
O.E. Contributions	92,000	.35	/Sq. Ft. GLA
Tax Contributions	80,600	.31	/ Sq. Ft. GLA
Dept. Stores Contri.	72,000		
Total Gross Income	1,661,600	6.38	/Sq. Ft. GLA
Less % Vacancy (Minor Tents.)	54,600		
Stabilized Income	1,607,000	6.17	/Sq. Ft. GLA
Operating Expenses	243,000	.94	/Sq. Ft. GLA
Real Estate Taxes	130,000	.50	/Sq. Ft. GLA
Total OE & T	373,000	1.44	/Sq. Ft. GLA
Net Income Before Deprec.	1,234,000		
Depreciation @ %	180,000		
Net Income After Deprec.	1,054,000		

15.2 % Stab. Inc.
8.2 % Stab. Inc.
23.4 % Stab. Inc.

Capitalized @ 10.5% = $11,750,000
Capitalized @ 10.5% = $10,038,000

Location: Northwest corner of I-42 and Route 38 in Midwest City 4 miles east of the central business district. The site is in the path of the city's growth. The trade area's population is 280,000 and has increased 30% since 1966. Freeway and local street access is excellent.

Improvements: A 2-story modern shopping mall with separately owned department stores at either end. The J.C. Penney store (183,000 sq.ft.) and the Associated Dry Goods Store (130,000 sq.ft.) bring the total GLA to 573,000 sq.ft. High quality construction and good mix of tenants.

Parking: 1,550 spaces, or 6.0 per 1,000 sq.ft. of mall GLA. Total center has parking for 3300 cars or 5.7 per 1,000

By Home Office Staff

Physical Valuation

Land @ _____ or $1.15 / Sq. Ft.
Bldg. @ 27.00 / Sq. Ft. Gross
Site Improvements
Total Physical Value
Value for Investment Purposes
Final Valuation of Leasehold
Land Allocation

Mortgagor's Investment
Land ( ) $1,400,000
Improvements 9,350,000
Fees 200,000
Total Cost $10,950,000

	Midwest
City	Midwest
State	Ohio
Land	27.65 Acres 1,204,277 Sq. Ft.
Year Built	1974-1975
No. Stores	Subject Leasing
Basement Area	None
Ground Floor Area	194,400
% Coverage Land	15.7%
Upper Floor Area	149,100
Mall Area	65,000
Kiosk Area	-
Office Space	-
Total Gross Area	344,000
Gross Leasable Area	260,000
GLA/Gross Area	76%

	$1,400,000
	9,288,000
	1,045,000
Total Physical Value	$11,733,000
Value for Investment Purposes	$11,750,000
Final Valuation of Leasehold	10,350,000
Land Allocation	1,400,000
	Equity $ 1,750,000
	17.8 % of cost

	Loan	Total
Return on Equity	$261,520	or 14.9
Value/Sq. Ft. GLA	39.80	$45.20
OE&T/Sq. Ft. Gross.	1.09	1.09
Debt Serv./Sq. Ft. GLA	2.96	3.65
Debt Serv. Coverage	1.6x	1.3x
DP/Sq. Ft. GLA	4.40	5.10
DP/Maj. Ten. Min.	2.3x	2.7x
Value/Gross Income	6.2x	7.1x
Value/Net Income BD	8.4x	9.5x
Loan/Gross Income	4.8x	5.7x
Loan/Net Income BD	6.2x	7.5x
Loan/Sq. Ft. Gross	21.40	26.75
Loan/Sq. Ft. GLA	29.60	35.60

Mortgagor: Able Developers Inc., experienced developers of several shopping centers and office buildings in the central and western states. Presently own six shopping centers and Manage four others. Total assets are $95,600,000 and stockholders equity is $16,000,000.

Rental Requirement: $6,700,000 floor loan and land purchased upon completion. Next $500,000 disbursed when 220,000 sq.ft. leased at not less than $5.30/sq.ft. Last $500,000 Disbursed when 220,000 sq.ft. leased at not less than $5.45/sq.ft. One year from initial closing to qualify.

Default Point: 82.5% of Gross Income Covers OE, T Debt Service and Ground Rent of $1,323,000

Fee Purchase and Leaseback - Land to be purchased for $1,500,000 and leased back at $180,000 (12%), plus 20% of minimum and percentage rents over $1,250,000. 40 year lease plus one 20 year renewal option. One repurchase option - during 15th year at greater of $3,000,000 or the average total ground rent (including % rent) for the prior 3 years

Midwest Shopping Center

Record of Leases

Area (sq. ft.)	Tenant	Term	Minimum Rental	Per Sq. Ft.	%	Sales to Reach % (per sq. ft.)	
	MAJOR TENANTS						
24,000	Dunhams	20	$96,000	$4.00	4	100	Womens & girls RTW. Strong local.
11,800	L-M Store	20	47,200	4.00	5-4	80	Mens & Womens RTW. Good quality regional.
11,800	Fashion Bar	10	35,750	3.25	4-5	81	Mens & Womens RTW. Good quality regional.
10,500	Lerner's	15	42,000	4.00	4	100	
10,000	Wyatt's Cafeteria	20	40,000	4.00	5	80	
6,658	Hunter's	15	33,290	5.00	6	83	Regional sport shop.
4,319	Singer	15	21,595	5.00	6	83	
4,189	Kinney Shoes	20	29,323	7.00	6	117	
3,936	Walden Book	15	23,616	6.00	5	120	
2,900	National Shirt	10	17,400	6.00	-	---	
2,842	Vorhees Shoe	20	19,894	7.00	6	117	(Brown Shoe Company)
2,670	Susan's Casual	20	16,020	6.00	6	100	(Kinney Shoe)
2,220	Zale Jewelry	15	16,650	7.50	4	187	
1,870	Green's	15	14,025	7.50	5	150	Regional jewelry store chain.
1,456	House of Nine	15	8,736	6.00	6	100	
1,074	Regal Shoes	15	10,740	10.00	6	167	
1,038	Florsheim Shoes	20	10,380	10.00	6	167	
640	Parklane Hosiery	15	8,960	14.00	8	175	
602	Russell Stover	15	6,020	10.00	8	125	
103,714	TOTAL MAJORS		$497,599	$4.80			

Midwest Shopping Center

Record of Leases

Area (sq. ft.)	Tenant	Term	Minimum Rental	Per Sq. Ft.	%	Sales To Reach $ (per sq. ft.)	
	MINOR TENANTS						
13,769	Midland Theater	10	$ 58,518	$4.25	10-12	43	Local chain
3,960	Evens' Gifts	15	26,730	6.75	6	112	
3,215	Meyer's Toy & Hobby	10	19,290	6.00	6	100	Medium price local chain
2,515	Runner Shoes	20	15,090	6.00	6	100	
2,467	Doctor's Pet	10	14,802	6.00	6	100	Women's fashions
2,200	The Lady	15	13,200	6.00	6	100	
2,168	Jane Barrie	15	13,008	6.00	8	75	Bath & linen
2,132	Bergholz Jewelry	15	15,990	7.50	6	125	
2,100	Hickory Farms	10	14,700	7.00	6	117	
1,736	Larry's Florist	10	9,548	5.50	6	92	
1,710	Record Shop	10	14,535	8.50	6	142	
1,050	Strong Shoes	20	9,450	9.00	6	150	
924	Buffy's Boutique	15	5,544	6.00	6	100	Women's boutique
796	Wicks & Sticks	10	6,368	8.00	6	133	
40,742	TOTAL MINORS		236,773	5.81			
115,554	TO BE LEASED		682,628	5.91			
103,714	TOTAL MAJORS		497,599	4.80			
40,742	TOTAL MINORS		236,773	5.81			
144,456	TOTAL LEASED		734,372	5.08			
115,544	TO BE LEASED		682,628	5.91			
260,000	TOTAL CENTER		$1,417,000	$5.45			

ANALYSIS: CASE STUDY 3—REGIONAL SHOPPING CENTER

The fifteen items referred to in the loan submission will, if property presented, provide sufficient information to fully analyze this loan. This is really a test of reviewing an analysis already prepared for you by someone else to see if you agree with it.

This case also illustrates a method of providing the maximum number of dollars desired by the developer. A land sale-leaseback (with the right to repurchase) together with a leasehold loan is the vehicle used.

The repurchase appears to include a rather substantial ''kicker'' based on performance, which could be most attractive to the lender.

Neighborhood and Convenience Shopping Center

Charles H. Thorne

A P P R A I S A L

West Bend Shopping Center
Located at
Alpha Street and Sherman Avenue
Capitol City, Kansas

Robert M. Thornton, Appraiser
ABC Appraisal Company
1016 Adams Street
Capitol City, Kansas
March 21, 1975

ABC APPRAISAL COMPANY
1016 Adams Street
Capitol City, Kansas
Phone: 489-8748

March 21, 1975

Mr. Arnold L. Mason, Vice President
XYZ Mortgage Company
1231 Washington Street
Capitol City, Kansas

Dear Mr. Mason:

In accordance with your request, I have made an appraisal of the
West Bend Shopping Center located at the northeast corner of Alpha
Street and Sherman Avenue, in Capitol City, Kansas.

I hand you herewith my report which describes my method of approach
to value and contains the supporting data gathered in my investigation.

I have appraised the property as a whole, owned in fee simple and
unencumbered by any indebtedness.

I hereby certify that I have no personal interest in the subject
property--past, present or contemplated--and that neither my employment nor my compensation for conducting this appraisal is contingent
upon the value found.

I further certify that I have personally inspected the property,
and that to the best of my knowledge and belief all statements
and information contained herein are true and correct.

Based upon the findings and conditions herein contained, it is
this appraiser's opinion that the fair market value of the subject
property as of March 21, 1975, is:

ONE MILLION SEVEN HUNDRED THOUSAND DOLLARS...$1,700,000.00

Respectfully submitted,

Robert M. Thornton

Robert M. Thornton, Appraiser

TABLE OF CONTENTS

EXHIBITS

A. Capitol City Map

B. Map of Subject Site

C. Land Sales Comparables Map

SUMMARY OF SALIENT POINTS

LOCATION: NE corner of Alpha Street and Sherman Avenue,
                   Capitol City, Kansas

ZONING: G-1 (Planned Commercial District)

SITE: 5.875 Acres (255,698 square feet)

IMPROVEMENTS: Three buildings - Convenience Shopping Center

                        A   43,050 square feet
                        B   14,560 square feet
                        Yum Yum Tree   2,632 square feet

                   Parking for 275 cars

APPRAISED VALUE: Land $ 332,400
                   Improvements   1,367,600
                      Total $1,700,000

APPRAISAL DATE: March 21, 1975

PURPOSE OF APPRAISAL

The purpose of this appraisal is to provide a supported opinion of the
fair market value, in fee simple, of the property described in this
report, as of March 21, 1975.

MARKET VALUE

Market value, as used in this report, is defined as "the highest price,
estimated in terms of dollars, which the property would bring (if
exposed for sale for a reasonable time in the open market) to a seller
willing but not compelled to sell, from a buyer willing but not compelled
to buy, both parties being fully informed of all the purposes for which
the property is being adapted and is capable of being used."

LEGAL DESCRIPTION

Lot One (1), Block Four (4), Sheraton Park Addition, in the NE¼,
Section 33, Tier 10 North, Range 7 East of the 9th Principal Meridian,
Capitol City, Kansas.

LOCATION

NE corner of Alpha Street and Sherman Avenue in Capitol City, Kansas.

ASSUMPTIONS AND LIMITING CONDITIONS

The results of this appraisal report are based on the following
assumptions and conditions:

1. The legal description, as given, is correct.

2. The title to the property herein appraised is good and
    merchantable, in fee simple, and without encumbrances.

3. The value is reported without regard to questions of title,
    boundaries, encroachments, or other matters of a legal nature.

4. Some conclusions reached in this appraisal are based on certain
    opinions, estimates, information and data furnished by others.
    These are correct to the best knowledge of the appraiser, but
    no responsibility for their accurancy is assumed.

5. The conclusion as to value was reached after examining all
    parts of the report, and any statement relating to the
    value of part of the property cannot properly be used
    without reference to all sections of the report.

6. Maps and data included in this report are for identification
    only.

7. The use of this report does not include the right to utilize
    the appraisal in court or to require testimony in connection
    therewith.

8. This appraisal is based on a preliminary site plan and
    tentative lease agreements. The appraiser reserves the
    right to review this appraisal upon completion of plans
    and specifications and upon receipt of signed leases, and
    to make any changes in this report resulting from new infor-
    mation received.

CITY DATA

The subject property is located in Capitol City, the capitol city of
Kansas (see Exhibit A).

Based on United States Bureau of Census figures, Capitol City has
exhibited the following population characteristics:

	1970	1960
Total Population	149,518	128,521
% Male	48.4%	48.2%
% Female	51.6%	51.8%
Median Age	25.3	27.6
Total Population 25 years of Age & Over	75,413	69,226
% of this group educated beyond high school	34.9%	29.2%
Mean school years completed by this group	12.6	12.4
Total Number of Households	48,608	41,108
Population per household	2.85	2.98
Mean Family Income (Annual)	$11,209	$ 6,032
% of total families earning $10,000 or more per year	49.4%	----
% of total families earning $6,000 or more per year	----	50.4%
Total Labor Force	70,354	55,355
Unemployment	3.0%	3.4%

With a current population of approximately 155,000, Capitol City is
the second largest city in Kansas. This reflects substantial growth
from a population of 107,000 in 1950. The City-County Comprehensive
Plan forecasts county-wide population to be approximately 176,000 at the
present time. More significant are the urban area population projections prepared by the City Planning Commission that predict a population of 185,000 for Capitol City by the end of 1976. Included in this
urban area are all residents located within three miles of the city's
corporate limits. Urban area projections for 1980 and 1985 are
209,000 and 231,000 respectively. It is this appraiser's opinion that
such corporate growth will be predominantly toward the west and northwest during the next decade.

Located midway between the east and west coasts on I-5, Capitol City
offers a well-established network of transportation facilities. Five
Class 1 railroads provide rail and piggyback service, while Trans-Am
Airlines, the nation's largest trunkline, and Lindburgh Airlines,

the fastest growing local service carrier, give adequate air freight
and passenger service. In addition, two excellent air charter facilities
are also available.

Eight of the nation's largest truck lines supply Capitol City firms
with nationwide, single-line motor carrier service. Over 40 regional
and area truck lines offer reliable and speedy overnight delivery
within 400 miles. Two transcontinental buslines plus several intrastate lines give Capitol City many schedules of bus passenger and small
express service.

Complementing these facilities are three federal highways, Nos. 9, 11
and 21, plus a state highway (No. 7), as well as Interstate 5.

Historically, the city's economy was based on the agricultural wealth
of the surrounding area. Since World War II, a trend toward indus-
trialization has brought several nationally-known companies to Capitol
City, such as Addressograph-Multigraph Corp., American Stores Packing
Co., Brunswick Corp., Control Data Corp., Cushman Motors Co. (a division
of Outboard Marine Corp.), Dorsey Laboratories, Goodyear Tire and Rubber
Co., National Biscuit Co., Norden Laboratories, Pegler and Co., Pepsi-
Cola Bottling Co., Ralston Purina Co., and Square D Co., to name a few.

Being the capitol city of Kansas, as well as the county seat, Capitol
City is "home" for many State and Federal offices and agencies. In
addition, Kansas' largest university, along with two private institutions
of higher learning (Liberal College and Theological Seminary), contribute
to Capitol City's reputation as a scholastic center. All of these schools
provide four-year baccalaureate degrees and State University and Liberal
College provide advanced degrees as well. Their combined fall enrollment
in 1974 totalled approximately 25,000. The public elementary and secondary school system is widely recognized as one of the finest and most
innovative in the country. In addition to the public school systems of
33 elementary and 15 secondary schools, the city boasts a sizeable
parochial school system composed of 11 elementary and 3 secondary schools.

The city is governed by a modified manager plan consisting of a strong
fulltime Mayor and seven councilmen who are elected for four-year terms
on a non-partisan ballot by the voters at large. The councilmen, as
part-time officials, established policies that are administered by
full-time department heads. The Mayor and councilmen have the power
to pass, amend and repeal any and all city ordinances.

Capitol City owns and operates its own water and sewage facilities
and electrical distribution system. In addition, natural gas is
available to all sections of the city and the gas, water and power
rates enjoyed by Capitol City residents are among the lowest in the
country.

Sports and recreational facilities, essential for the preservation of
the "great place to raise a family" image that Capitol City enjoys,
consist of 48 parks with over 4,500 acres, 3 zoos, 8 golf courses,
numerous indoor and outdoor swimming pools, 28 public and 9 private
tennis courts (both indoor and outdoor), and 6 bowling alleys.

The climate is typically mid-continental, hot in the summer and cold
in the winter, but the extremes are greatly tempered by the generally
low humidity. Average annual rainfall is about 27-1/2 inches.

It is this appraiser's opinion that the broad diversification of
agricultural and business activity, combined with the stabilizing
influence of the state-supported governmental and educational institutions, provides a sound economic base for the city's continued growth.

NEIGHBORHOOD DATA

The subject property is situated at the intersection of Alpha Street
and Sherman Avenue in Capitol City, Kansas. Both Alpha Street and
Sherman Avenue constitute county section lines and, as such, carry
vehicular traffic beyond the corporate city limits into the adjoining
rural area. Sherman Avenue was at one time considered to be Capitol
City's western boundary; however, residential growth now extends to
County Line Road. The impetus for western growth of the city in the
area immediately north of Main Street was triggered by the Westmont
subdivision during the mid 1950's. Further impetus to the western
growth of the city occurred with the construction of the Fellow
Travelers Life and Mutual Casualty insurance buildings, Capitol City
Plaza, Midstate Federal Savings and Loan and other ancillary buildings
in the area surrounding the Essex Drive and Main Street intersection.
During the past two decades, over 50% of the new housing units constructed
have been in the land area west of Forest Avenue.

More directly affecting the immediate neighborhood is the recent opening
of Capitol City's Spartan High School and the projected opening of Methodist
Hospital both fronting on Sherman Avenue between Alpha Street and Main
Street. Several builders have been successful in acquiring and subdividing
vacant land in the quadrant lying north and west of the subject site
for single family residential and multi-family developments.

In this appraiser's opinion, there is no existing zoned land that would
constitute serious competition to the proposed development. Oakridge
Center, located near the intersection of Essex Drive and Alpha Street,
is approximately one and one-half miles directly east of the subject
site. It is understood that this center had marginal acceptance during
its initial phase but can now be considered as extremely successful
from ownership's viewpoint. In visiting this center, this appraiser
reached a conclusion that because of the density of use, the developer
has created a shortage of on-site parking. Ingress and egress also
must be described as extremely difficult during peak shopping periods.

Shermantown, an existing center located just south of the intersection
of Sherman Avenue and Ivy Street, also might be interpreted to constitute a secondary competitive facility. However, the location two
miles due south of the subject site obviates any serious competition
between these two facilities.

Capitol City Plaza is a regional center comprising approximately
700,000 square feet of retail commercial buildings situated on a 50-acre
site and located just west of the intersection of Essex Drive and Main
Street. The concept of the convenience center as described in the
following pages sets forth a basis for the development of the convenience
center. In this appraiser's opinion, the existence of Capitol City
Plaza approximately two miles from the subject site does not interfere
with the projected economic feasibility of West Bend, but could conceiv-
ably be an asset since the subject site is situated in an intercept
location to traffic that may be attracted to the Plaza originating in
an area north or west of the subject site.

SITE DESCRIPTION

The subject site is near rectangular in shape except for a 190 foot square parcel occupying the corner of the intersection of Sherman and Alpha. The west boundary of the parcel faces Sherman Avenue, fronting 380 feet thereon, extending to an average depth of 520 feet to the west. The south boundary is 330 feet fronting on Alpha Street, extending to a depth of 570 feet. The property encompasses 255,698 square feet in all, or approximately 5.875 acres. Both Sherman Avenue and Alpha Street are four-lane, hard-surfaced arterial streets. Both street frontages have been improved with a public sidewalk. All public utilities are conveniently available to the site.

The elevation rises from a low point on the south boundary in a level plain some 20 feet greater at the north property line. An abrupt swale occurs in the extreme northwest corner where the property rises an additional 7 feet to street grade. In general, the natural lie of the land will not require any major earth movement to accommodate the proposed development but should instead constitute an ideal topography from a visual and physical standpoint.

ZONING

The property is zoned G-1 Planned Commercial District, which is a zoning classification for neighborhood commercial. It is the opinion of this appraiser that zoning regulations permit the operation of a convenience shopping center at this location.

TAXES

Within Capitol City, ad valorem real estate taxes are levied by both city and county governments.

The County Assessor has placed the assessed value of commercial property at 35% of its appraised value. The appraised value is calculated using the Marshall, Stevens Valuation Method.

City tax rates are set by the City Council and County tax rates are set by the County Treasurer. Both City and County tax rates are based on the assessed value as determined by the County Assessor. In 1974 all property within Capitol City was taxed at the following rates:

City Tax Rate	$24.500	per $1,000 of assessed valuation
County Tax Rate	$10.685	per $1,000 of assessed valuation
School Tax Rate	$47.198	per $1,000 of assessed valuation
Other	$ 1.770	per $1,000 of assessed valuation
Total	$84.153	per $1,000 of assessed valuation

DESCRIPTION OF IMPROVEMENTS

The improvements will consist of two major buildings (see Site Map, Exhibit B). Building A will be a 43,050 square foot, concrete block brick veneer, one story, basementless building, designed for multi-tenant use. Building B will be a 14,560 square foot, one story building of similar construction. A 2,632 square foot Yum Yum Tree will, in addition, be designed to meet franchise specifications. The parking lot will be paved and lighted, with parking for 275 cars.

Building A, a merchandising building designed for a food super market, drug store, clothing store, hardware, furniture store, etc., will be of English Tudor design with shake shingle overhang extending over three sides of the structure. The roof is to be flat, built-up, supported by steel bar joists with steel posts and girders 24 feet to 30 feet on center. Each tenant area will contain roof-mounted heat and air conditioning units and space will be fully sprinklered. Interior decorating will be provided by individual tenants.

Building B will be of similar construction and designed primarily to accommodate professional and business services such as medical offices, accountants, beauty shop, dry cleaning, financial office, etc.

The Yum Yum Tree will meet the franchise operators new concept for merchandising incorporating seating for approximately 70 patrons.

The parking lot will be asphalt paving, well lighted, with pole-mounted arc lights. Parking stalls will be striped and approximately ten feet wide.

There will be a planning strip approximately forty feet wide on both street frontages.

THE CONVENIENCE SHOPPING CENTER CONCEPT

The Convenience Shopping Center is not a random collection of stores, but instead a merchandising entity designed to meet the day-to-day needs of the suburban household. The primary need, of course, is food, and the supermarket is invariably the biggest, single tenant in the center. The family drug store, hardware and multi-line soft goods store constitute the remaining major tenants supplemented by the beauty parlor, barber shop, dry cleaner and liquor store.

Complimenting the tenant mix in a well-conceived neighborhood center is a branch bank or savings and loan office as well as a limited number of professional offices, notably for doctors and dentists. Generally, business offices are inappropriate unless the tenants provide a service to residents living in the trade area.

The proximity of the center to schools, recreational facilities or a location in an intercepting position to vehicular travel will broaden the market base for the convenience center. The income level of the area resident will have an impact on the tenant mix. The higher income families will be better able to support the beauty parlor, gift shop, home furnishing center or service oriented tenants than could be expected in a similar center situated in the lower income quadrant of the city.

Convenience centers will typically range in size from 30,000 to 80,000 square feet of building area occupying four to six acres of land. The primary market will depend on the accessibility of the site to the surrounding residential areas. Generally, automobile driving time is more important than distance. Residences within a three to five minute time zone can be considered prime customers depending on the location of competitive centers. This will normally cover a radius of $1\frac{1}{2}$ to 2 miles from the site. With customer mobility comes problems. Problems relating to accessibility to the site, vehicular traffic patterns on the site and parking. Expensive land means expensive parking. The parking lot is an integral part of the center and is no less valuable than the land on which the buildings rest. A proper development requires sufficient land for customer parking, drives and walkways, as well as some "green space" to frame the picture. Less desirable stalls on "off site areas" should also be available for employee parking.

The Urban Land Institute has published studies which indicate that, where there is little walk-in traffic, 5.5 parking stalls per 1,000 square feet of gross leaseable area are adequate. This report also states that up to 20% of the gross leaseable area could consist of office space without upsetting this ratio.

Finally, and possibly most significant of all, are the design features of the various store buildings, such as architectural style, material composition, customer circulation and servicing facilities related to the day-to-day merchandising activity of the tenants. Compatability of the individual merchants with each other and the center's management will be reflected in the degree of the financial success of the center.

In conclusion, the successful convenience shopping center is not just a "happening" but is the result of determining the economic needs of the consumers in a given market area and satisfying those needs by providing the proper site, physical improvements, merchandise and services to insure continued customer acceptance.

Source:

Nelson, Richard L., The Selection of Retail Locations, F. W. Dodge
Corporation, N.Y., 1958.

Lowden, James A., "Valuation of Shopping Centers," The Appraisal
Journal, April, 1967.

"The Village Shopping Center," House and Home, October, 1968.

HIGHEST AND BEST USE

Highest and best use is defined as that use which at the time of the appraisal is most likely to produce the greatest net return over a given period of time. In determining the highest and best use of raw land, it is imperative that such use meet the following tests:

1. The use must be legal.
2. The use must be within the realm of probability; that is, it must be likely, not speculative or conjectural.
3. There must be a demand for such use.
4. The use must be profitable.
5. The use must be such as to return to land the highest net return.
6. The use must be such as to deliver the return for the longest period of time.

It is this appraiser's opinion that the proposed development of a convenience shopping center meets all of the prerequisites outlined above and therefore constitutes the land's highest and best use.

ESTIMATE OF LAND VALUE

In order to estimate the value of the subject land, the records have
been checked for sales or leases of comparable land. The transactions,
listed chronologically below, are designated by number on the map
attached as Exhibit C.

Number 1: Lots 205 and 206 in the SE¼, Section 21, Tier 10 South,
Range 7 West of the 3rd Principal Meridian, Capitol City,
Kansas. Warranty Deed dated July 27, 1970. Grantor,
Lester Flowers conveying 1/2 interest to Reliable Life
Insurance Company. Consideration, $500,000. Size,
466,528 s.f.

Number 2: Lots 26, 27 and 28 of Addison's Subdivision, NW¼, Section
20, T10S, R7W, Capitol City. Warranty Deed dated June 1,
1971. Grantor, Paul Graham, et al to National Savings
Bank. Consideration, $375,000. Size, 272,727 s.f.

Number 3: Lots 198 and 199, NW¼, Section 21, T10S, R7W, Capitol City.
Warranty Deed dated November 5, 1971. Grantor, Joseph and
Mary C. Doe to Richard D. Jones, trustee. Consideration,
$1,060,000. Size 914,760 s.f.

Number 4: Lots 70 and 71, NE¼, Section 22, T10S, R7W, Capitol City.
Warranty Deed dated November 22, 1971. Grantor, Commercial
Realty Company to Robert B. Hall and wife, Sally A.,
Consideration, $200,000. Size, 130,680 s.f.

Number 5: Lot 183, Irregular Tract, NW¼, Section 21, T10S, R7W,
Capitol City. Warranty Deed dated May 25, 1972. Grantor,
Plaza Development, Inc. to Consolidated Department Stores,
Inc. Consideration, $750,000. Size, 871,200 s.f.

Number 6: Lot 1, Block 1, Jackson's Replat, SE¼, Section 20, T10S,
R7W, Capitol City. Lease commencing November 1, 1973.
Lessor, State Investment Company to Hypermarche, Inc.
Prime term, 30 years, with two 10-year renewal options
at rentals based upon the Consumer Price Index. Prime
term rent, $24,400 per year, absolutely net. The lease
refers to the annual rent being equal to "8-1/2% of value".
Using this as a capitalization rate, a value of $287,000
is indicated. Size, 265,900 s.f.

Number 7: Lot 71, NE¼, Section 22, T10S, R7W, Capitol City.
Warranty Deed dated December 10, 1973. Grantor, Robert
B. Hall and wife, Sally A., to Iowa Associates, Inc.
Consideration $141,000. Size, 81,457 s.f.

Number 8: Lot 71, NE¼, Section 22, T10S, R7W, Capitol City.
Warranty Deeds dated (a) December 21 and (b) December
22, 1973. Grantor, Iowa Associates, Inc. to (a) Fast
Foods, Inc. and (b) Conservative Financial Corporation.
Considerations (a) $50,000 and (b) $122,000. Size
81,457 s.f. (a and b combined).

Transaction Number	Date	Indicated Value	S. F.	Value per S.F.	Zoning
*1	7-27-70	$1,000,000	466,528	$2.14	A-2: Single Family
2	6-01-71	375,000	272,727	1.38	H-1: Hiway Bus.
3	11-05-71	1,060,000	914,760	1.16	G: Local Bus.
4	11-22-71	200,000	130,680	1.53	G
**5	5-25-72	750,000	871,200	.96	G-1: Planned Comm.
6	11-01-73	287,000	265,900	1.08	G
7	12-10-73	141,000	81,457	1.73	G
***8(a)	12-21-73	50,000	81,457	2.11	G
(b)	12-22-73	122,000			G

* Assumes that the $500,000 price for a 1/2 interest reflects
a value of $1,000,000 for the whole interest.

** Value per square foot of $.96 is based upon an _effective_
area of only 784,080 s.f. due to zoning regulations which
require a 150' buffer strip along Paris Avenue.

*** Because these two Warranty Deeds were granted at about
the same time by the same Grantor, I have combined them
to arrive at one value per square foot that will readily
compare with Transaction No. 7.

The transactions recorded above indicate a square foot value for
comparable land ranging from $.96 to $2.14.

Transaction 1 is zoned for single-family dwellings and is, therefore,
considered to be less comparable to the subject site than are some of
the other transactions.

Transaction 2 is quite comparable to the subject site in terms of
potential use, size and location along a major thoroughfare. It is
situated in a more highly-developed area than is the subject site,
however, and it enjoys about 900 feet of frontage along Capitol City's
busiest street. Thus, it is considered to be somewhat superior to the
subject site. It is currently improved with a full-service motel
facility, and, with the passage of time, the value of the land has
probably appreciated to at least $2.00 per square foot.

Transaction 3 is not considered to be very comparable to the subject
property because it is so much larger and enjoys a great deal more
exposure with nearly 2,500 feet of street frontage, over 700 of which
is on Main Street. Despite its superiority in size and exposure, however,
it is somewhat inferior to the subject property in that it would
need extensive site preparation before the land could be put to commercial use. In addition, prolonged controversy with respect to
whether or not this parcel is appropriately zoned has made it something of an "unknown quantity". These deficiencies are reflected
in the slightly low purchase price of $1.16 per square foot and in the
fact that the land remains untouched to this day.

Transaction 4, though irregular in shape and only half the size of the
subject site, is considered to be superior because of its location.

Transaction 5 is not considered to be comparable to the subject site
primarily because of its size and the circumstances surrounding its sale.
It was sold at a below-market price by the owners/developers of the

adjacent regional shopping center in order to induce the buyer to build
a major department store thereon.

Transaction 6 is comparable to the subject site in nearly every respect.
Its only deficiencies are that it is located in a slightly less affluent
section of town and it enjoys actual frontage on only one major thorough-
fare--Ivy Street. It is, however, very close to--and visible from--
Forest Avenue, another major thoroughfare which enjoys a high degree of
commercial development. Its time-adjusted value would probably approximate $1.15 per square foot.

Transactions 8(a) and 8(b) involved portions of the parcel involved in
Transaction 4 and are included here to demonstrate the effects that the
passage of time and further subdivision have had on land values in this
area.

After studying all of the above data, it is this appraiser's opinion
that the value of the subject land is approximately $1.30 per square
foot, or $332,400.

LAND AND IMPROVEMENTS - COST APPROACH

Section 13 of the _Marshall Valuation Service_ lists several types of
retail stores and restaurant facilities. The classifications that are
most descriptive of the improvements proposed for the subject property
are "Good Class C" for the retail stores and "Average Class D" for the
restaurant facility. Using the _Marshall Valuation Service_ information
in conjunction with other data, results in the following estimate of
value via the Cost Approach:

IMPROVEMENTS:

Restaurant:
  Basic Cost $26.60/s.f.
  HVAC   .80
  Sprinkler   .92
                      $28.32/s.f. x 2,632 s.f. $ 74,538

Retail Space:
  Basic Cost $19.10/s.f.
  HVAC   .85
  Sprinkler   .64
                      $20.59/s.f. x 57,610 s.f. $1,186,190

  Parking (Asphalt) $ .50/s.f. x 180,000 s.f. $ 90,000

TOTAL IMPROVEMENT COST $1,350,728

INTANGIBLES:

  Leasing Fees (5% of Gross Effective Income) $ 10,640
  Construction Interest (10% of Average Balance
    of a 75% Construction Loan)   50,600
  Loan Fees   20,000

LAND:

  255,698 s.f. @ $1.30/s.f.   332,400
                                                    $1,764,368
                                      Say, $1,750,000

I have been advised that the proposed contractor, Jiffy Construction Company, estimates that he could build the retail space for approximately $1,000,000. Using their figures, the following is projected:

Buildings A & B @ $18/s.f.	$1,037,000
Parking @ $0.50/s.f.	90,000
Yum Yum Tree @ $27.50/s.f.	73,000
Intangibles	81,000
	$1,281,000
Land @ $1.30/s.f.	332,400
	$1,613,400

This estimate is approximately $150,000 less than the estimated cost of improvements using the <u>Marshall Valuation Service</u> and is a fair representation of the owner's estimate of brick and mortar cost as of this date. Not reflected in the contractor's estimate is entrepreneurial profit. In my opinion, this "entrepreneurship" has a value equal to most of the difference.

ECONOMIC APPROACH

Shopping centers in the Capitol City area rent for prices ranging from $2.00 to over $6.00 per square foot, the lower rent being paid by larger, well-capitalized firms renting the larger spaces on long-term, substantially net leases. Higher rents are paid by the smaller tenants occupying smaller spaces for shorter periods of time.

Based upon a review of comparable properties--namely those plotted on the map attached as Exhibit A--it has been determined that the rents established by the owners of the subject property are competitive. In some cases, the leases require payment of the minimum rent or a percentage of gross income, whichever is greater. No attempt has been made by the appraiser to estimate overages in arriving at the following value by the Economic Approach.

	S.F.	Lease Term	Rent per S.F.	Gross Rent	Percentage
Building A:					
Grocery	16,650	25 yrs.	$2.50/yr	$41,625	1.75%
Hardware	10,200	15 "	2.80 "	28,560	4.00
Drugs	6,000	10 "	4.05 "	24,300	4.00
Furniture	4,800	5 "	3.75 "	18,000	6.00
Clothing	4,200	10 "	3.90 "	16,380	6.00
Miscellaneous	1,200	--	3.75 "	4,500	--
SUB-TOTAL	43,050			$133,365	
Building B:					
Financial	2,688	10 yrs.	$5.50/yr	$13,440	--
Liquor	1,344	10 "	6.25 "	8,400	3.00
Cleaners	1,000	5 "	4.05 "	4,050	7.50
Beauty Shop	1,000	5 "	5.00 "	5,000	8.00
Barber	670	5 "	6.25 "	4,188	8.00
Miscellaneous	7,858	--	5.00 "	39,290	--
SUB-TOTAL	14,560			$ 74,368	
Restaurant	2,632	15 yrs.	$5.00/yr.	$ 13,160	7.00%
GROSS FIGURES:	60,242			$220,893	

Gross Income $220,893

Less Vacancy as follows:
  25 year lease -- none = $ -0-
  15 year leases --   2%   =   834
  10 year leases --   3%   = 1,876
   5 year leases --   4%   = 1,250
  Miscellaneous -- 10%   = 4,379   8,339
Effective Gross Income $212,554

Less Expenses:
  *Taxes, 40¢/s.f. $24,097
   Insurance, 5¢/s.f.   3,012
   Management, 5% of Eff. Gr.   10,620
   Maintenance, 6¢/s.f.   3,615
   Common Area Reserve in excess
     of tenant's contribution   3,000
   Merchants Assoc. Dues   1,200
   Miscellaneous   1,000 $ 46,554
Net Income $166,000

Charge Land at 8-1/2% on $332,400 $ 28,254
Net Income Attributable to Improvements $137,746

    $137,746 capitalized at 10% $1,377,460

Add Land $ 332,400
                                                                  $1,709,860
                                                             Say $1,700,000

    *Note: Taxes are estimated at 40¢ per square foot
        of improvements based upon the following infor-
        mation:

        Oakridge Shopping Center
          53,043 s.f. 1974 taxes = $18,565   35¢/s.f.

        Shermantown Shopping Center
          40,730 s.f. 1974 taxes = $15,870   39¢/s.f.

        It is felt that the subject property will be
        superior to both of the above-mentioned centers in
        terms of size, location and embellishments. Hence,
        a slightly higher tax rate has been projected.

SUMMARY

Estimate of Value by the Cost Approach $1,750,000
Estimate of Value by the Economic Approach $1,700,000

CORRELATION AND CONCLUSION

The subject property is very well located in the heart of an excellent
trading area. As the city continues to grow toward the North and
Northwest, this area will become an even better trading zone.

The streets on which the property fronts have been recently widened
to accommodate four lanes of traffic, and access to the site is
very good.

The owner is experienced in this field, having spent over 20 years in the business of developing, for others, various types of commercial and residential properties on a regional basis.

The subject property is an income-producing property and, consequently, the Economic Approach is adjudged to be the best indicator of current value. This approach is based upon minimum rents with percentage leases which are typical for the industry, and while the excess rents were not capitalized into the value, the fact that there is a strong possibility of overages being paid considerably enhances the quality of the income stream.

Therefore, as a result of my investigation and my general experience, it is my opinion that the market value of the property described in this report, as of March 21, 1975, is:

ONE MILLION SEVEN HUNDRED THOUSAND DOLLARS...$1,700,000.00

Respectfully submitted,

Robert M. Thornton, Appraiser

EXHIBIT A

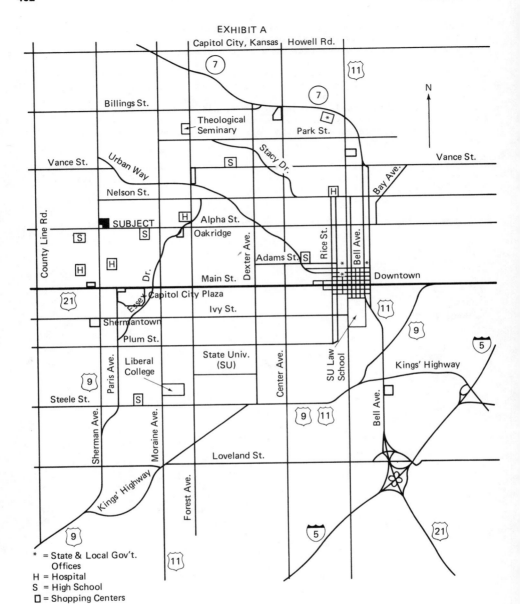

EXHIBIT B

Site Map

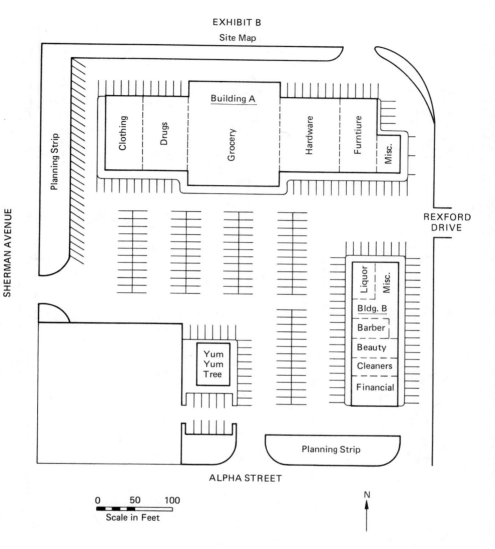

EXHIBIT C

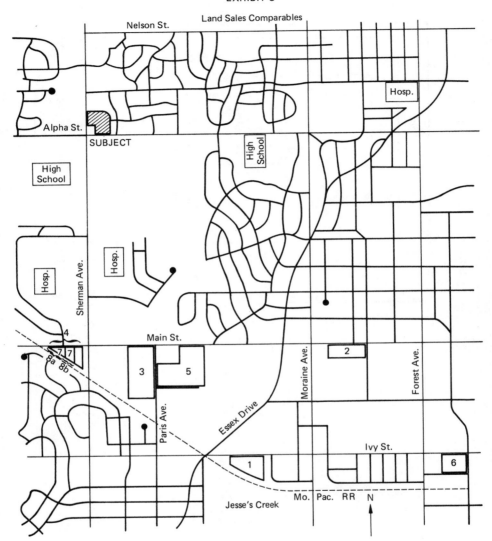

FOLLOW-UP CORRESPONDENCE

SOUTHEASTERN LIFE INSURANCE COMPANY
State and Madison Streets
Chicago, Illinois

John T. Allgood
Vice President

April 10, 1975

Mr. Arnold L. Mason
XYZ Mortgage Company
1231 Washington Street
Capitol City, Kansas

Re: Robert Johnson d/b/a West Bend Shopping Center
     60,242 S. F. Convenience Shopping Center
     Alpha Street and Sherman Avenue
     Capitol City, Kansas

Dear Arnie:

Thanks for the package on the West Bend Shopping Center in Capitol
City, Kansas. From our initial review, it looks like we can show
a positive interest in taking this loan application to our Finance
Committee, which will be meeting next Friday, April 18.

We do have some concern, however, in recommending this loan, with
the less than normal parking index. Could you give me comparable
parking information on the four other centers located in Capitol
City which were used in your Schedule of Comparable Rentals.

Arnie, it would also help if some of the "tentative" leases you
talk about in your letter have been finalized. Has any progress
been made in this regard since the signing of the application?

I am suggesting you give me a call relative to the parking data
since I would like to resolve this question before our Finance
Committee meeting.

Sincerely,

John T. Allgood

JTA:sdt

XYZ Mortgage Company
1231 Washington Street
Capitol City, Kansas
Phone: 464-7412

April 15, 1975

Mr. John T. Allgood
Vice President
Southeastern Life Insurance Company
State and Madison Streets
Chicago, Illinois

Re: Robert Johnson d/b/a West Bend Shopping Center
    60,242 S. F. Convenience Shopping Center
    Alpha Street and Sherman Avenue
    Capitol City, Kansas

Dear John:

This will confirm our phone conversation of this morning in
which I advised you of the results of our parking survey,
as follows:

Oakridge Convenience Center	3.9	cars per 1,000 s.f. of gross leaseable area
Shermantown	5.2	"
Urban City	4.8	"
Bellfort	6.2	"

The Oakridge Center is admittedly handicapped by its inadequate
parking index. The Bellfort Center is a phase development, and
the final parking index will probably be reduced to less than 5.0
per 1,000 when completed.

Our subject center, at 4.6, appears quite adequate; however,
ownership, upon our suggestion, has negotiated with a church on
adjacent property to provide parking for employees during the
week as consideration for allowing ingress and egress to the church
parking lot from the northeast corner of our Center. This concession
was made by the church after realizing the benefit that the parishioners
would have by having additional access to the lot for their Sunday
morning services.

I am also enclosing a lease summary for the Perry's Grocery lease,
which was executed last Friday. This lease is conditioned upon
Robert Johnson being able to obtain financing at the 9-5/8% rate
applied for. We should have, within the next few days, similar

Mr. John T. Allgood
April 15, 1975
Page 2

leases with National Hardware, Friendly Drugs, and U-Sav-Mor
Savings and Loan, at the project rentals indicated.

Let me stress once again how strong we feel about both Mr.
Johnson and his West Bend Shopping Center project. This site
is an absolute natural from a real estate standpoint and Mr.
Johnson has created what we feel will be an instant success.
Needless to say, this loan application, as submitted, carries
our full endorsement.

Please give me a call immediately following your Friday
Finance Committee meeting.

Sincerely,

Arnie

Arnold L. Mason

ALM:xxx

Enclosure

<u>LEASE ANALYSIS</u>

LESSOR: Robert Johnson d/b/a West Bend Shopping Center

LESSEE: Perry's Grocery

DATED: April 11, 1975
            FROM: April 1, 1976 or occupancy date, whichever is earlier
            TO: 2001
            TERM: 25 years

SQ. FT. AREA: 16,650 square feet

GUARANTEED $41,625/year
RENT: ($2.50/s.f./year)

PERCENTAGE: 1.75% of annual gross in excess of $2,378,570

MAINTENANCE: Lessor: Outside walls, roof, sewer, curbs, sidewalks,
                      paving, plumbing, HVAC
             Lessee: All interior walls, flooring, ceilings, lessee
                      improvements and fixtures.

SUBORDINATION: Full

INSURANCE: Lessor: Fire and extended coverage on building
             Lessee: $100,000/$300,000/$50,000 Liability plus coverage
                      on contents

TAXES: Lessor: Base year real estate taxes
             Lessee: Tax increases only

UTILITIES: Lessee pays all

ASSIGNMENT: Lessor's consent required

RENEWAL OPTION: One 5-year option with a rental increase tied
                 to the Consumer Price Index

USE CLAUSE: Supermarket only

EMINENT DOMAIN: If all or a substantial part is taken, lessee may cancel lease.

MISCELLANEOUS: If repairs take longer than 150 days, lessee may cancel lease

Reviewed by _Arnold L. Mau_

Date: _April 14, 1975_

THE LOAN APPLICATION

XYZ Mortgage Company
1231 Washington Street
Capitol City, Kansas
Phone: 464-7412

April 2, 1975

Mr. John T. Allgood, Vice President
Southeastern Life Insurance Company
State and Madison Streets
Chicago, Illinois

Re: Robert Johnson d/b/a West Bend Shopping Center
60,242 S.F. Convenience Shopping Center
Alpha Street and Sherman Avenue
Capitol City, Kansas

Dear John:

Having received a mortgage loan application (Exhibit D), with deposit, on the above-referenced property, we are pleased to enclose the following for your consideration:

LOAN SUMMARY AND ANALYSIS

SECURITY: Proposed 60,242 s.f. convenience shopping center, situated on a 5.875 acre lot, and consisting of 3 buildings:

Building A - Retail/Professional	43,050 s.f.
Building B - Retail/Professional	14,560 s.f.
Fast Food Franchise (National Chain)	2,632 s.f.

Parking is available for 274 cars.

LOCATION: NE corner at Alpha Street and Sherman Avenue (except corner piece measuring 190' x 190') in Capitol City, Kansas.

BORROWER: Robert Johnson d/b/a West Bend Shopping Center. Net Worth = $475,000. Experience - Over 20 years as a real estate developer, specializing primarily in apartments with some diversification into office buildings and small shopping centers. He generally builds for sale to other parties, but he intends, for the first time, to retain ownership of this project.

LOAN
REQUEST:

Amount:	$1,275,000
Term:	25 years
Amortization:	27 years
Rate:	9-5/8%
Servicing:	1/8 of 1% to XYZ Mortgage Company
Net Yield:	9-1/2%
Prepayment:	Closed 10 years. Open at 5% premium, declining 1% per year to minimum of 1%

LOAN   Loan to Value Ratio: 75%
ANALYSIS: Loan/S.F. of Bldg. Area: $21.16
              Annual Debt Service: $132,728 (Constant - 10.41%)
              Debt Service Coverage: 1.25 to 1
              Breakpoint: 81%
              Balance after 25 years: $240,975 (Land value = $332,400)
              Parking Index: 4.6 spaces per 1,000 s.f./building area

FUNDING: Second quarter, 1976.

LOCATION

The subject property is situated on the Northeast corner of Alpha Street
and Sherman Avenue in Capitol City, Kansas, diagonally across the intersection from the Spartan High School complex. This location is in the
heart of the city's Northwest Growth Corridor and is surrounded by a
rapidly-developing, well-maintained, upper-class residential neighborhood.
Homes in the immediate vicinity are in the $60,000 - $75,000 range, and
it would be necessary to travel at least two miles from the shopping
center to find a home valued as low as $30,000. As you can see, the
income level of the nearly 16,000 residents living within this center's
marketing area is sufficiently high to support a tenant mix which includes
a beauty parlor, a gift shop, a furniture store, and several professional
service-oriented businesses.

County Line Road, about one mile west of the subject shopping center,
forms Capitol City's western boundary, beyond which more upper-class
residential development is just commencing.

In addition to benefitting from the significant further growth potential
of the immediate area, the center is ideally located to attract patrons
from rural areas to the north and west. This is because both Alpha
Street and Sherman Avenue constitute county section lines and, as such,
are major carriers of vehicular traffic from beyond the corporate city
limits. Ingress and egress is excellent from both of these four-lane
arterials.

IMPROVEMENTS

The enclosed appraisal fully describes the physical characteristics of
the improvements so I will be brief in my comments concerning them. I
would merely like to point out that available parking, at 4.6 spaces per
1,000 s.f. of leaseable area, while below the Urban Land Institute's
"5.5 per 1,000" standard of adequacy, should nevertheless be sufficient
for the West Bend Shopping Center since very few of the businesses
require long-term parking.

VALUE

The cost estimate given by Jiffy Construction Company, and mentioned in
the appraisal, can be considered fairly firm as it was made in the form
of a fixed-cost bid by the highly reputable local contractor, who has a
great deal of experience in this type of construction. Adding a reasonable amount of entrepreneurial profit to their bid results in a cost
estimate which closely approximates, and thus corroborates, that derived
from the Marshall and Swift Valuation Service.

As for the project's economic value, we have conducted our own survey of comparable rents in the Capitol City area (a summary of which is attached as Exhibit B to this letter) which substantiates the validity of the tentative lease agreements reached with prospective tenants thus far. Details of these tentative leases are set forth in Exhibit A.

BORROWER

The borrower, Robert Johnson, is a life-long resident of Capitol City and is well known throughout the community. Although this project constitutes his first venture, personally, into the long-term ownership of a sizable commercial property, we feel completely confident in recommending him highly to you because of his twenty-plus years of experience in successfully developing such properties for others. We have attached his personal financial statement to this letter as Exhibit C, but we suggest that you approach this investment opportunity more from the real estate, than from the credit, angle.

SUMMARY

Based upon our underwriting criteria, we feel that this proposal contains the ingredients desired in a high quality loan offering. Our optimism stems from the following:

1. The excellence of the real estate, located in a high-income neighborhood, with tremendous growth potential.

2. A well-substantiated value, both from an economic and a cost standpoint, which is fully capable of supporting projected debt service and expenses.

3. Tentative lease agreements with good local credits which result in the property's being 85% pre-leased before construction has even begun. Letters of intent will be made available upon request.

4. An owner/developer who is highly experienced in the analysis and underwriting of such investments and who intends to retain his ownership interest in the property.

We therefore confidently recommend this loan for your favorable consideration, based upon a loan amount of $1,275,000, a loan term of 25 years, with a 27-year amortization, and a gross yield of 9-5/8% with 1/8 of 1% servicing.

Thank you very much for your consideration in this matter. We look forward to receiving your commitment for permanent financing.

Sincerely,

Arnie

Arnold L. Mason

Enclosures

ANALYSIS OF TENTATIVE LEASES

| | | MIN. ANNUAL RENT | | | |
Tenant	S.F.	Total	Per S.F.	% Rents	Prime Term
Perry's Grocery	16,650	$41,625	$2.50	1.75%	25 yrs.
National Hardware	10,200	28,560	2.80	4	15 yrs.
Friendly Drugs	6,000	24,300	4.05	· 4	10 yrs.
Sleepy Time Furniture	4,800	18,000	3.75	6	5 yrs.
Men's Wear, Ltd.	4,200	16,380	3.90	6	10 yrs.
Huey's Off-Sale Liquor	1,344	8,400	6.25	3	10 yrs.
Spot Check Cleaners	1,000	4,050	4.05	7.5	5 yrs.
Slyvester's Beauty Salon	1,000	5,000	5.00	8	55 yrs.
Yankee Clipper (Barber)	670	4,188	6.25	8	5 yrs.
U-Sav-Mor S & L	2,688	13,440	6.00	10	10 yrs.

Renewal Options	Lease Sub-ordination	Taxes	Maintenance	Insurance	Utilities
one 5-yr.	full	Lessor with 1st yr. stop	Lessor-Ext. Lessee-Int.	Lessee: Contents & Liability only	Lessee
two 5-yr.	"	"	"	"	"
two 5-yr.	"	"	"	"	"
two 5-yr.	"	"	"	"	"
one 5-yr.	"	"	"	"	"
one 5-yr.	"	"	"	"	"
two 5-yr.	"	"	"	"	"
one 5-yr.	"	"	"	"	"
one 5-yr.	"	"	"	"	"
two 10-yr.	"	"	"	"	"

EXHIBIT A

SCHEDULE OF COMPARABLE RENTALS

		Tenant Type	Prime Term	Renewal Terms	Annual Rent/SF	% Rents	Expenses Lessee	Lessor
(1)	Oakridge Essex Dr. & Alpha St. Capitol City, Kan.	Major:	15-20 years	two (+) 5 yr.	$2.65	1-2%	Utilities Tax Incr. Contents Ins.	All Other
		Minor:	5-10 years	0-two, 3-5 yrs.	$3.75- 6.50	3-7%	Liab. Ins.	
(2)	Shermantown Ivy St. & Sherman Avenue Capitol City, Kan.	Major:	20 yrs.	up to 10 yrs.	$2.50- 2.60	1-3%	All Exp.	None
		Minor:	5-10 years	up to 5 yrs.	$2.00- 6.00	4-6%		
(3)	Urban City Forest Avenue & Urban Way Capitol City, Kan.	Major:	25 yrs.	5 yrs.	$2.60	1%	Utilities Contents Ins.	All Other
		Minor:	5-10 years	very flexible	$3.50- 6.50	4-8%		
(4)	Bellfort Belmont Avenue & Calvin Street Capitol City, Kan.	Major:	20-25 years	two 5-yr.	$2.45 2.60	1.5%	Utilities Contents Ins. Int. Maint. Tax Incr.	All Other
		Minor:	3-10 years	0-three 3-5 yrs.	$3.60 6.50	3-8%	Liab. Ins.	
(5)	SUBJECT Alpha Street and Sherman Avenue Capitol City, Kan.	Major:	15-25 years	5-10 years	$2.50- 2.80	1.75- 5%	Utilities Contents Ins. Liab. Ins. Tax Incr.	All Other
		Minor:	5-10 years	5-10 years	$3.75 6.25	4-8%	Int. Maint.	

EXHIBIT B, Page 1

EXHIBIT A

Capitol City, Kansas

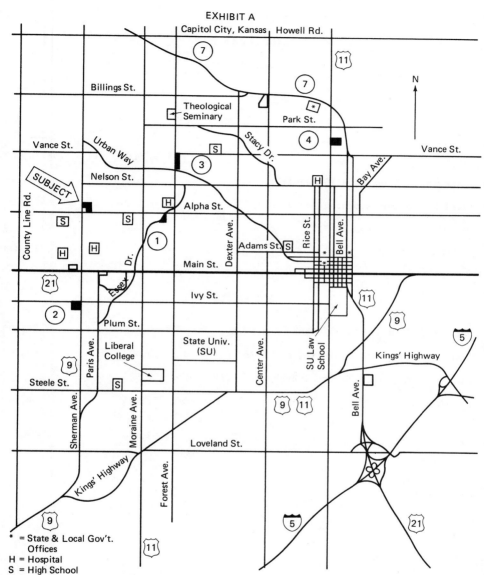

* = State & Local Gov't.
    Offices
H = Hospital
S = High School
■ = Location of Comparable Rental Properties

ROBERT JOHNSON

Balance Sheet
as of
December 31, 1974

ASSETS

	Cost	Market
Cash	$ 50,000	$ 50,000
Marketable Securities (Schedule 1)	80,929	74,479
Real Estate Investments (Schedule 2)	268,500	424,400
Other Assets (Schedule 3)	147,000	165,000
TOTAL ASSETS	$546,429	$713,879

LIABILITIES

	Cost	Market
Personal Note - National Bank, due 8/75	$ 37,500	$ 37,500
Personal Note - C. A. Smith, due 5/76	90,000	90,000
Mortgage on Land - National Bank, due 12/81	108,945	108,945
TOTAL LIABILITIES	$236,445	$236,445
EQUITY	$309,984	$477,434

SCHEDULE 1

MARKETABLE SECURITIES

		Cost	Market
2100 Shares	Blue Chip, Inc.	$ 33,600	$ 29,400
6000 Warrants	Blue Chip, Inc.	24,000	21,000
300 Shares	Ozark Distillers	6,000	4,500
1500 Shares	International Airport	5,000	5,250
Bonds	Capitol City Air Authority ('94)	24,750	25,000
	New York City, N.Y. ('97)	48,500	50,000
	Chicago, Illinois ('98)	24,750	25,000
		$166,600	$160,150
Less Amount Due Broker		85,671	85,671
Total Marketable Securities		$ 80,929	$ 74,479

EXHIBIT C, Page 2

SCHEDULE 2

REAL ESTATE INVESTMENTS

	Cost	Market
Unimproved Land Alpha St. & Sherman Ave. Capitol City, Kansas	$225,000	$332,400
Land and Retail Building Nelson St. & Belmont Ave. Capitol City, Kansas	24,500	38,000
Residence 3310 Stacy Drive Capitol City, Kansas	19,000	54,000
	$268,500	$424,400
Less Mortgage on Unimproved Land	$108,945	$108,945
Total Real Estate Investments	$159,555	$315,455

EXHIBIT C, Page 2

SCHEDULE 3

OTHER ASSETS

	Cost	Market
Art - Paintings	$ 30,000	$ 40,000
Employee Profit Sharing Plan	50,000	75,000
Cattle	20,000	20,000
Automobiles (2)	12,000	10,000
Furniture and Other Personal Belongings	25,000	10,000
Cash Value Life Insurance	10,000	10,000
Total Other Assets	$147,000	$165,000

EXHIBIT C, Page 3

MORTGAGE LOAN APPLICATION

(All questions must be answered in order to insure prompt consideration)

Application is hereby made to ___XYZ Mortgage Company_____

for a loan of $1,275,000.00___ for a term of _25_ years, _0_ months, on

which applicant(s) agree(s) to repay the sum of $11,057.44 to apply to

interest and principal _X_ monthly, ____quarterly, beginning no sooner than

the 1st_ day of ___April____, 19_76_. Interest is to be paid at the rate

of ___9-5/8%____ per annum monthly/quarterly on the 1st day of each ___month____.

SEE ADDITIONAL PROVISIONS

As evidence of said loan applicant(s) agree(s) to execute a mortgage or trust
deed note signed by all parties in interest and to secure said note by a
first mortgage or first trust deed on the following described real property
in the

City of __Capitol City_____ County of ___Gem_____ State of ___Kansas__

Legal Description: ___Lot One (1), Block Four (4), Sheraton Park Addition,___

in the NE¼, Section 33, Tier 10 North, Range 7 East of the 9th Principal

Meridian, Capitol City, Kansas._____

_____

being on the _east__ side of __Sherman Avenue_____, and the _north__

side of ___Alpha Street_____. The lot has frontage of __380__ feet

on Sherman Avenue and _330___ feet on Alpha Street, with a maximum depth of

_570_ feet and is improved with (give brief description of buildings)

_two__ one-story brick and block retail buildings and one one-story restaurant,

with parking._____.

Age of Buildings _proposed__ years. Occupied by OWNER_____ TENANT(S) __X____

$ 212,554 (proposed) ANNUAL RENTAL

EXHIBIT D, Page 1

MORTGAGE LOAN APPLICATION

(All questions must be answered in order to insure prompt consideration)

Application is hereby made to ____XYZ Mortgage Company_____

for a loan of $1,275,000.00____ for a term of _25__ years, _0__ months, on

which applicant(s) agree(s) to repay the sum of $11,057.44 to apply to

interest and principal _X__ monthly, ____quarterly, beginning no sooner than

the _1st_ day of ___April____, 19_76_. Interest is to be paid at the rate

of ___9-5/8%____ per annum monthly-quarterly on the 1st day of each ___month____.

SEE ADDITIONAL PROVISIONS

As evidence of said loan applicant(s) agree(s) to execute a mortgage or trust
deed note signed by all parties in interest and to secure said note by a
first mortgage or first trust deed on the following described real property
in the

City of __Capitol City_____ County of ___Gem_____ State of ___Kansas___

Legal Description: ___Lot One (1), Block Four (4), Sheraton Park Addition,___

in the NE¼, Section 33, Tier 10 North, Range 7 East of the 9th Principal

Meridian, Capitol City, Kansas._____

_____

being on the __east__ side of __Sherman Avenue_____, and the __north__

side of ___Alpha Street_____. The lot has frontage of __380__ feet

on Sherman Avenue and __330___ feet on Alpha Street, with a maximum depth of

__570_ feet and is improved with (give brief description of buildings)

__two__ one-story brick and block retail buildings and one one-story restaurant,

with parking._____

Age of Buildings __proposed__ years. Occupied by OWNER_____ TENANT(S) ___X____

$ 212,554 (proposed)   ANNUAL RENTAL

EXHIBIT D

Present Owner __Robert Johnson d/b/a West Bend Shopping Center__

FOR THE PURPOSE OF INDUCING FAVORABLE CONSIDERATION OF THIS APPLICATION
APPLICANT(S) MAKE(S) THE FOLLOWING REPRESENTATIONS:

Record title will be in the name(s) of ___Robert Johnson d/b/a West Bend___

Shopping Center

PROPOSED CONSTRUCTION: Applicant(s) purchased the land __December 10, 1971__

for $ _225,000.00_ . (Insert __actual__ purchase price). The estimated

costs for the proposed buildings, architects fee and land improvements are

$_1,432,000_ . Total cost of land and buildings $_1,657,000_ .

FINANCING ARRANGEMENTS: Of the cost, $_382,000.00_ will be cash equity,

$_1,275,000.00_ will be first mortgage, and $_-0-_ second mort-

gage. If trade or other financing is involved, explain _____

PRESENT MORTGAGES: Held By

			Year Made	Matures	Rate	Delinquencies
1st	National Bank	now $108,945.00 was $135,000.00	1971	1981	11%	None
2nd	NONE	now $ was $				

Is this loan requested to assist in redemption from foreclosure? ___No___

Do you intend to incur any other indebtedness in connection with this property?

___No___ If so, explain _____

For what purpose is this loan wanted?_Permanent Financing - land and buildings_

Are there any unpaid taxes, special assessments, claims for the construction,

improvement, alteration or repair of the property? (If so give statements of

amounts and claimants) ___No_____

ADDITIONAL PROVISIONS: (Insert Prepayment Privilege and all special conditions.)

No prepayment of principal shall be allowed during the first ten (10) loan
years. Privilege is reserved of making additional payments on principal on
any payment date, after the tenth (10th) loan year, of amounts equal to the
principal portion of one or more of the required installment payments that
are next due, but not in lieu thereof, provided thirty (30) days written
notice of the intention to make such payment and the amount to be paid is
first given to Bankers, provided that there shall be paid therewith, as
consideration for the privilege of making such payment, a sum equal to a
percentage of the principal balance so paid on a scale beginning with five
percent (5%), decreasing by one percent (1%) each loan year, to a minimum
of one percent (1%). The term "loan year" as used in this paragraph means
any twelve-month period beginning with the date of the first required installment payment due hereunder, or any anniversary thereof.

Monthly Tax Deposits Required ___Yes___

EMPLOYMENT STATUS:

1. Mortgagor

    Employer's Name: <u>Self-employed</u>
    Employer's Address: <u>3310 Stacy Drive</u>
    Type of Business: <u>Real Estate Development</u>
    Position Occupied: <u>President</u>
    Name and Title of Superior: <u>Not Applicable</u>
    *Number of years in present employment: <u>22</u>

    *NOTE: If less than 2 years, attach rider giving same details with
           respect to prior employment status

LIFE INSURANCE: Age of Mortgagor   <u>53</u>
                                                         Age of Spouse   <u>49</u>

Total in force $ <u>200,000.00</u>   Cash Value $ <u>110,000.00</u>
Less Amount of Loans on Policies: $ <u>100,000.00</u>
Net Cash Surrender Value: $ <u> 10,000.00</u>
                                                    Dependents (Other than Spouse)
                                                              Age   <u>26</u>
                                                                     <u>21</u>

ANNUAL INCOME:

Base pay of mortgagor $35,000.00
  Overtime or other employment earnings   ----
Net Income from Real Estate   15,000.00
Income from Other Sources (List sources and amounts):
      Stock Dividends   3,000.00
      Bond Interest   6,000.00
      Consulting Fees   2,500.00
      Speaking Honorariums   1,500.00
                                        TOTAL INCOME $63,000.00

Applicant(s) hereby warrant(s) to be in peaceable possession of the premises,
and that title thereto has never been questioned, and that no liens or claims
affect said premises, except as herein stated. Applicant(s) hereby agree(s)
that all liens of whatsoever character, except taxes not delinquent, shall
be fully paid and discharged of record out of the proceeds of the loan
applied for when and as said loan is completed, and that the mortgage or
trust deed given to secure said loan shall be a first and prior lien on the
land and improvements described therein. The representations and statements
made herein and in any accompanying documents or supplemental letters are
for the purpose of inducing the granting of said loan; and it is understood
the company making such loan, its officers, agents, and representatives, are
relying on said statements and representations, and the same are true in
every particular.

Applicant(s) agree(s) to furnish at its expense: a suitable photograph of
the property, a credit report issued by a credit information agency satisfactory to lender, a survey by an approved surveyor showing the location
of the completed buildings on the land, and any easement thereon, and an
appraisal in an amount, and by an appraiser, both satisfactory to lender.

In addition to a note and first mortgage or deed of trust, applicant(s)
will furnish all such legal papers and title evidence as lender's counsel
may require. Applicant(s) agree(s) to execute an assignment to lender of
its interest in each lease covering any portion of said property, and/or,
at lender's option, a general assignment of income derived from such
property; the right to receive regular income thereunder to be operative
only upon default in the payment of said note or in the performance of said
mortgage or deed of trust securing the same; lender may give notice of the
assignment to any tenant. Executed copies of all written leases shall be

deposited with lender. Applicant(s) agree(s) to execute the instruments necessary to give lender a first lien on all chattels and fixtures now or hereafter used in the operation of said property.

All legal papers and title evidence required by lender's counsel must, in both form and substance, be satisfactory to lender's counsel before closing. Applicant(s) agree(s) to pay all taxes and assessments due on the date of closing, and all recording fees, registration taxes, title insurance premiums, attorneys' fees, appraisal fees, and all other expenses of closing the loan. Applicant(s) will also pay all expenses incurred if the loan should fail to close on account of its inability or refusal to meet lender's requirements.

Applicant(s) agree(s) to furnish fire insurance with extended coverage endorsement and coverage against other hazards as requested from time to time by lender, covering all buildings and personal property used in the operation thereof, in amounts and in such insurance companies as may be acceptable to lender. All insurance policies shall contain standard mortgage clauses (without contribution) in favor of lender and shall be deposited with lender as evidence of such insurance until the loan is fully paid.

Lender shall not be obligated to close the loan when the buildings, improvements and any other security are incomplete due to damage by fire or other casualty unless provision satisfactory to it is made to restore such damage and for maintenance of the loan obligations, and funds are held by it to effect such restoration and provide such maintenance.

Applicant(s) agree(s) to deposit with XYZ Mortgage Company a standby fee in the amount of $25,500.00   to be held by lender without interest. It is understood that acceptance of such fee by lender shall not constitute an approval of this application. In the event that lender shall not issue a commitment on the basis of this application, said standby fee shall be refunded to applicant(s). In the event that such commitment shall be issued but the loan shall not close, through no fault of the lender, lender shall be entitled to retain said standby fee as an offset against the liquidated damages provided for below.

If a firm commitment is issued by the lender to grant this loan, but the applicant(s) fail(s) to close this loan, applicant(s) shall pay to lender as liquidated damages 2% of the amount of the commitment.

Applicant(s) agree(s) to pay to XYZ Mortgage Company a commission of $ 12,250.00 for services in securing a commitment for this loan.

Signed this _22nd_ day of _February_ , 19 _75_ .

WITNESS:

Arnold J. Mason

Natalie J. Smith

ROBERT JOHNSON d/b/a WEST BEND SHOPPING CENTER

Robert Johnson

Applicant(s)

This application taken by:

XYZ Mortgage Company
1231 Washington Street
Capitol City, Kansas

ANALYSIS: CASE STUDY 4—NEIGHBORHOOD
AND CONVENIENCE SHOPPING CENTER

This case, as contrasted to the previous ones, illustrates the problems that can arise in any actual case. It showed the concern the lender had on the limited parking available and then showed the way this was handled by the correspondent. A question you might ask yourself is whether or not you would be interested in making a construction loan on this center as well as a permanent loan. Where will the borrower obtain the equity funds necessary for completion? What is the status of the leasing? Should this be structured with a floor loan with additional monies to be advanced upon the achievement of certain rental requirements? There are arguments both pro and con for approving this loan.

This case demonstrates a clear separation between the appraisal process and the loan submission in the total underwriting of the offering.

Case Study 5

Condominium Complex

Jess S. Lawhorn

Southeast Mortgage Company
MORTGAGE BANKERS

April 2, 1973

Mr. John H. Tool, Mortgage Analyst
South Realty Investors
Post Office Box 1011
Mobile, Alabama

RE: Proposed 60-Unit Condominium Apartment Building
     100xx West Bay Harbor Drive
     Bay Harbor Island, Florida

     $2,700,000 - 24 Months - 4.5% above Old South Prime

Dear John:

We have received a first mortgage loan application with deposit in connection
with the proposed seven-story luxury condominium apartment building and, in
that regard, enclose the following for your favorable consideration:

    1. Mortgage Loan Submission with Supporting Exhibits
    2. Appraisal Report by Jess S. Lawhorn, SRA
    3. Building Plans
    4. Aerial Photographs
    5. Dade County Map

Incidentally, this is the property that David Bell and Peter Albright inspected
when they were in Miami a few months ago. Based on their site inspection and
meeting with the applicant, I am sure they will concur with my feelings as to
this project having all the necessary ingredients for a top-quality loan for
your portfolio.

LOCATION

The subject site is bounded on the West by Bay Harbor Waterway, which connects
approximately 1/2 mile North to the Intracoastal Waterway. Immediately North,
South and East of the subject are existing apartment buildings and condominiums.

The location of the subject is extremely prime being on the water and on Bay
Harbor Island, which has long been considered an excellent rental and condominium
area. SEMCO has financed several rental apartment buildings on the Island with
all buildings remaining virtually 100% occupied at all times. In addition, rents
in this area have increased rapidly during the past several years.

Mr. John H. Tool
April 2, 1973
Page Two

Approximately one year ago, SEMCO arranged a condominium construction loan
with the First National Bank of Richmond on the Longworth House, a 50-unit
condominium apartment building located $\pm$ 1 mile Southeast of the subject.
This building is selling extremely well with over 50% sales at the present
time. Prices have risen sharply since the project began and the owner of
the project, Mr. Russ Mann, indicates to us that he plans to increase the
prices again prior to completion.

IMPROVEMENTS

The appraisal report and accompanying plans fully describe the physical
characteristics of the improvements.

The building will consist of two towers connected together on the first
floor by the lobby entrance. An exceptionally large amount of common area
will be provided for the occupants with separate recreation room and kitchen,
card room and billiard room. The pool and deck area is very large and offers
a view directly on the Bay Harbor Waterway.

Mens and Womens showers, saunas and gyms will be conveniently located adjacent to the pool and patio area. Most of the parking will be provided
underground which provides a very desirable feature in selling condominium
apartments while creating a much better-looking building, since parking will
not be visible from ground level.

Each of the two apartment towers will contain two high-speed hydraulic elevators.
This is not a requirement of the building code, but rather a requirement of
the developer who feels that having two elevators will offer a distinct
selling advantage over his competition and provide the people purchasing
apartments with a much-desired feature.

All apartments are large and spacious with both bedrooms having walk-in
closets and separate baths. The layout of each unit is well designed and
provides a high degree of efficiency with little wasted space.

Wall-to-wall carpeting will be included in the sales price of each unit and
closed circuit television cameras in each apartment will allow the occupants
to monitor the lobby entrance at all times. The carpeting and security
system are two features not offered in many of the competition condominiums.

In addition to having adequate storage space in each apartment, additional
storage will be available for each condominium owner in the underground
garage area of the building.

PRINCIPAL

As evidenced by the accompanying financial statement, Mr. Barrett enjoys a
rather substantial financial position. Originally from Bogota, Colombia, he
moved to Miami in early 1968, establishing a permanent residence in Miami.
His first venture in the real estate field was to build a 15-unit condominium

Mr. John H. Tool
April 2, 1973
Page Three

apartment building on South Miami Beach which was completely sold out just shortly after completion of the building. Due to his high tax position, Mr. Barrett then decided it more advantageous to construct rental apartment buildings for depreciation purposes. He built two buildings, both of which are shown in the "Borrowing Corporation" section of the enclosed presentation. In 1972, SEMCO arranged financing on the Royal Bay Harbor Plaza, a 25 - unit luxury apartment building located at 9701 East Bay Harbor Drive. This building is over 50% complete at present and quality of construction is excellent with no problems encountered whatsoever in our loan. Mr. Barrett is highly regarded by SEMCO as one of our best clients, and we fully anticipate that we will be providing the majority of his financing needs in the future.

LOAN REQUEST

The loan requested represents 75% of the borrower's projected sales price and slightly more than 75% of our appraisal valuation. Mr. Barrett presently has $80,000 cash equity invested in the land and the enclosed cost breakdown indicates that he will be investing another $80,000 over and above the construction loan. This should prove to be more than adequate for the type of financing requested. The enclosed mortgage loan submission contains the terms and conditions requested in the "Loan Application" and "Loan Summary" sections.

The principals will secure a commitment from local savings and loans to finance 75% of the units on the basis of 80% loan to sales price for a term of 25 years at interest rates to be determined based upon local market conditions at the time the units are sold and the individual loan applied for. Based upon the number of cash sales and experience by other condominiums in the Bay Harbor area, 75% coverage should be adequate to provide those purchasers who wish permanent financing end loans.

Since the application was very closely negotiated with our knowledge of two competitive loan offers, we were not able to require that the applicant pay your site inspection fee; therefore, it will be paid by SEMCO, and I would appreciate your letting me know when this fee is due.

SEMCO is pleased to fully recommend this loan to South Realty, and we look forward to your commitment on this proposal in the very near future. If you have any questions regarding this case, please do not hesitate to call me.

Sincerely,

Jess S. Lawhorn
Senior Vice President

JSL/cl
Enclosures

LOAN SUMMARY SHEET

AMOUNT: $2,700,000

RATE: 4-1/2% floating above the prime rate established by the Old South Bank of Mobile.

TERM: 24 Months

BORROWER: A-1 CONSTRUCTION CORP.

Tom Barrett - President
Joyce Barrett - Vice President

ADDITIONAL PROVISIONS: See additional terms and conditions of "Application for a Construction Loan Commitment".

The $2,700,000 loan represents the following:

Loan per Square Foot of Gross Building Area	$16.53
Loan per Net Saleable Square Foot	$31.51
Loan per Unit	$45,000
Loan per Room	$8,182
Ratio of Loan versus Sales Price (Borrower's Projection)	75%
Ratio of Loan versus Sales Price (Appraisal)	75.8%
Ratio of Loan versus Rental Value	98.8%

FINANCIAL STATEMENTS

The enclosed Financial Statement for Mr. Barrett reflects sufficient liquidity to provide the equity required above the loan amount.

Enclosed is verification from the Republic National Bank of Colon, Panama, as to Mr. Barrett's cash balance at the present time. Under Schedule 5 (real estate), Eastview Construction, the lien of $353,190 is the amount of present indebtedness due on the construction loan, payable to Southeast Mortgage Company. The present market value is our estimate of value of the uncompleted project at this time.

PERSONAL FINANCIAL STATEMENT

Name Tom Barrett   To: **Southeast Mortgage Company**

Address 250 Surfside Drive (Miami Beach)

I make the following statement of all my assets and liabilities as of the ____21st____ day of ____March____ , 19 _73_, and give other material information for the purpose of obtaining credit with you on notes and bills bearing my signature, endorsement, or guarantee, and agree to notify you promptly of any change affecting my ability to pay.

(PLEASE ANSWER ALL QUESTIONS USING "NO" OR "NONE" WHERE NECESSARY)

ASSETS		LIABILITIES AND NET WORTH	
Cash (See Sched. No. 1) On hand, and unrestricted in banks.	$ 195,000.	Notes Payable to Banks, Unsecured Direct borrowings only. (See Sched. No. 1)	$ 60,000.
U. S. Government Securities		Notes Payable to Banks, Secured Direct borrowings only. (See Sched. No. 1)	
Accounts and Loans Receivable (See Sched. No. 2)		Notes Receivable, Discounted With banks, finance companies, etc. (See Sched. No. 1)	
Notes Receivable, Not Discounted (See Sched. No. 2)		Notes Payable to Others, Unsecured	
Notes Receivable, Discounted With banks, finance companies, etc. (See Sched. No. 2)		Notes Payable to Others, Secured	
Life Insurance, Cash Surrender Value (Do not deduct loans.) (See Sched. No. 3)		Loans Against Life Insurance (See Sched. No. 3)	
Other Stocks and Bonds (See Sched. No. 4)	1,420,000.	Accounts Payable	
Real Estate (See Sched. No. 5)	3,115,690.	Interest Payable	
Automobiles Registered in Own Name.		Taxes and Assessments Payable (See Sched. No. 5)	
Other Assets (Itemize)		Mortgages Payable on Real Estate (See Sched. No. 5)	1,533,190.
Import-Export, Inc.	25,000.	Other Liabilities (Itemize)	
Jewelry, Inc.	285,000.		
		Net Worth	$ 3,447,500.
Total Assets	$ 5,040,690.	Total Liabilities and Net Worth	$ 5,040,690.

SOURCE OF INCOME		PERSONAL INFORMATION	
Salary	$	Business or occupation	Age
Bonus and commissions	$	Investor	32
Dividends	$	Partner or officer in any other venture	
Real Estate income	$		
Other income—itemize	$	Married Yes	Dependent Children 3
		Single	Other Dependents
TOTAL	$		

CONTINGENT LIABILITIES		GENERAL INFORMATION	
As endorser or comaker	$	Are any assets pledged? No	
On leases or contracts	$	Are you defendant in any suits or legal actions?	
Legal claims	$	No	
Provision for Federal Income Taxes	$	Have you ever made a composition settlement? Explain: No	
Other special debt	$	Have you ever taken bankruptcy? Explain: No	

SUPPLEMENTARY SCHEDULES

No. 1 Banking Relations.   (A list of all my bank accounts, including savings, and loans)

Name and Location of Bank	Cash Balance	Amt. of Loan	Maturity of Loan	How Endorsed, Guaranteed or Secured
United Bank of Miami Beach	50,000.	60,000.		
Republic Nat'l Bank of Colon, Rep. of Panama	145,000			

(SEE OTHER SIDE)

P-29

No. 2. Accounts, Loans and Notes Receivable. (A list of the largest amounts owing to me.)

Name and Address of Debtor	Amount Owing	Age of Debt	Description of Nature of Debt	Description of Security Held	Date Payment Expected

No. 3. Life Insurance

Name of Person Insured	Name of Beneficiary	Name of Insurance Co.	Type of Policy	Face Amount of Policy	Total Cash Surrender Value	Total Loans Against Policy	Amount of Yearly Premium	Is Policy Assigned?

No. 4. Other Stocks and Bonds.

Face Value (Bonds) No. of Shares (Stocks)	Description of Security	Registered in Name of	Cost	Present Market Value	Income Received Last Year	To Whom Pledged
100%	United Americanas	T. Barrett		220,000.		Television Manufacturing
100%	Condo S.A.	T. Barrett		800,000.		Export - Lima, Peru
35%	I. Panama	T. Barrett		400,000.		Import - Colon, Panama

No. 5. Real Estate.

Description or Street No.	Dimensions or Acres	Improvements Consist of	Mortgages or Liens	Due Dates and Amounts of Payments	Assessed Value	Present Market Value	Unpaid Taxes Year	Unpaid Taxes Amount
Ace Const. 145 Miami Ave Miami Beach		Building under const.	353,190.	Southeast Mortgage		655,690.		
109 Canal Dr. Miami Beach		16 unit apt. bldg.	240,000.	Washington Federal		425,000.		
250 Surfside Drive		32 unit apt. bldg.	500,000.	Metropolitan Life Ins. Co.		750,000.		
Tarde Ave. Lima, Peru	Residence	Residence	40,000.	Chase Federal		185,000.		
Lot 3 & 4 TQI Street		24 unit apt. bldg.	------	------		500,000.		
Lot 1 & 6 W. Bay Harbor Dr.			400,000.	Southeast Mortgage		600,000.		

No. 6. I buy goods principally from:

Name	Address	Name	Address

The undersigned certifies that each side hereof and the Information inserted herein has been carefully read and is true and correct.

Date.. March 29, 1973 _____   Signed_____

REPUBLIC NATIONAL BANK
Post Office Box 1117W
Colon, Rep. of Panama

March 1, 1973

Mr. Tom Barrett
Miami, Florida
USA

Dear Sir:

We hereby confirm that your actual balance of your

Time Deposit up to October 31, 1972 is US $148,600.37

plus interest.

                              Very truly yours,

                              REPUBLIC NATIONAL BANK

AL/mt

Arling Business Credit Corporation of America

Correct Name and Address   Name and Address Given

Tom Barrett
250 Surfside Drive
Miami Beach, Florida 33154

March 8, 1973

1. Date of birth?	1. 1940
2. Married or single?	2. married
3. Number of dependents?	3. 4
4. Employed by or affiliated with?	4. A-1 Construction Corp., Ace Construction
5. Business address?	5. Mana Residence Corp. & Frast Corp.
6. Line of business?	6. Construction
7. Length of time with present employer?	7.
8. Position and/or title?	8. President and part owner
9. Approximate yearly salary or wages?	9. $55,000
10. Other employment: state nature and amount of compensation?	10.
11. If self-employed state nature and approximate net annual income from same?	11. See #4, 6, 8, 9
12. Other income and source?	12. $ From
13. Previous employment affiliation?	13.
14. Does subject rent living quarters, board, or own home?	14. ___Rents ___Boards ___Owns
15. If rents/or boards, what type of accommodations?	15. ___Room Apartment _x_ House
16. If rents/or boards, what is amount of room or board?	16. $ Weekly Monthly
17. If owns home, what is its value?	17. $2000,000
18. What other assets does subject possess?	18. $5,000,000 total assets
19. Any mortgages on home?	19. Yes - $40,000
20. What other debts does subject owe? (Describe and estimate amount)	20. $1,6000,000 total liabilities
21. Estimate of net worth?	21. $3,4000,000 net worth
22. How long at present address?	22. Five years
23. Former address?	23. Panama, South America
24. Does subject live within his income?	24. Yes
25. What is the subject's reputation for paying bills?	25. Good
26. Character and general reputation?	26. Good

Is subject a desirable credit risk?   Explain

Give your reasons in full:

Subject is president of four local well established businesses and is connected with several other businesses in South America. Derives good income and pays bills well.

FINANCE:

Home has mortgage of $40,000 and is worth $200,000. Subject reported total assets $5 million and liabilities of $1,6000,000 giving the subject $3,4000,000 net worth.

BANKING:

Subject has four loans at bank totaling a high five figures. Bank reports relations are excellent. Checking account at one bank has medium 4 figures.

HISTORY:

Barrett was born in 1940 and is married. He is President of Mana Residence Corp., chartered in 1971, Ace Construction Corp., chartered in 1971, A-1 Construction and Frast Corp. The subject also has interests in Import-Export, Inc., an exporting company, and Fair Constrcution Company of Miami Beach.

Enclosed is a resume for James Faus, who is the
architect and general contractor for A-1 Construction
Corp. on the proposed 60-unit condominium.

Southeast Mortgage Company has financed several of
Mr. Faus' projects, and we recommend him highly to
you concerning his knowledge and ability as an
architect as well as quality of work as a general
contractor.

Personal Resume of James Faus

Born in New York, New York, June 30, 1912

Graduated New Utrecht High School in 1929

Graduated New York University in 1933 with a Bachelor of Architecture
Degree

Worked for several architects and also was self-employed until 1960.
Joined the New York office of Morris Lapidus Associates in 1960, at
which time I was the job captain and supervising architect for the
Americana Hotel project. In 1961, I came to the Miami Beach office of
Morris Lapidus Associates as an associate in charge of the office.

During the period between 1961 and 1965, under my supervision, the
office designed many high rise and low rise apartment buildings, office
buildings, religious buildings, schools, banks, hotels and motels.

In 1965 I left Morris Lapidus Associates and started my own design
consultant firm. I have designed several high rise and low rise apartment buildings, single family homes, a mobile home park, office buildings,
interiors and various proposed projects. Some of the buildings are as
follows:

1.	Offices for the "17" Meridian Building, M-B	
2.	Ocean Garden Apartments, Ft. Lauderdale	24 units
3.	Manhattan Towers, Miami Beach	228 units
4.	Park View House, Miami Beach	54 units
5.	Alton Palms, Miami Beach	51 units
6.	Kohlmeyer & Co., Miami Beach, Interiors	
7.	Oakwood Manor Mobile Estates, Sarasota	670 pads
8.	25 Bay Tower, Miami	61 units
9.	700 Brickell Office Building, Miami	95,000 Sq. Ft.
10.	Various proposed apartment buildings, office buildings, convalescent home, shopping center, etc.	

I am licensed to practice architecture in the state of New York, Georgia
and Florida and I am certified by the National Council of Architectural
Registration Boards. I am also a licensed general contractor in the state
of Florida.

Within the past 6 months I have designed the following new projects:

1.	Royal Bay Harbor Plaza	25 units
2.	Marina Apartments of Sarasota	160 units
3.	Alteration to the Parkleigh Hotel, Miami	150 units
4.	Selma Towers, Miami	211 units
5.	West Avenue Condominium Apartments	150 units

Manhattan Towers, 6770 Indian Creek Drive, Miami Beach, Florida. 228-Unit Apartment Building. Financed by SEMCO in 1969 through its correspondent, Mutual Benefit Life Insurance Co.

25 Bay Tower, 175 S.E. 25 Road, Miami, Florida. 61-Unit Apartment Building. Financed by SEMCO in 1971 through its correspondent, United Insurance Company.

Southeast Mortgage Company
MORTGAGE BANKERS

P R O P O S E D   S A L E S   S C H E D U L E

Total Sales Price — $3,600,000

SOUTH BUILDING		NORTH BUILDING	
Apt. #		Apt. #	
201	$ 57,500	201	$ 57,500
202	57,500	202	57,500
203	57,500	203	57,500
204	57,500	204	57,500
205	57,500	205	57,500
301	58,500	301	58,500
302	58,500	302	58,500
303	58,500	303	58,500
304	58,500	304	58,500
305	58,500	305	58,500
401	59,500	401	59,500
402	59,500	402	59,500
403	59,500	403	59,500
404	59,500	404	59,500
405	59,500	405	59,500
501	60,500	501	60,500
502	60,500	502	60,500
503	60,500	503	60,500
504	60,500	504	60,500
505	60,500	505	60,500
601	61,500	601	61,500
602	61,500	602	61,500
603	61,500	603	61,500

Southeast Mortgage Company
MORTGAGE BANKERS

2.

SOUTH BUILDING		NORTH BUILDING	
Apt. #		Apt. #	
604	$ 61,500	604	$ 61,500
605	61,500	605	61,500
701	62,500	701	62,500
702	62,500	702	62,500
703	62,500	703	62,500
704	62,500	704	62,500
705	62,500	705	62,500

OWNER: **A-1 CONSTRUCTION CORP.**   Requisition # _____

CONTRACTOR: _____ Date _____

PROPERTY ADDRESS: _____

Subcontractor or Supplier	Contract	(A) Contract Amount	(B) Total Paid on Contract to Date (D-C = B)	(C) Amount of this Draw	(D) Job Complete to Date (B+C=D)	(E) Balance to Complete Job (A-D=E)
	1. CLEARING/GRADING & FILL	40,000				
	2. EXCAVATION & BACK FILL	80,000				
	3. PILING	20,000				
	4. RENTAL EQUIPMENT	--				
	5. CARPENTRY	20,000				
	Labor					
	Forming Lumber					
	6. MILLWORK					
	Labor					
	Finish Lumber					
	7. CABINETS & VANITIES	41,000				
	8. MASONRY					
	Labor	60,000				
	Material					
	Special Finish					
	9. REINFORCING STEEL	120,000				
	10. STRUC. STEEL					
	11. ORNAMENTAL IRON	20,000				
	12. CONCRETE					
	Material					
	Labor (Placing & Finishing	500,000				
	13. SHEET METAL					
	14. STEEL STAIRS					
	15. BALCONY RAILING					
	16. PLUMBING					
	Rough	180,000				
	Fixtures					
	Water Heaters					
	Septic Tanks					
	Lawn Sprinklers					
	17. ELECTRICAL					
	Rough	100,000				
	Fixtures					
	Switch Gear					
	Panels					
	18. HEATING, VENT. & AIR COND.	85,000				
	19. ROOFING	22,000				
	19a TRUSSES					
	20. LATH & PLASTER AND DRYWALL	155,000				
	20a STUCCO, MARBLETITE					
	21. TILE & MARBLE					
	22. FLOOR SURFACING					
	Vinyl Tile	40,000				
	Terrazzo					
	Carpet					
	Special Finish					
	23. WINDOWS	40,000				
	SLIDING GLASS DRS.					
	EXTERIOR &					
	INTERIOR DOORS					
	MIRRORS					
	24. PAINTING	30,000				
	25. FINISH HARDWARE	15,000				
	26. STORE FRONTS OR MODULAR WALL SYS.					
	SUB-TOTAL	1,568,000				

Subcontractor / Supplier	Contract	(A) Contract Amount	(B) Total Paid on Contract to Date (D-C = B)	(C) Amount of this Draw	(D) Job Complete to Date (B+C=D)	(E) Balance to Complete Job (A=D=E)
	27. KITCHEN APP.					
	Ranges & Ovens	80,000				
	Hoods & Fans					
	Refrigerators					
	Dishwashers					
	Disposals					
	Laundry Equip.					
	(if leased-indicate)					
	28. INSUL'N-THERMAL					
	and ACOUSTICAL					
	29. ELEVATORS	98,000				
	30. LANDSCAPING	12,000				
	31. PAVING					
	32. DRAINAGE					
	33. SWIMMING POOL	20,000				
	34. WALKS					
	35. FENCES					
	36. MAIL BOXES	2,000				
	37. TV ANTENNAS	4,000				
	38. LUMINOUS CEILING					
	39. FINAL CLEANING					
	40. CONTINGENCIES .	60,000				
	41 Land Satisfaction	345,000				
	42 Advertising	60,000				
	Lobby & Rec Room Furniture	49,500				
	Trash Chutes	4,000				
I)	TOTAL DIRECT COSTS					
	BUILDER'S OVERHEAD and/or SUPERVISION	30,000				
	BUILDER'S PROFIT					
	TOTAL DIRECT COSTS OVERHEAD/SUPER.PROFIT					
	Less 10% Retained.					
	AMOUNT DUE or ADVANCED					
II) INDIRECT COSTS	Interest during construction					
	1. Legal, Title Ins. & Rec. Fees)					
	2. Perm.Loan Comm.Fee)	321,500				
	3. Taxes during Construction					
	4. Ins. during Construction	8,000				
	5. ARCH. & ENG. Fees					
	a. Design $_____)	55,000				
	b. Inspection _____)					
	6. XXXXXXXX Demolition	30,000				
	7. xxxxxxxxxxxxxxxxxxxxxxxxxxx					
	8. Sales Exp.or Int.(Rentup Per.)					
	9. Permits,Survey,Soil tests	10,000				
	0. Other Fees or Costs	22,700				
	TOTAL INDIRECT COSTS					
	AMOUNT DUE OR ADVANCED					

III) LAND (VALUE) $_____ $_____

TOTAL COST OF PROJECT (I+II+III) $ 2,779,700   GRAND TOTAL $_____
DEDUCT LOAN AMOUNT $_____   Less EQUITY $_____
EQUITY REQUIRED $_____   Less AMOUNT
                                                  PREVIOUSLY
                                                  DISBURSED $_____

SOURCE OF EQUITY

. Land Value (Minus Land Debt)
        $_____   _____
. _____   _____
. _____   _____   TOTAL AMOUNT •
. _____   _____   DUE THIS
. _____   _____   DISBURSEMENT $_____

APPRAISAL REPORT
FOR
A-1 CONSTRUCTION CORP.

Proposed
7-Story, 60 Unit
CONDOMINIUM

100xx West Bay Harbor Drive
Bay Harbor Island, Florida

March 13, 1973
Jess S. Lawhorn
SOUTHEAST MORTGAGE COMPANY
1390 Brickell Avenue
Miami, Florida 33131

Southeast Mortgage Company
MORTGAGE BANKERS

CORRELATION AND CERTIFICATION

MARKET VALUE INDICATED BY THE COST APPROACH	$ 2,698,200
MARKET VALUE INDICATED BY THE INCOME APPROACH	$ 2,731,600
MARKET VALUE INDICATED BY THE MARKET DATA APPROACH	$ 2,635,000 - $ 2,823,000
MARKET VALUE INDICATED BY THE AGGREGATE VALUE OF THE INDIVIDUAL APARTMENT UNITS	$ 3,564,000

The first three approaches to value indicate a Market Value of $ 2,700,000 if the improvements were to be used as an apartment building where the profits would be received over the economic life of the improvements. But, the subject is to be utilized as a condominium and the profits are to be derived from the sale of the individual units, therefore, these three approaches to value are included for ancillary purposes only.

Ample sales of individual comparable condominium units were available. As can be observed on Page 11 the adjusted area of each condominium unit is multiplied by the appropriate sales price per square foot, thereby indicating the Market Value for the particular apartment. The accumulative total of the Market Value of the individual units is $ 3,564,000.

After considering all the forces that influence value, it is my opinion that the Market Value indicated by the aggregate value of the individual apartment units, as a condominium as of December 13, 1972, is $ 3,564,000.

THIS IS TO CERTIFY that I have inspected the subject site, examined the preliminary plans and specifications and that I have no past, present or contemplated future interest in the subject property.

Subject property: 100xx West Bay Harbor Drive, Bay Harbor Island, Florida. (Looking northwesterly at subject property. Existing buildings are being razed).

Street scene: Looking north along West Bay Harbor Drive from 100th Street. (Note: Rent Comparable #3 in background.)

Comparable condominium #1: Island Manor, 9660 W. Bay Harbor Drive, Bay Harbor Island, Florida.

Comparable condominium #2: Montego Club, 10180 W. Bay Harbor Drive, Bay Harbor Island, Florida.

Comparable Condominium #3: Bay Roc, 9180 West Bay Harbor Drive, Bay Harbor Island, Florida.

Comparable Condominium #4: Stuart House, 1050—93 Street, Bay Harbor Island, Florida.

Southeast Mortgage Company
MORTGAGE BANKERS

Rent comparable #1: Belmont, 10101 E. Bay Harbor Drive, Bay Harbor Island, Florida.

Rent comparable #2: Guilford House, 9800 W. Bay Harbor Drive, Bay Harbor Island, Florida.

GENERAL COMMENTS

Bay Harbor Island is located due west of the Cities of Surfside and
Bal Harbour, separated by Indian Creek.

The City of Bay Harbor Island consists of two islands, the island to
the west is improved with single family residences, and the island where
the subject is located is where all the commercial buildings and apartments
are located. This separation of residences and commercial properties into
islands insures against encroachment of non-compatible uses of the islands,
thereby, increasing the amenities of this exclusive city.

As of December, 1972, in Bay Harbor Island, there were 26 condominiums
with a total of 566 units in existence, and one under construction containing
56 additional units for a total of 622 units.

In addition to the condominiums there are 20 co-ops with 326 units, and
141 apartment buildings containing 1,698 units.

According to Mr. Preble, City Manager of Bay Harbor Island, there have
been only 4 or 5 rental apartment buildings built on the island in the past 5
years, whereas, there have been approximately 18 condominium projects completed
in the same period. Indications are that this trend will continue in the foreseeable future.

Bay Harbor Island's population as of the 1970 census was 4,619, an increase of 42% over the 1960 population of 3,250.

Bay Harbor Island, one of the most affluent residential communities in
Dade County, demands a premium rental as compared with other areas of the
County. The minimum net rental area for a one bedroom apartment is 900 sq. ft.
and for a two bedroom apartment is 1,150 sq. ft.

GENERAL COMMENTS - Continued

SHOPPING: The local, exclusive shopping area is located just 1 block south
of the subject along Kane Concourse (96th Street). The Bal Harbour Shops,
the most exclusive shopping center in Dade County, is within one mile and
some of the better known shops, to name a few, located in this center are:
Abercrombie & Fitch Co., Schwartz Toys, Sandra Post, Martha West, Adrian
Thal Furs, and Neiman Marcus Department Store.

CHURCHES: Churches of all demoninations are within a five minute drive.

SCHOOLS: The Bay Harbor Elementary School is within six blocks of the
Subject.

TRANSPORTATION: The M.T.A. Route "S" bus runs along Kane Concourse.

The construction cost estimate was based on known costs of similar structures,
and the land value estimate is based and considered to be well supported by
the Comparable Land Sales set forth on Page 17.

The rental projection is based upon the Rent Comparables set forth in the
schedule on Pages 18 and 19. It was concluded that the subject improvements
are superior to all the comparables listed.

The estimated expenses were based upon known expenses which I have on file.
High quality rental properties have been selling for 7.0-7.5 times their
effective gross income. Therefore, based upon the subject's projected
effective gross income of $ 376,400, the indicated Market Value Range indi-
cated by the Market Data Approach is $ 2,635,000 - $ 2,823,000.

Southeast Mortgage Company
MORTGAGE BANKERS

GENERAL COMMENTS - Continued

The Market Value Estimated as a condominium was based upon the four condominiums listed on Pages 12 and 13.

Since the subject improvements will have much larger recreation facilities, two elevators per tower, extra 1/2 bath, a garage, and a washer and dryer in each unit, it was concluded that the subject is superior to all four comparable condominiums.

The Valuation opinion rendered herein is contingent upon the successful completion of the improvements according to the preliminary plans and specifications submitted to me at the time the appraisal was requested. It is further contingent upon the issuance of a certificate of occupancy by the proper governmental agency.

SITE ANALYSIS

LEGAL DESCRIPTION:

Lots 11, 12, 13, 14, and 15, Block 3, BAY HARBOR ISLAND, as recorded in Plat Book 46, Page 5, of the Public Records of Dade County, Florida.

The subject site which is retangular in shape is located on the west side of West Bay Harbor Drive, with a frontage along West Bay Harbor Drive of 375.00 feet, and a depth along the north and south property lines of 150.00 feet; the rear property extends 375.00 feet along Bay Harbor Waterway containing a total of 56,250 sq. ft.

HIGHEST AND BEST USE:

The highest and best use of the subject site is for a condominium, as set forth in this appraisal report.

ZONING:

R-E Multiple Family.

UTILITIES:

Electrical, telephone, gas, water and sanitary sewers are available at the sites.

STREETS:

The zoned right of way is 60 feet wide. Thirty-three feet of this right of way is utilized as a two-laned road, and on either side of this road there is a two foot wide gutter, and between this gutter and this site there is an eleven and one half foot wide asphalt paved area which is utilized for parking.

Southeast Mortgage Company
MORTGAGE BANKERS

DESCRIPTION OF IMPROVEMENTS

TYPE	Proposed 7 story, 60 unit, condominium with 60 2BR/2-1/2B units containing 1,428 sq. ft. each.
BASEMENT	Garage with 90 spaces.
1st STORY	Lobby, Recreation, Card and Billiard Rooms, Saunas, Gym and Storage Rooms; 20 ft. x 40 ft. Pool and Deck; 30 on site Parking Spaces.
2nd to 7th STORIES	Twin towers containing 5 units per floor in each tower.
FOUNDATION	Precast concrete pilings and pads.
FLOORS	Reinforced concrete slabs.
WALLS	Exterior – Concrete block stucco
	Interior – Drywall on metal studs.
ROOF	Concrete slab with a tar and gravel surface.
WINDOWS	Aluminum framing.
KITCHEN EQUIPMENT	Dishwasher, double door (side by side) 19 C.F. Refrigerator, Americana double Oven and Range, hood and fan.
LAUNDRY	Each unit has a Washer and Dryer.
SECURITY	Closed Circuit T.V.
ELEVATOR	4 Hydraulic – 2 in each tower.
AIR CONDITIONING	Individual reverse cycle central units.
SWIMMING POOL	20' x 40'
PARKING	120 on site spaces of which 90 are under cover.
LANDSCAPING	To be adequately done.
REMARKS:	The existing structures are in the process of being razed.

Southeast Mortgage Company
MORTGAGE BANKERS

SCHEDULE OF MARKET VALUE OF INDIVIDUAL UNITS

(Based on Direct Comparison Method)

Floor	Location	Type	Net Sq.Ft. Living Area	Sales Price Per Sq.Ft.	Estimated Market Value	No. of Units	Totals
2nd	CW	2BR2-½B	1,428	$ 40.97	$ 58,500	4	$ 234,000
	CS	"	"	39.22	56,000	4	224,000
	I	"	"	38.87	55,500	2	111,000
3rd	CW	"	"	41.67	59,500	4	238,000
	CS	"	"	39.92	57,000	4	228,000
	I	"	"	39.57	56,500	2	113,000
4th	CW	"	"	42.37	60,500	4	242,000
	CS	"	"	40.62	58,000	4	232,000
	I	"	"	40.27	57,500	2	115,000
5th	CW	"	"	43.07	61,500	4	246,000
	CS	"	"	41.32	59,000	4	236,000
	I	"	"	40.97	58,500	2	117,000
6th	CW	"	"	43.77	62,500	4	250,000
	CS	"	"	42.02	60,000	4	240,000
	I	"	"	41.67	59,500	2	119,000
7th	CW	"	"	44.47	63,500	4	254,000
	CS	"	"	42.72	61,000	4	244,000
	I	"	"	42.37	60,500	2	121,000
			(85,680)	($ 41.60)	($ 59,400)		

ESTIMATED TOTAL MARKET VALUE OF INDIVIDUAL CONDOMINIUM UNITS $3,564,000

Southeast Mortgage Company
MORTGAGE BANKERS

SCHEDULE OF COMPARABLE CONDOMINIUMS

	Name and Location	No. of Units	No. of Stories	Type		Sq. Ft. Area	Sales Price	Sales Price Per Sq. Ft.
(1)	Island Manor 9660 West Bay Harbor Drive Bay Harbor Island, Florida	36	7	2BR/2-½B 2BR/2-½B 2BR/2-½B	(C-W) (C-S) (C-W)	1,402 1,673 1,680	$ 54,000-57,000 63,000 68,000-74,000	$ 38.52-40.66 37.66 40.48-44.05

(C-S) — Corner Street

(C-W) — Corner Water

COMMENTS: This building was completed in 1972. The above is based upon 11 known sales. Based on the new sales schedule, the asking prices range as follows: 1,402 sq. ft. units $ 56,990-62,990; 1,673 sq. ft. units $ 63,900-69,950; and the 1,680 sq. ft. units $ 68,950-74,950. Each unit has a fully equipped kitchen, and a washer and dryer. Boat Dockage. Small recreation room. Some covered parking but no garage. Only 1 elevator in each tower. Fewer amenities than subject. Carpeting not included. Located 3 blocks south of subject.

	Name and Location	No. of Units	No. of Stories	Type		Sq. Ft. Area	Sales Price	Sales Price Per Sq. Ft.
(2)	Montego Club 10180 West Bay Harbor Drive Bay Harbor Island, Florida	15	6	2BR/2-½B 2BR/2-½B	(C)	2,191 2,203	$ 65,000-85,000 76,000-81,500	$ 29.67-38.80 34.50-37.00

COMMENTS: This building is approximately 1-½ years old, and the units were sold between May 1971 and August 1972. All units have a waterway frontage. Kitchens were fully equipped. Laundry facilities on each floor. There is a pool and a small recreation room, and boat dockage. Units much larger than subject's. Some covered parking but no garage. Located 1 block north of subject.

SCHEDULE OF COMPARABLE CONDOMINIUMS - Continued

	Name and Location	No. of Units	No. of Stories	Type		Sq. Ft. Area	Sales Price	Sales Price Per Sq. Ft.
(3)	Bay Roc 9180 West Bay Harbor Drive Bay Harbor Island, Florida	18	7	2BR/2B 2BR/2B		1,475 1,555	$ 42,200-47,000 45,500-51,500	$ 28.61-31.86 29.26-33.12

COMMENTS: This building was completed in 1971, and the units were sold between March 1970 and May 1970, but the sales campaign started in 1969. Kitchens are fully equipped. Boat Dockage. Units are comparable in size to subject's, but building has fewer amenities. Some covered parking but no garage. Sales over 2 years old. Located 9 blocks south of subject.

	Name and Location	No. of Units	No. of Stories	Type		Sq. Ft. Area	Sales Price	Sales Price Per Sq. Ft.
(4)	Stuart House 1050 93rd Street Bay Harbor Island, Florida	56	8 Conv. Conv.	1BR/1-½B 1BR/2B 1BR/2B 2BR/2B 2BR/2B 2BR/2B 2BR/2B	(S) (C-S) (C-S) (C-S) (C-R) (C-R) (C-S)	916 1,148 1,108 1,185 1,325 1,458 1,272	$ 33,500-37,000 44,500-45,000 44,500-45,000 - - - - - 48,000-50,000 55,500-57,000 48,500-52,000	$ 36.57-40.39 38.76-39.20 40.16-40.61 - - - - - 36.23-37.74 38.07-39.09 38.13-40.88

COMMENTS: This building is approximately 80% completed and 27 units are under contract at the above prices. The new price schedule is as follows: 1BR/1-½B Units range in price from $35,000-37,500; 1BR/2B Conv. units $ 44,000-47,000; 2BR/2B units (C-S) $ 45,000-52,500; and the 2BR/2B (C-R) $50,000-57,500. There are laundry facilities on each floor. Fully equipped kitchens with top of the line appliances. Small recreation room, pool, and patio. Sales prices increase $500 per floor. Some covered parking but no garage. One elevator in each tower. Good comparable but inferior to subject's location. Located 8 blocks southeast of subject.

(S) - Street

(C-S) - Corner Street

(C-R) - Corner Rear

COST APPROACH

Main Building Area	112,200 sq. ft. @ $ 11.50 sq. ft.	$ 1,290,300
First Floor	12,955 sq. ft. @ $ 10.00 sq. ft.	129,600
Garage Floor	38,175 sq. ft. @ $ 7.50 sq. ft.	286,300
	BASE BUILDING COST	$ 1,706,200

EXTRAS

1)	4 Hydraulic Elevators	$ 98,000
2)	Closed Circuit Security T. V.	10,000
3)	Central Air Conditioning Units	85,000
4)	Pool	10,000
5)	Landscaping & Paving	25,000
6)	Indirect Costs	205,000

TOTAL EXTRAS 433,000

REPRODUCTION COST $ 2,139,200

Appliances, Carpeting and Miscellaneous Furnishings 137,000

Land 375' X 150' on Waterway = 56,250 sq. ft. @ $ 7.50 422,000

MARKET VALUE INDICATED BY COST APPROACH $ 2,698,200

INCOME APPROACH COMPUTATIONS

GROSS INCOME:

APARTMENT RENTALS

No. Apts.	Type	Sq. Ft. Area	Room Count	Per Month	RENTAL Sq. Ft. per Mo.	Room per Mo.	Annual	
24	2BR2-½B (W)	1,428	5.5	$ 560	39.2	$ 101.82	$ 6,720	$ 161,300
36	2BR2-½B (S)	1,428	5.5	525	36.8	95.45	6,300	226,800

60 Units   330.0 Rooms

TOTAL GROSS INCOME FROM APARTMENTS $ 388,100

MISCELLANEOUS INCOME   (Per Year)

Parking: 90 @ $ 90 = $ 8,100   8,100
   (90 garage sites @ $ 120 x 75%)

TOTAL GROSS INCOME FROM ALL SOURCES $ 396,200

VACANCY: 5%   19,800

EFFECTIVE GROSS INCOME $ 376,400

EXPENSES: (See next page)   116,900

NET INCOME BEFORE INTEREST AND RECAPTURE $ 259,500

CAPITALIZE AT 9.5%

TOTAL or MARKET VALUE INDICATED BY THE INCOME APPROACH $ 2,731.600

EXPENSES

<u>Taxes:</u>	Real Estate & Personal Property	$ 43,000
<u>Inusrance:</u>	Fire & Extended Coverage, Workman's Compensation & Elevator & Public Liability Coverage	6,600
<u>Salaries:</u>		19,000
<u>Utilities:</u>	Water, Sewer, Public Lighting	10,000
<u>Extermination:</u>		500

<u>Repairs & Maintenance:</u>

A)	Lawn Maintenance	$ 1,200	
B)	Air Conditioning Maintenances	1,100	
C)	Pool Maintenance	1,000	
D)	Elevator Maintenance	2,000	
E)	Building, Appliances, Carpeting & Paving	<u>7,000</u>	
	Total Maintenance		$ 12,300

<u>Supplies:</u> Janitor, Garden and Office		3,500
<u>Miscellaneous:</u> Legal, Licenses, Advertising Auditing, etc.		3,000

Reserves for
Replacements:

1)	Air Conditioning Mechanical Equipment 15 year life or .067 x $ 34,000 =	$ 2,280	
2)	Elevators 30 year life or .033 x 98,000 =	3,230	
3)	Appliances 15 year life or .067 x 67,000 =	4,490	
4)	Closed Circuit TV 10 year life or .10 x 10,000 =	1,000	
5)	Carpeting 8 year life or .125 x 40,000 =	5,000	
6)	Miscellaneous 10 year life or .10 x 30,000 =	3,000	
	$(279,000)	$(19,000)	
			19,000

TOTAL EXPENSES	$ <u>116,900</u>

SCHEDULE OF COMPARABLE LAND SALES ON WATERWAY

Legal Description	Location	Date of Sale	Indicated Sales Price	Size & Area	Sales Price Per Sq. Ft.
(1) Lot 25 Block 3	9760 West Bay Harbor Drive	September 1971	$ 83,300	75 x 150 11,250 sq. ft.	$ 7.40

COMMENTS: Site presently improved with a one story duplex. Estimated cost to raze is $ 1,000. Waterfront site, located within same block as subject. Site has much less utility.

| (2) Lots 5 and 6, Block 3 | 10180 West Bay Harbor Drive | March 9, 1970 | $ 150,000 | 150 x 150 22,500 sq. ft. | $ 6.67 |

COMMENTS: Located within same block as subject. Site has less utility. Presently improved with the 15 unit Montego Club Condominium.

| (3) Lots 31 and 32, Block 4 | 9701 East Bay Harbor Drive | December 4, 1971 | $ 150,000 | Av. 150 x 150 22,500 sq. ft. | $ 6.67 |

COMMENTS: Site presently being improved with a seven story, 25 unit apartment building. Located 2 blocks east of subject. Site has less utility.

NOTE: All sales are located in the City of Bay Harbor Island within BAY HARBOR SUBDIVISION Plat Book 46, Page 5.

SCHEDULE OF COMPARABLE RENTALS

Comparable Property and Location	Type and No. of Apts.	Monthly Rentals	Sq.Ft. Area of Apts.	Room Count	Monthly Rental Per Sq.Ft.	Per Room
1) Belmont 10101 E. Bay Harbor Drive Bay Harbor Island Florida	6 - 1BR1-½B	$ 300-350	975	4.0	30.8-35.9¢	$75.00-87.50
	18 - 2BR2B	435-485	1,275-1,300	5.0	33.5-38.0	87.00-97.00
	36 - 2BR2B (W-F)	475-550	1,275-1,300	5.0	36.5-43.1	95.00-110.00
	1 - 3BR3B (P-H)	1,000	1,700	6.0	58.8	166.67
	1 - 3BR3B (W-F/P-H)	1,200	1,700	6.0	70.6	200.00
	62 Units					

COMMENTS: This is a + 4 year old, 7-story waterfront building. $10.00 per month additional for undercover parking space. Located two blocks east of subject. The 2BR apartments are smaller than subject. Utilities $20.00 additional. Most comparable to subject.

Comparable Property and Location	Type and No. of Apts.	Monthly Rentals	Sq.Ft. Area of Apts.	Room Count	Monthly Rental Per Sq.Ft.	Per Room
2) Guilford House Apartments 9800 W. Bay Harbor Drive Bay Harbor Island, Florida	48 - 1BR1-½B	$ 290-340	935	4.0	31.0-36.4¢	$72.50-85.00
	24 - 2BR2B	375-425	1,260	5.0	29.8-33.7	75.00-85.00
	2BR2B (W-F)	390-440	1,260	5.0	31.0-34.9	78.00-88.00
	72 Units					

COMMENTS: This is a + 5 year old, 7 story waterfront building. $10.00 per month additional for undercover parking space. Located two blocks south of subject. Area reported is gross area. Units much smaller than subject's. Indicated rentals are + 7 months old. Owners are planning to sell as condominium. Fair comparable.

(Continued)

SCHEDULE OF COMPARABLE RENTALS - Continued

Comparable Property and Location	Type and No. of Apts.	Monthly Rentals	Sq. Ft. Area of Apts.	Room Count	Monthly Rental Per Sq. Ft.	Per Room
Lancelot Hall 10350 W Bay Harbor Drive Bay Harbor Island, Florida	108- 1BR1B	$ 270-310	940	4.0	28.7-33.0¢	$67.50-77.50
	18- 1BR1-½B	- - - -	980	4.0	- - - - -	- - - - -
	59- 2BR2B (W-F)	370-430	1,330	5.0	27.8-32.3	74.00-86.00
	185 Units					

COMMENTS: This is a $\pm$ 7 year old, 11 story waterfront building. $10.00 per month additional for undercover parking space. Located 3 blocks north of subject. Area reported is gross area. Units smaller than subject's, and improvements are inferior to subject property.

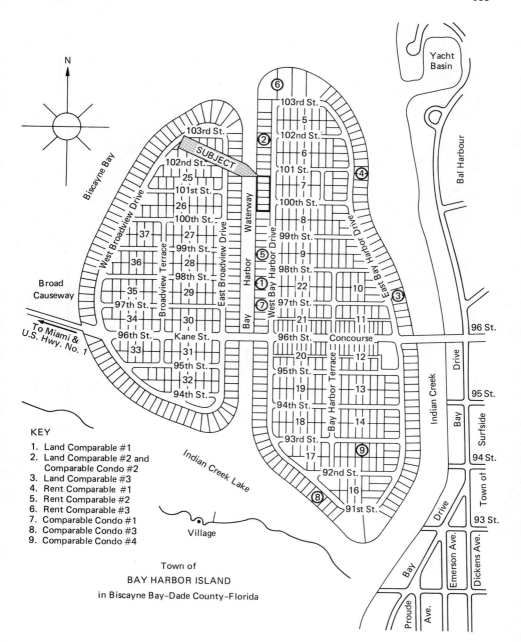

KEY

1. Land Comparable #1
2. Land Comparable #2 and
   Comparable Condo #2
3. Land Comparable #3
4. Rent Comparable #1
5. Rent Comparable #2
6. Rent Comparable #3
7. Comparable Condo #1
8. Comparable Condo #3
9. Comparable Condo #4

Town of
BAY HARBOR ISLAND
in Biscayne Bay–Dade County–Florida

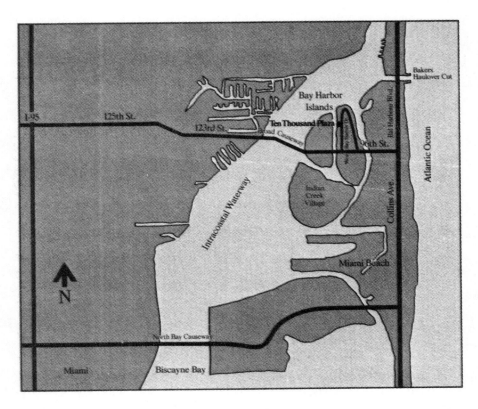

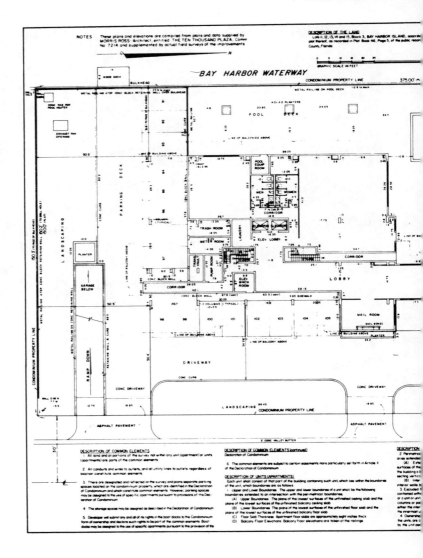

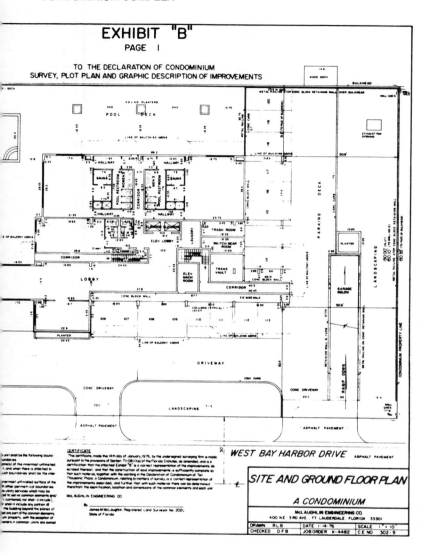

EXHIBIT "B"
PAGE 1

TO THE DECLARATION OF CONDOMINIUM
SURVEY, PLOT PLAN AND GRAPHIC DESCRIPTION OF IMPROVEMENTS

WEST BAY HARBOR DRIVE ASPHALT PAVEMENT

SITE AND GROUND FLOOR PLAN

A CONDOMINIUM

McLAUGHLIN ENGINEERING CO.
400 N.E. 3RD AVE : FT. LAUDERDALE, FLORIDA 33301

| DRAWN RLB | DATE 1-14-76 | SCALE 1" 10' |
| CHECKED DFB | JOB ORDER K-4482 | C E NO 302-9 |

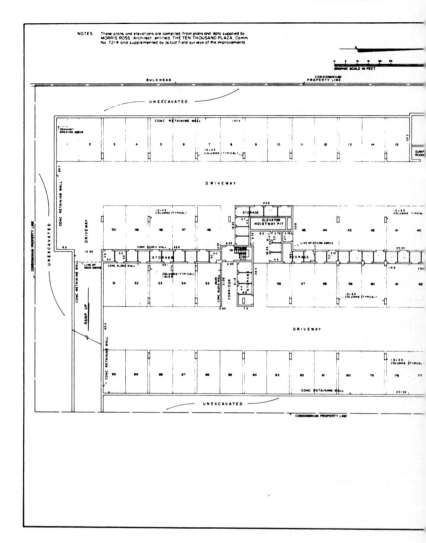

EXHIBIT "B"
PAGE 2

TO THE DECLARATION OF CONDOMINIUM
SURVEY, PLOT PLAN AND GRAPHIC DESCRIPTION OF IMPROVEMENTS

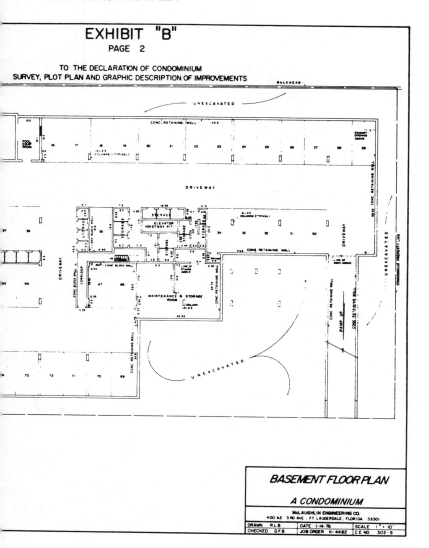

BASEMENT FLOOR PLAN

A CONDOMINIUM

McLAUGHLIN ENGINEERING CO.
400 N.E. 3 RD AVE., FT LAUDERDALE, FLORIDA 33301

DRAWN	RLB	DATE 1-14-76	SCALE 1" • 10'
CHECKED	DFB	JOB ORDER K-4482	CE NO 302-9

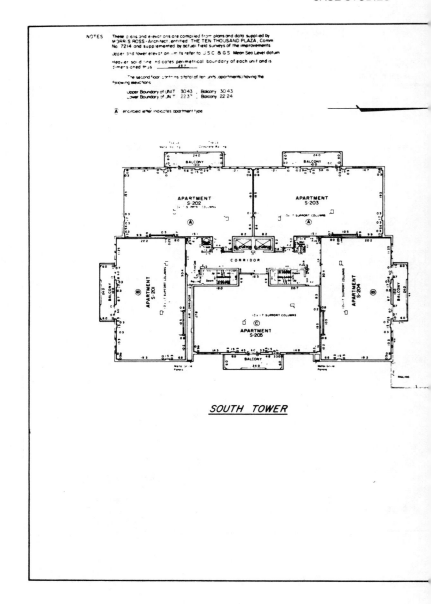

NOTES These plans and elevations are compiled from plans and data supplied by
MORRIS ROSS - Architect, entitled THE TEN THOUSAND PLAZA, Comm
No. 7214 and supplemented by actual field surveys of the improvements

Upper and lower elevation limits refer to U S C & G S Mean Sea Level datum

Heavier solid line indicates perimetrical boundary of each unit and is
dimensioned thus ———

The second floor contains a total of ten units (apartments) having the
following elevations

Upper Boundary of UNIT   30.43 ; Balcony   30.43
Lower Boundary of UNIT   22.37 ; Balcony   22.24

Ⓐ encircled letter indicates apartment type

SOUTH TOWER

EXHIBIT "B"
PAGE 3

TO THE DECLARATION OF CONDOMINIUM
SURVEY, PLOT PLAN AND GRAPHIC DESCRIPTION OF IMPROVEMENTS

GRAPHIC SCALE IN FEET   1" = 10'

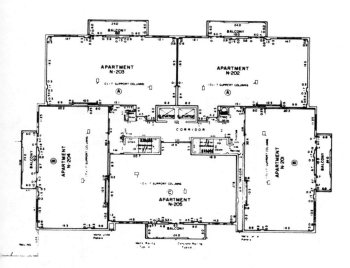

NORTH TOWER

FLOOR PLAN		
A CONDOMINIUM		
McLAUGHLIN ENGINEERING CO.		
400 N.E. 3 RD AVE., FT. LAUDERDALE, FLORIDA 33301		
DRAWN RLB	DATE 1-14-76	SCALE 1" = 10'
CHECKED DFB	JOB ORDER K-4482	CE NO 302-9

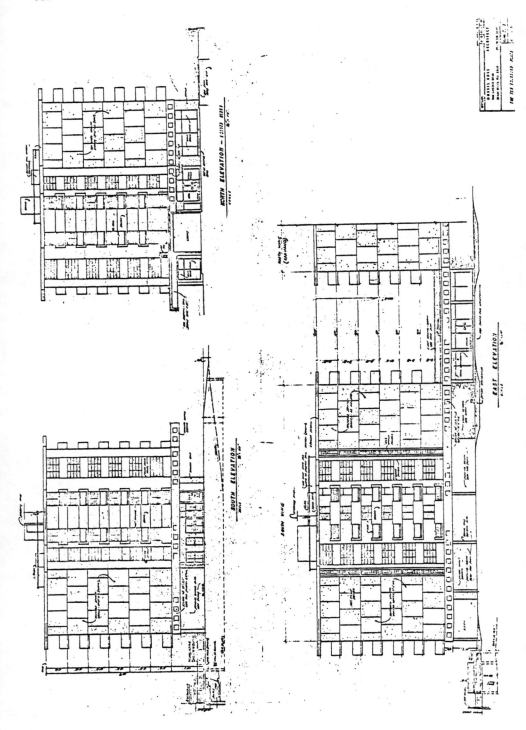

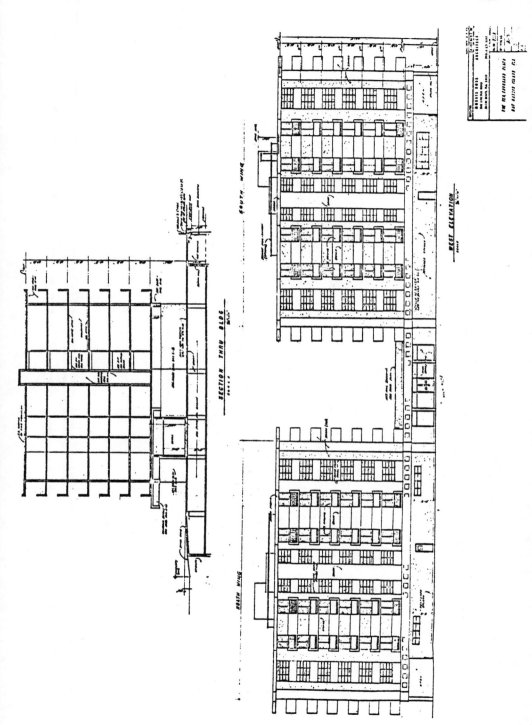

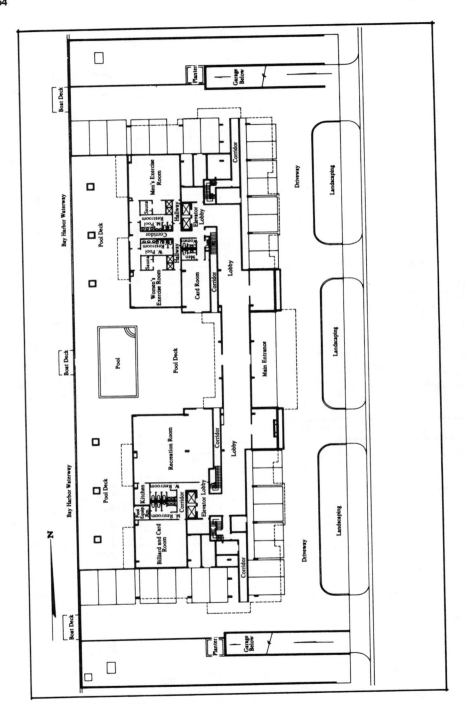

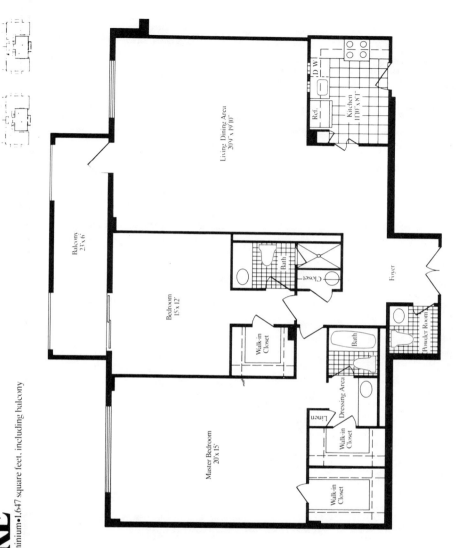

THE PIERRE

2-bedroom, 2-1/2-bath Waterfront Condominium • 1,647 square feet, including balcony

Features:

The Premises:

Prestigious Bay Harbor location on quiet, picturesque waterway.
No land or recreation leases; no management contracts.
Intercom system in each residence.
Uniformed doorman-valet.
Key required for all building entrances.
Bay Harbor police pass by every 6 minutes.
Sound-resistant and fireproof construction.
Lushly landscaped grounds.

The Residences:

Entry foyer with powder room.
Central air-conditioning and heating in every room
  including kitchens and baths.
Enormous living and dining areas.
Room-sized walk-in closets.
24-foot long balcony opening to living room and second
  bedroom/den.
Dead-bolt security lock on both exterior doors; peephole
  knocker on front door.
Fully-equipped eat-in kitchen with top-of-the-line
  General Electric appliances.
  21.6 cu. ft. side-by-side frost-free refrigerator-freezer
    with through-the-door dispensing of cubed or
    crushed ice.
  "Americana" range with self-cleaning oven.
  Range hood with variable-speed exhaust fan.
  Sound-shielded 2-speed automatic dishwasher.
  Custom-built cabinetry and countertops.
  Stainless-steel sink.
  Luminous ceiling.
Decorator-designed baths (featuring dressing area in
  Master Bath).
  Vanity with cultured-marble one-piece vanity top and
    integral basin.
  Huge vanity mirror.
  Luxurious fixtures.
  Ceramic-tiled floor.
Room-width windows in Master Bedroom.
Master color television outlet (also for B&W).
Pre-wired telephone outlets.

The Recreation:

Entire ground floor devoted to recreational and sitting areas.
Men's and women's gymnasiums with exercise equipment,
  saunas, and showers.
Private waterfront sun terrace with heated swimming pool.
Private boat docks and fishing area.
Billiard and game room.
Card room.
Party hall with full-service kitchen.

APPLICATION FOR A MORTGAGE LOAN COMMITMENT

The undersigned hereby applies for a permanent first mortgage loan commitment and requests Southeast Mortgage Company to issue or secure a commitment to make such loan on the terms and with the security hereinafter set forth:

AMOUNT: $ _2,700,000_ TERM: _30 months_ INTEREST: $4\frac{1}{2}$% floating over the prime rate _established_ % per annum

REPAYMENT: $_simple interest as_   drawn   by the Old South Bank of Mobile to be applied first to the payment of interest at the aforesaid rate and the balance to the payment of principal.

BORROWER: A-1 CONSTRUCTION CORP.
(If Corporation, list Officers)

       Tom Barrett, President

SECURITY: A first mortgage will encumber: (Address and Legal Description)

    100xx West Bay Harbor Drive, Bay Harbor Island, Florida

    Lots 11-15, Block 3, Bay Harbor Island, PB 46/5

IMPROVEMENTS: Existing ( )   Type: _Proposed 60-Unit Condominium_

       Proposed (x)   _Apartment Building_

DISBURSEMENT OF LOAN: The loan is to be disbursed to the Borrower prior to expiration of the loan commitment upon compliance with all terms of this application and of the loan commitment.

ESTIMATED CLOSING COSTS:

Commission	$ _27,000.00_
Mortgage Title Insurance)	
incl. Disbursement Service)	_--_
Photographs	
Recording Fees)	
Documentary Stamps)	_18,500.00_
Florida Intangible Tax)	
Credit Report	
Appraisal Fee	_Included_
TOTAL	$ _45,000.00_ Plus Abstracting and Surveys&Costs.

• The above stated commitment fees are due and payable when Southeast Mortgage Company has issued or secured the loan commitment requested herein. The applicant consents to any placement and/or servicing fee which the permanent lender may pay to Southeast Mortgage Company. A standby fee may be required by the permanent lender and the payment thereof shall be in addition to the above costs.

REMARKS:

SEE ADDITIONAL TERMS AND CONDITIONS (Page 3)

In addition to the above costs, it is understood the following may be required at borrowers expense:

1. Sums necessary to pay prior liens and to establish evidence of good title to the premises.

2. ~~Monthly tax deposits in an amount equal to 1/12th of the annual real estate taxes~~

3. ~~An amount sufficient to pay the real estate taxes, special assessments and hazard insurance premiums, if any, then due~~ ~~X and payable, plus an amount which when added to the monthly payments will be sufficient to pay the current year's X~~ ~~X real estate taxes, assessments and insurance when due and payable.~~

4. The insurance premiums for fire and extended coverage policies in amounts and in such companies, as may be acceptable to the lender and such other risks in the amount and kind required by the lender, including but not limited to Workmen's Compensation, Public Liability and Contents, and Rent insurance. The Borrower agrees to pay promptly all premiums when billed ~~directly by the insurance company or companies to the borrower~~

5. ~~Recording satisfactions of mortgages and payments of fees~~

6. Inspecting architect and/or engineer acceptable to permanent lender.

7. Rework of legal documents, if caused by borrower.

8. Flood insurance will be required if applicable.

9. Commitment Fee increase in event of major modification of Loan terms.

APPLICATION FOR A CONSTRUCTION LOAN: The undersigned hereby applies for construction financing ✗✗✗✗✗✗✗✗and ✗✗✗ ✗✗✗✗✗✗✗✗✗✗ Approval of interim construction financing shall be subject to the following conditions:

1. Simple interest on the outstanding balance, payable monthly at the annual rate of _____ $4\frac{1}{2}$% _____% above the prime rate of Old South Bank.
2. Construction/interim loan period to be concurrent with the permanent loan commitment period.
3. Approval of the cost breakdown, disbursement schedule, General and sub-contractors by Southeast Mortgage Company.
4. Execution of construction loan documents required by lender's counsel.
5. A completion building fund or a satisfactory completion bond.
6. Full compliance with the ✗✗✗✗✗✗ loan commitment terms and application.
7. Personal liability of principals during construction loan period.
8. Inspecting architect, engineer and/or cost consultant acceptable to lender, at borrowers expense.

EXCLUSIVE APPOINTMENT: In consideration of efforts to secure the loan commitment requested herein, including the organization and evaluation of loan data and the submission of this loan request to lenders and/or investors, the applicant hereby irrevocably gives Southeast Mortgage Company the sole and exclusive right to issue or obtain said loan commitment for a period of sixty (60) days from the date of receipt of all necessary exhibits to support this application and thereafter until Southeast Mortgage Company receives ten (10) days written notice of termination.

If the applicant has misrepresented or failed to disclose material facts, Southeast Mortgage Company may cancel the loan commitment without liability on its part. If the mortgage loan commitment applied for or a commitment in an amount and upon terms acceptable to the applicant is obtained and said mortgage loan is not closed because the Borrower has not fulfilled his part of this agreement, or for any reason has elected not to accept the loan, the applicant agrees to pay to Southeast Mortgage Company as liquidated damages, and not as a penalty, the amount of the commitment fee as aforesaid, but in no event less than 2% of the amount of the loan, without credit for any amount forwarded as a standby fee to the aforesaid lender or investor. In the event the services of an attorney are required to collect such damages, applicant agrees to reimburse Southeast Mortgage Company for reasonable attorney's fees paid by it, including fees incurred in appellate proceedings. If an acceptable commitment is not obtained, the mortgage loan application deposit will be refunded✗✗✗✗✗✗✗✗✗✗✗✗✗✗✗✗✗✗✗✗✗✗✗✗✗✗✗✗✗✗✗✗✗✗✗

March 1, 1973	_____(SEAL)
Date	A-1 CONSTRUCTION CORP.
	Tom Barrett, President

By signature hereon, borrower acknowledges receipt of a copy of this application.

Mailing Address:_____

101 South First Street

Miami Beach, Florida

Telephone: 446-1213

(Note: If Borrower is a corporation, please provide copy of Certificate of Incorporation showing state and date or incorporation, amendments and officer designation.)

In consideration of the sum of $ 10,000.00 , receipt of which is hereby acknowledged, and in compliance with Chapter 494 of Florida Statutes, SOUTHEAST MORTGAGE COMPANY agrees to organize and evaluate the loan data furnished by you and to use its best efforts to obtain the loan applied for herein by submitting it to lenders and investors. This deposit will be credited toward closing costs.

March 1, 1973
Date

SOUTHEAST MORTGAGE COMPANY
(License No. 2314)

By:_____
Jess S. Lawhorn

THIS IS AN APPLICATION FOR A MORTGAGE LOAN; IT IS NOT A LOAN COMMITMENT

ADDITIONAL TERMS AND CONDITIONS

1. Construction Loan to be fully endorsed and guaranteed by Mr. Tom Barrett and his wife, Joyce.

2. The construction lender shall not be required to join in the Declaration of Condominium Agreement until 50% of the individual units are sold to bona fide purchasers. At the time of the individual real estate and/or mortgage loan closing to purchasers, the construction lender will require that 115% of the loan amount or 90% of the sales price from an individual unit be applied toward the reduction of the construction loan, whichever amount is greater.

3. Borrower to furnish current survey of property.

4. Borrower to furnish copy of current building permit.

5. Borrower to furnish copy of authorization for sewer hook-up which shall be in compliance with the pollution regulations of Dade County and the State of Florida.

6. The loan will be closed by Southeast Mortgage Company on behalf of South Realty and Southeast Mortgage Company shall approve all disbursements, such disbursements to be made through Lawyer's Title Insurance Company.

7. A valid sales contract will constitute a minimum of 10% down, such down payment to be escrowed with a mutually agreeable escrow agent and these monies will not be used in the construction of the building.

8. 100% of each draw requested will be disbursed during construction with the final 10% not disbursed until South Realty has made site inspections and a Certificate of Occupancy is issued on the building.

9. The construction cost breakdown entitled "Schedule A" is made a part of this application.

Southeast Mortgage Company
MORTGAGE BANKERS

THE BORROWING CORPORATION

A-1 Construction Corp., a Florida Corporation

Tom Barrett	President
Joyce Barrett (wife)	Vice President
Sam Costa	Secretary/Treasurer

Mr. and Mrs. Barrett own 100% of the stock in A-1 Construction Corp. Mr. Sam Costa is their attorney and has no stock interest.

Since South Realty Investors has not experienced previous relations with the borrower, a brief resume of Mr. Barrett is included. The pictures are of the three apartment buildings which he now owns.

1754 Meridian Avenue, Miami Beach, Florida. 16-unit apartment building.

1990 Marseilles Drive, Normandy Isle, Miami Beach, Florida. 32-unit apartment building.

Southeast Mortgage Company

MORTGAGE BANKERS

9701 E. Bay Harbor Drive, Bay Harbor Island, Florida. 25-unit apartment building.

RESUME - TOM BARRETT

Mr. Tom Barrett, 33 years of age, is an extraordinary person who has achieved a high degree of success through his work and diligence. Born in Bogota, Colombia, he moved permanently to Florida in 1968 because of political instability in South America that was affecting his business operations. Since moving to Florida, he has been actively engaged in real estate development, as well as the import-export business. Future plans call for concentrated effort in developing real estate, and Southeast Mortgage Company regards him highly as one of our repeat borrowers.

Based upon meeting with Mr. Barrett, I am sure that you concur with our opinion as to his sincerity and ability for formulating plans for the future, as well as by his financial capability. He possesses a sincere desire to be associated with quality projects and enjoys a great amount of personal satisfaction when discussing his prior interests. Obviously, this is the type of client with whom our Company wishes to establish a lasting relationship.

In March, 1972, Southeast Mortgage Company obtained a $750,00 permanent first mortgage loan on the Royal Bay Harbor Plaza Apartments, a proposed 25-unit luxury rental building located at 9701 East Bay Harbor Drive. Southeast Mortgage Company provided the construction loan, and the building is approximately 60% complete at present. Based on progress inspection reports from our Appraisal Department, Mr. Barrett is on schedule and the quality of materials and labor is excellent, with no problems encountered with our loan.

In August, 1972, Southeast Mortgage Company provided a $400,000 land acquisition loan covering the subject property and two dry lots approximately ½ block east of the subject. At the time our loan was committed, we valued the subject property at $425,000. The amount of indebtedness on the subject site is presently $345,000, the amount indicated in the cost breakdown as land satisfaction.

Mr. Barrett's future plans call for construction of condominium and apartment buildings on Bay Harbor Island and he is presently negotiating with several people on the Island for purchase of their property.

ANALYSIS: CASE STUDY 5—CONDOMINIUM COMPLEX

This is more than a case study. It is a classic example of some of the cases of the condominium failures in the mid-1970s. Carefully note the financial statements of the borrower for sources of liquidity. Where is his "staying power" in the event sales are not completed at the same time as the building? Note how little prior building experience he has. Study the layouts for liveability. Note the dining area arrangements and the balcony opens off the second bedroom rather than the master bedroom. Study room sizes and shapes.

What happens to the lender's security if this doesn't make it as a condominium and is converted to rentals? How and when does he get his money back?

Photos, plans, and other exhibits that normally accompany a loan submission are included in this case to demonstrate their effectiveness in the presentation.

Low-Rise Office Building

G. Wayne Fleck

PDQ MORTGAGE COMPANY
710 Broad Street
Nashville, Tennessee

October 14, 1973

Mr. John Doe, Vice President
ABC Life Insurance Company
100 Main Street
Atlanta, Georgia

                          Re: The XYZ Company
                                Proposed Office Building
                                N/W/C Poplar Avenue
                                and Sweetbriar Road
                                Nashville, Tennessee

Dear Mr. Doe:

Enclosed is a full submission for a first mortgage loan in the
amount of $1,500,000 at 8-3/4% interest for 20 years with the
monthly principal and interest payment based on 30 year amortization. The subject property is the third office building in
this complex with your Company having financed the first two
buildings. We are excited with the long term potential of this
area. As you know, a 400 room Hyatt Regency Ridgeway Hotel, an
enclosed mall shopping center, and approximately 200 condominium
units and single family units will be constructed upon this tract
of ground. The site is the former Ridgeway Country Club and all
buildings should be completed when this loan is ready for
funding.

The principals are experienced developers and managers of real
estate particularly office buildings and apartments. The XYZ
Company will own and manage the property and will personally
sign the Note. Their latest financial statement showed a net
worth of $11,392,000 which is enclosed. All of the necessary
permits have been obtained and PDQ Mortgage Company has agreed
to make the construction loan.

Please let us know if you need any additional information.

                          Sincerely,

                          G. Wayne Fleck
                          Assistant Vice President

GWF:dc

TABLE OF CONTENTS

<u>SALIENT FACTS AND CONDITIONS</u>

Amount:	$1,500,000
Rate:	8.75% Gross - 8.625% Net - (1/8% Service Fee)
Term:	20 Years (9.45 Constant - Based on 30 Year Amortization)
Term of Commitment:	24 Months
Prepayment Privilege:	Closed 10 years, 105% penalty declining 1/2% per annum to a minimum of 101%
Appraised Value:	$2,000,000
Loan to Value:	75%
Ownership:	XYZ Company - Experienced office and apartment building developers and managers with a net worth of $11,392,000
Improvements:	A three story masonry office building containing 51,800 gross square feet and 44,025 square feet N.R.A.
Loan Per Gross Sq. Ft.:	$28.96
Loan Per Sq. Ft. N.R.A.:	$34.25
Rent Per Sq. Ft.:	$6.75
Net x Debt Service Coverage	1.31
Loan x Net:	8.09
Loan x Gross:	5.05

Prepayment Privilege No. ___20-A___

CITY INCOME PROPERTY
Application for First Mortgage Loan

Broker ___PDQ Mortgage Company___

(Applications will be considered for multiples of $100 only)

___XYZ Company___, the undersigned, desires to procure a loan of $ ___1,500,000___ at ___8-3/4___% {interest and principal} beginning at

{monthly ~~yearly~~ ~~semiannually~~} for ___240___ {mos., ~~yrs.~~} with payments of $ ___11,812.50___, payable {monthly ~~yearly~~ ~~semiannually~~} on account of {interest and principal}

in~~terest~~ payable {monthly ~~yearly~~ ~~semiannually~~} {mo. year} from

Based on a 30 year amortization

the end of ___12/75___

secured by first mortgage on the following property, title to which is perfect.

N

PAVED?

E

PAVED?

S

PAVED?

W

Attach hereto dated photographs (approximately 3½"x5½") show-ing (1) front view of h o u s e; (2) street view of building with buildings adjoin-ing on side.

Date, name of applicant and ad-dress to be typed on reverse side of each photograph.

Indicate location of lot, and distance from street corner and location of alley, if any.

LEGAL DESCRIPTION
Lot, Block and Addition or Metes and Bounds

Size of Lot ___2.84 Acres___ X

_____ from center city.
(Distance and direction)

Being on the ___north___ side and known as Building No. ___Poplar Avenue___ Street / Avenue

City of ___Nashville___, County of ___Davidson___, State of ___Tennessee___

Is building on same line with other buildings on block? ___No___ Occupied by Owner or Tenant ___multi-tenant___ Street paved with ___concrete___

Sidewalks ___concrete___ Driveway: Surfacing ___asphalt___ Independent ___Mutual___ ___asphalt___. Lot on, above or below grade ___on grade___

Approximate distance to nearest fire plug ___500___ ft. ___ Insured for, Fire $ ___1,737,000___ Tornado $ ___1,737,000___

(All insurance to be assigned to this Company as Mortgagee)

DESCRIPTION OF BUILDING AND IMPROVEMENTS
___multi-tenant office___ Type. Outside Materials ___brick & glass___ Independent Walls? ___yes___

___three___ Story

MATERIAL: Foundation? concrete   Roof? composition built up   Side Walls? steel frame   Exterior Finish? brick w/bronze reflecting glass

		No.	Total Sq. Ft.	1-Room	2-Room	3-Room	4-Room	5-Room	6-Room	Apt. Units	or Garages
	-	-	- - -	-	-	-	-	-	-	-	-
			44,025	-	-	-	-	-	-	-	-

Inside Finish:

	floors?	Terrazzo vinyl carpet	Walls? vinyl & wood panel	Trim?
1st Story	"	"	Walls?	Trim?
2nd Story	"	"	Walls?	Trim?
Others	floors?		Walls?	Trim?

No. Bathrooms 6   Floor? tile   Walls? tile   Wainscoting? tile   No. of Toilets 24

Built-in Features and Extras: (1) Plumbing? steel & copper fixtures ceramic class A   Basement Toilet? no   ; Kind of pipe? steel copper ; (2) Building heated by electricity

Oil Burner? -   Gas Burner? -   Automatic Stoker? -   (3) Insulated? yes   Weatherstripped? yes

(4) Built-in Kitchen Cabinets? -   Air Conditioned? yes - central   (5) Metal Lath? no   Steel Sash? yes

Car Capacity of Garage? -   Are there living quarters in Garage? -

Size of main building, exclusive of porches? irregular x 51,810 gross   Size of cellar? - X -   Size of L or extensions, proposed

exclusive of porches? - X -   Height of extensions? -   feet. When was building completed? proposed
(Submit sketch showing dimensions of building)

Remodeled? no   When? -   Cost -   When did you buy this property? 1971   What did you pay for: Land -
(Advise by letter extent)

$280,000 Improvement -   Total -   What do you value: Land $375,000 Improvement proposed Total

Present First Mortgage: Original Amount $ -   Present Amount $ -   Interest Rate - %, Date of Maturity -

Present Second Mortgage: Original Amount $ -   Present Amount $ -   Interest Rate - %, Date of Maturity -

Will there be any Second Mortgage or Junior Liens on this property subordinate to the first mortgage above applied for? no   If so, how much?

By whom held or to be held?   Any other encumbrances

or special street assessments on property? - -   Amount $ - - -   How payable?   Names of holders of above

encumbrance - - - - -   Why do you desire to secure this loan? first mortgage loan

proposed Condition of improvements (Give general condition and state repairs needed) - - - -

Net Square Feet rentable in mercantile and office buildings: Ground floor -   sq. ft., Upper floor -   sq. ft., Total 44,025 sq. ft.

Apartments: Automatic Refrigeration -   No. Units -   No. Stoves -   Gas or Electric   Does owner furnish heat? -

Number of elevators in building? 2 hydraulic

(In case of apartment buildings the Company will require separate instrument or instruments creating first lien on such equipment as building contains for maintenance, use and occupancy of tenant or tenants.)

STATEMENT IN REGARD TO LEASES AND RENTALS

Portion of premises leased	Year lease was made	Year lease matures	Right of renewal, if any, and for what period?	Does tenant pay taxes, water rent or make repairs?	Gross Annual Rental Less All Concessions
			19........	19........	19........	19........	Current year 19........

TOTAL GROSS RENTAL CHARGEABLE	297,169
Less vacancies and loss of rents	14,859
1. ACTUAL NET COLLECTIONS	282,310
Operating Expenses—Payroll	
XXX	
Electricity – utilities	19,811
Repairs and Redecorating	24,214
Supplies miscellaneous	2,201
XXX elevator	2,201
Management	15,410
TOTAL OPERATING EXPENSES	63,837
Fixed Charges—Taxes—State & County ($........ Assessed Value)	28,616
City ($........ Assessed Value)	
Other	4,402
Insurance	33,018
Depreciation	96,855
Total Fixed Charges	185,455
Total Expenses	

...feet and are at least square feet vertical of each roof of office buildings. All concessions granted must be itemized in this statement.

We will require copies of all leases where the original term and right of renewal extends over a period of five years.

NOTE—All applications for other than commitment loans stand approved for 120 days only, and such approval is automatically canceled after that period. A survey made by a competent civil engineer or surveyor will be required in all cases. All necessary expenses are to be paid by the borrower, including the charge for examination of title and the charge for title insurance, if the latter is required. It is understood that disbursement of the loan by the Provident will be made within 90 days after approval of title and all papers by its Law Department, provided that title showing and other necessary papers are received and approved by the Law Department within the 120-day approval period.

APPLICANT'S FINANCIAL STATEMENT

ASSETS

Property securing this loan _____ $

Other Real Estate _____ $

Stocks and Bonds _____ $

Other Assets _____ $

Total Assets _____ $

Total Liabilities _____ $

Net Worth _____ $

LIABILITIES

Mortgage on Property securing this loan _____ $

Mortgage on Other Real Estate _____ $

Unsecured Bank Obligations _____ $

Other Debts _____ $

Form G-2198 ML.

CITY DATA

Subject property is located approximately eight miles due east of downtown Nashville. The city's primary path of growth has historically been
in an easterly direction along the Poplar corridor. This has resulted
in a steady expansion of high quality residential and commercial developments along this route. The Ridgeway Office Park lies in the heart of
one of the finest residential areas in the city of Nashville. The River
Oaks area just to the north of the subject includes estate type homes
with values ranging from $100,000 to $500,000. Other subdivisions in
the immediate area, including Briarwood, Eastwood Manor, Kirby Woods
and Balmoral contain well kept homes ranging in value from $50,000 to
$100,000.

There is 1,240,000 square feet of retail space two miles to the west of
the subject on Poplar Avenue with two major shopping centers, Briarwood
and Eastgate, along with various strip commercial developments. Approximately 265,000 square feet of retail space will be provided in the overall
development of Ridgeway.

The subject property is in the southeast quadrant of Poplar Avenue and
Interstate 240, the circumferential highway expressway system around
Nashville. A lot of new construction activity has taken place in this
area the past few years. The Holiday Inn which lies west of the subject
on the opposite side of the I-240 interchange was built in 1969 and
operates at 90% occupancy. A 150 unit Quality Court has just opened
directly across westbound Poplar from the subject. Construction is now
being completed on the 450 bed Memorial Hospital located on Park Avenue
just to the south of the subject. Several high quality garden and
townhouse projects having approximately 950 units have also been
developed to the south of the subject and have traditionally commanded
high rents. A 140,000 square foot high fashion mall is scheduled to
begin construction shortly one mile east of the site.

The proposed improvements are part of the first phase of development
of the Ridgeway Country Club property purchased by the XYZ Company.
Initially, 180 acres will be developed and this land has already been
rezoned for office, commercial and residential use. Exhibit # B is
a plot plan showing the proposed long range plan of development for the
property. Construction on the 26 story, $15,000,000, 400 room Hyatt
Regency Ridgeway Hotel has already commenced and should be completed
mid 1975. The commercial areas will border I-240 and Poplar Avenue with
the single family residential and condominium phase to be constructed
on the extreme northern and eastern portion of the site to provide a
buffer zone for the existing residential community.

SITE DATA

The subject site consists of 2.84 acres located on the north side of Poplar Avenue west of Sweetbriar Road. The building will blend aesthetically with the other two office buildings just completed, the Home Office building of XYZ Company and their second building. The site is approximately eight feet above Poplar Avenue and will remain so to allow maximum visability from Poplar. The site is zoned 0-2 which permits the proposed improvements and all utilities are available.

DESCRIPTION OF IMPROVEMENTS

The subject property is a three story elevatored, multi-tenant office
building containing 51,810 gross square feet and 44,025 square feet of
net rentable area. Briefly, the building is composed of:

Structure:	Steel I beam with poured concrete over reinforced steel bar joists.
Exterior:	Brick with polished bronze reflecting glass windows.
Roof:	Composition built up.
Elevator:	(2) Hydraulic
Floors:	Terrazzo in lobby entrance, vinyl in halls and general office space, carpet in offices (100 sq. ft. for every 1,000 sq. ft. G.L.A.)
Walls:	Vinyl and Wood Panel
Parking:	200 spaces - Cross parking easements to buildings 1 and 2 having 128 and 207 parking spaces. Parking for subject - 4.5 spaces per 1,000 sq. ft. N.R.A. - Overall parking 4.2 spaces per 1,000 sq. ft. N.R.A.
Landscaping:	All buildings are part of a master plan and must be approved by the Ridgeway Board.

SITE VALUATION

The following comparable land sales were located in the immediate area of the subject. (See map, exhibit # **C**, for location of sales.)

Sale No. 1

Location:	5150 Poplar
Zoning:	R-1 (Single Family)
Sq. Ft. Area:	13,600
Date of Sale:	August 22, 1972
Sales Price:	$60,000
Price/Sq. Ft.:	$4.41
Comment:	Single family residence bought for speculative purpose.

Sale No. 2

Location:	4929 Block Road
Zoning:	C-2
Sq. Ft. Area:	7,500
Date of Sale:	February 15, 1972
Sales Price:	$26,000
Price/Sq. Ft.:	$3.47

Sale No. 3

Location:	4930 Block Road
Zoning:	C-2
Sq. Ft. Area:	7,500
Date of Sale:	September 8, 1971
Sales Price:	$25,000
Price/Sq. Ft.:	$3.33

Sale No. 4

Location:	4948-4966 Block Road
Zoning:	C-2
Sq. Ft. Area:	30,000
Date of Sale:	October 24, 1969
Sales Price:	$120,000
Price/Sq. Ft.:	$4.00
Comment:	Improved with South Central Bell Bldg.

Sale No. 5

Location:	S/S Poplar between Yates and Oakview
Zoning:	C-2
Sq. Ft. Area:	118,047
Date of Sales:	October, 1971
Sales Price:	$353,120
Price/Sq. Ft.:	$2.99
Comment:	Property was immediately resold to Northwestern Mutual for $400,000 or $3.39 sq. ft.

SITE VALUATION (Cont'd)

Sale No. 6

Location:	4956 Poplar
Zoning:	C-2
Sq. Ft. Area:	39,600
Date of Sale	February 29, 1971
Sales Price	$155,000
Price/Sq. Ft.:	$3.91
Comment:	Improved with a carwash.

Sale No. 7

Location:	S/S Poplar Ave., West of Massey
Zoning:	O-2
Sq. Ft. Area:	63,567
Date of Sale:	January 2, 1973
Sales Price:	$225,000
Price/Sq. Ft.:	$3.54
Comment:	Improved with 3 Story Office Bldg.

Sale No. 8

Location:	Ridge Lake Boulevard Ridgeway
Zoning:	O-2
Sq. Ft. Area:	100,623
Date of Sale:	January, 1973
Sales Price	$301,000
Price/Sq. Ft.	$3.00
Comment:	To be improved with 32,000 Sq. Ft. N.R.A. Office Bldg.

Sale No. 9

Location:	Poplar and I-240
Zoning:	C-3
Sq. Ft. Area:	174,240
Date of Sale:	1972
Sales Price	$740,520
Price/Sq. Ft.	$4.25
Comment:	Site west of Quality Inn on Poplar. Property was bought subject to C-3 zoning.

RENT AND TAX COMPARABLES

BUILDING	MAP # (LGE NOS. ON MAP)	SQ FT NRA	RENT	% OCC.	TAX/SQ FT	COMMENTS
XYZ Bldg A	1	52,300	$6.50-7.00	95	N/A	Just Completed.
XYZ Bldg B	1	32,800	6.50-7.00	70	N/A	Under Construction, Occupancy 11/1/73
Clark Tower	2	575,000	6.00-7.50	75	.38	Leasing is approximately 9 months ahead of projections. Partial year assessment.
White Station Tower	3	244,500	5.50-7.00	100	.57	Approximately 5 years old.
Executive Square	4	50,000	5.50-6.00	100	.50	1-1/2 years old.
1st American Bank Bldg.	5	51,000	6.00-6.50	65	N/A	Shell completed 7/1/73.
Eastgate (11)	6	32,000-O	5.25-6.00	100	.42	Tax includes 40,000 retail space that is leased for the higher of $1.06 sq. ft., or 3% sales. Approximately 7 years old. (Consider as Rent Comparable Only).
Oak Hall Bldg.	7	30,000	5.25-6.10	100	.60	Approximately 6 years old.
Poplar Towers	8	108,000	6.50	Under Constr.	Under Constr.	Construction began 1/1/73, will be 11 stories. Estimated occupancy 1/1/75.

O- Office
R- Retail

1. <u>XYZ Building A</u>

Location: Sweetbriar Road and Poplar Avenue

Net Rentable Area: 52,300 Sq. Ft.

Current Rents: $6.50 - $7.00

Completion Date: June, 1973

Occupancy: 95%

Comments: Attractive office spaced. 95% leased in
                       first 4 months.

1. <u>XYZ Building B</u>

Location: Poplar Avenue

Net Rentable Area: 32,800 Sq. Ft.

Current Rents: $6.50 - $7.00

Completion Date: June, 1973

Occupancy: 70%

Comments: Adjacent to XYZ Building A. Similar design
                     and finish.

2. <u>Clark Tower</u>

Location   North Side Poplar West of White Station Road

Net Rentable Area: 575,000 Sq. Ft.

Current Rents: $6.00 - $7.50

Completion Date: 1973

Occupancy: Estimated to be 75% Leased

Comments: Very attractive inside and out. Parking and
                      traffic are a problem. Parking garage with paid
                      parking.

<u>COMPARABLE RENTALS</u>

3. <u>White Station Tower</u>

Location: North Side Poplar West of White Station Road

Net Rentable Area: 244,500 Sq. Ft.

Current Rents: $5.50 - $7.00

Completion Date: 1968

Occupancy: 100%

Comments: Nicely finished space. Exterior is unattractive.
                         Traffic congestion and parking is a problem.

4. <u>Executive Square</u>

Location:	South Side Poplar East of Yates Road
Net Rentable Area:	50,000 Sq. Ft.
Current Rents:	$5.50 - $6.00
Completion Date:	Summer, 1972
Occupancy:	100% Leased
Comments:	Good location, fairly good curb appeal. Standard interior finish is basic. No elevator to second floor space.

5. <u>First American Bank</u>

Location: North Side Poplar West of Valleybrook

Net Rentable Area: 51,000 Sq. Ft.

Current Rents: Proposed $6.00 - $6.50

Completion Date: 7/1/73

Occupancy: Under Construction - 65% Leased

Comments: Ground floor occupied by Bank Branch.

6. Eastgate Office Building

Location:	Eastgate Shopping Center at Park and White Station Road
Net Rentable Area:	32,000 Sq. Ft. Office
Current Rents:	$5.25 - $6.00
Completion Date:	1966
Occupancy:	100%
Comments:	Attractive, well maintained building. Commercial (Julius Lewis) on first floor and basement. One floor occupied by owner.

7. Oak Hall Building

Location: Poplar Avenue at Perkins

Net Rentable Area: 30,000 Sq. Ft.

Current Rents: $5.25 - $6.10

Completion Date: 1968

Occupancy: 100%

Comments: Older building. Parking a problem, however
                     100% leased.

8. <u>Poplar Towers</u>

Location: W. Massey and Hwy. 7?

Net Rentable Area: 108,000 Sq. Ft.

Current Rents: $6.50

Completion Date: Estimated 1/1/75

Occupancy: Under Construction

Comments: Construction began 1/1/73.

PRO FORMA INCOME APPROACH

Gross Annual Income	44,025 Sq. Ft. @ $6.75	$297,169
Less 5% Vacancy Allowance		14,859
Effective Gross Income		$282,310

Expenses	$ Sq. Ft.	
Taxes	$ .65	$28,616
Utilities	.45	19,811
Janitor & Cleaning	.40	17,610
Management	.35	15,410
Elevator	.05	2,201
Insurance	.10	4,402
Decoration & Repairs	.15	6,604
Miscellaneous	.05	2,201
Total Expenses	$2.20	$96,855

Net Income		$185,455

Capitalized @ 9.25% - $2,004,919

Rounded   - $2,000,000

PRO FORMA COST APPROACH

Shell @ $20.75 Sq. Ft.	$1,075,000
Interior Finish	365,000
Architect/Engineer	50,000
Legal Fees	20,000
Permits, Licenses, Insurance	8,000
Title Policy	4,000
Interim Interest (Net)	135,000
Financing	30,000
Contingency	50,000
Building Only	$1,737,000
Land (2.84 acres @ $3.00 Sq. Ft.)	$ 375,000
Total Building and Land	$2,112,000

VALUE BY MARKET DATA APPROACH

Date of Sale	5/3/71	12/6/71	6/27/72	8/21/73
Sales Price	$3,100,000	$1,765,000	$2,335,000	$2,115,000
Mortgage Terms	8.25%-75% 25 Years	8.5% - 75% 26 Years	8.125%-75% 27 Years	9% - 75% 25 Years
Price Per Sq. Ft. N.R.A.	$42.00	$43.79	$45.15	$46.05
Price Per Sq. Ft. Gross	$33.60	$38.10	$38.38	$37.76
Efficiency	80%	87%	85%	82%
No. of Stories	5	3	3	3
Location	100 Executive Park, Nashville	400 Executive Park, Nashville	Dome Bldg. 1410 Lamar Dr., Nash.	7 Park Blvd. Nashville
Age of Structure	4 Years	5 Years	2 Years	4½ Years
Gross Income Multiple	7.1 x	6.75 x	6.96 x	6.95 x

Say - Gross Income Multiple of 7.0

$297,167 Gross Income x 7.0   = $2,080,000

Estimated Value Conclusion by the Market Data Approach = $2,080,000

<u>CORRELATION AND FINAL VALUE</u>

Estimated Value by Income Approach $2,000,000

Estimated Value by Cost Approach $2,112,000

Estimated Value by Market Data Approach $2,080,000

The value by the Cost Approach is generally the highest
of the three values. Since most income producing properties
are sold by the Income Approach, the value by this approach
is the most realistic. As a result of my appraisal and
analysis it is my opinion that when the property is completed
the fair market value of the property will be $2,000,000.

G. Wayne Fleck
Assistant Vice President

Date: October 14, 1973

CONSOLIDATED BALANCE SHEET
The XYZ Company and Subsidiaries

| | December 31 | |
Assets	1972	1971
Cash	$1,670,913	$1,121,913
Escrow Funds Held as Trustee - Contra	4,499,544	6,930,666
Marketable Securities - At Cost		
(Approximate Market: 1972 - $2,070,000		
1971 - $1,962,000)	1,245,201	1,192,719
Mortgages Held for Sale	13,563,363	12,119,925
Receivables:		
Construction Loans	9,550,218	8,173,671
Trade Notes and Accounts	11,387,253	5,907,747
Allowance for Doubtful Notes and Accounts	(138,000)	(93,000)
	$20,799,471	$13,988,418
Properties:		
Investment and For Sale Property		
including Development Construction		
in Progress	$21,383,493	$16,981,443
Other Properties (Primarily Rental):		
Land	3,631,578	2,900,205
Buildings	20,440,785	19,880,694
Furniture, Fixtures and Equipment	1,161,570	994,968
Leasehold Improvements	192,873	192,873
	$46,810,299	$40,950,183
Less Allowances for Depreciation and Amortization	8,293,398	7,271,238
	$38,516,901	$33,678,945
Investments in and Advances to Unconsolidated		
Subsidiaries and Affiliates	448,641	759,222
Investments in Joint Ventures	2,220,591	1,734,924
Other Assets:		
Utility and Other Deposits	1,306,725	704,883
Employee and Other Notes and Advances	955,677	491,352
Deferred Charges and Other Assets	646,764	578,895
	$ 2,909,166	$ 1,775,130
	$85,873,791	$73,301,862

CONSOLIDATED BALANCE SHEET
The XYZ Company and Subsidiaries

	December 31	
Liabilities	1972	1971
Notes Payable		
Notes Payable to Banks,	$28,186,041	$21,486,807
Notes Payable to Officers - Unsecured	1,186,500	1,219,803
Other Notes Payable - Unsecured	8,779,671	6,898,077
Mortgage Notes Payable	22,530,432	20,215,491
	$60,682,644	$49,820,178
Escrow Funds Held as Trustee - Contra	$ 4,499,544	$ 6,930,666
Accounts Payable and Accrued Expenses	6,990,165	6,225,621
Federal and State Income Taxes	1,029,699	788,580
Due to Affiliate	870,588	385,998
	$74,072,640	$64,151,043
Minority Interest in Consolidated Subsidiaries	$ 408,669	$ 268,368
Stockholders' Equity:		
Preferred Stock, 8% Cumulative, Non-Voting,		
Par Value $100 a Share:		
Authorized 150,000 Shares - None Issued		
Preferred Stock, 5% Cumulative, Par Value		
$10 a Share:		
Authorized, Issued, and Outstanding		
3,000 Shares	$ 30,000	$ 30,000
Common Stock, No Par Value, Non-Voting:		
Authorized 9,000 Shares - None Issued		
Common Stock, Par Value $100 a Share		
Authorized 4,500 Shares		
Issued and Outstanding 1,500 Shares	$ 150,000	$ 150,000
Retained Earnings	$11,212,482	$ 8,702,451
Net Worth	$11,392,482	$ 8,882,451
	$85,873,791	$73,301,862

VIEW IN FRONT OF SUBJECT SITE LOOKING EAST.

VIEW LOOKING WEST ALONG RIDGEWAY PARKWAY IN FRONT OF
SUBJECT SITE TOWARD THE SIDE OF HYATT REGENCY RIDGEWAY.

SUBJECT PROPERTY IN BACKGROUND FROM LEFT TO RIGHT ARE
XYZ BUILDING A, THE NEW ST. JOSEPH HOSPITAL UNDER
CONSTRUCTION AND THE RECENTLY OPENED QUALITY COURT
MOTOR INN.

VIEW LOOKING WEST TOWARD SUBJECT PROPERTY.

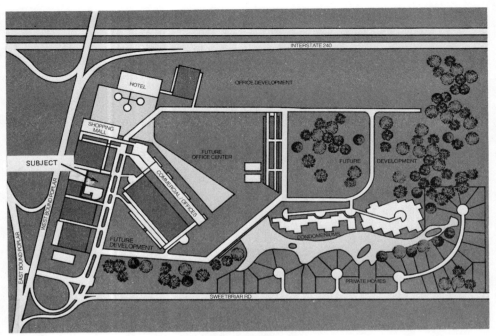

RIDGEWAY SITE MAP

ANALYSIS: CASE STUDY 6—LOW-RISE OFFICE BUILDING

Is this "full" submission truly a "full" submission? This is the third building in an office complex and we financed the other two. But nothing is said as to how successful they have been. Rental comparables indicate that there exists some vacancy in other office buildings, but we are not told how competitive they are with the subject. It would appear that this suburban location would attract tenants from the downtown area, but this theory is not developed.

This is an example of the "form" type of submission. Observe how comparable rental properties, land sales, real estate taxes, and office building sales are developed. Examine them for their comparability. Could these exhibits be laid out in a more meaningful form? Are we convinced that there is sufficient demand to make this project economically feasible?

The weakness of this case appears to be in the lack of analysis on the part of the mortgage banker. Basically, it is a presentation of data without underwriting, and this is one of the major problems encountered by institutional investors.

High-Rise Office Building

Clem C. Glass

Financing high-rise office buildings requires the same basic criteria used in the financing of all types of income-producing real estate; the project must include: good location, economic feasibility, "sound and knowledgeable" developers and owners, good management (or have the assurance it will be), and proper maintenance and "updating" to stave off obsolescence.

The above criteria are so simple to say, but so difficult to obtain! We must be careful not to be misled by computer printout sheets as *the* answer. The output is only as good as the input, and the input may not (or cannot!) include answers relating to some of the basic criteria set forth above. In the final analysis, management abilities and future market conditions will not light the "tilt" sign on the computer.

Office buildings obviously vary tremendously in type, size, and shape. General classifications might include:

"Skyscrapers" (say, 15 to 105 stories) located in
    Downtown
    Airport
    Suburban areas

High-rise located in
> Downtown fringe areas
> Downtown
> Airport
> Suburban
> Industrial areas

Office Building Parks with a
> Possible combination of high- and low-rise buildings

Within the above classifications falls the important factor of *use*, that is, owner-user, single-tenant, and multitenant use. It is not uncommon for an owner-occupied or single-tenant building to be economically unsound for an investor. For example, the prestige office of a bank, insurance company, or savings and loan may run higher in costs than comparable economic rents in the area can justify. However, it may be an excellent investment for the owner-user considering the prestige, public relations-advertising, and the extreme long-range goals of institutions.

Nowadays we are faced with rapid economic changes caused by energy crunches and ecological pressures which can change the feasibility of different types of buildings—for better or worse. For examples, a continued gasoline crunch would put a premium on buildings located near public mass transit; and environmental impact pressures could make it more difficult to develop outlying office buildings.

Office building tenants are going to continue to demand more aesthetic amenities. The fact that an older downtown office building can rent for less than one-half of its new, modern counterpart in the same general area still may not create a demand for cheaper space. Tenants tend to pay higher rent for a better, more prestigious product. The company prestige and demands of their employees put considerable pressure on the management to select better environments than the management's desire for low rental.

The office building world is full of many rules-of-thumb, many of which are probably satisfactory for quick analysis, but should never be used for in-depth analysis. Each project should be financed and developed on its own merits. There are no two projects exactly alike. As costs rise, rents must also rise or else the project becomes economically unsound. To underwrite the financing on a strictly "rule-of-thumb" basis became outdated long ago. However, for the sake of the record, let's look at a few rules-of-thumb:

1 Percent of land costs to total costs varies considerably—but check carefully if it is much over 15 percent.
2 Ratio of parking to net rentable area:

> Zero or one car per thousand in downtown
> One car per 200 or 250 square feet in suburban areas
> One square foot parking to one square foot of gross area in industrial office parks

3 Operating costs tend to be approximately 20–30 percent of effective gross scheduled income, and taxes another 5–25 percent (but varies considerably in specific areas).

4 Vacancy and rental loss tends to be 5 percent over the economic life of the building (but is this realistic with existing and *projected* conditions in a specific area?).

5 "Efficiency" of building (that is, percentage of NRA to gross area), should be 85 percent or better, but odd-shaped floor plans, such as triangular, "boat-shaped," and other departures from a balanced rectangle will drop efficiency, sometimes considerably.

There is (and should be) a tendency for lending institutions to increase loan amounts on a better project, that is, one with good aesthetics, better ratio of land to building to provide attractive setbacks, green area, etc. In the past there has been a tendency to loan a set amount per square foot. This practice encouraged a developer to construct more cheaply, later to be reflected in higher maintenance charges.

However, in these days of more rapid inflation and changing costs, it *is* most important that the developer hold to budgets and costs. Overruns in construction costs can be not only disastrous for the developer and equity participants, but for the lender as well.

HIGH-RISE OFFICE CONDOMINIUMS

To date, there seems to be more talk than action. The following may be some reasons why:

1 The tax advantage may be negative. As a tenant, *all* rental is deductible. As a condominium owner, there is no depreciation on land or deductions for principal payments.

2 Flexibility for expansion (and contraction) may be less; a key point—since relatively few office tenants have *exactly* the same space requirements five or 10 years after original occupancy. If too much space, you can sometimes sublease, but expansion is most often difficult.

3 Capital funds may be tied up in equity. Many businesses make a greater return on use of capital funds in their business than on investing in real estate.

4 The politics of management can be perplexing or frustrating when you have the multiple ownership of owner-occupants.

5 Sale or subleasing a condominium tends to be more difficult.

Advantages might include:

1 More secure occupancy and stable occupancy costs.
2 More voice in management.
3 Chance for capital value increase.
4 Pride in ownership.

REFINANCING

The financing of existing buildings gives the lender the advantage of working with *actual* income and expenses. However, much high-rise refinancing is required to modernize and therefore budgeted costs and pro forma income and operating expenses are necessary.

The appraiser must be alert to *real* expenses and *deferred* maintenance. Further, in financing old buildings there may be problems with city ordinances and building code requirements that can require drastic changes if just a few small alterations are made. The actual construction of the building versus the present-day codes and requirements should be carefully checked with the city and county to make sure there are no code or pending code violations.

A careful study of the location is essential. Is the existing building in a deteriorating area? A fine building physically can become obsolete due to a change in surrounding area, causing security, parking, or transportation problems.

Other considerations important in financing high-rise office buildings include:

1 Efficiency of space (as to public areas, window areas, depth, columns, etc.).

2 Absorption rate (a good guide would be the annual amount of additional office space that has been absorbed by the community for the past few years). Absorption rate can be changed by a general desire for a new space and an optimistic economy causing leasing now for future needs (or cutting back in a slack market) or change in types of tenants for the area, such as accountants, realtors, insurance agencies, manufacturers' representatives versus a demand for bulk space for insurance companies, credit companies, etc.

Figures have been worked out showing that the need for office space is related to population. Such guidelines can be very misleading. It depends on the *type* of population. For example, a bedroom community to a central area requires little office space in proportion to population. The demand may also depend on the *type* of industry in the area, that is, in Hartford, Connecticut, where the insurance industry is strong, there is a lot more office space required per person than a similar-sized community whose basic industry is manufacturing.

3 Vacancy factor—care should be taken in determining the "vacancy factor." A fair factor may not be justifiable by the actual vacancy of office space. For example, a new building with all the amenities could be 100% leased, while an adjoining old building of identical size is 50% vacant. Vacancy for the area = 25%.

4 Compatibility of tenants—some types of offices cater more to executive-oriented businesses, or executive departments of businesses, which may not mix well with users of bulk space. Doctors, as a rule, are not a good mix with office space users, although a few doctors in the building may be satisfactory. Doctors usually like to be in medical buildings where they can have a pharmacy, laboratory, and other facilities.

5 Office buildings are usually better off with convenient shopping facilities nearby. In fact, sometimes the disadvantage of locating offices in outlying areas is the poor selectivity of eating, shopping, and club facilities.

6 Leases—if a building is financed for an owner-occupant, the financing may rely heavily on the credit of the occupant through the terms of a lease. In many states it is difficult to get deficiency judgments or personal liability from a mortgagee—but you

can sue on the terms of the lease. We can be led astray by a tenant with not too strong credit requesting high-percentage financing based upon marketable terms in the lease. The lease must be competitive—otherwise, if the tenant fails, the loan is in trouble. In such cases, a "real estate" underwritten loan should be made instead of a credit loan.

A long-term lease has strength only if it is signed by a credit tenant. There is no advantage in having a long-term lease with a tenant of small net worth. In many office buildings one is better off with short-term leases (less than five years) in order that rents can be periodically readjusted. Chances are a long-term lease with a credit tenant will cut the profits to the owner considerably and, therefore, in most instances it is better to have a combination of, say, 30–50% long-term credit tenants and have the rest of the building on short-term leases.

Options for lease extensions are usually not satisfactory to the owner, but sometimes must be made for negotiating purposes. If options are in the lease, the future rental should be based upon the then current market on the basis of first refusal rather than tying the future to today's income and costs. Options are purely a one-way street for the owner, for if rents are lower at option time, the tenant will obviously negotiate for a lower rental—but if the rentals have increased, the tenant will stick to the option price.

Office building leases of three years or more must have escalation clauses. Escalation can be based on several methods:

    a Tenant pays a share of the increase in operating costs and taxes, based on a percentage of tenant's net rentable area to the total NRA (net rentable area). Operating escalation on this formula can be unfair if the management of the building is inefficient, because the rental charges cover the inefficiency of the management! Inasmuch as taxes are usually beyond the control of lessor, a "share" plan is fair.

    b Tenant pays increase in operating expenses based on something beyond the control of landlord, such as the percentage increase in union scale for maintenance workers.

    c Increase (or decrease) related to the increase in percentage charge of a "cost of living" index. There are many such indices. A recommended one is related to the local area, for example: "Los Angeles Consumer Price Index—All Items."

A further checklist of things to consider when financing high-rise office buildings might well include the following items:

    1 Location:

        a Accessibility—easy ingress and egress for pedestrians, automobiles, local transit, rapid transit, airport, helistop or heliport.

        b Visibility—from freeways, main arteries, well-known street address.

        c "Trend" in area (improving or deteriorating).

        d Nearby facilities—shopping, restaurants, clubs, parking, etc.

        e Aesthetic features such as adequate land for landscaping, adjoining parks, views, etc.

    2 Demand for use:

        a Adequate population to support need for office space.

        b Past and projected absorption rate.

   c   Special conditions (that is, supporting a major industry or use in the area, type of proposed tenancies—corporation space, computers, insurance agencies, lawyers, CPAs, real estate brokers, etc.).

3   Physical—site advantages or disadvantages:

   a   Soils, blasting required, or pilings needed?

   b   Room for surface parking versus cost of underground or above ground.

   c   Adequate area for setbacks, malls, patios.

   d   Height limitations, such as airport flight paths, local codes, as a cost factor.

   e   Surrounding "compatible" neighborhood.

   f   Earthquake faults.

   g   Flooding.

   h   Adequate sewers and utilities (underground?)

4   Improvements:

   a   Compatible with site and location.

   b   Properly planned (experienced architect in high-rise field).

       1   Efficiency of building (relation of rentable space to mechanical and public space).

       2   Attractive.

       3   Practical (depth of bays), location of mechanical and core areas, width of hallways and their relation to space use.

       4   Mechanical:

           a)   heating and air conditioning (economical? Relation to window space, sun heat, loads, etc.). Provision for air conditioning specific floors or offices without "turning on" the whole building.

           b)   Elevators. Adequate to handle peak loads? Mechnically sound? Fire safety controls?

           c)   Floors, walls, ceilings, windows built for most efficient maintenance.

5   Engineering—best available to be structurally sound:

   a   On-site parking—needs special planning by parking expert.

   b   Proper security controls.

   c   Safety precations. With recent publicity, real and ficticious, pertaining to high-rise building, this is an important consideration. Fires, earthquakes, winds, or just plain mechanical failures.

       1)   Sprinkler systems—throughout building?

       2)   Closing off and pressurization of fire stairways.

       3)   Elevator rooms fireproof?

       4)   Storage rooms fireproof?

       5)   Secure exterior windows (if blown out of a high-rise, the falling glass is a deadly missile).

6   Economic:

   a   Adequate rental, expense, and tax comparables for the area.

   b   Feasibility for demand (rate of absorption, etc.). Existing vacancy.

   c   Proper relationship of project cost to rental rates and expenses in the area.

   d   Rate of return. Is there adequate income to support?

       1)   Taxes. What are past and anticipated local tax policies?

      2)   Operating expenses properly explained and justified.

      3)   Ground rent (if any) on leasehold. How does it relate to a fair return on value of the fee?

      4)   Interest on debt.

      5)   Amortization of debt. The all-important "constant."

      6)   Reserves for replacements and repairs, including remodeling for new tenants and old tenants upon renewal.

      7)   Leasing commissions.

      8)   Vacancy factor.

      9)   Adequate return on the equity investment.

   e   Estimating future growth, inflation, both for expenses and taxes, as well as income.

7   Leasing:

   a   Calculation of area. Use of standards of Building Owners' & Managers' standard, summarized as follows:

      1)   Multiple tenancy—computed by measuring to the inside finish of permanent outer building walls, or to the glass line if at least 50 percent of the outer building wall is glass, to the office side of corridors and/or other permanent partitions, and to the center of partitions that separate the premises from adjoining rentable areas. No deductions will be made for columns and projections necessary to the building.

      2)   Single-tenancy floor—computed to outside walls as above, plus including all area within outside walls, less stairs, elevator shafts, flues, pipe shafts, vertical ducts, air-conditioning rooms, fan rooms, janitor closets, electrical closets—and such other rooms not actually available to the tenant for his furnishings and personnel— and their enclosing walls. Toilet rooms within and exclusively serving only that floor shall be included in rentable area.

   b   Adequate rental increases to compensate for future tax and operating expenses (essential on leases of three years or longer).

      1)   Based on actual (as a percentage of whole).

      2)   Based on cost of living index.

      3)   Based on labor cost increase.

   c   Options for extensions (or purchase).

   d   Superior or subordinate to financing? Rule of thumb: credit tenant superior, weak tenant subordinate.

   e   Rules for use of common area.

   f   Proper condemnation clause. Is mortgage adequately protected? Be careful of tenant's rights in "superior" leases. These will vary from state to state depending on local jurisdiction.

   g   Insurance clauses. In conflict with leases?

   h   Evidence of owner's ability to lease (or to engage professionals to lease) space.

8   Overall costs that create physical value:

   a   Land:

      1)   Actual cost or if owned for a period of time may include increased or decreased value determined by comparables.

      2)   Site improvements (on and off).

     3) Carrying charges—interest and taxes.

     4) Costs for zoning changes, environmental approvals, and feasibility studies.

   b Plans and specifications.

   c Engineering.

   d Actual costs of improvements.

   e Carrying charges during construction, interest, insurance, taxes.

   f Finance charges—interim and permanent.

   g Legal fees.

   h Survey (before and after construction).

   i Title costs.

   j Recording fees.

   k Lease commissions (paid and anticipated to full occupancy).

   l Other "costs to fill up" such as promotional, operating losses from completion to occupancy adequate to break even (usually around 85%).

  9 Wholesale versus retail value: The developer's profit should be related to an ability to put all the physical costs together to equal less than the *economic* value. The development produced at wholesale should now be worth the retail (economic) value.

High-rise building development and financing is complicated and has many pitfalls. Feasibility studies are vital. There are many fine local and national firms to provide this service. The Building Owners and Managers Association International (224 South Michigan Avenue, Chicago, Illinois 60604) has an excellent service for prospective high-rise developers through its Building Planning Service. It brings to the planning function a type of experience of demonstrated value—the experience of years of first-hand acquaintance with every aspect of building operation—the experience of successful building management. In brief, it is a meeting where an individually selected panel of building managers and representatives of the owners, architects, and engineers involved in a building project get together and discuss every part of the new building. Its aim for the general office building: to maximize income by arriving at the most efficient utilization of the space available and to minimize costs by eliminating or altering those features of the building that do not meet the high standard of operational efficiency the panel expects.

The many sophisticated methods of financing are described elsewhere in detail. Suffice it to say, high-rise financing runs the gamut.

Land leasehold—subordinated and unsubordinated. Before and after construction (land sale-leaseback). Land can be sold and leased back after financing (subordinated land purchase).

Leasehold—land and improvements.

Joint ventures.

Parnterships.

"Kickers" as percentage of gross or net, on entire rent roll, or after stabilized projected reached, etc.

Wraparounds.

Bank (credit).

But, let's take a particular case and apply some figures to it.

Proposed   13-story (including four floors of garage) office building.

Location   Suburban, five miles from downtown and three miles from airport on main thoroughfare, near a major retail center. Good visibility. Good access. Good demand for general-tenant modern office space. Building will dominate the area. The land is 51,300 square feet in area. All utilities to the site. Zoning is okay and environmental impact report approved. Local government cooperative.

Improvements   Quality of construction good to excellent. Steel frame, thermopane mirror glass exterior. Above-average floor loads and heating, ventilating, air conditioning (HVAC) system.

Parking 488 enclosed   — 1 per 440 square feet rentable area (RA)
       68 open   — 1 per 3,155 square feet rentable area (RA)
    556 total   — 1 per 386 square feet rentable area (RA)
223,100 square feet of garage area—1 car per 457 square feet.
Four elevators—Upper floor RA to each elevator = 52,700 square feet.

Note: Sometimes Rentable Area (RA) is referred to as Net Rentable Area (NRA).

Gross area (excluding garage)—		257,200 (GA)
Rentable area— Ground floor stores	8,100 SF	
Upper floor offices*	208,280 SF	
		216,380 (RA)

*Calculated per BOMA multitenancy.

Efficiency (RA ÷ GA)		84%
Office RA per floor (216,380 ÷ 9)		24,040
Cubic content (not frequently used but should be known)		5,471,700 CF

Land	51,300 SF @ $29.33 per SF		1,500,000
Building	257,200 SF @ $40.44 per SF	$10,400,000	
Garage	223,100 SF @ $12.10 per SF	2,700,000	
			13,100,000
			$14,600,000

Office income	208,280 SF @ $9.00 per SF	$ 1,875,000	
Parking income	@ $25 per space per month	169,000	
Retail income	8,100 SF @ $10.00 per SF	81,000	
Gross Income		$ 2,125,000	=$9.82/SF
Less 5% vacancy and collection		106,000	
Stabilized income		$ 2,019,000	=$9.33/SF
Operating expenses	@ $1.82 per SF = $394,000 (20% Stabilized Income)		
Real Estate taxes	@ $1.16 per SF = 250,000 (12% Stabilized Income)		
Total O.E.& T.	@ $2.98 per SF = $644,000 (32% Stabilized Income)		
Stabilized income		$ 2,019,000	
Less operating expenses and taxes		644,000	
Net income before depreciation		$ 1,375,000	
Capitalized @		9.35%	
		$14,700,000	

Allowing for the difference between "wholesale" and "retail," the value of the project for loan purposes is $14,700,000, which is $67.94 per square foot, 6.92 × gross income, and 10.7 × net income.

A commitment was issued for a loan of $11,000,000 (75%), 8.8% interest, 9.3% constant, 20-year due date, leaving a balance at maturity of $8,015,480, or $37.04 per square foot RA. No prepayment allowed for 10 years (closed for 10 years). Prepayment allowed in the eleventh year at 105 (5% × balance = prepayment penalty), and declining ½% per year. Lender to receive in addition 10 percent of all gross income over stabilized of $2,019,000 (if leases were net or partial net, the difference between gross and net imputed).

The lender required a holdback of $1,650,000 (15%) to be disbursed in three stages of $550,000 each at 40, 70, and 82.5 percent (approximate break-even point) occupancy at *scheduled* rents. The borrower to have two years after closing of floor loan to qualify for holdbacks. (This gives the lender assurance that the projected rents and leasing of the building will be equal to or better than the borrower's promises before all money is disbursed.) A further holdback of $6.00 per square of 95 percent of RA (basis of stabilized income per 5% vacancy factor) to be released when floor loan closes on basis of $6.00 per square foot RA improved ready for occupancy, and thereafter at $6.00 per square foot in increments not less than $180,000 (except last draw) as space is improved ready for occupancy. (This is obviously to protect lender from having a loan on an uncompleted building. In most cases, tenant improvements in a new building are made when space is leased. The building was appraised including tenant improvements, so therefore the lender is entitled to them being in place).

The annual debt service (monthly principal and interest × 12) will be $1,023,000, which leaves an indicated cash flow to equity of $352,000.

The full loan to gross income is..	$5.18×
The full loan to net income is	$8.00×
The full loan to square foot gross area is..	$42.77
The full loan to square foot rentable area is	$50.84
The full loan to cubic feet is...	$2.00

The default point (the point that gross income will not carry operating expenses, taxes and debt service, that is, $1,667,000) is 78 percent. In other words, the building must be 78% rented at projected rentals to break even.

If the stabilized gross rent increases 10 percent, lender will receive another $20,000, about 18 basis points for a yield of almost 9%.

The borrower's cash investment in the project (assuming full disbursement) was estimated at:

Land purchase	$ 700,000	(assembled over 3 yrs.)
Actual improvement costs	11,200,000	
Fees and other costs	1,800,000	
	$13,700,000	
Less loan	11,000,000	
Equity	$ 2,700,000	or 20% of cost

Divided into cash flow to equity of $352,000 = 13% return.

With high-rise office vacancies being at high levels in most U. S. cities, financing for this type of building would be difficult even without a money-short economy. However, in some cities, absorption of existing space overcomes new space coming on the market. At one instant in time, Pittsburgh's absorption seems to be in that group, Cincinnati and Washington, D.C., are strong, with San Francisco apparently the strongest—but cities like Miami, Minneapolis-St. Paul, Dallas, and Boston seem to be slated for a few years of rising absorption trying to chip away at overbuilt situations. New York City, of course, is still whittling away at some 30,000,000 square feet of available space. In Los Angeles, the great majority of available office space is in one location, downtown, resulting from a movement of its financial district to several large new bank buildings. Orange County seems strong, while San Fernando Valley and several other suburban locations seem to be improving.

The energy crisis raised a lot of discussion about greater suburban office trends, but suburban office movement was strong before that and the over-all effect of energy on office location is still questionable.

Whatever conditions exist—overbuilding, rising construction costs, energy problems, or even problems we have not yet foreseen—the fundamental ingredients of financing office buildings, location, economic feasibility, sound ownership and good management, still must be treated—and met.

ANALYSIS: CASE STUDY 7—HIGH-RISE OFFICE BUILDING

In this case the author does the analysis for you. The first few pages which precede the actual case are as thorough a review of the elements of underwriting a high-rise office building as can be found. Although there is little documentation on the facts listed in the case, the facts appear to be accurate and concise.

Also, this case study is a commentary on a series of suggested guidelines for underwriting office buildings, and could easily be adapted to other types of income-producing property.

Industrial Property

Robert F. Plymate

First mortgage, in the amount of $260,000, to be secured by the property located on the South Side of Clearbrook Drive from the Northeast Corner of Lot 8, 170 feet West in the Clearbrook Industrial Park, Arlington Heights, Illinois, to bear interest at the rate of 9⅞% per annum, payable monthly, the loan to mature as follows:

$2,383.33 per month, to be applied first to the payment of interest and second to the payment of principal; the loan to be completely amortized in twenty-three (23) years and three (3) months.

LOCATION

The subject property is located in Clearbrook Industrial Park in suburban Arlington Heights, a community 25 miles northwest of Chicago's Loop. A rather large suburb, containing an area of over fifteen square miles, this principally residential community is one of the "finger" communities paralleling the Chicago & Northwestern Railroad's right of way.

In 1973, the estimated population of Arlington Heights was 51,000, which represented an increase of 24,000 during its last six years.

Arlington Heights is bounded on the west by Rolling Meadows, on the south and east by Mt. Prospect and Prospect Heights, and on the north by Palatine and Wheeling.

A good highway system is easily accessible, with entrances to the Northwest Toll Road and Tri-State Tollway located just south and west of the town. In addition, speedy commuter service is afforded by the Chicago & Northwestern Railroad and remains the primary method of transportation between Chicago and the suburb.

The large population growth in recent years is principally due to the rezoning of substantial areas of the suburb for apartment use. Large planned unit developments have brought rental units to over 15,000 and provide an excellent labor base for the town's rapidly growing industrial districts.

Clearbrook Industrial Park is a relatively new industrial subdivision developed by Gottlieb/Beale & Co. It is located at the southwest part of Arlington Heights along the Northwest Expressway and Algonquin Road (Route 62). Its proximity to O'Hare International Airport being approximately five minutes away further enhances the desirability of this location.

In addition to the subject building, there are other industrial facilities in the subdivision occupied by the following companies:

Acme Hamilton Manufacturing Co.
Amersham Division of G. D. Searle.
Arlington Heights School District 59.
Gale Industries.
Micro-Plastics, Inc.
American Telephone and Telegraph Co.
Right-Mold Division of Micro-Plastics, Inc.

Some of the nearby major industrial developments include Western Electric, Pure Oil Company, United Airlines, General Electric, as well as numerous small plants and the Rolling Meadows Industrial Park, Plum Grove Industrial Park, Schaumburg Industrial Park, and, of course, Centex Industrial Park, located in nearby Elk Grove Village.

The area to the north of the subject is developed with some single-family residential properties as well as a large apartment complex. The property is bounded on the south by the Northwest Tollway, and the area on the east and west of the subject will also be developed for residential use.

There were originally 33 acres of land in this development. As of the date of this offering, approximately 23 have been sold, further evidencing Mr. Gottlieb's success as an industrial developer.

LAND

The land consists of an irregularly shaped parcel having a frontage of 170 feet along the southeast corner of Clearbrook Drive and consists of 136,820 square feet. There is a frontage of approximately 433.53 feet along the Northern Illinois Tollway and the property is zoned for industrial use.

Clearbrook Drive is a fully improved street with a cul de sac for turn-around being located approximately 60 feet from the edge of the subject parcel. All utilities are in and to the site and there are no apparent subsoil conditions which would prohibit the construction of the proposed improvement.

Land fronting on the Illinois Tollway has, of course, a great value because of the exposure a tenant can have for advertising purposes. We have seen a real estate sales contract which was prepared for Cincinnati Milling Machine Company wherein they agree, if the developers did not choose to build and lease back the property to the company, to purchase said land for approximately $1.00 per square foot or $135,000. We feel this contract is evidence of the fair market value, since it was an arm's-length offer and we are therefore utilizing this value in the analysis and appraisal.

IMPROVEMENTS

The improvements will consist of a one-story warehouse and office building containing 11,170 square feet to be constructed.

The property is to be used as a regional sales office and will be constructed of quality materials because of the image the company wishes to create through the structure.

The front exterior will be of face brick with 5'' stone coping, remainder of the exterior will be attractively painted block. Sash to be core wall with dark bronze permanodic finish. There will be a canopy above the entry with 1'' asbestos cement panels and aluminum cap as well as a two-foot-high brick wall at the entrance for aesthetic effect.

The warehouse area will have an 8'' concrete slab with 6 × 6 weld and wire reinforcing. There will be an overhead door for drive-in access so machine tools can be moved in and out without difficulty.

The office area will have 5'' concrete slab floors and will contain a general office, reception room, conference room with wire kitchen unit, men's and women's washrooms and lounges, and three private offices. All wood doors within the building will be 1¾''-wood flush walnut veneer with the exception of the entrance, which will be in aluminum frame with solar bronze plate glass. Room finishes will include carpeted offices, ceramic tile walls in bathrooms and lounges, vinyl asbestos tile in the mail room and laboratory only, quarry tile in entrance vestibules. Walls basically to be dry wall in the offices and exposed concrete painted or vinyl covered in all areas except lounges and storage areas. Ceilings in the office area will be acoustical tile with recessed fluorescent light fixtures using 2' × 2' lay-in type tile.

The building will basically be of masonry and steel construction and will have a 4-ply built-up tar and gravel roof over 2″ of rigid insulation over ½″ plywood supported by 2 × 10 joists. All flashings and counter flashings will be copper and all aluminum doors and windows are to be kawneer or of equivalent quality. Further details of the proposed construction may be seen on the enclosed plans. It should be noted that there will be parking for approximately 44 cars and the balance of the lot will be graded and landscaped.

PHYSICAL APPROACH TO VALUE

The borrowers have provided us with the following estimate of the physical value of the improvement:

Land	136,820 sq. ft. @ $1.00 sq. ft.	$136,820
Building:	1,170 sq. ft. office @ $30	
	10,000 sq. ft. warehouse @$15	185,100
Paving, landscaping & other indirect costs:		39,180
Total physical value estimate		361,100
		Say, $360,000

ECONOMIC ANALYSIS

The property is to be leased on an absolute net basis for 15 years for $38,500 per year or $3.45 per square foot net. Because of the credit of the Lessee and the location of the property and quality of construction, we feel an overall capitalization rate can be used. This is particularly true because of the high land value in proportion to the total project cost.

Capitalizing the above income at the aforesaid rate indicates a value from the economic approach of $360,000.

Additional Interest

As additional interest, your Company is to receive 2% of the collections from the operation of the real estate. Utilizing the aforesaid income of $38,500 per year, your participation will equal $770.00. This will raise your effective yield by 29.6 basis points the first year, increasing same to 10.171%. Naturally as principal is repaid, the yield will increase.

Prepayment Provision

The loan may be prepaid in its entirety after the 10th loan year on any interest date, upon giving 60 days prior written notice and upon the payment of a premium of 4% in the 11th loan year, premium reducing ¼ of the 1% per annum thereafter.

Valuation

A satisfactory M.A.I. Appraisal will be furnished.

Assignment of Lease

A specific 15-year lease between LaSalle National Bank as trustee in a land trust to be formed, as Lessor, and Cincinnati Milling and Grinding Machines, Inc., an Ohio corporation, the parent of the Lessee, will be assigned and deposited as additional collateral for the faithful performance of the covenants of the trust deed to be used only in the event of default.

This lease will call for a monthly rental of $3,208.33 and be for a 15-year term commencing the first day of the month following substantial completion of the building and improvements. The lease will call for the Lessee to pay all taxes, insurance, repairs and replacements, maintenance, utilities and all other costs involved in the operation of the real estate and as such which is a net lease. The lease has two 5-year options for renewal with rentals increasing on the basis of the consumer traders' industry of Chicago, Illinois, with August 31, 1975 being the base month.

You will also note that the rider to the lease, known as Article XXIII, calls for an addition to be constructed at the option of the Lessee, provided, however, that the Lessor can secure financing and/or release from his obligation under the existing first mortgage. No request for this agreement is being made at this time. The borrowers have agreed to negotiate such lease terms, should the Lessee desire such addition.

Funding

It is anticipated that this loan is to be funded the last quarter of 1975; however, funding can be deferred until the first quarter of 1976 at your option.

Annual Reports

Within 90 days of the borrower's fiscal year, you will be furnished with a copy of the borrower's financial statement covering the mortgaged premises, prepared by an independent certified public accountant, and accompanied by complete supporting schedules.

Tax Deposit

Monthly tax deposits will be included in the mortgage payments. However, inasmuch as this is a net lease, you will give the borrower a letter waiving such tax deposits as long as the net lease is in effect and the loan is not in default.

REMARKS

Title to the subject property will be held by a land trust to be formed at the LaSalle National Bank and Trust Company of Chicago, the beneficiary of which will be the Clearbrook Industrial Park Joint Venture, a group of investors, and Mr. J. R. Gottlieb of Chicago. Mr. Gottlieb is extremely well known to this office, as he has been one of the most prominent industrial developers in the metropolitan area for the past 12 years. Members of this firm have provided him with loans for numerous industrial, commercial, and residential properties throughout the years.

Attached to this offering is a list of some of the industrial facilities built, leased, and/or developed by him and his former company, as well as a brochure of his present partnership with Mr. Joseph Beale, known as Gottlieb/Beale & Co. A glance through the list will show that most of the largest companies in the United States are included.

In addition to handling leasing negotiations, Mr. Gottlieb and his company were responsible for the development of the facilities leased to such well-known firms as Armour & Company, Masonite Corporation, Honeywell, Inc., General Motors, Chemetron, Inc., Radio Corporation of America, Studebaker Corporation, and Litton Industries, to name a few.

In addition to the subject park, Mr. Gottlieb also has controlling interest in the Dansher Industrial Park which is in the community of Countryside, approximately fourteen miles southwest of Chicago's loop, Centex North Industrial Park in Elk Grove Village, Illinois, in which Mr. Gottlieb is a joint venturer on a portion with Equitable Life Insurance Company of Iowa and others.

Through his experience, Mr. Gottlieb qualified as an outstanding developer—well qualified as a borrower of your company.

Cincinnati Milling Machine Company, which was formed in 1884, is one of the top 500 companies in the United States, as listed in *Fortune* magazine.

Enclosed is their annual report and their financial statement for the year ended December 28, 1974, which is the latest financial information available. This shows the net worth of the company to be approximately $100 million, although we have been advised that at present it is approximately $125 million. Sales for that latest year were $2 billion with a net profit of over $102 million.

We do not feel it is necessary to go into a long and complex description of the credit, as it speaks for itself.

We are indeed pleased to recommend this loan to you, as we feel it has all of the attributes of a truly prime investment. We have knowledgeable and sophisticated borrowers, an outstanding location with exposure on the Illinois Tollway in an attractive industrial park location.

The credit of the tenant is unusually good for this size deal, and the unpaid balance at the expiration of the lease terms approximates the present land value.

Combining all of the above with the high initial rate of return and the long prohibition on repayment, together with a participation in the income for an increasing yield feature, makes this an unusually attractive investment.

We heartily recommend your purchase of same.

OFFERING

This loan is being offered to you at par. We are to service same, and participate in the interest to the extent of ⅛ of 1%. Also, we are to share equally with your company in the bonus to be paid by the borrower in the event the loan is paid off prior to maturity.

APPRAISAL OF

South Side of Clearbrook Drive and the

North Side of the Northern Illinois

Tollroad

Clearbrook Industrial Park

Arlington Heights, Illinois

PURPOSE OF APPRAISAL

The purpose of this Appraisal is to estimate the Market Value of the property herein described, to be built in accordance with plans and specifications in fee simple, free and clear of all encumbrances as of August 11,1975 or, in other words, to determine the present worth of all the future benefits arising out of ownership to typical users.

DEFINITION OF VALUE

The term "Market Value" as used herein, is defined as the highest amount of money that can be obtained in the open market within a reasonable period of time, between a prudent and well-informed buyer and a prudent and well-informed seller, neither acting under compulsion, and both exercising intelligent judgment.

LOCATION: The South side of Clearbrook Drive, and the
North side of the Northern Illinois Tollway,
of the Clearbrook Industrial Park, Arlington
Heights, Illinois.

COMMUNITY: The subject property is located in the Village
of Arlington Heights approximately 20 miles northwest of downtown Chicago, Illinois.

Arlington Heights is one of the northwestern
suburbs paralleling The Chicago and Northwestern
Railroad. Like many of the surrounding communities such as Mt. Prospect and Des Plaines,
Arlington Heights' rapid growth did not occur
until the 1950's when the population increased
some 375 per cent.

Today Arlington Heights has a population of
63,000 and its neighbors, Des Plaines and Mt.
Prospect, have estimated populations of 60,000
and 33,000 respectively. The medium income in
the area exceeds $10,000 per family per year and
the area is improved with moderate to expensive
homes ranging in age from new to 75 years old.
In addition, numerous apartment developments are
located nearby and experiencing extremely low
vacancy factors of less than 2%.

Randhurst Shopping Center is located 4-1/2 miles
northeast of the subject property in Mt. Prospect
and consists of a regional shopping center in excess of 1,000,000 square feet of rentable area,
being the world's larges shopping center under one
roof.

Arlington Heights has also developed several
industrial parks, one of which is the subject,
Clearbrook Industrial Park. Industrial facilities
in the Park are presently occupied by Micro-Plastics,
Inc., Acme Hamilton Manufacturing, G. D. Searle,
Gale Industries, American Telephone and Telegraph Co.,
and the Arlington Heights School District. There are
other inventory buildings which have been erected
in the park and a proposed multi-tenant incubator
type building is also being planned as well as a
four story office building completed for occupancy.

The area to the north of the subject is developed
with single family residential properties as well as
a large apartment complex.

Excellent commuter transportation is provided
by the Northwestern Railroad with a station
in Mt. Prospect four miles north of the subject

COMMUNITY: property. This service provides 30 minutes
(Cont'd)   express service to downtown Chicago in modern
              air-conditioned trains.

              The John F. Kennedy Expressway connects down-
              town Chicago to O'Hare International Airport
              and the Illinois Tollway System. The Elmhurst
              interchange of the Tollway is located two miles
              southeast of the subject property and traveling
              time from downtown Chicago to the interchange
              is approximately 30 minutes in normal traffic.
              An additional interchange is under construction
              at Arlington Heights Road, ½ mile west of the
              subject park.

              As previously mentioned, the Illinois Tollway
              provides direct access to the Kennedy Express-
              way as well as the Tri-State Tollway, Eisenhower
              Expressway, the Stevenson Expressway, Chicago
              Skyway and the Indiana Tollroad without encounter-
              ing cross traffic or traffic lights.

              Additional highway facilities convenient to the
              subject property include Elmhurst Road (State
              Highway No. 83) one mile east, Algonquin Road
              (State Highway No. 62) one block north, Northwest
              Highway (US No. 14) three miles north and Dempster
              Street, ¼ mile east.

              In the opinion of the Appraiser, based upon the
              improvements presently located in this area,
              the close proximity to O'Hare International
              Airport, excellent highway facilities and housing
              available, this area will increase its present
              desirability in future years.

LAND: Legal Description:

              Part of Lots 7 and 11 in Owners Subdivision and
              Lots 7 and 8 in Clearbrook Industrial Park Subdivision
              In Sections 15 and 22, Township 41 North, Range 11,
              East of the Third Principal Meridan, in Cook County,
              Illinois.

              Lot Size:

              An irregular parcel of land having a frontage
              along the South side of Clearbrook Drive of
              170 feet and along the North side of the
              Northern Illinois Tollroad of 433.53 feet.
              The lot contains approximately 137,664 feet
              and is zoned light industrial. Clearbrook
              Drive is paved and all utilities are in and
              available to the site.

IMPROVEMENTS: The land will be improved with a one-story
                       fully air-conditioned, no basement masonry
                       and steel office, and warehouse building which
                       will contain a gross floor area of 11,361
                       square feet. The valuation, as set out in
                       this report is contingent upon the completion
                       of the improvements in accordance with plans
                       and specifications.

                       The building will have a concrete foundation,
                       5 inch reinforced concrete slab floor in the
                       office area and 8 inch in the warehouse area,
                       masonry exterior walls consisting of face
                       brick with 8 inch concrete block back up on
                       front all elevation, aluminum window sash with
                       $\frac{1}{4}$" solar bronze plate glass with stone trim
                       and glass weld panels, and stone aggregate trim.

                       The roof will consist of tar and gravel roof-
                       ing over two inch ridged insulation on 1-1/2
                       inch metel deck over open web steel joists
                       supported by steel beams and columns, 13'3"
                       clear ceiling heights to the underside of the
                       open web steel joists in the display area, and
                       10'3" clear ceiling heights in the office area
                       providing finish ceiling heights of 12' and 9'
                       respectfully to the underside of the acoustical
                       tile ceilings. Heat will be provided by a gas-
                       fired boiler with distribution by means of hot
                       water baseboard radiation and ceiling duct work
                       for exhaust and air circulation; air-conditioning
                       units utiliazing the above duct work will provide
                       cooling in office only. Space heaters in warehouse
                       area.

                       The main entrance to the building is located
                       along the west elevation which will have access
                       from a canopy covered walk leading from the paved
                       parking area and will lead into the lobby area
                       which will have carpeted floor covering and
                       painted sheetrock and wood paneled walls and
                       acoustical ceilings. The remainder of the
                       office area will be partitioned into a general
                       office area, 3 private offices, men's and
                       women's toilet rooms, interview room, labora-
                       tory and mail room.

                       Finish in these areas will generally consist
                       of asphalt and carpeted floor covering, painted
                       and vinyl covered sheetrock walls, painted con-
                       crete block and acoustical ceiling. The remain-
                       portion of the building will be used for warehouse.
                       The finish in this area will consist of painted
                       concrete floors, painted walls and exposed ceilings.

IMPROVEMENTS: Shipping and receiving facilities will be pro-
(Cont'd) vided by a depressed truck dock at truck bed
level with a one truck capacity and located at
the north side of the building, with access
off Clearbrook Drive. A 10'x 12' steel rolling
overhead door will seve this entrance. An
asphalt paved parking area will be located along
the west and north elevations which will provide
off-street parking for approximately 44 cars.

CONDITION: At the date of the Appraiser's inspection,
construction had begun. The foundation was
completed and underground work and masonry
walls were in process.

OCCUPANCY AND Cincinnati Milling & Grinding Machines, Inc.
LEASE: will lease the entire building when completed
under a specific 15-year lease in the amount
of $38,500 annually, with two 5-year options
and guaranteed by the Cincinnati Milling Machine
Co.

TAXES: The property is currently assessed as part of
a larger tract of land and, therefore, the
assessed valuation and general real estate taxes
of this property are not available.

REMARKS: The availability of land for industrial development in the immediate Chicago area has
diminished quite rapidly and industrial concerns contemplating expansion and moderniza-
tion had to move to suburban or unincorporated
areas. The northwest area of Chicagoland
has been the fastest growing section in the
past decade. This area is rich in a supply
of labor and management.

Upon completion, the improvements will consist
of an attractive modern, one-story office and
warehouse building with off-street parking for
44 cars, well-located in one of Chicagoland's
most appealing industrial parks, with tollroad
frontage and exposure.

The above described 15-year net rental of
$38,500 per annum amounts to $3.45 per square
foot per year. In the Appraiser's economic
approach to value, the rental for the entire
property was accepted for the facilities
offered, which is consistent with other rentals
being received in the area.

The subject property will offer good office
and demonstration facilities readily adaptable
to a wide variety of usages. There is a demand for properties of this type and size and
in the opinion of the undersigned, the excellent location will improve as continued development takes place.

In estimating the physical value of the subject
property, the Appraiser used various costs
sources available. Costs were based upon wages
being received by the building trades in Cook
County, Illinois.

COST APPROACH TO VALUE

BUILDING:

Office, 1,170 sq. ft. @$30.00 =	$35,100	
Warehouse, 10,000 sq. ft. @$15.00=	150,000	$185,100.

Lot Improvements:

25,000 sq. ft. blacktop, lighting, striping @$.75	$18,750	
Concrete patio, 1,593 sq. ft. @$10.00	15,930	
Landscaping	4,500	
Total Lot Improvements –		39,180.
Total Estimated Cost of Improvements–		$224,280.
Land– 136,820 sq. ft. @$1.00		136,820.
Estimated Market Value Via Cost Approach		$361,100.

SAY $360,000

ECONOMIC ESTIMATE OF VALUE

Contract rent	$38,500.
Less 2% Management Allowance	770.
Net Income	$37,730.
$37,730 capitalized @10.5% overall =	$359,333.

SAY $360,000

MARKET DATA
APPROACH:
There is scant data available on sales of modern
industrial buildings in the area of the subject as
most have been built for use and kept for investment purposes.

It is possible, however, to relate a gross rent
multiplier to the subject property by estimating
the 11,170 square foot building with a rental
of approximately $3.45 per square foot which
amounts to $38,500 on a gross rental basis.
Similar buildings have been known to sell in
the Chicagoland area from 9 to 9.5 times the
gross income whereas the subject property
with an estimated $360,000 valuation amounts to
9.35 times the gross income as previously
estimated. Therefore, the appraiser estimates
a market value at 9.25 times the estimated
gross income of $38,500 or approximately
$356,000.

9.25 x $38,500 = $356,000.

CORRELATION AND CONCLUSIONS

A summary of the estimates of Market Value is as follows:

Cost Approach to Value	$361,100.
Income Approach to Value	$359,333.
Market Data Approach to Value	$356,000.

The preliminary estimates of value via the Cost Approach represents the highest price it will bring in the open market, assuming no one will pay more than its costs to duplicate the property.

The Market Data Approach has many variables due to the numerous adjustments made with the comparables; hence less credence is given to this approach.

The Income Approach is a more accurate indicator, because the economics are paramount to the typical investor.

In view of the relatively close range of values, it is the opinion of the Appraiser that the Market Value of the subject property, in fee simple, subject to completion as outlined herein as of August 11, 1975 was:

THREE HUNDRED SIXTY THOUSAND AND NO/100 DOLLARS

($360,000.00)

ADDENDA

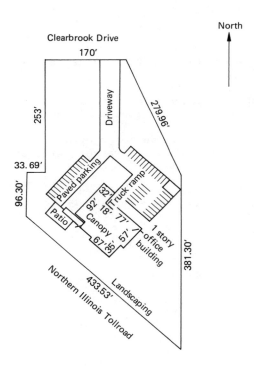

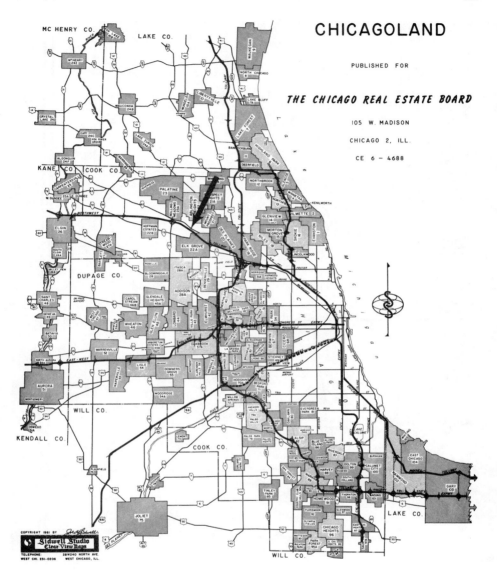

CHICAGOLAND

PUBLISHED FOR

THE CHICAGO REAL ESTATE BOARD

105 W. MADISON

CHICAGO 2, ILL.

CE 6 - 4688

ANALYSIS: CASE STUDY 8—INDUSTRIAL PROPERTY

This case is similar to thousands of industrial-type properties built in the United States in the past 20 years. Most are located in industrial parks of modern, one-story, attractively landscaped buildings. They usually contain a small amount—say, 10 to 15 percent of total area—of office space with the remainder of the building utilized for warehouse facilities or light manufacturing. An important consideration to the lender is to ascertain that the building is not so carefully tailored to the original tenant's specifications that it precludes use by other potential future users. In other words, is this a single-purpose building?

Another consideration is the financial strength of the tenant and the initial term of the lease. Check to see what the loan balance will be at the end of this lease. Many lenders feel the remaining balance should not exceed the present land value and that the cost of the buildings and improvements should be fully amortized. A further consideration in this case is the loan "kicker" where the lender is to receive 2% of the net rentals collected.

This presentation makes judgments for sales purposes which are not clearly substantiated by the facts presented.

FHA Multifamily

Alvin Zelitzky

An ever-increasing tool to developers of multifamily residential real estate in this country is the National Housing Act, which has various Sections. The Sections of the National Housing Act having to do with real estate are administered by the Federal Housing Administration (FHA), which is part of the Department of Housing and Urban Development (HUD).

Unless conversant with the benefits offered by the National Housing Act, a mortgage banker cannot offer a full choice of alternatives to a client when evaluating the feasibility of an apartment package.

At this writing, all the multifamily programs of the National Housing Act insure loans with 40-year amortization ranging between 90 and 100 percent of replacement cost. In addition to the advantage of the longer amortization period, the FHA mortgage amount is determined by a capitalization of 90 percent of the net income (as later explained). Also, a 40-year loan carries a constant which makes some loans economically feasible which would not be feasible with shorter amortization periods. In a conventional loan, capitalization of the net income would provide a value, not a mortgage amount. As in conventional loans, the economics of the development must be such that the proper percentage of replacement cost is supportable by the net income.

FHA vs. Conventional Financing

Lakeside Apartments

Rentals: 1 BR—$205, 2 BR—$245, 3 BR—$295

		221 (d)(4) FHA		Conventional
Gross income		$ 298,800		$ 298,800
Less vacancy (7%)		20,916	(5%)	14,940
Net effective income		277,884		283,860
Less expenses & taxes		115,000		110,100
Net income		162,884		173,760
Mortgage amount (90%		$1,842,300	(75% of Value)	$1,422,750
Debt service	(Constant—7.96)	146,595	(Constant—10.08) (25 yrs.—9%)	143,413
Cash flow		16,289		30,347
Mortgage amount (90%)		$1,842,300	(75% of Value)	$1,422,750
Less FHA fees & discount		106,853		—
Available mortgage funds		$1,735,447		$1,422,750

The above shows a comparative analysis of our FHA hypothetical case versus conventional financing. Note the greater mortgage amount that FHA makes available.

The 100 percent loans are utilized in the not-for-profit Sections of the Housing Act (exclusive of not-for-profit nursing homes, which are 90 percent), and the 90 percent loans are used in other sections. Since less and less emphasis is being placed on not-for-profit developments, and since most of the developments financed by the FHA are for profit, this case study will be devoted to the most widely used Section—221(d)(4).

While this case study covers only one Section of the National Housing Act, the principles are similar to all other Sections. Greater information on other Sections can be obtained from various Government publications, specifically FHA Form No. 2575, which provides a digest of insurable loans.

Section 221 (d)(4)

Section 221(d)(4) is a market interest rate program designed to finance construction or rehabilitation of nonluxury multifamily rental housing. There are no tenant income limitations set under this program. (This is true of all market rate programs.)

Initial rental rates are limited only by the market and FHA's "Rental Formula" which is shown on a later page. Tenants must meet the normal management criteria, but management must have a program for equal housing opportunities.

The requirements for FHA insurance for developments requiring rehabilitation vary substantially from the requirements for new construction and will not be discussed in this case study. The procedures, however, are similar.

The FHA mortgagee should be thoroughly versed in the FHA rules, regulations, and procedures, and for a set fee not to exceed 2 percent of the mortgage amount, will do all the processing necessary to obtain an FHA firm commitment; provide interim

FHA FORM NO. 2013
Rev. 8/72

U.S. DEPARTMENT OF HOUSING AND URBAN DEVELOPMENT
FEDERAL HOUSING ADMINISTRATION

Form Approved
OMB No. 63-R0676

APPLICATION - PROJECT MORTGAGE INSURANCE

Project No.

FHA assigns No.

Project Name

Lakeside Apartments

TO: **Insured Mortgage Company**   and the FEDERAL HOUSING COMMISSIONER.

The undersigned hereby requests a loan in the principal amount of $ **1,842,300** to be insured under the provisions of Section **221(d)(4)** of the National Housing Act, said loan to be secured by a first mortgage on the property hereinafter described.

Insurance of advances during construction [X] is, [ ] is not desired. [ ] Feasibility [ ] Conditional [X] Firm

Type of Mortgagor: [X] PM [ ] LD [ ] B-S [ ] NP   Permanent Mortgage Interest Rate **7** %.

A. LOCATION AND DESCRIPTION OF PROPERTY:

1. Street Nos.	2. Street	3. Municipality	4. Census Tract	5. County	6. State and ZIP Code
4200 East	**Wacker Drive**	**Chicago**		**Cook**	**Ill. 60606**

7. Type of Project: [ ] Row (T.H.) [X] Walkup [ ] Semi-Detached [X] Elevator [X] Detached

8. No. Stories	9. Foundation:	9.a Basement Floor:
2	[ ] Slab on Grade [X] Full Bsmt. [ ] Partial Bsmt. [ ] Crawl Space	[X] Structural [ ] Slab [ ] Slab on Grade

10. | 11. Number of Units | 12. No. Bldgs. | 13. List Accessory Bldgs. and Area | 13. a List Recreation Facilities and Area

[X] Proposed [ ] Existing

Revenue	Non-Rev.
100	

12. No. Bldgs. **5**

13. List Accessory Bldgs. and Area **none**

13. a List Recreation Facilities and Area **none**

SITE INFORMATION

14. Dimensions: **6 acres** ft. by **0261,369** sq. ft.

15. Zoning: *(If recently changed, submit evidence)* **Multifamily**

BUILDING INFORMATION

14. [ ] Conventionally Built

16.a [ ] Manufactured Housing [ ] Modules [ ] Components

16. Yr. Built	17. Structural System	17.a Floor System	18. Heating - A/C System
n/a	**Masonry-Wall Bearing**		**G/FHA**

16. Exterior Finish **Brick veneer**

B. INFORMATION CONCERNING LAND OR PROPERTY:

19. Date Acquired	20. Purchase Price	21. Additional Costs Paid or Accrued	22. If Lease-hold, Annual Ground Rent	23.a Total Cost	23.b Outstanding Balance	Relationship - Business, Personal or Other Between Seller and Buyer

From Site

Water [X] ___   [ ] Cuts   [ ] Fills   [ ] Rock Formations   [ ] Erosion

Sewers [X] ___   [ ] Poor Drainage   [ ] High Water Table   [ ] Retaining Walls

   [ ] Other (Specify) ___   [X] None

   [ ] Off Site Improvements

C. ESTIMATE OF INCOME:

27. No. of Each Family Type Unit	Living Area (Sq. Ft.)	Composition of Units	Unit Rent Per Month	Total Monthly Rent For Unit Type
25	645	1 Bedroom – 1 Bath	$ 205	$ 5,125
50	850	2 Bedroom – 1 Bath	245	12,250
25	1050	3 Bedroom – 1½ Bath	295	7,375

28.   TOTAL ESTIMATED RENTALS FOR ALL FAMILY UNITS $ 24,900

29. No. Parking Spaces—

[ ] Attended   Open Spaces **150** @ $ **n.c.** per month   -----

[X] Self Park   Covered Spaces **---** @ $ **---** per month   -----

30. Commercial

Area-Ground Level **coin laundry** Sq. Ft. @ $ **1.50** per sq. ft./mo.   150

Other Levels ___ Sq. Ft. @ $ ___ per sq. ft./mo.

31.   TOTAL ESTIMATED GROSS PROJECT INCOME AT 100% OCCUPANCY $ 24,900

32.   TOTAL ANNUAL RENT (Item 31 x 12 months) $ 298,800

33. Gross Floor Area— **94,300** Sq. Ft.

34. Net Rentable Residential Area— **84,875** Sq. Ft.

35. Net Rentable Commercial Area— **none** Sq. Ft.

36.

NON-REVENUE PRODUCING SPACE

Type of Employee	No. Rms.	Composition of Unit	Location of Unit in Project
none			

D. EQUIPMENT AND SERVICES INCLUDED IN RENT: *(Check Appropriate Items)*

37. EQUIPMENT

- [X] Ranges *(Gas or Elec.)*
- [X] Refrig. *(Gas or Elec.)*
- [ ] Air Cond. *(Equip. Only)*
- [X] Kitchen Exhaust Fan
- [X] Laundry Facilities

- [ ] Disposal
- [ ] Dishwasher
- [ ] Carpet
- [ ] Drapes
- [ ] Other *(Specify)*

a/c Sleeves only

38. SERVICES

GAS: [X] Heat [X] Hot Water
[X] Cooking [ ] Air Conditioning

ELEC.: [ ] Heat [ ] Hot Water
[ ] Cooking [ ] Air Conditioning
[ ] Lights, Etc., in Unit

OTHER FUEL: [ ] Heat [ ] Hot Water
[ ] WATER [ ] OTHER

39. Special Assessments:

a. [ ] Prepayable
   [ ] Non-Prepayable

b. [ ] Principal
   Balance **$ none**

c. [ ] Annual
   Payment **$** _____

d. [ ] Remaining
   Term _____ Years

E. ESTIMATE OF ANNUAL EXPENSE:

ADMINISTRATIVE—
1. Advertising	$	800
2. Management		9,500
3. Other		500
4. TOTAL ADMINISTRATIVE	$	10,800

OPERATING—
5. Elevator Main. Exp.	$	n/a
6. Fuel (Heating and Domestic Hot Water)		13,500
7. Lighting & Misc. Power		9,500
8. Water		2,500
9. Gas		4,500
10. Garb. & Trash Removal		3,500
11. Payroll		---
12. Other		900
13. TOTAL OPERATING	$	34,400

MAINTENANCE—
14. Decorating	$	5,500
15. Repairs		3,500
16. Exterminating		600
17. Insurance		3,500
18. Ground Expense		500
19. Other		---
20. TOTAL MAINTENANCE	$	13,600
21. Replacement Reserve (.0060 x total for structures Line 41)	$	7,937
22. TOTAL EXPENSE	$	66,737

G. ESTIMATED REPLACEMENT COST:

▲ 36a. Unusual Land Improvements	$	
▲ 36b. Other Land Improvements	$	
▲ 36c. Total Land Improvements	$	54,270
	STRUCTURES—	
▲ 37. Main Buildings	$1,322,801	
▲ 38. Accessory Buildings		
▲ 39. Garage		
▲ 40. All other Buildings		
▲ 41. TOTAL STRUCTURES	$1,322,801	
▲ 42. General Requirements	$	41,393
	FEES—	
▲ 43. Builder's Gen. Overhead @ 2 %	$	28,370
▲ 44. Builder's Profit @ --- %	BSPR	
▲ 45. Arch. Fee-Design @ 4 %		56,739
▲ 46. Arch. Fee-Supvr. @ 1.33 %		18,866
▲ 47. Bond Premium .0075		10,639
▲ 48. Other Fees		
▲ 49. TOTAL FEES	$	114,614
50. TOT. for all Imprmts. (Lines 36c, 41, 42 & 49)	$	1,533,078
51. Cost Per Gross Sq. Ft.	$	16.26
52. Estimated Construction Time	15	Months
	CARRYING CHARGES & FINANCING—	
▲ 53. Int. 15 Mos. @ 7 % on $ 921,150	$	80,600

TAXES—

23. Real Estate: Est. Assessed
Val. $1,023,500 @
$ 21.30 per $1000— $ 48,000

24. Personal Prop. Est. Assessed
Val. $ @
$ per $1000— -0-

25. Empl. Payroll Tax - - - - - - - 263
26. Other - - - - - - - - - - - - -0-
27. Other - - - - - - - - - - - - -0-
28. TOTAL TAXES - - - - - - - $ 48,263
29. TOTAL EXPENSE & TAXES - - - - - - - - - $ 115,000

F. INCOME COMPUTATIONS:

30. Estimated Project
Gross Income (Line C32 Page 1) - - - - - $ 298,800

31. Occupancy (Entire Project)
Percentage- - - - - - - - - - 93 %

32. Effective Gross Income (Line 30 x 31)- - - $ 277,884
33. Total Project Expenses (Line 29) - - - - - $ 115,000
34. Net Income to Project (Line 32 − Line 33)- - $ 162,884
35. Expense Ratio (Line 29 ÷ Line 32)- - - - - 41.4 %

H. TOTAL REQUIREMENTS FOR SETTLEMENT:

1. DEVELOPMENT COSTS (Line 71)- - - - - - $ 1,927,000
2. LAND INDEBTEDNESS (or Cash required
for land acquisition)- - - - - - - - - 120,000
3. SUBTOTAL (Line 1 + 2) - - - - - - - - $ 2,047,000
4. Mortgage Amount - - - - - - - - $ 1,842,300
5. Fees Paid by Other Than Cash - $ 175,181

---

54. Taxes - - - - - - - - - - - 9,000
55. Insurance - - - - - - - - - 15,500
56. FHA Mtg. Ins. Pre. (0.5%) x2 18,423
57. FHA Exam. Fee (0.3%) 5,527
58. FHA Inspec. Fee (0.5%) 9,211
59. Financing Fee (2 %) 36,846
60. AMPO (%) - - - -
61. FNMA/GNMA Fee 1.5% 27,634
62. Title & Recording - - - - - 6,500
63. TOTAL CARRYING CHGS. & FINANCING- - $ 209,241

LEGAL AND ORGANIZATION—

64. Legal- - - - - - - - - - - $ - - - -
65. Organization - - - - - - - $ - - - -
66. TOTAL LEGAL AND ORGANIZATION- - - - - $ 9,500
57. Supplemental Management Fund - - - - - - $ - - - -
68. Consultant Fee - - - - - - - - $ - - - -
69. Builder and Sponsor Profit & Risk- - - - - $ 175,181
70. Contingency Reserve - - - - -
71. TOTAL EST. DEVELOPMENT COST *(Excl.of*
Land or Off-site Cost) (50+63+66+67+68+69+70) $ 1,927,000
72. LAND (Est. Market Price of Site)
261,360 sq. ft. @ $ 0.46 per sq. ft. $ 120,000
73. TOTAL ESTIMATED REPLACEMENT
COST OF PROJECT *(Add 71 + 72)*- - - - $ 2,047,000

Source of Cash to meet Requirements:	Amount
Cash	$ 140,057
	$

7. CASH INVESTMENT REQUIRED (Line 3 – 6) - $	25,315
8. INITIAL OPERATING DEFICIT - - - - - - - - $	- - - -
9. ANTICIPATED DISCOUNT - - - - - - - - $	73,692
10. Working Cap. (2% of Mtge. Amount) - - - - - - - $	36,846
11. Off-site Construction Costs - - - - - - - - $	none
12. **TOTAL ESTIMATED CASH REQUIREMENT** (Lines 7 + 8 + 9 + 10 + 11) - - - - - - - - $	140,057

$
$
TOTAL $ 140,057

I. ATTACHMENTS: (Required Exhibits)

1.	Location Map	9.	Environmental Statement
2.	Evidence of Site Control (Option or Purchase) and Legal Description of Property	10.	Personal Financial & Credit Statement of Sponsors
		11.	Form 2530 Previous Participation Certification
3.	Form 2010 Equal Employment Opportunity Certification	12. ▲	Form 2328 Contractor's and/or Mortgagor's Cost Breakdown
4.	Form 3433 Eligibility as Non-Profit Corporation	13. ▲	Archetectural Exhibits - Preliminary
5.	Evidence of Last Arms-Length Transaction Price	14. ▲	Architectural Exhibits - Final
6.	Sketch Plan of Site	15. ▲	Survey and FHA Form No. 2457
7.	Management Plan	16. ▲	Evidence of Architect E & O Insurance Coverage
		17. ▲	Copy of Owner Architect Agreement
8.	Affirmative Marketing Plan	18. ▲	Management Agreement

financing, process payouts, and place the end loan. A discount on interim or end loans may be charged to bring the rate to current market criteria. While it is true that preliminary applications for feasibility analyses may be submitted by the sponsor directly to the FHA local insuring office, the final submission must be made through an approved mortgagee. It is logical to get the mortgagee involved as early as possible, since he has processed a number of FHA loans and has insight into the problems which are unique to FHA loans.

FHA PROCESSING PROCEDURES

Exact processing procedures required by the FHA change periodically. For example, a process called Site Appraisal Market Analysis (SAMA) is now being followed. However, the steps are similar to those described here.

Preliminary Meeting

The mortgagee should meet with the developer(s) and architect to discuss the project prior to any contact being made with FHA. The mortgagee will review all procedures to be followed by the FHA (see subsequent steps), and should to some extent act as the "Devil's Advocate." In other words, introduce all possible deficiencies that might make the project unfeasible. Obviously, to the extent the sponsor is unable to answer these problems, the mortgagee should then change "hats" and help the sponsor obtain the answers to all the questions which could be raised by the FHA.

It is possible that answers are not obtainable because a particular project is simply not feasible. It should be pointed out that the FHA mortgagee is not arbitrary in making a determination of unfeasibility, since he does not receive a fee if the loan does not go through.

The mortgagee, however, should review alternative Sections of the National Housing Act, alternative compositions of units, check expense ratios, and so forth, prior to making an absolute determination of project unfeasibility.

The mortgagee will, after this meeting, draft FHA application for Mortgage Insurance (Form 2013), and prior to the prefeasibility conference, review this form with the developers.

Prefeasibility Conference

At this conference the developer, mortgagee, and architect present the 2013, market data, site plan, and preliminary drawings to the FHA technicians for their review. The technicians review the data and ask questions in an effort to get a feel for the proposed development. After the FHA technicians find that the proposed development meets the FHA requirements, a letter inviting a submission for feasibility is transmitted to the sponsor.

Processing for Feasibility

When a letter inviting a submission for feasibility is received, the contents should be examined very carefully. Work should immediately start on gathering all the required documents requested by the FHA, since the invitation has a termination date of 90 days or less. While the documents required will vary, one requirement that remains constant is evidence of site control. Once all the documents have been submitted to the FHA, the mortgagee should follow up periodically to see how the review is going and to find out whether any additional documentation is necessary.

The feasibility processing takes longer than any other review by the FHA, since the documents are examined thoroughly by the underwriting divisions: Architectural, Valuation, Mortgage Credit and Management.

Processing for Firm Commitment

After the FHA has completed the feasibility review, and that review is favorable, they will invite a submission for either a conditional or firm commitment and indicate in this feasibility letter the general terms and conditions, but not the mortgage amount. An amount equal to 0.3 percent of the proposed mortgage amount must be paid to the FHA with the firm submittal. Under current practice, three payments of 0.1% are paid at each processing step.) Any variance in a firm submittal from the terms and conditions of the feasibility letter permits the FHA to reject the application and demand a new submission for findings of feasibility. The firm application is reviewed by the appropriate divisions of the FHA to see that it is in conformity with the feasibility letter. The most time-consuming step in the commitment processing is a review of the working plans and specifications. This time period, however, can be minimized, since the FHA assigns an architect to work with the project architect in preparing the working plans.

Initial Endorsement

It is at initial endorsement that the loan is opened and the FHA endorses the mortgage note. Obviously, prior to initial endorsement the mortgagee must make arrangements satisfactory to the developer for interim and end financing. All funds necessary for project completion, which are not in the loan, must be in the hands of the mortgagee. The mortgagee, working closely with the FHA Regional Counsel, should assist in the preparation of the required FHA documents for initial endorsement. A list of initial closing documents is not herewith exhibited, because this list is subject to constant change. The latest FHA requirements on initial endorsement should be reviewed on each case. Generally speaking, construction does not start until the FHA has endorsed the mortgage note; although under certain circumstances, construction can start with FHA approval after the firm commitment has been issued and prior to initial endorsement.

An interesting variance between conventional financing and FHA financing is the fact that as much as 15 percent of the loan proceeds are disbursed by FHA at the time of initial endorsement.

Construction Period

As construction progresses, regular construction advances are made. The contractor submits to the mortgagee a requisition on an approved FHA form. The mortgagee then prepares an Application for Insurance of Advances and Mortgage Proceeds for the mortgagor and sends the requisition and this form to the FHA. This latter form incorporates not only the construction advances, but such other payments that come due during the month such as construction interest and supervisory architectural fees. The FHA checks the request to see if all its requirements have been met, and upon approval, the amount of the FHA insurance is increased in the amount of the payout. Naturally, the mortgagee will not automatically make a payout upon receipt of FHA's approval application for Insurance of Advances of Mortgage Proceeds and a contractor's requisition. Other normal checks for construction financing must be met, which include, but are not limited to, increasing title insurance to incorporate the payout.

Final Endorsement

After construction has been completed, cost certification submitted by the sponsors, and the contractor has been approved by the FHA, the mortgagee, again working closely with the FHA Regional Counsel, assists and advises in the preparation of final closing documents. At final endorsement the mortgage note is endorsed a second time by the FHA. The mortgagee should then be ready to deliver the loan to the permanent investor, assuming all of the lender's additional requirement (if any) have been met. FHA insurance remains in effect for the life of the loan.

In the section which follows, an FHA Form 2013 Application—Project Mortgage Insurance has been filled out. The calculations showing how the 2013 was completed, using two approaches (the cost approach and the income approach), follow the 2013 along with the formulas for finding excess proceeds and maximum rents.

221 (d)(4) Calculations

1 Preparation of 2013 Using the Cost Approach

Item 50—Total for all improvements	$1,533,078
Item 54—Taxes	9,000
Item 55—Insurance	15,500
Item 62—Title and recording	6,500
Item 64—Legal	6,500
Item 65—Organization	3,000
Subtotal (Knowns)	$1,573,578
Subtotal $1,573,578 × 1.1 =	$1,730,936
(10% BSPRA Adj.)	
Item 70—Land Value	120,000
Total of knowns adjusted for	
Builder and sponsor profit & risk adjustment	(a)1,850,936
Item 53—Interest rate ÷ 2 × Const. time	
(.07 ÷ 2 × 1.25)	4.375%
Item 56—Mortgage ins. premium	1.000%
Item 57—Examination fee	.300%
Item 58—Inspection fee	.500%
Item 59—Financing fee	2.000%
Item 61—FNMA/GNMA fee	1.500%
Subtotal (Unknowns)	9.675%
Subtotal 9.675% × .99 (10% BSPRA Adj.) =	9.578% (Total Unknowns adjusted for BSPRA)

100%—Total adj. unknowns 9.578% = (b) 90.422%

$$\frac{\text{adjusted knowns (a)}}{100\%\text{—adj. unknowns}} = \text{total project cost}$$

$$\frac{\text{(a) }\$1,850,936}{\text{(b) }90.422\%} = \text{Total project cost } \$2,047,000$$

Total project cost × 90% = $1,842,300 max. mtge.
   Assume 90% mortgage

The amount of the unknowns can now be found by multiplying the percentage of each unknown by the mortgage amount.

Example:
  a) Interest during construction—15 mos. @ 7%
      (125 × .07) = 8.75 ÷ 2 = 4.375
      4.375% × $1,842,300 = $80,600
      Solve for the remaining unknowns

---

2 Preparation of 2013 Using Income Approach

Step 1. Estimate project gross income	$298,800
Occupancy percentage	93%
Effective gross income	$277,884
Minus total project expenses	115,000
Net income to project	$162,884
90% debt service loan	90%
Total for Debt service divided by	$146,595
Constant (7.957176)	

The constant is determined in the following manner:

7.00000 Maximum interest allowable by FHA as of 5/25/73
 .50000 Mortgage Insurance Premium
 .457176 Curtail rate (changes with the interest rate)
7.957176 Total

$146,595 ÷ 7.957176 = $1,842,300 Max. Mtge. Amt.
$1,842,300 ÷ 90% − $2,047,000 Replacement Cost

Step 2.   Find dollar amount of Unknowns

a) Interest during construction 15 mos. @ 7%	
4.375% × $1,842,000	$80,600
b) Mortgage Insurance premium	$18,423
(.205 × 2) 2 years .01 × $1,842,300	
c) FHA exam fee	$ 5,527
.003 × $1,842,300	
d) FHA inspection fee	$ 9,211
.005 × $1,842,300	
e) Financing fee	$36,846
.02 × $1,842,300	
f) FNMA/GNMA fee	$27,634
.015 × $1,842,300	

Formula for Finding Excess Proceeds/Additional Equity

Step 1.	
Replacement cost	$2,047,000
Minus mortgage amount	1,842,300
Total of Step 1	$ 204,700

Step 2.

BSPRA	$175,181
Plus land cost	120,000
Total of Step 2	$295,181

Step 3.

Total of Step 2	$295,181
Total of Step 1 (minus)	204,700
Excess proceeds	$ 90,481

This is the dollar amount available to the sponsor of this project at the time of initial endorsement after he has delivered clear title to the land.

FHA Basic Rent Formula

Project No. (FHA Assigns Number)

1	Total estimated cost of property		$2,047,000
2	Ratio of total cost to Dwelling Unit Cost 100%		100%
3	Cost applicable to dwelling use (Line 1 divided by Line 2)		$2,047,000
4	Cash working capital (2% of mortgage amount)		$ 36,846
5	Total investment in dwelling units (Line 3 plus Line 4)		$2,083,846
6	Interest rate	7.00000%	
	Initial curtail	0.457176%	
	FHA-MIP	0.500000%	
	Override	0.500000%	
	Total	8.457176% on Line 5—Allowable return	
		on investment	$176,234
7	Total annual expense, taxes and reserves		$115,000
8	Expense applicable to dwelling units (Line 7 divided by Line 2)		$115,000
9	Allowable gross income applicable to dwelling structures and tenant parking, not including vacancy and collection losses (Line 6 plus Line 8)		$291,234
10	Occupancy estimate	93%	
11	Maximum allowable annual gross income applicable to dwelling structures and tenant parking adjusted for vacancy and collection losses (Line 9 divided by Line 10)		$313,154
12	Maximum allowable monthly gross rental applicable to dwelling structures and tenant parking		$313,154
13	Monthly income from tenant parking		$ —
14	Maximum allowable monthly rental for all family units		$ 26,096

ANALYSIS: CASE STUDY 9—FHA MULTIFAMILY

This is not so much a case study as it is an introduction to the methods of financing multiunit residential projects with government-insured loans. In the words of the author, ''Unless a mortgage banker is conversant with the benefits offered by the National Housing Act, he cannot offer a full choice of alternatives to his client when he evaluates the feasibility of an apartment package.''

The author then goes on to illustrate side by side the differences between conventional and government-insured lending on the identical project. Perhaps he is partially prejudiced in not emphasizing the much longer time element involved with government financing.

High-Rise
Apartment Building

William C. Lutz

As in any type of investment offering, there is a direct relationship between the completeness of your submission and the time it takes an investor to express an interest, issue a commitment, or indicate a rejection. Only delays and frustrations result when one persists in trying to force feed the simplified procedure of a correspondent on an institutional investor who has formal committees through which to process investment offerings. Moreover, since the complete package required by the larger investors usually reflect their more sophisticated exposure, one would be prudent to make this the standard for all submissions. Not only would that impress less sophisticated investors, but it would simplify the immediate referral of the case to another investor should the first choice decline interest.

The following case study assumes more than a casual knowledge of commercial mortgage loan procedures and an understanding of the investor's prevailing underwriting requirements. If so, a formal submission would include the following:

1   Letter of transmittal.
2   Loan summary.
3   Application and good faith deposit.
4   Appraisal.
5   Borrower's financial statements, together with credit and/or D & B reports.
6   Plans and specifications.

Letter of Transmittal (See Exhibit A)

Note that it gives the type and location of property, lists enclosures submitted, explains negotiations that have taken place and if there is an existing loan, whether or not it can be paid off. Often an investor will express an interest in an investment offering, only to then learn that the existing loan cannot be paid off. The natural result in such situations is a waste of everyone's time.

The balance of the letter is self-explanatory, giving principal highlights of the case, background and ability of the borrowers, and a recommendation for the loan.

Loan Summary (See Exhibit B)

This is simply a brief synopsis of the security and underwriting terms. This could just as effectively be included in the letter of transmittal, but doing it this way avoids retyping this material if another letter of transmittal is necessary. The sole purpose of the loan summary is to summarize the salient features of the loan submission.

Application (See Exhibit C)

This is one form of application. There are as many forms of application as there are lenders, but substantially the same information will be required in all of them. The most important issue where applications are concerned is to *answer all the questions*. Only in this way does the application become an effective contract and lessen the possibilities of future litigation over ambiguities. Investors by their very nature are skeptical and leaving a question unanswered immediately arouses suspicion. It is also worthy of comment that the application should be signed by the borrower and any checks covering good faith deposits, etc., should likewise be drawn by that borrower; otherwise, it is possible to take a defense that the checks accepted were not an obligation of the applicant and a suit could be initiated for return of the good faith deposit. When submitting the application over the correspondent company signature on behalf of the applicant, it is expected that company checks will accompany the application. Should the commitment ultimately issued by a lender differ from the application, get the application changed and signed by the borrower to conform with the commitment before releasing the commitment to him.

Appraisal (See Exhibit D)

In the interest of brevity, this exhibit is simply a summary of salient facts and critical assumptions taken from the appraisal report. Always completely read the appraisal report before sending it to the lender, since there may be "surprises" (like a statement to the effect that there is an overabundance of similar vacant apartments on the market, etc.), and any submission should comment on such negative facts in the appraisal report.

Suffice it to say, a good appraisal report will fully support the conclusion of value with facts or reliable opinion on such important issues as the need for the facilities; justification of land values; support for projected income and expenses; and a clear picture of the vacancy situation in comparable buildings, together with an estimate of the absorption rate of new units under construction or planned. A well-documented appraisal report will enable the investor to readily accept a value conclusion even if it's based on higher projected rents than prevail at the time of appraisal. For example, this might come about because present rents are on the low side coupled with the fact that there are limited competing facilities with a restriction on further apartments being built because of inadequate sewer or other facilities.

One cannot overemphasize the need for good exhibits—not just good photographs of the subject property and competition but also site plan, together with area and city maps clearly showing the location of the improvements on the site, the neighborhood environment surrounding the property and the city transportation routes, schools, churches, recreational and shopping facilities, museums, parks, etc.

Borrower's Financial Statements

The financial statements supported by credit and D & B reports should clearly show the creditworthiness and financial stability of the applicant. The financial statements should also show sufficient liquidity to cover the equity needed. By equity is implied the difference between the loan amount requested and the total cost (not appraisal) of the property. Where a platform loan subject to leasing is involved, always show the source of such additional equity. This could, for example, involve additional equity partners, gap financing, the proposed sale of other assets shown in the financial statement.

It is good practice to attach a cover sheet on the borrower's background to the financial statement, credit reports, etc., outlining in depth the experience of the borrower and/or developers, elaborating on their property management experience or explaining what reputable firm they plan to engage to manage the property. This summary should be designed to fortify an investor's conclusion that the borrowers can acquire the property without undue financial strain and that they either have the experience or have hired capable management to maintain the property's competitive position.

Plans and Specifications

These were not necessary in this case, since it is a completed project. As such, its faults or shortcomings, if any, can be determined by random discussions with selected tenants, competing apartment building managers, etc. But where there is an offering involving proposed construction, one should have complete plans and specifications with any submission. If only preliminary plans are available, be sure they at least contribute something to the submission by showing the location of the buildings on the site, their dimensions, and examples of the proposed apartment layouts and room sizes. The location of parking and recreational facilities, such as swimming pool, tennis court, should also be indicated on preliminary plans. Above all else, be certain to send the correct plans and specifications for the specific property being submitted. Surprising as it may seem, there have been actual cases submitted to investors with the wrong plans, or even worse, plans for a shopping center included with an apartment offering. Above all, don't weaken a submission by enclosing reduced photo scale drawings that cannot be read without the aid of a magnifying glass.

Committee Brief (See Exhibit E)

This document is a copy of an investor committee brief, and simply shows how one major lender briefs the available data for presentation to the committee members. While self-explanatory, there are some areas that need explanation:

The loan amount is broken down into loan per apartment, per room, and per square foot. The percentage factor following the total loan (75%) refers to the relationship of the loan to the total appraisal.

Under TERM there is reference to a recast option which is simply a protective underwriting device where the term is longer than the investor would prefer to give on an average apartment loan.

Under MONTHLY PAYMENTS, the 9.45% in parentheses refers to the constant factor for a 30-year loan.

OPERATING HISTORY—this paragraph applies only in the case of an existing property. Its purpose is to show committee members how effectively the property has coped with rising expenses, taxes, etc.

Alongside the appraiser's projections of income, expenses, etc., certain key ratios are illustrated, such as (GM) following income—this refers to the gross rent multiplier. The (51.3%) following taxes and expenses refers to the ratios of taxes and expenses to gross income. The (CAP) indicates the capitalization rate used. The (DCR) following the annual interest and principal charges shows the number of times net covers debt charges.

If the CITY AND AREA DATA indicated a loss in population, single-industry town, high unemployment in relation to the national figures, etc., such shortcomings would have to be explained in this paragraph.

COMPETITION AND DEMAND explain any adverse factors, such as, higher-than-normal vacancies, or many competing buildings either planned, under constructions, or coming on the market. No salesman accents the negative, but it serves no purpose to ignore it either. There are often genuine reasons to offset concerns over such competition. For example, superior location across from a park; more convenient to schools, churches, transportation, or shopping; unobstructed view of lakes, ocean, mountains, etc.; superior layouts both as to room size, number of baths for apartment; exceptional recreational facilities, such as enclosed pool, exercise rooms, saunas, tennis courts, bowling alleys, etc.

While market conditions determine what can be negotiated, an investor expects any offering to be equal or superior to prevailing terms available in the area. If recommending lower rates, longer terms, shorter closed prepayment clauses than are available in the market, one should have ample justification for such recommendations; otherwise they reflect on judgment and invite declination.

In the final analysis, it is in a fiduciary capacity that the lender makes a decision as to whether he will follow recommendations. If he comes back with a counterproposal, it is the correspondent's obligation to strive to sell that counterproposal, and if not successful, to come back with an alternative. A good negotiator is more comparable to a fencing foil than a machete.

                            LETTER OF TRANSMITTAL

                                    (Date)

(Addressee)

                                    Tower View Apartments
                                    Street Address
Dear   :   City, State

    This submission covers a first mortgage loan offering
of $1,800,000 at 8-3/4% interest for a 30-year term. The
security is an existing 22-story, high-rise apartment
building. Included in this submission are the following:

    1.   Loan summary.
    2.   Application.
    3.   Check for $18,000 covering non-refundable fee.
    4.   Credit and D & B reports.
    5.   Financial statements on owners showing source of
          equity.

    In our negotiations we made every attempt to get a
contingent interest participation in any increases in gross
income but were not successful. We did negotiate a closed
prepayment privilege for a 15-year term with the right to
pay in full in the 16th year at a 5% premium, declining
each year thereafter 1/4 of 1%. The applicant understands
that in the 12th year you may at your option on 6 months'
notice accelerate this loan to be paid in full over 25 years,
but in that event he would have the right to pay the loan in
full without penalty.

    This loan, if committed, will be available for funding
within the next 45 days. We have confirmed that the present
mortgage which is held by a local savings and loan company
can be paid in full without penalty.

    This property is located in one of the most desirable
high-rise apartment sections of this city. The improvements
are well designed with good apartment layouts and room sizes
and quality workmanship. The building has been well maintained
and its better than 98% occupancy over the past two years
demonstrates its acceptability in the market.

    The applicants are experienced apartment developers and
managers. They own and manage over 1800 apartment units,
having an average occupancy of 97½%.

    We recommend this loan for your approval.

                                    Sincerely,

LOAN SUMMARY

Tower View Apartments

ocation   Street Address, City, County, State

lot Size   Irregular 226.98' x 84.03' x 239.28' x 83.0' - 19,350 sq.ft.

mprovements   Twenty-two story and basement elevator apartment building
               containing 78 apartments, 455 rooms and 121,500 rentable
               square feet. Parking for 73 cars (51 cars in basement,
               22 cars on surface). Built - 1965.

oan Request   Amount   - $1,800,000 (75% of appraisal)
               Rate   - 8 3/4% (constant 9.45%)
               Term   - 30 years. Lender's option to recast in
                                 12th year as a 25-year payout. If exercised
                                 owner has 6 months to pay in full at no char
               Monthly payment - $14,175 to interest and principal plus tax
                                 and insurance deposit.

ees $18,000 (1%) non-refundable commitment fee.

repayment
rivilege   Closed for 15 years in full in 16th loan year with 5% charge,
               declining 1/4 of 1% per year thereafter.

ppraisal   7/16/73 Land $640,000 Bldg. $1,760,000 Total $2,400,000

nalysis   Loan per apartment $23,077.
               Loan per room $ 3,956.
               Loan per square foot $ 14.81
               Rent per room per month $ 87.61
               Rent per square foot $ 3.94
               Break-even rent per room per month $ 75.17
               Break-even rent per square foot $ 3.24
               Debt coverage ratio   1.37

unding Date   Within 45 days after commitment.

NEW YORK LIFE INSURANCE COMPANY

EXHIBIT C
MORTGAGE
LOAN APPLICATION
(INCOME PROPERTY)

Please sign and submit in triplicate. All questions must be answered.

The undersigned hereby applies for: ☐ a direct loan from New York Life Insurance Company or ☒ a loan to be purchased by assignment by New York Life Insurance Company upon the terms and conditions set forth below,

To be secured by:

☒ a first mortgage or deed of trust on the marketable **FEE SIMPLE TITLE** to the property described below:

☐ a first mortgage or deed of trust on the lessee's interest in the following **LEASEHOLD ESTATE:**
(Give lessor, lessee, annual ground rent, initial term, renewal options, lease maturity date, contingent rental)

and on the easements appurtenant thereto and on all improvements to the property, free of prior mechanics' or materialmen's liens or special assessments for work completed or under construction on the date of the closing, and, if the Company requires, as additional security, it shall receive a chattel first mortgage (free of title retention agreements) on all fixtures and articles of personal property now or hereafter attached to or used in connection with the management, maintenance, and operation of the property, and an assignment of the lessor's interest in each occupancy lease of or affecting any part of the said property as additional security for the loan, which assignment shall be recorded and copy of which shall be served on the tenant; as to each lease to be assigned, the lease shall be in full force and effect, there shall be no offsets or defenses to enforcement of the lease, the tenant shall have accepted its premises, confirmed the commencement of its lease term, be in occupancy and paying rent on a current basis, evidence of which shall be furnished the Company.

LOAN

Amount: $1,800,000   Interest Rate: 8 3/4 %   Term: 30 years
Your option to recast in 12th year as a 25 year loan subject to 6 months' notice, during which notice applicant has option to pay in full without penalty.
Repayable in monthly installments of $ 14,175   due on the 10th of the month to be applied first to interest and then to principal, and monthly deposits for real estate taxes and hazard insurance.

Additional compensation to New York Life: NONE

Rental requirement for loan advance(s):   NONE

Prepayment Privilege: Closed 15 years. Payment in full in 16th loan year with 5% penalty declining ¼ of 1% per year.

Estimated Funding Date: 10-15-73

MORTGAGOR

Give name and address of borrower, (if borrower is a partnership or a corporation, give name and addresses of partners or stockholders and their respective interests. If borrower is a trust, give full designation thereof, and identify beneficiary(s) with address(es).
Tower View Apartment Company, Street Address, City, State
Principal Stockholders are:
1st owner's name and address   % of ownership
2nd owner's name and address   % of ownership

3400 4-72

MORTGAGOR'S BANK REFERENCES

Name of Bank	Account Officer	Address & Branch of Bank
Both applicants bank at		
A.B.C. Bank	(Name and Title)	Street - City - State

LOCATION AND PHYSICAL DESCRIPTION OF SECURITY

Street Address (When identifying location, even if not asked, always show where the property lies between major cross streets so it can be readily identified between what major cross streets on site maps.)

City   County   State

LAND: Dimensions Irregular 226.98' x 84.03' Sq. Ft. Area 19,350 sq.ft.
x 239.28' x 83.0'

BUILDING: Type, Use, Size and Stories: 22-story and basement apartment building containing 78 apartments.

YEAR BUILT: 1965   REMODELED (YR. & COST): No

(The property is to be insured as required by New York Life Insurance Company and the policies will be delivered to the Company with mortgagee loss clauses attached.)

MORTGAGOR'S STATEMENT OF COST

Existing construction: Date purchased *option to purchase Cost $ 2,500,000
*option expires in 30 days

Proposed construction: Starting date   Est. completion date   Cost $

Land: Date purchased or optioned   Purchase price $

Est. Current Value: Land $ Improvements $ Total $

Are there any mortgages against the property at this time? If none, so state. If so, give mortgagee, interest rate, maturity, loan balance, payments and prepayment options. Are there any other mortgage applications or mortgage loan commitments presently outstanding against this security? If none, so state:

Savings and Loan $1,515,000 at 6 3/4%, matures 1986, Loan Balance - $1,265,125 - $11,527 = monthly payment to interest and principal. Loan can be paid in full without penalty on 30 days' notice.

Submitted herewith is our check in the sum of $ 18,000   as payment for your study and consideration of this loan application. If you do not issue a commitment, this amount will be refunded to us.

On confirmation of your commitment and as consideration for your holding funds available until this loan is closed, we will deposit with you $ 36,000   which shall be non-interest-bearing. When the loan is closed by you, it is understood you will refund $ 36,000   , otherwise you will retain the entire deposit.

We understand that it shall be our obligation to enter into a buy-sell agreement with you and an interim lender satisfactory to you.

The undersigned further agrees that the form and substance of each and every document evidencing the loan or the purchase thereof and the security therefor and title and evidence thereof must be satisfactory to the Company, and any and all obligations incurred by the Company by reason of commitment issued for the loan shall be subject to such approval. The undersigned further agrees to pay all fees and expenses incurred in connection with closing the loan or purchase thereof including fees and expenses of local counsel, if any, employed by the Company in connection therewith, title insurance charges, cost of survey, recording and filing fees, documentary stamps and other taxes payable in connection with the closing of the loan. The undersigned will arrange with the occupants of the premises for full inspection by the Company's appraisers.

_____	_____
Broker's Signature	Signature of individual, partnership, corporation, etc. to whom commitment is to be issued.
Address	Address
Date	Date

ATTACHMENTS: ☐ Legal Description and Survey showing location and description of all easements. ☒ Plot Plan. ☐ Building Plans and Specifications. ☒ Owner's Financial Statements. ☒ Operating Statements. ☐ Pro-Forma Statements. ☒ Photos. ☐ Cost Breakdown. ☒ Owner's Detailed Statement of Equity Source. ☐ Copy of Ground Lease. ☒ Rent Roll showing name of tenant, designation of space, square foot area, minimum annual rental, renewal options, date of lease, dates of commencement and expiration and conditions which permit tenant to cancel for any reason other than landlord's breach. ☒ Copies of ~~principal Lease.~~ standard Lease.

660

APPRAISAL SUMMARY OF SALIENT FACTS AND CRITICAL ASSUMPTIONS

LOCATION: Street - City - County - State
TYPE: Twenty two story elevator apartment building
LAND: 19,350 ± square feet

IMPROVEMENTS: 22 sty. apartment of concrete & steel, 8 yrs. old,
160,000 s.f. gross area, 121,500 s.f. rentable area.

APARTMENT LAYOUT: (6) 1 bedrm. & 1 bath - rental $250 to $275 per mo.
                   (33) 2 bedrm. & 1 bath - rental $325 to $425 per mo.
                   (33) 2 bedrm. & 2 bath - rental $450 to $575 per mo.
                    (6) 4 bedrm. & 3 bath (Penthouse) - rental $750 per mo.
                 78 apts. - 455 rooms

Parking 73 cars. Parking ratio .92 spaces per apartment with ample public
and on street parking in the neighborhood.

OWNER'S OPERATING STATEMENTS: (Fiscal Years Ending 4/30)

YEAR	GROSS INCOME	TAXES	EXPENSES	NET
1971	$435,664	$60,833	$156,799	$218,032
1972	$443,109	$61,851	$166,101	$215,157
1973	$478,339	$75,434	$170,432	$232,473

RENTAL DATA: Leases are for 2 to 3 year terms. Vacancies in competing
projects are less than 2%. One new competing 95 unit high-rise is under
construction in the neighborhood.

APPRAISER PROJECTIONS 1974:

TYPE	UNITS	STABILIZED RENT RM./MO.	GROSS STAB. RENT 100% OCCUPANCY
Apartments	78 apts.	$88.32 avg./mo.	$484,522
Parking	73 spaces	$32.47 avg./mo.	$ 26,449
Other Income			$ 3,368
		Total	$514,339
		Vacancy 7%	$ 36,000
		Effective Gross Income	$478,339
		Expenses $170,432	
		Taxes $ 75,434	$245,866
		Net Income	$232,473

Net Income $232,473 ÷ capitalization rate .0969 = $2,400,000

VALUATION CONCLUSION:

Land	$ 640,000
Improvements	$1,760,000
Total	$2,400,000

COMMITTEE BRIEF

NEW LOAN OFFERING
APARTMENT

LOCATION	Street Address - City - County - State
LAND	.44 acres - 19,350 s.f.
IMPROVEMENTS	Existing 22 story and basement, reinforced concrete elevator (3), air-conditioned apartment building. Basement garage for 51 cars plus 22 outside stalls. Total parking for 73 cars. Layout: (6) 1 bedrm. & 1 bath; (33) 2 bedrm. & 1 bath; (33) 2 bedrm. & 2 baths; (6) 4 bedrm. & 3 baths. Total Units 78 - Rooms 455 - Rentable sq. ft. - 121,500 Built 1965 Commitment Expiration 45 days
FEE LOAN	$1,800,000 (75%) $23,077 apt. $3,956 rm. $14.81 sq. ft.
RATE	8 3/4% SERVICING FEE .106% YIELD 8.64%
NON-REFUNDABLE FEE	$18,000 OVERALL YIELD 8.76%
TERM	30 year payout - our option to recast in 12th year as 25 year payout. If exercised, owner has 6 months to pay in full without charge.
MONTHLY PAYMENTS	$14,175 (constant factor 9.45% p.a.) to interest and principal plus tax and ins. deposits.
PRIVILEGE	Beginning 16th loan year in full with 5% charge declining ¼ of 1% p.a.
APPRAISAL	7-16-73 LAND $640,000 BLDG. $1,760,000 TOTAL $2,400,000
MORTGAGOR	Tower View Apartment Company - Principal Stockholder: (Name) % of Ownership (Name) % of Ownership
REMARKS	The project is currently 100% rented - Leases are for 2-3 years with tax and expense escalation.
YR. & LOAN BAL. (000)	15 yr. - $1,417 20 yr. - $1,130 25 yr. - $686 30 yr.-0

OPERATING HISTORY

Year	Gross Income	Expenses	Taxes	Net
1969	$414,934	$150,356	$59,494	$205,084
1970	$415,675	$163,460	$58,214	$194,001
1971	$435,664	$156,799	$60,833	$218,032
1972	$443,109	$166,101	$61,851	$215,157
1973	$478,339	$170,432	$75,434	$232,473

APPRAISER   Mr._____(correspondent appraiser) projections less
$36,000 (7% vacancy)   Approved by Chief Appraiser

*INCOME	$478,339	GM 5.0	Room Rent p.a.	$87.61
EXPENSES $170,432			Sq. Ft. Rent p.a.	$ 3.94
TAXES 75,434	245,866	51.3%	Break-even room rent p.m.	$75.17
NET INCOME	$232,473	CAP 9.69	Break-even sq. ft. rent p.a.	$ 3.24
INT. & PRIN.	169,932	DCR 1.37		
CASH FLOW	$ 62,541			

*Includes garage income of $26,449 and other income of $3,368.

CITY OR AREA DATA

The property is located in (City - State) approximately 2 miles north of the
Central Business District. This section is characterized by luxury high-rise
apartment buildings and old brownstone mansions, and is considered the city's
finest apartment area. Neighborhood shopping, public bus and subway, access
to town, sailing and fishing are all within 2 to 6 blocks.

	City	County	SMSA
1960 Census	3,611,497	5,129,725	6,220,913
1970 Census	3,366,957	5,492,369	6,978,947
1973 Est. (E&P)	3,333,287	5,569,262	7,161,229
Household Avg. Inc.	$13,015	$14,166	$14,366

Principal Employers: Manufacturing (934,700), Primary Metals (68,300),
Wholesale Trade (223,900), Retail Trade (444,900),
Contract Constr. (118,500), Non-electrical
Machinery (123,400)
Area Unemployment is 3.8% versus 4.7% nationally.

COMPETITION AND DEMAND

A current survey of apartments in the area of the subject indicated an overall
occupancy of 98% in high-rise buildings. The subject has experienced 98.5% occupancy
or better for the past two (2) years. Another survey by the appraiser indicates
that even with a raise in the rentals, the subject units are still well within the
range of the competition. This is also true of the monthly charge for indoor and
outdoor parking spaces. The location, easy accessibility to downtown and shopping,
and its amenities should assure its continued popularity in the rental market. Only
one new apartment building with 84 apartments is under construction at this time.

APPLICANT

Mr. (Name) and Mr. (Name) are experienced apartment developers and managers. They
presently own and manage 1837 units with 97.5% occupancy. They have been involved
in real estate, and particularly apartment development since 1959. Combined net
worth of the principals is $1,508,075.

CONDITIONS

1. Subject to our Counsel's approval of title and all legal
documentation.
2. In addition to the commitment fee, Company to receive
$18,000 to be returned when loan closes.

APPLICATION
RECEIVED   July 25, 1973
SOURCE   (Name of correspondent)
BRANCH OFFICE (Name of branch office)

APPROVED 8/3/73

Definitions of Abbreviations:
GM - gross multiplier
CAP - capitalization rate

DCR - debt coverage ratio
SMSA - standard metropolitan
statistical area

ANALYSIS: CASE STUDY 10—HIGH-RISE APARTMENT BUILDING

As an example of an investment, this is near perfect. It emphasizes the requirements which an investor seeks from a loan submission prepared by his correspondent. Of particular interest is Exhibit E at the very conclusion of the case study. This very effectively illustrates all of the information which the investor requires when presenting a loan for the approval of the investment committee. This should provide a good checklist for the correspondent.

As pointed out, this is an excellent model which could be used with any lender.

Case Study 11

Downtown Office Building

John M. Hart

Mr. John Jones
Vice President
Mortgage and Real Estate Department
Large Life Insurance Company
Eastern City, U.S.A.

                              Re: Proposed Office Building
                                  Center City Complex
                                  10th Street
                                  Monument Builders, Inc.
                                  Southwest Metropolis City
                                  Southwest, U.S.A.

Dear John:

We are enclosing appraisal on Monument's proposed 32-story building
which includes a survey of major downtown office buildings, rates of
absorption downtown over a ten-year period, and the history of the
Center City Complex.

There is only one significant downtown building now under construction
which will come on stream in October of this year in our market area.
It is Monument Builders, Inc.'s other Center City Complex building which
is essentially a duplicate of the proposed project. Monument Builders, Inc.
has already leased to others approximately 80,000 square feet (25%) in
this building with first occupancy scheduled for October. The Forth
Street building is now about 90% occupied and United Bank Building is
virtually 100%. Therefore, starting a new downtown office building
seems to be a reasonable prospect.

An office building deal of this size in the current market in our area
will not allow for a participation and we, therefore, recommend a loan
of $20,000,000, 8¼%, fully amortized 35 years. There would be a 15%
holdback with full payout at 85% occupancy. Several New York banks
would provide construction money at prime plus 1½. Our local bank
would provide it at prime plus 2½.

Best regards.

Very truly yours,

A N A L Y S I S

Location:	Center City Complex Southwest Metropolis City
Size of Land:	34,000 square feet
Proposed Improvements:	A 32-story office building of pre-cast concrete and structural steel construction containing 349,000 square feet NRA office area, 52,000 square feet NRA retail area and 230 inside parking spaces.
Physical Valuation:	$26,700,000
Economic Valuation:	$26,700,000
Fair Market Value:	$26,700,000
Loan Recommended:	$20,000,000
Interest Rate:	8-1/4%
Term:	35 years
Annual Constant:	8.75
Loan to Value:	75%
Loan Per Sq. Ft.:	$31.64 Gross Area
Annual Debt Service	$1,750,000
Net Income:	$2,438,000
Cash Flow:	$ 688,000

SOUTHWEST METROPOLIS CITY

Southwest Metropolis City, the commercial capitol of the region, encompasses a 3-county metropolitan area of 2,100 square miles and ranked 20th in population and retail sales, 21st in effective buying income and 3rd in economic growth rate in the nation in 1973. This 3-county Southwest Metropolis City Standard Metropolitan Statistical Area (SMSA) as of April 1, 1973 contained an estimated 1,200,000 persons, an average annual increase of 32,000 persons since the 1970 Census Count.

Southwest Metropolis City ties in 4 legs of two major interstates and the perimeter highway which was completed in 1971. The city is served by three railroad lines of two systems. The Southwest Metropolis City International Airport ranked as the fifth busiest airport in the nation in 1972 in passenger enplanements handling in excess of 13 million passengers, up two million from 1970. ·The airport is served by seven major passenger carriers, nine air freight carriers and two local passenger services. Freight and passenger carriers moved 316,000 tons of freight and 229,000 tons of mail through airport facilities during 1972.

As of 1972, 9,422 businesses have operations in Southwest Metropolis City and of Fortune Magazine's 500 Top Industrial Firms 405 operate in Southwest Metropolis City. National concerns continue to locate here because of Southwest Metropolis City's strategic location in relation to major southwest and western cities. In addition, Southwest Metropolis City offers an excellent labor supply with a civilian work force of 580,000 in 1971, tax structure, dry climate and land for future expansion.

Retail sales for the Southwest Metropolis City SMSA for 1972 were $2,900,000,000 with an effective buying income of $14,100 per family and a per capita effective buying income of $4,600.

The city's growth rate may be attributed to the quality of local government and its cooperation with private industry for planned expansion as well as its excellent geographic location, magnificent dry climate, abundant natural resources, and recreational amenities.

DEVELOPER

The property will be developed by Monument Builders, Inc. whose Major developments are as follows:

Center City Complex Western Hotel - a 900-room hotel in Center City Complex developed by Monument Builders, Inc.

Center City Complex Office Buildings - Four office towers containing 1,800,000 square foot NRA. The Buildings were developed by Monument Builders, Inc. A fifth building is under construction.

A 850,000 square foot G.L.A. shopping center on 2 levels and including two major fashion department stores which are part of this complex.

Monument Builders, Inc. includes a competent organization of entrepreneurs construction men, engineers, architects, leasing people, and office building managers.

CENTER CITY COMPLEX

Center City Complex began in 1964 with the opening of the 170,000 square foot Center City Complex I Office Building.

Existing Buildings	Area
Center City Complex 1	170,000 sq. ft.
Center City Complex 2	159,000 sq. ft.
Center City Complex 3	200,000 sq. ft.
Center City Complex 4	307,000 sq. ft.

Buildings Under Construction	Area
Center City Complex 5	408,000 sq. ft.
Shopping Complex	850,000 sq. ft.

Proposed Building

Center City Complex 6 (Subject)	349,000 sq. ft.

At present there is 836,000 square feet of completed office space with the current occupancy being 96%. The following table summarizes the rental rates including office and retail on each building.

Building	Rate Achieved During First Year of Occupancy	Current Rate	Average Rate As of 1/1/73
Center City Complex - 6	$8.50	---	---
Center City Complex - 5	7.80 (projected)	$7.60 Low Rise	$7.85
		7.90 High Rise	
Center City Complex - 1	5.50	7.00	6.16
Center City Complex - 2	4.75	7.00	5.60
Center City Complex - 3	3.50	6.50	5.05
Center City Complex - 4	6.75	7.50	7.10

The Center City Complex-5 building will be ready for occupancy in the fall of this year. As of December 1, 1973 they have signed leases for 70,000 square feet and an additional 40,000 square feet is in the final stages of negotiation, bringing the total to 110,000 square feet.

Center City Complex has leased approximately 840,000 square feet over an 8 year period for an annual rate of absorption of 105,000 square feet and the rental rate has increased from $3.50 per square foot to $7.85 per square foot. Their absorption rate would represent about 30% of the downtown office market (seven major downtown buildings).

MAJOR OFFICE BUILDINGS CONSTRUCTED SINCE 1965

Name and Address of Building	Gross Square Footage
A Building 3068 1st Street	100,000
B Building 3074 1st Street	100,000
C Building 2080 Main Street	79,000
D Building 2 Broad Street	90,000
E Building 10 Broad Street	64,000
F Building 9 Broad Street	57,000
G Building 710 9th Street	260,000
H Building 680 9th Street	80,000
I Building 555 9th Street	160,000
J Building 650 9th Street	158,000
K Building 810 9th Street	340,000
L Building 410 9th Street	300,000
Center City Complex 1 Building 900 10th Street	170,000
M Building 710 10th Street	200,000
Center City Complex 2 Building 915 10th Street	159,000
N Building 440 9th Street	707,360

Name and Address of Building	Gross Square Footage
O Building 460 9th Street	190,000
P Building 1100 10th Street	127,500
Q Building 1500 10th Street	1,055,000
R Building 750 Main Street	132,550
Center City Complex 3 Building 650 Main Street	200,000
Center City Complex 4 Building 918 10th Street	306,726
S Building 300 Main Street	350,000
Center City Complex 5 Building 680 Main Street	408,000
T Building 4000 Johnson Road	655,426
U Building 5100 Johnson Road	300,000
V Building 720 9th Street	344,000
W Building 900 9th Street	500,000
Z Building 944 9th Street	344,000
AA Building 1 Olive Street	350,000
BB Building 12 Olive Street	351,000
CC Building 40 Olive Street	248,200
DD Building 400 10th Street	500,000
EE Building 450 10th Street	220,000
FF Building 550 10th Street	489,554

Assuming 85% efficiency and 90% occupancy in these office buildings, Southwest Metropolis City's average annual rate of absorption since 1965 has been 1,200,000 square feet per year.

MAJOR DOWNTOWN OFFICE BUILDINGS

Property	Area	Occupancy	Current Rate/sq. Ft.
Q Building	1,055,000 sq. ft.	99%	$6.75-$7.25
DD Building	550,000 sq. ft.	100%	$8.35
N Building	650,000 sq. ft.	95%	$6.25-$7.25
P Building	950,000 sq. ft.	96%	$7.50-$8.25
K Building	240,000 sq. ft.	99%	$7.50-$8.25

During 1972 800,000 square feet was leased in 28 suburban office parks and 400,000 square feet was leased in the seven major downtown office developments. Suburban rents on the north side are $6.25 per square foot for first class office space and range from $6.25 per square foot to $8.25 per square foot for the first class downtown office space. A survey conducted in October, 1972 by Building Owners and Managers showed that the occupancy in all downtown office buildings was 90% up 2% from May, 1972. The Center City Complex - 6 Building is the only major office building now under construction in downtown Southwest Metropolis City. Office leasing agents report that inquiries have increased in recent months and prospects for a strong office leasing market are excellent for the coming year.

<u>VALUATION OF FEE INTEREST</u>

Subject site contains 34,000 square feet and is entirely owned and controlled by Monument Builders, Inc.

The current market value of similar properties located in the area is 50 dollars per square foot.

We believe the current fair market value of the property to be $1,700,000.*

* Assume that this value is supported by a list of land sales of similar parcels over a 5-year period ranging from $35.00/sq. ft. 5 years ago to $57.00/sq. ft. this year.

APPRAISAL CERTIFICATE

Location:	Center City Complex Southwest Metropolis City
Land:	34,000 square feet
Improvements:	A 32-story office building of precast concrete and structural steel construction containing 349,000 square feet NRA office area, 52,000 square feet NRA retail area and 230 inside parking spaces.
Valuation:	Fee $ 1,700,000 Improvements 25,000,000 Total $26,700,000
General:	Subject will be the sixth office building in Center City Complex bringing the total office space to 2,093,000 square feet. At present there is 840,000 square feet NRA completed and 408,000 square feet NRA undercon-struction in the Center City Complex-5, which is the only major office building under construction in down-town.

INCOME AND EXPENSE STATEMENT

Location: Center City Complex - 6
                      Southwest Metropolis City

Income: Office - 349,000 sq. ft. @ $8.50/sq. ft. $2,966,500
                      Retail - 52,000 sq. ft. @ $12.00/sq. ft.   624,000
                      Parking - 230 spaces @ $30.00 /month   82,800
                              Total $3,673,300

                      Less 7.5% Vacancy Allowance   275,500
                      Gross Stabilized Income $3,397,800

Expenses: Taxes(1) $350,000
                      Insurance   15,000
                      Leasing & Management (5%)   170,000
                      Cleaning(2)   160,000
                      Repairs & Maintenance   30,000
                      Painting & Decorating   10,000
                      Elevator Contract   20,000
                      Heating & Air Conditioning (2)   130,000
                      Water   10,000
                      Lights & Power   15,000
                      Other   15,000
                                              $ 925,000

Net Income: $2,472,800

Debt Service: $20,000,000, 8-1/4%, 35 years   1,750,000
                    (8.75 constant)

Cash Flow: $ 722,800

(1)   Assume a series of tax comparables on similar buildings support
      this figure.

(2)   Retail leases are net of Cleaning and HVAC.

PHYSICAL VALUATION

Location: Center City Complex - 6
                       Southwest Metropolis City

Land: Fee $1,700,000

Building: A 32-story office building of pre-cast
                       construction containing 660,000 square
                       feet Gross Area at $29.00 per square
                       foot   19,140,000

                       Interest during construction,
                       architectural fees, taxes, legal
                       fees, financing and miscellaneous
                       charges   5,860,000
Physical Value: $26,700,000
                       The net income of $2,472,800 capitalized
                       at 9.25% indicates an Economic Value of
                       $26,700,000.

                       From the foregoing, the Fair Market
                       Value of the property upon completion
                       according to plans and specifications
                       will be $26,700,000.

EXPENSES ANALYSIS

Taxes: We based our tax estimate of $350,000 on the comparables
                                shown herein. The estimate is adjusted for 1974 completion.

Insurance: Three prominent insurance brokers estimate the premium
                                to be $15,000.

Leasing &
Management: 5% is typical for comparable office buildings in downtown.

Cleaning: Maintenance contracts are running $0.37 per square foot
                                for office buildings.

Repairs &
Maintenance: These expenses average $0.05-$0.06 per square foot on
                                high rise buildings.

Painting &
Decorating: These expenses average $0.02-$0.03 per square foot.

Elevator Contract: Our estimate of $25,000 (no major parts) is based on
                                discussions with Westinghouse.

Heating &
Air Conditioning: Based on discussions with building managers and the utility
                                companies we have estimated the cost of heating and air
                                conditioning at $0.35 per square foot.

Water: This expense is generally $0.015-$0.02 per square foot.

Lights & Power: Based on discussions with building managers and the utility
                                companies we have estimated this expense to be approxi-
                                mately $0.025 per square foot.

Other: Estimated to be $0.03 per square foot.

The expenses on this building are estimated to be $2.45 per square foot. The
expenses in the suburban office parks range from $1.70 per square foot to $1.80
per square foot and on downtown buildings from $1.90 per square foot to $2.20
per square foot. We feel the estimate for subject of $2.45 go be adequate to
cover any increase in expenses.

<u>OUTLINE OF BUILDING SPECIFICATIONS</u>

<u>Frame</u>:	Structural steel
<u>Exterior Walls</u>:	Precast concrete
<u>Windows</u>:	1/4" bronze glass in neoprene gaskets
<u>Roof</u>:	Flat built-up
Heating and <u>Air Conditioning</u>:	Carrier or equal double duct system with multiple zones
<u>Floors</u>:	Marble in lobby. Concrete on other floors with carpet covering
<u>Interior Walls</u>:	Gypsum board with vinyl covering
<u>Ceiling</u>:	Suspended acoustical lay-in tile with flush fluorescent
<u>Elevators</u>:	Eight - including three low rise 3,000 pound capacity speed 500 feet per minute, four high r 3,000 pound capacity 700 feet per minute and one service elevator 3,000 pound capacity speed 700 feet per minute. Westinghouse. Low rise elevators service through 16th floor. There are two elevators serving the parking levels.

Underwriting Guidelines
Downtown Office Buildings

1. BACKGROUND ON CITY AND AREA

   a. Economic base and strength - What makes the area tick, is it heavily
      dependent on few large employers, is it service oriented or
      manufacturing oriented, what is its geographical location relative
      to its region. Try to get a feel for its futures.

   b. Growth Statistics - over past 10 years and recent trends. Include
      population, bank deposits, retail sales, per capita income.

   c. Growth areas - where is population growth, where is wealth housed
      manufacturing or industrial areas, black areas, blue collar areas,
      major employers, arterial system and its impact - overall, get a
      handle on the layout of the city, where it seems to be heading and why.

2. DOWNTOWN

   a. Who is downtown - financial, insurance, Fortune 500, etc.
   b. What is happening downtown - what projects are planned, what is in
      the offing, who owns what land and what are their plans - any recent
      projects - how successful.
   c. Downtown traffic - patterns, bottlenecks, major arteries.
   d. Rapid transit possibilities - timing, layout, potential impact.
   e. Where is growth heading downtown and who is leading it.
   f. Significance of new space in pioneering locations - keep in mind who
      is involved. Is a heavyweight developer likely to start a trend in
      a new direction.
   g. Redevelopment possibilities.
   h. Strength of civic leadership, past performance.

3. CONCEPT

   a. New or established - in terms of type of product, design, market
      appeal, etc.
   b. Within scope of previous development in the area.
   c. Identify what you are dealing with and place it in framework of what
      is already there.

4. LOCATION

   a. In growth pattern; futures, established or obsolete location - is there
      action in the area.
   b. Address prestigious.
   c. Street and traffic pattern around site.
   d. Interior site or corner site - visual prominence.
   e. Relationship to established financial area.
   f. Proximity to good retail and hotel facilities and public parking facilities.
      How about the convenience to rapid transit if appropriate.
   g. Views

5. PRODUCT

    a. Plans and specs - looking for non-technical quality indicators i.e., lobby and corridor finish, standard door finish, reflected ceiling plan, bathroom finish, exterior finish and appearance.
    b. Sufficient elevators - number, speed; elevators/sq.ft.GLA.
    c. Floor plan - bay sizes, depth of space, corridor layout - oriented to large or small users - floor size is an indicator here. - NRA - how calculated - efficiency. Floor load.
    d. Retail layout versus pedestrian traffic flow.
    e. Standard tenant finish.

6. PARKING

    a. Number of spaces in building and ratio to NRA.
    b. Other spaces controlled by borrower and subject to our lien - are they convenient.
    c. Are these arrangements competitive - are they priced competitively.
    d. Available municipal parking.
    e. Does the city plan to go into the parking business in a big way - are they competitive to project.
    f. Are spaces large enough - is it uncomfortably tight - how is the flow.
    g. Any transient spaces planned - can people get in and out easily.
    h. Elevator access from parking to office area.

7. DEVELOPMENT TEAM

    a. Developer - experience in product and in area; financial strength, cash or real estate assets; other active deals or plans for new ventures, over-extension; what are his strong suits; does he have an adequate staff, age; does he have leasing and management capabilities; is he respected by area brokers and leasing men.
    b. Leasing and management - is this an experienced arm of the company; will it be a third party and will they be hustling competitive buildings; do th have an established clientele.
    c. Architect - experience and industry reputation - do they design good competitive buildings or monuments - role in the development and construction stages.

8. MARKET DEMAND

    a. Absorption study of new downtown space
        1. Over past 10 years and recent trend per year basis.
        2. Divide between major user space versus spec.
        3. Outsiders coming in and/or expansion from within.
        4. Based on what's happened, does what is planned seem realistic.
        5. Is there any movement from suburbs to downtown or is it vice versa.

9. ECONOMICS

    a. Rents

        1. Office Space - How is rentable area calculated - whole floor or multi-tenant basis - what areas included in rent - is this practice standard-BOMA? Check rents on comparable buildings through correspondent, our own experience, operating statements, lease renewals, etc. - are leases stopped - usual term. What is included in rent i.e., typical tenant finish allowance - are the rents today's rents or definitely futures.

2. Retail – check comparables – also determine what sales volumes tenants must do to justify the rents – how about traffic – is there enough to generate those sales – consider building population.

3. Parking – all monthly – if so check comparables – if some transient problem becomes complicated; check supporting data for transient income – turnover, rent/space/hour, average stay, etc.

b. OE&T (Operating Expenses and Rates)

1. If office, retail and parking income involved, must analyze each separately – follow same info gathering procedure for comps.
2. Compare on per square foot basis and as a percentage of stabilized income.
3. Have you allowed for inflationary gains between now and building opening.
4. What has OE&T done over the past few years.
5. Who pays the increases. Are OE&T stopped in the lease.
6. Analyze each component. Is the basis for this realistic.

c. NIBD (Net Income Before Debt Service)

1. Capatilize at market rate to determine value.
2. What is NIBD/cost.
3. What is cash flow to developer after annual debt service.
4. What is cash flow/equity.

10. COST

a. Is property worth more than it costs – has the developer created value above his cost.
b. How does total cost compare with other competitive buildings.
c. What is the cost breakdown. What are the actual out-of-pocket costs – Are profits to the developer included.
d. Based on market analysis and likely absorption of the space, is the operating deficit figure sufficient.
e. What is the tenant finish allowance – given the future leasing market, is this figure realistic.
f. Break costs down into their components.
g. What are the exposures on cost – Is contract a fixed price quote – are operating deficits the only exposure.

ANSWERS TO QUESTIONS IN
DOWNTOWN OFFICE BUILDING CASE STUDY

<u>Possible Answers</u>

It should be understood and appreciated that in the analysis, appraisal, and financing of real estate there probably are not exactly right answers and that final conclusions will ultimately depend on the project, the principals involved, and the market conditions at the time. Therefore, these answers should really be viewed as guidelines.

1. It would appear, given the assumptions stated in the case study, that this mortgage banker has done a very good job of (a) giving support to his recommendation, (b) he has supported the investment made, (c) he has answered generally most of the questions raised by the guidelines. However, there is one apparent weakness in his presentation. He has not really dealt with a careful analysis of the design and layout of the rentable area in relationship to his market; i.e., is this building really designed for large space users or small tenants. How much waste is there if a floor has to be subdivided many times, or are the floors really large enough to make an attractive deal to a major space user without forcing him to spread his operation inefficiently over a series of floors. Demand is not merely a function of space; it is clearly also a function of various types of space and efficient use of the space for particular types of markets. This presentation is basically silent on this subject. It also does not deal directly with the pluses and minuses of the convenience of location vs. the intangible of "prestige space." One further point would be that there could have been much greater emphasis on the future trends for the community and area as they might positively affect the subject property dealing with such things as municipal parking and direct competition, is the city evolving into a major regional distri- bution center where large corporations must have major offices, etc.

2. The ultimate test of how the lender could have made such a deal when the request was so different is that it was accepted by the borrower under open market conditions where the borrower had the choice of making the deal with others. Apparently in this situation the lender was able to be better compensated through his participation in gross income and met his needs to hedge against inflation and receive higher potential yields and because of the extra funds provided this was worthwhile for the developer, because he did not have to give up a meaningful portion of the ownership to draw in equity investors.

3. By the sheer fact that the deal was made, as is pointed out in #2, it appears that this was at the time a good deal for both developer and lender for basically the reasons outlined in #2. The lender was apparently willing to provide the extra dollars to achieve a greater yield on the greater risk for these extra dollars and the developer was assured of the funds needed to develop his building and carry it through the leasing period.

4. To answer this question properly you would simply have analyzed the rental structure, the cost structure, and the money markets at your present time to determine whether the appropriate adjustments would still indicate that the project should go ahead. You would have to carefully analyze that there was a sufficient return to the developer to justify taking the major risk involved in developing such a project.

5. Since there are a myriad of ways to structure any deal, you would
   simply have to apply the compounding inflation rate assumptions to
   your situation at the time and see first if the deal makes sense
   at that basis and then, with the economics of the money market, allow
   it would be viable after dealing with the cost of capital. Perhaps it
   might need structuring more as a joint venture because of the apparent
   increasing capital demands and higher costs of money where the lender
   could be a source of real equity money and participate in the risk and
   hopefully higher returns by putting money in as an equity partner rather
   than through a fixed obligation debt instrument.

6. There do not appear to be obvious major errors in this presentation
   but perhaps, as mentioned in #1, there are some errors of omission
   rather than commission. The greater the scope and contribution and the
   greater the depth of the analysis by the mortgage banker, theoretically,
   the greater assistance he can be to both the developer and his lender
   and therefore the greater his worth to both partners, and then, hopefully,
   the greater the source of his own earnings. The more professional he
   becomes, the more the developer will seek him out as a consultant and
   arranger of financing and also the more credence the lender will put on
   his recommendations and, theoretically, his percentage of deals made in
   relation to number of deals worked on will greatly increase and,
   therefore, his time will be far more productive to him.

Center City Complex-6 Office Building

Payout Date	2 years in future	
City—	S/W Metropolis City	
State	S/W State	
Land	.68 Acres	34,000 Sq. Ft.

Location: North east corner of 9th and Powell Streets in the most prominent corner of the Center City Complex in downtown Southwest Metropolitan City. Site adjoins the retail complex and the site of a future 1,100 room convention hotel.

Improvements: A 32-story office building with 3 levels of retail at grade and below. Steel frame construction with precast concrete and solar bronze glass exterior. A highly energy efficient building of quality construction. Excellent modules and layouts for large users.

Parking: 230 garage spaces with security plus 4,000 spaces in public garages and surfaces lots with a 6 block radius.

Year Built	x Proposed
No. Stories	32
No. Elevators	8
Basement Area	110,000
Office Area	340,000
Retail Area	52,000
Total Gross Area	660,000
Total Rentable Area	392,000
% Efficiency /x Garage	72%
GARAGE AREA	110,000
RENTABLE/FLOOR	

Economic Valuation / Amount

Amount:	$20,000,000 1st Mortgage
	2,000,000 2nd Mortgage
	$22,000,000 Total Loan
Term: 32 Years	**Interest Rate:** *8.250% 0 months 9.110% constant

Method of Repayment: Combined annual debt service of $2,004,200 with all principal payments applied to 2nd mortgage until paid in full.

Prepayment Option: Closed for 12 years. Open in 13th year at 105 declining 1/2 of 1% per year to 101.

Purpose: To provide 100% of out of pocket cost. Developer will leave in all their fees and services

Physical Valuation

Land @ 2,500,000/ acre or 50.00 Sq. Ft.	1,700,000
Bldg. @ 37.80 /Sq. Ft.	25,000,000
Total Physical Value	26,700,000
Value for Mortgage Purposes	26,700,000
Correspondent's Final Valuation	26,700,000
Correspondent's Land Allocation	1,700,000

GARAGE AREA		0
	Cash Equity $	

Mortgagor's Investment:
Land (1970)	400,000
Improvements	16,400,000
Fees	5,200,000
Total Cost	22,000,000

ECONOMIC VALUATION

By Home Office Staff		
Office Income	$8.50 /Sq. Ft. RA	$2,966,500
Parking Income	30.00 /Space/Month	82,800
	12.00 /Sq. Ft. RA	624,000
Gross Income	9.36 /Sq. Ft. RA	3,673,300
Less 7.5 % Vacancy		275,500
Stabilized Income	8.66 /Sq. Ft. RA	3,397,800
Operating Expenses	1.48 /Sq. Ft. RA 16.9 % Stab. Inc.	575,000
Real Estate Taxes	.89 /Sq. Ft. RA 10.3 % Stab. Inc.	350,000
Total OE&T	2.35 /Sq. Ft. RA 27.2 % Stab. Inc.	925,000
Net Income Before Deprec.	Capitalized @ 9.25% = $26,700,000	2,472,800
ANNUAL DEBT Service		2,004,200
Cash Flow to Equity		468,600

Mortgagor: Monument Builders, Inc. - A major commercial developer with a fully intergrated quality staff. (All principal individuals have ownership). Market value of real estate equities $22,000,000.

Cash flow $2,600,000. They have developed the entire Center City Complex of 5 other office buildings and the intown regional shopping center.

Rental Requirement: Floor loan of $19,000,000. Balance disbursed as follows:

	Office Rent	Retail Rent	Garage Rent	Amount
% Occup.				
85%	$ 8.25	$11.50	$25.00	$20,000,000
90%	8.50	12.00	30.00	22,000,000

Default Point 79.6 % of Gross Income Covers OE, T and Debt Serv. of $ 2,929,200

Summary: *Additional interest of 20% of gross income above $3,250,000.

Value/Sq. Ft. RA	$68.25
OE&T Sq. Ft. GA	$ 1.40
Debt Serv. Coverage	1.23x
DP/Sq. Ft. RA	$ 7.45
Value/Gross Inc.	7.28x
Value/Net Inc. BD	10.80x
Loan/Gross Inc.	6.0x
Loan/Net Inc. BD	8.9x
Loan/Sq. Ft. GA	$33.40
Loan/Sq. Ft. RA	$56.20
Loan/Value	82.5%

B3599 Rev. 6-72

ANALYSIS: CASE STUDY 11—DOWNTOWN
OFFICE BUILDING

This material offers an example of a full presentation from a mortgage banker to a large lender, a set of underwriting guidelines used by the lender, and an investment analysis form reflecting the investment made by the lender and accepted by the developer. Points that should be considered are:

    1 Does the mortgage banker's presentation, assuming it included financial statements, plans and specifications, aerial photographs, etc., give all the necessary information to:
        a Support the recommendation?
        b Support the investment made?
        c Answer the questions raised by the guidelines?
    2 How could the lender make the deal when the request was so different?
    3 Assuming the market at the time was 8 to 8.5% for good quality 75 percent loans, is this a good deal for the developer; for the lender; for both?
    4 In your current money market, would this deal make sense?
    5 If you assume a 5% inflationary increase in rents and expenses, how would you otherwise structure this loan?
    6 Are there any obvious errors in the mortgage banker's or lender's analysis?

Glossary

Acceleration clause A common provision of a mortgage and note providing that the entire principal shall become immediately due and payable in the event of default. Without this clause, the mortgagee may have to file separate foreclosure suits as each installment of the mortgage debt falls due and is in default.

Advance In real estate, a partial disbursement of funds under a note. Most often used in connection with construction lending.

Advance commitment (conditional) A written promise to make an investment at some time in the future if specified conditions are met.

Alienation clause A special type of acceleration clause that demands payment of the entire loan balance upon sale or other transfer of the title.

ALTA American Land Title Association. A national association of title insurance companies, abstractors, and attorneys, specializing in real property law. The association speaks for the title insurance and abstracting industry and establishes standard procedures and title policy forms.

Amenity As aspect of a property that enhances its value. Off-street reserved parking within a condominium community, the nearness of good public transportation, tennis courts, or a swimming pool are examples.

Amortization Gradual debt reduction. Normally, the reduction is made according to a predetermined schedule for installment payments.

Appraisal A report setting forth an opinion or estimate of value. The process by which this estimate is obtained.

Appraised value An opinion of value reached by an appraiser based upon knowledge, experience, and a study of pertinent data.

Appraiser One qualified by education, training, and experience to estimate the value of real and personal property. The estimate is based on a process in which the appraiser judges the facts discovered in an investigation of the property.

Appreciation An increase in value, the opposite of depreciation.

Architect's inspection certificate A document, usually issued by an independent architect, verifying that a certain portion of construction on a project has been completed in accordance with approved plans and specifications. This document is often required by construction lenders when advances of funds are to be made at specific stages of construction. Also known as an architect's progress certificate.

Assessment The value placed on property for the strict purpose of taxation. May also refer to a levy against property for a special purpose, such as a sewer assessment.

Assignment The transfer of a right or contract from one person to another.

Assignment of leases The absolute or conditional transfer of the rights of either party to a lease.

Assignment of mortgage A document that evidences a transfer of ownership of a mortgage from one party to another.

Assignment of rents An agreement signed between the property owner and mortgagee specifically fixing the rights and obligations of each under a lease affecting the property.

Average (rate of return) The return on an investment calculated by averaging the total cash flow over the years during which the cash flow is received by the investor.

Base rent The minimum fixed guaranteed rent in a commercial property lease.

Basis point One one-hundredth of one percent. Used to describe the amount of change in yield in many debt instruments, including mortgages.

Basket provision A provision contained in the regulatory acts governing the investments of insurance companies, savings and loan associations, and mutual savings banks. It allows for a certain small percentage of total assets to be placed in investments not otherwise permitted by the regulatory acts.

Break-even point In residential or commercial property, the figure at which occupancy income is equal to all required expenses and debt service.

Builder/sponsor profit and risk allowance (BSPRA) The developer's remuneration for assuming the risks involved in building government-assisted low-income rental housing. It is regulated by the government.

Builder's risk insurance Fire and extended coverage insurance for a building under construction. Coverage increases automatically as the building progresses and terminates at completion. Such a policy should be replaced by permanent insurance when the building is ready for occupancy.

Building code The local regulations that control design, construction, and materials used in construction. Building codes are based on safety and health standards.

Building efficiency A percentage ratio of net rentable area to gross building area.

Buy-sell agreement An agreement entered into by an interim and a permanent lender for the sale and assignment of the mortgage to the permanent lender when a building has been completed.

Capital The money and/or property comprising the wealth owned or used by a person or business enterprise. The accumulated wealth of a person or business. The net worth of a business represented by the amount that its assets exceed liabilities.

Capitalization The process of converting into present value a series of anticipated future installments of net income, by discounting them into a present worth using a specific desired rate of earnings.

Capitalization (as applied to appraisal) The process of ascertaining the magnitude, worth, or value of a capital good through the use of a rate that is believed to represent the proper relationship between that capital good or property and the net income it produces.

Capitalization rate The rate which is believed to represent the proper relationship between real property and the net income it produces.

Carrying charges Costs incurred by a developer or builder. Principally, interest on land and construction loans and property taxes to cover expenses until the point of sale.

Cash flow The spendable income from an investment after subtracting from gross income all operating expenses, loan payments, and the allowance for the income tax attributed to the income. The amount of cash derived over a certain measured period of time from the operation of income-producing property after debt services and operating expenses, but *before* depreciation and income taxes.

Cash-on-cash return The rate of return on an investment measured by the cash returned to the investor based on the investor's cash investment without regard to income tax savings or the use of borrowed funds.

Certificate of occupancy Written authorization given by a local municipality that allows a newly completed or substantially completed structure to be inhabited.

Closing The conclusion or consummation of a transaction. In real estate, closing includes the delivery of a deed, financial adjustments, the signing of notes, and the disbursement of funds necessary to the sale or loan transaction.

Commitment An agreement, often in writing, between a lender and a borrower to loan money at a future date subject to compliance with stated conditions.

Commitment (builder) An agreement by a lender to provide long-term financing to a builder, secured by an existing or proposed building. The commitment usually provides for the substitution of a to-be-approved owner-occupant at a higher loan amount than committed to the builder.

Commitment fee Any fee paid by a potential borrower to a potential lender for the lender's promise to lend money at a specified date in the future. The lender may or may not expect to fund the commitment.

Common areas Land or improvements for the benefit of all tenants and property owners. Shopping center parking lots and residential parks and playgrounds are generally common areas. All the space within a development can be used by all the tenants in that development.

Comparables An abbreviation for comparable properties used for comparative purposes in the appraisal process. Facilities of reasonably the same size and location with similar amenities. Properties which have been recently sold, which have characteristics similar to property under consideration, thereby indicating the approximate fair market value of the subject property.

Completion bond A bond furnished by a contractor to guarantee completion of construction.

Compliance inspection report A report given to a lender by a designated compliance inspector indicating whether or not construction or repairs have complied to conditions established by a prior inspection.

Constant The percentage of the original loan paid in equal annual payments that provide for interest and principal reduction over the life of the loan.

Construction contract An agreement between a general contractor and an owner-developer stating the specific duties the general contractor will perform according to blueprints and specifications at a stipulated price and terms of payment.

Construction costs Broadly, all costs incurred in bringing a building to completion, not including land acquisition costs, nor finance and sales costs.

Construction loan A short-term interim loan for financing the cost of construction. The lender makes payments to the builder at periodic intervals as the work progresses.

Construction loan agreement A written agreement between lender and a builder and/or borrower in which the specific terms and conditions of a construction loan, including the schedule of payments, are spelled out.

Construction loan draw The partial disbursement of the construction loan, based on the schedule of payments in the loan agreement. Also called takedown.

Contract rent Actual rent as called for in a rental or lease agreement without regard to estimated rental value in the open market.

Correspondent A morgage banker who services mortgage loans as a representative or agent for the owner of the mortgage or investor. Also applies to the mortgage banker's role as originator of mortgage loans for an investor.

Cost approach to value A method in which the value of a property is derived by estimating the replacement cost of the improvement, deducting therefrom the estimated depreciation, then adding the value of the land as estimated by use of the market data approach. Also called physical indication of value.

Cost certification A condition often placed in the contract requiring a certification of cost by the architect, contractor, or owners; must sometimes be audited by a third party.

Cost overrun The amount of money required or expended over and above budgeted costs, including such items as labor, interest, materials, and land.

Cost-plus contract A construction contract in which the contract price is equal to the cost of construction plus a profit allowance to the builder; as opposed to a fixed price contract.

Coupon rate The annual interest rate on a debt instrument. More generally, the annual interest rate on any indebtedness. In mortgage banking, the term is used to describe the contract interest rate on the face of the note or bond.

Covenant A legally enforceable promise or restriction in a mortgage. For example, the borrower may covenant to keep the property in good repair and adequately insured against fire and other casualties. The breach of a covenant in a mortgage usually creates a default as defined by the mortgage and can be the basis for foreclosure.

Debt-coverage ratio The ratio of effective annual net income to annual debt service.

Debt service The periodic payment of principal and interest earned on mortgage loans.

Deed restriction A limitation placed in a deed limiting or restricting the use of the real property.

Default A breach or nonperformance of the terms of a note or the covenants of a mortgage.

Default point See break-even point.

Density The ratio between the total land area and the number of residential or commercial structures to be placed upon it. Local ordinances usually regulate density.

Depreciation allowance The accounting charge made to allow for the fact that the asset may become economically obsolete before its physical deterioration. The purpose is to write off the original cost by distributing it over the estimated useful life of the asset. It appears in both the profit-and-loss statement and the balance sheet.

Developer A person or entity who prepares raw land for building sites, and sometimes builds on the sites.

Development loan A loan made for the purpose of preparing raw land for the construction of buildings. Development may include grading and installation of utilities and roadways.

Disbursements   The payment of monies on a previously agreed-to basis. Used to describe construction loan draws.

Easement   Right or interest in the land of another entitling the holder to a specific limited use, privilege, or benefit such as laying a sewer, putting up electric power lines, or crossing the property.

Economic rent   The rent that a property would bring if offered in the open market, the fair rental value. Not necessarily the contract rent.

Economic value   The valuation of real property based on its earning capabilities.

Effective gross income (property)   Stabilized income that a property is expected to generate after a vacancy allowance.

Egress   To go out. It is used with the word ingress to describe the right of access to land.

Encumbrance   Anything that affects or limits the fee simple title to property, such as mortgages, leases, easements, or restrictions.

Environmental impact statement (EIS)   A statement required by many federal, state, and local environmental and land use laws. It contains an analysis of the impact that a proposed change may have on the environment of a specific geographic region. It examines a wide variety of physical, social, and economic conditions that would be affected by the proposed development. The analysis covers effects that cannot be avoided, alternatives to the proposed change, short-term vs. long-term uses and long-term productivity, irreversible commitments of resources, and the benefits to be derived.

Equity   In real estate, the difference between fair market value and current indebtedness, usually referring to the owner's interest. It is also the difference between purchase price and the amount financed.

Equity participation   Partial ownership of income property, given by the owner to the lender, as part of the consideration for making the loan.

Escrow agent   The person or organization having a fiduciary responsibility to both the buyer and seller (or lender and borrower) to see that the terms of the purchase/sale (or loan) are carried out.

Exception   In legal descriptions, that portion of land to be deleted or excluded. The term is often used in a different sense to mean an objection to title or encumbrance on title.

Fair market value   The price at which property is transferred between a willing buyer and a willing seller, each of whom has a reasonable knowledge of all pertinent facts and neither being under any compulsion to buy or sell.

Feasibility study   A study or analysis that determines whether a real estate project, proposed or existing, successfully meets desired objectives.

Fiduciary   A person in a position of trust and confidence for another.

Financing package   The total of all financial interest in a project. It may include mortgages, partnerships, joint venture capital interests, stock ownership, or any financial arrangement used to carry a project to completion.

Financing statement   Under the Uniform Commercial Code, a prescribed form filed by a lender with the registrar of deeds, or secretary of state. It gives the name and address of the debtor and the secured party (lender), along with a description of the personal property securing the loan. It may show the amount of indebtedness.

First mortgage   A real estate loan that creates a primary lien against real property.

Fixture   Personal property that becomes real property upon being attached to real estate.

Floor loan A portion or portions of a mortgage loan commitment that is less than the full amount of the commitment. It may be funded upon conditions less stringent than those required for funding the full amount. For example, the floor loan, equal to perhaps 80 percent of the full amount, may be funded upon completion of construction without occupancy requirements, but substantial occupancy of the building may be required for funding the full amount of the loan.

Front-end money Funds required to start a development and generally advanced by the developer or equity owner as a capital contribution to the project.

Future advance Disbursement of funds subsequent to the execution of a mortgage. Obligatory future advances are found in construction loans and normally take preference over another encumbrance which is recorded prior to disbursing the next construction loan advances. Optional future advances are found in open-end mortgages and do not take preference over another encumbrance recorded prior to the disbursement of the advance.

Gap financing An interim loan given to finance the difference between the floor loan and the maximum permanent loan as committed.

General contractor A party that performs or supervises the construction or development of a property pursuant to the terms of a primary contract with the owner. The general contractor may use its own employees for this work and/or the services of other contractors (subcontractors).

Graduated lease A lease providing for a variable rental rate sometimes set forth in the lease, sometimes determined by a reappraisal using a predetermined formula.

Ground rent The earnings of improved property allocated to the ground itself after allowance is made for earnings of the improvement. Also, payment for the use of land in accordance with the terms of a ground lease.

Guaranty A promise by one party to pay a debt or perform an obligation contracted by another in the event that the original obligor fails to pay or perform as contracted.

Hard dollars Cash money given in exchange for an equity position in a transaction for real property.

Highest and best use The available present use or series of future uses that will produce the highest present property value and develop a site to its full economic potential.

Holdback (1) That portion of a loan commitment not funded until some additional requirement such as rental or completion is attained. (See floor loan.) (2) In construction or interim lending, a percentage of the contractor's draw held back to provide additional protection for the interim lender, often an amount equal to the contractor's profit given over when the interim loan is closed.

Income and expense statement The actual or estimated schedule of income and expense items reflecting net gain or loss during a specified period.

Income approach to value The appraisal technique used to estimate real property value by capitalizing net income.

Ingress To go in, to enter. Used with egress, to describe the right of access to land.

Inspection certificate Certification by a correspondent or designated agent that a property has been inspected and is accurately represented in a submission.

Institutional lender   A financial institution that invests in mortgages and carries them in its own portfolio. Mutual savings banks, life insurance companies, commercial banks, pension and trust funds, and savings and loan associations are examples.

Insurable interest   An interest of such a nature that the occurrence of the event insured against would cause financial loss to the insured. Such interests, for example, may be that of an owner, a mortgagee, a lessee, or a trustee.

Interim financing   Financing during the time from project commencement to closing of a permanent loan, usually in the form of a construction loan and/or development loan.

Involuntary lien   A lien imposed against property without consent of an owner. Examples include taxes, special assessments, federal income tax liens, judgment liens, mechanics' liens, and materials liens.

Joint and several note   A note signed by two or more persons, each of whom is liable for the full amount of the debt.

Joint venture   An association between two or more parties to own and/or develop real estate. It may take a variety of legal forms including partnership, tenancy in common, or a corporation. It is formed for a specific purpose and duration.

Kicker   A term describing any benefit to a lender above ordinary interest payments. It may be an equity in a property or a participation in the income stream.

Land loan   A loan for the acquisition of land to be held in anticipation of zoning and until plans are drawn and construction financing can be obtained.

Lease   A written document containing the conditions under which the possession and use of real and/or personal property are given by the owner to another for a stated period and for a stated consideration.

Leasehold   An estate or interest in an estate in real property held by virtue of a lease.

Leasehold mortgage   A loan to a lessee secured by a leasehold interest in a property.

Legal description   A property description recognized by law, which is sufficient to locate an identify the property without oral testimony.

Lessee (tenant)   One holding rights of possession and use of property under terms of a lease.

Lessor (landlord)   One who leases property to a lessee.

Leverage   The use of borrowed money to increase one's return on cash investment. For leverage to be profitable, the rate of return on the investment must be higher than the cost of the money borrowed (interest plus amortization).

Lien   A legal hold or claim of one person on the property of another as security for a debt or charge. The right given by law to satisfy debt.

Limited partnership   A partnership that consists of one or more general partners who are fully liable and one or more limited partners who are liable only for the amount of their investment.

Line of credit   An agreement by a commercial bank or other financial institution to extend credit up to a certain amount for a certain time to a specific borrower.

Loan submission   A package of pertinent papers and documents regarding specific property or properties. It is delivered to a prospective lender for review and consideration for the purpose of making a mortgage loan.

Loan-to-value ratio   The relationship between the amount of the mortgage loan and the appraised value of the security, expressed as a percentage of the appraised value.

Major tenants   A term used in shopping center, office building, and commercial property dealings to describe nationally recognized lessees with high credit standing, the amount of space they occupy, and the percentage of the development's gross rent they pay.

Market rent   The price a tenant pays a landlord for the use and occupancy of real property, based upon current prices for comparable property.

Maturity   The terminating or due date of a note, time draft, acceptance, bill of exchange, or bond. The date a time instrument of indebtedness becomes due and payable.

Mechanics' lien   A lien allowed by statute to contractors, laborers, and suppliers on buildings or other structures upon which work has been performed or for which materials are supplied.

Mortgage portfolio   The aggregate of mortgage loans held by an investor, or serviced by a mortgage banker.

Negative cash flow   Cash expenditures of an income-producing property in excess of the cash receipts.

Net income   The difference between effective gross income (property) and the expenses including taxes and insurance. The term is qualified as net income before depreciation and debt service.

Net lease   A lease calling for the lessee to pay all fixed and variable expenses associated with the property. Also known as a pure net lease, as opposed to a gross lease. The terms *net net* and *net net net* are ill-defined and should be avoided.

Net rentable area   The actual square footage of a building that can be rented. Halls, lobbies, stairways, elevator shafts, maintenance areas and the like are not included.

Net yield   That part of gross yield that remains after the deductions of all costs, such as servicing, and any reserves for losses.

Nondisturbance agreement   An agreement that permits a tenant under a lease to remain in possession despite any foreclosure.

Notice of commencement   A document used in some states and recorded after a construction loan mortgage has been recorded. All mechanics' liens relate back to the date of recording of the notice, thereby enabling the mortgage to remain a first lien, not subordinated to any labor, supplier, or other claim for nonpayment of bills.

Notice of completion   Notice recorded after completion of construction. Mechanics' liens must be filed within a specific period thereafter.

Obsolescence   The loss of value of a property occasioned by going out of style, by becoming less suitable for use, or by other economic influences.

Occupancy rate   The percentage of space or units which are leased or occupied.

Offsite improvements   Improvements outside the boundaries of a property, such as sidewalks, streets, curbs, and gutters, that enhance its value.

Onsite improvements   Any construction of buildings or other improvements within the boundaries of a property that increases its value.

Operating expenses   Generally regarded as all expenses of a property with the exception of real estate taxes, depreciation, interest, and amortization.

Operating ratio   The percentage relationship between budgeted or actual operating expenses, plus taxes, and effective gross income.

Origination fee   A fee or charge for the work involved in the evaluation, preparation, and submission of a proposed mortgage loan.

Overimprovement   An improvement that is not the highest and best use for a site by reason of excess size, cost, or inadequate return.

Parking index   A standard comparison used to indicate the relationship between the number of parking spaces to the gross leasable area or the number of leasable units.

Participation loan (1) A mortgage made by one lender, known as the lead lender, in which one or more other lenders, known as participants, own a part interest; (2) A mortgage originated by two or more lenders.

Percentage lease   A lease in which a percentage of the tenant's gross business receipts constitutes the rent. Although a straight percentage lease is occasionally encountered, most percentage leases contain a provision for a minimum rent amount.

Permanent loan   A long-term loan or mortgage that is fully amortized and extended for a period of not less than ten years.

Per unit allocation   The method of allocation costs over the total number of units affected.

Physical approach to value   An appraisal method whereby property value is derived by estimating the replacement cost of improvements, less estimated depreciation, plus estimated land value by use of market data.

Plans and specifications   Architectural and engineering drawings and specifications for construction of a building or project. They include a description of materials to be used and the manner in which they are to be applied.

Plot plan   A layout of improvements on a site, including their location, dimensions, and landscapes. It is generally a part of the architectural plan.

Prepayment privilege   The right given a borrower to pay all or part of a debt prior to its maturity. The mortgagee cannot be compelled to accept any payment other than those originally agreed to.

Prime tenant   A tenant, or related group of tenants, that is the largest single occupant of a building. Such occupancy is generally for 25% or more of the aggregate square footage.

Priority   As applied to claims against property, the status of being prior or having precedence over other claims. Priority is usually established by filing or recordation in point of time, but may be established by statute or agreement.

Pro forma statement   A financial or accounting statement projecting income and performance of real estate within a period of time (usually one year) based upon estimates and assumptions.

Purchase money mortgage   A mortgage given by the purchaser of real property to the seller as part of the consideration in the sales transaction.

Real estate owned (REO)   A term frequently used by lending institutions as applied to ownership of real property acquired for investments or as a result of foreclosure.

Recapture   An owner's recovery of money invested in real estate, usually referring to a depreciation allowance.

Recording   The noting in the registrar's office of the details of a properly executed legal document, such as a deed, mortgage, a satisfaction of mortgage, or an extension of mortgage, thereby making it a part of the public record.

Rental concession   A landlord's agreement to forego part of the advertised rent in an effort to attract tenants.

Rental requirement   A condition in the commitment letter stipulating that a specific number of units must be rented at a minimum rental rate before the entire loan amount will be funded.

Rent-up period   The time after construction that a rental property requires to achieve projected stabilized income and occupancy levels.

Reproduction cost   The money required to reproduce a building under current market conditions less than allowance for depreciation.

Retainage (retention)   The amount withheld out of payment to contractors or subcontractors as per contractual agreement to insure a final and satisfactory completion of the job.

Sale-leaseback   A technique in which a seller deeds property to a buyer for a consideration and the buyer simultaneously leases the property back to the seller, usually on a long-term basis.

Sandwich lease   A lease in which the ''sandwich party'' is a lessee, paying rent on a leasehold interest to one party, and also is a lessor, collecting rents from another party or parties. Usually the owner of the sandwich lease is neither the fee owner nor the user of the property.

Servicing agreement   A written agreement between an investor and mortgage loan correspondent stipulating the rights and obligations of each party.

Soft costs   Architectural, engineering, and legal fees as distinguished from land and construction costs.

Soft dollars   The amount invested in the development or purchase of a property that is immediately deductible for tax purposes, such as prepaid interest and fees.

Speculative construction   Construction of a building without prior rental, lease, or sale agreements.

Standby commitment   A commitment to purchase a loan or loans with specified terms, both parties understanding that delivery is not likely, unless circumstances warrant. The commitment is issued for a fee with willingness to fund in the event that a permanent loan is not obtained. Such commitments are typically used to enable the borrower to obtain construction financing at a lower cost on the assumption that permanent financing of the project will be available on more favorable terms when the improvements are completed and the project is generating income.

Standby fee   The fee charged by an investor for a standby commitment. The fee is earned upon issuance and acceptance of the commitment.

Subordination   The act of a party acknowledging, by written recorded instrument, that a debt due is inferior to the interest of another in the same property. Subordination may apply not only to mortgages, but to leases, real estate rights, and any other types of debt instruments.

Survey   A measurement of land, prepared by a registered land surveyor, showing the location of the land with reference to known points, its dimensions, and the location and dimensions of any improvements.

Surveyor's Certificate   A formal statement signed, certified, and dated by a surveyor giving the pertinent facts about a particular property and any easements or encroachments affecting it.

Takeout commitment   A promise to make a loan at a future specified time. It is most commonly used to designate a higher cost, shorter term, back-up commitment as a support for construction financing until a suitable permanent loan can be secured.

Tenancy   A holding of real estate under any kind of right of title. Used alone, tenancy implies a holding under a lease.

Tenant contributions   All costs that are a pro rata responsibility of the tenant over and above the contract rent specified in the lease, such as area maintenance.

Term mortgage   A loan having a specified term during which interest is paid but the principal is not reduced. The entire principal plus any unpaid accrued interest is due and payable at the end of its term.

Title insurance policy   A contract by which the insurer, usually a title insurance company, agrees to pay the insured a specific amount for any loss caused by defects of title to real estate, wherein the insured has an interest as purchaser, mortgagee, or otherwise.

Title search   An examination of public records, laws and court decisions to disclose the past and current facts regarding ownership of real estate.

Track record   The previous operating results of the sponsor (or developer) of a real estate program.

Underwriting   The analysis of risk and the matching of it to an appropriate rate and term.

Vacancy and rent loss   Vacancy refers to any type of rental property or unit thereof that is unrented. In the estimate of gross income of a property an allowance or discount for vacancy is usually made. Rent loss can result from a number of reasons, such as a loss in rental income during periods of remodeling or rehabilitation of a project, low occupancy rates, rent loss because of the tenant's inability to pay, and other such occurrences.

Vacancy factor   A percentage rate expressing the loss from gross rental income due to vacancy and collection losses.

Voucher system   In construction lending, a system of giving subcontractors a voucher in lieu of cash that they may redeem with the construction lender. The opposite of a fixed disbursement schedule.

Waiver of lien   The written evidence from the contractor (or supplier of material) surrendering the right of lien to enforce collection of debt against property.

Warehousing   The borrowing of funds by a mortgage banker on a short-term basis at a commercial bank using permanent mortgage loans as collateral. This form of interim financing is used until the mortgages are sold to a permanent investor.

Wraparound   A mortgage which secures a debt which includes the balance due on an existing senior mortgage and an additional amount advanced by the wraparound mortgagee. The wraparound mortgagee thereafter makes the amortizing payments on the senior mortgage. An example: A landowner has a mortgage securing a debt with an outstanding balance of $3,000,000. A lender now advances the same mortgagor a new $1,500,000 and undertakes to make the remaining payments due on the $3,000,000 debt and takes a $4,500,000 wraparound junior mortgage on the real estate to secure the total indebtedness.

Yield   In real estate, the term refers to the effective annual amount of income which is being accrued on an investment. Expressed as a percentage of the pricing originally paid.

Yield to maturity   A percent returned each year to the lender on actual funds borrowed considering that the loan will be paid in full at the end of maturity.

Zoning   The act of city or county authorities specifying the type of use to which property may be put in specific areas.

Index